JUSTICE & NATURE

Kantian Philosophy, Environmental Policy, & the Law

JUSTICE & NATURE

Kantian Philosophy, Environmental Policy, & the Law

JOHN MARTIN GILLROY

GEORGETOWN UNIVERSITY PRESS / WASHINGTON, D.C.

Georgetown University Press, Washington, D.C.
© 2000 by Georgetown University Press. All rights reserved.
Printed in the United States of America

10 9 8 7 6 5 4 3 2 1   2000

This volume is printed on acid-free offset book paper.

Library of Congress Cataloging-in-Publication Data

Gillroy, John Martin, 1954–
    Justice and nature : Kantian philosophy, environmental policy, and
the law / John Martin Gillroy.
        p. cm — (American governance and public policy)
    Includes bibliographical references and index.
    ISBN 0-87840-795-2 (cloth : alk. paper)
    1. Environmental policy. 2. Environmental law—Economic aspects.
3. Kant, Immanuel, 1724-1804.   I. Title. II. Series.

GE170.G52 2000
363.7'056—dc21   00-027254

Contents

PART II
A KANTIAN PARADIGM FOR
ECOSYSTEM POLICY ARGUMENT

PART III
ECOSYSTEM ARGUMENT:
APPLICATIONS AND IMPLICATIONS

EPILOGUE

List of Tables and Figures

Foreword

It is often asserted that environmental policy should be based on sound science. This is true enough, but the unidimensionality of the assertion often belies a considerable misunderstanding of effective environmental policy design and decision making. Science is necessary to the making of environmental policy, but at the same time is far from sufficient. Environmental policy also requires appropriate political and administrative processes, consistent philosophical principles, careful value analysis, and an overarching ethical logic. Science alone, however competently and thoroughly done, is never enough. This book offers a grounding in this "other dimension" of environmental policy development.

Environmental policy decision makers face innumerable value issues and another array of value issues whenever environmental policy initiatives must compete within the larger political and societal realm. Succinctly stated, environmental values include (1) wilderness, biodiversity, and habitat (in a word, nature); (2) the reduction of pollution and the protection of human health; and (3) "resource" conservation and sustainability. Each of these sets of environmental values is associated with several environmental sciences that are now widely familiar to most citizens (more so than they were as recently as three or four decades ago). Bright grade-school children often know something of the ecology of rainforests or the chemical composition of air pollution and smog. Attentive adult citizens soon learn the basics of toxicology and epidemiology, especially if their groundwater is threatened with contamination.

Scientific knowledge is thus ever more widely disseminated, but even sophisticated environmental scientists and policy analysts are not always comfortable with the value analysis and philosophical reasoning that are essential to good environmental policymaking. Very important value issues requiring analysis and public debate too often become hidden assumptions, unconsidered and unresolved. It needs to be more widely understood that such issues cannot be resolved by science, but rather by fact (given limited contemporary scientific capabilities) or, more often, by principle (because they are beyond the scope of science). It is within this world of often avoided value discourse that many highly contentious environmental issues arise.

Policy decisions that avoid these concerns or presume that there is some simple and somehow automatic way to resolve them frequently fail the test of time and are later regretted and seen as unwarranted expediences. Gillroy, in contrast, offers an approach that places value issues and ethical analysis front and center in the environmental policy process and looks for an overarching logical structure within which scientific findings and value analysis can be effectively integrated. In this Foreword I hope to convey why this approach is important and why it is likely to become more important in the future.

Why Science Is Not a Sufficient Basis for Policy

Perhaps the best way to appreciate the limits of environmental science as a basis for environmental policy is to briefly consider concrete cases. I have selected four cases that are not among the particular cases that Gillroy emphasizes (though several are discussed). I hope to show that policy analysts and practitioners across a range of policy subfields and government departments should consider the general analysis that Gillroy offers. The four cases are (1) nuclear power, (2) biodiversity, (3) climate change, and (4) genetically modified organisms. The policy subfields include energy policy, parks and wilderness policy, agricultural policy, and trade policy. Gillroy's analysis is even more obviously appropriate to policies that address air and water pollution and resource conservation.

Regarding nuclear power, a great deal is known scientifically about the human health effects of radiation exposure. That knowledge was developed in conjunction with considerable human suffering, primarily in unrelated occupations such as at Hiroshima, in relation to workplace exposures in uranium mining, and the painting of watch dials with radium. The early tendency in related policy decisions was to overestimate safe exposure levels. These errors were not so much a result of scientific ignorance per se as the absence of an ethical commitment to worker safety and to the precautionary principle. In some cases the potential for environmental caution was overridden by other, seemingly higher, societal objectives and values—the development and advancement of nuclear weapons capability at the height of the cold war, for example. The long-term (and not always fully understood) environmental health risks were judged to be less immediate concerns—in effect, a value judgment more than a scientific judgment.

Many predominant value issues remain regarding nuclear energy, however, and although science cannot answer these questions, it can contribute to a process of informed decision making. Science cannot, for example, determine with any precision the overall risk of system failure within a nuclear power facility (the likelihood of the occurrence of another Three Mile Island or Chernobyl). Experienced scientists can make informed guesses, but ultimately, the question is extra-scientific. So, too, is the broader matter of whether or not the risks associated with nuclear power are worth taking. It is an ethical and philosophical question as to whether a small risk of a collective, involuntary, catastrophic outcome is acceptable (even if citizens are routinely prepared to take higher risks every time they, as individuals, choose to drive an automobile). It may, of course, ultimately turn out that the full array of collective risks associated with nuclear energy are worth taking, given the alternative risks of climate warming. But, while again these are questions that demand scientific information, they cannot be resolved by science alone.

Science tells us most of what we know about endangered species, but policymaking regarding biodiversity also involves other issues. Some of these additional matters result from insufficient science or insufficient time—as in the case of the ecological characteristics of second and third growth forests in some settings and circumstances (uniform species and age replanting, for example). But science is also not enough because decision makers may face ethically loaded trade-offs between ecological and economic values, or even (especially within developing nations) between biodiversity and human well-being. This is not to say that economy should prevail over ecology, but it is to say that these are ethical, not scientific, questions. It is also true that the questions themselves must be considered in a context of centuries of human development that has favored humans and economies over ecological protection.

Other relevant questions may even concern trade-offs within the ecological world, as distinct from trade-offs with economic or other human values. Some examples include: Which is more important, the continued existence of an already decimated species or the preservation of remaining extant ecosystems? Or, are some species more valuable than others? and how does one decide? Or even, when does a tiger cease to be a tiger? Is a tiger in a zoo really a tiger? What about a species that exists only in sperm and egg banks? Gillroy's analysis cannot provide an easy answer to these types of questions. He does, however, make very clear why the intrinsic values of nature are worth considering and how they are inevitably relevant to the world of environmental policymaking.

When we turn from matters related to pollution, radiation, and biodiversity, we come upon environmental policy realms that are even more obviously fraught with ethical and philosophical concerns—and less easily guided solely by the science of the day. Climate warming was brought to the attention of the world, or at least confirmed, by very careful science, including the heroic retrospective reconstruction of climate data from the past. Clearly, humankind continues to alter the proportion of carbon dioxide in the atmosphere. It is probable as well that the change has altered the climate of the planet. We, however, know next to nothing about the pace or the exact character of the changes that are likely to ensue. It is also arguable that we will not know such things with great precision until well after the point at which we could undo the outcome within a reasonable time period through emissions reductions alone.

Where does that leave us, especially given the economic and social implications of significant changes in human contributions to the carbon cycle? It leaves environmental policymakers, and indeed all of us as citizens, with an array of ethical questions and philosophical dilemmas. But, science can only do what it can do. It cannot be "scientifically demonstrated" that fuel-inefficient sport utility vehicles (SUVs) should be illegal, or even radically discouraged. Nor can science alone decide whether government should increase subsidies to energy-efficient public transportation systems, or tax carbon, or change zoning practices to discourage suburban sprawl. Science could, perhaps, find radical new ways to sequester carbon (in biomass or oceans or soils), but it may not be able to determine with confidence, within an appropriate time frame, whether the risks associated with the cure are more or less worrisome than those associated with the disease (climate change).

Environmental decision making faces many ethical issues, so it needs a framework, or several frameworks, within which to even appreciate which questions to ask first, or which questions *must* be answered by society before policy decisions ensue. The fact that environmental policy has profound implications for many other policy realms, from transportation policy to agricultural policy to energy policy, make resolution of these ethical issues more rather than less compelling and urgent. What science has suggested thus far in a virtual consensus is that there is no avoiding the asking of such questions. It is also true that the absence of decisions about carbon cycle changes is also a decision. So, too, is a delay in asking the ethical questions, or in failing to think about how to formulate and address the real issues at hand. Gillroy's discussion in this volume is, in my view, highly pertinent to such tasks.

Finally, what about the environmental and ethical implications of genetically modified organisms? This headline-grabbing and trade nightmare is presently a challenging issue because it resides almost wholly within the realm of value-based controversy regarding appropriate criteria and procedures. The concern is in large part about the burden of proof regarding scientific evidence of environmental and human health effects. It is less a scientific controversy because there is not a lot of science (regarding possible impacts) to consider. It is a very public transatlantic ethical debate regarding the appropriate and prudential conduct and use of science itself.

Some other aspects of this debate may go beyond concerns that normally fall within the sweeping heading of environmental policy and into the realm of pure ethics and even spirituality. Do human beings have the right, in any way or for any purpose, to intervene directly in the process of evolution? Is doing so within or without the bounds of prudence? Does nature as a whole, as distinct from any particular species or ecosystem, not have intrinsic rights? Who will resolve such questions and how will they be resolved? Or, will we simply imagine that since they cannot be resolved scientifically, they should not be asked publicly? Or, more simply, that they are beyond our ken and collective capacities as a species and therefore best ignored?

Regardless of how one answers these questions, there are and will be many more "practical" questions that genetic modification will doubtless raise in the years to come: How much testing of what effects and by whom is sufficient for approval for what degree and character of use? Few of our leading institutions are accustomed to considering the type of questions that are likely to be raised in such an exercise. An EPA more versed in the questions and concerns of the sort that Gillroy advances might in time come to be a suitable venue, but presently, not even our spiritual institutions broach the appropriate considerations. North Americans are perhaps so accustomed now to pragmatism that we do not even recognize fundamental questions of ethical principal when they stare us in the face. How many political candidates, one might ask, would campaign on the need for a national debate about the ethics of genetic engineering?

Increasingly and interestingly, however, everyday policy decisions seem to raise questions about the language of ethics and political philosophy. I recall a statement I heard long ago in a wide-ranging discussion about the politics of pollution and resource depletion sponsored by Environment Canada. The apt assertion was that humankind was "racing to the moon in Moses' moral underwear". Three decades later, those who would insert moral debate into contemporary politics focus on such matters as abortion, capital punishment, same-sex marriages, and the restoration of "family values"—all questions focused on individual behavior, primarily sexual. The broader, and arguably more important and societally oriented, ethical issues are at the same time taken to be matters best left to economists, scientists, and other technically oriented experts, as if those who professionally eschew ethical matters were somehow especially gifted in this regard. As a society we seem to have agreed to pretend that the many genies that are so obviously out of their bottles are simply not there.

Ethics in the World of Three-Dimensional Politics and Policy

One other way to appreciate the importance of environmental ethics within political and policy discourse is to recognize the ways in which that discourse has evolved in the latter part of the twentieth century. Such debates have moved from what was often a two-dimensional contestation between equity and privilege (between left and right) to a three-dimensional debate among equity, economy, and environment. The addition of environmental considerations at this level has necessitated a rethinking of some fundamental aspects of ethics and political philosophy. Gillroy thus appropriately roots his very contemporary environmental policy discourse in the fundamentals of ethics, including in a central way the insights of classical ethicists such as Immanuel Kant.

At the same time that the dimensions of policy discourse have broadened the jurisdiction of policymaking, following the path blazed by corporate and financial decision making, a shift is occurring from the nation-state to a global scale. This latter shift, some argue, threatens to re-narrow policy discourse from two or three dimensions to one—a focus that might be called "economism," wherein policy and politics are always and only about the maximization of economic growth (a technical exercise largely devoid of ethical reflection and discourse). Gillroy recognizes and emphasizes the importance of an autonomous (noneconomistic) valuation of environmental risks and benefits and suggests in some contexts a requirement of science to demonstrate safety rather than harm. I have come to the view that such a perspective is essential if the long-term net effects of globalization are to be positive.

In a global era, policy and even societal performance must be judged fairly and comprehensively in economic terms but also assessed independently using noneconomic measures and within independent institutions in terms of social and environmental outcomes. In a phrase, there are three bottom lines, not one, and Gillroy makes an eloquent and careful case for the third, environment. He does so both within broad philosophical terms and within concrete case studies that include wildlife management issues, risk management in Florida's Biscayne Acquifer, NIMBY situations, California's Proposition 65, and other important contemporary issues in environmental policy and administration. He stresses that economy and environment must be treated in a balanced way, without a presumption of "core status" for economic efficiency within environmental law and policy. Private property, for both Kant and Gillroy, is an important societal value, but not an "overriding" value.

Balanced ethical analysis and clear fundamental principles appropriate to the contemporary age are Gillroy's territory. Effective environmental policy demands nothing less. We cannot assess risk fairly and effectively unless we understand and consider invisible risks as well as obvious risks, collective risks as well as individual risks, "technical" concerns such as latency and irreversibility as well as the fundamental democratic need for citizen activism and public trust. Such principles and distinctions are easily as important to successful environmental policy as are science and prudent attention to the economic well-being. Most polities and policy processes remain a good distance from getting this balance right, and some are rapidly losing ground in this era of economism and trade-driven globalization. This book can help to guide us back to the first principles that could allow us to go forward without losing ground.

Robert Paehlke
Trent University

Preface

Philosophers and policy practitioners need one another, but they are currently working at cross-purposes. The philosophers are not helping to provide practitioners with the simplified "tools" necessary to easily integrate complex moral and philosophical ideas into daily decision making. The practitioners are reluctant to use nonmarket normative values in their evaluation and justification of policy. This reluctance is not entirely their fault. Even if they had the inclination, their training leaves them one-dimensional and dismissive of the normative complexities of public choice, which they are taught to leave to others (e.g., legislators, citizens).

Specifically, the role of philosophical and ethical argument in policy evaluation and analysis is controversial. Few graduate policy programs offer an "ethics" course and fewer still require students to take it. Those who do get "ethics" are not required to read philosophical classics like Thomas Hobbes's *Leviathan*, David Hume's *Treatise of Human Nature*, or G. W. F. Hegel's *Philosophy of Right*, in the search for integrated alternative models of policy choice and argument. Instead, they examine modern interpretations of a small subset of ethical concepts like utility, right, and freedom, as isolated ideas divorced from the underlying philosophical systems that defined them. After all, freedom or utility mean different things to each of the individuals mentioned above, which only a comprehension of their full arguments allows one to understand. Today's student of policy is not encouraged to study these alternative normative systems and policy is the worse for it.

The only integrated argument paradigm taught to every single student of policy is that provided by Economic Policy Argument. There is an underlying skepticism in our age, compounded by the quest for "science" and the illusion that economics has no normative implications, that nonmarket principle is applicable to public choice. After all, Hobbes, Hume, and Hegel could not have anything constructive to say about global warming, atomic energy, negative income taxation, or handguns. I hope to make a dent in this preconceived and, I believe, uncritically accepted dogma.

My effort here is to take a preexisting philosophical system, that written by Immanuel Kant, and apply it to environmental politics, policy, and law. I make no claim that Kant's philosophical system is the only one relevant to public policy choice, but I believe that we do a great disservice to public policy studies by not exploiting the vast array of ethical argument that has already been done by philosophers.

But the only way nonmarket ethical principles will find acceptance in day-to-day policy evaluation is if the assumptions and concepts behind these principles give them as clear and widely applicable a foundation as efficiency does for economic argument. The market paradigm has produced a simple methodology (i.e., cost-benefit) from a complex philosophical foundation, and this helps the practitioner to handle many jobs with a single "tool." Today, the practitioner, with the market paradigm as his sole established "tool," is a person with only a hammer, to whom all public issues look like nails. One does not have to deny the importance of understanding economic analysis to also promote the alternative principles of freedom, equality, or fairness as a potentially sound basis for paradigms of argument. I intend this Kantian paradigm to be an additional "tool" for the analysis of public policy, and I encourage other philosophers to provide a service to policymakers by utilizing my logical framework (chapter 1), or one of their own, to turn other philosophical systems into additional normative "tools" for setting and improving our understanding of the public interest.

Our job is simple; those who have done the study of these systems of thought should help to create alternative methodologies for the practitioner, and the practitioner, both in her training and execution of policy choice, should take the time to consider the range of "tools" available given the policy job that stands before them. Together, we must take the work already done by centuries of philosophical study and move it a step ahead, so that it can become part of the concrete search for better public law.

Some of the words and ideas present in this book were first set out in shorter essays, published elsewhere. Specifically, chapter 1 had a previous incarnation as "Postmodernism, Efficiency and Comprehensive Policy Argument in Public Administration: A Tool for the Practice of Administrative Decision-Making," which was published by Sage Press in the *American Behavioral Scientist* 41:163–90 (1997). Chapter 3 appeared as "Environmental Risk and the Traditional Sector Approach: Market Efficiency at the Core of Environmental Law?" in *RISK: Health, Safety, and Environment* 10:139–76 (1999). Chapter 5 saw first light as "Kantian Ethics and Environmental Policy Argument: Autonomy, Ecosystem Integrity and Our Duties to Nature," published by JAI Press in *Ethics and the Environment* 3:131–58 (1998). Part of chapter 8 appeared as "When Responsive Public Policy Does Not Equal Responsible Government," which was chapter 12 in *The Ethics of Liberal Democracy: Morality and Democracy in Theory and Practice*, edited by Robert Paul Churchill and published by Berg Publishers. Finally, in chapter 10, I utilized some of my words and concepts from "Environmental Risk and the Politics of Assurance: Alternative Approaches to Waste Facility Siting," which was co-authored with Barry Rabe, and published by ITP Journals, London, in *Risk, Decision and Policy* 2:245–58 (1997). I wish to acknowledge the permission granted to me by the editors and/or publishers of these essays to reprint them here.

All of the quotations from Kant are translated by the author and are cited by the title of the work in short form (see bibliography) and their Prussian Academy page or section numbers. These translations reflect my best efforts to get at Kant's meanings and include my work with the German text, feedback from colleagues on my translations, and the study of numerous other translations of Kant's works. I wish to thank the many colleagues and Kant translators, living and deceased, whose lasting work has helped me synthesize Kant's arguments into English. These individuals include Alan Donagan, Helen Morris-Keitel, Mary Gregor, John Ladd, H. J. Paton, Allen W. Wood, Lewis White Beck, H. B. Nisbet, James W. Ellington, Ted Humphrey, W. Hastie, Peter Heath, Werner S. Pluhar, Theodore M. Green, Hoyt H. Hudson, Echart Förster, Michael Rosen, and Gary Steiner.

Acknowledgments

This book is the product of fifteen years of Immanuel labor. It began in graduate school at the University of Chicago as an investigation of Kant's practical philosophy and continued as a concern for air and groundwater policy at the Environmental Quality Laboratory of the California Institute of Technology, where I learned that ethics, political theory, and environmental policy were necessary to one another. Its theory was tempered by practice during my time working in the U.S. House of Representatives and at the Center for Philosophy and Public Policy of the University of Maryland. It was integrated into its first complete exposition during a term in the Department of Government at the University of Texas and came to fruition during my study of environmental law at the Vermont Law School.

Being a multidisciplinary argument, it has been built slowly, over time, into the most complete analysis and reassessment of the foundational argument behind environmental risk in particular and environmental policy and law in general, of which I am capable. During its development I was tempted to publish it in parts, but have held out so that the reader could see the entire development of my constructive argument from my critical concerns about market assumptions in public policy and the application of a Kantian alternative to environmental law.

I have many teachers, colleagues, friends, family, and students to thank for their attention to and feedback on the ideas and logical structure of what is presented here. It would add many pages to an already lengthy text to thank them all properly. Let me simply say that my contact with them and our exchanges of ideas have allowed me the rare experience of feeling truly alive.

In particular, however, I wish to thank Brian Barry for teaching me to write, and to appreciate the intricacies of theory and the importance of finding ways to apply it to my life. Russell Hardin introduced me to collective-action theory and was generous in his encouragement of my unconventional use of games, which his help and patience have made more rigorous. Toby Page introduced me to the field of environmental risk and challenged me to do the work necessary to understand it in all its complexity as a moral, social, economic, political, and scientific dilemma. Mark Sagoff and Douglas McLean helped me to understand the needs and expectations of scholars and practitioners alike and encouraged me to maintain my dedication to both philosophy and policy. David Braybrooke reached out to give me opportunities that allowed me to create the first completely integrated argument that led to this book; he also came up with the name "Justice from Autonomy" to describe what I was doing and introduced me to the importance of deontic logic in policy analysis. Celia Campbell-Mohn and Dick Brooks taught me to appreciate both the letter and the spirit of the law, and my time as Marsh Teaching Fellow at Vermont Law School gave me and my manuscript a new lease on life. Finally Thomas Donaldson, K. S. Shrader-Frechette, and Bryan Norton provided needed encouragement to this effort at critical times. I thank them.

One can number true personal friends on one hand. The most true of these, next to my wife Margaret Murray, is Maurice Wade. His unwavering support, intellectual acumen, and willingness to stick with me when the cost to him was high, makes him a rare scholar and a rarer human being. This argument is better for his having read it. I thank him.

This book would not be possible without the mentorship of the late Alan Donagan. Alan was a philosopher whose love of words and ideas transmitted to me the highest standards of dedication to both prosecute an argument to its conclusion and then amend it on the basis of the results of that prosecution. Truth was important to him, but he saw the route to truth though innovation, not through dogmatic loyalty to preconceived notions. Few established scholars would have allowed a graduate student to synthesize arguments in opposition to what they thought initially true and to allow that graduate student to convince them otherwise. Alan always treated me as an equal, and in our discussions I learned more about Kant in particular and the philosophical process in general than I could have gleaned from a thousand books. When everyone else told me I could not apply Kant to environmental policy, Alan encouraged me to ignore them; for this, and for his friendship, I thank his memory.

Margaret Murray, my dearest friend, read and edited this entire manuscript and was a constant sounding board for all of its ideas. I love her and I hope to be as supportive and influential to her writing as she has been to mine.

I will also thank Marlon Quintanilla, Rishi Kapur, David Zettlemoyer, Cathy Fahey, Todd Gleason, Tracey Sochor, Rachel Ward, and my other students at Trinity College, Vermont Law School, University of Hartford, and Bucknell University who have helped me to refine my ideas in the classroom, especially all those who took the various incarnations of my "Public Policy Analysis" class and who opened their minds, sometimes reluctantly, to new ways of looking at old problems.

Bucknell University and the MacArthur Foundation have also been very supportive and helpful, giving me the first and best home I have ever had. This project could not have been completed without them. I also wish to acknowledge the many journal editors who took a chance on me, and John Samples, Barry Rabe, and others at Georgetown University Press, who provided me with the opportunity to publish this effort in its entirety as one volume.

I am a lucky man and I am indebted to you all.

INTRODUCTION

Practical Reason, Moral Capacities, and Environmental Choices

Good theory is like good fiction, not in form, but in purpose and effect. Fiction is not empirically factual, but good fiction says something about human beings and their circumstances that is transcendentally true beyond context. Good fiction also explains the motivations of individuals in singular or collective action in a more intimate way than nonfiction is able to do.

Theory is likewise capable of more intimate and greater truth than empirical research, and is, in fact, the foundation upon which empirical research depends. Theory can anticipate and make recommendations about future action based on assumptions about the connections between human motivation and purposes; it is our primary tool for creating the world around us.

Retrospective empirical research exists to confirm and improve theory, but not to replace it. The theory at the foundation of a discipline is that which defines, integrates, and creates that discipline, and it informs any empirical research and observational undertakings within the area of study. However, in order to be of value this theoretical foundation cannot be static. For as we evolve socially and politically, so do our motivations and reactions to the world that surrounds us. Theory must keep pace with this evolution.

Theory keeps pace by constantly questioning the basic assumptions of a discipline and by never allowing theoretical assumptions to become axioms with a status and validity that are assumed to be true without reflection or analysis. In law and public policy, theory remains useful only if it remains conscious of the fundamental assumptions we, as citizens and decision makers, take into our consideration of what a "good" policy is and what are "reasonable" means to these public ends.

In my focus on policy as argument (Majone 1989; Fischer and Forester 1993),[1] I assume that public choice begins with theoretical principles and assumptions that inform arguments that then create discourse about public issues that leads to political choice and concrete law. Under these conditions, the theoretical principles and assumptions, and how they lead to both ineffective and innovative practice, are the core of my analysis.

To examine environmental policy as both theory and practice, this book contains a critical as well as a constructive argument and a series of case applications. In part I we shall critically establish that the market paradigm and context model is a dominant tool in present environmental law and policy analysis and that its use as an analytic point of departure for public choice is inadequate to the proper regulation of environmental risk.

In part II we will constructively demonstrate that an alternative body of theory exists within Immanuel Kant's moral and political thought that would better inform public policy argument, and we will synthesize the Justice from Autonomy paradigm and context model.

In part III, to test the feasibility of our alternative paradigm as an evaluation tool for policy analysis, we will apply it to six cases: wilderness, wildlife, NIMBY, comparative risk, FDA regulation, and NEPA planning policy.

Over the course of the entire argument I intend to provide a concrete and practical alternative to market efficiency as a core principle in environmental policymaking.

The Critical Argument: Moving beyond Market Assumptions

An essential notion within the confines of conventional public policy theory is that the state's purpose is to improve the material welfare of its citizens. Based on the ideal that the state and its ends are identical with, and ought to mimic, those of the market, this stricture has come to be interpreted in various ways, most notably through the use of cost-benefit methods. Common to all interpretations, however, are the ideas that, first, the "good" of the person is some function of personal preferences regarding present, past, and future physical conditions, and second, that the market (or the state as its surrogate) has no higher goal than to realize a social condition where the greatest proportion of consumers have their preferences for personal welfare satisfied. This state of affairs is considered efficient and therefore just.

No set of policy problems vexes this established framework of public choice analysis more than do issues involving environmental risk. Each day citizens are faced with the uncertainty posed by collective risks transmitted by technology and its by-products through the environment. Although physical science is increasingly able to detect smaller and smaller concentrations of chemical agents in environmental media, the regulatory issues transcend the numbers and involve questions of justice, moral principle, and respect for nature, individuals, and their communities.

Two stages of political choices must be made. First, normative and empirical standards must be found upon which to judge whether a risk should be allowed into the environment in the first place. Second, we must arrive at institutional arrangements that allow us to set comparative social, scientific, and moral priorities among the risks that exist for the purposes of political action, abating those deemed necessary but dangerous.

Although a considerable amount of human energy is exercised in an attempt to confront the issues presented by environmental risk, results to date have been largely negative (e.g., banning *ex post* a few chemicals that have proven, over time, to affect our health, or preventing the construction of storage and disposal facilities for the risk-producing wastes of our technology). Whether it is the production stage of the technologies that cause risk, the distribution of risk across the population, the disposal of products that generate toxic waste, or the more general attempt to determine standards for the comparative assessment of the variety of environmental risks that face us, our priority has been to allow markets for risky products to exist. Technologies are regulated, if at all, only after evidence is conclusive that the comparative risk of hazard has become a real cost and that these costs from risk outweigh the material benefits of the technology or market product.

To date, the burden of proof for environmental-risk policy, produced by this application of market theory to political practice, has been on those who would regulate risk and not on those who create it. The established regulatory concern is to prevent false positives (i.e., finding an innocent technology a hazard), which empowers economic trade, rather than to prevent false negatives (i.e., finding a guilty or hazardous technology innocent), which would require that a potential risk-generating technology prove its necessity and/or safety before it could enter the market or the environment. The dominance of market assumptions and the search for welfare allocations that satisfy human preference have promoted the vibrancy of the risk economy over the regulation of risk. Concentrating on the satisfaction of preferences as the basis for assessing the comparative seriousness of risks has defined the "public interest" in the continued generation of environmental risk.

Within policy analysis however, the phenomenon of the error of the third type (E_{III}) exists. As citizens and public administrators, we may have incorrectly formulated the problem because the assumptions, principles, and methods that we begin with are improper as representations of environmental-risk decisions. Consequently, the stalemate and failure of risk regulation resulting from our deference to markets in the confrontation over risk may not only be the logical result of individual preference and instrumental rationality, but a dysfunctional result of the failure of the policy process to recognize the essential stakes of risk situations.

If we have committed a type-three error, by applying the market paradigm to risk policy, then a competing theoretical framework (or paradigm) is necessary to analyze risk anew. To construct this alternative policy argument,[2] for environmental risk, the assumptions and principles of this alternative must accommodate what the previous conventional "welfare" approach to policy did not. But what is it, specifically, that conventional "market" policy analysis cannot accommodate?

The market paradigm, as used in the formulation of public choices in general and environmental-risk policy choices in particular, lacks two critical ingredients: first, concern for the moral integrity or autonomy of the individual and the intrinsic value this internal capacity grounds for each human being as a person; and second, a concern for the intrinsic value or functional integrity of the environment (Freeman 1993, 485).[3] Critical to moral integrity, as well as to the human responsibility toward the functional integrity of natural systems, is the promotion of *practical reason* in policy choice. Therefore, to establish an alternative approach to environmental risk we must move beyond a reliance on self-interested preference, welfare, and instrumental rationality; we must concentrate on the ramifications of individual practical reason as this translates intellectual imperatives into human choices and physical actions involving the natural environment.

The book contends that, in environmental-risk cases, a type-three error has been committed and suggests that it is not an individual consumer's welfare per se that is, or ought to be, the primary responsibility of law and the state, but the conditions necessary and sufficient to a citizen's use of practical reason to decipher and anticipate the affects of risk on the moral integrity of humanity and the functional integrity of the environment.

The Constructive Argument: Kantian Ethics and Practical Choice

Practical reason, that intellectual reflection and deliberation that moves the individual to action, includes more than mere instrumental rationality. The promotion of practical reason, as the point of departure for policy argument, allows one to establish a bridge between ought and is, between intellect and action, between humanity's duties to itself and to the environment, and between internal autonomy and the external moral agency of the individual. In order to understand and make proper environmental-risk choices, one must assume practical reason in the citizen, make it the goal of collective political action, protect it in law, empower it through a just state, and, in all ways, integrate it as both the motivation and goal of policy argument.

Shifting from concern for welfare to concern for moral autonomy means a complete reorientation of social theory as it relates to the characterization of the individual agent, the strategic framework[4] within which collective action takes place, the character of moral constraints originating and maintaining collective action, the standards by which policy ends are legally justified *ex post*, and the process variables that are accepted as proper means to those policy ends *ex ante*.

If one describes a person as an agent capable of practical reason and therefore of the development of full moral capacity, rather than as just a rational, self-interested welfare maximizer, the strategic format of collective action shifts from a prisoner's dilemma to an assurance game. Moral constraints cease to be strictly conventional and externally imposed, but also become analytically critical and part of the internal practical reason of the individual agent. The ends of policy are no longer the welfare of the material person but the autonomy of the moral agent, and the means to policy ends change from the preferences or utility functions of the individual to the baseline material conditions necessary to protect and empower one's moral agency. Public policy standards shift from producible material ends to nonproducible ethical ends and concentrate, not on the subjective physical condition and wants of the consumer, but on the objective physical and environmental needs that protect and empower that freedom necessary to enable agency and full moral development of the person. Focus shifts from the efficiency of social choice, to the rights and duties citizens owe to one another, to natural systems, and to the just state, as well as to what the policymaker owes to his constituents. The arena of public choice also changes; now the state has a distinct definition of the citizen and a distinctly "public" task that separates it from markets and their consumer transactions. The public interest becomes defined as that baseline of collective goods necessary to the full moral development of each and every citizen.

A new orientation brings new theoretical categories and questions. Instead of dealing with the dilemma of encouraging self-interested consumers to act for the collective good, the policymaker should assure all citizens that their expression of autonomy, their predisposition toward moral agency, will not be exploited by others but protected in law. From preferences and aggregation, concern shifts to the distinctions between those policy choices that address the autonomy of the citizen through their outward moral agency and those that do not.

Just as the market paradigm builds its policy methods on the fundamental assumptions and ethics of economic preference utilitarianism, a competitive paradigm can be constructed on the ethical base of Kant's philosophical politics. Kantian exegesis will provide the building blocks to offer the policy analyst an alternative tool for her trade. A full and structured exposition of Kant's moral and political thought enables us to move beyond mere aggregation of preferences to specific normative definitions that provide an alternative to the market paradigm. Specifically, Kant defines what moral principles ought to motivate action, how these specify what values are at stake, and how a practically reasoning citizen is more than an instrumentally rational consumer. Public interest defined by Justice from Autonomy integrates the individual moral agent into a human community and a greater natural environment that, once harmonized, constructs a "common life" for the individual that exhibits neither the dominance of social convention nor atomistic isolation.

Why Kant?

We are concerned with how arguments that justify, formulate, and implement a collective choice through the standards of Justice from Autonomy are synthesized and how this synthesis, in turn, changes environmental policy and law. But why use Kant?

First, to build an argument paradigm on the basis of an established philosophical system gives strength and resilience to that policy tool. Second, this nonconsequentialist philosophy is a natural point of departure for a policy theory designed to be an alternative to a market preference—utilitarianism (Donagan 1977; Gewirth 1978). Third, Kant provides, not only a "point of departure," but a full ethical foundation for public choice that focuses on the moral autonomy of practical reason as it finds voice in the politics of a just state.

For years, policy texts, when they treated the subject at all, have divided the normative dimensions of policy analysis into two alternative approaches: utilitarian and Kantian (Dunn 1981; Bobrow and Dryzek 1987). Utilitarianism has received a variety of treatments that range from the predominant and "traditional" concern for economic preference utilitarianism and cost-benefit analysis (Posner 1983; Mishan 1982a; Mishan and Page 1992; Haigh, Harrison, and Nichols 1984) to the rarer use of classical utilitarianism in its rule and act varieties (Barry 1990; Donagan 1968; Braybrooke and Lindblom 1970, Page 1983a).

To date, there has not been a comprehensive attempt to apply Kant's writings to policy argument in general, let alone to a specific policy dilemma (Gillroy 1992c). A "Kantian" approach is commonly assumed to be nonconsequentialist, concentrating on human dignity with a focus on concern for the noninstrumental value of the individual and one's status as an end-in-oneself (Donagan 1977). However, it has been assumed that a direct, detailed, and systematic application of Kantian scholarship to policy dilemmas is either unnecessary or impossible. For example, although both Rawls (1971, 1993; Freeman 1999; Gillroy 2000) and Habermas (1971, 1984, 1996) develop theories that claim Kant as an ancestor, they assume that Kant is silent on the issue of the relationship between morality, justice, and concrete policy choices. I will present evidence to the contrary.

But are my efforts here merely an argument "in the spirit of Kant" or is the exegesis of Kant's ethical thought a raison d'être for Justice from Autonomy? The single most critical barrier to the second approach, and the reason why it is dismissed as impossible, is the claim that Kant's ethics is at worst empty and formal, and, at best, an absolute imperative completely internal to the intellect of the individual and therefore not susceptible to physical conditions or political choice.

These claims of impossibility regarding the application of Kant's ethics to concrete issues are overstated. Kant provides a unique understanding of morality, practical reason, and political affairs that allows an approach to environmental-risk issues that takes full account of the intrinsic values involved. The connection between Kant's ethics and politics, as made by his definition of practical reason (which, unlike Hume's or Aristotle's concept of reasoning is epistemically, legislatively, and constitutively practical [Audi 1989, 71]), is sufficient to provide specific content to political decisions that create the social conditions within which we live. Further, while these conditions do not determine one's freedom, they do influence whether one is a fully empowered moral agent or not.

I shall make three points regarding the status of Justice from Autonomy at this early stage of its exposition. First, all theory is formal in that it attempts to derive general and transcendent "truths" about human affairs. To this extent, Kant is no more or less formal than any other theorist. Second, my focus is on the application of practical, not theoretical, reason to public choice. I am therefore concerned primarily with the capacity and ability of the moral agent and not with metaphysical truth. Any theoretical reason employed will be in the service of practical action and will have a conditional truth related to the logic and rigor of the argument put forth as Justice from Autonomy.

Third, this book is by necessity an *interpretation* of Kantian exegesis because, first, the connections Kant draws between individual autonomy, social cooperation, nature, and policy are scattered throughout his work, and, second, since Kant did not write in terms of collective action and public choice, it is incumbent upon this author to organize and visualize Kant's eighteenth-century ethical and political writings through the eyes of a twenty-first-century political scientist.

My "interpretation" of Kant's ethical and political thought, I believe, upholds both the spirit and the letter of Kant's philosophy because Justice from Autonomy honors and integrates Kant's views on individual autonomy, positive and critical law, interpersonal cooperation, our duties to humanity and nature, property, and the ideal contract, to give them new meaning and applications beyond those previously realized. Justice from Autonomy does not depart from the underlying logic of Kant's exegesis, but clarifies and synthesizes it for application to actual policy problems. Essentially, the logic of Kant's social and moral principles is extrapolated into the context of public choice and environmental decision making.

Extrapolation, however, does not mean that the act of synthesizing the normative and positive political theory necessary for Justice from Autonomy is a random process. A variety of Kant's texts are utilized throughout my argument, and the full prosecution of Kant's political project, as viewed through Justice from Autonomy, is a direct application of his definition of the categorical imperative or the moral law as it applies to public choice. The arrangement of the Kantian components is therefore determined by the requirements of the moral law in the construction, through practical reason, of the phenomenal world necessary to the full development (protection and empowerment) of the noumenal (essentially moral) self.

Therefore, I am convinced that my efforts are more than simply "Kantian in spirit." However, if the reader is happier to approach the following as an independent public choice theory that is simply Kantian in spirit and not in detail, then so be it. Detailed exegesis will facilitate the process of integration and synthesis that gives Justice from Autonomy its content and strength in policy argument. The specificity and strength of the paradigm will, in turn, be useful as an aid in making decisions from the "policy point of view" as long as its argument stands as an integrated and logical foundation for public choice.

Kant's Policy Point of View

Whereas Thomas Nagel (1986) states that the moral point of view is the "view from nowhere," the view within this study is the view from the collective, or rather from the individual making public decisions. This can, but does not have to, be that of a policymaker. The deliberation may also be that of a citizen attempting to understand the law as it exists to determine what policy choice is required by a specific collective dilemma. Any individuals consciously making decisions that they know will affect others, who may not be participating in the decision, are pondering a public choice; all such choices are made by individuals for collectives. Each individual may not be as decisive in the final result, but each must approach the decision with the consideration that if he or she were, the best choice among alternatives should consider both the status of individuals as well as the future of the political community as a whole and its construction of a common life.

The policy point of view assumes that the question the decision maker must ask is not the moral question, "Should I do A rather than B?" but the public choice question, "Should I use the coercive power of the state to make everyone do A rather than B?" The distinct question grants the policymaker a unique point of view, while it emphasizes the role of coercion in political decision making. The subject of coercion and the imperative to "make everyone do A" should be addressed first.

Justice from Autonomy as an "agency-focused" theory is intended to compete with the traditional preference utilitarian model of welfare economics which relies on markets for allocation, and claims, for this reason, not to be coercive. But coercion itself is not the decisive variable. In making collective choices, we cannot decide between coercion and no coercion. Any "public" choice, even those made by market mechanisms, coerces some for the advantage of others (e.g., making one person richer and another poorer). The central concern is the justification for regulating (i) to advantage (j). The underlying definition of justice and the standards of action rank as matters of the highest concern and distinguish what it is critical to regulate, protect, and/or empower in any collective choice.

Considering the policy point of view, and making choices for other individuals, one must ensure the standards of choice represent everyone affected by the decision. These moral standards of justification should persuade others that the choice, the coercion, is reasonable (i.e., a choice they would have made themselves). Specifically, the Kantian policymaker will decide with only one thing in mind: the requirements of state action in the provision of just circumstances for the full empowerment of the autonomous moral agent.

From the policy point of view, because one is making decisions for others, but must do so by standards these individuals would accept, a policymaker must make simplifying assumptions about who people are and what is important to them. From this vantage point, the characterization, and not the character per se of the individual, as well as the formulations of the collective-action problem and the role of law and the state assumed by the decision maker, are critical to avoiding type-three errors. To make public choices one needs to draw a picture of the policy space, and select standards of judgment and prescriptions as if the behavior and motivation attributed to each component of that policy space (i.e., individual, collective, state) are true *ex ante* (Friedman 1953, part I).

Even from within the market paradigm, the policymaker creates a model as a metaphysical stipulation of who the individual person is, what is important about him or her, and why. She cannot poll all individuals affected by the collective choice, even for their costs and benefits, so she assumes that policy argument ought to be made as if individuals, their values, and motivations corresponded to market presumptions. In this sense, the theoretical demands of the concept of environmental justice set out in this book are built on those assumptions about humans and their social interactions that form the model of the policy space that I claim is Kant's.

Fundamentally, Kant's model contends, first, that it is impossible for persons to be agents if they do not initially assume that they are free, and second, that individuals must act as if they have the capacity for formation of an autonomous character if their agency has the potential for moral expression (i.e., more than mere animal expression) in the material world. A Kantian decision maker must design policy as if individuals were free and capable of autonomous moral agency.

In arguing that the autonomy of the individual is a capacity that is a prerequisite to each person's humanity and necessary to his or her moral agency, I could claim that this model of the individual, collective action, and the active state is true of humanity in general, and applicable to any issue area of public debate. However, I need not make so general a claim for the purposes of this project. The argument does not dissolve if it is agreed that its scope is more restricted. The overall value of Justice from Autonomy must await empirical application of the model to many areas of public concern. My responsibility is to show that the connection between moral agency, environmental law, and environmental risk grants new insight into these issues while protecting and encouraging individual moral autonomy and environmental integrity.

Therefore, I contend that by creating a model of the policy space (individual/collective action /state) based on Kant's definitions of these concepts, the individual making a public choice will be better able to design a public policy, as well as an argument to support it, that better appreciates what is at stake in risk issues by empowering core human and natural capacities. The validity of the policy argument that follows is therefore based on its ability to trace its principles, and the entailments of these principles in law, to its basic operating assumptions about the policy space. I think these are true, *ex ante*, but if they are only a stipulation for the purposes of approaching environmental risk from a new angle, that will suffice for now.

But even if Kant can provide a theory of autonomy that puts the intrinsic value of humanity back into policy deliberation and choice, can he do the same for nature? Does his writing allow us to synthesize a more comprehensive environmental ethics that takes the integrity of natural systems seriously?

My contention is that, preconceptions notwithstanding, Immanuel Kant does offer an environmental ethics that uniquely contributes to two current debates in the field. First, he transcends the controversy between individualistic and holistic approaches to nature with a theory that considers humanity in terms of the autonomy of moral individuals and nature in terms of the integrity of functional wholes.

Second, he diminishes the gulf between conservationism and preservationism. He does this by constructing an ideal-regarding conception of the former that values nature not as "merely" a thing to be used by human preferences and translated by markets, but as an essential component and prerequisite to the intrinsic autonomy of human beings. Simultaneously, he argues for a definition of preservation that places responsibility on humanity to harmonize moral agency with the functional integrity of natural systems. Here humanity and nature become the two unique and equally important components of what we might call the greater "Kantian Ecosystem."[5]

At minimum, Kantian ethics is an anthropocentric theory that creates duties to nature arising from one's perfect duties to one's self and others to achieve autonomy, create happiness, and strive toward the "Kingdom of Ends." I call this "Kantian conservationism."

In addition, there is a stronger sense of duty to nature that can be created by an ecocentric reading of Kant's philosophy. In this reading, nature has intrinsic value and independent functional integrity, which creates moral duties in humanity, independent of the relationship of their autonomy or welfare to nature's resources. Here, our duty is to preserve, protect, and empower that of which we are an "ultimate expression" because of its inherent value as a self-generating, functioning, and evolving system and to create a state of affairs in which the world of causality and the world of freedom coexist harmoniously. I call this "Kantian preservationism."

In addition to the theoretical contributions of Kant's approach to our appreciation of the duties we owe to our natural environment, I will also suggest that Kantian conservationism and Kantian preservationism provide a sound moral basis for public policy arguments that wish to take the intrinsic value of humanity and nature into account. By requiring decision makers to consider citizens as ethical ends and nature as a functional end-in-itself, public choice becomes a process of restricting the use of the "Kingdom of Nature" to the essential requirements of a "Kingdom of Ends."

The foundation of Kant's ethical and political thought, in duties to both humanity and nature, creates a new regulatory model for the formulation, justification, and implementation of environmental-risk policy. The current model of the relationship between humanity and nature utilizes an economic perspective and divides the environment into species and minerals for extraction and into distinct media (i.e., air, water, land, groundwater) for disposal. This model, which we shall name the Traditional Sector Approach (TSA), promotes the instrumental-use values of the market paradigm.

With the Justice from Autonomy paradigm a new regulatory context model can be defined on the basis of the recognition that human and natural integrity are interdependent. Defining an Ecosystem as composed of the interaction of human and natural systems, the Ecosystem Design Approach employs a Resources to Recovery context model, using an environmental perspective to divide the economy into sectors pertaining to resource extraction, manufacture, and disposal. The new regulatory model reorients the priorities of regulation away from facilitation of economic efficiency and toward consideration of the moral and social requirements of "integrity" in making policy decisions. The reorientation of policy argument offers a reconceptualization of environmental risk and all subsequent law and policy.

Justice from Autonomy and Ecosystem Policy Argument

Environmental law and policy should reflect the scientific reality of natural systems, the social ramifications of risk, and the moral dimensions of its regulation. In order to free the decision maker from the "prison" of the market paradigm (Dryzek 1987, 245), a transition to a dialectic between the ideals of Kantian ethical principle and the constraints of practical environmental policy choice is necessary.

This transition moves from an established approach to policy design (Economic Policy Argument), made up of the market paradigm and its TSA policy context model, to an alternative policy design approach (Ecosystem Policy Argument), based on the Justice from Autonomy paradigm and its Resources to Recovery context model.

Both public choice paradigms are empirical and normative; their value is established by logic, consistency, and persuasiveness in political and legal discourse. The empirical verification of a policy argument is a function of our estimation of its essential grasp of the characteristics of the issue, the nature of the individual, his collective reality, and the proper standards of environmental choice.

For Kant, the value of the individual is her moral autonomy. The collective reality of the moral agent is one where her practical reason is confronted with environmental constraints as well as duties regarding natural systems that may support and/or exploit her agency. The proper standards of collective choice, which consider the demands of practical reason, require the legal protection and political empowerment of the internal moral capacity of humanity and the functional integrity of nature through the provision of the external conditions of social justice.

We begin by defining the paradigm and context model of the market approach to policy design and argument. In the process we will create a generic logical structure of questions for policy argument paradigms that can be used not only as I will use it (to derive the Kantian paradigm) but with many philosophical systems to provide additional tools for the analysis of public policy and law.

Notes to Introduction

1. My concentration on policy as argument is in no way meant to devalue or dismiss the importance of power, class, and other variables in their determination of policy. It seeks only to address the most fundamental level at which human beings consider and derive policy ends and means, privately or publicly, and to understand the moral principles that find application in concrete choice (consciously or unconsciously). Although argument is essential in democratic societies to operationalize policy, I do not assume that persuasive argument is the only route to law. I do contend, however, first, that for any collective course of action, one must begin with principle, with a plan, and convince oneself of its inherent logic and persuasiveness, and, second, that having a persuasive public argument for a particular course of action makes it much easier to coordinate collective action and achieve its ends, even in nondemocratic political systems.

2. In the last few years, an effort has been made to move from traditional Multiple-Use Management (Laitos 1985) of the environment to what has come to be known as Ecosystem Management (Yaffee et al. 1996). This effort has met with limited success in that agencies have tended to treat Ecosystem Management as another sector of Multiple Use rather than a new policy design perspective (Kessler and Salwasser 1995). I have made a specific argument elsewhere (1998) that this lack of success is because the theoretical underpinnings of Multiple Use and its principle of Sustainability have not been replaced by an alternative principle and new policy design paradigm that would properly evaluate and operationalize a concern for whole ecosystems (which unlike current Ecosystem Management defines ecosystem not as just a natural system but as the interface between humanity and nature) and their health and integrity over their instrumental use. Although my synthesis and application of Kant's philosophy focuses on environmental risk and not on public lands and resource policy, the Justice from Autonomy paradigm and its Resource to Recovery context model as components of a new Ecosystem Design Approach to policy argument may provide a fit theoretical foundation for the full and proper operationalization of Ecosystem Management by environmental agencies. My analysis of wilderness and wildlife policy in chapter 10 comes to many of the same conclusions described as goals of Ecosystem Management (Gordon 1993, 242–43).

3. While economic theory is devoid of any attempt to consider anything but the instrumental value of nature, even philosophers and practitioners alike have struggled with the notion of "rights" or "integrity" for nature (Thoreau 1985; Leopold 1977; Nash 1989). The most significant dilemma is the attempt to have but a single "moral" definition of the ethical terminology that applies to both humanity and nature. This is a dilemma as long as the locus of value for human beings is their individual integrity while nature's integrity is holistic. In addition, the application of moral terms and responsibilities to nature seems to lack logical sense. How can individual animals have rights without duties? How can they have rights without moral capacities? If it is not the individual animal, then how can natural systems have group integrity or rights while the term is only applicable to individuals? A good example of the trouble with this concept of ecosystem integrity can be seen in Laura Westra's book *An Environmental Proposal for Ethics: The Principle of Integrity* (1994).

Westra attempts to make nature's integrity a centerpiece of environmental ethics and generates many problems for policy applications in the process. First, her ecosystems do not include humanity (xiii), her focus is primarily on pristine wilderness (41; 59; 217–18), her concept of integrity is both too complex (separating structural from functional integrity, chapter 2) and too simple (trying to apply a single moral definition of integrity designed for human individuals to whole natural systems [67; 156–57]), forcing her to float uncomfortably between bio- and ecocentric environmental ethics (122; passim). These problems make it very hard to understand the complexity of the human–natural system interface and can only recommend, in the end, a hands-off policy toward nature and "buffer" or "integrity zones" to separate humanity from nature (216–19).

Her palpable struggle to come to terms with the concept of integrity as it bridges human and natural worlds begs further argument and also attention to how the concept might find greater use as an evaluative tool in making policy for whole systems that include humanity and nature, in "pristine" and not so pristine conditions, and where duties might be derived that would guide human collective and individual choice in the wide cross-section of issues facing environmental politics. One way to create a new and more useful definition of integrity is to begin with established philosophical systems that have already done much of the work to integrate concepts and derive principles (e.g., Kant's philosophical politics).

Westra addresses Kantian ethics in her efforts, first dismissing him as a possible foundation for her argument (81; 96–97), and then contending that Kantian ethics might be sympathetic to her work (175; 211). In the end she calls for further research and writing and a complete examination (175) of Kant's philosophical system as a possible foundation for a theory of the "integrity" of nature.

My concern here is to present a "complete" examination of Kantian ethics and politics which may take care of many of the dilemmas suffered by Westra and provide a new argument paradigm for policymakers attempting to include the intrinsic value of both humanity and nature, with distinct but interdependent definitions, in environmental policy about nature as a whole, both where humanity has disturbed it and where it has not. My effort is offered in the spirit of utilizing Kantian philosophy to move one more step in the evolution of the concept of integrity as a practical policy tool.

4. During the course of the argument in this book, the strategic context of human collective action will be analyzed through the use of "games" like the prisoner's dilemma, chicken, the assurance, and pure coordination games. These game formats will be used as heuristic devices for an understanding of the process through which individual choice becomes collective policy (Luce and Raiffa 1957; Hardin 1982a; Mueller 1979).

5. Ecosystem is written with an uppercase E because it represents the interaction of both human and natural systems and not just the internal working of natural systems. See chapter 4 for details.

PART I

Economic Policy Argument and Environmental Metapolicy

The dogmas of the quiet past,
are inadequate to the stormy present . . .

1

The Market Paradigm and Comprehensive Policy Argument

Law is codified policy. Policy is persuasive argument. Argument is a combination of theory and experience bound together with moral principles. The law, as it applies to environmental risk, represents policy argument in its most concrete form: that of statute and written regulation. These "laws" are not static, however, but evolving, and they find their direction within the alternative theories that exist in the background policy discussions of which they are a concrete component. As a court decides a risk case, or as an agency writes regulations to apply a statute, they integrate both the letter and spirit (or metaphysics) of the law in an effort to produce a result that is both morally relevant and responsive to some definition of the public interest. The standards that measure moral relevancy and our definition of the public interest are policy standards, for policy is an ongoing debate meant to adequately define and represent the interest of all parties in collective choice. Policy argument, made in public forums, before courts, and in administrative procedures, defines both the law and its application. Law is therefore a creature of policy argument and a product of the process by which we deliberate over public choices.

If all policy arguments combine current practice and background theory, bound together by moral principle, then, before we examine the theory and practice of environmental risk (in the next two chapters), we are obliged to examine the formal aspects of policy argument itself. Only then can we fully analyze the power of efficiency in current environmental policy and law while also establishing a template for alternative nonmarket arguments.

Practical Reason, Argument, and the Policy Process

Within *The Critique of Pure Reason*, Immanuel Kant (C1) is credited with a "Copernican" Revolution in philosophy (Cassirer 1981, VII and forward; Appelbaum 1995, 6, 11; Allison 1983; Deleuze 1984, 1–11). Specifically, Kant contends that humans have a tendency to create categories and schemas, so that we may sort and name the physical world in ways that simplify complexity, aid understanding, and correspond to our intellectual predispositions. Our status as the ultimate expression of nature (Kant C3, §§ 83–84) grants us the sole privilege of being that species who names and categorizes the rest of nature to increase our knowledge of it.[1]

Humans are conceptualizers; we need models of how things work. Kant identifies this predisposition to create and categorize reality as the basic means by which we cope with the complexity of the world around us. In terms of our sociopolitical lives, public policy is the expression of our attempt to deal with complexity, and to collectively address present uncertainties and the unknown future by establishing standards of cooperation. Public policy therefore requires schema.

Creating policy, like all of our attempts to deal with the material world, requires us to name, sort, and categorize in order to obtain a general conceptualization of a complex issue, ideas about what ought to be done about it, and a sense of how these objectives can be achieved. The simplest issue is too elaborate to handle in its specificity and entirety; we need a shorthand with which to organize its inherent complexity. The assumptions we take into our decision making determine our responses, expectations, and the standards by which we will accept justification and judge success in public policy.

In the next two chapters of this book we will be involved in a critical argument about the fit between market-efficiency assumptions and the theory and practice of environmental risk. I will argue that efficiency represents the core principle of risk law and policy and that a concern for an efficient economy has quite consistently trumped concerns for environmental quality. We need to consider how a principle, like efficiency, gains a *core* status in policy argument that allows it to determine policy. If we think of the environment in terms of efficiency, why is this so?

The answer to this question is found, first, in the way that human reason struggles with understanding, second, in the importance of argument to policy, and third, in the critical role that one's conceptualizations of reality play in the definition of a "reasonable" policy argument. A "reasonable" argument has three phases. First, humans understand through their theoretical capacity to simplify, that is, categorize and name or model reality. Second, these simplifications are tested through argument. Third, the resulting arguments, in order of their persuasiveness, determine what we consider to be "practical" or "real." What we consider conventional, or realistic, is a function of which policy arguments are most persuasive, while the persuasiveness of a policy argument is itself a function of the "common sense" of the theoretical conceptualizations and practical models that inform, either obviously or surreptitiously, those policy arguments.

Therefore, in order to appreciate the power of the principle of efficiency, we must understand the way its underlying assumptions reflect a perceived set of persuasive truths that provide it a foundation. With this undergirding, we can analyze how the concept of efficiency is translated into material conditions, decision maxims, and methods of application that further translate theory into practice, or "truths"[2] into reality. Efficiency is, in this way, the centerpiece of a schema or paradigm of argument: the market paradigm. We need to understand how this paradigm creates a persuasive model of reality before we can apply it to the characteristics of environmental risk and make judgments about the practical context in which risk regulation is argued and decided.

In applying cost-benefit methods to environmental-risk issues, an administrator may not fully comprehend or analyze the fundamental assumptions and individual components of classical economics that support the market paradigm or fully understand or analyze the model thus created for the context of environmental decision making. But these fundamental assumptions, models, and conceptualizations that are accepted as truth representing common sense subsequently grant efficiency power as a "reasonable" standard to determine public choice, even in situations where it is not entirely appropriate. The "power" of efficiency is in the "power" of the market paradigm as a strategy of policy design. By defining persuasiveness the market paradigm places the burden of proof on other competing principles to establish conditions where the default principle of efficiency ought not be applied.

This may explain why nonefficiency options are frequently characterized as "fuzzy," uncertain, unclear, and unscientific, while efficiency analysis is considered moral, scientific, and factual as a policy tool (Stokey and Zeckhauser 1978). The market strategy is a "convention" in David Hume's sense ([1740] 1975, 489–91). It represents an evolved set of expectations with known persuasive advantages. Market strategy holds the status of a social habit or custom that requires little conscious thought, only practiced acts, to maintain its validity. Even though many voices are left unsatisfied that efficiency is the proper principle for environmental policy, the tenacity of the "common sense" of the market paradigm as a conventional conceptualization of public policy holds the moral high ground in the debate. The most recent manifestation of this is the attempts by the Republican Congress, since 1994, to apply risk-cost-benefit analysis to all health, safety, and environmental regulation as representing a common sense and scientific approach to regulation (Breyer 1993; Graham and Wiener 1997).[3]

If the dominance of efficiency is a result of the persuasive strength of the market strategy, then the power of an alternative principle will rise or fall on the basis of its provision of a complete and persuasive alternative strategy; that is, an alternative paradigm and context model that meets all of the formal requirements that the market strategy now serves. In addition, only by studying the structure of the market paradigm will we be able to understand the fundamental assumptions of the economic approach and critically analyze each of its components. Here, we may convert those who support market assumptions by showing how ill-fit these assumptions are to questions of environmental concern. Conscious analysis is the first step in forcing convention to change.[4]

If our ultimate task is to replace market values with environmental values, then our primary concern must be to construct an integrated nonefficiency-based strategy to replace economic precepts in environmental policy design.

But this task requires that we first understand what is meant by policy design and its place within the policy process.

Policy Design: The Strategy and Tactics of Public Choice

According to Schneier and Gross, "[f]ollowing Clausewitz, *strategies* are usually regarded as the general plans and allocations of resources designed to achieve broad policy objectives; *tactics*, as the specific maneuvers designed to achieve these and other immediate advantages" (1993, 4). Bobrow and Dryzek argue that policy "[d]esign is the creation of an actionable form to promote valued outcomes in a particular context. It is the emphasis on clarified values and context sensitivity that promises amelioration of [policy] problems" (1987, 201).

If policy design is the clarification of values and context, whereas strategy is delineated from tactics in terms of the distinction between that which is general and theoretical versus that which is specific and practical, then it may help us to understand the demands of policy strategies if we see them as part and parcel of policy design and its strategic and tactical processes.

Design takes place within, and acts as fuel for, the policymaking process. Let us begin with what Steven Kelman (1987, 6–8) calls a "roadmap" of this process. First is the policy idea, which is "a proposal for some change in government action." Next, ideas compete with one another in the political process and a political choice is made among them. Next, these public choices must be implemented by government. In production, more policy choices are made (e.g., in the process of writing regulations from statutes) and "just as political choices specify and modify policy ideas, so too does the production process specify and modify political choices that have been made." The fourth step in the process is final government actions (e.g., the final rule), which produces real-world outcomes. "The connection between government policies and a set of real-world outcomes is always a hypothesis by policymakers about the effect of certain actions on those at the receiving end."

Kelman describes a process by which the general is made specific, by which tactics are attached to developed strategies so that ends can be realized. We can utilize this model of the process to isolate the strategic dimension of policy design and also to recognize the overall process by which one may create policy through schema, moral principle, and argument. As we trace the development of policy ideas to the final actions of government, policies develop more specific features than they had when they first began (Kelman 1987, 8).

Policy design has both a tactical and a strategic phase (see fig. 1.1). The strategic phase begins with the real-world outcomes of final government action on any issue. If one perceives that *is* does not measure up to what *ought* to be, then one returns to the policy idea(s) at the beginning of the process and analyzes them for their relevance to the issues at hand and their outcomes. This feedback loop, imposed upon Kelman's roadmap, gives us the genesis of a policy design strategy in the first step of the policy process: the policy idea.

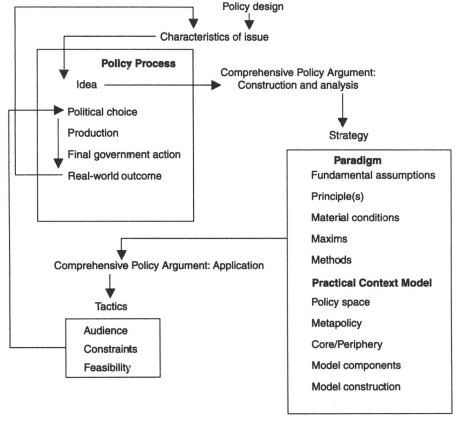

FIGURE 1.1
An Anatomy of a Policy Design Approach

The tactics of policy design can be described within the other steps of Kelman's roadmap. Tactics begin with a set of strategic assumptions (i.e., paradigm) and a model of the world drawn from these assumptions (i.e., context model). A context model orders the world in terms of the principles and priorities set up by the paradigm. As informed by the strategic conceptualization of the policy idea in its paradigm and context model, the tactics actualize the strategy, in light of the contingencies of political choice, production, government action, and the real-world outcomes that will again be compared to the standards of success prescribed in the design strategy itself.

Strategy defines tactics as tactics define reality, and this chain of causality is what must be understood if we are to construct a competitive design strategy for environmental risk. We must think about policy within a schema so that when we apply reason to policy it is within this structure that we are both analyzing present law and synthesizing alternative public policy (fig. 1.2).

The analytic process starts with real-world outcomes and moves from these specifics, inductively, to the broader parameters of the ideals and strategy that gave us present law. By contrast, the synthetic policy process begins with the

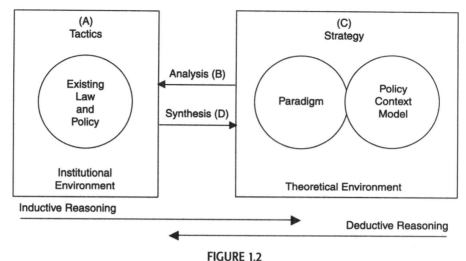

FIGURE 1.2
The Strategy and Tactics of Comprehensive Policy Argument

(*A*) The current state of law and policy. We begin with the existing final government action produced by past tactical process steps (e.g. political choice, production, final government action); (*B*) Inductive reasoning, which starts with the specific law and policy, and, through analysis, derives its more general core paradigm and practical context model. Here, during the critical analysis phase of comprehensive policy argument, one makes the first trip from the institutional to the theoretical environment; (*C*) Analysis and redefinition of current strategy to change the paradigm and context model that is into a new strategy (paradigm and context model) for what ought to be. Here the binding agent of moral principle is added to integrate an overall strategic plan that will be able to prescribe the proper ground-level tactics to apply theory to practice; (*D*) The deduction of alternative policy from a new paradigm and context model. Here during the constructive synthesis phase of comprehensive policy argument, one makes the second, return trip, moving anew from the theoretical to the institutional environment by starting with the general theory and deriving specific recommendations for policy choice.

general parameters of the present strategy and, by deductively searching and changing the character of its component parts, redesigns strategy and tactics. As the ends of policy are characterized in strategy, so acceptable means are defined within tactics. Together these describe present law and give imperatives to future policy change.

Kelman's definition of the policy idea can be further articulated if we think of it as the strategic phase of policy design. This strategic phase has two component parts: the theoretical paradigm at its foundation and the practical context model of the world that this paradigm creates for the decision maker (see fig. 1.1). The policy strategy now offers a point of departure both for understanding present policy and for synthesizing alternatives.

In discovering the generic structure of a policy paradigm and context model, we can understand what formal properties the Economic Design Approach contains. Then we can acknowledge the logical, moral, and structural requirements for an alternative design approach that could compete for core status in environmental law and policy.[5] My assumption is that any principle, within any integrated system of thought, has the potential to offer a fully integrated, three-dimensional, and competitive line of argument with its own definition of "good" policy.[6] Our concern is to construct a design strategy appropriate to environmental risk, while simultaneously finding the proper scope for instrumental economic value.[7]

The structure of the market argument is paramount, not because form alone gives the economic approach its power to determine policy, but because the structure organizes the components of the market into a powerful and persuasive model for policy choice. Although the structure of paradigm and context model at the foundation of policy design and tactical policy outcomes is insufficient to grant dominance to a principle in policy debate, it is a necessary prerequisite for that principle to gain the position of a legitimate and competing line of policy argument.

By studying the content and structure of the market paradigm and context model, we will construct a framework for what I will call "Comprehensive Policy Argument" and then use this framework to analyze both market efficiency and our Kantian alternative paradigm for policy choice.

The Economic Design Approach and Comprehensive Policy Argument

The idea of a paradigm will be addressed before considering the components of the practical context model.

What Is a Paradigm?

The concept of a "paradigm" comes from the physical sciences in general and from Thomas Kuhn's book *The Structure of Scientific Revolutions* (1962) in particular. Although within this exposition of the historical and methodological process of scientific inquiry, Kuhn may have as many as twenty-one different definitions of paradigm (Masterman 1970), paradigm has come to represent the integrated theoretical conceptualization of a field of inquiry. Paradigm defines and synthesizes the beliefs, ideals, observed facts, and normative principles of a worldview. In the words of Jong Jun, a paradigm is "[a] theoretical framework for understanding the world, based on assumptions that are taken for granted[8] as valid" (Jun 1986, 57).

Within a field of study, like physics, Kuhn suggests that a single or dominant paradigm comes to define our conceptualization of reality until its theory no longer can be verified in reality. Then, in the process of "scientific revolution" a new paradigm, which integrates theory and observation more closely, replaces the old paradigm. The Newtonian paradigm, for example, dominated our view of the world until replaced by the conceptualization of time and space given to us by Einstein.[9] In this manner, the history of science might be described as a series of paradigm successions where one integrated worldview is dominant in terms of its power through evidence until another comes along that is acknowledged to better represent observed or theoretical reality.

Paradigms are comprehensive and influential within the "thinking" and "action" of actors who function within their worldview. A paradigm dominates others by its capacity to define what is a "fact" and to influence not only what is seen as important to a decision, but what decisions need to be made and how.

> A paradigm is a fundamental image of the subject matter within a science. It serves to define what should be studied, what questions should be asked, how they should be asked, and what rules should be followed in interpreting the answers obtained. The paradigm is the broadest unit of consensus within a science and serves to differentiate one scientific community (or sub-community) from another. It subsumes, defines, and interrelates the exemplars, theories, methods and instruments that exist within it. (Ritzer 1975, 7)

In the humanities and social sciences the idea of a single paradigm or worldview being dominant and then being replaced by another, in succession, seems less sensible. Bernard Williams describes the difference between science and ethics in terms of the latter's lack of convergence upon a single definition or explanation of reality.

> In a scientific inquiry there should ideally be a convergence on an answer, where the best explanation of that convergence involves the idea that the answer represents how things are, whereas in the area of the ethical, at least at a high level of generality . . . there is no such coherent hope. (Williams 1989, 68)

If "convergence" is considered "unrealistic" in the field of ethics, the concept of a series of single dominant paradigms is argued to be unworkable in the policy studies context.

> It is doubtful that the public administration field can ever validly be viewed as having successive paradigms, simply because the discipline will never become that much of an actual scientific community. Rather, the field will continue to have competing paradigms (or theories) that exist simultaneously, with some tending to be more popular than others. (Jun 1986, 61)

However, despite the drawbacks noted, the concept of paradigm is still of use to us, both in its capacity to describe the milieu in which policymakers and public administrators make choices, and in explaining the power of economic principle in policy analysis. First, I contend that a paradigm based on market assumptions and the principle of efficiency is the "dominant" paradigm defining public policy choice. This book is an attempt to put this influence in relief and suggest that we need new ways of looking at policy in general and environmental risk in particular. Second, the concept of paradigm can be redefined for the ethical/public policy realm without losing the basic idea that, within policy argument, one particular principle and its essential assumptions tend to hold the "moral high ground" in relation to its competitors (Gillroy 1992a).

Within a field of policy discourse, competing parallel lines of arguments can exist even as one dominates the field providing "the" most fundamental standard for policy analysis.[10] This approach reflects Jun's point that a plurality of theoretical conceptualizations or paradigms exists within a policy area at the same time, but also allows for dominance within this pluralism.

Not all policy actors in a particular issue area converge upon the ethics of a single paradigm to the exclusion of all others, but distinct constituencies form around a set of paradigms that influences all who participate in the deliberation over and debate of a public issue. One paradigm, or line of argument, can still achieve dominance, because it is more persuasive or influential in policy argument and because it contains assumptions and principles "that are taken for granted as valid."

Although the assumed validity of the dominant policy paradigm makes it the trump card in policy choice, it can be replaced by any of the existing competitive arguments when another set of assumptions comes to provide a more persuasive consensus on the issue. However, a "revolution" in policy choice requires, first, that the assumptions, principles, and ends of the trump paradigm be analyzed for their true relevance and not simply "assumed to be valid." Second, any fit competitor will have to match its predecessor in logic, consistency, and completeness. Paradigms will be replaced only by other complete paradigms.

What Is a Paradigm's Generic Structure?

How is it that we make collective decisions? What assumptions do we make about individuals, their collective action, and the role of the state in producing justice? How do these theoretical assumptions generate moral principles? How are these moral principles applied to the material conditions of human lives, and how can these conditions create ethical maxims for decision making and methods for the application of theory to practice?

Recently the literature of policy analysis has begun to include concern for two dimensions of collective choice that allow for a fuller and more comprehensive examination of public issues. The first of these dimensions concerns inclusion of normative as well as empirical information in policy choice (Sagoff 1988; Gillroy and Wade 1992). The second dimension moves toward a focus on argument in addition to technical analysis (Majone 1989; Bobrow and Dryzek 1987; Forester 1993; Fischer and Forester 1993) as a prerequisite to the expression of policy as power to coerce.[11] Both these dimensional shifts in approaching public policy have influenced each other, for the move to include normative considerations in the core of policy assessment has forced the focus on technical analysis to expand to include normative and comprehensive policy argument as the basis of decision making.

In an attempt to understand the logical structure of policy paradigms, one needs to discover the logic of questions, the categories, and the schemas of a generic policy argument. In this way, we can understand how arguments in this specific issue area can be better structured so that they address the critical components of these public choices.

I will assume that all policy argument has a similar structure as part of the process of policy design and that this structure has two component parts: theoretical foundations (mostly normative) and practical constraints (mostly empirical). The first of these will be the subject of the paradigm and the second will be addressed by my definition of the context model which follows shortly. I suggest that only by combining these two elements is a policymaker able to fully comprehend the transition between theory and practice in the argument she designs. I will call this logical framework, or model, for argument paradigm construction, "Comprehensive Policy Argument" (CPA). I argue that the theoretical structure has five components: (1) fundamental assumptions about individuals, collective action, and the role of the state; (2) operating principles; (3) the material conditions of these principles; and (4) maxims of action, yielding (5) methods of application. In addition, I contend that these components provide categories for answers to a series of applied questions drawn from deontic logic. These questions facilitate an understanding of (1) *why* an issue ought to be considered a public policy dilemma, (2) *what* end we ought to pursue in solving it, and (3) *whether* one option or another is the proper means to that end.

The authority of efficiency as a principle in environmental-risk decisions is a result of two factors: first, it is derived from a pre-existing, systematic, and complex normative foundation, and second, it has the ability to derive a relatively simple and concrete methodology from this complex normative foundation. Specifically, I contend that the strength of efficiency as a principle or standard of judging and justifying environmental-risk decisions relates to the assumption, by the user, that behind the principle lies a complete and persuasive normative logic from which efficiency is derived and, further, that efficiency so justified can then produce a cost-benefit method that is relatively simple and straightforward in applying a rich theoretical paradigm to specific instances of policy practice. If the strength of efficiency is in its combination of complex normative theory and simple applied method, this may explain why no major alternatives have become available.

Although scholars have approached policy methodology and analysis with distinct logical frameworks (Fischer 1980; MacRae 1976; Meehan 1981, 1990; Dryzek 1983, 1987), this work lacks either sufficient normative complexity in the foundation of alternative principle(s) or simplicity of method in turning theory into practice. Those suggesting alternative principles to efficiency have not integrated pre-existing normative systems into their arguments to lend broader foundational definitions to isolated values (Williams 1989, 72 passim). Neither have these theorists been concerned with the formal framework within which policy argument must be carried on, giving incomplete guidelines for defining questions or failing to identify requirements that answers must accommodate.

Working separately, those who have created alternative logical frameworks and methods of argument have neglected to anchor these "formal" representations of thought with normative foundations, and further, have presented such elaborate formal models that they confuse and dissuade the practitioner from using them. Overall, alternatives to the dominance of the market paradigm in policy argument have presented the policymaker with theory that is either too morally vague to be of use in concrete application or too formally elaborate and clumsy to be readily accessible to the average practitioner. Two examples will suffice to make this point.

Mark Sagoff has suggested nonmarket principles upon which environmental policy should be built (1988, 7). Sagoff encourages the decision maker to make categorical distinctions between preferences and values, consumer and citizen, and private and public interests, as well as between methods and virtues. The problem lies in the rich texture of the "market" side of these distinctions and the less clear or precise meaning of Sagoff's "nonmarket" alternatives. What does "value" mean in this context? How is one specifically a "citizen"? What distinct responsibilities, for individual and policymaker alike, result from conversion to these terms? What is meant here by a unique "public" interest? Is it just the sum of individual interests or a specific condition of the whole that is greater than the sum of its parts? What is the specific value in this condition? How can virtue be defined for the policymaker? Whose virtue? How can one make collective decisions without method? These distinctions can and must be made if proper environmental policy decisions are to result. Such distinctions, however, beg for a rich, systematic, normative foundation to make them workable and integrated concepts within an alternative policy paradigm.

Frank Fischer (1980) offers an example of a logic too complex to operationalize. He prescribes a logic of questions for the policymaker that allow her to integrate nonefficiency values into the choice process. However, to use this new "methodology" the individual must ask as many as thirteen logical-process questions arranged in four categories each time a decision must be made. In addition, there are no categories or guidelines for the specification of answers that might aid in integrating them into a normative system, simplifying the process. Were a decision maker to seriously want to adopt Fischer's methodology, she would have to commit a great amount of time and effort to asking questions and providing answers and would face this same maze for each policy issue. Fischer's "method" lacks the concreteness and formal simplicity of balancing costs and benefits while it makes the search for alternatives to the market unduly complex and too theoretical to be easily applied to practical cases.

Sagoff and Fischer, among many others, recognize that a competitive foundation for policy choice that seeks to break the market's hold on the analysis of public issues requires both a set of new principles and a logic of questions. However, any alternative principles must be erected upon an integrated system of normative supports; at the same time, any formal logic of questions must be less complex while providing a schema of categories that better define what the "proper" range of answers must address. Only with these requirements will it be possible for the decision maker to get at the core of the policy issue and turn normative principles into usable empirical methods.

A call for a policy strategy with principle at its foundation is the call for normative or moral theory.[12] The advantage of the market is that it is built upon a systematic and widely accepted normative base of classical economics. The principle of efficiency in policy argument utilizes this normative microeconomic/moral theory to define terms, relationships, and values so that efficiency becomes a foundational concept from which methodology can be rendered. Cost-benefit methods, derived from the normative market assumptions of welfare, preference, and Kaldor improvements, therefore utilize an existing ethical system of definitions, standards, and relationships to justify their validity within the process of policy design (Gillroy 1992a).

If the power of efficiency lies in its adoption of a pre-existing normative system of relationships within classical economics or the private market, then, if one wishes to offer an alternative basis for choice, one ought to adopt another pre-existing normative system utilizing the framework of CPA to render principles from assumptions and method from these principles. CPA is expressly designed for this purpose.

The strategic approach to policy argument and design intended to set up paradigms of thought to compete with the principle of efficiency and its market foundations can utilize pre-existing integrated systems of moral theory to provide alternative foundations for public choice principles and accessible methods of application from those principles. CPA will aid the policymaker in making these selections. Using any pre-existing normative system (from Locke's to eco-feminism), she can segregate those assumptions and principles related to public choice and tie them to concrete material conditions, maxims of choice, and methods of application. In effect, CPA allows a person to construct paradigms with both normative texture and methodological simplicity by answering questions and filling in predefined categories. The result should be a wider variety of paradigms (as tools) at the disposal of analysts and citizens alike.[13]

Using CPA, we will see both the inherent normative structure of efficiency analysis and how alternative normative systems can be brought to the consideration of environmental-risk choices.

The Market Paradigm and Comprehensive Policy Argument

The process of policy research has many stages and actors, but at each stage any actor who wishes to analyze a public choice, in order to affect it, must understand its constituent parts and the worldview with which choices are made. To accomplish this, the decision maker may use research as a series of actions aimed at a complete (or near-complete) accumulation of knowledge (fact and value) about the issue (Majchrzak 1984, 12).

Although we may all recognize, on a transcendental level, that normative concerns are central to this evolution, and that indeed they may determine the way in which an issue is described and its policy solutions constructed, the overt inclusion of normative concerns in policy analysis is, for many, still unrealized. Here, I will suggest a specific map of the normative and logical substructure of policy argument so that one might understand the central place of normative concerns in the process and how theory evolves within the research itself toward a comprehensive argument that includes nonmarket principles as standards of choice and accountability. CPA can contribute to the methodological analysis of policy argument, sorting inconsistent from logical assumptions and dogmatism from legitimate normative principles in order to integrate principles with empirical evidence. In this way CPA can be applied, persuasively, to public dilemmas.

The Logical Process Questions

In describing the process of thinking about policy, according to the deontic logic of rules, David Braybrooke (1991, 1–2) defines a policy as being composed of three elements.[14] These elements are " a *volk* or demographic condition, specifying to whom it applies. . . a *wenn* condition, which describes the circumstances in which the prohibition that is at the heart of the rule applies, [and] a *nono* part, which specifics the actions or sequences of actions that are prohibited by the rule." In addition to the deontic logic of rules describing a policy, Braybrooke (1991, 2) also creates a logic of questions that define a policy argument. Braybrooke distinguishes what he calls an "issue simpliciter" question, "shall we have a flat rate income tax or a proportional income tax or a progressive income tax?" from an "issue-circumscription" question, "what shall we do about taxing income?" He argues that the "issue-circumscription sort of issue" is "of a higher order" than issue-simpliciter sort of issues.

These two issue-questions, added to a third of my own construction, define the logic of questions required by CPA. My third question, and the most basic of all, is the "why" or "issue-identification" question. Why is it important to consider (X) a proper subject for collective choice? Before we can ask simpliciter and circumscription questions we must gather our intuitions about why a current state of affairs is not what it ought to be and why the public realm is the correct venue for finding a solution. Together, these three questions create a bridge between theory and practice by establishing the basic questions about practical matters that require normative analysis and theoretical constructions in their answers. With direct answers to these questions, we have identified the underlying logic of paradigms in the policy design process.

If policy design can be considered the "activities and attitudes that shape the transformation of policy inputs into outputs and impacts" (Dunn 1981, 333), then this transformation hinges on an answer to the issue-circumscription question. This central and complex question builds on the basic intuition that an issue is the proper realm of public choice (issue-identification question) and then sets the stage for a choice between alternatives (issue-simpliciter question) in which whatever alternative is chosen becomes ideal-regarding (Barry 1990) as it sets policy and the standards by which the results of action will be judged.

The normative bookends that are the issue-identification and issue-simpliciter questions are controlled by the argument developed in the issue-circumscription stage of the process. Here, moral principles and their material conditions are defined as the inherent standards of the paradigm and the greater design strategy. Ultimately, the empirical dimensions of the strategy and the applied tactical success of the policy will be judged by the moral principles in this stage of paradigm definition. Here we ask: What is important about the policy problem and what should be done about it?

The formal schema is made up of three stages of issue-questions over three levels of analysis (see fig. 1.3). The three levels of analysis include the individual, the collective, and the state; the three process questions ask *why* an issue qualifies as a public concern, *what* ends hold moral imperatives, and *whether* one ought to choose X, Y, or Z solution as appropriate means to actualize these ends.

Each stage is defined by the categories within which the answers must be confined. The *why* question must be answered by reference to what the fundamental assumptions of the argument are concerning the characterization of our three levels of analysis. The characterization of the individual, the collective-action problem, and the definition of the "legitimate" state answer the question of why this issue is fit for public policy argument. The rigor of thought necessary to make these connections replaces noise, confusion, and uncertainty with argument, analysis, and persuasion.[15]

In the second stage, once the issue is classified as a public one, the question is *what* ought to be done to provide a solution to the policy problem. The answer to this question involves setting imperatives and moral standards by deriving operating principles from the fundamental assumptions and then assigning those material conditions that will make the moral principles of the argument manifest in people's lives. It is these manifest conditions that the policymaker will be able to allocate, distribute, or in some way provide as a means to the realization of principle in policy practice.

Finally, in stage three, the *whether* question requires the policymaker to choose the "proper" alternative. She must formulate specific maxims and meth-

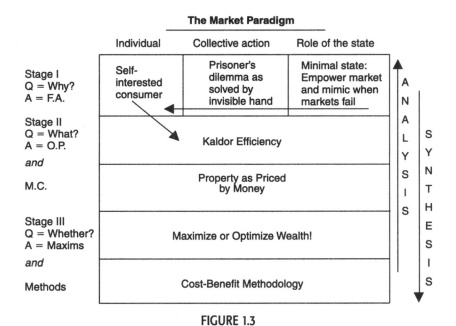

FIGURE 1.3
Comprehensive Policy Argument
F.A. = fundamental assumptions; O.P. = operating principle(s); M.C. = material conditions of principle(s).

ods of application to produce the guidelines with which she can make actual policy that agrees with the normative imperatives of her argument. The answer to the third-stage question lies in these maxims and the application methods derived from them. The methods will become a shorthand for the decision maker. In applying the method one is representing all the normative and empirical considerations that are foundational to it within the argument paradigm.

These steps, whether traditionally called policy development (Majone 1989, 145) or the structuring of a policy problem (Dunn 1981, 106), identify a policy dilemma and form the argument that will limit the choices and provide the moral imperatives through maxims of choice. This approach assumes that rational arguments can be made about normative issues (McLaren 1989; Snare 1992; Anderson 1979; Amy 1984) and that the traditional dominance of empirical description in policy decision-making is inadequate to answer the issue/process questions (Dryzek 1990, 142–48).

Schema Stage I: Question = Why? Answer = Fundamental Assumptions

The first step in using CPA is recognition of one's intuitions about a policy issue and the fundamental theoretical assumptions one makes across the three levels of analysis involved in policymaking (the individual, the collective, and the state).

The characterization of these "levels of analysis" must justify practical action by the policymaker, and therefore must satisfy two areas of concern: first, as pertains to a perceived distinction between *is* and *ought*, and second, in the conviction that this gap should be filled by "public" or "collective" action. If the policymaker assumes that policy issues are characterized by public means to the production of social and individual ends as collective goods,[16] her realization that some "thing" exists that should be provided or protected, but is not being addressed, would satisfy the first area of concern.

For a particular issue we must conclude that what *is*, is not what *ought* to be. This fundamentally normative intuition is the point of departure for the construction of rational policy argument. Next, definition and substance must be added to these intuitions by specifying or characterizing the actors and levels of analysis that the policy result must satisfy. Here the focus of the model becomes change. The purpose of policy is to detect where law is inadequate and where government can correct the situation. This definition of policy rejects the contention that policy is working within and to support the status quo (Stokey and Zeckhauser 1978, 4). From the vantage point of CPA, existing law is adjusted by policy argument.

The issue-identification question demands that one construct a three-dimensional analysis of the policy problem. Intuitions about the normative importance of the issue and the collective role in sponsoring change do not specify the details of the problem or how to solve it. But, sorting intuitions into three categories or levels of foundational assumptions helps to define a "rational" policy by forming the framework for the expression of operational principles that, in turn, inform practical methods of analysis and provide imperatives to the policymaker to decide what policy is chosen for analysis, how it is analyzed, and what results are seen as producing a "socially better" policy reality.

1. The Individual: The basic component of all foundational assumptions in policy analysis is the characterization of the individual. Here the analyst must be concerned with how the individual acts and why. What motivates the individual and how is the characterization of the individual critical to the solution of the problem? Who is the person? What concerns him or her? By what standards will he or she judge policy problems and solutions? Will preference, interests, rights, or other variables close the gap between is and ought, solving the policy problem?

For the market paradigm, with its foundations in classical economics, the individual is assumed to be a rational consumer. The individual's preferences for material goods and the provision of these products by the market are inhibited by central regulation which should not have precedence over the market. Classical economics assumes that the individual is a self-interested welfare maximizer concerned with little but personal satisfaction (Sen 1979). The individual's wants as a consumer and his or her overall welfare will matter most in any policy choice. Further, no one can judge the wants of the individual better than that individual (Sen 1970; Mishan 1982b). Self-interested motivation is both a want-regarding description of individual behavior and an ideal-regarding assumption that individuals are the best judge of such considerations (Barry 1990). The policy analyst, employing a normative base in classical economics, must render policy prescriptions that benefit the self-defined welfare preferences of the individual consumers who are his constituents.

2. Community and Collective Action: In addition to the isolated consideration of the individual, the dynamics of interpersonal choice and interaction should be considered in making public choices. The policymaker should specify what dynamic role the community plays in defining a "good" policy. Does the collective action of the political community and its interests represent more than the sum or aggregate of individual interests? What is the goal of collective action? What problems do individuals face in establishing cooperation? Is society a necessary level of analysis or concern? How do the community and the way it coordinates the actions of individuals give rise to the problem necessitating public action? How can attention to the collective-action problems of the society help to provide answers to the logical-process question?

Within the formal foundational assumptions of any policy analysis lies a general description of the problems inherent in convincing individuals to cooperate toward a common end: political community. This foundational assumption builds on the formal definition of the self that precedes it, while it informs the parameters of the "legitimate" state that will be subsequently defined. In the political community and the terms of collective action, we see the transition point between assumptions about the individual and about the state. Here, the importance of the community and the dilemmas of collective action help the decision maker to locate and clarify her intuitions about what a "socially better" policy is and how she might achieve it.

The market paradigm builds a collective level of organization with no distinct character independent of the individuals of which it is an aggregate. The whole is no more than the aggregate sum of individual wants and preferences, while collective action is primarily concerned with establishing just enough cooperation to satisfy the material interests of the most people possible without force or fraud connected to trade.[17] This represents a collective-action problem akin to a prisoner's dilemma (Goodin 1976; Axelrod 1984; Hardin 1982a), which is iterated in order to find an aggregation rule that can avoid either continuous exploitation or complete cessation of trade.

The solution to the prisoner's dilemma assumed by the market paradigm begins with a functioning "invisible hand" (Smith [1776] 1937, bk. 4, chap. 2) that coordinates the self-interested acts of each person toward the collective well-being of all. The effectiveness of the invisible hand, however, wanes when we move from a pure market context to the public sector. The collective-action problems involving over- or under-supply of common goods, free riders, and pollution effects external to markets cause the market to fail. This is where the market paradigm comes in. If we cannot have markets because of externality and commons[18] problems, then we can have administrators utilizing market assumptions making collective decisions for us. The market paradigm solves collective-goods problems by having policy argument mimic the solutions markets would produce, were they able to function.

Whatever the solution, community must be formed out of consumers through the terms of market exchange and, where these fail, through the aggregation of individual preference into a social ordering that reflects individual wants in collective choices (Mueller 1979; Gillroy and Wade 1992). The state may act as an aggregation mechanism, but no specific definition of a distinct political community exists to concern the analyst.

3. The Legitimate/Just State: The requirements of solving the collective-action problems faced by policymakers, and the normative attributes of the individual citizen as described above, help to define the last level of fundamental assumptions concerning the role of the just state. Policy design is concerned with the basic assumptions that define what makes a government legitimate (Fishkin 1979).[19] When considering legitimacy, one is concerned with what standards define social justice. What are the form, role, and objective of a just state achieving the overall goals of policy? What are the legitimate ends and moral limits of state action?[20]

For the market paradigm, the state has only two functions: to police and adjudicate contracts and to provide a surrogate decision process that can substitute when markets fail and allocations cannot be made without the involvement of government (Mishan 1982a, 1982b; Feldman 1980). The normative system underlying the market therefore defines the legitimate state as the "minimal" state (Nozick 1974; Posner 1983), maintaining the background legal institutions that protect market exchange and substituting when markets fail. The state is therefore active only to the extent it mimics market allocations (Gillroy and Wade 1992, 8). The paramount moral role of the legitimate state is to maintain existing markets, the property of the individual, and her right to trade it.

The institutions of the "minimal state" function to facilitate individual want-satisfaction and regulate behavior only to further this end. For the market paradigm, as a policy-analysis tool, the character of political institutions has been produced by a confrontation between the individual consumer and the need for government to facilitate cooperation, solve the prisoner's dilemma, and provide collective goods as the market would itself.

The market paradigm defines all three of its fundamental assumptions in terms of intuitions about how the conditions and results of private choice can be translated into public choice. It searches for an answer to the "why" question by transferring the assumptions of a competitive market into the public sphere. With these assumptions as a base, the analyst clarifies normative priorities and sets up a foundation for comprehensive policy argument that will influence the rest of the process and the resulting policy recommendations.

Schema Stage II: Question = What? Answer = Operating Principles and Material Conditions

In applying CPA, we derive operating principles from the fundamental assumptions and then define the material conditions of these normative principles. We need to understand what principles set the best standard of choice, given the fundamental assumptions, and then what material conditions, accessible to the decision maker, make the imperatives of the principle(s) physically real within the political community.

1. Operating Principles: To inform the developing policy argument and produce actual alternative public choices, it is critical to simplify the theoretical assumptions into principle(s) that can provide a shorthand for what is normatively essential in whatever policy is eventually produced. The operating principle sets the standard that will define what is right or good as well as what is and is not a "reasonable" policy or a "persuasive" argument. Defining a "rational" policy requires operating principles to form the basis of the policy imperative for the decision maker and then the creation of techniques or methods that the policymaker can easily use to apply these principles to practical decisions.

For the market paradigm, the protection and facilitation of each person's voluntary economic trade is the essential concern. Policy does not focus on community or state except to the degree to which they aid the individual in protecting his property and satisfying his wants. The levels of analysis (individual, collective, state) do not each render a distinct principle, but all are represented in a single one. The normative operating principle of the market is efficiency as it aggregates and satisfies individual preferences for wealth. Within the market, efficiency is defined by the Pareto condition, which asserts that a new state of affairs is more efficient than the status quo only if everyone is as well off or better off. This strong condition, that there exist no welfare losers in efficient trade, is not practical in public policy choice (Andrews 1999, 8–9). In public decisions there are likely to be both winners and losers and therefore efficiency is redefined there as the Potential Pareto Improvement. Otherwise known as Kaldor efficiency, a new state of affairs is now efficient if the winners gain enough that they could "hypothetically" compensate the losers and make everyone as well off or better off. Using Kaldor efficiency, one aggregates personal costs and benefits in order to maximize collective wealth but is basically indifferent to wealth distribution within the society (Gillroy and Wade 1992; Feldman 1980; Stokey and Zeckhauser 1978).

Although some may argue that profit maximization or other principles trump efficiency in the market paradigm, I contend that Kaldor efficiency not only is basic to profit, production, and consumption, but also, in its application, is assumed by the classical economist to protect the freedom of the individual and to maximize his utility. This claim will be the subject of the next chapter, where I argue that "freedom" or "autonomy as consent" is a liberty to consume where choice defines the efficient and material "good" of the person (Gillroy 1992a).

Kaldor efficiency is derived from the characterizations of the individual as a self-interested welfare maximizer, the definition of collective action as a preference aggregation problem, and the concern for a minimal state that charges the policymaker to protect property and voluntary trade. The imperatives are to satisfy as many individuals as possible and to provide as wide and growing an economy as possible so that the maximum number of individuals can find preference satisfaction. Using Kaldor efficiency as the operating principle of the market paradigm indicates the policy objective of maximizing aggregate social welfare.

2. Material Conditions: Merely defining the operating principles of a policy is insufficient. One should also define what material conditions can be manipulated by the policymaker to make these principles manifest in the day-to-day lives of constituents.

For the market, the sole material condition is wealth. This can be defined in many ways including property and possessions, but within markets all such concerns must be defined within the common metric of money. Price is the prominent sensor of the market and money is the currency of the price system. The signals of price are the only ones recognized and responded to by markets; it becomes critical for an entity or "thing" to have a proper price, reflecting its economic or instrumental value to the individual, so that it is properly counted in trade and evaluated as part of wealth maximization (Posner 1983; Feldman 1980).

The generation of profit in markets through Pareto efficiency is transferred into the public sector as wealth maximization through Kaldor efficiency. The material conditions of interest from the market point of view, therefore, are those where economic production is maximized and the most goods are produced for consumption, thus maximizing wealth, trade, and preference satisfaction as public policy.

We have now answered Braybrooke's issue-circumscription question for the market paradigm. The boundaries of acceptable policy alternatives have been set by establishing the operating principles and material conditions of these principles. Only one question remains, and it will provide maxims for day-to-day decision making and a methodology that citizens and administrators can use to apply the paradigm without direct reference to its principles or fundamental assumptions.

Schema Stage III: Question = Whether P1, P2, or P3? Answer = Maxims and Methods of Application

Stage III deals with those imperatives and rules of thumb, or methods of application, that each decision maker uses in order to make the moral force of the underlying normative system "real" for citizens and other policymakers wishing to apply the same normative standards without detailed considerations of their foundations. The central concern of the policymaker at this crucial point in the generation of an argument paradigm is to create a maxim, or imperative, that combines the operating principle and its material conditions. From this maxim one then derives a method of application that can eventually select tactical policy instruments (e.g., taxes, standards, liability law) that reflect the fundamental assumptions of the paradigm.

We understand, from Majone (1989, 116), that a policy instrument is a means to achieve the ends of the policy. Even though choosing specific instruments is a tactical choice determined by the context model of the paradigm (examined below), I would argue that the proper choice of means requires, first, that the ends of the policy be represented by the moral imperatives of decision maxims as these have been defined by the fundamental assumptions and principles of action. Then the methods of application, built upon these maxims, can render the complex framework of moral theory underlying a choice into simple and accessible methodological tools for decision making. In this way, the maxims define the choice and the methods implement them through the selection of proper policy instruments (e.g., taxes, standards) (Majone 1989, chap. 6).

1. Maxims: By combining operating principle and the material conditions it defines, one can produce an imperative or maxim for policy that helps the decision maker distinguish which alternative policy choices are compatible with the argument (those that promote the principle) and which are not compatible (those that reject the principle).

The market paradigm has but one maxim for the decision maker: Maximize Wealth! Kaldor efficiency is represented by maximization, and the material conditions, by wealth. The maxim implores the policymaker, in every choice she makes, to satisfy individual welfare preferences by maximizing net social welfare across the population. Under certain conditions, fully treated in chapter 3, the imperative may be to optimize instead of to maximize wealth, but in either case, the maxim seeks a state of affairs where it is not critical how the wealth is distributed as long as it is properly aggregated with as little government interference and cost to the economy as possible.

2. Methods: The purpose of CPA is to provide a framework or schema of categories that allows an individual policymaker either to recognize what underlies a method that he conventionally applies to his collective choices or to utilize an existing moral theory for the purposes of changing a public choice. I have argued that the key to doing both analysis and synthesis is to have a schema that combines normative strength in complexity of theory with practical strength in simplicity of method.

After one has constructed the CPA from a moral theory, or recognized the underlying normative and empirical conditions of an applied operating principle, this CPA is readily accessible to anyone, without reconsideration of its details. This easy access comes from a methodology that is derived from the maxims, which are derived from material conditions and principles that are ultimately derived from fundamental assumptions of the paradigm. With only an application of the methods, one represents the entire paradigm in policy choice.

Using the principle of efficiency, the market paradigm evolves the methodology of cost-benefit analysis (Mishan 1982a)[21] so that the ends and means of public issues are submitted to the Kaldor efficiency test in order to be recommended as reasonable public policy. Cost-benefit methodology acts as practical shorthand for the decision maker and allows her to apply the principle of efficiency and protect her foundational assumptions, from which the principle is derived, with a minimum of intellectual effort. Without having to answer any questions or retrace her steps through the logical schema, she has set the ideal-regarding standard for policy choice through concern for the definition and balancing of cost and benefits and she can decide among policy alternatives.

Once the market paradigm has rendered its maxim and a method of application through CPA, the policy analyst is ready to utilize the market paradigm to address the specific policy and choose an appropriate alternative that fits within the normative and empirical constraints of his or her argument. Each principle is then connected to a policy instrument through the maxims and methods rendered by those principles.[22]

For the market paradigm, the choice between alternative policies must reflect the principle of Kaldor efficiency as it relates to the control of pollution and the regulation of the economy. The analyst's maxim to Maximize Wealth causes him to make connections between choice and welfare, on the one hand, and between preference and welfare maximization on the other (Sen 1982, 66–67). These connections are realized in the effort to maximize social benefit through the use of cost-benefit methods. In efficiency analysis, alternatives will be acceptable to the degree they involve cost incentives and protect voluntary trade. Of primary concern is the allocation of goods related to the satisfaction of individual preferences and how these may be curtailed by the state in its third-party regulation of the economy to limit production of goods and externalities in favor of a cleaner environment. The burden of proof is on those who regulate the market, and in this way, interfere with its capacity to satisfy preferences. The use of economic incentives to affect consumer behavior informs the choice of alternative policy and answers Braybrooke's "whether" question, making one alternative (e.g., P2) more appealing than the others. The standard of evaluation demands that policy which minimizes government regulation while it maximizes benefits over costs and therefore most efficiently satisfies more individual wealth preferences than it disappoints.

Overall, for the market paradigm, the self-interest of the individual consumer, as made manifest in expressed preference, forms the touchstone for all environmental-risk policy decisions. The material satisfaction of these preferences is assumed to be of central importance and government policy should therefore be limited so as not to interfere with that material production that is meant to maximize satisfaction across the population.

Environmental risk, in this context, can only be regulated subject to individual preference and choice, and markets for risk are the best policy instrument, while the state mimicking risk markets will suffice as sound policy when risk markets fail (Aharoni 1981; Viscusi 1983, 1992). A risk market requires the sole assumption that individual choices for instrumental wealth accumulation must be respected regardless of the risks involved (Sagoff 1982). If we can assume that individuals will recognize and weigh risk within the strategic framework, where individual self-interest is the rational motivation, the collective-action problem allows only maximum trade of risk between actors with minimal third-party interference. Risk, like all things in the market, is a commodity, the disposition of which is left up to each trader, who is assumed to have sovereignty over her risk choices.

The concern of the policymaker, therefore, is to maximize wealth in an atmosphere where environmental risk is weighed symmetrically with all other risks, as a potential cost to the individual. The minimal state, and the administrator employing cost-benefit analysis, are only there to mimic the market allocation of risk by maximizing social welfare with minimal interference from nonmarket forces.[23]

Overall, the market paradigm finds a means to the ends of efficient preference aggregation in the policy instrument of a surrogate-market price system that would allow individual as well as collective risk generators to accept and/or impose risk on the basis of their "willingness to pay" for it. This internalizes the cost of any hazard, supports an expanding economy, and places one's preferences for a risky environment on an identical level with all other preferences, so that environmental quality is established at the point where the overall aggregate costs exceed the benefits. People will get the environment they are willing to pay for.

The details of choosing appropriate tactical policy instruments for the full application of the market paradigm, given the characteristics of the particular issue, require that we next consider the second component of policy design strategy. This is the phase of CPA that involves the construction of a practical context model from the principles and methods produced by the theoretical paradigm. Only with both components in hand can the policymaker enter the tactical phase of the policy process with the assurance that essential ends will not be compromised by inappropriately chosen means.

A Context Model for the Market Paradigm

Public policy is a combination of theory and practice or strategy and tactics. The tactical enactment of the policy is in administrative institutions, implementation instruments, and "real world outcomes" (Kelman 1987, 7). Public policy is also the strategic conceptualization of ends, standards, ideals, and plans that create justification for choice and means of evaluation and accountability. In describing the strategy of a policy, one is not only considering the theoretical argument paradigm that forms the foundation of the policy idea, but also the context model that is formed by defining what components create the particular policy space (Majone 1989, 158–59) under consideration, and how these components are evaluated and ordered relative to one another. In contemplating the tactics of a policy in the political choice and production stages of the process, one is considering the feasibility of the strategy, its possible constraints, audiences, and implementation instruments, which will themselves be defined in terms of the context model or worldview of the person employing the paradigm.

Both the strategy and tactics of a policy can be described as involving policy argument (Majone 1989, chap. 5). In the strategic phase of policy design one constructs one's CPA from the normative foundation of the paradigm, whereas in the tactical phase of policy design one uses the context model to judge feasibility and to adjust one's argument to empirical political contingencies.

The importance of a theoretical paradigm and its designation of methods from fundamental assumptions is that it forms the foundation for a worldview. Returning to natural science, we note the Newtonian paradigm created a mechanical worldview that affected how the human being and his environment were pictured outside the realm of science. Thomas Hobbes, for instance, builds his views of human nature, collective action, and the politics of the state from within a Newtonian view of the world (Hobbes [1651] 1968, bk. 1), as does Kant (C1).

When Einstein's vision replaced Newton's as the pertinent paradigm, the worldview it spawned changed the way in which philosophy and politics were perceived. The perceived failure of foundational theory in moral discourse and the growth of deconstructionism, post-modernism, and relativist ethical thought, with its concern for the context of politics in theories of justice (Walzer 1984; Larmore 1987, 1996; Rawls 1971), might be considered a pertinent implication of scientific relativity applied to social thought.

Although policy paradigms in public administration may not be as influential as paradigms in natural science, it is reasonable to suggest that one of the critical entailments of a paradigm as applied to environmental regulation is the model of the social and natural environment that is produced. I will call this worldview the practical context model, and define it as rendered from the par-

---

adigm's conceptualization of how it interrelates to, and arranges, both other paradigms within a designated policy space and the components of the world (i.e., humanity, nature, government, economy) around it.

The context model defines the worldview of the paradigm and is the practical intermediary between the theoretical paradigm and the tactical operation of the policy process in political choice, production, final action, and real-world outcome. The practical context of choice defines what components make up the world and which one has priority in collective decisions.

In chapter 2 of this book we will examine, in more detail, the application of the market paradigm to environmental-risk theory. In chapter 3, we will examine the practice of risk law and policy through the worldview, or context model, of the market paradigm. Before proceeding, we will introduce the vocabulary of policy space and establish how its ideas and logical relations are a natural outgrowth of the market paradigm applied as a context model or economic worldview. Giandomenico Majone's (1989) concepts of metapolicy (146–49), core/periphery (150–52), and policy space (158–59) will help to construct and map the theoretical landscape of the practical context model, within which our policy argument about the defining principles of environmental law will take place.

The Concept of Metapolicy

The most fundamental concept in defining a policy worldview is metapolicy. The concept of metapolicy can be traced to Majone (1989, 146–49), who provided policy with a dynamic and self-critical capacity by claiming that "our understanding of a policy and its outcomes cannot be separated from the ideas, theories and criteria by which the policy is analyzed and evaluated" (147). On the basis Berman's (1983, 8) definition of a "meta-law," where argument, analysis, and internal standards for evaluation are tied to the development of law and legal institutions, we can establish a dialectic for policy as a self-defining phenomenon through the concept of metapolicy.

Each metapolicy combines the existing debates, institutions, and processes regarding a public issue and encourages multiple or parallel lines of argument concerning an issue's collective disposition. This totality of argument and institutions represents the dynamic and ongoing debate about what is and ought to be in any area of public concern. Each line of argument within a metapolicy represents an alternative paradigm about what ought to be, and while one paradigm may dominate discourse as the most persuasive for any period of time, the other lines of argument remain in the metapolicy as options for the adjustment or change of that metapolicy over time.

Inherent in any metapolicy, and the most critical component of this concept, is the idea of the foundational moral principle within the dominant paradigm, which sets the internal standards of evaluation and justification for each metapolicy. Whatever line of argument is currently defining the metapolicy, its success as law will be judged by the principles internal to its persuasive argument. As long as these principles find actualization in the institutional application of policy through law, and these results cause what *is* to measure up to what *ought* to be (as defined by the principle), then the 'dominant' line of argument within the metapolicy holds its persuasiveness and law remains dynamic but constant.[24] That is, the law is constant in that the rules and expectations remain true to the operating principle of the dominant paradigm but dynamic in that the ongoing debate establishes options and distinct competitive moral standards which can be brought to the metapolicy as time and need require. What "is" the current law, is not the only option, even though it remains the most persuasive paradigm to us at any one time.

The operating principle of the dominant paradigm can be considered the *core principle* of the metapolicy. It is singular and not plural for a specific reason. Although a plurality of principles is useful for deliberation in public policy, in terms of choice and administrative consistency over choices, one principle inevitably will come to trump the others. As long as two or more principles and their corresponding paradigms can be assumed to have any conflicts in determining law, a single principle is necessary to define the essential character of the metapolicy and set the public expectations for those who are affected by it.

A single, fundamental core principle defines a metapolicy and cannot be sacrificed without the wholesale change of the character of that metapolicy. The "trump" principle is critical to decision making and must be repeatedly applied over time in order to set expectations and establish consistency in the public administration of the metapolicy. If competitive paradigms gain in persuasiveness, their core principles will also gain more power in the deliberation process until they trump the status quo principle and change the conventional metapolicy.

Change in policy and law occurs when we are no longer persuaded that the dominant context model, its underlying paradigm, and inherent moral standard are best for the issue. We then consider the alternative paradigms within the metapolicy (e.g., environment) for a better definition of what is at stake, how it should be handled, how the ends of the policy should be defined, and what the proper worldview looks like. This process of change can be gradual, as one line of argument is found, over time, to be progressively more persuasive as the dominant standard fades, or it can be sudden, as the dominant line of argument is abruptly replaced by a competitor. One might define the former as evolution and the latter as revolution, but no matter what they are called, the metapolicy is the sum total of the "ideas, conceptualizations and proposals advanced by policy actors, analysts, academics, and bureaucratic experts who share an active interest in that policy" (Majone 1989, 147).

The final dimension of a metapolicy that is important to our analysis of environmental law is the dialectic established between policy as theory and as practice. The institutions that translate metapolicy into law are themselves the product of policy arguments (Majone 1989, chap. 5). Institutions that we accept as authoritative (Hart 1961, chap. 6) or legitimate (Fishkin 1979) encapsulate those processes and practices that are persuasive to us. The parallel lines of argument within a metapolicy, in this way, have an effect upon the evolution of the institutions and process by which they are transformed into law. The development of metapolicy, as well as its ongoing dynamic quality, are therefore the result of an interactive process between competitive theories about what ought to be and the institutions and political processes that write and interpret these arguments as law: where *ought* becomes *is*. In Majone's words, "the relationship between policy and its intellectual superstructure, or meta-policy is a dialectic one" (Majone 1989, 166).

The Concepts of Core and Periphery

Metapolicy contains the elements of continuity and change, and in order to conceptualize the components that provide for both, it is useful to make the distinction, as Majone does, between core and periphery (1989, 150–54). Majone defines these two elements of a metapolicy to distinguish between "the relatively stable and rigid part of a policy and its more changing and flexible components" (150).

For our purposes it is useful to describe the core as that part of the metapolicy which contains its fundamental principle. The core principle provides the policy with its character and sets the standard for judging ends, means, accountability, and success. Therefore, it is the essential element in defining the dominant paradigm within the metapolicy. The core principle, with its dominant argument, gives the metapolicy its identity. Although not unchanging, the core resists change, and successful change represents a fundamental shift in the standard, and therefore the basic character, of the metapolicy. By our working definition of metapolicy, change takes place when a parallel argument and its essential principle, which exist within the metapolicy (although not in its core), replace the dominant or status quo principle of the metapolicy in the core. Here we agree with the spirit, if not the letter of Majone's definition.

> To say that the core represents the rigid part of the policy is not to suggest that it is immutable, but only that it changes more gradually and continuously than the elements of the periphery that are its transitory end-products. A radical transformation or abandonment of the core signifies a major change in policy—revolution rather than evolution, so to speak. (1989, 150)

In contrast to the core principles that create the essential standards and the identity of the dominant policy argument, the periphery contains the other elements of the metapolicy that are less directly critical to the integrity of the dominant argument but that contribute to the operationalization of the core principle.

> If the core provides continuity, the periphery—largely composed of programs and other concrete administrative activities that are intended to give effect to the core principles—provides flexibility. The need to adapt the particular programs through which the policy operates to ever-changing economic, social, and political conditions keeps the periphery in constant flux, but peripheral changes do not usually affect the core, except perhaps through their cumulative impact. (Majone 1989, 151)

The periphery also can be described as containing those parallel lines of argument that compete for dominance within any metapolicy. So, in addition to the institutions and processes that are to implement the core principles, the periphery also contains alternative paradigms and principles that can be a part of the deliberation over means and ends within the metapolicy but that do not give the current policy its justification, identity, or immutable standards. The idea of alternative principles in the periphery supports the dynamic quality of our definition of metapolicy and also creates the image of a persistent discourse about proper ends and the standards by which these should be judged within metapolicies.

Majone's image actually consists of a core surrounded by "concentric circles" or levels of periphery (1989, 151), but it will suffice, for our purposes, to make the distinction between what principle supports the dominant or persuasive paradigm within the metapolicy (the core) and those principles that present alternative arguments but have less persuasive power and are therefore, for the present, consigned to the periphery. In effect, what we are describing is a three-tiered metapolicy (figure 1.4).

As part of our worldview, the top tier, the *periphery*, contains the law, institutional, and administrative apparatus, with its rules and regulations, that define the status quo metapolicy and that operationalize the dominant or persuasive policy paradigm. At this level we find the public rhetoric associated with a debate over how a metapolicy is legislated, executed, and evaluated by experience. Here, law is codified and tested by the dominant metapolicy argument and its core principle.

The middle tier, which we shall call *deliberative*, is broader than the first, and is the reservoir of alternative principles and arguments for the policies that do not define it as a status-quo metapolicy but that represent opportunities for future change and redefinition. Given the effects of the status quo metapolicy, here is where a debate about the "reasonable" or "proper" ends of policy takes place. Here judgments are made about the difference between what is and what ought to be. This deliberative zone contains the competitors for the core paradigm and the backup lines of argument that can be called upon when the core no longer persuasively serves the metapolicy or its constituents.[25]

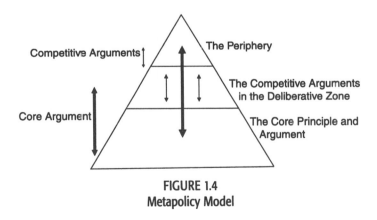

FIGURE 1.4
Metapolicy Model

The third tier, containing the *core* principle and its policy paradigm, is foundational and defines the character of the metapolicy, providing the stable standard for the pyramid. The core principle determines the context and constraints for the deliberation in the second tier and the proper tools and legal arguments for the public processes, debate, and institutional framework of the first tier.

Pride of Place in the Policy Space

In addition to each metapolicy having an internal structure that is defined in terms of a core and periphery, one also needs to be able to characterize the external relationship of one metapolicy to another within a policy "space," which is defined by that "set of policies that are so closely interrelated that it is not possible to make useful descriptions of, or analytic statements about, one of them without taking the other elements of the set into account" (Majone 1989, 158–59). The policy space is the map of relationships between associated metapolicies (e.g., health policy, pollution abatement policy, risk policy). In order to understand my conception of the policy space, we shall utilize the example of environmental metapolicy and define three concepts that, I will argue, characterize the history of environmental law and policy: *overlap*, *germination*, and *position*.

Overlap is a special dimension of interrelations within the policy space where one metapolicy which, by its subject matter, or on its surface, is separate, in fact essentially overlaps with the core principle and argument of another metapolicy. *Germination* describes the situation where the overlap results from the genesis of one metapolicy within the core of another, and *position* recognizes that if one metapolicy germinates another, its core principle is at least initially decisive in the new metapolicy through pride of place. These three concepts add a chronological or historical dimension to the idea of policy space and give a normative pride of place to that paradigm that represents the dominant argument of the first metapolicy to occupy the space, especially if it germinates or generates the other metapolicies in that space.

The policy space now seemingly occupied by distinct metapolicies related to health, natural resources, and pollution abatement was first occupied by the metapolicy of national economic growth and prosperity. This economic metapolicy, with its core principle of efficiency, germinated the environmental and natural resource metapolicies as they became necessary for long-term efficiency and continues to overlap and determine them. Further, the pride of place gained by the market paradigm, and by efficiency as the core principle of economic metapolicy, has caused all of the subsequent metapolicies related to the natural environment, and to the human position within it, to be dominated by the core principle of Kaldor efficiency, whether or not it is the appropriate principle with which to discern and design policy in these areas.

Because efficiency was the foundation of the first economic metapolicy in the space, and its paradigm (because of pollution and resource concerns) caused new areas of environmental policy to be created, efficiency continues, as the dominant or core principle in the policy space, to be the trump card in the theory and practice not only of its original metapolicy (economic prosperity) but also of any ensuing policies (e.g., environmental-risk policy). The resulting environmental metapolicy, with all its imperfections, is a direct outgrowth of the dominance of the market paradigm in its development and conceptualization.

When one metapolicy grows out of and overlaps an established, persuasive precedent, its fundamental principle will be dominated by the core of the parent metapolicy, in effect causing the core of the new metapolicy to replicate the core of the parent. The new metapolicy, at least on its surface, has a distinct focus of concern, distinct institutions and goals but, essentially, is dominated by a core principle that is not necessarily relevant to the new metapolicy, even though this moral standard will be decisive in the formulation of law and institutions for the prosecution of the ends within the new metapolicy.

Fundamentally, it is possible for one seemingly independent metapolicy to in fact have been built upon a previous metapolicy's paradigm and core principle (i.e., efficiency). Although this assumes that the core of the parent has been persuasive in the new metapolicy, it may be the case that the parent's core is applied without great thought or analysis. New areas of metapolicy may be perceived as derivative and made necessary by the parent; therefore, they are judged within the context of the parent's core principle. In this case, the success of efficiency in the parent metapolicy carries efficiency into the new field where it has yet to be determined as appropriate.

More importantly, the core principle is the basis for the conceptualization of the policy, and although the new metapolicy may be unique in content and truly involve distinct components like endangered species and natural systems, it is assumed that the critical dimension of these components can be captured within the parent's core (as environmental policy is conceptualized as a branch of economic policy). The core principle of the parent metapolicy is assumed, without analysis, to be relevant to the new metapolicy, as it is generated from the parent and overlaps with it.

But, as in this case, the transplanted core may fail to capture the critical components of the new metapolicy and be more vulnerable to change than it was in its original context. For however well efficiency represented what was at stake in the original metapolicy, it may not take into account the vital dimensions of concern that prompted the formulation of a new metapolicy argument, and therefore, the law and policy created by the parent's principle will be dysfunctional in the new context. The recognition of inappropriateness may be slow, however, especially as those with a vested interest in the transplanted core can rely on the power of the original persuasiveness of the principle as well as on its pride of place in the policy space. The uphill battle of any competitive principle will be great, even if its logic and practical ties to the issue are more profound. The longer the parent's core principle remains the defining characteristic of the new metapolicy, the more conventional and embedded it will become.

The analogy of an iceberg may best exemplify the pride of place efficiency holds in the "environmental" policy space. With the naked eye one might perceive five separate ice mountains floating in the ocean. Upon closer examination, however, one discovers that, in their essence, underwater, all the separate islands are part of one huge iceberg that has five perceptible peaks that break the surface of the sea. In essence, all are manifestations of the same core, but to the eye, they appear separate. In that same way one might describe five separate metapolicies dealing with economic prosperity, natural resources, agriculture, health and safety, and pollution/risk abatement. In policy terms, they are products of the same core normative principle and paradigm applied to a variety of public issues within the same policy space.

If we see the many manifestations of metapolicy in the general space of environmental law as an ice flow with several distinct peaks breaking the water, we may then ask what an analysis of the subsurface of these metapolicies will reveal. Do all these seemingly independent metapolicy arguments have a common core principle? Is this principle economic efficiency?

If the formation of a single metapolicy is derived from a core that represents standards that reflect the essence of the issue area, then the periphery can be understood as forming around this persuasive core, representing its principles in the formulation and implementation of law. In the case of one hybrid metapolicy growing from another, this process is not so clear or one-directional.

The hybrid metapolicy, like all policy, is created by a perception that what is does not measure up to what ought to be. However, the core principle derived from the essence of the parent metapolicy is transferred into the hybrid and preexists as an established or conventional standard and justification mechanism responding to the new concerns. The core has been applied without first considering whether it makes sense in the new issue area. Therefore, with overlap, germination, and position in the policy space, it is critical to analyze the true core of each metapolicy no matter what perceptions meet the eye. One cannot assume that environmental metapolicy has its own core principle that has been selected for its relevance. One must critically analyze the law-and-policy argument of the status quo in order to understand, first, if the metapolicy is independent within the space or is the offspring of another metapolicy, and second, if its core standard and motivating principle is native to its issue area or is inherited from a parent.

In some cases an inherited core principle may be appropriate to the new hybrid metapolicy. It may be that law and policy in this new issue area can also be best prosecuted by the dominant core principle and its conceptualization of the new issue. Perhaps if the core of health policy was the integrity of the person, then a new metapolicy concerning labor safety might profit from being born of the same core. However, the concern should be for the conscious analysis of what principle defines a policy and determines the law, and for an understanding that what is superficial or assumed may not be the essential "truth" about a metapolicy.

Model Components, Priorities, and Construction

The policy space created by the market paradigm distinguishes among the policy issue areas of economic prosperity, natural resources, agriculture, pollution abatement, health and safety, and environmental risk, but all have a single set of fundamental assumptions and a core operating principle of Kaldor efficiency. The result is a policy space dominated by efficiency and cost-benefit methods and one in which all policy bends to the demands of market assumptions and ends. Economic metapolicy, built upon efficiency and the market paradigm, defines the core of each policy issue it influences in terms of these priorities. This means that the market argument paradigm has default status in environmental policy deliberation and choice.

Envisioning a policy space where environmental decision making proceeds from within the context of the market paradigm creates an anthropocentric worldview based upon the instrumental evaluation of nature for its use properties to humanity. I contend that this application of the market paradigm to environmental law and policy has gone through two phases, each with a distinct context model. As I will fully argue in chapter 3, the definition of efficiency has evolved from the maxim of Maximize Wealth to the maxim of Optimize Wealth, as the limitations of the natural world have been realized.

First, the efficient use of the environment by the market required the government to play the role of facilitator of maximum wealth generation, allowing unregulated pollution of the environment and transferring as much public land as possible into private hands. As pollution increased and inventory of resources decreased, the government took on a new role, setting the levels of optimal efficiency so that market use could proceed over the long run. I will call this first context model the *Traditional Sector Approach I: Maximum Use Model* and the second variant the *Traditional Sector Approach II: Optimal Use Model*.

Both context models have three basic components, with priority among them determined by the market paradigm's worldview. The first component is the market itself. Here efficiency holds the moral high ground in both model variants, and the continued persistence of the market is the ultimate standard for all policy and administrative decisions. The second component, also second in priority, is the government, existing to facilitate market decision making and to mimic market allocations through cost-benefit methods when the market itself fails. The third component, and last in priority for both the maximum use and optimal use models, is the natural environment, which exists to be used and can be divided into a set of raw materials, or eco-inventory, for input into the market and a series of environmental media as sinks for disposal of waste generated by the market.

I called these context models the *Traditional Sector Approach* (TSA-I and TSA-II) since the market worldview perceives the economy as a whole while it divides the natural environment into *sectors* for use. It is also the case that the market paradigm is traditional in this context since it held pride of place in the policy space before there was any law or policy-protecting nature, and through overlap and germination, became the parent-dominant paradigm of the new area of environmental metapolicy.

One can argue that the difference between TSA-I and TSA-II is one of emphasis, since the definition of efficiency evolves in order to maintain market persistence. The evolution from maximum use to optimal use necessitates that the government component of the model shift its role from one of maximum facilitation of market processes with public resources and media to a more regulated use of resources and media, to prolong their effective life and provide for an optimal economy over a longer period of time. The priority of the market and the regulation of nature for use does not change; only the role of government, which must intercede to respond to the evolving definition of efficiency, changes.

From Strategy to Tactics

Using both the paradigm and the context model, the policy analyst can map the strategic dimensions of policy design and create a full comprehensive policy argument (CPA). What remains is to take this analytic model of theory and practice and apply it to the subject of environmental risk.

In terms of Kelman's map of the process, we have created a detailed model of what we mean by a policy idea and can use the paradigm and context model to define the standards, ends, and appropriate means as we make political choices, implement decisions, transform statute law into final government action, and evaluate real-world outcomes (see fig. 1.1).

A full tactical analysis of an issue would require that we now consider the feasibility of the policy idea; its institutional, technological, and economic constraints; the audience problems it may encounter; and the overall feasibility of the policy as effective law. Although most policy texts and almost all public administration courses concern themselves exclusively with these tactical concerns, it is my contention that they are a product of the theory and argument that support them. All of these "tactical" variables, as well as how they are handled, are dependent on the standards set by the policy paradigm as strategy. By studying the paradigm and its entailed context model, we can not only establish priorities and moral standards for both the ends and means of the policy issue but also identify counterarguments and anticipate constraints, feasibility questions, and audience problems.

For example, in the strategic dimension of policy design we concern ourselves with ideas and ideals, but in the development of our policy argument we also gain the ability to define a real constraint, how feasibility will be measured, what audiences may have more to lose or gain than others, and how they might be approached successfully. A well-defined metapolicy that is theoretically rigorous will provide a tactical advantage to the decision maker by defining its own ends clearly so that compromise and shifts in emphasis necessitated by tactical contingencies can be understood in terms of their core or peripheral impact and their consequent importance.

The strategic component of policy design, that is, the paradigmatic thinking made evident in the analysis of existing policy and the synthesis of new alternative arguments, is the most fundamental dimension of the policy process. Without an understanding of what our fundamental assumptions are, what principles represent them, and how maxims and methods derive from these and generate a worldview or context model for the study of an issue, we can never hope to have any control over the tactical process of law and policy nor any standards by which to judge a predicted outcome from an unintentional one, or success from failure. Argument is critical to achieving sound policy, and the normative standards of an argument are its essential component.

The logic of policy analysis, as well as most of the writing, research, and teaching of policy technique, has centered on the promotion of the language of efficiency to the exclusion of nonmarket normative standards. However, adopting the logical framework of CPA allows new methods of analysis for nonmarket principles to be established that may successfully challenge the market paradigm in terms of both rigor and ease of application. Overall, it is up to those who write and think about public policy choices to facilitate the utilization of the entire range of normative thought and existing moral theory in the law-and-policy context. In this way, a variety of distinct alternatives may become part of conventional policy thinking and produce alternative methodological answers to the demands posed by increasingly difficult policy problems like environmental risk and the complex policy arguments these issues entail.

But before I use CPA to create an alternative Kantian paradigm for environmental policy, let us analyze the dominance and shortcomings of the market paradigm and context model as it is presently applied to the theory (chapter 2) and practice (chapter 3) of environmental risk.

Notes to Chapter 1

1. Genesis's second account of creation, verses 19–20, states: "So from the soil Yahweh God fashioned all the wild beasts and all the birds of heaven. These he brought to the man to see what he would call them; each one was to bear the name the man would give it. The man gave names to all the cattle, all the birds of heaven and all the wild beasts," and as we know we have not stopped there!

2. For our purposes, truth can be considered that argument that is persuasive to the individual. In terms of public policy, the truth is the status quo policy: what "is" the law. In this sense, law as codified policy can be assumed to be true in collective terms, that is, what remains presently and conventionally persuasive across a society. As a competitive line of argument, which is private truth to some, gains sociopolitical momentum and the argument becomes persuasive, or the truth, to more individuals who then convince others, it also becomes majoritarian and conventional. In this way core arguments represent and define the predominant definition of the truth about the "public interest" for their metapolicy.

3. See *Congressional Quarterly Yearbook* (1995/1996/1997/1998) for a discussion of the risk analysis bills before the 104th and 105th Congresses. From within the context of this chapter we might say that Congress has attempted to re-establish TSA-I as the pertinent context model for environmental policy.

4. If environmental values have no central place in current policy design strategy, but just free-float without context or consistent/extensive underpinning, this may be why we perceive them as "unscientific" and vague and may explain why they have not been determinative in policy and law even though they may better represent what is at stake in environmental decisions.

5. Alternative philosophical systems, including Kant's, can then be organized and applied on the basis of this model and the metaphysical foundations or possibilities for policy choice and argument expand exponentially. In chapter 2, I will argue that even the market paradigm has both a metaphysics of self and a metaphysics of

choice. All policy analysis has a metaphysical foundation in the fundamental assumptions of its paradigm.

6. Kelman (1987, 210–13 and 227–30) defines good policy as that which promotes human dignity.

7. This is not to say that all policy is based upon efficiency, but that all policy analysis begins with the premise that efficiency is the reasonable and dominant principle and therefore that it ought to be the standard by which the "proper" action is defined. It is true that there are many areas of policy where efficiency is less of a concern (e.g., constitutional rights) but it is even truer that policy is and has been viewed first, and principally, through an economic lens, represented by what I call the market paradigm.

8. "[F]or granted" is critical, as the hegemony of a paradigm allows practitioners to apply it without undue reflection or analysis upon its metaphysical roots. This disconnection leads to its misapplication.

9. Einstein's paradigm has since been challenged, but not yet replaced, by quantum theory.

10. If schools of public policy are any indication, efficiency/cost-benefit methods, based upon the market paradigm, play this role. I once had a student, from the Kennedy School of Government at Harvard, declare that what we call the market paradigm was the "only legitimate paradigm for policy analysis."

11. Argument in policy comes from a democratic tradition that assumes persuasion to be an important component in creating law. However, argument works no matter the form of government as even within a limited circle at the top of a totalitarian regime arguments are made to conceptualize and implement policy. Policy is ultimately an expression of power, but the degree of coercion necessary to establish cooperation and to solve collective-action problems will vary inversely with the persuasiveness of the policy argument made by a government to its people.

12. Although the current debate between philosophers concerning the role of moral theory in making individual ethical choices may result in victory for the claim, made by antitheorists, that moral theory is not necessary to moral behavior, I wish to claim that in making public decisions (choices related not to why I should do X but why the coercive power of the state should be used to make everyone do X), moral theory plays a more important and necessary role in formulation of argument, justification of principle, recommendation of alternatives, and implementation of choice.

13. Within courses I have given, my students have constructed CPAs from the moral theories of Hobbes, Locke, Rousseau, Hegel, Hume, and J. S. Mill, as well as from deep ecology, sustainability, and eco-feminism, among others.

14. One could argue that the "why" question maps onto the "volk" condition, the "what" question onto the "wenn" condition, and the "whether" question onto the "nono" part.

15. Which addressees the problems defined by Lindblom (1990) without piecemeal incrementalism.

16. Using Hardin (1982a) I will define a collective good as any public or private good (by definition of jointness and nonexclusion) that is distributed or allocated by the state through policy. See chapter 2 for a fuller explanation.

17. In terms of force or fraud, this is primarily focused upon that which is external to the market. One can argue that force and fraud are part and parcel of market operations in that unequal economic power and ability, as well as false claims and information, are prevalent within market operations. What the market paradigm does require is a state sufficient to limit fraud without its action forcing or restricting personal preference (Feldman 1980).

18. The original description of a "commons" problem is attributed to G. Hardin (1968), who described the tendency to overgraze a collective or public commons

by self-interested welfare maximizers. The problems confronted by private welfare calculations confronting collective goods (fully covered in chapter 2), and the propensity for consumers to free ride, undersupplying the good, has been examined as the generic problem of "common pool resources" (see Ostrom 1990 and Buck 1998, for a global perspective).

19. I use both justice and legitimacy to describe the state because in constructing a paradigm, one needs to consider what role legitimizes the state within the paradigm as well as how this role reflects the operational principle and, in this way, defines justice.

20. It is this fundamental assumption that is occupying the Republican Congress and which will be discussed in the epilogue to this book.

21. It must be kept in mind here that cost-benefit methods are not cost-effectiveness methods, as the former places both means and ends under the principle of efficiency, whereas the latter limits efficiency to the means and allows other principles to determine ends (see Gillroy and Wade 1992, 5–15).

22. This matching process can be seen as a test of the argument's feasibility. If the argument requires an instrument that is not available, it is of little use. For example, a principle requiring cheap and effective solar energy to be operationalized may be for the future, not the present. In addition, if it requires institutions or political structures that do not exist, this, too, divorces it from adequate policy instruments (e.g., if it requires the unconstitutional use of power by one arm of government to be operationalized).

23. The problem with a minimal state is: if the market is a prisoner's dilemma and the failure of the "invisible hand" (a piece of market metaphysics) causes less than collectively optimal outcomes, then authoritarianism is not far away. This conclusion would support the argument that true markets best survive in totalitarian environments, and it would be supported by some interpretations of market theory (Posner 1983; Nozick 1974).

24. The concept of dominant argument is related to the degree of persuasiveness one argument has in comparison with the others available in the policy debate. Some arguments within a metapolicy may have short lives and some long; some may remain alternatives, and as they become more persuasive, and the status quo argument wanes in persuasion, they gain dominance. Some lines of argument may never become full-fledged paradigms within comprehensive policy arguments.

25. For example, if we decide that efficiency is not producing an adequate environmental policy, as it ought to be, we may find within the deliberative zone an alternative argument, based upon the principle of integrity, to act as a replacement core for environmental metapolicy.

2

The Theory of Environmental Risk: Preferences, Choice, and Individual Welfare

Public policy choice regarding man's relationship with his natural environment is concerned with human life and health, the value of natural resources, the quality of the ecology as a dynamic life-support system, and aesthetic considerations. The predominant approach when evaluating environmental policy emphasizes the methodology of cost-benefit analysis and the principle of market efficiency. Let us examine the theoretical framework of environmental–risk policy to determine if the justification-and-evaluation structure of economic thought is morally adequate to define risk situations and to propose "socially better" policy alternatives for this area of environmental law.

I contend that the logical and the strategic structure promoted by cost-benefit method causes nonprovision of the collective good of environmental quality. The value scheme promoted by applying efficiency to public choice cannot address the intrinsic values at stake in the regulation of environmental risk. To address these intrinsic values, we should move beyond the "thin" theory of autonomy present in economic thought and toward a "thick" concept of autonomy like that in Kantian ethics. Therefore, I propose to begin the formulation of a Kantian risk paradigm with a critical analysis and application of the cost-benefit methodology derived from the market paradigm (chapter 1) to the political theory (this chapter) and practice (next chapter) of risk regulation so that we may build a constructive argument about what *ought* to be the law from a thorough consideration of what *is* our present policy.

The essential dilemma is whether one can adequately compensate for involuntary transfer of external effects (Page 1973; Pigou 1932) by treating them as renegade market considerations within a value system based on instrumental economic efficiency, or whether they ought to be considered collective-action problems, external to markets and best handled by government with a distinct set of moral principles stressing intrinsic value.

Before drawing a conclusion about the need for environmental (i.e., non-efficiency-based) principles to accommodate the special moral and strategic character of environmental-risk problems, we must analyze the market paradigm, examine the strategic ramifications of traditional cases of pollution and the distinctive institutional, strategic, and moral nature of environmental risk. How do cost-benefit methods measure up to the demands of environmental-risk dilemmas? Can the market paradigm prescribe both the moral solutions and the political institutions necessary to respond to environmental risk? Finally, does the ethical poverty of the economic approach require new justification for, and evaluation of, environmental policy and reorientation of the ethical arguments at the foundation of risk decision making?

The Economic Viewpoint: From Private Exchange to Public Choice?

Economic reasoning is concerned primarily with efficient voluntary exchange. Anything relevant to the analysis of a policy problem is defined as either a cost or a benefit to human individual preference satisfaction. Cost-benefit tradeoffs define the most rational, and therefore moral, policy choice (Leonard and Zeckhauser 1986). Under real-market conditions, private benefits and costs equal aggregate joint or social benefits and costs; the efficient outcome (a solution that is Pareto optimal [Feldman 1980, chap. 7]) can be found purely through private and isolated voluntary trade. However, when the principle of efficiency enters the realm of public choice, the replacement of fungible private goods with collective goods causes the market to fail and replaces actual trade in a market with bureaucratically calculated cost-benefit decisions that mimic market solutions (Feldman 1980; Tresch 1981). Here, choosing cost-benefit methods over cost-effectiveness analysis is an attempt to use efficiency to judge both the ends and means of a particular policy, and not just the least costly means to policy ends chosen on the basis of nonefficiency principles (Gillroy 1992a; Gillroy and Wade 1992).

For environmental policy, conditions are not "normal" from a market point of view. The collective nature of environmental goods causes social costs and benefits both to be greater than individual valuations and to be involuntarily traded to others (Page 1973). Cost-benefit methods, functioning where these externalities and commons problems have forced the market to collapse, must compensate for the involuntary nature of transfers and the collective, nonmarket nature of generated costs and benefits. The public administrator must reinterpret these nonmarket costs and benefits into economic language so that she can judge efficient outcomes and choose policy that mimics what the market would have done had it been able to operate. All relevant variables are therefore translated into equivalent monetary costs and benefits for the purposes of seeking, not Pareto, but Kaldor efficiency (Feldman 1980, 142–44; Leonard and Zeckhauser 1986).[1] In seeking Kaldor efficiency the nonmarket dimensions of environmental goods are reintegrated into the price system, subjecting them to voluntary transfer (or allocation by willingness to pay), where social and aggregate individual costs and benefits are again equal.

For pollution regulation, the administrator's task is to set the conditions under which the pollution externality is absorbed within private cost and benefit calculations ($b_i - c_i = v_i$), so that she can aggregate individual values into a social valuation ($\Sigma v_i = V$) that recommends "efficient" policy. If social and private costs are fungible, individuals will pollute an environment until the costs of pollution (health, aesthetics, etc.) outweigh the benefits (waste costs avoided). Ethically, expression and aggregation of individual cost-benefit preferences are products of the optimal, efficient operation of market forces as translated by public decision makers; they are preferable to any state-imposed solution based on nonmarket principles.

In the economic approach to policy any and all government solutions are "second-best," falling short of the ideal outcomes markets produce (Lipsey and Lancaster 1956; Tresch 1981, 4). Therefore, normal market processes should handle as much of any pollution problem as possible, leaving government intervention at a minimum. This ensures limited involvement for the public sector and co-opts decision making to market ends and means so that efficiency remains the sole motivating principle of both public and private choice.

Justified by the market ideal, cost-benefit methods recommend government intervention only when it responds to the sovereignty of individual preferences. Its role is to redefine the sociopolitical and moral elements of collective-goods problems (that cause markets to fail) so that environmental quality considerations become accessible to private welfare calculations, trade, and preference satisfaction. Cost-benefit analysis is, therefore, a systematic and comprehensive decision procedure used to mimic markets when these fail. Normatively, cost-benefit calculations reduce both the ends and means of public policy to the task of seeking efficient social welfare improvements for individuals with private consumer preferences.

The Strategic Nature of the Polluter's Dilemma

The natural environment is joint and nonexcludable. It is joint in that it is not transferable or fungible in the economic sense, but exists for use by one and all simultaneously. Providing clean air for one person does not significantly diminish clean air for others. Nonexcludability means that environmental quality is not a private good claimable by one person to the exclusion of others. The environment as property is attenuated (i.e., nonexclusive, incompletely specified, and privately unenforceable).[2] As a good, environmental quality exhibits joint nonvoluntary transfer and nonexcludable rights—traditionally described as the two characteristics of a public good (Snidal 1979; Feldman 1980, chap. 6). Russell Hardin (1982a, chap. 1) uses the term "collective good" to characterize provision of goods through solving collective-action problems. For our purposes, it is the fact that a good is considered to produce a "collective" action problem, rather than merely its degree of jointness and/or nonexcludability, which makes government regulation necessary to its provision.

Although a variety of game or strategic formats can be used to discuss a collective-goods problem (Taylor 1976, 1987; Ostrom 1990), we will characterize it as a prisoner's dilemma (Hardin 1971, 1982a), where individual self-interest causes a collective nonoptimal provision of the good. For example, public television is a collective good: individuals do not want to pay for this joint and nonexcludable good when they can watch for free. But, if no one contributes, the station will fold for lack of funds. In order to persist, the television station needs to encourage a critical mass of individuals to fund it. If all free ride, no collective good will exist; if a critical mass (k of N viewers) supports the station, others can free ride without destroying it for all. Here, (k) can be one person or one million, but the term represents the minimum number of cooperators necessary to ensure the provision of the collective good in a situation where individual strategic rationality tells everyone to free ride on the cooperation of others.

For environmental policy, the quality of the environment represents the collective good under consideration, and pollution of this environment by individuals causes its quality to diminish. Using the assumption, as the economic policy model does, that individual self-interested preferences are the core of collective policy choice, we can place this economic model into a strategic framework and examine pollution within the context of game theory. The game format helps us understand the inherent logic of individual preferences, choices, and the resulting joint outcomes that are inevitable, given those market preferences and choices. The prisoner's dilemma involved here is the polluter's dilemma.[3]

Row (R) and column (C) (fig. 2.1) offer a choice between two strategies: to cooperate in the provision of environmental quality by not polluting [(R1) (C1)], or to pollute and free ride on the quality of the environment provided by others [(R2) (C2)]. Individuals, considering their own self-interest in isolation, prefer environmental quality but fear exploitation by others. The collective result of individual rational choice is an equilibrium at (R2,C2), where both actors play their dominant strategy and continue to pollute, free riding on each another and causing the continued erosion of the environment. [4] In this strategic interaction, it is assumed that the actors are making economic cost-benefit calculations that result in the nonoptimal provision of the collective good.

> The question is simply whether the individual ought to add his own little bit of pollution to that vast amount that would be in the environment anyway. A man always gains something from polluting (he reduces costs of waste disposal), so there is a *prima facie* case for the rationality of preferring universal polluting to unilateral restraint. (Goodin 1976, 167)

From the standpoint of cost-benefit evaluation, (v_i), the self-interested efforts of individuals to satisfy their preferences, choosing in isolation, will result in an aggregate (V) that favors universal polluting. The cost-benefit analyst, reflecting these preferences, will recommend a policy that tolerates a nonoptimal (if not zero) collective provision of environmental quality.

THE THEORY OF ENVIRONMENTAL RISK

We assume two actors, in isolation, weighing the subjective costs and benefits of a decision to pollute. Further, we assume that each has the expectation that the other will act rationally, in that she will try to achieve the highest utility payoff by satisfying her highest preference. The actors are assumed to have the following preference order:

	(utility to i)	(preference)
(best)	1	unilateral polluting
	2	universal restraint
	3	universal polluting
(worst)	4	unilateral restraint

For all (i): $u_i(1) > u_i(2) > u_i(3) > u_i(4)$ and $1 P_i 2 P_i 3 P_i 4$.

These rational (complete, transitive) preference orders or individual payoffs are contained in the following strategic matrix:

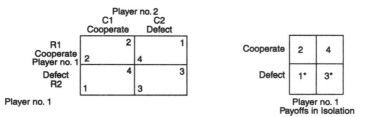

In this matrix, row (R) and Column (C) have two strategy choices (S): to cooperate in the provision of the collective good of environmental quality by not polluting ($R1$ and $C1$), or to continue to pollute and free ride on the quality of the environment ($R2$ and $C2$). The contention is that individuals, considering their self-interested preferences in isolation, will have a tendency to pollute on the basis of the assumption that in comparing the personal costs and benefits of unilateral restraint versus pollution, the latter will win out, since waste management will always be a cost, while polluting will always be a benefit. From within this strategic context, as we can see if we look at player no. 1's payoffs in isolation, it is the *dominant strategy** for each player to defect whatever choice the other makes (*1* is preferred to *2* and *3* is preferred to *4*). With both agents playing their dominant strategy, the resulting payoffs will be (*3, 3*). This is a dilemma for the polluters as long as they independently prefer universal cooperation to universal defection but collectively end up with the latter (Goodin 1976, 166–68).

FIGURE 2.1
The Polluter's Dilemma

To provide the collective good, a critical mass of individuals must overcome their self-interested predisposition and cooperate so that a standard of environmental quality can be established and regulated to persist over time. Hume concludes that, within an N-person society, this requires central coordination through government.[5]

> There is no quality in human nature, which cause more fatal errors in our conduct, than that which leads us to prefer whatever is present to the distant and remote, and makes us desire objects more according to their situation than their *intrinsic* value. Two neighbors may agree to drain a meadow, which they possess in common; because 'tis easy for them to know each others mind; and each must perceive, that the immediate consequence of his failing in his part, is, the abandoning of the project. But 'tis very difficult, and indeed impossible, that a thousand persons shou'd agree in any such action; it being difficult for them to concert so complicated a design,

and still more difficult for them to execute it; while each seeks a pretext to free himself of the trouble and expense, and wou'd lay the whole burden on others. Political society easily remedies both these inconveniences. (Hume [1740] 1975, 538, emphasis added)

Hume recognizes strategic rationality and what happens when one's economic preferences are processed through a strategic situation characterized by the need to provide a collective good (the meadow). Humans are strategic animals: they are capable of waiting or using indirect means to their elective ends (Elster 1979, 18; 1983). Also, the collective reality in which we live is not the product of what each chooses separately; rather, it is what is rendered by the integration of many individual choices into a single joint outcome. For example, when we get to work is a function less of when we leave home and how fast we drive than of how many people leave home at once and how slow and congested the resulting traffic pattern is.

Hume suggests that government is responsible for the provision of collective goods through coordination of individual choices.[6] Government relies on the concept of critical mass (Goodin 1976, 168) to define the degree of coercion and coordination necessary for the adequate regulation of private choice and, therefore, for the provision of the collective good.

For public television, the good can be provided by k of N individuals, the minimum number necessary to see that the good exists at an optimal amount, allowing all others to free ride without affecting the provision of the good. The collective good of environmental quality requires a different concept of critical mass. One or a specified number of individuals cannot and ought not to be required to provide a sound and quality environment for us all. On the contrary, persistent environmental quality requires that a sizable proportion of individuals, k/N, cooperate in order to provide for the collective good; we all have a joint "moral" responsibility for the social provision of a sound environment.

In addition to establishing a proportion of cooperators, there is also an absolute number of defectors (N-k) who will be able to free ride at any level of environmental quality. But as many free riders as possible must be allowed in order to both maximize social benefits (Goodin 1976, 181) and maintain the persistence of the environment as a collective good (Goodin 1976, 151).[7] This proportion of free riders to cooperators sets the critical mass necessary to establish and maintain any level of environmental quality (Q).

$$Q = \frac{N-k}{k}$$

For critical-mass maintenance, the state needs both to set the standard for environmental quality (Q), and to coordinate enough of the population so that this standard can persist as population increases. Encouraging (k) to cooperate is insufficient without considering that the rest of N will efficiently free ride; if (N-k) is large enough, the quality of the environment will be substandard. When the absolute number of defectors is critical to maintaining environmental quality, more central coercion is necessary to produce the collective good.

Critical-mass requirements, combined with the strategic deadlock of the polluter's dilemma, support state intervention in private preference transactions to establish environmental quality standards and ensure that a required proportion of individuals cooperate to provide the collective good. Solving the polluter's dilemma requires institutions greater than the minimal state in order to establish a critical mass for the collective good of environmental quality.[8] Unlike the normal prisoner's dilemma, in which the noncooperative equilibrium is static, a polluter's dilemma without cooperation causes environmental deterioration. In this situation, the nonmarket establishment and maintenance of critical mass is a prerequisite for the provision of the good.

The logic of cost-benefit methods depends on the ethical contention that individuals ought to be "willing to pay to have pollution reduced in order to consume clean air" (Bish 1971, 122). But this moral symmetry between polluter and polluted ignores the nature of the polluter's dilemma. Ethical asymmetry between polluter and polluted is a central concern when one questions why he or she should have to pay someone, or be extorted, to stop current and prevent future harm. If the strategic reality among polluters is akin to that in the polluter's dilemma, where individual action breeds collective harms, then the role of government as representative of the public interest in the provision of collective goods must be assumed to be ethically real and necessary. If we move from the strategic consideration of pollution to environmental risk, this asymmetry becomes even more exaggerated and critical to public choice.

Environmental Risk and the Imprisoned Rider

> A new type of environmental problem is emerging which differs in nature from the more familiar pollution and resource depletion problems. This type of problem, which may be called environmental risk, has rapidly increased in importance over the last few decades and may indeed become the dominant type of environmental problem. (Page 1978, 207)

In the twenty years since Page wrote these words, his prediction has come true. No area of environmental policy so vexes traditional patterns of government regulation as matters of collective risk. But what is the strategic nature of environmental risk? What are its particular moral ramifications? What policy arguments and institutions are necessary to manage them? What are the elements of a justification-and-evaluation system that can properly handle administrative decision making in this area?

The Unique Character of Environmental Risk

Talbot Page (1978) wrote the seminal article distinguishing environmental risk from traditional cases of pollution. He arrived at nine distinct characteristics of environmental risk, four related to its uncertainty, and five more that concern its institutional management.

The first distinction is technical *ignorance of mechanism*. Traditional pollution cases (litter, detergent in water, smoke and particulate in the air) are understood by science in terms of their generation, transmission, and effect on human and natural systems. Often the technically unsophisticated observer can detect the presence of traditional pollutants with the naked eye, and one can normally tell immediately that they are being affected by them.

With environmental-risk cases (toxic chemicals in groundwater; generation of nuclear power and disposal of its waste; the production, storage, and use of synthetic chemicals and pesticides; as well as genetic research and experimentation), the effects of a suspected agent, alone or in reaction with others, may produce carcinogenic, teratogenic, or mutagenic effects that go unnoticed and undetected even by a trained eye. Overall, "[t]he mechanisms of generation, transmission, and response are understood so poorly that any management of these problems is truly decision making under pervasive uncertainty" (Page 1978, 209). Risk-assessment science involves complex methodology and quantitative testing (Natural Research Council [hereafter cited as NRC] 1983), but pervasive uncertainty remains and is the primary evidence for the argument that environmental-risk policy transcends science (Brickman, Jasanoff, and Ilgen 1985; Jasanoff 1990; Breyer 1993).

Page's second distinction is the *potential for catastrophic costs* associated uniquely with cases of environmental risk. A scientific understanding of the mechanism of traditional pollution such as suspended solids or eutrophicants makes it possible for decision makers to judge both the degree of risk involved in pollution incidents and the potential costs of "worst case" scenarios. But the "pervasive uncertainty" related to environmental risk makes costs unknown and "worst cases" hard to define. Usually, the costs or harms of risk are assumed to be much higher and less incremental than those associated with traditional pollutants. The synthetic nature and large number of prospective toxins, for example, and the potential synergistic effects of mixing them, plus the fact that smaller doses of environmental-risk contaminants may pack higher concentrations of potency, suggest that any bad effects of environmental risk could be catastrophic. "But what is not known about mechanisms precludes specification of just how catastrophic and likely the costs might be" (Page 1978, 209). The obvious and incremental nature of most traditional pollutants is juxtaposed with the clandestine and cumulative nature of environmental risk that may catastrophically harm human and environmental persistence. This asymmetry of potential effect needs to be considered in the formulation of distinct environmental-risk policy.

Relatively modest benefits are the third mark of environmental risk. Some may argue that the benefits of nuclear power, synthetic chemicals, pesticides, or recombinant DNA are substantial, but any positive aspects pale beside the potential harm, in "worst case scenarios," to long-term human and environmental persistence. A large-scale release of radioactive contaminants, a toxic chemical spill, or an atmospheric leak of toxins, might suggest that "there appears to be at some level a strong asymmetry between potential costs and benefits" (Page 1978, 210). Any of these occurrences could lead to widespread death, destruction of entire natural systems, extinction or long-term mutation in the genetic code of humans and other life forms.

Low subjective probability is the final characteristic connected to the uncertainty of environmental risk.

> Due to the fragmentary knowledge of mechanism, the likelihood of the catastrophic hypothesis cannot be determined objectively, but must be assessed subjectively, based upon whatever knowledge is available. (Page 1978, 210)

The subjective probability connected with environmental risk is normally low, introducing a second asymmetry.

> [L]ow subjective probability of the catastrophic outcome . . . tends to counterbalance the asymmetry of potential high costs and modest benefits. . . . Whether the greater likelihood of the favorable outcome compensates for its smaller relative size is a fundamental question of environmental risk management. (Page 1978, 211)

The reality of low (near zero) subjective probabilities of infinitely harmful costs labels environmental risk as a *zero-infinity problem* (Page 1978).

In addition to the distinctions from uncertainty, Page also defines five additional characteristics that affect the institutional management of environmental risk. The first two concern the generation of costs and benefits in environmental-risk cases: specifically, the *internal transfer of benefits* and the *external transfer of costs*.

For environmental risk, the small benefits of accepting the gamble both exist within the market and are allocated through its mechanisms (e.g., the greater profits of firms, greater consumer satisfaction). These markets produce and sell technological innovation within the price system of supply and demand. However, the costs generated by the same innovation are collectively transferred, nonvoluntarily, throughout society. The biosphere directly absorbs costs since "the adverse effects of environmental risk gambles usually are transferred directly through the environment rather than through the market" (Page 1978, 212). The risk gamble is being imposed upon the general population while the economic benefits are limited to those with market access or control of the technology and products involved. Zero-infinity cases have much higher potential cost, borne by a population that collectively has not accepted it by any definition of a voluntary choice. The *collective nature* of risk is the next unique feature of environmental-risk management.

Unlike private market transactions, which affect principally those involved in the exchange, environmental-risk transactions affect wide populations of people with or without their knowledge or consent. The diffusive effects of environmental risk pose severe questions about traditional administrative ways of protecting individuals from risk gambles in public policy. Such protective mechanisms as insurance, liability law, or other compensatory systems, are *ex post* remedies that, by their nature are inadequate to the task of protecting, *ex ante*, the millions of people potentially affected by an environmental-risk hazard (Page 1978, 213).

Page suggests that the policy tools related to all market conceptions of "socially better" are inappropriate for environmental-risk law. Markets, seeking Potential Pareto Improvements, can only promise *ex post* remedies, which do not require *ex ante* participation or consent and are not adequate to the protection of people or nature before the imposition of the risk. The only guarantee in a market-driven policy insures *ex post* economic compensation, or an attempt to pick up the pieces after the risk has been generated and has had an effect.

Because of the stealth quality of environmental risk, its potentially high costs, and collective nature, this guarantee may often be inadequate. Individuals may need to be protected before the fact so that any risk is distributed fairly, especially to those who reap the economic benefits. Any *ex ante* action, however, must be justified by values other than economic ones, which can only sanction *ex post* satisfaction of preferences. The need for political institutions and a nonefficiency-based set of values to inform the definition of "socially better" and to shape policy *ex ante* is further supported by the final two management characteristics of environmental risk: *latency* and *irreversibility*.

> [T]he extended delay between the initiation of a hazard or exposure to it, and the manifestation of its effects . . . is sufficiently long and the risk sufficiently diffuse so that the risk is borne involuntarily, if not unknowingly . . . [and may] be masked by other factors. (Page 1978, 213)

The collective nature of risk, with its stealth quality, produces situations where one may be affected by a toxin generated by other persons, miles away, without one's knowledge and not know it until ten or twenty years later when health effects surface. Latency may stretch over many generations who will be faced with changes in the genetic code that cause hazardous mutations over time.

The effects of environmental risk are also irreversible. They are not privately irreversible, like consuming a hamburger, but collectively irreversible. One individual or firm may impose an irreversible stealth harm on the community that may not become evident for years or generations.[9]

The policy ramifications of environmental risk are what is of concern. Page concludes that the collective nature of these risk characteristics "have profound ethical and institutional implications. . . . They raise questions concerning fair distributions of risk over time and how institutions can be designed to anticipate adverse effects, rather than merely to react to existing known effects" (Page 1978, 214).

These ethical and political questions are arguments about moral principle, systems of valuation, and the proper ethical justification of political institutions. They speak to the reality of environmental risk as a species of collective-action problem requiring a distinct set of values to shape policy argument and institutions, while they relate directly to the character and requirements of human beings and their natural environment, independently of efficiency considerations.

To the characteristics of environmental risk deciphered by Page, I will add three more, related to its strategic nature, which produce the *imprisoned rider*. The strategic reality of the zero-infinity gamble will be like and unlike those of other environmental collective-action problems but completely distinct from those of markets and their assumptions.

Environmental-risk regulation requires a solution to a collective-action problem. To anticipate and distribute risk fairly, central guidance should coordinate actors, against their subjective welfare preferences, in order to establish a critical mass to ensure that environmental quality is achieved and maintained over time. We can use the polluter's dilemma, with certain adjustments, as the basic model of the strategic reality of environmental-risk situations.

The first unique strategic characteristic of the environmetal-risk dilemma lies in the goal of coordination. The central authority is not really providing a collective good but preventing a public bad from rendering collective and irreversible harm.[10] Providing a collective good and preventing a public bad can be distinguished strategically by their unique concepts of critical mass.

In the case of provision of the collective good, it is the goal of the coordinating authority to get k or (N-k)/k players to override their subjective self-interest and cooperate, establishing a critical mass. Although the number who defect will lower environmental quality, it is possible for a sizable proportion to free ride, raising general welfare without lowering the level of good provided below an acceptable level. In preventing a public bad, however, free riders cannot be as graciously tolerated, and the coordinating authority must use N-k as the proper critical-mass concept. The imperative of political institutions is to keep N-k to a morally justified minimum, as close to zero as possible.[11]

With environmental risk small doses of highly toxic material can have catastrophic effects on a large number of actors. A small number of free riders can render widespread harm. The low threshold for free riding on the critical mass, cooperating to prevent the public bad, makes it harder to achieve the cooperative solution. If the goal is to minimize the number of noncooperators, it will only be in any person's interest to be part of the critical mass if all others (or nearly all others) also are. Central institutions must have established and justified standards, the power and resources to apply them, and must detect defectors from cooperation swiftly to prevent long-term harm to the community and ensure widespread cooperation. The definition of acceptable risk must be public and clear. The system of justice, which distributes risk, must have proper moral authority that is understood to set the expectations with which everyone joins the critical mass (Gillroy 1992b, 1992c).

The second characteristic is that the environmental-risk dilemma is a second-stage strategic choice. The solution to the polluter's dilemma has already set a standard for environmental quality. The authority faced with a potential environmental risk needs to impose stricter cooperative requirements, minimizing or eliminating free riders and preventing the breakdown of the collectively optimal solution (R1,C1).

A third strategic distinction producing the imprisoned rider involves the choices of the players. The normal polluter's dilemma gives each player two strategy choices: to cooperate in the critical mass providing environmental quality, or to defect and pollute. Usually, environmental-risk cases involve one actor (e.g., a corporation) that develops a technology or scientific process that presents the risk, and then natural systems and the rest of the human population, which share the collective dissemination of harms from any risk. But only one of these parties has the option to impose risk, while the other, without collective representation, can only accept the imposition of risk and its outcomes.

The stealth quality of environmental-risk dilemmas means that harms are often not evident to one's senses. One can live in a house full of radon, or drink water laced with toxic chemicals and not know it. Stealth, combined with a long latency period before physical ailment becomes evident, places the individual citizen-player in a position of dangerous ignorance: thinking she is safe when she is not. Without the collective energies and resources of political institutions to monitor the environment and to support everyone's full agency, the corporate player can use its dominant strategy without fear of immediate detection or retaliation.[12]

Citizens face risks that are potentially catastrophic, irreversible, have long latency periods that conceal hazards from their knowledge or perception, and are collective, so that no one individual acting alone (Row) has power against a firm (Column) that wants to use a risky technology or market a new product. If we return to the polluter's dilemma game matrix (fig. 2.1), and we assume that no background institutions exist, the environmental-risk equilibrium will not be at R2,C2 but at R1,C2.

Individual citizens must cooperate, for they have no threat power (i.e., defection and counterimposition of environmental risk) but require the collective good of environmental quality to continue to live. Specifically, the individual has no alternative but to choose the cooperative strategy (R1). The corporate entity is already inclined, by market assumptions, to play out its dominant strategy and defect in order to maximize its internal economic benefits. Column can also impose risk with stealth, that is, without the direct knowledge of the other player, who does not have the power, skill, or resources to identify or monitor an environmental-risk violation, nor the capacity to do anything about it if known. The firm can serve its self-interest by choosing to defect and impose the risk (C2) without immediate fear of detection or reaction from the other player, and with no disincentive from the other player, the firm can produce its highest preference, to defect while enjoying the full advantage of the good.

In cell R1,C2, an equilibrium is established where the individual is exploited by the firm, receiving his lowest payoff while the firm gets its highest. Given the strategic nature of the risk dilemma, I contend that this lone citizen is an imprisoned rider. Central political representation, based on the individual's interests as a member of the collective and existing to protect and define the public interest and to prevent the exploitation of isolated individual citizens, is a necessary prerequisite to freeing the imprisoned rider. Because the qualities of environmental risk make normal detection-and-response mechanisms for the individual player dysfunctional, only central authorities with organization, power, and resources can overcome the strategic asymmetries, minimize (N-k) coordinating the critical mass of actors, and solve the second-stage game in anticipation of any defections that could render harm to all. The state's responsibility is to protect the citizen from exploitation as an imprisoned rider, stop harm before it affects anyone, and preserve each citizen, *ex ante*, from any potential hazard to his or her strategic agency.

Only with a morally justified central authority to represent individuals as citizens is it possible to manage risk and distribute it fairly within and between generations. A conscious and rational attempt to discuss risk-generation in such a way that R1,C1 persists as a point of equilibrium is a prerequisite to the goal of ensuring that all citizens are protected from exploitation in R1,C2. Active state institutions are necessary for the row player to have a threat strategy against column, for each individual to have the capacity to protect himself from being exploited as an imprisoned rider, and for reestablishing a symmetry of strategic choice between players. Political institutions give individuals preemptive power to require the cooperation of firms that, in order to be efficient, may not have subjective interests in that direction. But anticipatory action in defense of the imprisoned rider requires moral justification beyond economic values; it is to the roots of this ethical argument that we now turn.

Beyond Monetary Cost: Harm to Intrinsic Value

As expected, the cost-benefit approach to policy decision making in cases of environmental risk is preoccupied with what it is designed to prevent, and what it is best capable of handling: instrumental monetary cost. The money that will be lost or gained and the opportunity cost of capital expended in the achievement of other ends are the permanent and sole concerns of anyone using cost-benefit evaluation, where a benefit is defined in terms of a dollar cost saved. This overriding interest in funds and their allocation is not solely a concern with the efficient allocation of capital, but it is deeply tied to a moral intuition that maximization of wealth in trade also provides for the autonomy of the individual and the good of the community (Nozick 1974; Posner 1983; Becker 1976).

In cases of environmental risk, there are indeed monetary costs to be considered, both real and in terms of economic opportunity. It costs real dollars to clean up a toxic dump, to properly dispose of waste materials, or to build safety into a nuclear reactor. There are opportunity costs when a firm must test extensively and hold back a new chemical or genetic technology, sometimes only to have it prohibited from sale. But are these the sole costs of environmental risk? If not, are they the most important costs? If not, what is truly at stake in a decision to accept an environmental risk?

The answers to all these questions lie in an examination of the last one: what are the true costs of environmental risk? Costs exist in the expected effects of "worst case" scenarios.[13] Although these differ and are, as we have seen, uncertain, it is possible to describe what is at stake when these zero-infinity risks inflict their maximum effects.

But, perhaps cost analysis fails to properly evaluate the capacity of humans and natural systems to persist and to have a reasonable opportunity to reach full potential within their social or ecological contexts. Are the "integrity" of human beings and the natural systems in which they exist, that is, the respective intrinsic values of human morality and a functioning natural environment, at stake in environmental-risk gambles?[14]

The natural environment is an intricate set of interrelationships and elemental cycles (Odum 1975, 1993) stressed by environmental-risk hazards. Owing to the synthetic nature of the technologies that produce risk, their irreversibility, and their mutagenic effects, environmental-risk contaminants are potentially more dangerous to natural systems persistence and natural selection than traditional pollution problems that, to some degree, can be accommodated by the internal cleaning cycles of the environment. The breakdown of a number of critical subsystems could potentially cause a dysfunction of the entire natural environment, a process of degeneration that might be irreversible.

Exposed to the effects of environmental-risk contaminants, humans have their ability to think and process information made dependent on the state of the natural environment (as a medium of transmission), where the assault of toxins, radioactive material, and new strains of synthetic disease directly affect the air we breath, the water we drink, the food we eat, and the land on which we live. The capacity to think for oneself, to have agency in the world, is the central component of each and every human being and is at hazard in the environmental-risk gamble (Gillroy 1992b). Without the capacity for self, the individual can have no independent character, no self-conscious thought or voluntary purposeful action, nor any possibility for preferences let alone a rational preference order that is, in any real sense, her own.

The word "cost," in this context, is inadequate, and perhaps a logical category mistake (Sagoff 1981, 1411; 1985). The human capacity for agency and the moral integrity of that agency as well as the functional capacity of natural selection to persist over time are concerns that ought to be put into terms that can reflect their intrinsic value. Cost properly evaluates only variables that have a monetary price and can be traded as fungible goods with exclusively instrumental value. Costs are calculations of uncompensated economic loss as means for the end of wealth maximization (Pigou 1932).

Harm, however, can be related to the destruction, damage, or incapacitation of that which has intrinsic value. Therefore, harm should be distinguished from cost as that result of environmental risk that negatively affects the intrinsic capacities of human or natural systems. With this definition, harm carries a moral connotation relating to damage of essential capacity, ability, and potential. The new vocabulary also grants asymmetric weight to preventing an essential harm as against providing an elective benefit. Harm is now more than a nonbenefit, which is the economic definition of cost (Feinberg 1973, 29–31).

In effect, costs and benefits cease to be positive and negative sides of the same coin: prevention of harm due to its effect on essential value has priority over provision of a benefit in welfare terms.

Contrary to this use of "harm," the cost-benefit criterion assumes that avoiding a harm of a certain magnitude is just as desirable as producing a benefit of the same size. I maintain that this symmetry is not consistent with the gamble in environmental risk. Harm to moral or functional integrity is essential; it is separate and more important than cost to the economy or to any individual in the market and is therefore not subsumed in the efficient maximization of wealth nor in instrumental preferences for welfare improvements. Capacity exists prior to preference in that, without a self, preferences cannot be created, and without essential capacity, there is no delineated self (Fried 1977, 185–88).

The harmful effects of environmental risk will not be prevented or remedied by the encouragement of subjective wealth maximization, for this behavior is what causes the strategic reality of the polluter's dilemma, the imprisoned rider, and the imposition of risk by the few on the many. Nor will environmental risk be rendered harmless by the noninterference of government, for the lack of an active collective agent for nature and the public interest allows the environmental-risk prisoner's dilemma to produce the phenomena of the imprisoned rider and degenerating environmental quality. Nor will cost-benefit evaluation be adequate to define "socially better," since it is not instrumental monetary cost primarily at stake but intrinsic harm to human and natural systems.

The capacity for human agency and the capacity of the natural environment to functionally persist should provide the core concerns of environmental-risk policy. These are basic, necessary, and comprehensive concepts of intrinsic value in that they have to do with the internal integrity of living and evolving organic, and, in the case of the human individual, moral capacities. Respecting essential freedom within the context of environmental risk necessitates that the central authority anticipate free riders and regulate their behavior so that constituent capacities are protected and empowered before economic externalities can harm them. Anticipatory regulation of economic market behavior through an active state requires a justification scheme that transcends preference, consent, and "willingness to pay" as a basis for policy choice.

But, while the market treats the environment instrumentally (Dorfman and Dorfman 1977), don't the ethical dimensions of the economic model protect both the maximization of utility and the preservation of human autonomy as an intrinsic value (Leonard and Zeckhauser 1986)?

Efficiency, Morality, and a "Thin" Theory of Autonomy

Two questions must be addressed: first, are the "moral foundations" of cost-benefit methods adequate to move efficiency analysis from the competitive market to the realm of public administration? Second, is there an argument for intrinsic value within the market paradigm's concern for the autonomy of the individual (O'Neill 1993, chap. 5)?

Efficiency is the central principle of markets and can always be used to judge the least-cost means to public ends.[15] But anyone proposing that the assumptions of the competitive market are adequate to judge public ends themselves is also assuming that efficiency has a deeper moral validity than merely its "rational" economic nature in order for it to hold moral sway outside of the pure market context.[16] For market decision and evaluation criteria to transfer into the realm of political decision making, their justification cannot be based solely on efficiency as an economic standard; an argument must be made that efficiency has moral weight, as a more universal and necessary ethical standard or principle that can evaluate both the instrumental and the intrinsic values at stake. Those recommending cost-benefit methods, for both the means and ends of public policy, must claim that this moral weight exists at a more fundamental level than the rational argument for efficiency. The two most probable bases for this moral weight are in the concepts of utility and autonomy. I will concentrate on the latter.[17]

Autonomy is a complex moral standard that has many definitions and exists within both consequentialist and nonconsequentialist ethical thought from Mill to Kant to Hegel (Christman 1989). For the purposes of this chapter, I will identify three theoretical definitions of autonomy, categorize them into "thin" and "thick" theories, and demonstrate that, while only the latter version can accommodate intrinsic value, only the former can be claimed by the principle of Kaldor efficiency.

A "thick" theory of autonomy representing the intrinsic value of the person[18] has three components; the first two are logical entailments of the third. First, it defines what is intrinsically important about the person (e.g., will, choice). Second, it distinguishes between autonomous and nonautonomous behavior (e.g. as a theory of the "good" or the "right"); and third, it provides a location for the moral worth of an act (e.g., the internal character of the act or its consequences).

Two categories of autonomy theory can be called "thick" by definition. The first alternative is nonconsequentialist in nature and defines autonomy as the internal capacity of the human will to control the agency of the individual. Here, the choices of the individual and their consequences are not as ethically critical; it is the freedom of the individual's will and one's intent that are prior to, and conditions choice. Central to this concept of autonomy is that one's will be controlled by one's capacity to reason. This capacity creates human character and a full concept of the "self" that defines what is "right," that is, what is necessary to enable or empower the will of the individual to legislate for himself and to be autonomous.

The second "thick" alternative is consequentialist in nature, and here, the internal will is not as important as the desires and wants revealed in individual empirical choice. The moral worth of these choices is defined by the consequences produced by them. To avoid tautology, all choices made by the individual cannot be considered autonomous, and a definition of the "good" is necessary to distinguish that which consequentially affirms the autonomy of the person from that which does not. The "good" must reflect the complexity (economic, moral, political, social) of the environment within which the individual exists and define what is of utility to his or her autonomy.[19]

Although the "thick" theories of autonomy are either consequentialist or nonconsequentialist, the "thin" theory is represented by a hybrid category that attempts to combine the consequentialist use of empirical preferences and choice with a nonconsequentialist focus on rights that sanctify these choices.

Autonomy, as a "thick" nonconsequentialist ethical concept, is normally thought of as one's control over one's own will (Kant GW; C2), as a "kind of higher order control over the moral quality of one's life" (Kuflik 1984, 273). But a disagreement exists between nonconsequentialists like Kant and Kuflik, who define autonomy as an internal qualitative consideration, and those (Wolff 1970; Nozick 1974) who consider autonomy an act of revealed choice, based on preference, and in terms of the noninterference of third-parties in the act of consenting. Here what is important about a person is consequentialist and instrumental (his or her empirical choices),[20] whereas what distinguishes between autonomous and nonautonomous choice (the "right" to have one's empirical choices respected by others), as well as where the moral worth of the act itself (the intent and desire of the individual) is located, are nonconsequentialist.

It is this "thin" hybrid theory of autonomy that lies at the root of the market paradigm. But by combining consequentialist and nonconsequentialist approaches to autonomy, one is left with a theory that cannot distinguish autonomous from nonautonomous choice, for it has neither the rich sense of "self" necessary to define an "intrinsic" metaphysical standard as the nonconsequentialist "thick" theory does, nor an enriched theory of "good" consequences that would support a consequentialist vision of autonomous action (Sagoff 1986).

Essentially, the "moral high ground" (Leonard and Zeckhauser 1986, 47) for cost-benefit methods is coextensive with, and no more powerful than, the "rational" or narrowly economic justification of cost-benefit. We shall see that, limited to instrumental valuation, the autonomy of individual choice outside of a market is an impoverished and morally "thin" theory of "autonomy as consent" that is unable to stand on its own, provide any definition or support for "intrinsic value," or justify the use of an efficiency standard, outside of a competitive economic market, for making political choices.

Cost-Benefit: The Rational and Ethical Justifications?

According to Mishan (1982a, 1982b), a cost-benefit criterion for public policy replicates market choice, but with externalities internalized.[21] The ethical appeal of markets is traced to the noninstrumental notions of freedom, consent, and autonomy. "It is only under a system of voluntary exchange that freedom is maximized" (Director 1964, 7). The alleged ability of the market to respect individuals "intrinsically," by one's liberty to maximize one's own personal welfare, provides a more fundamental moral basis for public choice than its mere efficient maximization of social welfare. Mishan and Page (1992, 63) set Kaldor efficiency upon the normative foundation of an "ethical consensus" about freedom and utility. In defining markets, Richard Posner appeals to Kant.

> [H]ighly congenial to the Kantian emphasis on autonomy is consent. . . . Suppose we consider consent an ethically attractive basis for permitting changes in the allocation of resources, on Kantian grounds. . . . We are led . . . to an ethical defense of market transactions that is unrelated to their effect in promoting efficiency . . . so that maximizing wealth and protecting autonomy coincide. (Posner 1983, 89–90)

Other supporters of the market approach to public policy choices connect the ethical appeal of markets (without externalities) and the allocations of cost-benefit analysis (integrating externalities). They argue that "[w]e know of no other mechanism for making such choices that has an ethical underpinning" (Leonard and Zeckhauser 1986, 33).

A cost-benefit test for policy therefore claims two levels of justification. Rationally, it is justified teleologically by the end of preference satisfaction and aggregation where Kaldor efficiency (the Potential Pareto Improvement[22]) acts as the foundational normative concept. Each person maximizes personal welfare assuming that individual rationality, in its drive to provide for one's self-interest, can be aggregated by the policymaker (using cost-benefit methods to mimic the market). This aggregation produces a social ordering that, simultaneously over all persons, renders an efficient collective allocation of goods.

Ethically, a cost-benefit criterion is justified on the basis of one's voluntary consent, where one's autonomy, or freedom of choice, is the foundational moral ideal. In the realm of public policy, efficient allocation is superficially a formal economic argument for the use of cost-benefit procedures that has no independent moral weight but must be justified by other moral principles (Gramlich 1981; Boadway 1979; Layard 1972; Lave 1981; Kelman 1981a, 1981b). So choosing cost-benefit methods rather than cost-effectiveness analysis in policy evaluation grafts the superficial "economic" claims of cost-benefit methods onto a deeper moral argument that market assumptions about individual self-interest, freedom of choice, and autonomy are normatively true *ex ante*. The "moral high ground" argument for cost-benefit procedures works or fails to the degree that the market justification system of "autonomy as consent" that motivates the use of cost-benefit evaluation in nonmarket situations has ethical strength in the public realm.[23]

The ethical justification for cost-benefit analysis, its claim to "ethical propriety" (Leonard and Zeckhauser 1986, 47–48), and the "moral high ground" is an argument based on two essential concepts that are used in the economic literature to define and support the idea of autonomy: consent (which defines its theory of the good) and preference (which acts as its theory of the "self").

Welfare and Hypothetical Consent: A Metaphysics of Choice

Autonomy, in the guise of consent and consumer sovereignty in the market (Posner 1983, 80–95; Mishan 1982a, 1982b), is one of the basic normative assumptions of cost-benefit methods. But does autonomy in this context represent an individual's intrinsic value in terms of his external choices?

In the literature, the individual is the sole repository of utility and welfare in the market mechanism. She is assumed to know her mind, what is best for her, and to have sovereignty over all judgments of welfare, which will serve, primarily, her own self-interest (Mishan 1982b, 33). In this way a type of integrity is posited for the individual by the degree of self-sufficiency and personal sovereignty he or she maintains. Such a concept of sovereignty disallows any but the most basic collective (third-party) interference in one's affairs, limiting government policy to the role of encouraging wealth-maximizing transactions. Exchange is an individual choice motivated by subjective preferences that are the point of departure for all judgments of welfare.

The market operates on the assumption that individuals are self-sufficient, and it sanctions transactions only on the basis of voluntary consent. *Webster's New World Dictionary* defines "autonomy" as "functioning independently without the control of others" (2nd ed., s.v. "autonomy"). In the sphere of economic concerns this has come to mean free exchange between individuals on the basis of their mutual consent and without the interference of government. Thus, a definition of "autonomy as consent" is created for the market. But can this idea of the autonomous trader be transferred into the realm of public environmental choice, which requires that we adequately represent at least human intrinsic value?

The economic definition of the "good" that supports "autonomy as consent" is the moral foundation of cost-benefit evaluation. This concept of the "good" draws its normative power from the components of consent: the idea of voluntary choice, the connection of choice to consideration of welfare improvement, and the preferences that inform and motivate one's sovereign choices.

Choice: The central concerns of "autonomy as consent" in a market are the voluntary choice of individuals and collective respect for that choice. The normative ramifications of choice rest on the assumption of individual self-sufficiency, while respect for these choices defines justice in a specific way that influences the role played by the status quo in market allocations.

First, in order for a choice to be voluntary, it must not be interfered with. The market approach is interested primarily in the interference of collective authorities in the individual maximization of wealth, but when we consider public choices, other individuals and their externalities can also be as interfering as any government. If one is enslaved or routinely exploited by another person or group of people, then one's wealth maximization will be curtailed as his utility function and autonomous choices become subject to the person who controls his life. When stuck on a bridge jammed with traffic, other individuals have interfered with one's voluntary choices, not any collective authority, whose regulation may in fact be the only way out of the jam. In the public context, the moral assumptions at the base of cost-benefit evaluation focus on the state as location of all principal interference, and therefore place maximum pressure on the noninterference of policymakers in the voluntary exchange of consumers. This blinds the policymaker to concern for the externalities of some individuals or groups as they affect the freedom of others. Such externalities are assumed to be internalized and free of transaction costs (Coase 1960).

But voluntary choice, even in isolation, is a function of the endowment of fungible goods one has, with which he begins trade, and the opportunity set of which he can take advantage. Status quo entitlement is the sole basis on which welfare improvements are judged, and they constrain power to maximize wealth in trade (It takes money to make money!). If the initial endowments of the individuals involved in an exchange are greatly asymmetric (which is very possible within a policy framework), then voluntary choice is also asymmetrically distributed.

Even if endowments are not asymmetrically distributed, opportunity may be, so that individuals have the economic power to improve but no occasion to make the actual exchange. In the public context, one may therefore be strategically exploited in two ways: by beginning with an asymmetrically small endowment, which restricts one's freedom to make voluntary choices; or, by having an asymmetrically small opportunity set that does not allow one the choices he would wish. Both of these complicate the meaning of voluntary action for the policymaker and blur the connection between one's act and the ideal of consent as a moral concept representing an equal and ideal-regarding definition of intrinsic value (Barry 1990, 39–40).

On the basis of the policy requirements of equal consideration of all citizens, the market lacks the necessary guidelines to ethically define the status quo point from which exchange begins and its results are evaluated. Dependence on an amoral status quo entitlement, self-sufficiency, and noninterference may be enough to define autonomy within the market, where instrumental value is all that is at stake. However, the environmental policymaker must assume that first distribution affects the freedom and voluntarism of his constituents and thus the ability of each individual to equally express his capacity in autonomous action, within which his intrinsic value as consent to policy is framed. Therefore, voluntary consent (autonomy in the economic sense) has neither a minimum universal foundation nor a mechanism to ensure its fair distribution.

What a public policy decision maker may consider an initially unfair or inadequate distribution does not, from the market point of view, morally cloud the autonomous capacity of individual consumers' choices. The individual valuations (v_i) aggregated by cost-benefit methods are counted equally, regardless of any one consumer's status quo endowment or opportunity set. With the Potential Pareto Improvement, it does not matter to whom the benefit falls, only that the net welfare benefit exceeds loss enough for the possibility of a hypothetical transfer from rich to poor to occur. Cost-benefit evaluation depends on the market assumption that aggregation and allocation protect individual autonomy. Any redistribution of entitlements, by third parties without consent, violates autonomy as a matter of definition.

However, a policy analyst using the market approach is not concerned with real autonomous choice but with attributing such choice to individuals, assuming, whatever their condition or environment, that they are self-sufficient and free to trade. Self-sufficiency, it might be argued, is the core of intrinsic value for the market paradigm. If self-sufficiency is the foundation of one's integrity, then it must be basic to one's autonomy, representing the essential value of the person. But, autonomy, especially in public policy, may not be equivalent to self-sufficiency. Individuals may require assistance, through distribution of information or entitlements, to empower their capacities for equal political/economic participation. One may not know what is best, and autonomy or intrinsic value may not be a function of self-sufficiency but may require the involvement of others to assure a morally relevant and fully capacitated decision.

> Autonomy is not to be equated with self-sufficiency. Indeed, in a complex world it is difficult to believe that anyone is always the best judge of every possible matter. Thus the morally reflective person is prepared to acknowledge that in certain cases someone else may be in a better position to gather morally relevant information or even to give disinterested attention to the facts. (Kuflik 1984, 273)

Autonomy, distinguished from self-sufficiency, is the ultimate power over one's capacity to be a moral person, which equally defines one's essential or intrinsic value in a way that may require the assistance of collective authorities in the definition and regulation of a fair first-distribution. If a deeper sense of justice than what any self-sufficient individual can choose is a necessary ingredient in an ethical definition of autonomy, for environmental-risk policy, then, we need more than Kaldor efficiency can provide.

Justice derived from the market definition of "autonomy as consent" does not address concerns about instrumental voluntary choice but sets them in concrete within cost-benefit methodology. Cost-benefit procedure requires that the choices and valuations of individuals be respected as they are and thus defines the role of the state in terms of the authority necessary to ensure that "from each as they choose, to each as they are chosen" (Nozick 1974, 160; Hayek 1976). This definition of justice grants the status quo entitlement the moral validity of a just endowment and narrows the possible range of redistribution to what is voluntarily undertaken by the wealthiest.

Any asymmetry in the initial entitlement will probably be perpetuated into the future, as any government interference to redistribute will violate "autonomy as consent," and wealth holders will set the terms of trade to maintain their advantage. Under these conditions, the first distribution, upon which all future allocations will be based, gains moral sanction, and de facto right to its contents becomes real and controlled by the owner. In reality, de facto right gains moral respect as the proper basis upon which voluntary choice will define autonomy. One's entitlement will now dictate the degree to which one's freedom or autonomy is expressed. "Autonomy as consent," however, with the assumption of self-sufficiency, will judge all exchanges as if they were made instrumentally by voluntary consent. Cost-benefit evaluation will not interfere or compensate for this assumption but will build on it as a fit point of departure for government-sanctioned public policy decisions. In effect, the only definition of intrinsic value accessible to "autonomy-as-consent" allows wealth to determine variations of worth and sanctions those with more "intrinsic" value to take advantage of those with less instrumental means and therefore less moral worth from the perspective of the market.

> Another implication of the wealth-maximization approach, however, is that people who lack sufficient earning power . . . are entitled to no say in the allocation of resources unless they are part of the utility function of someone who has wealth. (Posner 1983, 76)

Consent and Welfare: An inherent assumption in the economic analysis of policy decision making is that autonomous individuals will always consent to that allocation which will improve their welfare relative to their initial endowment. Each consumer is said to be interested in maximizing personal welfare and, to this end, will seek alternative allocations that efficiently advance his economic position. "Autonomy as consent" must necessarily be examined from within a theory of the "good" that is limited to this connection between consent and personal welfare.

However, in evaluating policy ends, there may be other variables of moral importance connected with a public choice that override increases in welfare. For example, one may be involved in a transaction in which, in the end, he is better off (in welfare terms) than he was to begin with, but in which the transaction involved extortion or exploitation of power or strategic advantage that may be considered inherently unjust. A miner with no education or other skill, indebted to the company store, may not be considered autonomous in "choosing" to go down in the mine, even though the work does improve his welfare and that of his family. In such a case, where one can be said to have a gun at one's head, the fact of the extortion has no effect on the judgment of self-sufficiency or consumer autonomy for the cost-benefit analyst. Consent only requires a trade or act of choice and that the gains from the act outweigh the net loss. One may object to occupying a position where exploitation causes trade, but this fact in itself does not affect the assumptions about autonomy in a market; it is not considered a cost and thus cannot devalue the welfare increase that is the basis of assumed consent.

One may also at times be motivated to act for reasons other than wealth maximization that are morally relevant to a definition of autonomous choice in the public realm. One may decide to cooperate in a prisoner's dilemma even though he knows that he will lose welfare (at least initially), or he may lower his personal time preference and save more for the future than is efficient, being concerned less with his own well-being and more with the welfare of others. In aggregating individual interests into public policy one cannot always make the assumption that welfare maximization is the most morally relevant concern in a person's autonomous actions. Even assuming self-interested behavior, one may not always consent to those transactions that improve wealth but may promote an ideal above instrumental wants as a standard of choice.

It may be an unpredictable and unquantifiable option, but nonwealth-based choices are an important moral dimension of autonomy for the policy decision maker to consider. To set public ends, both instrumental and intrinsic values need to be considered. A theory of autonomy that makes one's intrinsic value coextensive with one's instrumental wealth value is therefore deficient in evaluating what is at stake in risk decisions. If policy choice can be ideal-regarding as well as want-regarding in nature (Barry 1990, 38–40), our policy paradigm and context model must transcend the strictly want-regarding nature of wealth maximization and Kaldor efficiency.

Outside of markets, applying the market paradigm to public policy, real choice ceases to be the foundation of efficient aggregation. A central decision maker subscribes to the connection between consent and welfare as a sound definition of individual reason and an adequate basis for public choice. This is especially suspect in a situation where the Potential Pareto Improvement ensures welfare losers as well as winners.[24]

By assuming that all wealth-maximizing allocations gain the consent of all consumers who benefit, the policy decision maker is, in reality, taking sovereignty over subjective valuations and decisions away from the individual. Within the demands of the market paradigm for consumer sovereignty, this seems a violation of autonomy rather than a proper definition of intrinsic value.

If welfare improvements can gain consent, it may also be possible that welfare loss might gain or lose consent, or that consent and welfare are unconnected in any collective or individual sense. What is important about the individual is, therefore, not her instrumental welfare desires or the choices she makes, but her essential agency or capacity to choose. But this capacity is not part of the market argument for intrinsic value.

Hypothetical Consent: We also need to remember that cost-benefit analysis is not concerned with real-market Pareto Improvements, but only with Potential Pareto Improvements. Consequently, we are faced, not with real consent to guaranteed welfare improvements over the collective, but with hypothetical consent to overall social benefits outweighing costs, where many may suffer welfare losses. This entailment complicates the policy decision and places further stress on "autonomy as consent" as a definition of one's intrinsic value outside markets.

First, with Kaldor efficiency, consent ceases to be an intrinsic moral expression of voluntary choice to maximize subjective welfare. Because all will not receive a welfare improvement, the decision maker cannot rely on the voluntary consent of all unless hypothetical compensation (an assumption of the *Po-*

tential Pareto Improvement) is made actual, which is not necessary to Kaldor efficiency.[25]

The decision maker must rely on the metaphysical assumptions that voluntary choice and consent are connected, and that consent and welfare are also interdependent, to carry the weight of his policy decision. Only with these conceptual bridges can he assure himself that individual autonomy is the basis of market-paradigm public choice. With these assumptions, he is also assured that autonomy means consent to all welfare improvements (potential or real) and that these are the choices that moral individuals would make to ensure their continued personal autonomy or intrinsic freedom.

At this point a cycle begins to develop in the moral argument as one concept is defined in terms of the other (Sagoff 1986). An allocation that renders a Potential Pareto Improvement is assumed to gain the autonomous consent of the people, while autonomous choice is considered protected and revealed in those policies that render Potential Pareto Improvements.

But can one assume consent without compensating the losers? Yes, for a powerful sense of *ex ante* compensated consent also exists within the concept of Kaldor efficiency. If one is assumed to consent to efficient allocation, one is also said to consent to all outcomes of that new allocation, even if these turn out to be personally negative. *Ex ante* or hypothetical consent is then used as an assumption of prior compensation, relieving Kaldor efficiency from dependence on real *ex post* compensation to turn a Potential into a Real Pareto Improvement.

> It is my contention that a person who buys a lottery ticket and then loses the lottery has "consented" to the loss. . . . Many of the involuntary, and seemingly uncompensated, losses experienced in the market or tolerated by the institutions that take the place of the market . . . are fully compensated [for] ex ante and hence are consented to in the above sense. (Posner 1983, 94)

Again, in using an economic definition of autonomy outside a market the policy decision maker is metaphysically conflating self-interest, subjective welfare, and consent. He is assuming that any fair lottery that is even potentially a benefit to one, gains one's consent, and does not violate one's integrity, which is compensated *ex ante*, whatever the outcome.

But if welfare and consent have no necessary metaphysical or ethical connection in terms of one's intrinsic value, then counterfactual consent (Dworkin 1980) cannot be used as justification for a Potential Pareto Improvement. In no case, even if consent and welfare are connected, can it be said that individual consent is compensated for *ex ante* to an allocation that has uncertain outcomes. Although one may choose to be part of a lottery, one does not simultaneously consent to the outcome; this is a separate moral consideration requiring independent ethical justification and evaluation (Fishkin 1979, 70–71).

This distinction is especially true when the character of the choices at each stage of the lottery has distinct ramifications. For example, although one may agree, when measuring strictly instrumental value in a market, that buying a one-dollar lottery ticket for a chance at one million dollars implies consent to win or lose the million; both the cost of the ticket and the win or loss have a distinctly narrow, instrumental, and economic character. The same economic calculations are used to decide both spending the dollar and the probability of winning the million.

When lotteries involve the noninstrumental value of individuals and are part of the public sector, this may not necessarily be the case. For example, one may participate in the military draft lottery because one feels that *politically* one has a general obligation to his country and his fellow citizens to participate in the chance of nonvoluntary service. This choice does not *morally* obligate one to serve or fight if drafted. Each stage of the lottery has a distinct character related to the relationship between one's integrity of self and the moral obligations generated by this intrinsic value that has political and moral ramifications requiring separate evaluation, justification, and choice on the basis of distinct criteria. A duty to participate in a fair lottery to serve one's country as an abstract political consideration does not imply a moral duty to serve in any war, any place, any time, if drafted.[26] The decision to serve may be affected by the social, political, medical, and moral particulars of the agent and the military situation for which one is called, one's disposition to serve, and whether personal circumstances or the nation's plight necessitate one's active service. Such distinctions have even been acknowledged by the Selective Service Commission, after the draft was canceled, to encourage registration for the lottery as a distinct act, not implying service. The moral distinction is not between instrumental costs and benefits but between concerns about the responsibilities to self implied in registering for the draft and in actually being called: the former is the duty of all, the latter will be the duty of only some, under specific circumstances.

Overall, market consent has some inherent flaws as a noninstrumental foundation for autonomy. Resting on an impoverished theory of the "good," it is solely concerned with wealth maximization as the extent of autonomous expression. Specifically, self-sufficiency is not morally necessary to autonomy in public policy choice, and it is a bad metaphysical and ethical assumption in a social reality where individual endowments and opportunity sets dictate degrees of freedom and voluntarism. The sense of justice in the market definition of autonomy grants moral validity to de facto possession and places asymmetric initial endowments in cement as a sanctioned point of departure for all judgments of "socially better." In terms of the ends of policy, no absolute connection exists between welfare and consent, and the addition of the idea of hypothetical consent leaves the policymaker with an even less coherent justification for action, cycling between autonomy and the Potential Pareto Improvement.

To gain an adequate theory of intrinsic value, as a basis for judgments of instrumental value, such cycles cannot be tolerated, as they provide no fundamental metaphysical foundation or standard by which to distinguish autonomous from nonautonomous choices and good from bad policy. Overall, autonomy, within the market paradigm, lacks a sense of absolute or intrinsic value while it is subjugated to degrees of wealth and the instrumental search for welfare, which, by definition, are only measures of external and elective value.

In utilizing market assumptions to choose public ends, cost-benefit analysis is a centralized decision process based on a definition of autonomy that is antithetical to centralized regulation. Cost-benefit methods empower the policymaker only insofar as she protects and mimics market allocations. In addition, the public administrator's decision is not based upon real consumer choice but upon assumed metaphysical connections between welfare and consent that are then imputed to all social valuations (V) by the decision maker.

Preference: A Metaphysics of Self

The market argument for the "moral high ground" with autonomy at its core can be further reduced, in metaphysical terms, to individual preferences that form the basis of consent and the ultimate point of departure for a definition of the "intrinsic" self. Preference is the most basic concept in the autonomy-based moral defense of cost-benefit analysis and could compensate for an impoverished theory of the "good" with a more complex theory of the "self" that could support a "thick" version of autonomy able to first define and then account for the intrinsic value of the individual.

To understand consent as personal autonomy, one must first recognize the premise that all choices are based on subjective preference. We are interested in the metaphysical assumptions made about the self, the normative ramifications of the inability to distinguish between preferences (on an ethical plane), and the problems with reliance on revealed preference. Preference is the common core of both the rational and the ethical arguments for the use of cost-benefit procedures. We will see that it adds nothing of moral importance to the market sense of "autonomy as consent" and provides neither the capacity to incorporate intrinsic value nor an independent argument for cost-benefit's ethical significance outside of the market.

The Unified Mind and the Self: Basic to any discussion of preference as a fundamental moral concept in the argument for cost-benefit methods are the dimensions of the self assumed by the market paradigm. Here, we might expect that sufficiently complex assumptions about the mind and the evolution of character might be our best opportunity for a definition of intrinsic value. But the market paradigm assumes a unified mind and unidirectional human goals dedicated to the satisfaction of one's subjective desire for welfare maximization. Is this one-dimensional self too restrictive a vision of intellectual capabilities for a policymaker to assume when choosing public ends that must incorporate intrinsic values in risk decisions?

Individuals do have instrumental policy preferences for things that increase their welfare, preferences that they may wish to satisfy and that a policymaker may assume in policy choice. But it seems less than realistic to imagine that

---

these are the most critical and common component, let alone the extent of the human intellect, or its most basic moral capacity, that ought to define the public decision maker's responsibility.

If humanity's priorities and motivations are more complex than the theory that describes them, behavior will be hard to explain, and harder to predict, understand, or take into account in policy choice. The market reduces the individual to a rational maximizer of personal welfare where reason is indistinguishable from desire satisfaction. In making collective decisions it may be important to assume, contrary to market assumptions, that the mind has the internal capacity to originate as well as order preferences and to distinguish between "proper" and "improper" preferences, recognizing when a choice involves moral imperatives, and when it does not. A capacity to reason by intellectually approved moral principle may be basic to any definition of the self that has ethical validity and intrinsic value.

The internal decision process that results in one's personal cost-benefit valuation (v_i) is one where an end is defined that increases the person's welfare by matching it with one's preexisting subjective preferences. Reason is used to compute a public policy alternative as an instrumental means to the fulfillment of the desire that motivates a preference. This economic means-end rationality prescribes what philosophers call a hypothetical imperative (Hill 1973), and it limits the mind to processing only those desires that produce the highest personal welfare. In reality "economic rationality" betrays the fact that the mental processes of economic man must be more complex than assumed, if indeed he is capable of thinking in terms of hypothetical imperatives. If we define a hypothetical imperative as an elective imperative to do A if you desire B, it is necessary to presuppose that the individual is capable of more than mere desire maximization.

> [R]eason cannot be, in practice, the mere instrument of wants and desires. For the hypothetical imperative, which must be valid if reason is to have a practical function in the service of desire, itself imposes choices, which are often undesired, between adopting means and relinquishing ends. In short, nobody whose action really is determined by himself as a result of deliberation (i.e., willed), even if he embarks on a deliberation with nothing else in mind than to gratify desire, can be subject to those desires, for his deliberation can lead him not to gratify them. (Donagan 1977, 230)

If the individual is assumed by the policymaker to think ethically, to comprehend and acknowledge one's own intrinsic character and moral self, one needs to expand the concept of imperatives past the full use of the hypothetical variety and describe the individual making decisions independently of the influence of his desires, on the basis of intellectually approved moral principles arrived at through reflection. If one can reason practically, recognize one's intrinsic value as an autonomous moral agent, and judge when desire ought to play a role in decision making and when it ought not, then one may be said to have noninstrumental value and a complex sense of self. This dualistic mind, with both ethical and nonethical properties, is beyond the scope of the market paradigm and cost-benefit methods, which prescribe policy only for one-dimensional humans.

Moral Preferences: The standard by which the market justification identifies those preferences that will count in cost-benefit evaluations is through the idea of consumer surplus or *willingness to pay* (Mishan 1982a, 23; Friedman 1984, chap. 5). However, this concept is based on consent to welfare improvements within the rational justification and, in support of the concept of autonomy as a more powerful "moral high ground," adds nothing to the stature of cost-benefit evaluation. The market definition of autonomy is only capable of distinguishing surplus wealth and cannot "ethically" distinguish between preferences (Sen 1974). But being able to separate morality from monetary cost is critical in defining a noncircular concept of intrinsic value and for moving these efficiency assumptions outside of markets where more than "instrumental economic preferences" compete for attention and priority.

A public decision maker must be able to distinguish between preferences that empower the integrity of humanity or nature and those that do not. However, the "willingness to pay" standard can only decipher and rank instrumental economic choices and distinguish between economic and noneconomic preferences. This limitation is critical for environmental-risk policy and is too little to fully support intrinsic value. Willingness to pay offers no "moral high ground" or ethical priority to cost-benefit method in the public realm.

For example, willingness to pay treats a preference for cocaine the same as one for water in terms of an efficient allocation of welfare. Both are commodities, with consumer markets where preferences are fulfilled, making the recipient more satisfied than in his initial condition, thereby rendering a net benefit to him. That the former may impede one's capacity to think and act for one's self, whereas the latter may enhance those same capacities has no effect on market assumptions that support one's willingness to pay for cocaine and would proclaim either choice as autonomous.

In order to make a "moral" distinction between these two choices, one must transcend the concept of preference and create a standard that (in addition to the economic standard of "willingness to pay") draws moral distinctions between human wants. No "intrinsic" sense of "right" or "good" in the economic model offers such a distinction (Sagoff 1983, 1988; Page 1973, 1986).

The market assumptions allow ersatz consumer sovereignty to preclude the administrator from making any further distinctions among preferences using cost-benefit analysis. The decision maker takes individual cost-benefit valuations as given, and after the "willingness to pay" criterion has been applied, instrumental preferences have been quantified and are part of the aggregation of social welfare, the satisfaction of which, without alteration, is the job of the policymaker.

Not only does this definition of preference not include intrinsic value, but there is also no means of distinguishing between individual and collective preferences for various policy alternatives. Mark Sagoff (1988, chaps. 3 and 5) has suggested that a "citizen preference" may exist. A citizen preference is a desire, held by the individual, that what is good for the community should be chosen collectively, even if this diminishes his personal welfare. Sagoff's central example is of a citizen's preference for pristine nature winning out over the same person's private preference for recreation in the community decision to build a ski resort in the middle of a National Forest. The same person is assumed to hold both a preference for skiing and for wilderness and the power to override the latter for the former, as a matter of "public" policy.

The market and its surrogate, cost-benefit evaluation, recognize no strata of preferences or standards except the individual and his self-interested valuations. Therefore, no basis for policy choice at a political or group level exists that could override a subjective welfare preference without simultaneously violating the self-sufficiency of autonomous individual choice. The pertinent concern, in locating a morally sanctioned, collective policy choice, is to identify individual welfare preferences so that collective choice is instrumentally efficient in response to them.

Revealed Preference: The major concern of the policymaker who must use individual preferences to define policy choice is that he accurately represent the true welfare preferences of these individuals in his eventual decision. A definition of autonomy that included a concept of intrinsic value would also have an independent basis for the conceptualization of a true, that is, autonomy-based preference. But the market definition of autonomy depends on empirical judgments to define preferences. "The crux of the question lies in the interpretation of underlying preferences from observations of behavior" (Sen 1982, 54).

The only data readily available to the policymaker are the observed choices of individual consumers. Such expressed preferences are the necessary basis of all market policy choice. But do these empirical choices reveal autonomous policy choice, that is, the true preferences of the person? Can one make this judgment from within the concept of preference itself, as the moral core of the argument? If not, can choice define more than instrumental values? Remember, there is no independent nonpreference standard within the definition of the "self" or the "good" by which to judge the real interests of the individuals involved apart from the empirical choices revealed to the policymaker.

As a representative of a collective third party that responds to and translates preferences into policy, the cost-benefit analyst functions with two assumptions. First, any individual's valuation (v_i) or choice function reflects his or her autonomous preferences (i.e., what is made manifest is a true representation of desire) and therefore is worthy of respect. Second, the analyst assumes that there is a connection between one's preferences and one's physical welfare.

> This dual link between choice and preference on the one hand and preference and welfare on the other is crucial to the normative aspects of general equilibrium theory. All the important results in this field depend on this relationship between behavior and welfare through the intermediary of preference. (Sen 1982, 66–67)

A problem arises when one encounters expressed behavior that does not fit the choice that would produce the higher welfare increment, a common situation in public policy analysis.

An individual might be motivated by different principles than those that encourage her to maximize welfare. In these cases (e.g., cooperating in a prisoner's dilemma), one cannot fit revealed preference together with the economic assumptions basic to the market paradigm. One can assume that true preference is connected to personal welfare improvements and separate from that preference made manifest, or that a revealed preference is not necessarily welfare centered but nevertheless decisive. Either way gaps have developed among preference, behavior, and welfare that make revealed preference a shaky ground for theoretical investigation or the moral justification of collective choice.

The possibility that individuals live in a policy environment where a sense of political responsibility or moral duty, as essential elements of their intrinsic value, may lead them to choose outcomes that do not reflect economic assumptions illustrates the fact that the wider range of revealed preferences that are critical to public deliberation and choice cannot be accounted for by "autonomy as consent."

The policymaker faced with a complex society, and without the possibility of distinguishing between true and manifest preferences (without a moral standard), will make metaphysical assumptions about preferences to make the job easier. If she is convinced that Kaldor efficiency provides a "moral high ground" for the justification of policy as well as for market transactions, she will adopt a cost-benefit analysis relying on the assumptions that preferences, choice, and the Potential Pareto Improvement are all related. In effect, she will ignore the myriad of problems and the moral poverty of this assumption and proceed to set up a cyclical argument as a justification for the application of cost-benefit evaluation. Specifically, it will be argued that a Potential Pareto Improvement provides a moral policy alternative because it satisfies the assumed welfare preferences of the individuals involved. Kaldor efficiency is said to respect the preferences or the autonomy (intrinsic value) of the individual who would only consent to a Kaldor-efficient allocation of welfare.

Autonomy in markets, as translated into public deliberation and policy argument, is defined as individual instrumental preference for welfare improvements with little or no empirical evidence or argument that connections between preference, choice, and welfare exist. Problems with subjective evaluations, true or manifest preference, and individual consent are assumed away in the theoretical axioms that preferences are the basis of all welfare calculations, that these involve welfare improvements, and that on the basis of one's autonomous preferences for welfare improvements, one would always consent to a policy that renders a Potential Pareto Improvement (even if loss results). In effect, the aggregation problem of the policymaker is assumed away and autonomy co-opted in the search for wealth maximization.

Preference is the logically primitive foundation for economic argument and for efficiency as a policy principle. For a policymaker however, these "true" preferences have no distinct intrinsic moral character but are an unstable and unreadable basis for autonomous consent as a moral concept prescriptive to public policy. The theory of the "self" contained in this definition of autonomy is instrumental, one-dimensional, and tied neatly into the desire for wealth maximization. The market framework lacks a theory of the "self" with intrinsic value and cannot therefore make any moral distinctions between preferences that would establish a deeper foundation for the Potential Pareto Improvement than those that already exist for it as a formal rational concept. Efficiency lacks a "moral" sense of the self that could compensate for an impoverished vision of the "good."

When a rich sense of human reason informing a three-dimensional concept of the "self" is not considered applicable to ends, then only preferences remain as a basis for setting and attaining these ends; autonomy becomes a strictly want-regarding phenomenon containing only instrumental values. Morality becomes instrumental rationality, and ethics is reduced to efficient preference satisfaction. Autonomy is, therefore, not a distinct moral foundation for cost-benefit methods. It requires either a fuller sense of what is consequentially "good" to get policy that supports individual autonomy, or a richer concept of the "self" to describe what is necessary for a policy to respect the rights of autonomous persons and to impute a noninstrumental value to each person.

Autonomy, in the market ideal, services economic assumptions, metaphysically connecting preference to choice and choice to welfare improvements. Such a thin theory of autonomy, will fail to account for intrinsic value to the degree autonomy is not (or ought not be) defined by Kaldor efficiency. Cost-benefit analysis presupposes that welfare improvements define consent and preferences and that these in turn define the breadth of autonomy. This "thin" theory however is weighted by this contention, so that the ends of economic efficiency and allocation automatically become the overriding *ends* of all public policy to the demise of freedom, equality, wealth distribution, and political or ethical responsibility. Remember that cost-benefit methods seek to set ends as well as means and in this way preclude other principles from determining policy.

To say that costs and benefits, in welfare terms, are all that morally count in making a public decision is to say that any ethical variable that is not directly translatable into an instrumental monetary equivalent is of consequentially less importance to the outcome. To treat individuals strictly as consumers (rather than as citizens, for example) limits the evaluation system to questions of consumption, when the real moral concern may rest upon obligation or protection or distribution.[27]

Efficiency is an economic precept, not a moral principle, and therefore is not applicable outside the market context to public choice without additional prerequisite moral justification. Kaldor efficiency, as the operating principle for cost-benefit methods, is not a moral principle like autonomy, equality, or benevolence, which carry a definition of intrinsic value. If we consider the complexity and conflict within which political choices are made, efficiency cannot be allowed to set the ends of policy.

Risk policy must address the essential interests of human and natural intrinsic value and the public obligations thus engendered prior to consideration of elective instrumental welfare preference. Cost-benefit methods reduce autonomy to a rational argument for efficiency based on assumed consent and instrumental personal preference. If autonomy is important as a moral ground for defining intrinsic value and for judging the ends of public policy, it must be independently defined and justified within its policy context outside the market paradigm.

Public Choice, "Thick" Autonomy, and Respect for Intrinsic Value

The environmental policy analyst needs to step beyond the surface issues of wealth, consent, and preference to find the essential value of humanity and nature. With a theory of integrity, or "thick" autonomy, at the foundation of policy decision making, a new normative language of responsibility, right, and duty can be introduced into the evaluation and justification of policy. With this vocabulary, we will begin to see the problems of environmental risk as involving a lack of respect for the functional integrity of natural systems and the moral integrity of human agency. With integrity representing the intrinsic value of humanity and nature, the ethical standards informing public choice will focus on the protection of these values against those who would exploit the imprisoned rider and impose risk to further their private wealth preferences.

A right is now defined as a claim one actor makes for herself as an individual or as part of the political community for that which empowers or protects her internal capacity for agency. The consideration of an agent's capacity based upon integrity grants a specific character to right and duty. It is no longer merely a preference of the individual to be a capable moral agent, but a right that invokes a private as well as a collective duty to create and support those political institutions that regulate the costs, benefits, harms, and potential exploitation of the person.

Each claimed right involves a corresponding duty that one provide for his own integrity and the moral agency of others in his political community (on an individual or collective level, depending on where potential violation of the right is centered and which level is best equipped to handle protection or redress). Freedom involves obligation to ourselves and to others as intrinsically valuable entities in an environment that supports us, while it exists with a purpose, potential, and therefore an intrinsic value of its own.

> We can be truly free to pursue our ends only if we act out of obligation, the seeming antithesis of freedom. . . . [T]o be free is not simply to follow our ever-changing wants wherever they might lead. . . . [T]he highest purpose of human reason is to evolve a comprehensive understanding of mankind's place in the universe, not merely to serve as a detector of consistency and causality and thus as an instrument for morally blind desire. (Tribe 1974, 1326–27)

No longer should the policymaker be interested primarily in aggregating the diverse subjective ends of distinct individuals to maximize their wealth or happiness; she will be concerned to respect individuals as agents with the capacity to be of moral value in-and-of-themselves. Concern for duty and responsible policy replaces reliance on the consequences of preference aggregation and the Kaldor efficiency of social policy. The moral requirements of such a duty, that would empower the state to regulate in anticipation of free riding, must also require increased moral justification in order that public duty is fulfilled without tyranny (Fishkin 1979). Coercion must be mutual and morally grounded.

In order for the state to protect, *ex ante*, the essential capacities of individuals, it must regulate that which interferes with the full potential growth and use of moral agency or intrinsic value: those material conditions that empower or retard the integrity of its agent-citizens. The state is responsible for the provision of information, but also for the distribution of the material entitlement, opportunities, and a level of environmental quality that protects the ability of each person to utilize his freedom and autonomy in making choices and in acting in the polity. Such basic material conditions define that without which individual integrity (essential internal freedom) cannot flourish. Basic entitlement and opportunity provide the external conditions in which the internal capacity of the individual can find full range, ability, and potential expression, while the level of environmental quality protects one's rational freedom from the ravages of hazards. Overall, basic capacity is fostered and protected while the strategic nature of environmental risk necessitates political involvement in provision of environmental quality.

Environmental-risk decisions, therefore, ought to be made on the basis of how each policy alternative affects the intrinsic values at stake. Life should not be defined as a quantity of time, but as a quality of evolving or persisting mental and physical capacity. The goods, opportunities, and environmental quality necessary to essential persistence of both the individual's integrity as a human being and nature's integrity as a functional system[28] ought to be the essential foundation for environmental policy, and all tradeoffs should concern how one or both types of integrity are affected.

The environment will always contain risk. But do we consciously consider what collective risks are worth taking? Do we reflect on how any particular environmental risk will affect moral and functional integrity? Imposed risk ought to be judged through its effect on the rights and duties implied by a respect for integrity and not judged by cost as the primary factor in the determination of ends and means for environmental policy. But what does this mean?

In terms of environmental risk as a collective-action problem, each individual can be said to have a private right to respect for his integrity and a public duty to respect the integrity of others. He will be assumed to have a public right to his integrity and a private duty to participate in and support the collective institutions that protect and empower his capacity and the integrity of others, without which compliance in collective action can neither be expected nor morally required. In respecting himself and others, coordination to maintain environmental quality and regulate environmental risk should be collectively maintained to the individual advantage of each person's full integrity and to the functional integrity of the natural environment. In cases where these conflict, tradeoffs should be intrinsic value for intrinsic value (e.g., basic food for one less woodland or the sacrifice of higher crop yield for the functional integrity of a unique natural system).

Environmental quality is something we have a public right to expect and a collective duty to provide. We may rightfully expect that we and the environment will be protected from the externalities of others over which we have no personal control, especially when they could affect our essential freedom or the persistence of natural systems for instrumental efficiency reasons alone. On this basis, we are not privately expected to pay for what we have a right to expect as contributing members of a political community. Our public duty to respect others coincides with our private duty to participate in the political process that provides collective compliance, and this, in turn, defines what is required of each person, collectively, in order to ensure the freedom and integrity of all, individually.

The policymaker need no longer be concerned with what an individual is "willing to pay" for. Instead, it is critical that a decision maker understand what each person has a private right to expect and a public duty to provide for his fellow citizens and the natural environment. This sets the expectations of administrator and citizen alike, the range in which cooperation can be expected, and how this cooperation will be defined and any conflicts resolved.

Environmental Risk and Environmental Values

The critical foundation for economic cost-benefit analysis is its metaphysical assumptions and ethical prejudices that construct the way in which the economist views the world, what variables count in policy considerations and by how much, and, ultimately, how far the market can pursue efficiency (Rhoads 1985).

The strategic reality of environmental policy and the fate of the imprisoned rider requires that two moral asymmetries be considered in evaluating and justifying public decisions. First, we must distinguish the party to the strategic interaction that inflicts the uncompensated loss from the party that suffers harm from it. The isolated individual or firm whose economic decision making imposes the cost must be distinguished from the collective (all others, including nature), who are not always empowered to adopt defensive strategies against potential harm.

Second, and especially relevant in environmental-risk cases, an asymmetry between essential harm to intrinsic value and nonessential cost or benefit to instrumental value should be recognized. In the provision of a collective good like environmental quality both of these asymmetries entail policy considerations.

The first asymmetry requires the policymaker to identify those who inflict harm and either stop them *ex ante* or make them responsible to compensate those they inflict it upon, who have a proper expectation that such monitoring, protection, or compensation is forthcoming. A sound environmental policy demands that the evaluator define a "public" interest as a distinct entity, apart from the sum of individual preferences. The collective good will often conflict with individual choice and preference, and therefore political institutions must be constructed, and terms of conflict resolution established, so that

coordination can be set that is fair to both individuals and their collective interests.

Within the logic of market efficiency, the state may absorb transaction costs that inhibit market exchange but cannot regulate that exchange once it has been established. All value in a cost-benefit equation is fungible and of symmetric weight. When one determines public ends through cost-benefit methods, even the disposition of property rights is considered morally arbitrary (Coase 1960). The only acceptable state action is that which assigns these rights and provides expectations and contract enforcement, so that one's "willingness to pay" may set the price of the externality. No independent collective or public interest exists in this analysis, only the aggregate of individual economic choices that allocate, by each person's willingness or ability to pay, the price of environmental quality.

Such a limited level of state involvement in setting environmental policy is troublesome within the context of traditional pollution problems and the polluter's dilemma, but when one moves from the regulation of traditional pollution problems to environmental risk, this role is even more strained. With stealth, long latency periods, irreversibility, and the moral implications of the imprisoned rider, the collective "good" must take precedence over individual wants and the unfettered functioning of market processes. The proper distribution of burdens and risk is more important than ever when moral asymmetries place essential capacity at risk. The need for prevention of environmental risk becomes an essential ingredient in producing equitable policy, now and in the future, and a sense of fairness to those who might be harmed if it were not for the protection of anticipatory institutions. Cost-benefit methods, with their emphasis on instrumental value and *ex post* incremental change, seem "especially inappropriate to environmental policy" (Goodin 1976, 153).

By defining integrity, or "thick" autonomy, as internal capacity, we can generate a set of environmental values concerned with protection, preservation, and fair distribution, defining, in this way, the responsibilities of the active state. The natural environment and the human agents that both inhabit it and to some degree control its destiny need independent weight in the competition for wealth and preference satisfaction. But the imperative to represent intrinsic environmental and human values runs counter to the tradition of applying the market paradigm to decipher the proper means and ends of public policy.

> Policy analysts typically operate within a social, political and intellectual tradition . . . that perceives the only legitimate task of reason to be that of consistently identifying and then serving individual . . . preference. . . . This tradition is echoed . . . in environmental legislation which protects nature not for its own sake but in order to preserve its potential value for man. (Tribe 1974, 1325)

Cost-benefit evaluation assumes that the environment, like all other consider-ations, has value only as an instrument to man's want-regarding nature (Bagley 1961, 149–50). Consequently, if an artificial technology serves humanity as well as a natural competitor, then it is also a morally acceptable substitute (Tribe 1974). As long as the level of satisfaction is equitable, they are consid-ered fungible goods subject to trade.

The quest for Kaldor and the reliance on preferences exogenous to the mechanism of the cost-benefit evaluation relegates all ethical consideration to those in search of welfare-maximizing options where the environment is just another good, tradable until the costs to humanity outweigh the benefits.

> By treating individual human desire as the ultimate frame of reference, and by assuming that human . . . ends must be taken as externally "given" rather than generated by reason, environmental policy makes a value judgment of enormous significance. . . . [A]ny claim for the continued existence of . . . wilderness . . . or . . . species must rest on the identification of human wants. (Tribe 1974, 1326)

Cost-benefit evaluation is an economic technique for computing the ends and means of policy. Like all decision-making techniques, cost-benefit is "likely to bias conclusions in the direction of the considerations they can most readily incorporate" (Tribe 1972, 97). Those costs and benefits that normally appear in economic-monetary terms will therefore be more "readily incorporated" than qualitative variables like human agency, health, natural system damage, moral good or right, or aesthetic considerations that are not usually analyzed in terms of money. Everything that finds its way into the cost-benefit tradeoff will be considered a priced consumer good. No discontinuity or incom-mensurabilities between goods can be evaluated by the cost-benefit criterion.[29] All considerations that are part of the analysis are fungible and defined in trad-able currency. This leaves out

> values that are intrinsically incommensurable with human satisfaction . . . values with inherently global, holistic or structural features . . . [and] values that have an on-off character like . . . integrity, . . . ecological balance . . . or wilderness. . . . [O]ne should recognize that the techniques of policy analy-sis . . . will tend either to filter [these] out of the investigation altogether or to treat them in ways inconsistent with their special character. (Tribe 1972, 96–97)

Policy analysis ought to be responsible for the protection of humanity and our environment as ends in themselves. We may want to reject a policy that is inef-ficient, but we may also want a policy justification-and-evaluation system based on a set of environmental values that judges policy by how it affects in-trinsic values.

> Policies . . . that involve the destruction of wilderness may be condemned because they destroy what has intrinsic value . . . things which are valued in

---

THE THEORY OF ENVIRONMENTAL RISK

themselves and independently of uses to which they might be put. (Elliot and Gare 1983, ix)

In those policy decisions that involve human interaction with the natural environment, cost-benefit evaluation ignores the "special character" of both humanity and nature and therefore ought not be the primary decision-tool for policymaking. In effect, using the market paradigm to judge the means and ends of environmental policy

> embodies an unacceptable premise, namely that the question to be answered is "What is efficient for society?" rather than "What is good for society?" By all means use the most cost-effective way to achieve the end once the end has been determined, but do not use the cost-benefit analysis to determine the end. (Ashby 1978, 56)

The determination of public ends ought to take the intrinsic value of humanity and nature as is and set standards for externality control and the management of involuntary transfers on the basis of a set of environmental values that can properly evaluate the unique quality of what is at stake in environmental-risk policy, without devaluing it or ignoring its "special character."

Political theory can render environmental values from the principle of protecting and empowering the integrity (intrinsic value) of humanity and the natural environment. Such environmental values entail an active state with adequate terms of conflict resolution, responsible for the coordination and provision of the collective good of environmental quality. With these at the foundation of policy evaluation, the case of environmental risk, even with its requirements for stricter compliance made necessary by the concern for minimizing and anticipating free riders (N-k), may be more adequately debated and argued within the proper context of a stronger system of moral prerequisites.

Beginning with the strategic reality of the polluter's dilemma, we need to define a public interest based, not in the strategic stalemate of private preference seeking, but in anticipatory political institutions representing citizens with collective interests. Political institutions, by setting the terms of coordination and by articulating the collective good, "define the manner in which citizens are related to each other. . . . [P]olitical institutions constitute the citizenry in the sense of giving it an organized existence" (Elkin 1983, 260–61). Thus the general good, the collective welfare, acquires an independent existence that may be reflected in something akin to Sagoff's citizen preferences (1983, 2–7). Here the public interest is not a means to subjective consumer ends but represents a person's concern for the persistence and realization of his collective identity as part of a political community.

The logic of political rationality is distinct from its economic counterpart in that a policymaker is now interested in how the individual participates in the goals of the collective. After all, "political rationality is not concerned with scarcity in the sense of something being subject to consumption" (Elkin 1983,

268), but with individual and collective responsibility to the public good and the terms of coordination necessary to its provision.

For environmental quality, instead of the economic efficiency of a policy choice, the *responsibility* of that choice takes center stage. Such responsibility can be initially defined by political institutions taking the attenuated property rights of a clean biosphere in trust for its citizens. A joint and nonexcludable good ought to have joint and nonexcludable rights and a collective entity to oversee its protection, persistence, and provision over time.

Responsibility can be further defined by equality and fairness within and between generations. Political institutions must address the persistence of its citizenry over time and with the equal participation of all in collective decisions (in person or by representative). Because of involuntary transfers, the political system must coordinate fairly; that is, one person or subset of citizens cannot be allowed to bear an asymmetrically large burden in the provision of public goods. Fairness also requires attention to the distribution of goods and services, in addition to their reallocation by policy. Although different definitions of fairness and equality will arise, any definition will have to be justified with a systematic set of environmental values, defining what is an acceptable value asymmetry, how and to what extent future generations will participate in the decisions of today,[30] what degree of distribution is fair and just to all citizens, and how (within what bounds) the good of the collective is deciphered and promoted. Environmental values honoring the intrinsic value of humanity and nature will utilize politics to change the reality of interpersonal interaction from what it strategically is to what it morally ought to be.

Overall, for the twenty-first century, we need to redefine the scope of an active government and the particulars of individual and state responsibility on the basis of the degree of cooperative compliance necessary for the persistence of human and natural integrity within the common good. An "environmental values" approach will establish a decision-making system that creates a nonmarket ideal to solve collective-action and collective-goods problems responsibly and that takes essential human and environmental values seriously while being truly reflective of the strategic and moral character of collective-goods dilemmas.

Environmental risk requires the recognition of intrinsic value in human agency and ecological persistence and the replacement of preferences and instrumental consequences with inherent duties and rights. Only by replacing conventional and relative definitions of fairness and equality with definitions that relate to the intrinsic, universal, and necessary values at stake can we ascertain the unique character of environmental risk and justify a different role for government and a more essential definition of "socially better."

To empower and protect human and natural integrity, achieve compliance in the collective coordination of individual action, and ensure that the intrinsic value of the environment is part of policy, the policymaker needs a strong set of environmental values underlying policy decisions that justify case evaluations and recommendations. Market values compensate for harm by relying on *ex post* legal compensation (e.g., torts, liability law). Environmental values function *ex ante*, independently of liability law and *ex post* monetary compensation, protecting intrinsic value from harm.

The moral standards upon which institutional evaluation of policy is raised must allow for anticipatory decisions based on duty, before harm is transmitted through the environment. The rights and duties involved in protecting potentially imprisoned riders require that policymakers be responsible to the integrity of citizens and distribute environmental quality fairly and equally across generations, holding power in trust for both real and potential agents.

The burden of proof in the imposition of risk must shift from those who want regulation to those who would support economic behavior that produces a public bad. For the policymaker, it is not that the economy should function without interruption, but that individual agency and the functional integrity of the environment ought to be fostered and protected, while economic behavior is regulated, unless it can be demonstrated that the imposition of risk through the economy is necessary to the quest for full and equal access to individual or natural systems integrity.

This reorientation of choice standards cannot be achieved without a shift of essential values in the policy-making process. But before we can ask whether Kant's ethics and political theory adequately represent a set of environmental values that take account of the intrinsic status of both humanity and nature, we must show the need, within environmental law, for such a theoretical reorientation. Only then can we move on to consider Kant and his contribution to environmental ethics, law, and policy and give administrators a decision paradigm that is adequate and accessible while being sensitive to environmental values.

Notes to Chapter 2

1. The movement of efficiency from private to public choice requires that efficiency be redefined. The idea of Pareto efficiency being linked to a new state of affairs where everyone is either as well off as he or she was under the old one or better off has no relevance in a public policy world were every decision creates welfare winners and losers. For a complete argument on this point see Gillroy and Wade 1992, Introduction to part 1.
2. Although Coase (1960) has argued that as long as right is assigned its physical "reality" is not important, it is normally understood that a physical nonattenuated property right is a necessary condition of private market transactions, which makes air and water hard to trade. The more important question is whether any environmental medium (e.g., air, water, or land) ought to be treated as a private or as a collective good. The collective-action problems related to this distinction and its moral implications are critical to environmental law and policy. The debate over public lands is a good example of this type of deliberation (Lehman 1995).
3. "Pollution control is a coordination problem for all those who would rather no one (themselves included) pollute to everyone polluting. Independent decision making is guaranteed to lead to a situation in which everyone (or nearly everyone) pollutes with, of course, some polluting more than others. Joint decision making is required if actors are to achieve an outcome which virtually all prefer, everyone refraining from polluting" (Goodin 1976, 166).

4. The dominant strategy is that choice that gives a player the best payoffs no matter what choice the other player makes. For example, Row's dominant strategy is R2, because a payoff of 4 is better than one of 3 (if column chooses C1) and a payoff of 2 is better than one of 1 (if column chooses C2).

5. There has been much written and argued on the matter of whether or not a collective-action problem can be solved without central coordination. However, it will be assumed here that the collective-action problems involved with pollution and especially risk (because of its stealth character) cannot be solved by iteration of the game or by the evolution of convention (Axelrod 1984; Hardin 1982a; Taylor 1976, 1987). There is no evidence that environmental collective-action problems are solved without government regulation, and it would seem logical that central authority would be depended upon for monitoring, enforcement, and anticipatory action as well as detection (see note 10) of environmental risk.

6. It was also Hobbes's fundamental solution of the prisoner's dilemma with or without iteration (Gauthier 1969).

7. "The biosphere is characterized by self-renewing, self-cleaning mechanisms. . . . There are, however, quantitative limits to the biosphere's capacity for self-renewal. . . . Anything in excess of these limits will stay in the atmosphere, river or ocean and cannot be removed naturally" (Goodin 1976, 151).

8. See Nozick (1974) for the authoritative definition of the minimal state.

9. This factor results in many hazards being recognized only after the firm that caused them has gone out of business. Again, tort remedies are made more and more difficult when responsible parties, even if they are eventually identified, no longer exist. See Percival et al. 1992, 630–56.

10. For discussion of the concept of a public bad, see Hardin 1982a.

11. N-k is here assumed to be the total number of defectors or free riders on the collective good. These would impose risk that has not been justified *ex ante* but is considered contrary to the public interest. As I will make clear further on in this book, in no way does this contention assume a zero-risk society; rather, it assumes one in which all environmental-risk imposition is considered (*ex ante*) on the basis of what it will contribute to individual or collective duties and what harm it will bring.

12. According to Axelrod (1984) the ability to detect a defection from cooperation and to retaliate immediately are both necessary prerequisites to any hope of solving the prisoner's dilemma through iteration or the evolution of conventional expectations and without third-party or government regulation.

13. For a complete discussion of the role of worst-case hazards in risk analysis and the value assumptions science brings to them, see Shrader-Frechette 1993, 82–85.

14. The morally intrinsic value of a functional environment shall be more completely argued in chapter 5.

15. That is, economic analysis of public policy is limited to the use of efficiency as cost-effectiveness. Once we have decided, with the use of other principles, that X is a sound public policy end, we will employ an efficiency assumption to judge the least-cost means to that end. This definition of efficiency is employed by Anderson (1979).

16. Here one must distinguish between the use of cost-benefit method and its reputation. This procedure can be used only to judge both the means and the ends of a particular public policy and is therefore a comprehensive standard that is distinct from cost-effectiveness analysis. However, economists frequently maintain that cost-benefit is not comprehensive and leaves room for other types of more morally sensitive analysis. This is simply not the case. Cost-benefit methods are meant to be, and are used, as a comprehensive standard for policy choice. For a complete exposition of the economist's argument and its critical analysis, see Leonard and Zeckhauser 1986; Gillroy 1992a; Gillroy and Wade 1992, preface and 5–13.

17. There has been much written on the moral basis of efficiency in utilitarianism. See, for example, Page 1983a and Sen and Williams 1982. An especially devastating attack on efficiency as a consequentialist moral principle is given by Sagoff (1986). Here the consequentialist moral argument for efficiency as utility is argued to be circular.

18. I assume that efficiency cannot be and is not formulated to take account of the intrinsic value of nature, but that an argument does exist that it can represent the intrinsic value of humanity in its calculations (O'Neill 1993, 46–47).

19. One could say that theories like those of Bentham and Mill, which define the good in terms of happiness or liberty, would qualify as pertaining to this definition of autonomy, whereas a theory like Hume's, based upon social convention, would have no strong sense of individual autonomy.

20. Here I agree with Rosenberg (1988, 72) that: "Revealed preference theory in effect tells us that the starting point of economics is the consequences of, and not the causes of, individual choice."

21. Remember that the task of a decision maker, using cost-benefit methods, is to take each individual's personal valuation of a policy (v_i) as revealed to him and aggregate them into a social valuation (V). If this social valuation is a net positive, then he can say that the benefits outweigh the costs and recommend the policy as a Potential Pareto Improvement; if not, then the policy fails to provide more social benefits than costs and should be rejected. See Gillroy and Wade 1992, 5–13.

22. Kaldor efficiency assumes that the benefits of the winners will be enough that they could compensate the losers, turning the Potential into a Real Pareto Improvement. This compensation, however, need not even actually take place for efficiency to be maintained under this definition. See Gillroy and Wade 1992, 5–13.

23. The rational justification of cost-benefit methods is only that; it has no moral independence or weight. Efficiency as a "rational" and economic argument must be justified in terms of other moral concepts (freedom, equality) if it cannot show that it has an independent moral justification of its own.

24. The reality that Kaldor-efficient policy decisions result in winners as well as losers puts greater moral pressure on the policymaker to take more than allocation and wealth maximization as a basis for his choices. If one is to be a loser, it must be for a morally justifiable reason that one's rights, wants, or needs are being transgressed.

25. Most of the moral complexity of the public decision is lost if one assumes that all citizens consent to any outcome simply by their participation in the society. In the same way, to assume that a consumer consents to any outcome of a transaction in which he is involved is to simplify the aggregation problem without solving it.

26. Even Thomas Hobbes ([1651] 1968, chap. 21), who could not be considered a dove, stipulated that no sovereign could command a subject-citizen to "give his life to his country."

27. The weight, in autonomy by the thin theory, is given to efficient allocation, when we have seen that the pretrade distribution is politically critical to all eventual allocation outcomes. Distribution, a critical problem for public policy, is ignored. Equality becomes a less valuable principle when cost-benefit analysis can define autonomy and cooperation in welfare exchange without any reference to it.

28. In chapter 5, I will demonstrate how the baseline for human autonomy also provides basic functional integrity for nature.

29. For an excellent argument that consequentialism can deal with incommensurability through a quantitative method, see Ellis 1998.

30. See Sikora and Barry 1978 for a complete discussion of the effect of various moral principles on future generations.

3

The Practice of Environmental Risk: The Market Context Model and Environmental Law

The conceptualization of a policy issue and the principles that define and motivate this conceptualization are the primary influence on the "reality" of the law that the policy process produces. To analyze and understand the current state of environmental law, it is necessary to describe not just what statutes, precedent, and regulation reveal about the economy and the environment, but also what principles define our status quo conceptions of humanity and nature and thus set the standards by which we judge "good" or "reasonable" environmental law.

Environmental risk presents the public decision maker with a near-zero probability of producing an infinitely catastrophic outcome.[1] Does one regulate risk in anticipation of unlikely catastrophe, or does one stand back, allow risk into the environment, and deal with any hazard in a remedial fashion?

The choice here is value dependent. Is the use-value of accepting the risk as important as preventing any harm that may be caused? To answer this question requires that one assign values to risks, to humans, and to nature, and decide among them. The policymaker must establish a moral standard that defines what is most fundamentally at stake in the decision. She must establish the core principle that will determine what is valued and how.[2] But before she decides what principle ought to define environmental risk, she must first understand what principle presently determines our perception of it so she has a point of departure for her deliberations.

According to Celia Campbell-Mohn, Barry Breen, and J. William Futrell (1993), there are many problems with the current application of principle to policy.

Despite ever-growing public and private expenditures to implement environmental law, surprisingly few actual improvements occur. Often, spending large sums of money has only kept problems from worsening.

Meanwhile, the gap between environmental quality and the objectives of environmental law widens. Congress responds to environmental problems by adding more administrative law fixes, creating an acropolis of administrative structures. Still, the administrative capacity to resolve environmental problems diminishes. Eventually administrative institutions become overwhelmed by the piecemeal approach. (Campbell-Mohn, Breen, and Futrell 1993, vii)

If the current law defining our relationship with nature is not achieving the level of environmental quality that we think best (e.g., if it chases pollution from one medium to another without preventing it or cleaning it up, if existing law is inadequate to the task of defining significant risk to human or natural systems health), then the fundamental principle upon which our law is built may need reconsideration and reform. Most critically, the fundamental principle that sets the standards for "persuasive" policy argument and "reasonable" law may need to be changed.

Recently, the answer to improving the general state of environmental affairs is to blame government regulation, to argue for abandonment of "command and control," and to support the introduction of more market mechanisms to make environmental law efficient (Anderson and Leal 1991; Breyer 1982, 1993). If indeed efficiency had not determined our policy to date, this might be a reasonable course of action. But I argue in this chapter that efficiency is, and has always been, the core principle that brought us to this point.[3] So to introduce more market mechanisms would only add fuel to fire.

Before we make judgments about the future, before we can move ahead to new models and solutions,[4] before we can envision the requirements of any alternative principle for environmental-risk law and policy or construct competing arguments for what is "truly" at stake in risk decision making, we need to understand how the principle of efficiency has shaped the ways we view the environment and we conceptualize our place within it. Specifically, we need to understand how a concern for economic efficiency has created the environmental-pollution-abatement and risk law we now have.

To do so, we will trace the normative roots of risk law and argue that the predominance of economic principle in the origin and evolution of environmental law has had a defining and predominant influence in the conceptualization of risk and of the standards for its reasonable regulation. The core status of economic efficiency in environmental law and policy incorporates the prejudice toward *ex post* preference satisfaction and reliance on instrumental, to the exclusion of intrinsic, value to justify choice and set standards for successful policy. A reliance on *ex post* legal measures and a concentration on the instrumental value of the environment pervades the law, and any reorientation in order to incorporate the anticipatory regulation to protect and empower intrinsic values will require a fundamental shift in the core principles by which environmental law is conceptualized.

The change of perspective requires a transition from the status quo policy model founded upon market assumptions and the division of nature into sectors for use (e.g., species, minerals, land, air, water) to an alternative regulatory model that assumes the perspective of whole Ecosystems (made up of human and natural components) and divides the economy, as the interface between humanity and nature, into sectors (e.g., extraction, manufacture, disposal). I call the conventional model the "Traditional Sector Approach" (TSA) and examine its two variants (TSA-I: Maximum Use Model, and TSA-II: Optimal Use Model) in this chapter. Building on the work of others (Campbell-Mohn, Breen, and Futrell 1993), I name the alternative "Ecosystem Policy and Law,"[5] which we shall examine in chapter 8.

Before we examine the law of risk, however, we will analyze the transition from efficiency as maximum use of species, mineral, and media within the materials balance (TSA-I) to the governmentally regulated market where efficiency is defined in terms of optimal levels of extraction and pollution (TSA-II). With these context models in mind, we can examine, in turn, pollution-abatement law and then environmental-risk law itself.[6]

Efficiency and Environmental Law

Environmental law and policy was preceded into the policy space by the metapolicy of economic growth and prosperity, where market assumptions and principles held pride of place. The dominant ethic of the first hundred years of our nation's history concerned growth, expansion, and private wealth maximization, which caused us to conceptualize the environment as resource and as waste receptacle as the American economy expanded. This conceptualization also created the institutions and administrative apparatus of environmental and resource regulation and our present uncoordinated policy map that may be described as less than fully effective (Campbell-Mohn, Breen, and Futrell 1993, vii; Dryzek 1987).

According to Posner (1983), the core of economic efficiency as a motivating principle is its focus on the welfare preferences of the individual consumer and their maximization of wealth. He argues that this definition of efficiency is compatible with the Kaldor criteria and the basic assumptions of cost-benefit methodology (Gillroy and Wade 1992, 6–13). Posner contends that this principle lies at the core of economic policy and that it has an ethical imperative in the search for maximizing private and social prosperity through law (Posner 1977).

Applied to the context of nature, the goal of creating a national economy and expanding westward can be seen as motivated and justified by the principle of market efficiency. Within the market context all goods and services can be substituted for one another. Trade is based on the individual's preferences and proceeds until no further trade is profitable to any person. Efficiency, when transferred into the public realm from the market, gives government the imperative to mimic a functioning market seeking an efficient level of collective (or in this case environmental) goods.

This brings us to the market paradigm's first sector model: TSA-I. In this model the market dominates the policy space and the natural environment is

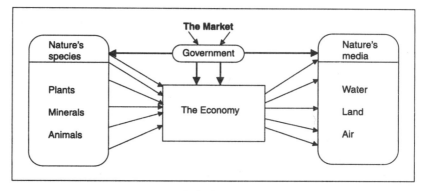

FIGURE 3.1
Traditional Sector Approach—Model I

Efficiency means the maximum use of the environment, by market forces, with government assistance, for both resource extraction and waste disposal.

simply one of its subsystems. As we can see (fig. 3.1), the core principle of the paradigm in this context is maximum efficiency, which is set up to expand the market and produce prosperity. Efficiency values everything instrumentally as it contributes to growth and the production of "wanted" things. From the market standpoint, the earth can be described as a wealth of material that gives no utility to the consumer in its "raw" state. The imperative is therefore to transform as much of this raw material as possible into products and services that can improve the economy and maximize the collective wealth.

The imperative of Kaldor efficiency is to maximize social benefit over cost, and the reality of the expanding economy in the nineteenth and early twentieth centuries was characterized by one relevant fact: the perceived zero cost of both environmental media as sinks and virgin materials as resources. This zero price for raw materials, and the government's concern to get as much land and resources into private hands as possible, encouraged the market system to absorb as much raw materials into the economic process as its technology could consume and transform.

In order to facilitate an expanding economy, nature was divided into separate species, minerals, and media. Economic use was then sought for each. We found immediate tangible market value in some (e.g., timber and fur), and potential in others (e.g., oil, ore), but ultimately we sought only maximum use for market value. This search for efficient, or maximum, use of nature created the foundation for present environmental law, policy, and institutions.

In addition to the categorization of species and minerals as "natural resources," this expansion of prosperity also conceptualized the use of air, water, and land for the disposal of wastes as a "legitimate" use of nature for the facilitation of efficiency. The near-zero price of resources was matched by the perceived zero cost of disposal into environmental media. Nature presented a seemingly bottomless capacity, and the imperative to seek maximum benefit was therefore aided by the zero price at both ends of the economic process: extraction and disposal.

TSA-I can be described as a market-driven model in which the perception of a boundless and inexpensive nature, combined with the driving force of the normative standard of efficiency,[7] encourages the maximum use of nature to fuel economic progress. In this drama, the government plays the role of making nature available to the economic process, securing and transferring land, protecting trade, and in all ways facilitating private commerce and its technological innovations.

However, by the late nineteenth century the perception of the free use of the environment was changing. As technology allowed for greater and faster use of resources, concerns arose about long-term sustainable efficiency and the supply of resources. Although science and technology were assumed to be their own saviors, able to replace any raw materials that ran out, for the first time in our history we began to consider the long-term use of nature's species and minerals. Meanwhile, with the growing density of urban areas, where most of the production was going on, the perception of free waste disposal also changed. The smoke, dirty water, disease, and odors of industrialization caused concern that maximum production created more use of environmental media as sinks than was optimal, in the long run.

From the market point of view, the near-zero price of species, minerals, and media in TSA-I, combined with the unregulated advancement of technology, which is the main governor of use in this market, led the market to fail by overuse. Without the true price of resources and pollution reflected in the economic calculation of efficiency, and with the growing sophistication of technology, the market did not take all the necessary contingencies into account in its maintenance of long-term efficiency and, as a result, extracted too much from the environment and put too much back in as pollution (Ruff 1977). When the collective-goods nature of public policy problems causes market failure and the true price of an item is not reflected in its market value, then the role of the government, in an efficiency-based regime, is to mimic the market and allocate accordingly, maximizing social benefit over cost.

In terms of the environment, instead of allowing the market to set the maximum rate of extraction from, and disposal into, the environment, it becomes the job of government to compensate for market failure and to set optimal rates of extraction and disposal, given the technology available and the natural contingencies of species, minerals, and media. This brings us to the second variant of the traditional sector approach.[8]

Examining the optimal-use model of TSA-II (fig. 3.2), one can see that instead of the many arrows of extraction and disposal that appear in TSA-I, we now have single controlled rates of extraction and disposal, regulated by government. For each species and mineral a single optimal rate of extraction has been calculated, and for each medium a corresponding rate of disposal has been set. In effect, efficiency is now defined not in terms of *maximization* but in terms of an effort to find the *optimal* long-term relationship between economy and nature (Pinchot 1947). Policy maxims establish the optimal level of extraction and the optimal level of pollution and risk, implying a government-

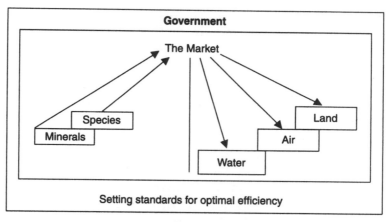

FIGURE 3.2
Traditional Sector Approach—Model II

centered search for what economists call the "materials balance" (Mills and Graves 1986, 8–18).

The materials balance describes all of nature as an inventory of natural resources. On the basis of the second law of thermodynamics (that matter cannot be created or destroyed), the economy is assumed neither to create nor to destroy nature but "merely" to transform it (Mills and Graves 1986, 8). All natural material is of value to the extent that it can be used to support human life, "fulfill human values" (Pearce and Turner 1990, 140), and create economic wealth. The materials balance, as an expression of the principle of efficiency applied to human use of nature, assumes that the environment can be considered either inventory, product, or waste. All material extracted from the environment equals that within the capital stock of products plus that returned to the environment as waste. This equivalence is the "balance." All natural material is a constant quantity in fungible symmetric states of being that change form to optimize human economic wealth. The importance of a materials balance, as an expression of efficiency, is the continued presumption of use.[9] The use of nature for human wealth maximization accounts for each resource in terms of its form and place in the overall consumption process (i.e., take, use, dispose).

For example, an optimal level of pollution requires one to assume that pollution is a natural by-product of the economic process and that not all pollution need be controlled. By defining pollution as "damage to the environment that impairs its usefulness to people" (Mills and Graves 1986, 18), media (e.g., air, water, land, groundwater) have definable tolerance levels that cannot be stressed without the breakdown of that media (Goodin 1976, 175–76).

"Tolerance," however, has a more pertinent meaning in terms of the perception of environmental quality by the individual consumer. For example, the airshed can only absorb X amount of pollution before it is organically incapable of absorbing any more, but it can also only absorb so much before consumers perceive a change in quality that causes them to lose utility. Both definitions of "tolerance" have a place in the discussion and definition of "optimal" levels of pollution.

For a market-based policy analysis, the environment is valuable as natural cleaning and storage media; the goal of the efficient system, as described by TSA-II, is to use this "facility" to its maximum without violating tolerance levels. "Discharge of limited amounts of wastes is a legitimate use of the absorption capacity of each environmental medium" (Mills and Graves 1986, 19).

The capacity of the environment to hold and purify pollution is here measured against the demands of individual wealth maximization that require as many individuals as possible to avoid the costs of pollution control. If each attempt not to pollute costs the individual, and all efforts to control pollution are not necessary to preserve minimal functioning of environmental media, then the trick is to minimize the costs of pollution control to the economy by allowing the maximum amount of pollution possible, while abating just enough so as not to exceed the tolerances of these media as storage and purification devices (Fisher 1981; Stokes 1994).[10]

The concept of using optimal levels of extraction and pollution to set and maintain a materials balance emphasizes, again, the instrumental value of the environment to humanity. Use by species, mineral, and media is the imperative; efficiency is the driving principle. The qualitative state of a natural entity or system is insignificant, as long as that state serves wealth accumulation. The economy neither destroys nor creates but merely transforms: trees into lumber, tigers into coats.

In TSA-I, efficiency is wealth maximization in a world of zero price for the environment; principle is defined by market imperatives that co-opt the government to encourage and facilitate the maximum use of nature by keeping prices low or nonexistent and providing/protecting technological innovation and infrastructure (e.g., trails, canals, timber roads, legal patents, etc.). In TSA-II, efficiency is modified by the imperative to seek optimal, not maximum, rates of extraction and pollution; the government compensates for market failure and defines the "optimal" rates of use and disposal in order to maintain a regulated "materials balance" over time.[11]

Within both TSA-I and II, efficiency remains the core principle of a regulated government market and the basis for the origin of environmental law. First, efficiency is the foundation for a law and policy of natural-resource extraction in the search for optimal efficiency in the use of nature's raw materials.[12] Second, efficiency produces a law and policy of pollution and risk abatement as the government regulated market seeks the optimal level of contamination. Both models of the traditional sector approach promote the dissection of nature into tangible economic values (i.e., raw materials and absorbent media); the models differ in the connotation of the principle of efficiency.

Let us focus on both traditional pollution-abatement law and then environmental-risk law and policy from the viewpoint of the market paradigm and TSA context model to see how efficiency dominates legal discourse and decision making.

Traditional Pollution: Finding the Optimum Level for Efficient Abatement Law and Policy

TSA-I applied to pollution-abatement law and policy originated with the attempt, in the early part of this century, to use the private law of nuisance to combat tangible pollution in the air and water of the United States.[13] Before this concern for excess pollution, by-products of industrialization were considered signs of prosperity and economic growth. As Bounderby states in *Hard Times*, "you see our smoke. That's meat and drink to us. It's the healthiest thing in the world in all respects, and particularly for the lungs" (Dickens [1854] 1961,130). The use of air, land, and water for the disposal of pollution was considered an acceptable and necessary use of nature for the well-being of humanity.

Using economic principle as the core of environmental metapolicy establishes an economic perspective on nature. It encourages the division of nature into distinct media, each with a capacity, not for function, but for waste assimilation at minimal (zero) cost. Environmental media are receptacles for, and in this way components of, market processes. The economic definition of pollution as an "externality" also sets nature into an economic context where its instrumental value is emphasized.

An externality is an external social cost, that is, a social cost imposed by market processes but not priced within the market system (Pigou 1932, 183). An externality has at least two interesting dimensions. First, an externality is an indirect effect of a process. It is assumed that the "external" effect or the by-product of manufacturing is that which causes the pollution and not the product itself. Pollution is secondary, at least from an economic viewpoint, and of less concern than the products that are the fuel of the market and the key to its expansion and persistence. In applying the principle of efficiency to environmental metapolicy, the production of goods is of primary importance, and secondary attention is paid to any by-products, good or bad. Therefore, external effects mean both outside of, and secondary to, the demands of the market.

Second, economic externality places nature outside of the market and outside its competitive pricing system. If markets are responsive to the degree that something has a real price, then if pollution is external to this price system, it will have no role in balancing supply against demand and will thus have no power in the calculations by which the market regulates itself. An external effect means a zero-cost effect. Here, the absence of price leads to the overuse of the environment as a sink and to the evolution of our need to redefine efficiency (from maximization to optimality) in order to keep it as our core principle. For pollution, the market cannot regulate itself by locating a price through exchange. Under these conditions the level of technology alone inhibits media use; the state must find a substitute or nonmarket price so that external effects can be internalized, a standard of regulation established, and natural media conserved from overuse.[14]

The revelation in the Progressive Era of our nation's history (1900–1920) was that maximum use of environmental media leads to considerable diminishment of perceptible environmental quality. Especially with the advent of the Depression and the New Deal in the 1930s, environmental economics became a companion field to natural resource economics and a major force in policy analysis and decision making. As natural resource economics concerned itself with that component of the materials balance related to the optimal rate of extraction, environmental economics found its origins and continuing mission at the opposite end of the materials balance in the search for a definition of an optimal rate of pollution (Goodin 1976; Mills and Graves 1986; Fisher 1981; Stokes 1994).

The history of environmental law and politics reveals that we have approached nature with two distinct bodies of regulation, one concerning natural resources and one applied to pollution (and more recently risk) abatement (Campbell-Mohn, Breen, and Futrell 1993). In addition, the government regulatory approach created to handle these issues has utilized TSA-II as its context model for an efficiency-based environmental metapolicy, concentrating on providing individual units of pollution-control law for each medium (e.g., the Clean Air Act, the Clean Water Act) that mimic the market by setting standards of optimal pollution. In doing so, abatement law provides a piecemeal approach to the conceptualization of nature as motivated by the use of distinct media for economic purposes. The resulting patchwork of environmental law expresses a metapolicy built upon efficiency, first in terms of maximum pollution (TSA-I), and then in terms of optimal abatement levels (TSA-II).

Recognizing that the technology was producing a nonoptimal rate of pollution, and acknowledging that without a real price the market was unable to internalize pollution and regulate the materials balance itself, government was recruited to "mimic" market outcomes. Beginning with attempts at the local and state level, government calculated "safe" or "healthy" levels of pollution and set standards for effluent (Percival et al. 1992, 116–22).

The federalization of abatement law occurred during the 1960s and 1970s as attempts by other levels of government to find the "optimum" failed. The core problem that necessitated the involvement of the state was, not that efficiency was considered an inappropriate principle upon which to base abatement policy, or that a concern for ecology became competitive with, or dominant to, economic ends, but that nonoptimal release of pollution had degraded environmental quality and made nature of less use to human communities. Legislation and subsequent regulations have been aimed, not at the protection of the environment,[15] but at the long-term protection of an efficient materials balance that provides for our long-term economic growth.[16]

The fact that environmental law has chased pollution from air to water to land is a direct outgrowth of applying the TSA model to the abatement of pollution. In addition, the concentration of our abatement law on point sources is consistent with an economic model of abatement law because point sources characterize the production economy and define the materials balance. If one approaches pollution from a natural systems standpoint, then point and non-point sources are equally important, as pollution is a comprehensive concern based upon degree of effect and not upon the phase of market processes that produce it. A government mimicking the market, however, sees only the production process and its externalities as point sources, responding with that specific legislation required to set optimal levels for each medium, one at a time. So a core of environmental values would not have produced the type or pattern of abatement law we now have.

Arguing for efficiency as the prevailing core of abatement policy does not deny that environmental values also exist and compete with efficiency for core status. In fact, many approaches to environmental policy focus on natural systems, not efficiency. But to approach environmental metapolicy without understanding the power and traditional pride of place in the policy space held by the market paradigm and its core principle, economic efficiency, is to fail to understand the true standards of justification and success that we are applying (consciously or unconsciously) to the law.

Although the rhetoric of abatement legislation focuses on a clean environment and appears ecocentric,[17] environmental values do not determine policy. The economy's health continues as the major focus of environmental regulation; not a single environmental law places natural systems first. Again, within the deliberative tier of a metapolicy, parallel arguments exist and compete with the status quo core principle. One competitor for efficiency is indeed ecocentrism, defined in terms of intrinsic, not instrumental, value. Although echoes of these environmental values haunt pollution-abatement law, they never define the status quo core.

From Traditional Pollution to Risk Abatement

An important area of environmental law, not yet fully understood or regulated, concerns environmental risk. As we have seen in chapter 2, Talbot Page (1978) distinguishes environmental risk, as a policy issue, from traditional pollution problems in terms of its pervasive uncertainty and the management difficulties presented to a decision maker trying to regulate a near-zero probability of an infinitely catastrophic harm. The regulatory structure of risk law, in present practice, is a direct outgrowth of market assumptions and the TSA context model. Risk regulation, as a metapolicy issue, like natural resources and pollution-abatement law before it, is built on the core principle of efficiency and the evolution of its definition from maximization under TSA-I to optimization under TSA-II.

The issues surrounding risk regulation highlight the problems of an efficiency-based environmental law. A core of efficiency has led to a counterintuitive and harmful treatment of environmental risk. Specifically, the burden of proof is placed upon regulators; there is a general failure to comprehensively anticipate the imposition of risk; unreasonable demands are placed upon science to bring authoritative data to decision making (Henderson 1993); and intrinsic value in policy calculations is neglected, so that the resulting law is inadequate when faced with the uncertainty and management difficulties of harm from environmental risk.

Since World War II the human race has increasingly produced natural and synthetic chemical agents to improve wealth and welfare (Trost 1984). Initially, in the United States, these chemicals were produced without any regulation in an atmosphere of competition meant to maximize their production (Percival et al. 1992, 435). In this era of TSA-I, risk agents were produced to create and expand markets and to increase prosperity and quantity of product. During this era the stealth characteristics of environmental risk allowed individuals to ignore the effects these agents might have in contaminating the environment around them.

With the publication of *Silent Spring*, by Rachel Carson, in 1962, this atmosphere changed. Although the specific concern of Carson's book was the toxic effects of pesticides, all chemical agents produced within the economy immediately became a concern for the general public. Before *Silent Spring*, the positive welfare effects of risk agents were assumed to far outweigh any hazard. However, as the calculation of social utility changed, and many began to appreciate that the risks might indeed be real and harmful, risk issues shifted from being considered primarily private market transactions to being considered subjects of "public interest" and deliberation. In issues as diverse as mining for radioactive ore, nuclear energy, and the chemical content of food, growing public concern required a redefinition of efficiency away from the maximum use of nature if it was to remain the core standard of risk metapolicy. The new conceptualization required a shift to TSA-II and its substitution of optimal risk, with its market assumptions and goals, for maximum risk.

Although risk regulation is multifaceted, with many agencies and bodies of law controlling various sectors of risk production and storage, the legal debate over the shift from TSA-I to TSA-II is evident and ongoing throughout. On the bases of an economic definition of a risk as "a known probability" of harm and a market definition of rationality as the ability to accept or decline risk in terms of individual preference (where environmental risk has no special character but is symmetric with all other risks—like driving a car or walking across a street), courts and public managers defined the optimally efficient risk as that which was "reasonable," given the core status of markets and wealth maximization in their assumptions about us and our social priorities (Posner 1983, 60ff).

This characterization of environmental risk has provided the standards and language for the legal, political, and policy deliberations about risk regulation and makes the core principle of Kaldor efficiency manifest in the legal search for a "reasonable" amount of risk in the environment. The economic approach to environmental risk assumes that the markets that generate risk are important to us and therefore have a moral standing prior to most environmental considerations. The question then becomes, not whether a certain risk ought to be accepted, for that is implicit in accepting the market paradigm, but how much and what kind of risk is acceptable so that an optimal amount is established as part of the greater materials balance.

Risk is assumed to be part of life; all risk is of symmetric instrumental value; and individual preferences in the market should be the only valid means of regulation for the existence of risk-producing technology. The shift from TSA-I to TSA-II, which is a reaction to the consciousness of excess environmental risk on the part of the public, does not seek to replace market efficiency in the definition of risk or the assumptions about its economic value. What change are the realizations that too much risk can be produced by the market and that regulation is necessary to optimize the risk so that its social costs will not outweigh its benefits to consumers. Government standards save efficiency from itself.

Environmental Risk, Efficiency, and the Federal Courts

A chain of federal court cases that trace the judiciary's struggle to establish the standards for optimal or "reasonable" environmental risk illuminate the evolution from TSA-I to TSA-II.[18] First is the case of *Reserve Mining Co. v EPA* (514 F.2d 492, 8th Cir. 1975).

Reserve Mining (Percival et al. 1992, 442–43) involves excess dumping of mining by-products into the air and into the water of Lake Superior and the court's decisions on how to regulate it.[19] In this case the court made two decisions that address maximum and optimal efficiency. First, it decided that agency (Environmental Protection Agency, EPA) expertise was sufficient to establish that too much risk was being produced in *Reserve Mining*. Second, the court concluded that the economic costs of immediate intervention, even with the existent hazard, would cause grave market costs and therefore, in its remedy, did not close the company but instead gave it "reasonable time" to find other ways to dispose of the by-products of its mining operation (*Reserve Mining*, 537–38).

In *Reserve Mining*, the court gave EPA sole authority to decide when an unregulated market had produced too much risk (*Reserve Mining*, 520). In our terms, the judiciary established that EPA would be decisive in delineating the demarcation between TSA-I and TSA-II for environmental-risk issues. In addition, once EPA had established that TSA-I was no longer an acceptable context model for metapolicy, the type of regulation considered "reasonable" would be only that which preserved the economic market and the specific industry involved in risk production (*Reserve Mining*, 537–38). The court rejected both closing the company for producing excess risk and reconsidering the role of the risk-producing product for society at large (*Reserve Mining*, 537). Instead, the court assumed that as long as Reserve Mining makes a "good faith" effort to dispose of its waste in a better manner,[20] the economy should proceed with as little interruption as possible (*Reserve Mining*, 504, 538).

The court in *Reserve Mining* recognized that "risk," unlike traditional pollution problems, presents a potential hazard rather than an actual one (*Reserve Mining*, 529); the opinion in this case addresses the fact that prevention requires *ex ante* regulation of risk. However, once the court confirms the agency's power to set the TSA-I/TSA-II threshold for risk, it treats the protection of human or natural integrity as secondary to the persistence of the market. For the first time the courts established that when EPA declares TSA-I to be inadequate, the search for optimal risk is ruled by the overriding consciousness that efficient market persistence is of primary, or "trump" importance.

In this decision, the court did not mandate a specific methodology by which EPA should determine the existence of excess risk (*Reserve Mining*, 529) as a prerequisite to declaring that TSA-I was invalid for policy argument and TSA-II was necessary. The court implied that assessment of risk was not a matter of objective or quantitative science but a policy matter that ought to be left to the discretion of the agency (*Reserve Mining*, 529). However, although the court recognized that risk was a distinct and harmful reality in the realm of pollution abatement, it also recognized that risk production was simultaneously so established in our economy and so uncertain that true remedies for protection against excess risk would require drastic (and inefficient) disruptions in the market economy (e.g., shutting down industry, banning products/processes, etc.). The court was unwilling to trade "clearly predictable social and economic consequences" for what it called "unpredictable health effects" (*Reserve Mining*, 536).

Although the trial court initially ordered the plant closed, an appeal from the company (which pledged to spend $243 million in antipollution measures) was finally persuasive in arguing that an individual working for the company would face more certain harm from unemployment than from environmental risk (Hoban and Brooks 1987, 49). In a seeming contradiction of its findings about the potential harms of environmental risk, the federal court retreated from the logical remedy and allowed the company to continue to pollute, granting it time to stop air and water discharges as if the harm from environmental risk were insignificant rather than irreversible, latent, stealthy, and potentially catastrophic.

Siding with the company by allowing it to continue operation despite a zero-infinity dilemma is reasonable only if the court saw its responsibility to be to preserve efficiency. If this represents the evolution from maximum to optimal efficiency, the courts would logically charge EPA experts with establishing the line between TSA-I and TSA-II but would allow manufacturing to proceed in the meantime. In this way, the courts allow government to set standards for optimal efficiency while it simultaneously moves to protect the market position of the industry through a "liberal" interpretation of "optimal" that included "good faith" by the industry and the expenditure of money to mitigate harm *ex post*.

Even with the court's focus on markets, however, it is significant that risk, as well as the threshold for market failure and the establishment of TSA-II, were considered policy questions and the responsibility of EPA in *Reserve Mining*. This would soon change.

Built on the findings of *Reserve Mining* is *Ethyl Corp. v EPA* (541 F.2d 1, D.C.Cir. 1976 [*en banc*]),[21] which redefined the EPA's authority to decide optimal risk levels (Percival et al. 1992, 444–45). In *Reserve Mining* the court allowed EPA to establish the point at which maximizing efficiency should be replaced with optimizing efficiency, but in *Ethyl Corp.* the court required more restrictive requirements of the agency, including the search for a safety threshold (*Ethyl Corp.*, 14), and the use of scientific evidence to justify regulatory arguments (*Ethyl Corp.*, 24, 26–27). The court agreed with its colleagues in - *Reserve Mining* that risk did not have to cause actual harm to be regulated, but, as if from a regulatory skepticism that TSA-I may not be outmoded when EPA says it is (*Ethyl Corp.*, 14–16), the court required the agency to make a specific connection between the probability of risk and the severity of the harm it causes (*Ethyl Corp.*, 14; Percival et al. 1992, 445).

To regulate environmental risk, the administrator was required to establish a "fixed probability of harm," defined by the severity of the potential harm and its specific probability of occurrence at dangerous levels (*Ethyl Corp.*, 17–19; Percival et al. 1992, 444). The variety and severity of risks became vital elements in the shift from TSA-I to TSA-II. To regulate risk markets the EPA would need more than expertise; it would also need data and argument about harm to prove its case. In both *Ethyl Corp.* and *Reserve Mining*, the court appears to be concerned that the definition of efficiency as maximization (TSA-I) be maintained as long as possible (*Ethyl Corp.*, 11). But, whereas in the first decision, the courts allowed EPA to declare TSA-II to be in effect without justification and then minimized its power by allowing a liberal interpretation of the concept of "optimal," in *Ethyl Corp.*, the court preempted EPA's declaration against TSA-I until the specific severity of the risk and its numeric probabilities were completely examined (*Ethyl Corp.*, 26).[22]

The EPA's discretion to unilaterally redefine risk efficiency as optimality, moving to TSA-II, was further limited by the Supreme Court in *Industrial Union Department AFL-CIO v American Petroleum Institute* (448 U.S. 607, 1980 or 100 S. CT. 2844, 1980). The *Benzene* case concerns the Occupational Safety and Health Administration (OSHA) efforts to set an acceptable benzene level for exposed workers. Instead of either deferring to the EPA experts to decide when maximum risk should be replaced by optimal risk (as in *Reserve Mining*), or establishing general guidelines requiring agency substantiation of excess environmental risk (as in *Ethyl Corp.*), the Supreme Court required that the EPA set an absolute threshold of "safety" before it could, in effect, replace maximum with optimal efficiency or move to regulate markets for risk (*Benzene*, 2864; Percival et al. 1992, 457–77).

The Supreme Court, in the *Benzene* case, established a definitive threshold between TSA-I and TSA-II by requiring that regulators persuade the Court that efficiency defined as maximization had produced too much risk and that harm was real before government intervention in risk markets was acceptable public policy (*Benzene*, 2864). Only after a threshold finding has been established showing that efficiency as maximization poses a "significant harm" can the administrator, now within TSA-II, set parameters for optimal risk generation, given the needs of the market and the materials balance.

> [The] Act . . . requires the Secretary, before issuing any standards, to determine that it is reasonably necessary and appropriate to remedy a significant risk of material health impairment. Only after the Secretary has made the threshold determination that such a risk exists with respect to a toxic substance would it be necessary to decide whether [the Act] requires him to select the most protective standard he can consistent with economic and technological feasibility, or whether . . . the benefits of the regulation must be commensurate with the costs of its implementation. (*Benzene*, 2862–63)

[W]e think it clear that the statute was not designed to require employers to provide absolutely risk-free workplaces whenever it is technologically feasible to do so, so long as the cost is not great enough to destroy the entire industry. Rather, both the language and structure of the Act, as well as its legislative history, indicate that it was intended to require the elimination, as far as feasible, of significant risk of harm. (*Benzene*, 2863–64)

Therefore, administrative agencies (e.g., OSHA, EPA) only have power to regulate risk that will pose an established and "significant" harm (*Benzene*, 2864). The government cannot declare unilaterally that efficiency as maximization in a free market has become dysfunctional unless it first shows that the threshold between TSA-I and TSA-II has been established and crossed in the form of significant harm to the public.

To set this threshold the Supreme Court, unlike the *Ethyl Corp.* court,[23] does not allow OSHA experts to employ any methodology they see fit, for again, this choice may wrongly declare TSA-I dysfunctional. In the *Benzene* case, the Court required that uncertainties become risks; that is, that "scientific" probability numbers be assigned to the uncertainty of harm (*Benzene*, 2871). In effect, the Supreme Court mandated that a specific methodology, *Quantitative Risk Assessment* (hereafter QRA), was necessary, first, to set a "significant risk" threshold where TSA-I fails, and then, to decide on standards for optimal risk under TSA-II if government regulation is needed. Although setting this specific test methodology seems merely an extension of the risk versus harm balancing test of *Ethyl Corp.*, it did more. A risk assessment became defined, not as a policy problem, but as a quantitative scientific calculation of symmetric and economically rational probabilities (*Benzene*, 2864–65).

Although the Supreme Court in the *Benzene* case did not mandate cost-benefit methods or specifically require OSHA to consider cost in its rule making, by protecting TSA-I from random regulation and mandating QRA in setting both the threshold of TSA-I and the definition of optimal risk within TSA-II, the Court accomplished the same end: risk efficiency. The *Benzene* case established the priority of QRA both in setting "significant risk" probabilities and in defining optimal or reasonable risk probabilities over that threshold. When the court maintained that "safe is not the equivalent of risk-free" (*Benzene*, 2864), it was building this legal aphorism on the foundation of economic rationality and market-efficiency criteria. The Court accepts the economic definition of risk and gives no special normative or empirical character to environmental risks, which it assumes are symmetric with all other risks in one's life.[24]

There are many activities that we engage in every day—such as driving a car or even breathing city air—that entail some risk of accident or material health impairment; nevertheless, few people would consider these activities unsafe. (*Benzene*, 2864)

Here we have the substitution of science for policy, the replacement of deliberation and choice based on normative and empirical considerations by a dedication to numbers and the rational preferences connected to the calculation of which probabilities generate what levels of welfare for the individual consumer. The establishment of QRA as a necessary and sufficient condition for defining the threshold for government interference in risk markets requires science to play the role of gatekeeper in the name of maintaining the primacy of maximum efficiency as the core principle of environmental-risk metapolicy. The Supreme Court assumes that people are economically rational consumers and that a market for benzene is evidence of its value in terms of those welfare preferences that set the standard for efficient and therefore "socially better" policy. The moral prerogative of established economic markets frames the deliberation of the Court and its definition of "reasonable" law (*Benzene*, 2862–63).

The Supreme Court, in approaching risk from an efficiency standpoint, wants unregulated markets for risk (TSA-I) to exist in as many cases as possible. A specific, quantitative ("scientific") test must be used so that preference calculations can be made to establish whether too much risk exists, and if it does, the same risk assessment must then determine, considered in the light of economic-feasibility analysis, the proper standards for optimal risk under TSA-II. The Court introduces QRA in defense of the market and maximum efficiency in order to establish the "risk severity" concerns of *Ethyl Corp.* both in the transition beyond TSA-I and in the definition of optimal risk within TSA-II. The interference of government in private economic calculations is deterred unless real harm from risk is established. As the chief justice states, "[p]erfect safety is a chimera; regulation must not strangle human activity in the search for the impossible" (*Benzene*, 2875; Percival et al. 1992, 473).

One year after the *Benzene* case, the Supreme Court, in *Textile Manufacturers Institute, Inc. v Donovan* (452 U.S. 490, 1981 or 101 S. CT. 2478, 1981), known as the *Cotton Dust* decision, appeared to establish a mandate against the use of cost-benefit measures in assessing risk and its remedy (*Donovan*, 2490; Sagoff 1988, 214). Writing for the court, Justice Brennan said that EPA "was not required" (*Donovan*, 2492) to complete a cost-benefit analysis in setting standards for cotton dust.

This case is important because it involves cotton dust, which is a risk agent that scientific data has shown to be a well-known hazard. OSHA and the Court agreed up front that "exposure to cotton dust presents a significant health hazard to employees" (*Donovan*, 2487) and so, in effect, QRA had already been used to argue that the threshold between TSA-I and TSA-II had been crossed. The Court, in interpreting the statute to mean that cost-benefit was not necessary, reaffirms the *Benzene* Court by requiring that QRA first set a threshold of "significant risk," which it, in effect, did (*Donovan*, 2489).

Unlike the Court in the *Benzene* case, the Court in *Cotton Dust* began deliberations within TSA-II with a quest for a standard to define the optimal amount of risk. For this task, the Court gives OSHA the option of cost-benefit but requires what it calls a "feasibility analysis" (*Donovan*, 2489–97). Although the specific costs and benefits of regulation do not have to be part of the decision process for EPA, this is precisely "because" feasibility analysis is required by the Court (*Donovan*, 2490). We have not, therefore, stepped away from efficiency-based policy. "Feasibility analysis" is used as a type of efficiency analysis within the context of TSA-II with the Court's blessing (*Donovan*, 2481–82). It is efficient in the same way that technological standards under the Clean Air Act (42 U.S.C.A. §§7411 and 7412) or Clean Water Act (33 U.S.C.A. §§1311 and 1316) are efficient in setting a standard for optimal pollution.[25] In effect, to find a feasible standard for acceptable risk, the EPA would have to identify that level of dust control which would not significantly hurt the business involved and be achievable through existing technology. For all practical purposes, the means and ends of regulatory requirements would have to be within the "optimal" tolerance range of the markets involved.

The *Cotton Dust* case is the first one in our chronology where the transition from TSA-I to TSA-II is assumed to have been completed; a standard is being set for a "known" excess risk. To set this optimal level of risk, the Court requires "analysis showing that performance is possible but not an analysis comparing the cost of compliance with the benefits" (Findley and Farber 1992, 187). But if "feasibility" requires that available technology (*Donovan*, 2491) be used and that "costs" to the market are not excessive, then what is the real difference? In both cases, optimal efficiency and the survival of the market dominate the decision. For both procedures, what is economically and technologically "feasible" is defined in terms of the market. We are not concerned with what may be feasible from the standpoint of the integrity of human or natural systems, but only with efficient outcomes.

The final case in this chain, *NRDC v EPA* (842 F.2d 1146, D.C. Cir. 1987 [en banc] and 804 F. 2d 710 D. C. Cir. 1986 [panel]), deals with EPA's regulation of risk from vinyl chloride. This case offers a natural conclusion to our legal-risk chronology as it mandates a definitive *two-step test* for efficient risk regulation (*NRDC v EPA* en banc, 1165, fn.11).

> [T]he EPA administrator must first establish an "acceptable" level of risk based solely on health considerations before setting standards that provide for an "ample margin of safety." In determining the ample margin of safety, the administrator may require further reductions in emissions to consider health risks, as well as costs and technological feasibility. (O'Leary 1993, 110)

"Health considerations" can be read to mean the use of QRA. The established way of assessing health risk through QRA has been codified as a specific procedure for federal agencies.[26] The curious idea here is that economic-feasibility criteria, in step two, would result in tighter regulations (*NRDC v EPA* en banc, 1158). It is more reasonable to assume that consideration of technology and economic cost would lead to more liberal standards from the market standpoint.

This case was rendered by two decisions in the D.C. Circuit Court: a 2-to-1 panel decision and a unanimous *en banc* decision that reversed the panel's findings. The panel's decision affirmed EPA's choice to forgo a long-term, zero-emissions goal as its regulatory strategy and, instead, rely on Best Available

Technology (BAT) "considering economic and technological feasibility" (*NDRC v EPA* panel, 722; Percival et al. 1992, 857).[27]

> By emphasizing available technology, the EPA has ensured the maximum regulation against uncertainty without the economic and social displacements that would accompany the closing of an industry or any substantial part of an industry. By ensuring that costs do not become grossly disproportionate to the level of reduction achieved, the EPA guarantees that the consuming public does not pay an excessive price for the marginal benefits of increasing increments of protection against the unknown. (*NRDC v EPA* panel, 722)

The *en banc* court reversed the panel by arguing that EPA could not "primarily" rely on BAT standards within §112 of the Clean Air Act (*NRDC v EPA* en banc, 1163). Instead, the court mandated its two-step process requiring the primary finding of a "significant level" of risk and then the consideration of technology and economic cost to find the optimal standard for control of any excess hazard (*NRDC v EPA* en banc, 1165).

From our point of view this reversal does not represent an antiefficiency decision, but rather the recognition by the *en banc* court that the panel decision did not recognize the necessity of establishing a threshold before setting an optimality standard. The *en banc* court reminds us that it is unacceptable to use technological standards to regulate risk before we have established that TSA-I has been transcended and government-set standards become necessary (i.e., that excess risk exists).

All the decisions in this chain of cases demonstrate an effort by the courts, within the uncertainty of environmental-risk issues, to require that the agency first persuade them that a "significant risk" exists; that is, the hazard potential of the risk is excessive and beyond the capacity of markets alone to regulate them adequately. Only when the threshold between TSA-I and TSA-II has been crossed and we have determined a definition of efficiency as optimality is it proper to use any type of government standard setting, for only efficiency defined as optimality requires state regulation of markets. This logic is confirmed in the two-step test, evolved over these cases, where step one concerns the TSA-I threshold and step two focuses upon TSA-II standard setting.

Both of these decisions about vinyl chloride are fascinating in that, while they superficially address the "ample margin of safety" language of §112 of the Clean Air Act, they actually concern, first, whether maximizing efficiency has produced too much risk, and, second, if so, then what tests should define the government-set definition of optimal efficiency. The court specifies the steps and the specific tests that agencies must use in this determination of "reasonable risk"; it is clear that the administrator must first determine if a "significant risk" exists before seeking "the level of emissions that will result in an 'acceptable' risk to health" (*NRDC v EPA* en banc, 1165).

These decisions are dominated by *ex ante* concerns for economic rationality and risk markets. The process of risk regulation, from the standpoint of the courts, concerns "what risks are acceptable in the world in which we live" (*NRDC v EPA* en banc, 1165, fn.11; 1153). In the opinion concerning vinyl chloride, the *Benzene* decision is quoted and the market paradigm is established as the valid principle and theoretical assumption for both parts of the two-step process (*NRDC v EPA* en banc, 1165).[28]

In step one, QRA turns the uncertainty of harm into the probability of environmental risk and places science in the role of gatekeeper for efficient outcomes as it is used to guard against state involvement in risk markets when these markets have not yet broken down. QRA is used to establish when, and at what level of concentration, a "significant risk" of severe harm exists, making the prevailing definition of "efficiency as maximization" dysfunctional. If significant risk is not established, TSA-I remains intact as the reasonable context model and risk markets operate unencumbered.

Cost-benefit methods represent efficiency, as the core principle of the metapolicy, in step two (*NRDC v EPA* panel, 164). Only if QRA establishes that TSA-II is in effect does efficiency require cost-benefit or feasibility analysis to judge the means and ends of government risk policy. In step two, as the state becomes a market surrogate in the policy process, the court allows the full use of technological and economic considerations to define optimal or reasonable risk. The court in the *Vinyl Chloride* decision defined the second step specifically for technological and economic feasibility, thereby routinizing the feasibility analysis first suggested in the *Cotton Dust* decision six years earlier.

Two critical variables in the evolution of environmental-risk law are the rise of QRA as a requirement of the courts to establish risk levels and the judicial banishment of cost-benefit methods in the first phase of the two-step process. QRA alone determines whether efficiency as maximization creates too much risk. The question for us is whether the legal institutionalization of QRA for the purposes of turning uncertainty into risk probability is a departure from our contention that market efficiency is the core principle of risk-abatement metapolicy. I argue that it is not.

QRA and cost-benefit methods are both based upon the same definition of economic rationality and operate on the same definition of risk as substitutable, tradable, and preference-based.[29] Both QRA and cost-benefit methods are normative decision procedures that employ a theory of comparative instrumental value that is necessary to make each risk tradable with all others. Efficiency is therefore represented by two distinct "decisionist" (Majone 1989, 12–15) methods with a common foundation of values and definitions: QRA (for step one) and cost-benefit (for step two).

The background assumptions of the market can be seen in the rise of quantitative risk assessment as a "scientific" basis for the assignment of probabilities to environmental uncertainty. If we characterize the economic project as one allowing individuals to trade symmetric risks in a market according to their preferences, then one must first assign probabilities to risks so that these rational calculations can commence. If cost-benefit method represents economic decisionism (Majone 1989, chap. 1) in general policy argument about standard setting under TSA-II, then quantitative risk assessment represents economic precepts as scientific decisionism for establishing threshold risk.

In both "decisionist situations," the actor is a unitary decision maker in an environment where there is no collision of interests or arguments, only logic, evidence, and truth. All policy is assumed to be applicable to proof from empirical observation and verification by experiment in the present context. Both also view policy choice as decision analysis where specific probabilities can be weighed and deliberated over before choice. Both are positivist in that the methodology is claimed to deduce conclusions from factual premises that are themselves based on general laws, verifiable by observation and experimentation. In addition, both are preoccupied with instrumental value and consequences, making no allowances for intrinsic character in either evaluation or justification. In short, both cost-benefit methods and quantitative risk assessment are nonpolitical, myopic, and ethically instrumentalist.

Efficiency as maximization in TSA-I relies on QRA to protect against instances where the market would be regulated without need; in other words, to protect efficiency as maximization against false positives. A fully functional and unregulated market under TSA-I is innocent unless QRA can prove it guilty; that is, prove that its products or by-products subject humanity to a "significant risk of harm." In terms of efficiency as optimality under TSA-II, the use of quantitative risk assessment allows a more precise mathematical feel for the "optimal" level of risk and guards against too much regulation encumbering the market. In both steps of the risk-regulation test, QRA turns uncertainty into risk by the assignment of probabilities. As long as economic precepts provide the background assumptions within which QRA operates, efficiency has the determinative power to utilize the products of QRA in support of risk markets.

I have argued (in chapter 2) that cost-benefit analysis, although ethically impoverished, is not value-free, and other writers (Shrader-Frechette 1991, 1993) have argued that the "scientific" process of QRA is also fundamentally normative in nature. I expand this argument by contending that QRA is a natural extension of cost-benefit methods, protecting efficiency as maximization in TSA-I from false positives and representing efficiency as optimality under TSA-II. In both instances, QRA minimizes regulation and maximizes the level of "reasonable risk" in policy standards.

The chain of federal risk cases illustrates that within environmental-risk regulation there has not been a full evolution from TSA-I to TSA-II. Even well after the publication of *Silent Spring*, we as a nation continue to argue about whether or not there is too much human-generated risk in the natural environment.

Environmental Risk, Efficiency, and Statute Law

The power of efficiency considerations is further supported by an examination of the statute law of risk regulation (Cranor 1993). As in the court decisions, which mandate a two-part test to first establish whether TSA-I still holds, and if it does not, then to set optimal standards for risk, considering technological and economic feasibility under TSA-II, the protection of efficiency as maximization appears to dominate risk statutes as well.

Three distinct sets of statutes are definable in risk-abatement law. One group of statutes defines the risk threshold between efficiency as maximization in TSA-I and optimal efficiency in TSA-II for manufactured products. A second set of laws attempts to provide market solutions for the disposition of risk-generated waste produced under TSA-I. A third group includes those laws that assume TSA-II and seek to integrate risk abatement into the preexisting regulatory regime established to set optimal efficiency standards for traditional air and water pollution.

These three categories all exhibit a profound effort, on the part of legislators, to fit risk abatement into the preexisting pollution-abatement model regardless of the differences that accompany the management of risk, with its profound uncertainty. We shall describe these statutes as they exist and are applied, and consider what normative principle sets the standards, and provides the basis for justification, of the metapolicy.

The first set of statutes illustrates how policy defends TSA-I against regulatory intervention, applying law to setting threshold risk standards concerning chemical agents and their manufacture. Historically, because markets for risk were originally in effect under TSA-I and efficiency was defined in terms of maximization, when synthetic chemicals were first created and marketed they were produced to maximize welfare with only market demand and technological capabilities determining their formulation and introduction into the environment.

However, because of the growing concern that these chemical agents might be producing too much risk and because of their economic value for our prosperity, legislation became necessary to protect against the production by maximum efficiency of excess hazard. The two statutes that set the threshold between TSA-I and TSA-II for chemical risk are the Toxic Substances Control Act (TSCA) (15 U.S.C.A. §§2601–96) and the Federal Insecticide, Fungicide, and Rodenticide Act (FIFRA) (7 U.S.C.A. §§136–136y).[30]

TSCA offers the possibility of a premarket testing scheme for the *ex ante* protection of the public health from hazardous chemicals. However, the dominant and decisive argument within this legislation defers to and protects an unregulated risk market by placing the burden of proof on the EPA to demonstrate that too much risk exists before it can write regulations. The EPA must first test to show that unreasonable risk exists and then the legislation limits both what EPA can demand from the industry, which has very few premarket requirements to meet, and when it can demand it.

The strongest part of this legislation, in which the EPA administrator is granted sole power to require testing of a chemical agent, relates only to those specific circumstances when a "chemical may pose an unreasonable risk to health" (§2603 [a]). In language reminiscent of the risk cases we have reviewed, EPA must establish a threshold of "significant" or "unreasonable risk"; only then can it regulate a chemical in order to find an optimal level of environmental risk.

As one might expect in legislation built on efficiency as maximization, the burden of proof for finding and stopping a hazard is entirely a responsibility of EPA.[31] The agency must test the chemical itself and prove that it presents an "unreasonable" risk to the public. EPA will define "unreasonable" in terms of QRA. Industry must notify EPA of the pending release of a risk into the environment, but after the EPA is notified (§2604) that a chemical will be marketed it has little power to stop it. The administrator can require testing mainly under emergency circumstances (§2607 [e]), and then only by going through a costly and time-consuming rule-making process, subject to judicial review, during which the manufacturer can proceed, unimpeded, to market the chemical unless another rule is written to suspend production until the rule for data analysis becomes law. Specifically, all testing must be done through the rule-making process (§2603), and if the agency does not decide to commit its time and energy to the investigation of the chemical and its effects, then the risk-generating chemical enters the market without regulation.

Therefore, the production of possible toxic chemicals proceeds in this nation without significant premarket regulation. Even economists (Portey 1990) admit that the rate of production in this market precludes the gathering of data on all the possible hazards and that "progress in reducing these data gaps has been quite slow" (Shapiro 1990, 236). Considered from the standpoint of protection for environmental or human qualities, this procedure may seem counterintuitive, but as an expression of protecting efficiency as maximization from the economic disaster of a false-positive risk assessment, it makes perfect sense.

The idea of premarket testing in TSCA exists for the one or two cases in a thousand where a known and very dangerous chemical is proposed for marketing (Cranor 1993, 27–28). In these odd instances, the EPA relies on preexisting knowledge and scientific studies and takes time to analyze the testing and write the necessary rules to regulate or ban the agent. But even if testing is done and "significant risk" established by rule, the actual regulation of the toxic agent, under TSCA, has been made very difficult by both the statute and the courts. Specifically, once EPA has established that TSA-I is no longer the context model and that the government must step in under TSA-II to set the level of optimal risk in the environment, the agency is constrained to adopt only the "least burdensome" regulation possible (§2605a [1]–[7]). This statute requirement, as interpreted by the courts, has made banning even a known toxic substance almost impossible (*Corrosion Proof Fittings v EPA*, 947 F.2d 1201 [5th Cir. 1991]), and has more generally and severely limited both chemical testing and more modest regulation of toxic agents with requirements for the economic and technological feasibility of agency actions (*AFL-CIO v OSHA*, 965 F.2d 962 [11th Cir. 1992]).

In the spirit of the market paradigm and TSA context models, we have established a false-positive risk regime[32] for almost all agencies of the federal government,[33] where a suspected risk agent is innocent of causing harm until the agency can prove it guilty. Under TSCA, chemicals are marketed first and questioned later, only if they exhibit, over time, evidence of widespread negative human health effects.[34] However, the fact that the EPA cannot begin to keep up with testing and has successfully regulated few chemical agents can only be characterized as a failure if the metapolicy was intended to protect human integrity and natural systems and regulate the economy *ex ante*. If, however, TSCA exists to allow free functioning of the market, except in that rare instance when a chemical blatantly produces too much health hazard for its economic value, then the statute's failure to regulate this market is actually, by market-efficiency standards, a great success.

TSCA expresses the principle of efficiency in risk regulation where the threshold between TSA-I and TSA-II is assumed not to have been crossed until the uncertainty of hazard is proven by the agency. The second piece of legislation, designed to license the commercial use of poisons as pesticides, defines this threshold more succinctly as it examines the question of "optimal" risk under TSA-II.

More restrictive than TSCA, FIFRA focuses on an optimal level of pesticide production, given the known hazards. In designing and implementing FIFRA, the EPA has maximized the scope of an efficient risk market within TSA-I. But this particular risk market is different because we are dealing with poisonous substances that are intended to kill plant life, and have been known to take unintended human and animal victims. Therefore, it is reasonable and efficient to have manufacturers of these substances acquire licenses in order to market their products.

FIFRA does this, but it protects the market by not allowing the EPA to make any judgments about either the need for a particular pesticide or its safety compared to other products in the field. Regulators within FIFRA can only demand that minimum product requirements be met. The EPA is not empowered to make any *economic* judgments. If a pesticide meets minimum functional and labeling requirements, it must be licensed and allowed a marketplace.

The policy history of FIFRA is a story of the growth of law from the demands of economic prosperity and technological innovation within agricultural markets (Bosso 1987).[35] The efficiency of these poisons, their comparative ease of use, and their improvement of crop yield define them as an issue within the law.[36] Motivated by the goal of efficient crop yield, the administration of pesticide regulation (like the administration of our forests) began within the United States Department of Agriculture. This pride of place for efficiency within the metapolicy has caused pesticide regulation, even when transferred to the EPA in 1970, to be designed so as to foster the market while attempting to establish safeguards against the production of excess risk (Bosso 1987, 152–53).

Again, as within TSCA, safeguards exist for that rare case when a particular chemical agent (e.g., DDT) is found to produce too much risk for its economic benefits, even when efficiency is defined as optimality. In a regulatory framework where the overwhelming imperative is to foster economic prosperity, it was only after there was no doubt that DDT had not only passed over the threshold between TSA-I and TSA-II but that it was impossible to find any level of use that did not cause widespread harm, that DDT qualified for further regulation.[37] FIFRA, like TSCA, is legislation in defense of the unregulated TSA-I market and efficiency as maximization; the only difference is that the subject of FIFRA is known poisons and therefore a degree of uncertainty is removed from the risk calculation. But this is a market for poison and more risk is tolerated as a matter of course. License requirements support a "free" market by allowing products to enter economic trade as long as they meet minimum registration requirements (§136 [a]). This licensing maximizes market entry while setting up a mechanism whereby very risky poisons are identified and banned. From an efficiency standpoint, FIFRA is successful.

In both cases, the regulation of the chemical agents grants the benefit of doubt to the market and lays (all or most of) the burden of proof on the regulatory agency. Within this false-positive risk regime, the burden of proof is both for the charge that any chemical has or will produce too much risk and for the degree of regulation required for that particular toxic agent in the environment.

In both cases the EPA cannot make any economic judgments about the need for, or comparative safety of, any potentially toxic agent and must allow the market to decide a chemical's fate unless it provides such an obvious and immediately known danger that it merits using the courts and the agency's time to remove it from the market. For example, since the passage of FIFRA in 1972, only DDT and ALAR have been successfully banned from U.S. markets, and only after years of service to the economy. DDT was the most important and widely used pesticide in the United States for thirty years, and it continues to be exported; in the case of ALAR, its exit from the market after years of consideration as a vital chemical to the apple industry was due to a voluntary withdrawal by the manufacturer owing to financial and market-status loss (Bosso 1987; Pimentel and Lehman 1996; Percival et al. 1992, 490–95). This predisposition toward minimal interference in risk production illustrates the success of the market paradigm in determining environmental-risk law.

A second category of risk statutes attempts to find market solutions to the transportation, disposal, and cleanup of preexisting toxic waste. In this category we have two legislative efforts: an original piece of legislation (like FIFRA and TSCA) and an attempt to graft toxic regulation onto an existing statute. The grafted legislation is the Resource Conservation and Recovery Act (RCRA), which was an amendment to the preexisting Solid Waste Disposal Act (42 U.S.C.A. §§6901–6992k), whereas the original legislation is the Comprehensive Environmental Response Compensation and Liability Act (42 U.S.C.A. §§9601–9675) (CERCLA), better known as Superfund.

In RCRA and CERCLA, the most stringent market measures are applied to risk, representing an effort, not only to trace all suspected toxics from cradle to grave, but to allow those "harmed" by toxic waste to sue the "responsible parties" for compensation (CERCLA at 42 U.S.C.A. §9607). Although regulation of toxic waste under these two legislative mandates has been criticized from the market point of view as heavy-handed and cumbersome, one would expect that the regulation of toxic waste would be the most cumbersome, even from the standpoint of efficiency.

First, toxic waste does not provide a positive market benefit that increases welfare but instead produces negative market costs in storage, disposal, and health effects. Whereas previously, during the production phase under TSA-I, the potential cost of risk-generating material or technology was outweighed, in efficiency terms, by its benefits, in storage as waste, risk is all external cost and requires more serious regulation to integrate it back into the price of the manufacturing process. Departing from traditional pollution abatement, where disposal involved direct release into nature at zero cost but was regulated by public standards, we have collectively decided that risk-generating toxins cannot be released but must be stored and monitored. For toxic waste, the TSA-I threshold has been passed and government regulation, within TSA-II, seeks optimal levels of risk from waste and ways to internalize externalities that are "known" hazards.

Second, the regulatory tools provided by these statutes to set the optimal levels of risk in the economy are efficiency-based. RCRA is merely sound accounting for specific wastes, representing the attempt to internalize a hazardous externality through follow-up and management of the transportation and disposal of potentially cost-generating compounds. CERCLA has an *ex post* liability mechanism that assigns responsibility to manufacturers and sends them the appropriate market signals that allow them to anticipate cost and figure it into production. Accounting and liability law are efficient means to measure and manage optimal levels of risk from waste, mimic the market, and integrate the cost of hazardous externalities.

In effect, both RCRA and CERCLA are afterthoughts of efficiency-based environmental law. Risk is maximized in production within TSA-I, which generates waste that requires disposal. Crossing into TSA-II, we acknowledge that, in protecting the market against false positives, we have created a situation where some harm will be done to individuals and nature. The efficient answer to these problems is to adopt a strict accounting system so that we can track the production and allocation of potentially toxic agents without interrupting their production, while we set strict, joint, and several liability as a legal standard and hold producers, transporters, and even financial underwriters responsible for any harm that does befall the odd individual (CERCLA at 42 U.S.C.A. §9607; Percival et al. 1992, 630–56).

Overall, the efficiency core of environmental law produces risk within TSA-I and requires that responsibility for any future harm from this risk be internalized into market price. RCRA and CERCLA do this. In addition, the framework of efficiency-based environmental law concentrates waste from air and water onto land and creates the disposal problems that RCRA and CERCLA try to address.[38]

The final set of statutes, or more properly amendments to existing statutes, attempts to deal with risk in air and water media by grafting hazardous-pollution provisions onto preexisting legislation. Efficiency is defined in terms of optimality under TSA-II, where the concern is not risk from market products but risk from by-products of manufacturing that might contaminate our air and water.

To provide for these concerns, §112 of the Clean Air Act (42 U.S.C.A. §7412) and §307 of the Clean Water Act (33 U.S.C.A. §1317) were created. In both cases, technology standards are designated for hazardous or toxic emissions. The same legislation and technological standards approach connected with the abatement of traditional pollutants are now, without significant amendment, being utilized in the regulation of environmental risk. Either environmental risk is the same as traditional cases of air and water pollution, which it is not, or its comprehensive quality and distinct characteristics are ignored in the codification of air and water risk policy. But let us look first at the statute treatment of traditional pollutants, upon which risk regulation is grafted.

The aims of clean air and clean water legislation are to protect the public health and to maintain a level of environmental quality that supports productivity (42 U.S.C.A. §§7401 [b1]). The objective of both pieces of legislation is for the government to set a "shadow price" for pollution through the establishment of standards specific to particular emissions in specific air- or watersheds. Setting an optimal level of pollution is accomplished both through setting ambient air and water quality standards and by using technology to control emissions. Both statutes therefore attempt to find the optimal level of pollution by a combination of quality-based and technology-based standards.

Whether they are National Uniform Ambient Air Quality Standards (42 U.S.C.A. §§7408 [CAA: NAAQS—§108]) or Water Quality/Effluent Standards (33 U.S.C.A. § 1311 [CWA: §301]), the quality standards represent an attempt to locate the proper level of pollution through establishing the minimal level of environmental quality needed to maintain human health and aesthetic qualities. Although the traditional "economic" approach to optimal, and therefore efficient, polluting makes a distinction between charging a "price" per unit of pollution and standard setting (Ruff 1977; Mills and Graves 1986), it can be argued that a performance standard and a price on polluting are efficiency-equivalent means to the same end: setting an optimal (i.e., efficient) level of pollution (Majone 1989, 126–33).

Specifically, the quality standard sets the optimal level by defining how clean the air- or watershed must be and then issuing permits for each type of pollutant equal to the level of waste disposal to achieve this environmental quality. In essence, setting uniform standards, especially when left to individual industries to meet these restrictions as they wish, is more efficient than setting a dollar price per unit of pollution, which would require much more monitoring and administration to achieve the same result (Majone 1989, 134).[39] But even if standards are efficiency-equivalent to prices for pollution with fewer administrative headaches, specific technology standards as opposed to general quality standards cannot be said to correspond to a principle of efficiency. Or can they?

Technology-based standards establish mechanical requirements for each industry and are an attempt to operationalize an efficient means to attain the ends set by the quality standards. With concern for Best Achievable Control Technology (BACT) or Maximum Achievable Control Technology (MACT) or Reasonably Available Control Technology (RACT) or Best Conventional

Control Technology (BCT),[40] legislation sets technological requirements for scrubbers and processes that clean waste before it is emitted into environmental media.

As quality standards set efficient ends for the condition of an environmental medium, technology standards mandate specific equipment that a plant must install as a means to higher quality air or water. In the beginning, with the Clean Air Act, the focus was on quality standards, but with the Clean Water Act just two years later, and in the recent rewriting of both air and water legislation, the trend has been toward the ascendancy of technological standards. Does this mean that efficiency has been forsaken?

The drift toward technological standards reflects, not the replacement of efficiency with another principle, but its redefinition. The problems faced by federal abatement law in the last twenty-five years are twofold. First, it had to retroactively clean up the excessive level of pollution produced and piled up by the market over many decades within the context of TSA-I. Second, federal law had to establish the means by which an optimal level of pollution (by industry and media) could be established and maintained over time, factoring in technological advancement.[41] The trend toward reliance on technological standards must be characterized by the principle that motivates it. If our primary concern were protecting natural systems and their intrinsic value, then technology standards could be seen as a means to that end, but this is not the case.

Under TSA-I, technology set the rate at which humans use the environment. Technology progressed so quickly that natural systems were stressed by pollution beyond an efficient level. The market answer was to let government set the optimal rate of natural systems use (under TSA-II); the means to this end was a technology of pollution abatement to counteract a technology of pollution production.

Technological standards are, in reality, a way to uniformly internalize the cost of pollution across any sector of the production economy by requiring that all current abatement procedures be used as the standard establishing an efficient optimum of pollution for any particular industry at any particular time. The law of technology standards focuses on "conventional," "reasonable," and "achievable" technology and does not judge the "necessity" of the polluting production process nor alternatives to it. No awareness exists in these standards that particular natural systems require particular degrees of environmental quality prior to our wants, or that human integrity must have a cleaner environment than present technology can produce. We employ available technology and pronounce the resulting air or water quality as clean enough. In effect, as technology standards have eclipsed quality standards, setting optimal pollution levels has shifted away from how clean the environment ought to be and toward how clean technology can make our manufacturing process, given current economic and scientific considerations.

One way to understand the seemingly counterintuitive propensity for decision makers and regulators to graft risk regulation onto existing abatement legislation, when it is characteristically distinct, is to assume that they believed they were doing nothing different in abating risk than in abating traditional pollution: finding efficient or optimal levels of contamination consistent with market functioning and an acceptable materials balance. On the basis of this conceptualization, technological standards for optimal risk are a conventional, logical, and efficient solution to toxic air and water contamination.

The only accepted difference (within TSA-II) is that toxic contaminants are characterized by greater uncertainty and potential harm, so a concession is made that mandates a more stringent technological standard for toxic than criteria pollutants. For example, hazardous air pollutants are regulated by the application of Best Available Control Technology (BACT) under §112 of the Clean Air Act. But even with the understanding that toxins are more hazardous, we still only require "best available" technology to regulate them.

On the basis of a principle of efficiency, which recognizes no special class of risk in environmental-risk dilemmas, it is necessary to allow the optimal economic use of environmental media. Section 112 of the Clean Air Act mandates that "in setting hazardous air pollution standards, EPA is to consider both the beneficial and adverse economic, environmental, and energy impacts associated with the standard" (Worobec and Hogue 1992, 121).

"Efficient" Environmental-Risk Law and Policy

Current environmental law has grown from a market paradigm metapolicy and a policy space where a core principle of Kaldor efficiency held pride of place. Within the context of risk abatement, the statutes and their legal interpretation by the courts have consistently defended markets from excess regulation whenever possible.

Although one can argue that the statutes examined here have both language related to a core of efficiency and language based on the value of natural systems and human integrity, and although I concede that both lines of argument are part of the legal deliberation of the courts, the core principle and trump card in legal and policy choice remains either maximum or optimal efficiency. By leaving the burden of proof on the regulators, treating each resource or medium noncomprehensively from within a market framework, and by considering all factors in terms of their effect on the ongoing economy, legal and policy choice leave efficiency to become the official standard and justification for environmental action and legal risk decision making.

With the conceptualization of environmental-risk law and policy from within the context of TSA-I and TSA-II, I have traced the gradual evolution of a range of principle from maximum to optimal efficiency, where the law defends TSA-I as long as possible and then only grudgingly concedes transition to TSA-II. With the uncertainty of risk policy questions, the courts have been preoccupied with establishing the parameters of the threshold between TSA-I and II. The science of risk assessment is used in defense of TSA-I, protecting the market from false positives, whereas efforts to find efficiency as optimality, when TSA-II is established, tend toward implementing traditional technological standards or using other efficiency tools, like accounting and liability law, that affect markets as little as possible while mimicking their results.

Environmental law and regulation is built on economic ideas and ideals. Whether the economic definition of rational choice, or the economic calculus applied to risks as symmetric and preference-based, efficiency requires that risk be regulated principally in the market. Within this false-positive risk regime, the public is protected only from extremely hazardous substances and then only by the application of current technology to establish optimal levels of risk that are the "least burdensome" to the economy.

Overall, the market paradigm has established environmental metapolicy, codified in statute law and reinforced by the courts. Perhaps Justice Marshall stated properly, in his dissent on the *Benzene* decision, that "today's decision will come to be regarded as an extreme reaction to a regulatory scheme that, as the Members of the plurality perceived it, imposed an unduly harsh burden on regulated industries" (448 U.S. 607 at 198).[42] But for now, efficiency dominates the arguments that form the deliberative strata of environmental metapolicy, and its core status allows it to define what is "reasonable" and set the standards for legal and policy argument, at least for a "plurality." The long-standing status of efficiency makes it conventional for legislators, administrators, and courts alike to think primarily of the economy when they regulate the environment.

If environmental law, as it exists, is ineffective and unfair, displacing pollution from air to water to land rather than eliminating it (Dryzek 1987, part 1), and suffers from a piecemeal approach by the division of nature into sectors for use (Campbell-Mohn, Breen, and Futrell 1993, 51–71), it is precisely because of the core status of the principle of efficiency in creating that law and policy which we now perceive is inadequate. Majone (1989, 150–54) contends that the core principle and how it leads one to conceptualize the policy problem is the most crucial factor in determining the design of any particular metapolicy. For environmental-risk law, efficiency defines, not only the justification for decision making, but also the standard for success and accountability. Therefore, if environmental-risk law is unreasonable and inadequate, it is because the fundamental principle of efficiency, at the base of its policy argument, is an unreasonable and inadequate foundation for the law of environmental risk.

But if what we have is unreasonable, what characteristics might a reasonable paradigm for environmental-risk regulation need? This is the subject of chapter 4.

Notes to Chapter 3

1. This is why environmental-risk problems are called zero-infinity dilemmas.
2. I use "principle" in the singular because as I argued in chapter 1, in making collective decisions about policy and law, one is faced with a situation where one must be fair and consistent to all constituents over time. Without this consistency, expectations could not be created and no one could define or anticipate the requirements of administrative law. Therefore, while one may consider a number of values in making a collective choice, one must, in the end, consistently allow one value to trump all others. This trump card becomes the core principle of the dominant policy argument for any area of policy/legal choice. Unless one either sacrifices consistency, or assumes that one value will never conflict with another, then a dominant core prin-

ciple will emerge, over time, to define "conventional" environmental law. While it is possible for a competing argument to replace a conventional one, this takes great effort and political capital.

3. One might counterargue that a statute like the Endangered Species Act (16 U.S.C.A. §§1531–44) provides an exception to my claim that market assumptions and the principle of efficiency are the foundations of environmental law. However, I would argue that although this statute comes the closest to representing different core values in the law, the instrumental value of nature for economic purposes remains a core and superseding value to any intrinsic value nature might have. Market-efficiency considerations appear throughout the Endangered Species Act, for example, in the determination of "critical habitat" (§1533 [b2]); in the establishment of the Endangered Species Committee (§1536 [e]-[p]); and in the allowances for economic hardship exemptions (§1539 [b]), to name only a few. Even within the Congressional Findings section of the statute that outlines the reasons for the act, only one of six values, "ecological" (§1531 [a3]) can be said to have a completely nonmarket definition.

4. Campbell-Mohn, Breen, and Futrell's solution, on the other hand, requires a conceptual reorientation away from a concentration on individual media or sectors of the environment (land, water, air, etc.) to a consideration of the economic process as a series of interfaces between human action and nature, beginning with the extraction of resources from the environment and ending with their reintegration into nature (1993, chap. 10). "Unlike traditional approaches to environmental law that either explain each statute or group the statutes by media, this [argument] reflects the fact that laws govern activities, not the environment. It develops a new approach, called resource to recovery, that explains all the laws that apply to an activity, from the time resources are allocated for extraction, through their manufacture into products, and on to their disposal" (1993, vii).

5. I am assuming here that Ecosystems are not just natural systems but contain both human and natural systems as components. I call this the Kantian definition of Ecosystems, and a fuller argument for this proposition is contained within chapter 5.

6. My argument will establish the predisposition toward economic principle which limits environmental regulation to concern for instrumental "use" value that then discounts the consideration of man and nature as intrinsically valuable variables in legal calculations.

7. Normative in the sense that it set the standards by which public choice and action are judged, justified, and evaluated.

8. The argument for TSA-II has been recently adjusted by supplanting the word "sustainable" for "optimal" (Costanza, Norton, and Haskell 1992; Gillroy 1998). Also, recently the field of "ecological economics" has been created (Costanza 1991; Costanza et al. 1997) as an effort to involve environmental values in economic decision making. Fundamentally, however, they are both efforts to rehabilitate the principle of Kaldor efficiency in the cause of optimal use within TSA-II. Elsewhere (Gillroy 1998), I have argued that sustainability is a type of optimal-use efficiency conditioned only by intergenerational concerns. Ecological economics seems, at first, to be a type of cost-effectiveness analysis, where Kaldor efficiency is limited to defining the "means" but not the ends of policy. What ecological economics does to define policy "ends" is substitute the principle of sustainability for Kaldor. However, if sustainability is just Kaldor in new clothes, then what we actually have is not cost-effectiveness analysis but cost-benefit methods from within the market paradigm, where Kaldor sets both the means and ends of policy, and we are no further toward environmental values in policy decision making than straight neoclassical economics, where efficiency is preference based and future people have no existing preferences. The dilemma here is that for the field to be economics it must hold Kaldor as its core principle, or the paradigm concedes the

metapolicy. To be ecological, it must forsake Kaldor efficiency as its core principle in order to properly value nature, effect distribution, and shift the burden of proof to polluters (all goals desired by ecological economics). Therefore it is either economics and business as usual under TSA-II, or it is ecological and not economics at all. I am currently completing research on both of these matters that will be the subject of my next book project, tentatively titled *Beyond Sustainability: The Imperative for Ecosystem Law and Policy*.

9. Even "conservationist"-oriented economic approaches to nature still assume use as the primary instrumental value of all natural attributes. To make room for natural systems with intrinsic value, we must replace the dominant argument.
10. This presents us with the polluter's dilemma examined in chapter 2.
11. The TSA models create a world where resource and pollution issues are separate concerns. It is not surprising that from this model two areas of law, one devoted to resources and the other to pollution and risk abatement, have developed.
12. See Gillroy 1998.
13. See, for example, *Missouri v Illinois*, 200 US 496 (1906).
14. Some mechanisms for integration are the shadow price or the individual's willingness to pay for a quantity of the condition (clean air, water). See Rhoads 1985.
15. In the United States, one might argue that it is more honest to call the EPA (Environmental Protection Agency) what it is: the Economy Protection Agency. See Landy, Roberts, and Thomas 1990 for another point of view.
16. This is also now the case internationally, where the major argument against global regulatory regimes is that they will inhibit economic development. See Hunter, Salzman, and Zaelke 1998, chaps. 2 and 4, for an analysis of this argument.
17. See, for example, in the Clean Air Act (42 U.S.C.A. §7401 [b][1]).
18. My argument is that the following cases provide the critical links in a chain of reasoning that has established our common law of risk regulation.
19. For an analysis of this case and the role of science and ethics in the law, see Bartlett 1980.
20. The "good faith" effort included a $34 million air-pollution-control program, a $100,000 contribution to the construction of a water-filtration plant, and construction of land-disposal facilities. See Bartlett 1980.
21. Even though the decisions on these cases are one year apart, *Reserve Mining* quotes *Ethyl Corp.* (*Reserve Mining*, 519ff.) and bases its decision on a similar logic and definition of "reasonable."
22. For a cost-benefit model that agrees with the court's mandate here, see Page 1978. In addition, it should be noted that this mandate by the court helped EPA to declare TSA-II in effect and to adopt a very conservative definition of "optimal" in the case of lead. It is less certain that, if the suspected toxic did not have the certainty of harm represented by lead, "maximization" would have remained the pertinent definition of "efficiency."
23. Who wanted agency use of science but did not specify methodology (24, 26–27).
24. For an argument that there are normative distinctions that make environmental risks asymmetric with other risks in one's life, see Gillroy 1992b.
25. This is fully argued in the next section of this chapter when I examine risk and the Clean Air/Clean Water Acts.
26. See both National Research Council 1983 and Rodricks 1992, for a complete explanation of QRA. Chapter 4 of this book contains my analysis of QRA and how it compares to CBA.
27. One could argue that this is the point of both the *Benzene* and the *Vinyl Chloride* decisions.
28. This process can be argued to reflect trends in federal policy launched by the Reagan administration (e.g., Executive Order 12,291, 3 C.F.R. 127 [1981]) but is argued here to be the establishment, by an "independent" judiciary, of the domi-

nance of market assumptions in environmental-risk policy choice. Here the market assumptions that had long held pride of place in policy argument are being carried over into the regulation of a new area of legal concern.

29. This can be seen in the definition of risk quoted from the *Benzene* decision.

30. I concentrate here on FIFRA before it was amended in 1996 by the Food Quality Protection Act. Although these amendments made some changes in the law, the essential definition of environmental risk and the fundamental assumptions about the application of market assumptions did not change. My argument, being about fundamental assumptions, is therefore largely unaffected. See Wargo 1998, 301–09 for a fuller analysis of the changes.

31. Chapter 10 of this book has a fuller comparative analysis of FDA versus EPA risk regulation.

32. This means an institutional practice where the government protects the market against false-positive risk results, that is, for example, finding a chemical agent to cause cancer when it does not.

33. The only agency that uses a false-negative risk regime, where a proposed product is guilty of causing harm until the manufacturer can prove its safety and good use, is the Food and Drug Administration (FDA).

34. The effects of toxic risk agents on natural systems eludes the law. The Clean Air Act (at 42 USCA §§ 7401–7671q, 1992) does state a competitive argument for the inclusion of ecosystem research (§7403 [e]) and ecosystem risk assessment (§7408[g]) in the establishment of national air standards.

35. I am told by the author that a revised edition of this argument is now being written.

36. "Pesticides may have provided farmers with a new technological edge in the battle against pests, but the economic imperatives made chemicals absolutely necessary. The new products were relatively cheap and promised to the farmer increased yields at lower costs. Such economic arguments were, if not totally compelling, highly persuasive" (Bosso 1987, 32).

37. Even at this point, after DDT was considered too risky for U.S. sale, foreign sales were allowed to continue.

38. "The hazardous waste problem faced by the United States is a by-product of an advanced economy and technological life-style. It is also the result of our other environmental laws, which have redirected health and environmental risks from air and water to the land. Coping with the risks of carelessly discarded wastes, while trying to maintain the other aspects of environmental quality and economic well-being, will require a flexible regulatory structure that tries to minimize the costs of transition between the status quo and the future" (Dower 1990, 189).

39. We should remember here that the market paradigm can only justify a minimal state that mimics the market but does not become intrusive in its operation. The bureaucracy needed to set these prices might be very intrusive indeed.

40. For example, under the Clean Water Act, Best Practicable Technology (BPT) is used for existing point sources; Best Control Technology (BCT) for conventional pollutants; Best Available Technology (BAT) for toxics; Best Available Demonstrated Technology (BADT) for new sources.

41. Both of these problems have intergenerational implications that are beyond the scope of this essay, and that of the principle of efficiency, to analyze.

42. Other dissenting opinions in major environmental cases also espouse lines of argument that are based on environmental values. It is in the dissenting opinions of the courts that we would expect to find noncore argument attempting to gain the persuasiveness necessary to become the core of a new environmental metapolicy. (See, for example, Justice Douglas's dissent in *Sierra Club v Morton* [405 U.S. 727 (1972)].)

4

Moving beyond the Market Paradigm: Making Space for "Justice from Autonomy"

Even if the practical tactics of the process present pitfalls or ultimately confound us, policy design attempts to control the standards and strategy with which we approach environmental law. I have already broken down the strategic phase of creating a policy argument into two components: the theoretical paradigm and the practical context model. These two component parts, combined with the tactical concerns of addressing constraints and audience problems, integrate into an overall policy design approach which can then be applied to the particular characteristics of an issue to derive specific policy recommendations.

The policy design approach is comprehensive in nature. So far the Economic Design Approach, containing the market paradigm and the TSA I and II context models, has dominated the theory and practice of environmental risk and its regulation. Now, in preparation for part II, we will reexamine the characteristics of environmental risk in order to identify concepts and connections that might provide a bridge between the status quo approach to policy design and an alternative paradigm and context model better suited to environmental-risk regulation. I offer one which integrates a Kantian paradigm (called "Justice from Autonomy" [JFA]) with a "resources to recovery" context model.[1] Together, I call this alternative the *Ecosystem Design Approach*.

With a new paradigm and context model we can approach questions of both environmental risk and environmental law from a new perspective. Our task is comprehensive: to provide analysts and citizens with an additional tool in the search for a proper relationship between humanity and nature. Our new tool must be as versatile, universal, and applicable as market analysis and methods. Our prescription for a new core paradigm in environmental-policy argument shall appeal to our "common" sense, and it should measure up to the requirements of comprehensive policy argument, as set out in chapter 1. Finally, our proposed alternative will address itself more effectively than the market paradigm to what is at stake in environmental-risk law and policy.

Although our immediate concern is environmental-risk law and policy, our study of economic thought and the environment, as well as our investigation of policy argument and the idea of "paradigm," place demands upon us that surpass application to risk issues. An alternative paradigm that can compete with market assumptions must also have the potential to be complete and comprehensive enough to set standards and methods for other types of environmental policy and other areas of public interest.

Although I cannot accomplish this greater task within the confines of this book, I can offer a fully developed Kantian paradigm, Justice from Autonomy. Following the generic categories and schemas of comprehensive policy argument, I shall devote part II to the fundamental assumptions, principles, material conditions, maxims, and methods of the Kantian paradigm as well to as the Resources to Recovery context model, which together will be the Ecosystem Design Approach. In part III, we will apply Justice from Autonomy to a range of environmental-policy dilemmas and set out a series of case studies where the Ecosystem Design Approach is used to justify policy and make public choices. One can then compare its collective recommendations with those of the market paradigm.

Creating an alternative and well-integrated paradigm begins with a simple step: setting the goals of a nonmarket environmental paradigm on the basis of the characteristics of environmental risk, the requirements these demand of environmental ethics as the substructure of policy argument, and the adjustments in practical environmental administration required for the actualization of these alternative public policies.[2]

We need to reconceptualize environmental-risk law and policy. Environmental risk is not a single issue, law, or policy, but a classification for a cross-section of environmental concerns characterized by pervasive uncertainty and management problems. Using Page's characteristics of environmental risk, as we did in chapter 2 to assess the failure of market assumptions, we can articulate the ethical and administrative requirements of any paradigm and context model seeking to handle risk issues.

First, we will identify some essential dilemmas in environmental ethics useful to address the uncertainty characteristics inherent in risk. These ethical debates include the distinctions between anthropocentric and nonanthropocentric theory, between intrinsic and instrumental values, between private and public goods, and finally, between conservationism and preservationism.

Second, we will concentrate on the administrative dichotomies faced by the environmental-risk manager. The particular management dilemmas of environmental risk will be addressed through another series of dichotomies: between responsive and anticipatory institutions, between efficiency-based and autonomy-based policy instruments, between public and private management techniques, and finally, between incremental and comprehensive policy planning.

Finally, we shall expand our working definition of "ecosystem" to focus on the interface between human systems and natural systems as these interact and affect one another. This new definition of "ecosystem" in *ecosystem policy design* will redefine the policy space and substitute *ecosystem law and policy* for economically motivated environmental decision making.

A Substructure: Uncertainty and Environmental Ethics

Environmental ethics attempts to apply normative philosophy to issues relating humanity to the environment. The application of the concepts of environmental ethics to public-choice questions raises significant challenges to the prevailing market conventions in environmental law and policy.

Some prominent debates in environmental ethics might provide us with a bridge from the market paradigm to the goals of an integrated alternative system of theory and practice. Ethical thought may allow us to transcend uncertainty without ignoring it.

Anthropomorphic versus Anthropocentric and Ignorance of Mechanism

One normally distinguishes a risk from an uncertainty by the fact that a reliable probability number can be arrived at for the former, but not for the latter. However the "science" of environmental-risk estimation (Quantitative Risk Assessment) has ignored this distinction by taking what amounts to a pervasive uncertainty and assigning a probability number to it. Stating that environmental risk is characterized by "ignorance of mechanism," Talbot Page (1978) means that the physical and chemical processes by which risk agents make their way through the environment and integrate into what we might call a "risk soup," with health effects for human beings and nature, is not traceable or predicable through current scientific methodology.

Although science generates numbers that characterize the probabilities that humans will be affected by "toxins" in the environment, these predictions are limited by a number of assumptions, including reliance on the singular (non-synergistic) effects of individual chemical or biological agents, the distinctions between low doses in humans and high doses in animals, the validity of linear models, and the existence or nonexistence of "thresholds" of effect (Rodricks 1992, chap. 10; Conservation Foundation 1985; National Research Council 1983; Shrader-Frechette 1993; Henderson 1993). Environmental-risk estimates are controversial because of these and other assumptions that are necessary in order to make the transition between unquantifiable uncertainty and quantifiable risk. The continued ignorance of mechanism, compounded by the necessity of making human-effect conclusions on the basis of animal data, causes the uncertainty of environmental risk to persist even with the assignment of risk numbers to possible hazards (Graham, Green, and Roberts 1988, 148–50, 176–78).

These numbers are especially troublesome when we translate risk from animals to humans. Scientific method is valuable because it takes nature on its own terms: as a functional system of inorganic materials and organic life. The ability to understand biological systems and how they ingest, metabolize, and react to potentially harmful chemical agents is not the primary concern of risk analysis; it is the translation of this knowledge into terms useful to making policy decisions concerning human health that causes the greatest uncertainty.

The certainty of science does not begin with, or even involve, humanity or its social, political, or moral dimensions, but begins and ends within natural systems function and evolution. An ignorance of biological, chemical, and physical mechanisms, compounded by the use of nonhuman findings to make human health estimates, results in policy decisions that are "choices under pervasive uncertainty" (Page 1978). This means that the numbers produced by quantitative risk assessment can be used only as data and not as definitive evidence for setting standards or regulating environmental risk (Graham, Green, and Roberts 1988). The gap between science and public choice requires that additional considerations be added to policy arguments about risk.

In the face of this uncertainty humanity has either made metaphysical assumptions in the lab (e.g., about the connections between high doses in animals and low doses in humans), or from within our economy (e.g., that more use of nature satisfies more preferences for wealth), or even from within philosophy (e.g. that nature has specific rights, as individual humans do), and in so doing we have ignored the distinctiveness of nature and failed to consider it on its own terms. Policy has therefore failed to make judgments that take the unique characteristics and requirements of humanity and nature into account.

To change this predisposition we would need to acknowledge three postulates: first, that humanity sets the terms of discourse and value for the assessment of humanity, of nature, and of their interaction; second, that humanity's intrinsic value is moral in nature; and third, that the intrinsic value of the environment has its roots in its capacity as a persistent living system that cannot be properly evaluated by the transference of human moral or intellectual attributes (e.g., thought, choice, strategy, rights, interest) to nature.

Environmental ethics traditionally takes a single moral vocabulary (e.g., rights, utility) and divides the general theory of valuation into two camps: first, ethical theory that denies, for example, rights or utility to nature and places humans as the sole or central character of value (anthropocentric theory), or second, theory that places nature in the prominent ethical role (bio- or ecocentric theory) by granting it, for example, greater rights or utility than those granted humans. This division is a false dichotomy because it ignores the three postulates above. First, it fails to acknowledge that the terms by which both humanity and nature are described and valued are human. Second, instead of assessing humanity and nature incommensurably, each in its own terms, and judging decision priorities on a case-by-case basis, it places one component of the greater world system in moral dominance over the other. Third, it assumes one vocabulary of moral evaluation so that in order for a tree, animal, or natural system to have moral standing it must have preferences, rights, or interests that are commensurable with human moral attributes.

What we might learn from science, applied in the risk context, is that, although human ignorance in the face of environmental mechanism is not good, it not as bad as a failure both to acknowledge the inherent incommensurabilities between humanity and nature and to analyze natural systems in their own functional terms. The natural world is neither scientific nor ethical; in fact, only one component of nature, humanity, has evolved these capacities. All analysis is from a human point of view and to a greater or lesser extent because of this, humanity is the center of discourse and thought in both its scientific and ethical forms. This does not mean, however, that we must place ourselves as the only "subject" of value, or that the moral terms in which we define ourselves (e.g., rights, interests, etc.) must be transplanted to nature in order for it to be properly (that is, commensurably) evaluated (Hargrove 1992).

The scientist, in her analysis of natural systems, evaluates each ecological entity, not in terms of human characteristics, but in terms of the functional character of nature. She neither imports human-centered vocabulary (e.g., intelligence, strategy, determination, choice) into components of nature, nor does she analyze each system primarily as to how it affects, or has value to, human beings. In this way, although the scientific process is human and defined in terms of human vocabulary, it neither devalues nature nor makes humanity or its attributes its centerpiece.

Ethical analysis is also a result of human design and execution. We should be capable of evaluating nature in its own terms, ethically, without either importing human characteristics onto nonhuman entities or making humanity the only creature of moral value in the universe. If all human analysis is anthropo-*morphic* in that it begins and ends with human categories, schemas, and vocabulary, then the distinction of importance in environmental ethics is not between anthropocentric and eco- or biocentric theory, but between anthropocentric ethical theory (which ignores nature's unique capacities and values) and merely anthropomorphic analysis (which does not). All ethical analysis is anthropomorphic, even that which places natural systems or the biosphere in the central place of value. The important question is not whether humans have decided the terms of analysis, but whether incommensurabilities are acknowledged in how distinct entities are evaluated, and in what terms they are valued.

Within present environmental-risk law and policy the economic models are both anthropomorphic and anthropocentric because nature is analyzed only as it has instrumental use to humanity. Nature is defined in terms of its resource value to individual preference, and its characteristics are described to facilitate human consumption (e.g., not a tree, or a component of a natural system, but a thousand board-feet of lumber). Humanity not only sets the terms of discourse for nature but is the sole standard of value in this analysis.

The approach of science, in contrast, is anthropomorphic but not anthropocentric because with it we attempt to understand the internal structure and function of nature, where humanity is seldom a character, never the central agent, or the singular value (Abrahamson and Weis 1997; Odum 1975). The pervasive uncertainty in policy risk estimates appears when science tries to translate environmental, nonhuman data into commensurable human risks. In effect, risk analysis fails to alleviate uncertainty because it assumes a commensurability between natural and human-health effects that may not exist.[3] Policy evaluation and environmental ethics may exacerbate uncertainty by assuming a similar commensurability in the terms of ethical discourse and valuation. Perhaps science should not apply environmental data to judge human capacities, but policy ought not to attribute human ethical designations to nature, as if it were also a moral agent.

Public policy, like science, may have to plead ignorance of exact mechanism in its evaluation of nature, but it must begin to consider nature within its own context and integrate it as a distinct but equally valuable component of our ethical deliberations about good and bad policy, right and wrong decisions. We should recognize that all ethical deliberation, even that which places central and greatest ethical value on the natural systems themselves, is anthropomorphic.

However, while we acknowledge our necessary role in the proper valuation of nature, we must also understand that our responsibilities to nature and the duties that flow from these responsibilities must be based on nature's functional characteristics and not on quasi-human rights, utilities, or interests. In addition, we need to realize that debating in human terms does not make humans the only proper subjects of moral duty. When making public choices, we should recognize the intrinsic functional value of the environment as a foundation that defines our duties to nature, just as the intrinsic moral value of humanity defines our duties to other persons.

If natural systems are to have a distinctive place in policy analysis, we must put them there. Our central concern should be to distinguish between those policy principles and paradigms that can accommodate only nature's instrumental value to man, and those where the functional or intrinsic value of natural systems plays a role. Only within this second group of theories can nature have a place of equality or prominence in our moral consideration of which environmental risks are acceptable and which ones are not.

Instrumental versus Intrinsic Value and Modest Benefits

Another characteristic of environmental risk related to its uncertainty is what Page (1978) calls its "relatively modest benefits." An ethical dilemma exists in how we judge the "modest" nature of the benefits and justify a decision that denies them to those with a market preference for them. The policy choice, as we have argued, requires that we justify why we will use the coercive power of the state to make everyone do X (Gillroy and Wade 1992, vii). In justifying a collective choice, coercion needs to bring cooperation without significant or systematic hardship or rights deprivation. Avoiding tyranny (Fishkin 1979) is of primary importance for political theory, but the justification of a decision that benefits some at the expense of others is also a necessary result of policy decision making and the primary reason why economic policy design must move from the Pareto efficiency criterion to the Kaldor (Gillroy and Wade 1992, 8).

However, economic policy design assumes the existence of only one type of value (instrumental), and the discussion of how much benefit is accrued by choosing one alternative rather than another is the major subject of deliberation for policy decision making. I contend that the importance of the uncertainty of risk issues to the decision process diminishes if we shift our analytic focus from the benefits themselves to the distinct types of values involved and to a tradeoff matrix where the winners and losers are sorted by what values are at risk.

Instead of a world of trade between instrumental human values, where the metric of money and willingness to pay defines the difference between "modest" and "greater" benefits, let us expand the world to include both instrumental and intrinsic value related to both humanity and the environment (see fig. 4.1). Now four combinatins of risk tradeoffs can be examined for their potential to result in winners and losers on two distinct levels of value and for two distinct "subjects" of concern. In cell *A*, the intrinsic value of humanity is weighted against the intrinsic value of nature. We may be deciding here between an old-growth forest system and our need of the lumber for national security reasons. In cell *B*, the intrinsic value of nature is weighted against what has only instrumental value to humanity. Should we trade essential damage to the ozone layer for the convenience of propellants in spray cans? In cell *C*, what is of instrumental value to nature is weighted against what is of intrinsic value to humanity. An example here might be the selective cutting of forests that are inconsequential to the persistence of the natural system but essential to provide human shelter. Finally, in cell *D*, what is of instrumental value to both humanity and nature is being traded. Shall we take an already used urban piece of land and build a mall?

The uncertainty of benefits and its implications for policy decision making is now more complex but also more approachable because we have anthropomorphically segregated what affects *essential* (intrinsic) value from what affects

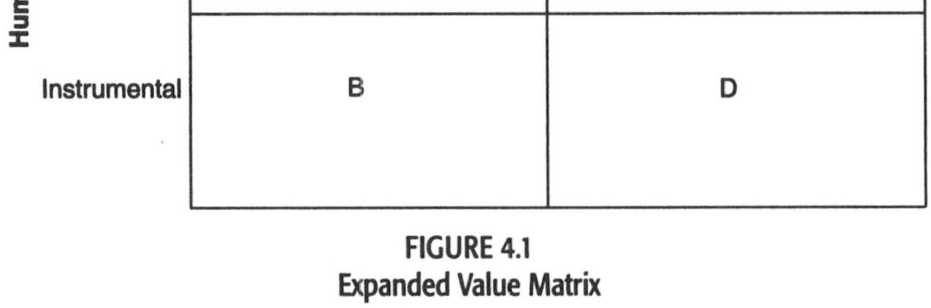

FIGURE 4.1
Expanded Value Matrix

elective (instrumental) value and are considering both humanity and nature in terms of their distinct characteristics and essential/elective requirements.

A taxonomy of ethical value replaces a single scale of instrumental welfare benefits. The uncertainty of symmetric outcome "benefits" is replaced by the certainty of intrinsic value and the responsibilities that occur with delineating the essential from the elective and setting priorities between these. Consequently, the judgment and justification of "benefits" can be analyzed to provide more options and arguments to the environmental decision maker. In addition, the idea of "tyranny" now becomes intertwined with how one's public choices affect what is essential about humanity or the environment; concern for trading away intrinsic value for instrumental becomes important.

Private versus Public Goods and Catastrophic Results

Another dimension of uncertainty regarding environmental risk is its potential for catastrophic harm. In addition to a concern for the difference between intrinsic and instrumental value in public choice, a consciousness of how a policy choice relates to degrees of private versus collective risk and voluntary acceptance versus involuntary imposition of risk can further eliminate uncertainty by defining "catastrophe" in risk decision making.

For market analysis, catastrophe has no meaning beyond that attributed to any considerable instrumental cost to humanity. Within our new multidimensional tradeoff scheme, however, the concept may be redefined by the distinction between private and collective goods. If we assume that a bad result is compounded if its effect is not only to intrinsic value but is also joint and nonexcludable (Snidal 1979), then a catastrophe is more than just a greater than normal material cost to the individual.

In addition, if an environmental risk places the universe of individuals in the way of harm, where one's subjection to it is joint with all and where one suffers without consent or voluntary choice (which compromises one's intrinsic value as a person), then one is discussing harm that is collective, immoral, and insidious. If one first assumes that harm to the intrinsic or essential value of humanity or nature is possible, and then contends that this harm may be collective and nonvoluntarily transferred, then this degree of harm can indeed be said to be potentially catastrophic. Uncertainty as to result may still prevail, but one can now place uncertainty about what is essential and collective in a separate class of considerations, *ex ante*, and justify the protection and empowerment of the constituents of that class in any risk analysis.

By examining risk questions from within the dichotomy of public and private goods transactions, we replace the free rider with the imprisoned rider and the various degrees of cost with essential and collective harm. This new taxonomy may not lessen uncertainty, but it places it within a more complete and fitting context for the policy and legal matters at hand.

For example, if we chart prospective risk-policy decisions on a graph where the range from a fully collective choice to a fully private choice is on one axis and a range from full voluntary acceptance to involuntary transfer of risk is

FIGURE 4.2
Environmental Risk Asymmetry and Government Regulation

charted on the other axis, one can see the relationship between choices of more or less government regulation of risk by the degree the decision concerns collective involuntary environmental risk (see fig. 4.2).

In the lower-left quadrant of this graph we have issues that involve voluntary private risks. Here, with smoking cigarettes, for example, the private choice requires little government regulation as the risk is private to the individual smoking (in the closed room) and voluntarily accepted (by the adult smoker). In the lower-right quadrant of the graph we have risks that are still predominantly private but which may be involuntarily transferred to the individuals involved. In these cases, like dealing with radon in the home, a bit more government involvement may be rational, at least to alert the individuals involved as to the private risks they are accepting by living in their home.

In the upper-left quadrant, where the risk may be accepted voluntarily (sitting in a smoking section of a restaurant but not smoking oneself), it is now collective, affecting everyone in the vicinity who breathes the air. Because of this, we may require more government involvement to mitigate risk to otherwise innocent parties and to protect collective interests. Lastly, in the upper-right quadrant of the graph are the true zero-infinity dilemmas that involve collective involuntary risks, like the emission of radioactive air pollution. In these cases, where catastrophe to the imprisoned rider is likely, government intervention to anticipate the risk, judge its necessity, and regulate it is essential.

Conservationism versus Preservationism and the Zero-Infinity Dilemma

A policy argument paradigm is of use in risk issues only if it can provide a sound ethical base that recognizes and can accommodate the complexities of environmental-risk issues. Environmental ethics applied to the characteristics of environmental risk can provide a language and a set of requirements for any such argument paradigm.

The overall uncertainty of risk policy can be most completely characterized in terms of the zero-infinity problem; that is, the almost zero probability of an infinitely catastrophic result. This idea, however, gains new meaning and greater complexity because of our recent analysis. By examining the zero-infinity dilemma within the ethical framework of the debate between conservationism and preservationism, we may find a bridge to better understand how risk's inherent uncertainty can be made more concrete to the policymaker (Taylor 1992).

The core distinction between conservation and preservation can be traced to the difference between a policy based upon an interest in the long-term violability of nature as an instrument of man's continued prosperity and one concerned with protecting and empowering the inherent capacities of the natural world.[4] These two views manifest the most basic dichotomy in ethical theory: consequentialist and nonconsequentialist thought (Smart and Williams 1973).

To the consequentialist, and I would argue to the conservationist, the value of a policy decision lies in its ability to produce certain consequences, specifically, the long-term persistence of nature's use value. Nature is resources that provide a sustainable yield of material in both the short and long term. Environmental media are also important resources and their persistence as a sink for pollution is also a consequence to be ethically desired in terms of humanity's continued use of nature. The ethics of conservationism is an ethics of consequentialism that values policy and law to the extent that it provides for whatever rate of resource use is proscribed by the theory.

The ethics of preservationism, in contrast, although partially concerned with consequences, places primary moral value on the act of preserving the functional integrity of natural systems themselves, regardless of the consequences. The moral value is independent of man's use of nature or its instrumental value to the economy or anything else.

The zero-infinity dilemma can be viewed through either a conservationist or a preservationist lens. Using the former, a consequences-based decision standard relies on the relative probabilities of different welfare outcomes to determine the proper choice. Outcomes, having their moral validity in a future unrealized state of affairs, exacerbate the role of uncertainty in the policy-decision process.

Through a preservationist lens, however, the uncertainty of outcome is limited in its effect as scientific probabilities diminish in their importance to moral decision making and the ethical value shifts to the concept of *ex ante* preservation, which is deemed of moral value regardless of the consequences. Add the anthropomorphic concepts of intrinsic value and public good to this preservationist imperative and we have the foundation for an ethical paradigm that moves beyond the market to place the uncertainty of environmental risk into a new and more complex moral context. Within this context, the uncertainty of environmental risk has less effect on the moral values involved in risk decision making, or on the definition of the "right" public choice, because it is the essential value of what is at stake that now determines the precautionary decision.[5] With this shift in focus, a new consideration of the essential ethical stakes of environmental-risk policy is illuminated for the policymaker.

We have examined the characteristics of environmental risk connected to its uncertainty in order to move toward a distinctive conceptualization of the issue of scientific uncertainty within the framework of a substructure of environmental ethics. We shall now consider the management characteristics of environmental risk and the demands of a new theoretical conceptualization on the superstructure of administrative decision making.

A Superstructure: Environmental Risk and Public Administration

In addition to the characteristics of environmental risk related to uncertainty, peculiarities related specifically to the management of risk policy also exist (Page 1978). Just as we bridged the conventional market paradigm and the requirements of an alternative with ethical dichotomies in the last section, we will now utilize a set of administrative dichotomies in order to address the practical management of environmental risk.

Responsive versus Anticipatory Institutions and Stealth

Among the most difficult issues regarding the administration of environmental-risk law and policy is the stealth quality of risk. Environmental risk affects individuals in intangible ways that make detection or individual defensive strategies nearly impossible. Dependence on the consciousness or preferences of the individual as a basis for policy, therefore, also becomes problematic.

Preference is the currency of economic decision making. Under the best of circumstances, it is difficult for an economist or policymaker to distinguish between a true preference and a manifest preference (Sen 1982, part 2; Gillroy 1992a). Is the expressed preference of the person her real preference or does it involve strategic behavior? The surreptitious quality of environmental risk makes it even more difficult for a responsive government to decipher the true risk preferences of its constituents (Page and MacLean 1983), which is essential to policy formulation and implementation within this paradigm.

The market paradigm assumes a responsive government. The sole function of government is to respond to the welfare preferences of consumers when markets cannot, and without the signals sent by preference, the market policy paradigm has no foundation for decision making. However, even if an administrator could properly read individual preference, the stealth quality of environmental risk exacerbates the difficulties of using them as a basis for public choice. If one cannot sense environmental risk, then one cannot form a preference order with risk as a factor. Even if informed of the existence of risk, one would find it difficult to measure cardinal or ordinal differences between risk preferences without an independent sense of each in terms of both presence and effect.

The stealth problem is further compounded by the connection between responsiveness and the burden of proof within the market paradigm. In addition to the assumption that the only "ethical" and justifiable public decisions are based on the state's response to aggregate welfare preferences, market axioms also assume that the burden of proof for action lies with those who would intercede in "natural" market functioning: the state. But the state cannot intercede until specific market failure occurs. Even then, the state can only do what the market would have done, that is, respond to unfulfilled preferences, and cannot depose preference in favor of more secure noninstrumental values. To do so would be an act of paternalism, as it would create state action without authorization from consumers. For the market *responsive* government is the only *responsible* government (Gillroy 1994).[6]

The dilemma of waiting for preferences to form while environmental risk affects people collectively and irreversibly, creates the imprisoned-rider scenario. In order to overcome the stealth quality of environmental risk, and to make proper policy, we must move beyond the idea of "responsive" government as the only responsible government. The ethical complexity of the concept of responsibility should be understood, and the "burden of proof" in matters of regulation ought to be shifted to those who would impose the environmental risk on society.

Specifically, in order to regulate responsibly, risk must be anticipated and action justified *ex ante*. The state, as the responsible party, must have a means to decipher what is of necessary value to its citizens and move to preserve these values from those who would place them at risk.[7] The burden of proof, in this approach to regulation, changes from those regulating risk to those imposing it. Their responsibilities are to justify the imposition of risk, to describe the potential effects on humanity and nature, and to gain political assent for each imposition of environmental risk.

To manage risk a decision maker cannot rely solely on the expressed preferences of consumers but must define and anticipate the values and needs of citizens in order to justify action *ex ante*. The state becomes more than a mere aggregator of market preferences. Anticipatory government functions to define and provide the fundamental requirements of its citizens, as well as of the natural world, requiring those who would risk these essential interests to justify the imposition in terms of the intrinsic values involved.

Efficiency-Based versus Autonomy-Based Policy Instruments and Internal Benefits versus External Costs

But how do we define the "essential" needs or interests of citizens? If we rely on the market paradigm, we cannot attribute any preferences to persons because the role of the state is to respond to existing preferences, not to create them. This stricture is compounded by the management characteristic of risk where most benefits are transmitted within the context of the market, while most costs are external and therefore not counted in market price computations (Page 1978).

Within the market paradigm, risk can only be addressed by internalizing the costs. But if these costs are unknown because of the stealth nature of risk, how can one internalize them? In addition, having the benefits of risk (e.g., spray cans, red apples) as immediate and tangible market factors prejudices the cost-benefit calculations because the economic benefits do not have the stealth dimensions that characterize the costs.

Efficiency-based policy instruments can respond only to expressed preferences and to the signals sent by price through the market. We face a serious dysfunction of these signals and an exaggeration of economic benefits when we consider environmental-risk policy. We need a new set of signals that provide for an anticipatory state rather than for the responsive market if the "external" costs of risk are to be appreciated. These new signals ought to allow both the negative and positive effects of risk on essential citizen interests to be read properly and reported publicly *ex ante*.

Essential citizen interests could be defined in terms of many philosophical concepts; I suggest that to identify what is basic to all individuals, one must focus on the concept of "humanity in the person" (Kant C2; GW). If one asks what is most basic about one's humanity, it is one's internal capacity to act as an agent. But not all actions confirm one's humanity. A specific type of agency, that is, moral agency, needs to become the focus of our definition of essential interest and intrinsic human value.

To move from dependence on efficiency-based policy criteria and gain a foothold against the stealth quality of environmental risk and its external cost problems, we need an autonomy-based administrative system. Why autonomy-based? Because autonomy defines "moral agency" as capacity and the practical reason necessary to use it. Agency involves action, but it can be defined to specifically address those actions that confirm and express humanity in the person. This allows one to define what is essential to the person in terms of what empowers or protects this essential autonomy. Further, responsibility to autonomy requires the state to set an *ex ante* standard of regulation on the basis of what collectively provided goods are necessary to the material conditions of each citizen's moral autonomy, that is, what is in every human's essential interest as a being of intrinsic value.

When applied to environmental policy, the concepts of essential interest and intrinsic value require the policymaker to also consider the capacities of nature. It is the interfaces between moral agents and natural systems that become the focus of concern and the field where values must be assessed and tradeoffs contemplated. Public responsibility is no longer responsiveness to, but protection and enhancement of, human and natural capacities as these compete with one another.

As we have already argued, all human analysis is anthropomorphic. Yet, we should construct a theory of human autonomy that includes what is unique and essential about nature without devaluing it. Anthropomorphically, nature can only have value as humans value it or recognize duties toward it, but it ought to have equal intrinsic value in policy deliberation and choice, even when no environmental crisis is looming on the horizon.[8] Autonomy-based criteria can take account of environmental risk and all of its effects as part of a management decision. To inform public choice in this way is the task of a new policy argument paradigm.

Private versus Public Management and Collective Risk

Another characteristic of environmental risk related to its management is its nature as a collective risk. Although individual persons or corporations can impose an environmental risk, the collective, including nature, is affected by it. The collective nature of risk-effects is characterized by the idea of nonvoluntary transfer (Page 1973), and the stealth nature of the risk further intensifies both the responsibility of government as an agent of the people's autonomy and the necessity to examine risk in terms of the collective-action problems it creates.

Public policy is about solving collective-action problems (Gillroy and Wade 1992) and presenting reasonable choices to citizens (Schattschneider 1960). Collective-action problems are normally thought of in two categories: coordination dilemmas and public choice issues. Coordination problems focus on encouraging a critical mass of individuals to cooperate in the provision or protection of adequate levels of collective goods (Hardin 1982a, 1982b; Axelrod 1984). Public choice is concerned with establishing aggregation regimes by which collective choices can be made by groups of individuals (Downs 1957; Buchanan and Tullock 1962; Green and Shapiro 1994).

There are many collective-action problems related to environmental policy in general. The "commons problem" that affects public lands (Hardin 1968; 1993; Lehman 1995; Ostrom 1990; Buck 1998) is one of the fundamental dilemmas in environmental literature; the use of the prisoner's dilemma and other "games" has been effective in defining the problems inherent in the provision of public goods, including environmental quality (Hardin 1982a; Gillroy 1992b, 1993).

One major contention of my argument is that economic assumptions and the market paradigm have greatly influenced, even determined, the history of environmental law and policy. Collective-action problems are caused, from within the market, by both commons problems and the existence of externalities. These dysfunctions cause markets to fail and create the market paradigm applied by public administrators to public-sector issues through cost-benefit methods. Public choice theory, with its concern for wealth preferences defining the citizen's interests and for efficient aggregation representing the objective of government, has become a major theoretical foundation of policy administration (Bobrow and Dryzek 1987, 44 passim; Laver 1981, 1986).

In terms of collective risk, distinctions ought to be made between risks that one imposes autonomously on oneself and those that are nonautonomously imposed on the group. The state is responsible to make this distinction and regulate the collective risk in the interests of its autonomous citizens.

For the public administrator to act as this imperative requires, she needs a concept of "public" management based on responsibility, distinguished from private management based on efficiency and the application of the market paradigm. Again, a dialectic is set up between the assumptions of the market and the requirements of environmental risk that illustrates the requirements of a proper risk paradigm.

Current public administration writing and research reflects a continuing belief in the argument that most tasks now assumed by government could be better analyzed and accomplished from within a private management framework (DiIulio 1994; Willig 1994; Gordon 1992). However, this analysis has not separated those issues and policies that bear directly upon individual autonomy and its essential empowerment and protection, which I would classify as a responsibility of public management, from those that relate to elective or instrumental preference as governed by efficiency, which may properly be the domain of private management and the market as applied by government administrators.

The practical concern of public managers should be to separate and publicly regulate risks to collective action. The responsibility here includes creating the background conditions where no imprisoned riders exist, and further entails that human and natural capacities be empowered in the actions of government to maintain cooperation and the provision of public goods. It also forces one's theory of public choice to be informed by citizens as moral agents who have capacities for practical reason behind their superficial interests and preferences and needs that must be fulfilled responsibly by government before wealth is increased efficiently.

This requires that collective action and public choice, as theory, be separated from dependence upon economic assumptions and the market paradigm and also obliges the decision maker to find an autonomy-based paradigm with which to define, not only the standards of public choice and collective action, but the proper venue for each type of decision. Only when this analysis is complete shall we be able to truly define the proper subjects, respectively, of public and private management.

Incremental versus Comprehensive Policy Planning within the Context of Latency and Irreversibility

The last two management dimensions of environmental risk have to do with the latency and irreversibility of the effects of risk on humanity and environment (Page 1978). As argued, the market paradigm is consequentialist in assessing moral value. Both latency and irreversibility confound this ethical orientation.

With latency, the effects of risk on humanity or nature will not be made evident for many years after exposure. This delay compounds the stealth quality of risk issues and makes the impacts of risks not only invisible but delayed. Latency means that negative consequences will not surface until it is too late, at least for those affected, to address the risk. If one adds the collective nature of the risk to this scenario, the potential exists for a universe of people to be affected by unsensed harm, with no tangible results for years to come. Within a strict consequentialist system of evaluation, not until after the outcomes are predicted or made actual can moral judgment be made. The pervasive uncertainty of environmental risk as a zero-infinity dilemma makes the assignment of probabilities to future outcomes even more problematic than it normally is. Waiting until outcomes and effects are made real also allows harm to be transmitted collectively and involuntarily throughout the population while "moral" response is delayed until well after any negative effects have already been initiated.

Add irreversibility of harm to latency, and these negative effects cannot be undone once they are finally recognized. Irreversibility is also collective and represents a causal chain that may be years or decades old and perhaps untraceable.[9] Within this context, a paradigm dependent upon preferences and consequences falls back upon a Kaldor definition of efficiency and adopts a policy of maximizing gross tangible welfare improvement, despite the actual preferences or interests of citizens (Gillroy 1992a). Since most environmental risk is generated by the same technology and economic processes that also generate wealth, and we assume that we are correct in saying that the present benefits of the latter will be much more certain and obvious than the future costs of the former, Kaldor will always define efficiency in terms of maximum economic growth and prosperity, no matter the eventual risk imposed.

The maximization of wealth (or its optimization) is justified by the claim that we cannot have a zero-risk society (Aharoni 1981; Viscusi 1983, 1992). The premise is that the attempt to regulate risk *ex ante*, and independently of markets, is an attempt to eliminate all risk in society, which is impossible. Questioning the maximization of wealth as a tradeoff for risk prompts the patronizing response that "all life involves risk." However, this worn maxim does not take into account the distinctions made in my argument about the differences in both environmental risk itself as a policy issue and what is at stake in its collective imposition. In addition, such a response fails to envision that between the impossibility of a no-risk society and the free-market, risk-ridden society is the possibility of the *risk-conscious society*.

In addition to the ability to be rational, a person has the capacities to identify morally important decisions and to apply intellectually approved principles to the assessment of right and wrong. Practical reason, applied to collective choice, can consider risk, not just in terms of its quantity, but in terms of its possible qualitative relationship to intrinsic value and collective responsibility. If practical reason is the application of moral reason to action, then moral consciousness can be applied to environmental risk using a standard that acknowledges both instrumental and intrinsic value and asks how the imposition of any environmental risk can be justified in these terms. This conscious deliberation over the moral quality of environmental risk is a middle ground between the economic justification for all risks that the market will bear and the fiction of a "no-risk" society.

Within the risk-conscious society, each potentially collective risk is analyzed and considered *ex ante*, before being imposed on society and nature. Utilizing our tradeoff matrix for intrinsic and instrumental value (fig. 4.1) as well as our graph of private versus public risk and voluntary versus involuntary transfer (fig. 4.2), the decision maker can now construct a policy argument for or against accepting a risk before it is marketed on the basis of essential values and collective responsibilities. Using the best science, along with ethical reason, we would strive to understand the potential risk, why it is necessary, and what is at stake in terms of value tradeoffs before we would agree to accept it. Any risk that passes these tests will then be one that has been consciously accepted by the citizenry for a particular collective reason.[10]

The responsible state, anticipating and regulating to empower and preserve autonomy, has a sizable planning responsibility. By placing the burden of proof on those who would impose environmental risk, the state is responsible to allow only those risks that, in the greater tradeoff between instrumental and intrinsic values, can be justified in terms of the autonomy of its citizens and the intrinsic value of nature. The state's imperative is to anticipate harm and therefore to plan.

But how comprehensive must the state's planning be? Within the scope of the market paradigm, each facet of environment law and policy is addressed incrementally, as if in isolation. Such an incremental approach to policy is antithetical to the proper administration of environmental concerns because policy choice regarding humanity and the natural world is required to cope with the interdependent biota and abiota of evolving systems that make up a comprehensive biosphere. These interconnected media and living species frustrate piecemeal analysis and punish segregated action that does not consider the connection between systems and their effects upon one another.

The key to conscious risk planning is comprehensive planning. To those who counter that it is administratively impossible to consider environmental policy comprehensively, I borrow a page from March and Simon (1958, 140–41), who contend that all administrative decision making exists within the limits of human intellect and information and is therefore doing the best one can with the knowledge one has. They call this goal of decision making "satisficing" (Simon 1982, part 8; 488–89). Within the context of environmental-risk choices, "satisficing" would require the risk-conscious society to make an effort to consider each individual policy within our knowledge of intersystemic causes and effects. We currently have greater knowledge of interactions between humanity and nature than we employ to judge the instrumental values of costs and benefits; this knowledge could be used to make the satisficing decisions sensitive to the intrinsic values involved in planning for environmental-risk choices. Planning, within this framework, requires a more complex definition of the policy space to anticipate the effects of a collective risk; planning must take into account the essential values at stake in the decision and must satisfice to choose growth and development strategies that are conscious of our duties to ourselves and to nature. We must segregate the ends of a policy from the means and keep thinking about these ends comprehensively even as we focus on the incremental implementation of specific tactical means to our overall strategic ends.

The imperative in risk planning is to remain conscious of the collective risk we impose upon ourselves and the environment. The state should first allow, and then move to monitor, only those risks that are persuasively argued to be worthwhile on the basis of the demands of our autonomy-based criteria.

Overall, in dealing with environmental policy one may begin with the substructure of environmental ethics addressing uncertainty and derive a concern for planning and autonomy-based public administration from it. But one must also be concerned with the enhanced definition and role of nature as viewed from this alternative policy perspective. What role should nature play in the deliberation and choice of public risk policy? How ought it to be defined to inform a move to Ecosystem Law and Policy design?

Ecosystems in Ethical Context

The Ecosystem[11] design approach draws on a more inclusive definition of ecosystem than that currently used. The sciences provide the predominant definition of ecosystem, attributed to Sir Arthur Tansley (1871–1955), an English botanist who "coined the term ecosystem for biotic and abiotic components considered as a whole" (Odum 1993, 38). Defined as a hierarchy within nature that includes both the organic (biotic) and inorganic (abiotic) components of the environment, ecosystems are assumed to be systematically interdependent (Odum 1975, 1993). For conservation biology, ecosystems are normally considered to be natural systems, that is, the environment within which animals, plants, and other populations of organisms live. It is the distinction between human and natural systems which provides the demarcation line for science between that which they study and that which they traditionally leave to the social sciences and humanities (Primack 1993).

To examine ecosystems as a tool of autonomy-based policy design, one must transcend science and determine what is important about the definition of "ecosystem" to a comprehensive policy argument. There are three ways in which one may understand the relationship between humanity and nature for the purposes of policy design. First, humanity is simply part of nature, integrated into various ecosystems and considered as a component part. Second, is the opposite view, that ecosystems are the natural components of the biosphere while humans and their artifacts are separate and distinct entities, outside the field of ecosystem studies. A third approach is to understand humanity as part of nature and interdependent, but also transcendent, where the special moral capacities and technological abilities of humanity impose specific obligations upon us to preserve and protect the natural world from which we came.

Placing humanity as merely another species within the natural world is the approach of many religious and tribal views of nature that assume a cosmology of man's awe of and dependence upon nature as a point of departure (Grim 1983, chap. 4). From this perspective, humanity is merely another species subject to extinction if it does not follow the "natural laws" of the ongoing natural order, together with which we either survive or die. Although this picture of a dependent humanity, one within the myriad of species, is basic and argues against technological evolution, humanity did arise out of the natural world and remains a species of animal that, in the largest sense, depends upon the functioning of the biosphere for continued existence. This perspective fails to acknowledge, however, that humanity, alone among the creatures of the earth, has moral capacity and extensive technological abilities that, taken together, impose specific responsibilities upon us as a particular species of animals with a unique capacity and ability to shape our environment.

The second approach, which describes humanity as a "natural alien" (Evernden 1985), argues that, even though humanity has grown out of nature, we have established ourselves apart from the systemic interdependence of natural systems. Our independence is based upon the human ability to utilize technology to create our own environment "outside" the natural order.

> The consequences of technology are subtle but extensive, and one such consequence is that man cannot evolve *with* an ecosystem anywhere. With every technological change he instantly mutates into a new—and for the ecosystem an exotic—kind of creature. Like other exotics, we are a paradox, a problem for both our environment and ourselves. (Evernden 1985, 109)

> [H]umans are, in effect, organisms without a niche. We are creatures without a predetermined role, who must create ourselves anew in each generation and in the process undergo what we call 'cultural evolution.' (Evernden 1985, 111)

The alienation of humanity from nature may be either a good or a bad situation. Most economists would view it favorably, since distinguishing humanity from nature allows us to use nature, without moral strictures, toward the material enhancement of human life. Evolving past nature and becoming "exotic" grants us our place at the top of the food chain, as that "creature" who has the power, and therefore the obligation, to make the best life possible utilizing current technology and the environment as a resource.

Those who view the alienation of humanity from nature as a bad thing have a variety of reasons for this judgment. Some view this situation as a "truth" with moral ramifications, while others ignore the ethical dimensions, isolate humanity, and focus on the ecosystems left behind by our exotic species as the primary subject of analysis. Among this latter group are most scientists who, when they speak of ecosystems, include humanity only as an afterthought or as a potential perturbation. Studies and experiments in natural science examine biological diversity of nonhuman plants and animals, and the interference of humanity in the otherwise ongoing evolution of natural systems, but do not fully integrate human and natural systems nor suggest that the former has specific obligations to the latter. The many subdisciplines of the life and physical sciences studying the patterns and complexities of natural phenomena do so without specific concern for humanity's place (Abrahamson and Weis 1997), while fields like conservation biology examine humanity only in terms of our separate functioning as whole populations or societies (Primack 1993; Odum 1993, chap. 6), not as integral parts of a larger whole and never as individuals with moral capacities and value.

Those who acknowledge the moral ramifications of human alienation from nature provide a bridge to our third approach to the humanity-nature question: humanity has obligations to nature specifically based upon our capacity to evolve past nature's internal mechanisms.

> Man remains in nature even if the range of choice he enjoys seems incomparably greater than that of other species. Others are made to their world, while man must construct one with constant risk of error. (Evernden 1985, 118)

Our third approach to the definition of "Ecosystem" is based on the "fact" that humanity is unlike any other product of nature on earth because we are both moral and technological. Unique in the moral discourse of life, we alone hold ourselves to self-generated moral and legal strictures or standards of interrelations. We are also technologically singular, for even if other creatures can be recognized as using tools for construction (e.g., beavers, monkeys, ants), we have evolved the most sophisticated technology on earth, creating our own complex artificial environments.

This third view of the humanity-nature connection accepts the uniqueness of human, as distinguished from natural, systems but also acknowledges that a complex two-way interdependence characterizes the interrelationship. We are subject to natural constraints, but we place more complex and potentially devastating constraints on natural systems than any other species of animals. Our alienation is both empirical and normative. We have transcended nature but bear duties to it, and our duties speak directly to how we utilize our knowledge, science, and technology to create a life for ourselves on earth while respecting the pattern of natural systems that surrounds us and which produced us.

But what provides the basis of our duties? If we refer to the four-way table of values in this chapter (fig. 4.1), we see our obligations do not just concern the instrumental value of man to nature or nature to man, but they must speak to what is essential, or intrinsically valuable, about ourselves and the natural world. Emphasizing the third perspective on the relation between humanity and nature, an Ecosystem for the policymaker needs to include the biotic and abiotic elements of both natural and human systems. These elements include humanity's moral agency and its artifacts, machines, and social, political, legal, moral, and economic constructions as well as plants, animals, and their nonorganic environment. The intersystemic nature of this Ecosystem is found in that balance between human and natural systems, but the key to this balance lies in the moral responsibility specifically allocated to humanity to define its creativity in terms of both our own and nature's intrinsic value.

From a policy point of view, an Ecosystem is the intersection of human and natural systems, which must be considered in public choice. Our alienation, from this perspective, forms an imperative to define our responsibilities as moral and technological creatures and to achieve that particular balance between human creativity and natural evolution that allows the essential intrinsic value of each to persist in harmony with the other.

Natural Systems: A Point of Departure

The Ecosystem approach to policy must begin where science begins: with natural systems. The policymaker has to understand the science of biological, chemical, and physical systems and how they persist and evolve, but more importantly than this, she must be able to primarily value them for what they are and not for what they can do for humanity.

To acknowledge the foundational imperative of natural systems is to acknowledge that all life begins with the evolution and progress of nature. The earth and its "life-support" systems (Drury 1998; Odum 1993) are a primary level of policy concern, not only because of the scientific or empirical functioning of these systems and processes, but for the purposes of making collective choices concerning them in terms of our evaluation. Both the fact and the value of natural systems form the foundation of the Ecosystem approach to policy design. But how are values and facts related? David Hume offers a good beginning.

Hume contends that a statement of fact cannot directly lead to a value statement because one is distinct from the other (Hume [1740] 1975, 469). If we apply Hume's contention to our subject matter, we may conclude that the fact of an Ecosystem's persistence cannot lead to a moral imperative that it ought to be preserved.

However, this perception of difference between *is* and *ought* is based on a very restrictive theory of morality that is not founded upon human reason, but on what Hume calls "the passions" ([1740] 1975, bk. 2). Hume's premise, as I interpret it, assumes that morality is based in sentiment and that sentiment is alien to reason. Since reason is limited to the definition of empirical fact while only the passions are associated with moral matters, it follows logically that *is* and *ought* are constituents of distinct lines of thought process and argument, and therefore, one cannot be deduced from the other. However, from our Ecosystem Design Approach one must, as a policymaker, move from situations of fact (e.g., that a natural system is empirically unique) to moral imperatives (e.g., it ought to be preserved by public policy). To do so we need to bypass the positivism inherent in Hume's assumptions and move toward the application of practical reason to public choice.

Hume assumes that reason applied to empirical reality is, by nature of the exclusive connection between moral value and sentiment, value-free. But is it? If practical reason not only delineates facts but assigns value (on the basis of those facts), could a policymaker not use a scientific assessment of a natural system to draw moral imperatives about that system? How might he or she do so?

Let me suggest that the functioning and persistence of natural systems represents the moral value at issue. Nature is assumed to have no morality, which is an anthropomorphic attribute, but it can have value as a self-generated, self-perpetuating web of natural components. Within this interconnected systemic whole, each subsystem could be assumed to have value as it evolves through various states of homeostasis. The fact of functionality, then, has essential or intrinsic value to the persistence of the whole. But here we are speaking of a functional integrity, not a moral integrity.

Nature, in its own terms, is a functional entity that predates us, produced us, and has the probability of continuing to exist long after us. This functional independence is a fact, but a fact that compels a moral duty to act on the part of humanity. Since we can disrupt this independent functioning, and also because we depend upon it, if we owe any duties to ourselves or others, then we owe duties to nature both in terms of the good of ourselves and the "good" of nature as an "other." Contrary to Hume's formulation, humanity's moral duties to nature can be deduced from the fact of natural systems functionality.

Pertinent from a policy point of view is that natural systems function on their own; the primary value of these systems, internally or externally, requires that they be protected, empowered, and allowed to persist over time. Since humanity is the only group of moral agents on the planet, it is left to our responsibility to assume this charge. Both the science of nature and the point of origin help define an intrinsic value that is not based on human contact or use of the environment but finds its foundation in the idea of nature as a functional end-in-itself. The empirical persistence of natural systems and their internal functions, which have value to humanity because they *are* is illuminated as a central value. Practical reason assigns duty to action in support of the persistence of nature as an empirical world of cause and effect, amoral within itself, but the subject of human responsibilities and obligations owing to our capacity as moral and technological beings to cause disruptions in its empirical persistence over time.

If reason is a moral attribute of humanity, and it is possible that we can deduce an obligation from a set of facts, then both *is* and *ought* are subject to the same logical framework and can be part of the same policy argument. This variant of the "naturalistic fallacy" (Moore 1903; Frankena 1967; Searle 1967) is—in reality, the fallacy that the sentiments are the only human capacity capable of moral motivation or action.

Human Systems: Artifice and Obligation

Humanity deduces its obligations to nature from the fact of the empirical existence and functioning of natural systems. This contention assumes that humanity, as another level in the total Ecosystem Policy Argument, is capable of moral thought that combines reason, duty—made imperative by moral principle—and action.

All human creation is artifice, an addition to nature. The creation of the artificial, however, carries with it a moral capacity, first, to set standards for our actions based upon our duties to ourselves and others (including nature), and second, to maintain these standards despite the possibilities suggested to us by our cumulative knowledge and our fabrication of technology. This ability to set standards suggested by duty and to maintain them could be defined as the possibility of deciphering the difference between what *is* possible and what *ought* to be done. Specifically, our knowledge and ability to take a certain course of action does not automatically invoke it as a proper course to be chosen. The ability to construct nuclear weapons may be a matter of scientific and technical expertise, but the actual construction of these weapons, and then their employment, are distinct moral choices.

To make this distinction between *is* and *ought* a person must possess the moral capacity to judge the difference. But what is the nature of this moral capacity? From where does it arise? What obligations does it place on the moral agent? I contend that this moral capacity is defined by the concept of autonomy, which is derived from and transcends our understanding of the persistent evolution of nature. From this moral principle obligations arise that require the person to respect not only her moral autonomy and that of other humans, but the functional integrity of nature.

Hume notwithstanding, Western philosophers have understood the role of empirical nature as a genesis point in human anthropology and ethics. The Greeks described nature as both the point of origin for ethical thought and the source of the teleological ends of moral action (Annas 1993, 214–20). Nature's role in the development of the person, as first described by the Stoics, gives us a sense of humans evolving, not only within the physical environment, but as moral or metaphysical beings (Annas 1993, 159–80).[12]

The Greeks "found nature figuring at the most general level of our lives" and our roots in the natural world represented "those aspects of ourselves that we cannot change but must work with" (Annas 1993, 214). In this way, "nature gives us a starting point for ethics" (Annas 1993, 215) by representing "what is natural [as] opposed to what is conventional" and "an ethical ideal that gives us the means to locate and correct the merely conventional elements in our moral thinking" (Annas 1993, 217). This correction is achieved by reflection on our intuitions and the moral theory with which we approach the world; the content of this reflection forces humanity to transcend nature while still remaining a functional entity of the natural world. For the Greeks nature is normative, foundational, and universal.

> To live naturally, in fact, involves an inner change, without which outer changes are useless; we must start to reflect on what kind of being we are, what our needs are and so on. Clearly we cannot do this in a way which keeps ethics right out of it. The appeal to nature gives shape to a demand to come to terms with ourselves from an ethical point of view . . . ethical improvement is seen in terms of my increased rational ability to come to terms with and modify the given aspects of my life. (Annas 1993, 219–20)

From nature we learn that we are functional entities with an existence that has purpose as part of the ongoing evolution of the natural world. We begin to reflect about our needs and how we can continue to persist within the environment around us. We can also divide the moral world into conventions and the critical reflection that amends these conventions.

We are, first, part and product of the causality that is nature, and this determinism dominates our thoughts, actions, and beliefs. From this we derive convention, as Hume pointed out. Our artifacts include justice as defined in terms of those conventions that allow us to anticipate the actions of others and cooperate toward shared goals (Hume [1740] 1975, 489–90).

134

However, as Kant argues, in addition to the determinism of nature that is our ancestry, we also inherit the possibility of critical reflection based upon the idea of freedom and the capacity to make decisions on the basis of one's own standards, not arising solely from convention, but from freedom, which is a universal and necessary assumption for human reason (Kant C1, C2). The realization of freedom by the person can be described as the true point at which the individual becomes the "natural alien" transcending the natural world. This is an ethical epiphany that results from the reflective process addressed by Annas. In the inventory of needs and interests, the person comes to understand that in addition to being within the causal reality of the natural world, he can also be a first cause himself in the satisfaction of needs and the creation of the world around him.

Kant contends that, in order to be a human being, one must acknowledge freedom as the capacity to be an agent-cause in an otherwise deterministic world. This acknowledgment of one's "moral" capacity to have an effect on one's own and other lives evolves into one's capacity for autonomy. Autonomy then becomes the capacity to reason practically about one's existence and to act by intellectually approved principle in order to further one's ability to have a higher order control over one's life (Kuflik 1984). Acknowledging freedom propels the person from the functional world of natural causality into the political and moral world of humanity and human communities. Because of the concept of freedom, one can assume obligations and duties to utilize this freedom in ways that are not contrary to autonomy in the person or to functionality in nature.

But how is nature part of a theory of human autonomy? As previously explained, all moral evaluation is human, or anthropomorphic. I suggest that one can acknowledge the anthropomorphic fact of moral value without devaluing the nonhuman world. The ideas of the evolution of morality and of freedom from nature give us a conduit to establish a theory that does just that: a theory that values nature as part of human autonomy without devaluing it.

If nature is the point of origin for human ethical thought, it is because the existence of nature as an independent and self-generating entity gives nature cause to continue and gives us reason to protect and facilitate this evolution. If our realization of freedom comes from our reflection on need, and this reflection itself begins with existence, then the first moral thought could be: because I exist, I ought to persist in that existence. This realization could not come without the experience of nature and our understanding of its systemic processes (e.g., life, death) from which we came. Functionality is both necessary and sufficient for the continuation of natural wholeness or integrity, but while the same can be said of humanity physically, its ethical dimension makes survival itself necessary (but not sufficient) to the full moral agency or integrity of the person, and therefore of *prima facie* moral value.

The advent of morality is the genesis of duty. Duty defines our obligations, but to what? If nature generates humanity, and we then transcend nature with our capacity to be free agent-causes, then the subjects of duty fall nicely into two primary categories: our obligations to humanity and our responsibilities to nature.

If, as Kant suggests, we are defined by our capacity to have and express freedom, and freedom is described in terms of autonomy as a higher order control of life, then our duties to humanity would be to autonomy in ourselves and in others. Our duty to nature could then be defined within either of these categories.

As a duty to ourselves, we might define nature as a necessary prerequisite to our freedom, as the context of our morality and the point of departure for both our physical and spiritual being. In these terms, nature is critical to who we are and therefore of vital importance to our freedom, or our capacity to be human. Our duty to nature is necessary to our autonomy; this instrumental value is not optional but essential; nature is valued as much as autonomy; both are equal components in defining one's humanity.

However, our duties to nature are also independent of the instrumental value of nature to our autonomy, if we define obligation to nature as an external entity falling under our duties to others. The duty to other humans appears straightforwardly as a duty to their autonomy. After all, if the standard of human morality in oneself is autonomy, it is reasonable that this same standard also marks others as moral ends-in-themselves and worthy of respect.

Respect for nature, however, since it lacks moral capacity or autonomy, must be defined by a distinct sense of intrinsic value, one that marks what is necessary and sufficient to the integrity, or whole intrinsic value, of nature. The functional integrity of nature offers such a definition. We have argued that nature is a whole entity in terms of systemic function; it is a self-generating, persistent, and evolving whole with many parts and subsystems. The wholeness of nature defines its intrinsic value and our moral obligation to respect the natural world independently of its instrumental use to us. The gauge of our success in evaluating and respecting nature, independent of its use by humanity, is in the persistence and evolution of individual natural systems.

Toward Ecosystem Policy Design: A Tension of Intrinsic Values

The characteristics of environmental risk have been examined and goals have been set for an alternative design approach. A new design approach must be based upon the central role of environmental ethics, autonomy-based administration, and an expanded definition of "Ecosystem" in the policy decision-making process.

"Ecosystem" has been redefined, not in terms of isolated natural systems and their interaction, but as the tension between natural and human systems. Having traced the origins of moral capacity in humans arising out of, and then transcending, nature, we subsequently suggested that there are two intrinsic values with which an Ecosystem approach must concern itself: human moral autonomy and the functional integrity of nature.

Environmental-risk policy is riddled with uncertainty. That uncertainty is as much an ethical as a scientific dilemma, and understanding the full range of ethical categories of value and the tradeoffs between those values is critical to making sound public choices. The administration of risk questions is a matter of sorting instrumental from intrinsic value and setting standards that protect the essential ethical and functional qualities of living things while placing the burden of proof on those who would put them in jeopardy, especially for the promotion of elective preferences.

The ethical demands of uncertainty in risk decision making require a theoretical paradigm that considers ethics as an anthropomorphic activity that regards nature in nonhuman terms without devaluing it. Further, uncertainty requires that policy analysis encompass intrinsic as well as instrumental value and the tradeoffs between these. The policy choice should be characterized by its concern with collective goods and what action will solve the coordination problems involved. Decision makers should elevate the inherent values of acts over the consequences they produce.

No sounder base for such an alternative paradigm exists than the ethics of Immanuel Kant. Within the context of what I shall define, in chapter 5, as Kantian conservationism and Kantian preservationism, we can define duties to humanity as well as to our intrinsic value, but also to the environment as both a necessary instrumental ingredient in human autonomy and an independent functional end-in-itself.

To build an alternative context model we turn, in chapter 8, to Celia Campbell-Mohn, Barry Breen, and J. William Futrell who, in *Environmental Law: From Resource to Recovery* (1993), define an alternative administrative structure or context model for environmental regulation that provides a framework for the complexities of Kantian philosophy in public choice. In this alternative, labeled the "Resources to Recovery" model, the relationship between environment and economy is reversed from what it was in TSA-I and TSA-II. No longer do we dissect the environment into resources and sectors from the point of view of the economy; rather, we divide the economy into extraction, manufacturing, and disposal interfaces from the point of view of the environment and examine all law that is relevant to a particular economic function simultaneously.

The demands of Kantian environmental-risk management are facilitated by this new context model. The requirements of risk anticipation and planning, within a context of autonomy-based policy standards, require the economy to serve the environment and not the reverse. Policy is refocused onto the intrinsic values involved. The risk-conscious society requires that each potential risk be analyzed as to its effect on the interface between humanity and nature, *ex ante*, before a product or technology is allowed into the environment.

Considering the stealth, latency, and irreversibility problems of environmental risk, our alternative paradigm requires a context model that defines the metapolicy in terms of a core of intrinsic value and its worldview in terms of the hierarchy of nature, state, and then market. The new paradigm will have an administrative model comprehensive enough to examine environmental characteristics and their economic requirements, given the specific function at hand (e.g., extraction, manufacture, or disposal). In this model, the political state co-ordinating human collective action is responsible to the essential capacities of humanity and nature. We will than have transcended a context model where economic principle and assumptions determine the boundaries of politics and the uses of the environment on a medium-by-medium or resource-by-resource basis.

The Resources to Recovery model assumes that the economy serves both humanity and the environment rather than the opposite, which is a founda-tional axiom of the market paradigm and TSA. It facilitates comprehensive planning for resource designation, use, and reuse without the presupposition that nature is only a resource. Although it does not imply a specific ethical core, the model does require a moral theory that can accommodate intrinsic as well as instrumental value and one that is not econocentric.

In order to answer the questions generated for the public manager (e.g., What can be designated a resource? What can be extracted? How will this be done?), the Resource to Recovery context model requires a prior paradigm that sets distinct and noneconomic standards for choice, making it more com-plex than the market paradigm. The questions above make no sense in a world where all material is subject to extraction by any efficient means, given willing-ness to pay. To the principle of efficiency within the market paradigm, every-one and everything is a resource and subject to extraction and use limited only by the preferences and technology available. Such a paradigm cannot accom-modate the preservation of a natural system from resource exploitation. It has no way of justifying a nonresource decision, and it cannot argue that our use is trumped by our duty to the intrinsic value of a natural system.

Justice from Autonomy, in its role as a Kantian, noneconomic foundation (Gillroy 1992c) for a risk-conscious society, will be utilized as an ethical foun-dation for the Resources to Recovery model. This new strategic model will then be employed to provide a standard for identifying and defining acceptable resource use and how and if nature ought to be extracted, polluted, or put at risk, given our dual responsibility to ourselves and to nature. The Resources to Recovery context model provides a fitting framework for the managerial de-mands of environmental risk and is accommodated and made whole by its con-struction upon an autonomy-based ethics.

The goal is now set: an Ecosystem Design Approach to policy. The task of taking us there begins where we have argued all comprehensive policy argu-ments start, with the fundamental assumptions of the alternative "Kantian" paradigm.

Notes to Chapter 4

1. Based upon the work of Celia Campbell-Mohn, Barry Breen, and J. William Futrell (1993).
2. Because the Economic Design Approach is the dominant paradigm for environ-mental-policy analysis, it is the point of departure for all constructive arguments about the application of environmental values to public choices like public lands,

pollution, and biodiversity (Norton 1987, 25–135; Wenz 1988, 5–22, 56–101, 210–31; O'Neill 1993, 44–82, 168–81; Lehman 1995, 56–228; Knight and Bates 1995, passim; Noss and Cooperrider 1994, 3–30, 67–98). The foundational and comprehensive nature of the market paradigm, and the superficial and relative nature of applied environmental values form an imbalance created by the conventional status of the former and the less concrete or accepted status of the latter. I do not mean to say that environmental values are superficial, or need be, but rather that without a systematic attention to environmental ethics as in and of themselves the foundational assumptions of policy analysis, the noneconomic normative content of environmental-policy argument plays the role of either a secondary concern of the decision maker or a "nonobjective," "nonuniversal," and "biased" set of concerns that are grafted upon the preexisting core efficiency criteria. This forced status limits environmental ethics to the role of critical comparative argument rather than to that of alternative core argument for a new environmental metapolicy.

3. Commensurability in the translation of animal data to human-health effects is understood here to involve mathematical factoring to compensate for the "differences" between the subjects. Even with this adjustment, however, the process still assumes ultimate commensurability between humanity and nature. See Henderson 1993 and Rodricks 1992 for a more complete explanation.

4. This core distinction comes from Passmore (1974, part 2) and remains essential to the analysis of both conservation and preservation. Bryan Norton (1986) has tried to redefine preservation by defining it as a policy outcome (setting aside wilderness) rather than as a principle providing distinct motives to action. I argue that this definition does not work. Specifically, I argue that it fails to appreciate the intrinsic value of natural systems as functional wholes and the many policy actions that are necessary to systems' persistence.

5. Both the precautionary principle and the prevention principle are currently topics of argument within international environmental law. See Hunter, Salzman, and Zaelke 1998, 360–61 and 364–65. Although my use of these terms is not contradictory of their meaning in international law, the difference here is that my use of both terms will be supported by a more detailed substructure of Kantian ethics that will allow them to inform a wider range of policy choices that consider the values at stake and the context of the choice. See chapters 9 and 10.

6. See chapter 7.

7. We need to remember that, according to Kant, to move to stop someone from executing an anti-autonomous choice is not in itself a violation of his or her freedom, while to move to protect and empower the autonomy of those who would be exploited in such a choice is a subject of duty to oneself and others (see chapter 7 of this volume for the detailed argument on this point).

8. Mark Sagoff (1997) argues that environmental policy is no longer faced with scarcity or crisis in its consideration of the public interest. Although this is a controversial approach to modern environmental ethics, my argument holds whether or not crisis or scarcity exist.

9. This is the major problem in toxic tort law (see Percival et al. 1992, 630–56).

10. This does not require that each potential risk be voted on. When the public administrator decides on the basis of essential qualities of humanity and nature, she will be able to justify her decision in terms of her responsibility to these intrinsic values and persuade her audience of its rectitude. This will at least be as sound a basis for decision making as the imperative to maximize wealth.

11. To distinguish what I mean by Ecosystem from the traditional meaning, I will capitalize it.

12. This moral evolution would be later used by Enlightenment philosophers to justify the transcendence of nature and the uniqueness of human freedom in a world of determinism.

PART II

A Kantian Paradigm for Ecosystem Policy Argument

The occasion is piled high with difficulty,
and we must rise—with the occasion . . .

Executive Summary

To facilitate moving from the critical argument about the market paradigm, in part I of this book, directly to the application of the Kantian alternative paradigm to environmental policy, I provide this executive summary which specifies how the Kantian alternative paradigm, Justice from Autonomy (JFA), fits the basic logical categories of Comprehensive Policy Argument, as defined in chapter 1.

JFA is distinct in terms of its fundamental assumptions, principle, material conditions, maxims, and methodology; a more complete and detailed argument for each component may be found within part II. Reading the entirety of part II fully enables one to understand the philosophical foundations and full justification of the Kantian paradigm for policy analysis, but this summary will provide guidance for those practitioners more concerned with direct application.

To apply the logical categories of CPA to Kant's thought, we begin, as we did with the market in chapter 1, with his fundamental assumptions about the individual, the collective-action problem, and the role of the state.

The Individual and Nature (see chapter 5)

For the market paradigm and its foundations in classical economics, the individual is a rational consumer with welfare preferences. Within the Kantian paradigm as Justice from Autonomy, the policy analyst responds to a complex individual who is more than a collection of wants, or different "levels" of wants (Olson 1971; Sen 1974). This person is assumed to be a practical reasoner struggling to form a moral character as an active agent on her own behalf. The internal character struggle is between the predisposition toward moral self-awareness and one's propensity to be a self-interested agent, which is the fundamental tension in Kantian ethics (Allison 1990, 146–62; Kant GW, C2, RL, PP, MJ, MV). This dual character describes a complex moral agent with the capacity and the predisposition to act in accordance with the maxim that she shall respect the moral autonomy or humanity in herself and others, but who is also a person in a material world of scarcity, uncertainty, and fear that will condition her expression of autonomy.

The "reality" of being neither god nor animal but a combination of both is the basic unit of normative currency within the Kantian moral system and describes the individual with which JFA begins its analysis of a public issue. The ends of individuals are not wants per se, but the empowering of their autonomy through the manifestation of their predisposition to act morally in the practical abilities of their moral agency (Kant C2). Here it is critical to understand that the moral agency of the individual is the focus of the policymaker. By providing for this agency, she protects and empowers the autonomy of citizens.

In addition to the moral integrity of the individual citizen, the policymaker must also consider the functional integrity of Ecosystems made up of human and natural systems and their interactions. Just as one's morally intrinsic value is based upon practical reason and one's capacity, ability, and purpose in becoming an autonomous person and a moral agent, so the functional integrity or capacity, ability, and purpose of nature must also be a policy priority. This presents humanity with obligations both to use nature carefully and without waste as necessary to human autonomy and agency (Kantian conservationism), and to respect the integrity of natural systems as functional ends-in-themselves and preexisting causal components of greater Ecosystems (Kantian preservationism).

Collective Action (see chapter 6)

The market paradigm builds a collective level of organization that is no more than the aggregate sum of individual wants and preferences, while collective action is primarily concerned with establishing just enough cooperation to satisfy the material need of the most people possible. JFA examines the political community as a distinct entity where individuals (the moral building blocks of collective action) and the just state (which ratifies and enforces the collective terms of cooperation to ensure the moral character of individuals) coordinate and reinforce one another. The problem with collective action is in encouraging each individual's predisposition to act morally. The strategic situation is not a prisoner's dilemma, but an *assurance game* (Gillroy 1991; Elster 1979) in which each citizen is assumed to be willing to cooperate in the production of morally cooperative outcomes within a just state, which is more than the aggregation of welfare preferences. Kant's state also has a duty to protect and treat each person as a moral agent. The political community, within a Kantian paradigm, is a necessary and vital actor.

In terms of collective action, the policymaker should assume that when faced with the fear and uncertainty of exploitation in a community where no "public" regulation exists, the individual's underlying propensity toward "evil" or self-interested behavior will dominate one's predisposition to act morally (Allison 1990, chap. 5). A policymaker needs to be aware that the "externalities" of others' behavior and the subsequent fear of exploitation by these external market effects may cause individuals to ignore their predisposition toward cooperative action and to move to protect their core of freedom in isolation, acting to exploit others before they are exploited themselves. This "mania for domination" (Kant AT) illustrates the government's failure to provide the conditions necessary to coordinate the assurance game and provides the decision maker with the priority to protect individual autonomy by regulating that behavior that would exploit this essential moral capacity in some for the instrumental benefit of others. The collective-action implications of the assurance game promote a distinct definition of "public interest" and are the reservoir of the moral precepts and traditions that define the "right" and the "good" and therefore "justice" itself.

The State (see chapter 7)

From the standpoint of the market paradigm the state has only two functions: to police and adjudicate contracts and to provide a surrogate exchange system that can step in when markets fail and allocations cannot be made without the involvement of a collective third party. For Kant the state is a distinct entity, functioning independently and prior to economic markets and existing to anticipate and regulate them in a way that contributes to the "harmony of freedom" for all citizens.

Kantian justice is rooted in the characterization of the individual and the collective-action problem held in JFA. Each individual is assumed to have the capacity to recognize herself as a moral being. The "just state" is therefore defined as that set of institutions and regulations that provide the material conditions for the protection and empowerment of the moral capacities of its "active" citizens (Kant MJ, §46). This responsibility requires the state to solve the assurance game and maintain cooperation over time. Here, the "just" state empowers the individual's predisposition to act morally and defuses, or prevents, the mania for domination.

From this viewpoint, the state is more than the sum of individual preferences and is established to maintain an independent and duty-based sense of justice that ensures its long-term existence and justifies its policy choices. The institutions in a just state are responsible to the individual; they support each citizen in seeking autonomy while protecting each against the immoral actions of others.

Here, in a search for an answer to the *why* question, the policymaker can utilize Kant's assumptions about the individual, collective action, and the just state to clarify his or her normative priorities and justify law that anticipates environmental risk and regulates it with the integrity of humanity and nature at stake.

Operating Principles (see chapter 7)

Our next concern is with the entailments of these foundational assumptions, once chosen. Defining a rational policy requires operating principles to form the basis of the policy imperative for the decision maker and the creation of techniques or methods that the policymaker can easily use to apply these principles to practical decisions.

For the market paradigm, the protection and facilitation of each person's voluntary economic trade is of prime concern, and the principle of Kaldor efficiency does this by supporting the maximization of aggregate social welfare. For JFA, the principle is *autonomy*, which, unlike efficiency, is divisible into three subprinciples, each corresponding to one of the levels of fundamental assumptions.

The assumptions about the individual require concern for the principle of *freedom* in terms of both its negative and positive manifestations. The solution of the assurance game requires concern for the principle of *equality* before the moral law, and the institution of a just and active state mandates concern for the principle of civic *independence*. Freedom, equality, and independence, which Kant calls the "juridical attributes" of the active citizen (TP, 290), are the operating principles of a policymaker applying JFA to a public choice in an effort to assure autonomous citizens that they will not be exploited in their expression of moral agency and practical reason.

The three principles, like the categorical imperative upon which they are based, all contribute to the same end: autonomy. Duty, individual rights, and community interests are balanced by an active state attempting to protect and empower individuals as ends-in-themselves with intrinsic moral value. It is critical that a "thick" sense of moral autonomy (Gillroy 1992a) or "a higher order control over the moral quality of one's life" (Kuflik 1984) be supported, but it is also important that both the private and public dimensions of autonomy be recognized in the three operating principles as they create a cooperative community of moral agents.

Material Conditions (see chapter 7)

Operating principles require material conditions that can be manipulated by the policymaker to make normative value practical in the lives of citizens. In the market paradigm, the sole material condition of the principle of Kaldor efficiency is tangible property or wealth. For JFA, each of the operating principles that provide for human autonomy is satisfied by a specific material condition. Freedom of the individual is promoted by the protection of Ecosystem integrity (which is the consideration of both natural and human intrinsic value in policy choice). Equality within the political community is guaranteed through the distribution and redistribution of the physical property necessary to the widespread expression of autonomy through moral agency. Lastly, civic independence is empowered in the public provision of those opportunities necessary in order for anyone to apply his or her practical reason to both personal and political choice. The Kantian policymaker is concerned with human and environmental integrity, collective and private property, and social opportunity to provide for the "active" citizenship of her constituents. I have now provided a circumscription of the issue, and only the question of maxims and methods remains.

Maxims (see chapter 8)

Each operating principle and the material conditions it defines can help the decision maker distinguish which policy alternatives are acceptable to the argument (promoting the principle) and which are not acceptable (rejecting the principle) by defining the maxims of decision making that will inform this choice.

The market paradigm has but one maxim for the decision maker: Maximize Efficiency! With its three principles and three material conditions, the decision maker using JFA will have three maxims. The first, on the individual level of analysis and originating from the concern for moral agency, for the principle of freedom, and for the material conditions of natural systems functioning, implores the decision maker to Protect Ecosystem Integrity! The imperative here is to protect and secure those environmental background conditions that are a prerequisite to individual autonomy and that we owe the natural world.

The second maxim, built on the collective level of analysis and from the circumstances of the assurance game, the principle of equality, and the material condition of property, is to Distribute Property! Here the imperative is to distribute and redistribute physical property consistently with the moral law.

The final and third maxim, on the state level of analysis and stemming from the need for an active state, the principle of independence, and the material condition of opportunity, is to Provide Opportunity! This invokes an imperative to guarantee those opportunities necessary to the expression of the moral or cooperative predisposition of each citizen and, in this way, her independence as an active citizen of a just state.

Methods (see chapter 8)

With the principle of efficiency, the market paradigm evolves the methodology of cost-benefit analysis so that the ends and means of public issues must submit to the Kaldor efficiency test in order to become policy. From JFA, the decision maker must seek to enforce the maxims to protect integrity, distribute property, and provide opportunity to empower independence by the use of what I will describe as the *baseline function*.

This baseline function contains three variables: Ecosystem integrity (E^I); property (p_i); and opportunity (o_i). The baseline (E^I, p_i, o_i) represents Kant's argument that justice in collective policy choice requires government to consider, not an equal measure to each, but the basic protection of freedom, distribution of property, and provision of opportunity that will solve the assurance situation and establish collective cooperation for the full expression of each person's practical reason and moral agency in the world. The charge of the policymaker is to create those circumstances in which each citizen's predisposition toward acting morally is empowered, creating autonomy in each and a harmony of moral agency for all.

Principles, Baseline Method, and Public Policy

Using these maxims to establish the baseline produces distinct policy choices and outcomes. For environmental policy, distributing the means to free expression, protecting equality, and empowering independence moves the burden of proof from the regulators to the creators of risk externalities and supports the use of standards to protect basic agency and autonomous capacity in the face of collective assaults from market extraction, production, and disposal.

Differences will exist between the nature of the standards, which, in this case, would be national and would consider Ecosystems as wholes, and the degree to which the market should be contained to provide for flourishing human and natural systems, rather than for their minimal existence. If the baseline function is used, the intrinsic value of functional natural systems, as it contends with the intrinsic moral value of humanity in the person and with one's autonomy as made manifest in one's moral agency, is at stake and defines justice for the policymaker and citizen alike. Preference or the superficial freedom of consumer choice is consequently not as important as empowering those components of the baseline function that assure each and every person's freedom in terms of his or her essential capacity to choose. To answer the issue-simpliciter question, all policy choices are subject to an ideal-regarding test: Is this alternative a means to the end of protecting intrinsic value?

For JFA, the autonomy of the individual as made manifest in his or her moral agency is of critical importance for the policy analyst. The intrinsic values of humanity and nature are essential in the environmental decision and must be protected and empowered by policy choice. Such an imperative produces duties and rights that take precedence over maximization of wealth and the processes that produce this wealth. In addition, the imperatives promote the citizen as practical reasoner over the consumer as rational maximizer.

The intrinsic value of the moral agent within JFA and the need for one's cooperative moral predisposition not to degenerate into the "mania for domination" require that the community's assurance game be solved so that the cooperation of moral persons can persist across generations. Environmental contamination is a collective threat to the intrinsic value of individual autonomy and must be considered a public phenomenon that can inhibit moral agency and trigger the mania for domination. Under these conditions, the policy priority is to regulate risk and other externalities *ex ante*.

For example, whereas the state promoted by the market paradigm can only approach risk through the private calculations of individual rational maximizers, the opposite is true for the state in the Kantian paradigm. No longer driven by market assumptions and principles, the state becomes independent and active in the provision and maintenance of collective action and in the protection and empowerment of individual moral agency. Risk becomes a "public" concern, not relegated solely to individual calculation. It is incumbent on the state to define which risks are collectively acceptable and which are not, on the basis of the requirements of the baseline function, to inform each citizen what the risks of any particular choice are, and to provide for the regulation of those risks that would inhibit moral agency and therefore the individual struggle for autonomy.

By considering the agency of the individual to seek her own autonomy as well as the maxims to protect freedom, to distribute property, and to provide opportunity, JFA elevates the intrinsic value of humanity and nature over the instrumental value of things and gives paramount importance to the creation of that public reality which empowers the expression of moral agency and the flourishing of natural systems integrity. The environment of the political community, its capacities to persist and to stop the exploitation of some of its citizens by others, may require that all risk-producing activity causing collective damage to environmental security be justified as supporting moral-baseline needs before it can continue. This is a prescription for a risk-conscious society, where each collective risk is analyzed for its capacity to empower individual autonomy and natural systems functioning before it is allowed into markets or the environment.

This sketch of the Kantian paradigm (see fig. 8.2) is meant only to introduce the full philosophical justification of Justice from Autonomy that will occupy us in the next five chapters. For those who see the contrasts well enough to proceed to applications, I recommend going directly to part III (chapters 9 and 10), where case studies and legal analysis apply the Kantian paradigm and context model to a number of current environmental issues. For those who wish to fully understand the theory before analyzing the practice, or who need to understand particular components of the CPA model, I recommend continuing with those sections of part II that might inform your questions and concerns.

5

Justice from Autonomy:
The Individual and Nature

Kant's fundamental assumption about the individual concerns his or her core capacity and potential to become a practical reasoner. Practical reason includes more than economic rationality alone, for each practical reasoner has strategic rationality and the ability to construct conditional choices but also the moral will to act with responsibility in ethical matters. Practical reason also means more than autonomy of will; merely knowing right is insufficient; one must be able to take action in order for reason to be "of itself practical," thereby affecting the material world to promote autonomous moral choice in oneself and others (Kant C2, MV). Practical reason is the application of moral imperatives in an environment of cross-currents, desires, wants, emotions, relationships, and human concerns, all of which may aid or interfere with our prosecution of what we know to be right. It is the practical reasoner who defines morality in terms independent of, and not coextensive with, these sensual and contextual considerations.

The Three Components of Practical Reason

Practical reason is not synonymous with self-sufficiency but is the capacity to assess the demands of the moral law, and the ability to act on its imperative, which always involves respect for others and sometimes may involve the aid of others (individually or collectively) (Kant GW, 397–99). Practical reason is, for the individual, the full expression of virtue in the material world, the ultimate goal of the autonomous person, and the full manifestation of one's status as an end-in-oneself. The state of practical reasoning is not a discreet condition but a continuous quest for full moral agency. A human seeking full moral agency strives, with a deontological (duty-based) purpose, toward that ideal condition of reason being practical in his or her life that admits to degrees of sophistication over a lifetime.

147

Practical reason is built upon the foundation of basic human freedom that all must assume in themselves and which, once acknowledged (Kant PP, 370), must ever be part of the choice process. It evolves with the expanding capacity of the individual to be an autonomous person and with the ability of the individual to express this moral autonomy in the actions and choices of a moral agent. But practical reason may be hobbled by the external effects of others' choices. Being a moral agent is therefore more basic, but also more complex, than being a human agent. It is more basic because one's true humanity will never be part of one's character and deliberative processes without the moral component of agency as a precondition. Simultaneously, practical reason is more complex because, to truly express one's rationality in a morally constructive and responsible way, it must be integrated with and built upon autonomous capacity, which makes Kant's definition of the individual moral agent more complex than, for example, the "rational" agent of his market counterpart (Gillroy 1992a; Gillroy and Wade 1992).

Practical reason defines the individual as an end-in-himself. Humanity in the person and its empowerment through practical reason grants the person intrinsic value and therefore inherent moral worth that becomes the subject of duty and the object of respect. In order to be an end, one must be a practical reasoner. To be a fully empowered practical reasoner requires that one have: (1) the internal *capacity* for autonomy, (2) the external *ability* to choose morally, and (3) a deontological *purpose* in the full integration and perfection of these components in one's moral agency. It is these characteristics that will become the focus of the Kantian policymaker.

The Internal Capacity to Will Autonomously

The first and most basic component of practical reason is one's internal capacity to have an autonomous will. What does this mean? What is autonomy?

Autonomy is a buzzword in our culture and in our ethical and political deliberation, implying independence, liberty, self-sufficiency, and the atomistic isolation of the individual (Locke [1690] 1988; Hobbes [1651] 1968). This definition of autonomy is evident in the contemporary works of Nozick (1974) and Wolff (1970), among others, and is assumed in the economic underpinning of market ideology as individual utility-maximizers express preferences for welfare (Posner 1983). This efficiency-based or "thin" definition of autonomy (Gillroy 1992a) is but one possibility. Although such interpretations often name Kant as an intellectual ancestor, Kant's theory of autonomy is at once more simple and more complex than these caricatures.

Kant's concept of autonomy is simpler because it describes, practically, how humans make choices in moral matters; it is more complex because it seriously considers the intricacies of the human intellect and the pressures placed upon it by the material world. Kant seeks the roots of autonomy, not in the choices one makes, but in one's prerequisite capacity to choose. For Kant, autonomy is the freedom provided by a "higher order control" over the quality of one's life and physical environment (Kuflik 1984), and it necessitates that one's decision process remain sensitive, not only to the internal demands of reason, but to the external conditions in which this reason seeks manifestation.

Autonomy is built upon a foundation of individual freedom. Kant posits that each person must first assume in himself, and then come to understand and completely utilize, a core capacity to will freely, consistent with the demands of reason in moral matters (Kant GW, C2, MV). This core of freedom cannot be destroyed but may lie undetected or unutilized or underutilized within the person. Everyone is born with the capacity to be free but not necessarily with the ability to acknowledge this freedom or with the resources to use it to his or her full ability (Kant PP, 370–72). Kantian morality, however, is based on the assumption that the freedom of the individual must be protected and empowered so that each person can come to acknowledge its presence and power in defining and creating his or her own life. The external ability to express autonomy will be discussed later; first, we shall examine autonomy as if it were already acknowledged by the individual, as the internal capacity to will in line with intellectually approved principle.

149

What does it mean to say that autonomy is the internal capacity to will consistently with the demands of reason in moral matters (Kant GW, C2, MV)? Autonomy is an internal causality that takes as its point of causal origin, not the stimulation, pressures, and inclinations of the material world in which one lives, but what duty demands of the individual independent of these contextual conditions. Although we live in a material world with all the accompanying pressures, when we have to make a decision that involves a moral choice, Kant suggests that we ought not to allow our environment and the pressures and fears it generates to *determine* our will. We should ask: What is the *right* thing to do? Ethically, we should not exploit another because of the pressure for money or the fear of insecurity. We should not abandon someone because we are cold or afraid. We should not amass wealth while depriving others of the basic necessities of life because we fear that without control of others, we will be controlled by them (Kant AT, 271–73). But why might reason deem such determination of action immoral? What is it, specifically, that reason demands of us?

The standard of justification and sole imperative to the will of an autonomous person is the moral law or what Kant calls the categorical imperative (Kant GW; C2; MV). An imperative is categorical when it is neither elective nor concerned with instrumental value. A categorical imperative is universal and necessary to the persistence and empowerment of one's humanity and involves the intrinsic value of humanity in the person. Its imperative to action therefore cannot be hypothetical, for Kant defines this type of imperative as dealing exclusively with means/end calculations of instrumental value in nonmoral matters (e.g., if I wish to go to college, I need to obtain a financial loan) (Hill 1973; Donagan 1977).

The categorical imperative provides the maxims by which one defines autonomy as a moral principle and gives reason power over external stimuli in moral decision making. It puts the "reason" in practical reason, as it is the means by which a human is able to decide, first, whether a matter has moral implications (that is, implications for intrinsic value) and, next, what these implications require in terms of practical action.

Because a human being is not a god with a holy will, and automatically and objectively good, each person must struggle for morality by applying his or her reasoning capacity to the practical world around him or her. This application of will is accomplished ever mindful that employment of one's will can be either moral or irresponsible and self-destructive to one's personal freedom. In order to preserve one's freedom (as well as the freedom of others), one must regulate one's will by the categorical imperative as a prerequisite of practical reason that serves as the critical moral standard to which all proposed alternatives of a decision must be subjected.[1]

First, Kant defines a moral principle as "nothing but a dimly conceived metaphysics, which is inherent in every person's rational constitution" (Kant MV, 376). Next, he defines the "good will" (Kant GW, 393) as the ideal, autonomous will of the practical reasoner.

> [P]ure reason can be practical, that is, of itself and independently of everything empirical it can determine the will. This it does through a fact wherein pure reason in us shows itself actually to be practical. This fact is autonomy in the principle of morality by which reason determines the will to action. At the same time it shows this fact to be inextricably bound up with the consciousness of freedom of the will, and actually to be identical with it. By this freedom the will of a rational being, as belonging to the sensuous world, recognizes itself to be, like all other efficient causes, necessarily subject to the laws of causality, yet in practical matters, in its other aspect as a being in itself it is conscious of its existence as determinable in the intelligible order of things. . . . [I]f freedom is attributed to us, it transfers us into an intelligible order of things. (Kant C2, 42)

Autonomy, therefore, is not just the isolated intellect willing morality, it is our capacity to deliberate independently of, but within, the intelligible world and affect that world through our expressions of principled, and therefore free, will.

Autonomy is empowered and protected by our self-application of the moral law to individual action that makes categorical imperatives of those choices that support freedom in ourselves and others. The focus on understanding and acting upon what is categorically imperative places an emphasis on one's duties and not one's rights. One's duty to the full expression of one's good or moral will (Kant GW, 393) is a duty to the protection and enhancement of one's autonomy and that of others; from this duty, rights find their genesis.

> [W]e know our own freedom (from which all moral laws and hence all rights as well as duties are derived) only through the moral imperative, which is a proposition commanding duties; the capacity to obligate others to a duty, that is, the concept of a right, can be subsequently derived from this [categorical] imperative. (Kant MJ, 239)

The categorical imperative, that is, the moral law, is unique in that it is *categorical* (i.e., necessary and universal). As it provides the ethical foundation for rights in one's duties, it also plays the role of a deliberative prerequisite to the moral dimension of one's agency. In order for an agent to preserve his freedom, the moral law must be acknowledged and followed through this categorical imperative.

The concept of the categorical imperative distinguishes autonomy from heteronomy (Kant GW, 433). In heteronomy, hypothetical imperatives command only conditionally, and are determined externally, from the pressures and context of the material world, on the basis of a multiplicity of elective ends. In contrast, the moral law one gives internally to oneself commands categorically, and its single end is to cause humanity to flourish in the person (Hill 1973, 1980). The difference is between choosing X in order to keep up with the neighbors or choosing X independently of the choices or wants of yourself or those around you. The moral choice is always one that defines what is right independently of the instrumental desires and inclinations of the person.

For Kant, the moral law has three components, each reflected in a different formulation of the categorical imperative. In order for a maxim or precept of the will (which we will examine later) to be compatible with the moral law and to generate a categorical imperative, Kant (GW, 436–37) states that it must have the following three components:

1. A form, which consists in universality; and in this respect the formula of the moral imperative requires that the maxims be chosen as though they should hold as universal laws.
2. A material (i.e., an end); in this respect the formula says that the rational being, as by its nature and thus as an end in itself, must serve in every maxim as the condition restricting all merely relative and arbitrary ends.
3. A complete determination of all maxims by the formula that all maxims that stem from autonomous legislation ought to harmonize in a possible realm of ends.

When one's deliberation over action includes these three components of the moral law, then one's choice can be considered a product of an autonomous will utilizing the categorical imperative in duty to individual freedom. Autonomy, in considering one's intrinsic value as an independent basis for moral choice, "is thus the basis of the dignity of both human nature and every rational nature" (Kant GW, 436).

The fundamental character of the moral law is that, in all its forms, it concerns how the intents and actions of one person, legislating for himself, affect the power of others to will or choose in the same way. The *form* of the law is its universal nature. Its *material* content is the necessary and basic "unconditional and incomparable worth" of each person, equally, as separate from all other material objects and ends (Kant GW, 436). The *full determination* of the moral law is a system of civil law in a realm or community of autonomous beings where all their choices harmonize, providing each with full access to his or her potential as human moral agents. But let's not try to fly before we walk. First, how does each formula aid in the decision process and build on its previous manifestation in order to create moral action from human deliberation?

In order to distinguish a moral from an immoral option, one applies the form of the moral law: *the universalization test*. Ought the maxim of my proposed action hold for all rational beings as well as for me? If not, then this alternative can be classified as immoral. However, if the answer is yes, two possibilities remain. Either the proposed act is a moral matter implying a categorical imperative and therefore can potentially affect autonomy in oneself or others, or the act is nonmoral, making it an elective, "subjective" end, neither required nor prohibited by morality and therefore the subject of a hypothetical imperative. The universalization test only segregates the immoral act and therefore only ensures that one complies with the moral law by not violating it.

In order to make the distinction between a moral and a nonmoral act, one must examine any proposed action in light of the material of the law: *humanity as an end-in-itself*. If the deliberation over action (or inaction) affects intrinsic value, that is, the status of human beings as ends, then it is a moral matter and requires behavior that respects (protects and empowers) humanity in the person or individual moral autonomy. If it does not involve autonomy, then it is an act without moral ramifications, or nonmoral, and therefore involves only elective ends and hypothetical imperatives.

Where the form of the moral law grants universality, the matter/material of the law establishes the necessity of respect for individuals as ends. The individual has a duty to act with respect for his own and others' capacity to reason and will autonomously, and for each person's capacity to shape his or her own life responsibly.

> Man is certainly unholy enough, but humanity in his person must be holy to him. . . . He is, the subject of the moral law which is holy, because of the autonomy of his freedom. . . . Such is the nature of the true incentive of pure practical reason. It is nothing other than the pure moral law itself, so far as it lets us perceive the sublimity of our own super sensuous existence and subjectively effects respect for their higher destiny in persons who are also conscious of their sensuous existence and of the accompanying dependence on their pathologically affected nature. (Kant C2, 87–89)

To understand the critical Kantian concept of an end-in-itself, one can begin by describing ends as "reasons for action." Heteronomy of choice, where externally generated desire determines the will and gives hypothetical imperatives, defines an end in terms of its instrumental use to the subject. If one desires it, one works out a means to obtain it. Autonomy of the will, however, concerns intrinsic value and is based in the moral law (categorical imperative) which defines "end" as the self-contained end-in-itself. Because of the intrinsic value involved, the demands of respecting ends-in-themselves in one's moral deliberations supersede both all subjective "desires-as-ends" and the means/end calculations that trade such "instrumental" values. The intrinsic end-in-itself becomes the point of departure for all calculations of instrumental value, for, to fulfill one's moral duty, no subjective desire or elective end should ever be allowed to exploit or diminish one's intrinsic value, that is, one's capacity for autonomy.

Because intrinsic value is a universal attribute of all individuals, granted by their humanity, and since it is necessary to uniformly respect this humanity in one's moral deliberation, will, and choice, it is critical that reason be self-reflective, that is, its own regulator, with the categorical imperative acting as the ultimate standard upon which ethical decision making is judged and justified. "[R]eason as legislative need only presuppose itself, . . . the rule is objectively and universally valid only when it holds without any contingent subjective conditions that differentiate one rational being from another" (Kant C2, 20–21). Another way to differentiate between a subjective end and a moral end-in-itself is to examine the difference between their producible and nonproducible characters (Donagan 1977, chap. 7).

A producible end, or condition, is one that exists as an instrumental means to some other end, perhaps unique to an individual's personal history, and attainable through appropriate action by that person. These ends give hypothetical imperatives that make them only of elective value to each person. In contrast, a nonproducible end does not generate a means/end (consequentialist) rationality, but an introspective concern with the protection and empowerment of one's capacity to legislate for oneself and to be autonomous. The introspective use of reason is the means by which one generates and defines those duties that are required in order to protect and empower autonomy. Self-reflection takes the nonproducible end, the intrinsic value of the individual, as a prior condition or point of departure for all consideration of subjective or elective ends.[2] One's reason to act becomes a consideration, not of what one will subjectively render to fulfill one's desires, but of what one owes humanity in his person: not what one wants, but what will support one's knowledge of himself and what is required for the individual's autonomous (moral) agency.

The moral law directs mental energies away from the primitive selfishness of desire satisfaction and toward development of the individual as an autonomous end-in-herself. In this way, selfishness can evolve on a basis of knowledge of one's rational nature into what Kant calls rational self-love (Kant C2, 72–75). At this point, one's autonomous will elicits the choice of subjective values in such a way as to support one's perfection. Reason subjugates producible ends with instrumental value to the service of the human being as a nonproducible end with intrinsic value. Kant does not argue that self-interest and desire satisfaction are not part of human affairs, but rather, that without autonomous direction, desire satisfaction is self-defeating, as one's life is no more than an instinctual existence where deliberation yields to determination by momentary subjective desires that, without consciousness of humanity in the person, will tend to shortchange this intrinsic value in its determination of choice.

> Pure practical reason merely checks selfishness, which is natural and active in us even prior to the moral law, but is restricted by the moral law to agreement with the law; when this is done selfishness is called rational self-love. . . . [T]he certainty of a disposition that agrees with the law is the first condition of any worth of the person. (Kant C2, 73)

With power to affect the world as an agent-cause intact, but lacking a moral dimension to this agency that recognizes one's "ethical" responsibility, one is likely to exploit his own and others' intrinsic value by not respecting it when making choices. He is then a "moral" hazard to himself and others.

Kant's second formula of the categorical imperative, addressing the concept of the end-in-itself, provides the necessary grounds for the moral law, and has both a negative and a positive connotation. *Negatively*, the second formula offers an imperative to refrain from interfering with ourselves or others as ends with intrinsic value; *positively*, it demands that each individual actively promote herself and others as ends. This latter positive manifestation is also interpreted as requiring that each person consider, in his or her choice of subjective or elective ends, how he or she might make choices that harmonize with the subjective choices of others. Kant argues that we must make the choices of others our own (Kant MV, 450, 462–65). We have a duty to condition our elective, want-regarding choices (Barry 1990) in such a way that they ultimately contribute to the establishment of a community of autonomous ends-in-themselves. This community is Kant's Realm or Kingdom of Ends (Kant GW, 436–40).

The Kingdom of Ends, as the third formula of the categorical imperative, provides a collective moral standard and a strong positive manifestation of the moral law that can be used to judge both our moral choices and our election of subjective ends. Of critical concern here is how all the choices of one person integrate into the choices and actions of all collectively. The Kingdom of Ends is the ideal-type (Weber [1922] 1947) for the Kantian political community. When intrinsic value is respected by each and all citizens, through their choices, this positively affects the environment in such a way that autonomy is empowered for everyone. The Realm of Ends is Kant's call for the individual to seek morality not only in his soul but in a community of souls.

Our consideration of individuals as ends highlights the importance of the protection and perfection of humanity in our person.[3] But this, in itself, is insufficient to a full understanding of the demands of the moral law. We must also strive toward a social condition where all individuals are able to achieve their complete moral autonomy and fully subjugate their subjective wants and desires to the enhancement of autonomy and practical reason in each and all simultaneously. Here, one's choice of subjective ends wills a positive contribution to the "community" of moral persons by making the creation of a Kingdom of Ends its duty. The Realm of Ends is the institutional harmony of autonomous individual wills and, as such, is both the collective ideal each person ought to strive for in his social life and the standard of "moral" or acceptable individual choice in any society. The ideal of the Kingdom of Ends represents a state of affairs that is a "totality or completeness" (Kant GW, 436), a collective standard by which individual ethical and elective expression is judged. One's autonomy is here placed into moral community, so that our exercise of practical reason encourages the use of practical reason in others, thus making the possibility of the Kingdom of Ends an ethical probability.

The Realm of Ends is also the basis for the imperative to create the just state, for it prescribes the moral requirements of autonomous agency and therefore the just boundaries of civil law. Although the Kingdom of Ends is an ethical state of affairs, as one's expression of internal capacity is empowered by one's community through choices of elective and nonelective ends, a just political state of affairs that coordinates choice by the standard of the moral law will empower individual autonomy and, therefore, the realization of this ethical kingdom. Thus, one's metaphysical capacity for autonomy is connected to material political reality through the idea of the Realm of Ends. Through this formula of the categorical imperative, as an ethical metaphor or standard for human affairs, duty necessitates and directs the application of the moral law to civil affairs and the creation of the just state as the collective political means to individual moral ends.

Overall the Realm or Kingdom of Ends is the ideal realization of the categorical imperative by all moral agents at once and therefore represents the community of the virtuous. It prescribes that only those external acts of will that promote the moral law, and therefore would be acceptable within a collectivity of moral persons, are worthy of respect by that collective as a true expression of individual practical reason.

Practical reason is a goal of the moral agent that can only be achieved if one acts under the duty to empower one's capacity for autonomous thought and action. When each single intellect and will acts freely, that is, in accord with the moral law, then one has the complete determination of the law in a Realm of Ends. Practically, this realm may never materialize but practical reason demands we search for and strive toward it, as a duty to ourselves and others under the categorical imperative.

The categorical imperative (see table 5.1) sets the standard for moral will and defines freedom in its full application to individual decisions. But it also makes important distinctions between the immoral, moral, and nonmoral decision-situations.

The categorical imperative defines an immoral choice as one that violates its first formula, and a truly moral choice as one that involves humans as ends-in-themselves (second formula) and that is willed as if in harmony with a Kingdom of Ends (third formula). However, the dialectic between the immoral and moral choice produces a third category of possibility: the nonmoral choice.

One violates one's autonomy only when one does not allow the categorical imperative to define one's will in a moral matter. If one's deliberations involve all three of the formulas, then the categorical imperative must be applied to generate the ethical solution. However, many if not most of the decisions an individual will make in a day are not moral decisions but nonmoral ones. Will I eat lunch today? What is the best choice on the menu? Shall I watch *Zulu* or *Rio Bravo* this evening? Do I need a sweater?

TABLE 5-1
The Logical Sequence of the Categorical Imperative

The assumption is that the categorical imperative (the moral law) is universal and necessary to the full development of practical reason in each person. It has three component parts, each building and strengthening the last.

1. The Form of the Moral Law (Universalization Clause):

The Law of Nature clause of the categorical imperative is a standard that ensures that one's maxims adhere to the moral law by not violating it. It is negative in that it tells one what is immoral without being able to distinguish between a moral and nonmoral act.

The Question Remains:
Now that one can distinguish what is immoral, what standard allows one to tell the difference between a moral act (required by the categorical imperative) and a nonmoral act (not so required)?

2. The Material of the Moral Law (Necessity Clause no. 1):

To supplement the universalization test and provide a thicker standard by which to make finer distinctions within the decision process, the concept of the individual rational human being as a nonproducible end-in-himself is introduced. The concept of the end-in-itself provides an independent and necessary grounding for the maxims of the will and adds enough strength to make the distinction between a moral act that promotes the persistence and perfection of ends-in-themselves and the nonmoral act that does not involve humans as nonproducible ends.

The material of the moral law, the end-in-itself clause, however, provides a necessary strengthening standard but two distinct incentives, both of which are necessary to the proper application of the categorical imperative in the real world:

    a) To refrain from interference with others as ends;
    b) To promote oneself and others as ends.

The Question Remains:
How can the negative and positive incentives of the materials clause of the moral law be harmonized and made real in one's decisions? How can one be sure he or she promotes the moral law?

3. The Determination Clause (Necessity Clause no. 2):

This clause provides the individual with the thickest version of the requirements of the moral law and a full manifestation of the duties of the individual toward himself or herself and others. If the maxim of an act of will (or the resulting choice) is not in harmony with one's ends and the ends of others (what is subjectively necessary to their full realization of objective capacity) so that it respects and promotes the ends of all in a harmony of freedom, as in a Kingdom of Ends, then it is not a moral act of will and cannot be expected to be respected as coming from the moral law. While the Realm of Ends is a moral realm and inaccessible to political institutions, it provides the moral ideal for justice and the legitimate state, which are themselves necessary to the full development of its moral ideal.

These are not necessarily moral choices involving a person's status as an end-in-herself but are subjective and elective choices that rightly involve only instrumental values invoking, not categorical, but hypothetical imperatives. These nonmoral deliberations are means/ends decisions. Such decisions will and ought to be determined by consideration of desire, preference, or other external factors as practical reason will have nothing authoritative to say about them.

Nonmoral decisions are elective and externally determined but, as such, do not interfere with the autonomy of the individual who must only apply the categorical imperative to classify and act upon a moral choice. In discussing autonomy, many critics of Kant, like Susan Wolf (1990), fail to consider the distinction of the nonmoral seriously. Recognizing the Kantian definition of autonomy in one's self-determination of will without external cause, what Wolf calls "after Kant, the requirement of autonomy," she correctly states that "our desires are a result of heredity and environment, they come from something external to ourselves," but then wrongly concludes that this fact is "incompatible with the satisfaction of the condition of autonomy" (Wolf 1990, 12).

If Wolf were correct, no category of nonmoral choice can exist, for while it is true that Kant rejects the idea that external desire should provide the imperative in moral matters, he does not deny either that desires are external to us or that we are shaped, to some extent, by external "heredity and environment." The important distinction for autonomous will is not the external/internal dimension of the cause but whether the decision is a moral or a nonmoral one in terms of the formulas of the moral law. The examples Wolf uses (i.e., desire for a pastry, a new sweater, writing my congressman [1990, 11]) do not involve humanity in the person and are not moral matters, but appear subjective and elective and therefore necessitate that desire and hypothetical imperatives hold sway in complete compatibility with one's autonomy, which is not at risk in these nonmoral matters.

The capacity for autonomy is therefore a capacity to distinguish between ends of the will and to estimate their moral impact through application of the formulas of the categorical imperative. Autonomy is the capacity to affirm one's humanity in the reasoning process and to make sure that what one wills empowers that humanity.

As one's highest moral priority is one's humanity, and since this humanity is confirmed in autonomous practical reasoning, one might expect that Kant's individual, other things being equal, will tend toward the perfection and use of practical reasoning in his daily life. This tendency is defined by Kant in terms of one's "predisposition toward good" (Kant RL, bk. 1 21–23; Allison 1990, 148–50; Kant MV, 419–20 and part 1, bk. 1, passim)

The internal causality of reason applying the categorical imperative to distinguish and act upon moral matters grants each person the predisposition toward good, that is, a tendency to act consistently with the duties prescribed by the categorical imperative. Kant's characterization of the individual assumes that each person has the predisposition to respect herself as an end, to see the moral value of others, and to act in such a way that practical reason is made manifest in her actions, confirming the intrinsic value of her humanity. However, this presupposes that one acknowledges the categorical imperative as the standard of moral deliberation in one's life (Kant PP, 370).

Acknowledging the categorical imperative as the moral law in one's life is necessary to control one's will; that is, recognition of the moral law is critical in allowing one's reason to control one's deliberation over ethical matters. Ethical self-respect and respect for others give one a predisposition to act in such a way that his or her capacity for autonomy, for freedom, is fully and most completely perfected through expression. But acknowledging the categorical imperative is an act of will, one that commits the individual to the duties, both private and public, that are part of its imperative. Once one has internally acknowledged the categorical imperative as the central organizing principle of one's life, capacity implies action, *ought* implies *can* (Kant PP, 370–72).

> Taken objectively, morality is in itself practical, for it is the totality of unconditionally binding laws according to which we *ought* to act, and once one has acknowledged the authority of this concept of duty, it would be utterly absurd to continue wanting to say that we cannot act as the moral law requires. (Kant PP, 370)

Without acknowledgment of the moral law in one's life, one does not have an active predisposition toward moral behavior. It is therefore critical that individuals come to acknowledge their autonomous capacity and to form their character in such a way that their predisposition toward good holds the field in moral deliberations. Although everyone has the basic capacity for autonomy, its acknowledgment may not be automatic. The existence of political justice, or its absence, may have a good deal to do with how widespread such acknowledgment is.

However, once one has acknowledged the categorical imperative as the moral law, one's will becomes the point of origin for all moral deliberation and action. "Will" is the internal causality that expresses autonomy in action through the application of practical reason to moral decision-situations. One's will is internal to the intellect of the individual and informed by the categorical imperative and the ethical respect one has for the intrinsic value granted to the individual with his or her status as an end. Autonomous will specifically involves *positive* freedom, or the freedom of reason to practically legislate through the will in moral matters. Autonomy is, in this way, not concerned with choice, but with one's capacity to choose. An autonomous will has the critical capacity to accept the categorical imperative as its guiding standard in judging the moral quality of action, thereby acting in the world so as to promote this quality. Such a will determines itself, that is, isolates itself from the pressures of the external world of sense for the consideration of right and wrong. The autonomous will first elects the categorical imperative as that set of decision maxims most universal and necessary to the persistence of humanity in the person. Then one applies the moral law to the decision situation, first, to see if the matter under consideration is moral, and second, to understand what action reason demands so that the principle of autonomy can find full manifestation and application through practical action.

With the concept of willing and its relationship to choice in the material world, reason, previously an internal, intellectual capacity, becomes external and practical. If one were a god, only will would be required. What one willed, would be. However, humans are spiritual/moral animals who require reason to be practical; that is, applicable to changing the conditions of their material environment. This "reality" means, among other things, that the will must be bi-furcated into internal willing and external choice and, further, that to apply practical reason to existing circumstances, individuals must use "maxims of ac-tion" to express their wills as making choices that are compatible with moral imperatives.

Because all humans are nonproducible ends with intrinsic value, one must consider one's behavior in terms of its effects on one's own and others' human-ity. The fact that individuals are both intellectual and material, and exist in an environment filled with other moral beings who must be considered in one's decision making, requires each person to deliberate in a way that protects the intrinsic value of all, or at least takes it into account. In turn, each person con-siders the moral imperative within the context of the material world, guided by what Kant calls a maxim (Kant C2, 19ff; GW, 400 fn, 413–25). The important dimension of Kant's conceptualization of a maxim is that it gives practical rea-son an independent yet context-sensitive definition. We now turn to the role of the context of choice in moral deliberation.

The External Ability to Choose Morally

Do circumstances matter to individual autonomy? Is the expression of the moral law in human action context-sensitive, or does Kant consider the indi-vidual to exist in an ethical vacuum where the material world has no connec-tion to the practical execution of moral imperatives in action? Kant first ad-dresses the issue of context, not in his political theory but in his ethics, with the concept of the maxim (Kant C2, 19ff).

> A maxim is in the first place a practical principle [precept], . . . of a particu-lar rational agent at a particular time . . . thus distinguishing [it] from *objec-tive principles* or *practical laws*, which are valid for all rational agents at all times. . . . The test of the Categorical Imperative is to show which maxims conform to practical laws. (Nell 1975, 34)

With the use of maxims the agent is, in effect, adopting a personal policy that, through precepts of behavior, connects the internal demands of principle (hy-pothetical or categorical imperatives) with the external context of choice in one's deliberation over courses of action.

> A minimally rational agent is one who forms interests on the basis of . . . re-flective evaluation . . . and adopts policies on the basis of these interests. Such policies are termed maxims and an agent that behaves in this way can be said to act "in accordance with the conception of laws, that is, in accor-dance with principles." (Allison 1990, 89)

Reason, through maxims, becomes practical, meaning "in the world" and "ap-plied to it" (Kant C2, 58–66) as it relates the internal or "noumenal" self with its external or "phenomenal" world.

In terms of how the maxim connects the noumenal and phenomenal worlds of the agent, I contend that the practical application of a maxim, as a precept or rule of behavior adopted by the agent, has three component parts: principle, context, and resultant values. The first component is the principle that lies at the base of personal deliberation and forms the standard by which the maxim evaluates choice. Sometimes, in nonmoral choice situations, the principle will be elective and without universal moral necessity. However, concerning autonomy, this role is always played by the categorical imperative, which defines and prosecutes all moral matters.

The application of the categorical imperative is necessary in order to define a moral matter, and, therefore, in all deliberations the implementation of the moral law allows the individual to judge whether his proposed maxim is immoral, morally required, or elective and nonmoral. Now, it is not controversial to posit that, in nonmoral choice situations, context matters. The external stimuli as well as the means/end nature of subjective preference requires contextual sensitivity. Controversy arises when trying to determine whether context has any effect on the prosecution of one's choice in a moral matter. We shall concentrate on this case.

The second component of the maxim is the context of choice. In what circumstances and environment will the principle of autonomy, this moral law, seek expression? How do these temporal conditions affect, not what is my duty, but what tools are available to implement my choice, so that the moral principle finds its truest and most complete expression in the material world?

It is important here to reaffirm that consideration of context in the maxim of moral action is not so that it can determine the will in these matters, for the moral law as principle has already filled this role. Nor is it the case that the context produces a "mere" morality of prudence as one seeks his own self-interest. The context component of the moral maxim matters only after the principle has informed the will, but before specific practical action is chosen to execute what one has already legislated for oneself. In order for the principle to affect the material environment and accommodate the demands of practical reason, context must be considered as the vehicle through which ethical principle finds practical fruition. Principle defines the imperative, not self-interest. The categorical imperative classifies the act and informs right and wrong, but the context provides the temporal stage upon which timeless imperatives must find proper language and action to prosecute moral ends.

The third component of maxims, and the result of this application of principle to context, are the values the individual derives as rules of thumb for practical action. Values are the temporal expression of timeless principle rendered by consideration of what is morally required within the practical context of individual choice. What one values, and therefore how one weighs alternatives in choice, must be responsive to the moral law or the categorical imperative as principle, but one must also ensure that the expression of this principle in choice of specific action is not disconnected from, or oblivious to, the context of that choice. One should choose the right action, in context, to operationalize the moral principle and make reason practical.

This is accomplished with the generation of values through maxims. Values are moral but also temporal. They change over time and respond to the circumstances of choice based upon, and always responsive to, the demands of the moral law. Values do not carry the moral weight of principle but allow principle to remain universal and necessary, independent of time and context, yet not ineffective because of this distance. The distinction between principle and value allows universal and necessary standards to remain effective as time and place change in the material world. This definition of a value acknowledges that even when the will is determined by reason through application of the categorical imperative to what must be done, there still needs to be consideration of which value best represents the principle and what actions will best implement one's duty, so defined.

The relationship between principle and value also remind us that although many values can be utilized in deliberation over practical action, only one can be decisive in choice. The choice of contextual *trump card* is a function of the moral force of universal principle seeking value in action. Under this definition of the relationship, a practical reasoner cannot assume that the implementation of a single value will always realize the moral law in practical context. One must reflectively consider what values express the application of principle in context and choose the one that has the best possibility of representing the end of autonomy in human interaction.

One is therefore constantly seeking, through his or her maxim, innovative means to the ethical ends of the moral law, which is decisive with regard to what values ought to inform practical action so as to fulfill one's duties to oneself and others. One makes a judgment about the best means to moral ends where one's maxim is a combination of moral principle and environmental context rendering values.

The categorical imperative requires that I respect humanity in myself and others. This is a timeless duty, but what does it specifically mean to respect humanity in any particular choice of action? What values are generated by the imperative to respect? What specific practical action does this imperative entail? Would the choice of value and action entailed be timeless, that is, the same action prescribed in 1863 as in 2003? Is the specific action context-neutral, that is, the same for a person in suburban Chicago, on a battlefield, or in a death camp?

There is no dispute that in all of these situations the categorical imperative requires that we act on the same principle, but for reason to be truly practical in each unique circumstance, the independent principle requires a context-specific evaluation of definitive action so that the principle has the most effective operationalization to actualize its moral ends.

For example, moral law required Lincoln to end constitutional slavery in the United States (Greenstone 1993, 18–26). Before he became president, he forthrightly prosecuted this imperative through public speaking. In the context of his prepresidential years, the proper means to moral ends were in the values of active debate and the communication of unconventional ideas to mainstream American audiences.[4] Because of a lack of personal political power, his actions were the best he could do to fulfill his moral duty. When he became president, the principle, emancipation, remained the same but the context values changed as the Civil War loomed on the horizon. His power, responsibilities, and circumstances were more complex and his implementation of the imperative became both more probable and less theoretical. With actual power to lead the country away from slavery, debate was replaced with action and he could no longer speak as forthrightly as before since he represented an entire nation violently divided on the issue and at war. He needed a tactic to implement a permanent end to slavery, which required the full prosecution of the Civil War as well as the minimization of the Confederacy by keeping the border states in the Union. The moral imperative was to end slavery but rash action could have doomed this moral end, as well as the integrity of the nation-state as a whole. He had to decide what values and sequence of policy choices would best and most permanently end slavery and reintegrate the United States, even to the point of waiting for a Union "victory" at Antietam to announce the Emancipation Proclamation. Good strategy requires context, and without well-defined tactics, moral principle will not find full and proper manifestation.

Lincoln did permanently end slavery in the United States, as he had preached before becoming president, but his success could be in large measure due to the shift of temporal values that came from his application of principle to context upon assuming the presidency. These circumstances did not determine his will, which, it can be argued, remained committed throughout the change of context, but did change his values in choosing the appropriate path and sequence of choices for successful implementation of practical reason in this *very* moral matter.

Personally, duty requires that I perfect humanity in my person. I have interpreted this imperative through the maxim that I should hone my intellectual skills by acquiring an education. What we have here is the moral law, through maxims, determining the subjective value choices of the person.

In the fifteenth century the maxim may have directed me to value religious orders as that place where I could best hone my intellect, whereas in the twenty-first century, placing value in the choice of religious orders may limit and defeat my quest for a critical intellect. In these cases, what I value as well as what specific plan of action I select is subject to variation, that is, subject to my changing values which are necessary to achieve the principle of self-perfection given my specific context.

In these examples practical reason demands that I clear my head of context and circumstance to judge, first, whether my decision-situation is a moral matter and then to judge what duty demands of me in relation to myself and others as ends. The specific requirements duty prescribes for me, however, require that I take where and what confronts me seriously in my choice of temporal values.

Considering context is one step removed from arguing that one's environment actively affects the degree of moral freedom enjoyed by the individual. Some argue that Kant's approach to the individual is encompassed in a strictconstructionalist reading of his ethical theory of autonomy, which is said to proclaim that nothing in the phenomenal world can affect the autonomous noumenal self (Nozick 1974; Williams 1985; MacIntyre 1981; Galston 1980, 1991). Ultimately, however, Kant is ambiguous on this point and, in his political and anthropological writings, he seems to contradict this picture of insulated ethical autonomy.

This "insulationist" school of Kantian scholarship bases their argument on two points: first, that the ethical freedom of the individual is something that is infringed by any interference from external authority. Second, they maintain that autonomy admits of no conditional strategies but is the mechanical application of the categorical imperative where the individual is compelled in choice to "always cooperate" (Elster 1989) regardless of context and circumstances. Without these assumptions, it is argued, Kant's absolute statement that moral action cannot be based on inclination is contradicted; categorical imperatives become hypothetical imperatives by the encroachment of the phenomenal world on the thought and actions of the noumenal self. This "Kantian" school of thought gives rise to a series of criticisms that attack Kant for dismissing such phenomenal factors as emotion, compassion, and commitment, which are argued to be critical components of ethical decision making and necessary to any theory of justice. Feminist criticism is prominent in this context (Larrabee 1993).

However, the "insulationist" approach to Kant is narrow and ignores his work in political theory and anthropology while setting up his concept of autonomy as a straw man for critics to attack. Such a straw man makes Kantian ethics seem impractical and invokes criticism from those, like feminists, who rightly assume that context matters to the expression of moral agency. This caricature of Kant will be addressed after I offer a more complex and complete account of his definition of the Kantian self and its relationship to the material world.

The first point of departure, for Kant's definition of the moral self, is his contention that human beings are neither gods nor animals but a synthesis of both (Kant MV, 379, 461; MJ, 222). He argues that because of this condition, humans are caught between a world of pure reason and one of instinct and desire motivating action. Humans are animals, but with spirit and intellect that gives them a moral dimension. They are gods, but without a purely metaphysical existence, burdened with the needs, wants, desires, and senses that make their material environment an important part of their lives. The condition of the person is therefore one of a "moral" animal who has a capacity for autonomy but who also exists in an environment that continually tests his or her predisposition toward good, his or her perfection of autonomous willing, and therefore his or her practical reason (Kant MV, 397, 464; RL, bk. 1.1, passim).

The juxtaposition between these worlds sets up a tension that Kant defines as the human struggle for character: *Gesinnung* (Kant RL, 25, 20; MV, 419–20; Allison 1990, 36–45). The intellectual struggle, or contest, is between one's internal predisposition to be moral and act autonomously, and the pressures of the animal environment to satisfy one's desires, act by instinct and inclination, and, in all ways, allow the fears and pressures of the material world that routinely determine one's nonmoral choices also to determine one's "moral" decision processes. The countermoral pressure, competing with reason to be decisive in moral matters, Kant calls the human "propensity toward evil" (Kant RL, 22–23; 18–19; Allison 1990, chap. 8; Korsgaard 1996, 109).

Kant defines "evil" as the tendency in terrestrial beings to allow senses and the stimulation received from the environment to determine their will in moral matters. This violates autonomy and makes the act immoral, for human reason is replaced as the source of ethical motivation by animal fears and sensations. Evil denies the humanity in the person and degrades autonomous capacity and practical reason.

The fact that humans exist in a material world of want, need, and desire is very much part of Kant's theoretical treatment of the individual's struggle for character development (Kant AT, 230–83; MV, 388). For this struggle to be meaningful, however, one must assume that in some cases reason is defeated by inclination in moral matters and that therefore external conditions and context determine the will and lead individuals to make decisions contrary to their autonomous predispositions. Kant argues that while moral predisposition exists, a countertendency excited in the individual by the external world also exists; this countertendency and how one responds to it are the most important elements in shaping individual character. Little struggle would exist if individuals had no choice but to act autonomously in mechanical response to the categorical imperative or if the external world could not influence choice. The "struggle" is reasonable only if external conditions are a powerful component part of one's decision process. Thus, acting autonomously is conditional (to a greater or lesser degree) on one's *ability* to overcome the propensity toward evil and act upon his or her *capacity* or predisposition toward good.

By understanding Kant's concern for the struggle between autonomy and heteronomy, by claiming that internal capacity can be conditioned by external ability, one does not have to replace Kant with Hegel and maintain that freedom is only granted to the individual by the existence of external institutions (Hegel [1821] 1978). The freedom of the individual, one's core of autonomous predisposition is, and always will be, part of one's essential humanity for Kant. However, there is a difference between having something and being able to use it, between capacity and ability, which I claim is the critical distinction within Kantian political theory (1992c, 1994).

The picture of an individual struggling between good and evil to form character is a complex vision of the person and one that speaks to human nature and the human condition. This is a world full of conditional strategies, choices, degrees of freedom, and other people whose behavior produces external effects on one's opportunity and ability to choose. Within this environment the individual strives to preserve and perfect his or her autonomy, to become a fully competent practical reasoner.

In this struggle a critical distinction is made. Kant does not deny that emotion, inclination, and compassion are part of the individual's world and exercise a strong pull on one's decision process. He does, however, argue that these factors are not a suitable basis for considerations of right or justice, which must protect humanity in *the* person and in *all* people simultaneously. Kant here distinguishes the ethical realm from the political or juridical realm of human experience (Kant MJ, 218–21, passim).

Kant might answer feminist criticism (e.g., Larrabee 1993) by arguing that a moral decision should not be based upon one's personal interrelationships because this would deny humanity in any person not part of this "compassion-circle." Kant argues that the core of morality is humanity in the person; that is, every person and each individual's capacity for practical reason is the only appropriate qualification for membership in the moral community. To base personal ethical reflection, let alone political justice, on the preestablished relationships people have with one another will, by design, allow, or even encourage, one to treat others not connected to his or her compassion-circle unjustly as a foreign or potentially threatening influence. The superstructure of justice would be built on a nonuniversal and nonnecessary foundation, invoke duty only to one's "relations," and violate the categorical imperative in one's internal ethical will and external juridical choice toward everyone else.

Distinguishing between the *ethical* and the *juridical*, Kant reinforces the difference between capacity to know right and ability to act upon it. Where the ethical realm is defined in terms of internal capacity, autonomy, and the moral will of the individual, the juridical realm is external and involves the physical arena in which the struggle for character takes place. The juridical is the environment in which one strives to be an agent-cause by expressing one's practical reason. The juridical realm focuses on the choices one makes and the freedom or ability to express these choices within the community.

Whereas the ethical realm is internal to the intellect of the person and its motives are forever shielded from external examination or control, the juridical realm is about external behavior and is subject to the regulation of civil law. Although moral freedom must always be assumed in the will of every person, each individual's ability to first acknowledge and then express this freedom in external choice will be a matter of degree. A being may not understand or acknowledge his or her freedom (e.g., because of ignorance), a free being may not be a free chooser (e.g., a slave or a person in prison), whereas an externally free chooser will be more able to internally perfect autonomy in his moral being and express his practical reason.

> For, in fact, the moral law ideally transfers us into a nature in which reason would bring forth the highest good were it accompanied by sufficient physical abilities; and it determines our will to impart to the sensuous world the form of a system of rational beings. (Kant C2, 43)

A policymaker's perspective is from the collective viewpoint, as a decision maker choosing for all, so the assumption must be that all individuals are, and ought to be, free moral beings who have the capacity to be autonomous persons. However, the moral dimension of the person is internal and not subject to determination by policy or the civil law; if it were, one could not be autonomous. The access point to the moral dimension of the individual, for the collective decision maker, is the just political circumstances in which this moral individual formulates maxims and makes choices as expressions of his or her autonomous will. Policymakers therefore are not involved with personal virtue but with collective justice and the civil law as these create the context for the juridical or public expression of one's humanity.

The juridical context of the person is not primarily focused on his or her motivation to be autonomous, but on his or her ability to first acknowledge, and then to choose in accord with the demands of his or her autonomy. By creating a just juridical environment, the policymaker creates that framework within which the greatest number of individuals can recognize and act in accordance with their autonomous capacities; to identify and show respect for humanity in themselves and in others. The just juridical environment empowers the morality of each person by creating those conditions that favor one's predisposition toward good and therefore allow the most widespread autonomous expression of will in choice. Justice constructs an environment in which the decision maker can have the highest expectations that individuals will generally behave morally. This higher level of expectation results from the creation of those external circumstances that best support responsible choice in accord with autonomous will and one's predisposition toward good and against evil in individual character development.

The policymaker needs to assume that his constituents are potential practical reasoners and that justice in policy and civil law will promote and empower practical reason in human affairs. The imperative is to create the best circumstances for the widespread expression of practical reason with an understanding that "practical reason is concerned not with objects in order to know them but with its own capacity to make them real (according to one's knowledge of them)" (Kant C2, 89–90).

Identifying the components of the just juridical condition and making them real is, therefore, the central ethical focus of the Kantian policymaker. The distinction between the ethical and juridical is supported by a further distinction between positive and negative freedom. As the ethical realm is concerned with the positive freedom of the will to legislate for itself, the juridical realm is concerned with the negative freedom of choice or the ability to execute the imperatives of practical reason.

I have argued that, when deciding a moral matter, the individual experiences a two-stage thought process. Once the ethical decision is made about right action, one must make a choice in line with this categorical imperative to actuate it through one's maxim in the material world (Korsgaard 1996, 18–19). Such choice involves the negative freedom of the individual to act practically: his or her degree of liberty. Negative freedom is freedom from the influence of others, or more specifically in the Kantian context, the externalities of others' choices (Kant MJ, 226; Pigou 1932, 183). The free person is one who can will autonomously and express his or her autonomy in choice. The external effects of one person's choices can interfere with the negative freedom of others, and this potential conflict is the focal point of political regulation for the Kantian policymaker (Korsgaard 1996, 19–20; 220 n. 36).

The environment in which we exist is collective, where the results of action are not so much the direct consequences of any single person's choice but the confluence of one's choices with the choices of others. Unregulated, externalities of choice will empower some and exploit others, creating the material environment of a less than juridical condition. The juridical condition is distinguished by its ability to protect the essential humanity of each person and to empower autonomous thought and action in each citizen by providing the opportunity and the collective support network for the coordination and harmonious expression of autonomous will.

From a policy point of view, one's positive freedom to express practical reason is a function of the degree of external negative freedom supported by the juridical conditions in which one finds oneself. These conditions, or the degree of negative freedom, are within the control of policymakers, who may channel and coordinate individual choices so that any externalities contribute to the ends of the moral law. A just state can create an environment in which an individual's full positive freedom is protected and empowered by the provision of those physical conditions in which the ability to choose consistently with the demands of practical reason is empowered by the enhancement of negative freedom in the material world. In this way, with the encouragement of internal moral autonomy through coordination of external free agency, the policymaker contributes to the widespread creation of citizens as full-fledged, practically reasoning, moral agents. It is here that the best external conditions are created for the realization of the Realm of Ends.

In the ethical/juridical distinction, Kant acknowledges that moral autonomy, as fully realized in an ethical Kingdom of Ends, is best promoted by juridical (political) justice. He also provides the concept of justice with a basis in the moral law or categorical imperative, for justice finds its definition in the creation of those external conditions in which the ethical capacity for autonomy finds its best and most widespread expression.

Kant also acknowledges the critical role played by politics in the struggle for character that marks the situation of the individual trapped between the demands of morality and the pressures and stresses of the material world. In the juridical state, with the politics of justice creating a material distribution of goods and services necessary to protect and empower morality, one finds the best external support network to encourage one's internal struggle for the victory of moral character in practical action.

In this way, critics who condemn Kant as being insensitive to emotion, compassion, and the role of the material world in the definition of justice miss his point. Kant does not envision people existing outside or alienated from these characteristics of the material world and their relations to others. Nor is it the case that these do not affect the individual; they form one of the two critical components in the struggle for character, the antithesis to the thesis of right that synthesizes in the evolution of practical reason. Kant is only warning us against the fallacy of determining ethical choice or justice on the basis of the fears, uncertainties, desires, or preferences prompted by the outside world.

Humans are physical and finite creatures whose need for mere physical existence sometimes threatens their better moral deliberation and action (Kant MV, 419–21). One's ability to act autonomously, to form an autonomous character, has a threshold where the choices of others so bind the individual that he succumbs to fear and inclination in order to protect his finite physical existence and thereby acts immorally (Kant MV, 382). One is always free, able to intellectually know what is right, but is one always able to act freely to express right in the world? Kant argues that the first requires only a "maxim" whereas the latter requires both internal "capacity and physical ability" (Kant C2, 36–37).

One may be able to intellectually "satisfy" the moral law in one's knowledge of right. However, as Kant also argues, "practical reason is concerned not with objects in order to know them but with its own capacity to make them real" (Kant C2, 89), and the ability to make an intellectual precept "real" requires that one be able to make choices, given the reality of the surrounding empirical environment. Autonomy only become heteronomy when the heteronomous world of the senses determines right in moral deliberation.[5] The challenge, therefore, is not just to know the maxim of the moral law but to realize it in the empirical world without interference from fear, lust, or emotion. Such a state uses justice as an organizer of the empirical world to diminish the influence of these variables and to aid in the realization of the categorical imperative as the moral law in practical affairs.

Kant contends that the absolute hold of the categorical imperative is in the ethical maxim, not in the practical action (Kant MV, 382, 392, 394, 410, 446). In distinguishing between the ethical and juridical, one is presented with a more complex universe where, for the moral law to determine action, more variables and material realities must be considered. If practical reason is not about knowledge but about realization, then the moral law is directly concerned with changing those dimensions of the material world that inhibit autonomous expression and with creating those conditions where empirical heteronomy has the least probability of determining action in response to maxims in moral matters, thus protecting the independence of autonomous will. Therefore, from our perspective, the execution of the moral law in action also requires "knowledge of the world."

The role of inclination is negative if it overpowers practical reason and causes heteronomous choices to be made in moral matters. The juridical conditions of a just state are not necessary to moral autonomy in its pure and metaphysical form but do empower practical reason in its execution of the moral law and lower the probability that heteronomous conditions will generally determine human actions in the physical world. For Kant, justice must be based on those material conditions that empower the universality and necessity of the categorical imperative, speaking to the humanity in each and every person, not on the "special" emotional or compassionate relationships that define a smaller circle of individuals. The fact that we can act justly toward someone we love is not in controversy. The pertinent question is whether we have to love someone to act justly toward him or her? Kant argues that we do not (Kant MV, 402–03, 448–50).

The motivation of the policymaker under the categorical imperative is to create a juridical state compatible with the material demands of humanity-in-the-person where practical reason has its highest probability of executing action as required by the legislative maxim of the autonomous will. These demands include that environment in which one's capacity for autonomy can find its widest and most complete expression. The proper end for policy is, therefore, those circumstances, context, and juridical conditions that protect and empower moral agency.

The Purpose of Moral Agency

For Kant, moral agency is the political or juridical equivalent of autonomy, which is his core ethical principle and the ultimate standard for social justice. Although the human autonomous agent is the primitive concept in Kant's ethical system, any future discussion of politics, and a Kantian approach to collective-action theory in the justification of public choice, begins with an investigation of what Kant meant by human agency and, in particular, the moral agency of the individual. Kant is interested in what the individual should strive toward, within the struggle for her character, to make herself at once as free and virtuous a human being as possible.

The single most important characteristic about a human agent is that she has the greatest intellectual capacity and moral power among other living things, which allow her to act, not only in regard to the external causality of nature, but from her own reason as an agent-cause. She can shape her life as well as have it shaped by circumstances. This capacity to shape one's own life responsibly is called human freedom and distinguishes the individual from other animals, providing the basis for ethical interrelationships.

We have established that Kant's fundamental assumption is that human ontology is both material and spiritual. However, the human is not just another species of animal, for he has more potential for intellectual activity and the capacity to affect the world around him through his deliberate actions. Man is more powerful because of his capacity for expression of freedom, which is a two-edged sword. On the one hand, because of such expressions of thought and freedom through technology and social interaction, humans can destroy the world in which they live. On the other hand, when these expressions of freedom are coordinated and harmonized, each human agent can protect himself and enhance free agency for all. In such a state of affairs, our great power over life on earth is combined with responsibility in its use, and mere individual agency becomes moral agency.

The human is a creature capable of morally affecting the world. He alone is capable of reason, transcending a world of instinct and sensory response. If one lives only by one's animal instincts and needs, relegating one's reasoning capacity to the service of short-term desire satisfaction alone, then one denies the responsible use of one's moral autonomy and, in this way, its long-term security. To act freely and responsibly, one need recognize the creative potential in reason and apply it practically to the world. One is required, by the moral law, to distinguish situations when one's freedom is at risk in a decision, and act, in such cases, in accord with principle that ensures that one's expression of agency will not adversely affect one's moral capacity to shape one's life and the world in which one lives.

Because the moral agent is said, by Kant, to have a capacity for freedom from determination in a causal world, she is capable of placing an intrinsic value on this freedom. In this way, not only can she use her reason to value objects instrumentally by the degree to which they fulfill her desires, but she can also judge the world by the intrinsic value of her human capacity to be free, and by how actions and states treat this noninstrumental/nonuse value.

> [H]e is not so completely an animal as to be indifferent to everything which reason says on its own and use it merely as a tool for satisfying his needs as a sensuous being. . . . But he has reason for a yet higher purpose, namely, to consider also what is in itself good or evil, which pure and sensuously disinterested reason alone can judge, and furthermore, to distinguish this estimation from a sensuous estimation and to make the latter the supreme condition of the former (material estimation). (Kant C2, 61–62)

This capacity to reason autonomously is at the center of Kantian ethics. By being intrinsically valuable itself, the capacity for autonomous agency makes the moral agent intrinsically valuable.

> The person, alone as a human, that is, as the subject of a morally practical reason, is exalted above all price. For as such a person (homo noumenon) he is not to be valued merely as a means to the ends of other people, or even to his own ends, but is to be valued as an end in himself. . . . [H]e possesses a dignity (an absolute inner worth) whereby he exacts the respect of all other rational beings in the world. . . . (Kant MV, 434–35)

The Kantian dichotomy is between human nature and autonomy, between mere human agency and moral agency. In order to understand the concept of human agency, one can begin by distinguishing between "things I did" and "things that befell me" (Davidson 1980, 43). Agency means that one is capable of forming intentions and acting on these, to "do" something (Davidson 1980, 45–47). Free agency in this definition is simply the ability of an individual to "get what he wants" (Watson 1975, 205). In some cases, one may not get what is desired; then one can say that the agency of this person has been restricted.

    The ability to intend, act, and achieve what one desires is not a sufficient definition of "moral" agency on a Kantian model. Kant views moral agency as a product of a complex and divided mind, as a tug-of-war between good and evil in the person struggling for dominance in the determination of one's intention to act and in the establishment of his or her character. One influence is desire, excited by the external world, which motivates the individual mind to action, determining intention. The other influence is reason, the capacity to judge by intellectually approved principle. Human reason does not depend

---

upon, but must be independent of, outside influences to maintain its separate identity and its moral determination of action. In many cases, it is not critical which of these two contenders wins out, for the freedom of the individual may not be at stake in the choice situation. When, however, the capacity of reason to determine intentions independently of sensuous input (i.e., autonomy) is at issue, a moral decision-situation exists that requires that one's intention to act be determined by reason.

Moral agency, therefore, can be defined as the capacity and ability of the individual reasoner to abstract from his subjective and short-term desires in cases where his objective and intrinsic value as a human being is at stake. A moral decision requires that reason create the individual's action so that it is free from determination by external inclinations that might cause the long-term disintegration of one's autonomy. What one "ought" to do can only be assessed when "freedom is made the regulative principle of reason" (Kant C2, 49) (i.e., when reason is self-regulative), allowing freedom to be expressed responsibly in moral decisions. One is not a moral agent simply by knowing what the moral law demands of his will, but only by fully expressing this autonomous knowledge as actions and choices in the material world.

A concern for both capacity and expression requires Kant to define the human will as having two components: willing and choice (Kant MJ, 213–14). The primary moral faculty is the will (*Wille*). Will legislates for the moral agent, rendering duties as a response to the moral law. The second faculty, choice (*Willkür*), has an executive function that follows the legislative requirements of the will and acts in the external world to produce change. Choice is the interface between the will, which is internal to the intellect of the individual, and the material world, within which the individual lives.

The two components of willing (*Wille* and *Willkür*) connect to the two definitions of freedom (positive and negative), which, as we have seen, correspond to the distinction between the ethical and the juridical realms of human experience. Through the provision of negative freedom and the coordination of choice in the juridical realm, we influence the expression of will and positive freedom in the ethical realm. The widespread expression of moral agency is therefore a collective political goal based upon individual ethical standards. Public policy focuses on the relationship between one's positive freedom of the will and one's negative freedom of choice.

One's positive freedom, as we have seen, is the "capacity of pure reason to be of itself practical" (Kant MJ, 213), or the "causality of reason in determination of the will" (Kant C1, B831). Positive freedom is therefore an internal capacity of the intellect to determine itself. Reason, in this way, can legislate morally for the individual, giving mere human agency ethical responsibility in the material world.

Negative freedom is the freedom of choice in the material world that allows the will to function unimpeded by the pressure of desire or impulses determined by external sources. It is specifically the "independence of choice from determination through sensuous impulse" (Kant C1, B526; MJ, 213). When one's will determines choice in a moral matter, then reason commands and the intrinsic worth of the individual is protected and empowered in one's material action. If however, the external pressures on one's choices are such that they determine the will instead of reason, then one's desires rule and mere agency incapacitates moral agency.

The logic of freedom in Kantian philosophy is such that, in order to have reason determine one's will in moral matters, the will must first be free from determination by causality in the material world. In order for an agent to be positively free and to express his own responsible causality in the world, he therefore must first be negatively free to allow reason primacy in the process of both willing and choosing (Riley 1982, 129–30; 1983, chap. 3).

Moral agency, by this definition, is concerned with ability as well as capacity, and with "being," not "wanting," with protecting and empowering intrinsic humanity, and not just with "getting what one desires" on a day-to-day basis. In this way, morality has more to do with the external conditions that promote internal freedom for each person than with those acts or states of affairs that promote the greatest happiness. Happiness is not the central motivation of moral agency, but it does play a role. "[P]ure practical reason does not require that we should renounce the claims to happiness; it requires only that we take no account of them whenever duty is in question" (Kant C2, 93).

Duty, which gives all actions moral worth (Kant GW, 397–400), is self-imposed to maintain and exploit one's potential for independent thought and action. One's duty is to one's self, to nurture the capacity to think independently and prior to immediate desires and preferences, putting them in proper perspective as subject to one's self-determination, not as the source of one's life and potential (Kant MV, 421ff).

Moral agency is a condition in which one acts for the sake of his humanity, which places moral worth, not in the consequences of the act, but in the duty fulfilled by the act itself. But, to use a maxim of action, I have argued that circumstances, context, and success matter. My point is that even in moral matters consequences count for Kant, but only in terms of the implementation of one's duty, not in terms of the moral worth of an intention or act, or the definition of the duty itself.

> [One ought] not *begin* with the consequences and say that because an action will have certain consequences which he desires, therefore he will regard the action as his duty. . . . Kant is right in saying that the expected consequences cannot be the *determining ground* of an action if it is to have moral worth. Nevertheless the good man begins with the *maxim* of a proposed action . . . "if I am in certain circumstances, I will perform an action likely to have certain consequences". . . . Nevertheless we must not judge the action . . . according as we like or dislike the consequence. (Paton 1948, 76)

Kant begins his study of ethics with the statement: "Nothing in the world can possibly be thought of which can be called good without qualification except a good will" (Kant GW, 393). The good will is necessary to separate moral agency from agency, and is the focus of the intrinsic value of a person, what is required for the persistence of his individual autonomy in the material world.

If one endeavors to develop and maintain a good will, then one is protecting and empowering one's core of positive and negative freedom and the full potential of one's capacity as a moral agent. Acting from a good will can never detract from or injure one's freedom and therefore is good without qualification. The test of a maxim, in terms of its support of one's good will, is whether the moral law is violated or fully operationalized in one's action. One's duty to oneself gives the individual the imperative to "aim at consequences because of the law . . . not to obey the law merely because of the consequences" (Paton 1948, 76).

With the introduction of the moral law as the sole principle for the maxims of a moral agent, pure reason, hitherto a theoretical abstraction, becomes practical reason, applied in the world in which the individual lives.

> The moral law adds . . . a positive definition: that of reason which determines the will directly . . . thus reason . . . can be given . . . an objective, practical, reality; its transcendent use is changed into an imminent use, whereby reason becomes, in the field of experience, an efficient cause through ideas. (Kant C2, 48)

Moral agency is the ability of each person to will and act autonomously. It is the ability to will, choose, and act without undue interference from other individuals or their choice patterns. Although agency is superficially attributed to any and all human action, moral agency is necessary for that action to have ethical content. To be a responsible agent-cause and act autonomously, that is, to strive toward being a virtuous person in the material world, one must be able to apply his or her reason practically. If Kant's individual is a practical reasoner, then each person's *purpose* is in the protection and perfection of his or her moral agency as the two ethical duties one has toward oneself (Kant MV, 386–88; 417–21). Purpose, in this context, has a deontological rather than a teleological connotation. Just as one determines one's will without considering consequences but is not oblivious to them, one must seek purpose in his or her duty toward one's nonproducible moral agency, one's intrinsic value as a person.

Moral agency synthesizes autonomy and agency. Through moral agency one finds, in the establishment of one's "moral" character, not only full internal moral capacity but the external ability to express it. The moral agent is Kant's practical reasoner, who, through reason and its expression, has dignity and intrinsic value. Within the context of empowerment of capacity and protection of ability, the individual will most likely aspire to follow his or her predisposition toward acting from the moral law: to do his or her moral duty and strive toward a good will, virtue, and a Kingdom of Ends.

For the individual in isolation, virtue is a function of autonomy, which in turn is dependent on the ability to will and choose freely. Freedom here is more than negative external liberty; it is the positive internal power to exercise and fully empower one's capacity to control and direct one's own life.

> Autonomy of the will is the sole principle of all moral laws and of the duties conforming to them. . . . The sole principle of morality consists in independence from all material of the law (namely, a desired object) and in the accompanying determination of choice by the mere form of giving universal law. . . . That independence. . . . is freedom in the negative sense, while the intrinsic legislation of pure and thus practical reason is freedom in the positive sense. (Kant C2, 33)

Basic autonomy of will is a prerequisite for moral agency and is empowered by it. We assume that all individuals are born with a core of positive and negative freedom, and an implicit potential for full expression of moral agency. Just as the human intellect can wither and die as a child grows into adulthood, wasting or crushing one's potential, the potential for full and mature moral agency can either be empowered to its full capacity or be grossly inhibited, for reason is not always successful in determining the will and executing choice in the material world. Fundamental harm to the individual must be considered in terms of external interference with intrinsic autonomous capacity, for the inhibition of autonomy can pose the most basic threat to any person's humanity. Although physical health is necessary to life, it is not sufficient, for without an empowered capacity for the expression of autonomous will in moral agency, the person has diminished human worth, and primarily an animal existence.

The duties made incumbent upon the individual by his or her capacity for moral agency are divided by Kant as follows:

> The subject who is obligated, as well as the one who obligates, is always nothing but a person. . . . [T]he duties to oneself, . . . admit of only one objective division, *formal* and *material*. . . . The former forbid[s] one to act contrary to his natural *end* and, accordingly, involve[s] nothing but his moral *self-preservation*; the latter bid[s] him make as his end a certain object of *choice* and such duties involve his *perfection* of himself. (Kant MV, 419, emphasis added)

One's duty is to preserve one's basic moral autonomy and empower it over time until it has reached its full potential as moral agency in constructing one's life in the material world. Moral agency is thus both the capacity of the individual to be autonomous and the ability of the individual to express this autonomy toward self-perfection. The development of one's moral potential is thus a function of seeking purpose in the full constitution and integrity of one's "moral" agency. Kant argues that one's moral agency provides both purpose and duty as each of us strives toward virtue and the full use of our practical reason.

Recall Alan Donagan's words that autonomy is a "nonproducible" end-in-itself that seeks virtue nonconsequentially in one's observance of duty.

Kant's ethics is duty-based, where rights flow from duties. Creating the circumstances and context in which the juridical environment empowers the ethical ends of internal autonomy and external moral agency is a unique obligation or purpose, for it is duty-based. One's duties involve the expression of one's positive freedom in moral agency: to create a human life out of a mere animal existence. One's goal is to arrange one's subjective wants and desires around preserving, protecting, and enhancing the core of positive and negative freedom equally inherent in each person. The freedom of the moral agent is a freedom to choose to act responsibly in the material world on one's own behalf, and a "good will" is one that does so to the greatest degree possible, understanding that the moral law requires that no individual express his agency in the exploitation of another.

The purpose of moral agency is not, however, teleological (Riley 1983), or goal oriented, in the sense of building toward a producible end on the basis of hypothetical imperatives, but concerns one's duty to perfect and protect one's autonomy as a nonproducible end on the basis of categorical imperatives. Moral agency is therefore a deontological purpose for the Kantian individual. The integration of positive and negative freedom within a juridical environment empowers one's internal capacity through coordination of external expression and choice.

The moral agent is distinguished from a mere agent by two factors: first, by the act of acknowledging that one has the internal capacity for autonomy; second, by one's understanding of the ethical/juridical distinction and the duty toward construction of a material environment in which one has the most practical ability to express and perfect one's internal autonomy in external moral agency. These factors allow the individual to create himself through his reason, with responsibility to his own worth as a person. Such is the ethical purpose one finds in moral agency.

Individual Autonomy and a Mutual Duty to Justice

The individual, to protect and enhance her core of positive and negative freedom, finds ethical purpose in development of her moral agency as it coordinates and integrates her internal autonomy and external agency into a combination that can truly express reason practically in the material world. This is Kant's goal, not the isolated autonomous "self" making moral choices without regard to their contingent reality, but the practical reasoner who knows what is right but also knows the best way to make what is right real in her particular context and physical circumstances.

The moral agent will not sacrifice long-term development for short-term gain nor will she fail her moral purpose in intrinsic character development by forsaking essential internal control of her will for the satisfaction of desire. She recognizes that good and bad are not characteristics of objects, but of human perceptions, and acknowledges that by applying maxims to connect internal principle with external context she will be able to construct a reality that protects and empowers moral agency not only in herself but in a wide cross-section of humanity. She will place ultimate value in her own moral agency, and that of others, and in the maintenance of equal access to those external conditions that support negative freedom and allow the development of inner autonomy and the expression of positive freedom. In this way, one can shape one's character, the individual self, which, in its expressions, will shape the collective material environment in which all live. Only a moral agent is a responsible agent-cause, a practical reasoner with a good will. All wants and desires of the moral agent are organized to protect and promote the objective end of human freedom, without ignoring the capacity for autonomy in others or their ability to express this autonomy in moral agency.

The internal capacity to be autonomous is inherent in all individuals, but when the individual interacts with others, autonomy can be affected through restriction of moral agency. If all were motivated to acknowledge and obey the moral law, then their multiple expressions of positive freedom would harmonize in a Realm of Ends.[6] In reality, however, some individuals will utilize their physical power of numbers to dominate others and deny the dominated the freedom they, the powerful, cherish for themselves. Humans, being animals, have a tendency to protect their physical natures at the expense of their autonomous wills. In such circumstances, the purpose of moral agency can be derailed or entangled. At this juncture, the policymaker can contribute to the protection and empowerment of a citizen's predisposition toward becoming a moral agent by working toward justice through public choice.

The primitive concept, or point of departure, for the policy decision maker, considering the individual in the Kantian model, is the freedom of the moral agent, that is, the particular freedom necessary to the expression of one's full autonomy in choice and action. Social justice is a collective means to the full moral agency of the individual. But how can law and politics fill this role?

For the answer we return to Kant's distinction between the ethical and the juridical, which the policymaker would appreciate as a difference between the incentive toward justice (*Recht*) and the incentive toward virtue (*Tugend*) (Kant MJ, 218–20). Virtue is the condition where one's incentive, as well as the act that results, comes from one's respect for the moral law. Justice, in contrast, is concerned only that the act and its external ramifications are compatible with the demands of the moral law. An external party cannot make others moral, but everyone can contribute to the construction of a just society that will institutionalize the demands of the moral law, as they affect external behavior by setting up the optimal framework in which one's positive freedom of the will is assured against the choices and the acts of others that directly interfere with it.

In effect, it is the realm of choice (*Willkür*) in which politics regulates the negative freedom of its citizens and, in this way, encourages the full potential of positive freedom (*Wille*) across a population of citizens. By distributing and regulating negative freedom, the policymaker can assure that each agent has that political and economic quality of life necessary to empower his or her full potential as a moral agent.

To express the political requirements of the moral law, a fourth component should be added to the categorical imperative. I will call this the *public choice formula* of the moral law.

4. Each person has a duty, in concern for his or her full and long-term moral agency, as well as for the moral agency of others, to establish or to contribute to a just society through private/collective choice and decision making in order to provide the optimal environment within which maximum equal negative freedom of choice can be assured to all citizens as a base upon which their full capacity and potential as morally independent and autonomous agents may find empowered ability for expression.

Public policy, through the establishment of justice, can assure each person that the construction of that material environment which best protects, empowers, and coordinates individual moral agency becomes a public responsibility of, and entitlement to, each citizen.

> . . . justice, insofar as it . . . is moral, applies . . . only to the external and . . . practical relationship of one person to another in which their actions can . . . exert influence, each on the other . . . (Kant MJ, 230)

Justice, therefore, finds its meaning in those policies that best apply the moral law to the positive law in regulating or coordinating individual choice so that individual moral agency is not exploited. This establishes Kant's law of freedom that contends that

> every action is just [or right] that in itself or in its maxim is such that the freedom of the choice of one can coexist together with the freedom of everyone in accordance with a universal law. (Kant MJ, 230)

Justice in public policy is therefore concerned with external coercion. Everyone's actions should show respect for the moral law and thus for humanity in the person. Justice transforms the question from "Why should I be moral?" to "Why ought I obey the just civil law and use it coercively to regulate and harmonize my freedom with the freedom of others?" (Gillroy and Wade 1992, vii).[7]

The task of justice is essentially distributive (Kant MJ, 297, 300, §41–42); to make it impossible for moral agency to become inaccessible to some by the design of others or the fortunes of nature. Although the state cannot grant freedom to the individual, it can either nurture it or inhibit it. One is morally responsible for all his decisions, but it is also important to consider that making the moral choice in conditions of restricted negative freedom may be a supererogatory act.

Justice coerces the individual with the moral law that assures his equal moral agency, treating him as a means, but also simultaneously as an end-in-himself. Guided by the categorical imperative, the construction of institutions through public choice should be based on the requirement that human beings be treated as ends-in-themselves and that their choices be harmonized, so that individual wills can be made fully autonomous by their own efforts. Each society is thus measured by the moral law, which as a critical morality (Hart 1961, 205–06; 1963, 20) "will ultimately have to provide the justification for setting up a system of coercive state law" (Murphy 1970, 96). Under this stricture, a slave society, or a civil arrangement where one race, gender, or class is routinely exploited for the sake of another, would not be just.[8]

Kant requires that the coercive power of the state be justified on independent principle that defines what is necessary and reasonable from the standpoint of the critical morality (justice as *Recht*), while it allows the particular manifestation of the positive law (*Gerechtigkeit*) to have various forms on a societal level (Kant MJ, §51).[9] The principle of the moral law does not dictate one type of institutional structure or political economy; it does disallow inherently racist or exploitive social orders as unjust and therefore immoral, and sets the positive standards and basic requirements for any "legal" system claiming to be just, and thus obligating its citizens (Hart 1961, 205–06).

Justice therefore does not require as much as virtue (i.e. that one is free to will for the sake of the moral law), but rather is concerned with what the moral law demands of a system of political constraints or incentives, the product of policy choice and legal adjudication.

In order to understand the role and origin of justice within Kantian political philosophy, the policymaker must begin with the moral law, specifically, the material basis and full determination of the categorical imperative. This material component is defined as the imperative to recognize the intrinsic value of humanity in oneself and others and respect it as the basis of ethical public choice.

> If there is to be a supreme practical principle and a categorical imperative for the human will, it must be one that forms an *objective* principle of the will, from the conception of that which is necessarily an end for everyone because it is an *end in itself*. Hence this objective principle can serve as a universal practical law. The ground of this principle is: rational nature exists as an end in itself. Man necessarily thinks of his own existence in this way; it is thus far a subjective principle of human actions. Also every other rational being thinks of his existence by means of the same rational ground that also holds for myself; thus it is at the same time an objective principle from which, as a supreme practical principle, it must be possible to derive all laws of the will. The practical imperative, therefore, is the following: Act so that you treat humanity, whether in your own person or in that of another, always as an end and never as a means only. (Kant GW, 428–29, emphasis added)

Although superficially one might see moral virtue as an isolated, internal quality, in one's personal struggle for the good will against desire, one requires that others act morally so that an expression of agency on the part of others does not prevent or exploit one's moral purpose in agency. The individual should respect not only himself but the autonomy of others in his political community; both are duties of the moral law (Kant MV, 385–89). An individual following the moral law and respecting his own autonomy is a kind of communitarian, striving to create a community of moral agents, aware that he and others have mutual duties in the preservation and perfection of autonomy and therefore mutual rights to respect for their own humanity.[10]

In this way, the material base of the moral law (humanity-as-an-end-in-itself) becomes the necessary end of each and all good wills. The administrative and institutional setting constructed to assure the mutual duty of each to individuals as ends in turn should create those just material conditions where the full determination of the categorical imperative in a Kingdom of Ends may find a more efficacious evolution and realization.

> By "realm" [of Ends] I understand the systematic union of different rational beings through common laws. Because laws determine ends with regard to their universal validity if we abstract from the personal difference of rational beings and thus from all content of their private ends, we can then think of a whole of all ends in systematic inter-connection, a whole of rational beings as ends in themselves as well as of the particular ends that each may set for himself. . . . Morality, therefore, consists in the relation of every action to that legislation through which, alone, a realm of ends is possible. (Kant GW, 433–34)

The moral law thus requires that the autonomous person will only that public legislation supportive of the equal actualization of all wills as autonomous and belonging to a realm of ends.

Private choices will be empowered and encouraged by the public choices we make as a community. Policymakers play a role here with the collective regulation of immoral action by the public coordination of choice through law. The regulation of law, based on just public policy, assures that each person's agency does not interfere with the moral agency of others.

But what about the natural environment? Does it play a role in this interrelationship of wills at the foundation of public choice?

Our Kantian Duties to Nature

Examining Kant's philosophical system[11] as a whole,[12] I will address the issue that Kantian moral and political philosophy is anthropocentric and has no environmental ethic, especially one that considers nature for itself. I will then contend that there are arguments for two sources of human duties to nature that exist within Kantian exegesis: one based upon our responsibility to conserve nature as humanity's duty to itself (individually and collectively), and another focused on our obligation to preserve natural functioning for its own sake, as humanity's duty to the highest good (Kant C3, 450) and the harmony between the realm of nature and the realm of ends considered as a whole biosphere made up of Ecosystems.[13]

Although the first of these justifications for our duty to nature values the environment as instrumental to humanity, Kant's definition of "instrumental," and what ends justify the "instrumental" use of nature, is unique and unconventional. For Kant, our instrumental duty to nature is brought about by our intrinsic duty to ourselves and is neither consequentialist nor want-regarding. Rather, it is concerned with the moral ideal of autonomy that requires a sound environment and regulated use of resources, as it requires justice, for the essential needs of all generations of human beings.

The second argument attributes a human duty to nature as a distinct component (with humanity) of Ecosystems as wholes.[14] Kant defines "Ecosystems" as the interface between human and natural systems that make up the whole biosphere or world system.[15] Our duty is to the intrinsic value of nature as a functional entity that has a capacity, ability, and purpose of its own, which has created us and of which we are the highest expression (Beck 1960, 161).

From within Kantian philosophy, humanity, being the most prominent moral and strategically rational species on the planet, has duties to nature not only because the environment affects human moral agency or autonomy but also in terms of nature's existence as a functional end-in-itself. Human consideration of autonomy and its moral demands on how one conducts individual and collective/political life will generate environmental policy that not only conserves nature as it essentially affects humanity but also preserves evolving natural systems, functioning independently of human concern.

Kantian Conservationism

Diverse schools of thought exist within environmental ethics (Zimmerman et al. 1993; Devall and Sessions 1985; Taylor 1986; Norton 1987; Johnson 1991; Nash 1989; Goodpaster and Sayre 1979; Elliot and Gare 1983).[16] These approaches offer a variety of standards and ends for human ethical deliberation that grant either individual animals, plants, or natural systems and the biosphere varying degrees of moral standing. Whatever the moral argument, however, humanity must play a central role, at least in the vocabulary and agency of moral choice.

Human beings have the technological capacity, are the agents of widespread and intergenerational change, and "matter" more than any other single species in whether or not life persists and in what form. We do not worry that beavers will destroy a forest, or that fish will contaminate a water supply. What humanity does is, and ought to be, our primary "environmental" concern. Positively, only human beings have the moral capacity to understand what *is* and what *ought* to be, and act to achieve it. We are moral agents; nature is not. Therefore, our actions, our technology, and the control of these by our sense of duty to ourselves and to the environment will determine our public policy and our own and nature's condition, now and in the future. These duties define our environmental policy.

Although some argue for the interests (Singer 1980, 1990; Johnson 1991) or rights (Regan 1980b, 1982) of nature and its components, these arguments are an effort to create nature in our own image with our own moral attributes. They fail to consider nature in its own terms and create a second-order moral class that is more remote and foreign than humanity and its moral responsibilities. By extending the human concepts of interests and rights to nature, do we simultaneously extend the concept to where it has no moral purchase or power in policy argument (Norton 1987; Hargrove 1992)?

While we argue about the "rights" of animals, species fail to thrive. While we argue about the spiritual character of old-growth forests, they are clear-cut. The rights, interests, or demands of nature simply do not matter if humanity feels no duty to respect those demands. Ethics is a human attribute. The predispositions of our practical reason, as we apply moral imperative to action, will create our view of the world and our definition of responsibilities to ourselves and nature. In the end, if humanity does not perceive that nature is vital, either in itself (on its own terms) or to the ends of persons, the necessary respect, reflected by a policy of protection or conservation, will not be forthcoming and environmental "rights" are moot.

Humanity can have many relationships with nature. Approaching the moral status of nature from the vantage point of intrinsic value, or autonomy of the human individual in Kant's moral philosophy, commits one to the contention that while humanity is *of* nature, we are also transcendent in terms of our moral capacities and can imprint and reshape both our own character and nature's in accordance with human agency as regulated by moral principle.[17] When the basis of justice is the intrinsic value of humanity in the person, then the pertinent question becomes: How does human autonomy invoke duties to nature?

A superficial reading of Kantian philosophy, as it regards nature and natural systems, begins with the contention that Kant is an anthropocentric or human-centered "rationalist" with an ethics that grants intrinsic moral value only to humanity (Attfield 1983, 20–33). Only humans are "moral" ends-in-themselves (Kant GW, 427–29), and therefore, we are the only intrinsically valuable life form. All other living systems exist to instrumentally support humanity in its search for moral perfection.

> Our duties toward animals are indirect duties toward humanity. (Kant LE, 27:459)

> If a man has his dog shot because the animal is no longer capable of service, he is not in breach of duty to the dog, for the dog cannot judge, but his act is inhuman and damages in himself that which he ought to exercise in virtue of his duties to humanity. (Kant LE, 27:459)

These assumptions about Kantian environmental ethics are essentially true, but it does not follow that an environmental ethic therefore does not exist, or that it grants no intrinsic value to nature. Kant does ascribe ethics to humanity alone. This is logical, for mankind is the only species whose capacity, ability, and purpose has "moral" content that allows him to "judge" and act ethically. Kant, as all moralists are, is anthropogenic in taking a human, that is, an *ethical* point of view. Only humans are ethical ends-in-themselves with the capacity to recognize their duty, and the ability to take on obligations and perform them purposively, to create a just world.

Kant's concern is the distinction between the realm of ends and the realm of nature. The former is the world of human systems where individuals count because they are the focus of intrinsic value. The latter is the world of natural systems where intrinsic value is concerned with functional wholes, which are the units of evolution and the focus of human duty. The individual animal or plant has functional value only as part of a greater system and not in-and-of-itself. This is why Kant states that our duties to individual animals can only be a duty to oneself. By discounting individual creatures, however, Kant does not simultaneously discount nature and its functional systems as being without intrinsic value.

The human moral purpose in perfecting one's freedom or autonomy is to take a higher-level control over one's life. The definition of human intrinsic value can attach concepts like duty, right, and justice to human conduct.[18] The second point however, that is incorrectly drawn from the first, is that owing to this moral distinction, all other species and natural systems are outside the pale of moral duty for humanity and can be used by mankind, at will, as instrumental values to supply his wants (Singer 1980, 231–32; Regan 1980a, 1980b). The important distinction here is between being inherently moral and being the subject of moral duty for those who are. Whereas nature can never be the former, this does not disqualify it from being the latter.

As the instrumental value argument goes, with "personhood" (McCloskey 1983, 59), the dominant force in ethics, "[e]verything other than a person can only have value for a person . . . if x is valuable and not a person, then x will have value for some individual other than itself" (Vlastos 1962, 48–49). Therefore any moral argument (including Kant's) that is based on the "dignity" or "intrinsic value of man" (Frankena 1962, 23) is antithetical to any environmental ethic that attributes a distinct and intrinsic value to the natural ecology and its component parts (Goodpaster 1979, 26–28).

Kant, although he grants no inherent "moral" status to nature, never recommends waste or exploitation of, or cruelty to the natural world considered as a system (Kant MV, 443). These are all immoral acts against our ethical duties to ourselves and others.[19] Within this reading of Kant, one can argue that nature is still only "instrumental" to human ends, but Kant's use of "instrumental" is unconventional because it is concerned with more that the mere *use* of nature to increase human utility.

For Kant, even if natural systems do not have intrinsic value (I will shortly argue that they do) but only instrumental value, this still does not allow humanity to treat nature and its components merely as means to any and all of their subjective preferences. Kant's individual is required to function within the categorical imperative and has ethical duties to herself that concern both her animal nature and her character as a moral being (Kant MV, 420). Within one's duties to these dimensions of human character, permissible and non-permissible uses of nature can be defined within Kantian conservationism.

When nature is "instrumental" to one's perfection and preservation as an autonomous moral agent, then one's relationship with nature is not want-regarding but ideal-regarding (Barry 1990) and predicated on the role resources play in empowering one's autonomy. The reinforcing and "transformative value" of nature (Norton 1987, 188–91) is critical here.

Nature plays a role in reinforcing humanity's value through empowering one's capacity to see beauty, show kindness and consideration, and act justly. When one acts so as to treat nature with respect, the use of practical reason in its application to the person is honed. In addition, nature empowers the autonomy of the individual by transforming his preferences to those more compatible with the moral law. If we believe

> that experience of nature is a necessary condition for developing a consistent and rational world view, one that fully recognizes man's place as a highly evolved animal whose existence depends upon other species and functioning ecosystems, [we] also believe that such experiences have transformative value. Experience of nature can promote questioning and rejection of overly materialistic and consumptive felt preferences. (Norton 1987, 189)

Instrumental use of nature, from a Kantian point of view, is not consequentialist but nonconsequentialist and finds its moral value in the maxims that recognize one's joint duty to seek excellence in oneself and justice for society. "[U]nresponsiveness to what is beautiful, awesome, dainty, dumpy, and otherwise aesthetically interesting in nature probably reflects a lack of the openness of mind and spirit necessary to appreciate the best in human beings" (Hill 1991, 116). The standards are duty to one's basic capacity, ability, and purpose and the role that nature plays in preserving and perfecting the human being.

From the standpoint of one's physical or animal being and its perfection, the use of resources must fall within the moral law. We are not concerned with human preference, economic efficiency, or one's utility but with the empowerment of moral autonomy. In addition, the use of resources must be planned from a timeless and nonrelative standpoint as all generations of humanity, all over the world, will require a similar resource base to preserve themselves and their opportunity to perfect their autonomy (Barry 1977, 1978b; Page 1977, 1983a). Therefore, the imperative is to conserve resources with one's duty to justice from autonomy in mind. Waste and abuse are immoral, and the long-term empowerment of present and future moral agents must regulate humanity's designation and use of nature as a resource.[20]

Within a political or policy framework, the role of nature in fulfilling human private and public right requires humanity to treat nature through justice. A just state is a necessary (but not sufficient) condition for the realization of the Realm of Ends, and these conditions include a sound and evolving natural world that provides the physical setting for human moral and political advancement. As justice provides the basic distribution of freedom, nature provides a sound and thriving environment to bring out the best in humanity.[21]

With the human consciousness of our role in nature evolves a further appreciation of the independent value of nature as an equal component in the "system of the whole earth," and here, with this realization, we have the essential conditions for the creation of Kant's Kingdom of Ends. "[A]s we become more and more aware that we are parts of the larger whole we come to value the whole independently of its effects on ourselves" (Hill 1991, 111). In the creation of a just political world and its reconciliation with the natural world, we find the roots for more than an evaluation of nature as it is instrumental to humanity. Kant did not write of the Kingdom of Ends as the sole consideration of human moral choice; he also wrote of a preexisting Kingdom of Nature and the harmony of the Realm of Freedom with the Realm of Nature as necessary to effectuate the "highest good" of the human condition. Here, the unconventional argument for humanity's instrumental use of nature evolves into an argument for human duty to the intrinsic value of nature as an independent element in the greater whole of human experience and moral ends. "Yet the opposition between nature and culture is to be finally overcome in the creation of 'the perfect civil constitution' that would mark the end of political history, creating a new harmony between reason and nature by reshaping the latter in view of the former" (Yovel 1980, 193).

Kantian Preservationism

When we posit that human autonomy requires the environment to sustain and perfect our agency, we must also remember that, for Kant, the realm of nature lives independently of us and is our progenitor (Kant C1; C3, 427; Zammito 1992, 342). Nature produced humanity, but now that humanity has morally transcended nature we have separated ourselves from the complete control of nature. We are agent-causes within a functionally causal world. But what about our duties to nature after human transcendence?

Inherent or intrinsic value can have more than one definition. The intrinsic value of nature is different from the intrinsic value of humanity. Humanity is of inherent value for its unique moral capacity, whereas nature is of inherent value in terms of its causality and systemic functioning. We can argue about whether nature has rights, but not with the assertion that it is a self-generating, functional system with the capacity for independent evolution. In its function, nature is an end-in-itself. Within the teleology of natural systems causality and evolution, nature has value, not only to humanity but independent of us.[22] "Darwin explained the teleological character of the living world non-teleologically. The evolution process is not itself teleological, but it gives rise to functionally organized [natural] systems and intentional agents" (DLH in Audi 1995, 791). Where humans have a particular capacity, ability, and purpose that grants them moral autonomy or integrity and intrinsic value, natural systems exhibit a distinct capacity, ability, and purpose that grants them *functional* autonomy or integrity (Kant C3, 373–75).[23] This grants nature an intrinsic value of its own and independent ethical standing in human policy decision making.

A KANTIAN PARADIGM FOR ECOSYSTEM POLICY ARGUMENT

A unique element of this Kantian argument is that valuing nature as a functional system not only grants it intrinsic value status, but defines intrinsic value not in human terms (rights, interests, etc.), but uniquely in terms of the specific physical, chemical, and biological characteristics of nature, making the Kantian approach neither anthropocentric nor anthropomorphic.[24]

Human beings are moral creatures. Kant suggested that humans have one foot in the material world and one in the spiritual (Kant RL, bk. 2, §1). Such placement gives human beings a moral quality; this moral dimension places requirements upon individual will and choice in our dealings with the material world (Yaffe 1995). The substance of the human moral quality is evaluation: the predisposition to place value on entities and make this evaluation the basis of our relationship with that entity. All valuing (produced through maxims) is human and all moral worth is a product of human deliberation and argument. Morality is measured in terms of duty; only humans can have or be responsible to moral duties. Therefore, only those persons and things that invoke moral duty will count in human deliberation and ethical choice. The moral realm is a human realm, but that does not mean that humans are the only subjects of moral duty, or that valuation must transmit human ethical characteristics to nonhuman life (e.g., rights).

Pushing past the surface of Kant's remarks about the duties to nonhuman forms of life (Kant MJ, 239–41; MV, 443–44) and examining the essential logic of his structural argument about intrinsic value, one finds a Kantian justification for humanity's relationship to natural systems, based on the intrinsic value of those systems, not as moral, but as functional, ends-in-themselves in the greater world system.

The Realm of Nature and the Realm of Ends exist as parallel and interconnected systems of life, each dependent upon the other for persistence.[25] The duty of humanity is to establish harmony between these realms and to find coordination and perfection in their common evolution (Kant C3). Here, one can utilize Kant's concepts of teleology and the "highest good" to their best results. Let us examine three dimensions of the inherent value of nature within the Kantian scheme: (1) the definition of the world system, (2) how nature gets a moral value for its functional purpose, and finally, (3) what specific duty humanity owes to nature in-and-of-itself.

The World System Defined: Kant states that "[t]he world can be regarded as a universal system of all ends, whether through nature or through freedom" (Kant LT, 143). The world is the combination or "complex of all natural beings" (Kant OP, 22:59) that forms an evolving and interdependent whole of organic life. First Kant defines an organic body.

> An organic body is one in which each part, with its moving force, necessarily relates to the whole (to each part in its composition). The productive force in this unity is life. This vital principle can be applied *a priori*, from consideration of their mutual needs, to plants, to animals, to their relation to one another taken as a whole, and finally, to the totality of the world. (Kant OP, 21:211)

Next we need to see these organic entities as connected and evolving, even beyond this planet.

> That its organizing force has so arranged for one another the totality of the species of plants and animals, that they, together, as members of a chain, form a system (man not excepted). That they require each other for their existence, not merely in respect to their nominal character, but (similarly) their real character (causality)—which points in the direction of a world organization (to unknown ends) of the galaxy itself. (Kant OP, 22:549 fn)

Within this world system there are two realms: the Realm of Causality, which is nature, and the Realm of Freedom, which involves human moral perfection. The former preexisted and created the latter, but the latter has the power to affect the ongoing internal progress and evolution of natural causality. The strategic and moral rationality of humanity, moving toward a Realm of Ends, has the power to disrupt, alter, and reshape the course of the Realm of Nature.

However, without the perfection of the Realm of Nature, the human condition cannot achieve ultimate value (Kant LT, 138–48). Therefore, our "reshaping"[26] of nature must function under moral imperatives that impose duties upon us in terms of the functional capacity, ability, and purpose of nature if we are to achieve not only the Realm of Ends[27] but the "highest good" of both physical and spiritual perfection.

"In the highest good the moral good and the natural good are combined according with the rule of worthiness to form the entire good of moral man" (Yovel 1980, 57). We are special within nature, but this does not give us privilege but responsibility to the whole and its joint perfection.

> The physical perfection of the world is the system of all ends in accordance with the nature of things; and is attained along with the rational creature's worthiness to be happy. It is only in this way that the state of a creature may obtain a preeminent value. Without such a physical perfection of the world, the rational creature might certainly have an excellent value in himself, but his state could still be bad; and vice versa. But if both moral and physical perfection are combined, then we have the best world. (Kant LT, 140–41)

If the "best world" is one where nature and humanity are in harmony, and each is considered to be an independent component with equal value both in itself and as a part of a greater whole, then any moral imperative to conserve nature or preserve its functional integrity, as we empower our own autonomy, must be considered within a Kantian model of Ecosystems.

The scientific definition of "ecosystem" (Odum 1975) tends to underplay the human role and focus on the systemic connections between organic and inorganic components of natural systems. For Kant, the Ecosystem is both an actual physical interface between humanity and nature and a metaphysical ideal of human and natural systems coordination.

Kantian Ecosystems can be considered to be made up of two major components: the sphere of humanity, with its physical and moral life (biota), and technological/sociopolitical organization (abiota), on the one hand; and functional nature, on the other. Therefore, it is the interfaces between human biota and abiota and natural biota and abiota that are of interest to justice and political theory and that become the points of practical consideration for human duties to nature. In addition, the metaphysical goal of perfection and harmony creates an end for Ecosystems and the ultimate justification for human ethics. Before we examine the duties humanity has to recognize and maintain the intrinsic value of nature, we must first proceed from nature's functional value in an Ecosystem to its moral weight as a subject of ethical value in and of itself. To the human evaluation of nature's inherent integrity we now turn.

The Intrinsic Value of Nature: The ideal of a harmonious natural and human world is connected with Kant's concept of the "highest good" of that system. The "highest good" is more fundamentally connected to both the purpose of man and the purpose of nature. Here the highest good is "the union of the purposiveness arising from freedom with the purposiveness of nature" (Kant RL, first preface). The causal characteristics of nature, as harmonized with the deontological character of humanity, set the standard by which humanity ought to value both itself and nature.

A theory of value should establish the basis upon which that value is judged. For humanity, the dignity of the individual is a function of the integrity of moral capacity, ability, and purpose: specifically, one's internal *capacity* to will in line with the moral law; one's *ability* to express moral predisposition in external agency; and one's *purpose* in perfecting internal autonomy in external moral agency and political justice (Kant GW; MV). Willing the categorical imperative (Kant GW, 419–20) is, for Kant, the basis of all moral (intrinsic) value, for humanity has dignity only "so far as it is capable of morality" (Kant GW, 435; Yaffe 1995). It is in the Realm of Ends that Kant makes the distinction between dignity and price (Kant GW, 435–36); only here is the motivation of each person moral. In a Realm of Ends (Kant GW, 433–39), where all have fulfilled their purpose, becoming fully articulate moral agents, each person's capacity, ability, and purpose grants him or her a good will (Kant GW, 393) and, therefore, moral dignity as individuals within just societies.

This is not to say that each person ought not always treat his fellows with respect as having intrinsic value, but that an individual earns dignity by submitting his will to the moral law and expressing this will through his choices in the material world. Civil law, through justice, empowers each person's capacity for autonomy, protects his or her ability to choose morally in the material world, and seeks his or her potential (purpose) as moral agents able to reason practically in civil discourse (Kant MJ, 311ff.). This defines human intrinsic value.

A natural system also has its own capacity, ability, and potential as part of the world of cause, effect, and natural selection. Nature predates us and has created the possibility of humanity and its future Realm of Ends. In this way, the

Realm of Ends is built upon the model of the Realm of Nature (Paton 1948, 190–91).

Nature's subsystems are characterized by their dynamic evolution and their intricate web of cycles, energy, and material flows (Golly 1993; Pimm 1991;

O'Neill et al. 1986). The mutualism of species and the interdependent subsystems of nature find their *capacity* in causality, their *ability* in natural selection, and their *purpose* or potential in evolving toward different moments of complexity and homeostasis (Abrahamson and Weis 1997; Williams 1966; Mayr 1976). The unique character of a natural system, to reach various points of change, is dependent upon its functional integrity remaining intact (Pimm 1991; Brooks and Wiley 1988). A natural system, therefore, is a functional whole, a well-balanced, dynamic, and evolving entity (Abrahamson and Weis 1997; Von Schilcher and Tennant 1984), that is a functional end-in-itself. Because it has an internal dynamic and intrinsic value that is distinct and worthy of moral respect independent of its uses by humanity (Kant C3, 380; MV, 443), it is an end for itself, as well as for us. But how can this functional value have moral impact as a human duty?

Nature has no inherent morality, only causality. Humanity, in order to synthesize its moral half with its natural half, reflectively imputes to nature a supersensuous quality, a teleology of natural purpose (Kant C3, §§82–84; Paton 1948, 149). This teleology provides a bridge between the moral and the functional sphere, where humanity is the ultimate expression of functionality in nature, and provides the means for the harmony of the moral and the natural as the "highest good" of the world system. Here, human duty finds voice, in terms of responsibilities both to oneself and to the whole.

The duty to the whole implies a duty to nature as the functional prerequisite of total harmony. We must use nature to achieve our perfection and persistence. But, as we ought not use other humans as mere means but simultaneously as moral means and ends, so to achieve harmony we must recognize the unique realm of nature and preserve its functionality as a prerequisite to our use and conservation. Only in this way can we achieve our moral goals within the limits of the demands of the moral law. As all things in nature are mutual means and ends of one another, so we must never consider nature as merely a means, but always simultaneously as a functional end-in-itself and, as such, as having moral value independent of humanity as a separate component in the Ecosystem and greater biosphere.

The goal of Kant's Ecosystem is "unity and harmony," which motivates us against "destroying all order in nature" (Kant LT, 157). Kant defines integrity as "not the opposite of depravity (perversity) but of loss (as of a limb) and of imperfection by deprivation" (Kant OP, 21:37). Both humanity, through the "freedom of man," and nature, through "Newtonian attraction through empty space," are said to be "categorical imperatives" (Kant OP, 21:35; Yaffe 1995). In addition, nature, as humanity itself, is said to have a "soul" (Kant OP, 22:418; also 21:18; Zammito 1992, 304–05). Here nature finds a unique capacity, ability, and purpose or an integrity that ought not be "deprived" in the interplay of means and ends through human calculation and choice (either public or pri-

---

vate). "The idea of organic bodies is indirectly contained a priori in that of a composite of moving forces, in which the concept of a real whole necessarily precedes that of its parts, which can only be thought by the concept of a combination according to purpose" (Kant OP 21:213). We consider nature to have inherent value in seeking its own ends. The system of natural law that is our environment is a fitting model for human moral law and also a teleological standard for human judgments of the ultimate ends both of nature and of humanity. The realm of natural law is essential to the formulation of human categorical imperatives and is, in this way, the basis for one's moral deliberations.

> [T]he system of natural laws applying to dogs and cats as well as human beings is to be understood as defining a *teleological* system—one in which events occur for the sake of realizing natural ends. In conceiving of nature this way we are imposing a rational order on it; we are conceiving of it as a fundamentally rational system. As so conceived, the formal structure of natural laws is not just analogous to the formal structure of rational laws: the formal structure is the *same* in both cases. Given this, the system of nature is *necessarily* an adequate model for a system of rational wills. (Aune 1979, 59–60)

Nature is that nonmoral purpose which created humanity (Zammito 1992, 327). Inherently, this is a functional value, but in relation to the origin and persistence of humanity as an end-in-itself, the human duty to its creator, and the persistence of the whole Ecosystem, it is an intrinsic moral value (Kant C3, 427). Therefore, the functional integrity of natural systems has standing as an end-in-itself, as necessary in-and-of-itself and independent of any elective ends humanity may have. Humanity alone recognizes and executes duty to that which has intrinsic value. Human duty toward the environment is to respect and preserve nature's functional integrity as an evolutionary and homeostatic end-in-itself, necessary to the realization of the "highest good." "The highest good is always conceived as a harmony of heterogeneous systems, where exact correspondence between the different constituents (. . . freedom and nature in general) takes place *by the autonomous laws of each system itself*" (Yovel 1980, 66).

One's Duty to Preserve Nature's Intrinsic Value:

> The highest good is no longer a separate, transcendent world, but becomes the consummate state of *this* world, to be realized through a concrete development in time. . . . The progressive power of history is ascribed not only to a hidden "cunning of *nature*," but also to the conscious work of practical *reason*. . . .[T]he concept of happiness loses its central position and is replaced by nature in general as the empirical component of the highest good. (Yovel 1980, 30–31)

The intrinsic value of nature invokes a duty that humanity not exploit the natural environment for mere personal convenience, and it directs the regulation of human behavior toward the end of the harmony of humanity and na-

---

ture as two distinct but equal entities, in a world system that it is the duty of humanity to create as the "highest good" of our efforts. Within this greater system, the Realm of Ends and the Realm of Nature are reshaped by the moral capacities of humanity with the understanding that each component of the greater whole has its own unique intrinsic value and role in mutual evolution.

> But if he is conscious of following his duty, then man is certain of being a member or link in the chain of the kingdom of ends. This thought gives him comfort and reassurance. It makes him inwardly noble and worthy of happiness. And it raises him to the hope that he may constitute a whole together with all other rational beings in the kingdom of morals, in just the same way that everything is connected and unified in the kingdom of nature. (Kant LT, 41)

Humanity is born of nature but moves beyond it in terms of moral capacities and the ability to reason strategically (Kant C1, C2, C3, MV, MJ; Elster 1979). Therefore, even when Kant states that human duties to animals and nature are indirectly duties to humanity, he is not discounting nature but reaffirming that our moral value, our duties to nature, are indirectly to ourselves as the sole products of nature capable of morality ("the dog cannot judge"). This means that, as our deontological purpose toward moral agency grows from the teleological and causal purposes of nature, this "moral product" builds a moral intrinsic value from a preexisting functional one. Kant's argument leads to a unity of humanity and nature where both humans and the natural systems in which they evolve can be said to have interdependent, albeit distinct, intrinsic values (Kant C3, 429–35).

Only humans create or owe moral duties, but the principle of this duty, its necessity to the moral perfection of humanity, applies not only to man as an ethical end, but also to nature as a functional or causal end-in-itself as equal components in the world system that is Kant's definition of the "highest good." Morality is a transcendent quality of nature; it cannot be of mere instrumental value if it created that which has intrinsic moral capabilities.[28]

> [O]nce we have discovered that nature is able to make products that can be thought of only in terms of the concept of final causes, we are then entitled to go further; we may thereupon judge products as belonging to a system of purposes even if they (or the relation between them, though purposive) do not require us to account for their possibility, to look for a different principle beyond the mechanism of blind efficient causes. For the idea of nature as a system of nature already leads us, as concerns its basis, beyond the world of sense, so that the unity of the supersensible principle must be considered valid not merely for certain species of natural beings, but just as much for the whole of nature as a system. (Kant C3, 380–81)

In the same way that humans have a deontological moral purpose in practical reason and moral agency, natural systems can be said to have a teleological purpose in their functional integrity and evolution. This is the same functional evolution that produced humanity as its highest teleological purpose:

> judging man . . . to be not merely a natural purpose, which we may judge all organized beings to be, but also to be the *ultimate* purpose of nature here on earth, the purpose by reference to which all other natural things constitute a system of purposes. (Kant C3, 430)

Under these circumstances practical reason ought to recognize that the unique capacity, ability, and potential of nature (its functional integrity) grants it intrinsic moral standing. The human duty is to preserve that which is required for the production of the highest good, especially since humanity can have detrimental effects on nature's basic functioning. Our strategic rationality requires us to be responsible to nature, in both the preservation of its integrity and the conservation of our resource use of it. The policy imperative is to respect the causality of nature while using nature primarily for moral purposes, that is, for those uses that are necessary to our autonomy, but not to the extent that its functional integrity is compromised.

In effect, as the "ultimate" expression of nature, humanity is charged with reshaping both itself and nature in terms of the moral law. Humanity's obligation is to produce the "highest good as the *overall* harmony of experience and morality, or as moral nature . . . created by human action (by man's reshaping of the sensuous world in light of a supersensuous idea, and by his creating new social and ecological systems)" (Yovel 1980, 50).[29]

Man protects his humanity through an active and just state. We are also responsible to protect and empower the environment as a functional end through an active policy of government regulation. This duty to nature comes from three practical realizations:

1. The moral integrity of humanity and the functional integrity of nature are interdependent in the greater "whole" or Ecosystem.
2. Human technology presents the greatest challenge to the persistence of this scheme of interdependence.
3. Humanity alone has both the moral capacity and the strategic rationality to express freedom responsibly and to innovate or adapt itself so that interdependence with the environment can persist over time and establish the harmony of human and natural realms.

Although humanity remains critical in its role as moral agent, in the realization of harmony, the duty one has is not only to nature in view of the end of man's autonomy but to nature as a separate and independent causal component of greater Ecosystems, where the interface between humanity and nature requires regulation and where the responsibility to establish harmony is humanity's alone. It becomes immoral for humankind to use a natural system as a means to its own ends without simultaneously treating it as a living, functioning, end-in-itself. Respecting nature does not mean that we never use resources or place the environment at risk or pollute it. Respect is the recognition that nature exists as a total system with capacity, ability, and purpose for perfection within itself, and by its own biological and chemical standards and processes, which command respect independent of us.

Individuals can morally "use" one another as long as they simultaneously respect humanity as an end-in-itself (Kant GW, 428). Through the test of the moral law, humanity can use a natural system if this use is responsible to the intrinsic value of that system and leaves its functional processes intact or enhanced or positively reshaped by the application of the moral law.[30]

> Man is no longer a member among other members in nature. Rather, by virtue of his rational consciousness, he now becomes the focal point of nature itself. . . . [R]eason . . . makes nature itself possible by imparting a logical structure to it. Human reason thus becomes a world-shaping power. (Yovel 1980, 136)

However, if humanity abuses the functional integrity of the environment so that natural cycles are permanently interrupted, species are lost forever, and natural energy and material cycles fail, natural systems will not persist as natural selection and, therefore, evolution ceases. This would be the result of immoral action on the part of humanity, independent of the fact that mankind will eventually cause its own demise by these perturbations (Goodin 1976, 176–77).

Therefore, humanity should be responsible and coordinate choices to establish harmony between natural and artificial worlds. As mankind is charged, through politics, to protect and empower the dignity of the individual, we must also, by the same means, endeavor to protect and empower the functional integrity of natural systems for their own sake as well as our own.

But the imperative to "reshape" nature has an active as well as a protective meaning. In order to reshape, we must first protect and preserve that functionality that allows natural systems persistence in the first place. But the duty to reshape is one to enhance the natural capacity, ability, and purpose of nature as we empower our own autonomy.

Humanity's destiny is tied to nature as nature's is to humanity's. With the governing of the moral law, in our consideration of both human and natural systems, we have a unique definition of environmental ethics that provides for human action, not only to conserve resources and preserve natural function, but also to empower natural evolution through the restoration and enhancement of natural systems' processes.

The imperative to protect and preserve the functional integrity of nature in environmental policy and law might involve any or all of the following: restoring "native" species (e.g., wolves in Yellowstone) and extracting "exotic" ones (e.g., purple loosestrife) from natural systems; not sacrificing nature merely for man's utility maximization; not inflicting synthetic compounds on the environment or technologies that cannot be processed by a system's natural cleaning mechanisms; keeping all pollution to the minimum necessary for supporting human moral integrity and always within the capacity of the natural system

---

to process waste and cleanse itself; recycling or reusing as much of what we need as possible so that the cost of our technological requirements rests on humanity and not on the productive capacity of natural systems; domesticating species necessary to our survival so that the biodiversity of wild species can pursue their functional end within nature; replacing what we take from the environment as compensation in kind for each ecological subsystem (land reclamation, reforestation, purification of the water cycle, etc.); placing the burden of proof on those who would use nature and not on those who would preserve it from use; "allocating natural resources to peaceful uses and to the real needs of man" (Yovel 1980, 196); and, most generally, never imposing a risk on a natural system that has a high probability of irreversible or irrevocable damage to its functional integrity when the elective wants or efficiencies of humans are the only issue.[31]

Although nature can destroy itself and has the capacity to allow one species to die and another to continue to evolve, this internal natural selection is part of the unique capacity and potential of nature, therefore part of its functional properties, and a mark of its intrinsic value that man has a duty to protect and empower. Humanity, in contrast, because it has both technologically and morally transcended nature, must innovate with minimal disturbance of the greater Ecosystem. The human capacity for freedom, and not nature's capacity for causal functioning, puts mutualism and the interdependence of integrities at greatest risk through human perturbation. This is also where our duty lies.

To show proper respect for nature is a subject of justice. Individuals can anticipate the irresponsible expression of freedom through the construction of political institutions within just states that protect and empower not only humanity, but the intrinsic value of nature. The mandate of the just state working for respect of natural systems can be characterized as the imperative to harmonize the freedom of humanity with the structure and function of nature so that the intrinsic value of each is appreciated and one complements the other harmoniously. In this way, the respect humanity shows itself and nature will be rewarded by the persistence of an environment that provides both an evolutionary home, equally, for all human beings, and the life-support system in which every person's practical reason is nurtured and perfected.

For the policymaker attempting to be just to both humanity and nature, the two duties can be simultaneously fulfilled by the same environmental law. In the process of properly conserving those natural resources that we need for our moral autonomy, humanity is ethically required, as a prerequisite, to respect nature as a duty to its unique causal capacity, evolutionary ability, and teleological purpose or potential, that is, its functional integrity. The functional integrity of nature is thus a necessary and primary component of the moral integrity of humanity.

When we make public choices that protect the environment and place the burden of proof on those who would use it to justify use as essential to human ends, we will coincidentally produce the best conditions in which the process of natural selection in nature and the quest for personal autonomy by humanity both find their "highest" expression.

The harmony of integrities gives the imperative to humans to regulate their behavior in such a way that we harm neither ourselves nor nature in any essential, that is, intrinsic way. In this consideration, however, nature has priority because it is vulnerable in the face of humanity's capacity to technologically

innovate.[32]

Kant's Environmental Imperative: Harmonize Humanity and Nature!

It may be that in "creating man nature has transcended itself" (Elster 1979, 16); that, in its "ultimate purpose" (Kant C3, §82), nature has put itself at a disadvantage to its progeny. But because only humanity has a moral dimension, natural systems have a strong call on humanity's moral sensibilities since nature has few options in its ongoing evolutionary gradient climbing but to adapt to what humanity imposes upon it.

The overall moral imperative, the duty of man to nature through political regulation, is to harmonize both types of life on earth: functional and moral. Only with proper self-regulation will humanity, nature, and the interdependent intrinsic values these represent persist into the future, where each enhances the other's quality of life. "It may be the persistence of life itself, of which the forms of life (including man) are multiple investments, which provides the environmental imperative" (Goodpaster 1979, 35 n. 26).

The only species that can be moral, that can assign value to anything, is humanity. Humankind, under the moral law, assigns an intrinsic value to humanity through the moral capacity to be autonomous and to perfect the self as a moral agent. Humanity is also part of the biota, evolved from within the process of natural selection. Placing Kant's theory in an ecological context, we acknowledge humanity is the most complex and perfect product of natural evolution; the highest or ultimate teleological purpose of nature is in humanity (Kant C3, §82). But without human self-regulation, nature can look forward to a continued diminution of its component subsystems until its evolutionary patterns begin to fail.

Overall, the integrity of nature is protected, both as an instrumental resource to humanity and as a functional end-in-itself, through the application of Kant's moral law to individual maxims and to collective juridical law (Zammito 1992, 332). In considering our freedom and the imperatives of morality and justice, we will understand not only how we ought to relate to one another but how we should best handle the Ecosystem interfaces between humanity and natural systems.

Kant states that "without man . . . the whole of creation would be a mere wilderness, a thing in vain, and have no final end" (Kant C3, 442). However, humanity's responsibility is also to ensure that *with* humanity the world does not become "a thing in vain," but is enhanced by the ethical conduct of its most versatile species.

> This dictum does not mean that the appearance of man as a *natural* being supplies the rest of nature with a teleological center to which all others are

subservient. On the contrary, if man were just another link in nature, creation would still be "a thing in vain and have no final end." The universe needs man so that he, as a free and conscious creature, can *confer* its final end on the world and change himself and nature in such a way as to realize it. (Yovel 1980, 179–80)

A Kantian environmental ethics is comprehensive because it grants morally relevant value to nature both in terms of the conservation of resources for human perfection and in terms of nature's intrinsic functional value as a component of greater Ecosystems. Kant supports an ideal-regarding concern for both human and natural perfection and steers policy toward those laws that would increase harmony between humanity and nature and consider the environment as a necessary element both to human freedom and to the "highest good" of biospheric evolution. Kantian philosophy provides just public policy for humanity and nature simultaneously. Beginning with two concepts of intrinsic value, he prescribes a policy that considers the environment as an entity unto itself and worthy of equal representation in the definition of justice and ethical perfection.

If Kant is a human-centered ethicist, he is able to provide the tools for a distinct and unique approach to environmental policy argument that respects Ecosystems as interfaces between humanity and nature where each has an integrity that is interdependent and critical to just public choice.

Nominally, Kant belongs with those for whom man is the center of creation. Yet for Kant man's preeminence is not given and automatically guaranteed; . . . man enjoys a central position not by virtue of what he is, but by virtue of what he *ought* to do and to become. He must *make* himself the center of creation by using his practical reason to determine its end and by consciously acting to realize it. (Yovel 1980, 180)

Kant's categorical imperative requires humanity to overcome fear with morality and to use intellectually approved principle to navigate in a world of uncertainty. In this search for moral autonomy, humanity finds not only itself and social justice, but also a respect for, and harmony with, nature. Our application of practical reason to environmental questions requires the equal and conscious consideration of nature as the prior functional component of a greater, ongoing, evolutionary process (Kant C3, 449 n).

With a definition of the Kantian world system and its component Ecosystems, containing human and natural systems as these interface and create a biosphere compatible with the demands of the moral law, a nonmarket standard results upon which to build alternative public policy arguments. This model defines a just environmental policy as one that equally considers the intrinsic requirements of both humanity and nature; that is, it considers what autonomous choice demands of moral agents in dealing with one another as well what that choice demands of the moral agent in dealing with environmental media and species.

This chapter has defined what it means to be a practical reasoner within an Ecosystem. We have argued that intrinsic value based on capacity, ability, and purpose is the source of respect for both nature and the practical reasoner, and we have derived Kantian duties to nature as well as to humanity in the person. If practical reason in moral agency is the deontological purpose of humanity and evolutionary function is the purpose of natural systems, then justice must consider both in its conceptualization, formulation, and implementation of environmental policy, if the eventual harmony of a Realm of Ends with a Realm of Nature (Kant's definition of Ecosystem) is to become a reality.

The basis for the legitimate use of policy toward this end, in view of Kant's fundamental assumption about how practical reason is made manifest in the strategic nature of interpersonal collective action, is our next subject of concern.

Notes to Chapter 5

1. This I will later define as a distinction between critical and positive or conventional morality (see chap. 8).
2. This would include the preferences of the person.
3. These are the two ethical duties one has to oneself: specifically a duty to the "preservation of one's nature" and a duty to one's "moral prosperity" or perfection of oneself as an ethical person (Kant MV, 419).
4. See especially the Lincoln-Douglas debates in Lincoln [1858] 1989.
5. Kant defines autonomy and heteronomy as follows: "The sensuous nature of rational beings in general is their existence under empirically conditioned laws, and therefore it is, from the point of view of heteronomy. The supersensuous nature of the same beings, on the other hand, is their existence according to laws that are independent of all empirical conditions and that therefore belong to the autonomy of pure reason" (Kant C2, 43). Here, I read "independence" in terms of the determination of the moral maxim.
6. I believe that Kant still sees a role for government, even within a Kingdom of Ends, as he recognizes that collective-action problems would still be a problem, even among the morally predisposed. This is the subject of the next chapter.
7. The answer is that to disobey a just civil law is to deny one's own humanity.
8. Other examples would include the Penal Laws in Ireland and South African apartheid.
9. This is the same mix of principle and value that I described in the maxim of action.
10. See my section on Kantian communitarianism at the end of chapter 6.
11. Most "modern" ethical philosophies (e.g., those of Locke, Rousseau, and Hegel) were written when human relations with the environment were marked by perceived plenty rather than scarcity, and when the idea that humanity could seriously affect nature was eclipsed by human fear of natural systems and their power over individual life. They, therefore, did not consider environmental ethics.
12. The reader should be aware that my argument is predicated upon a nonstandard definition of "intrinsic" or "inherent" value that is not identical to current usage and that makes no distinction between these two terms. I assume that "inherent" and "intrinsic" are interchangeable terms for the same concept of noninstrumental value, which is different only in its application to humanity (where it has an individual *moral* foundation) as distinguished from nature (where it has a systemic *functional* foundation). Therefore, the core distinction is between instrumental and intrinsic value. Moral status in human deliberation is a function of classification by

type of value (Plant 1991; Sagoff 1988). The individual (or collective) will orient itself toward everything it encounters in the world and grant it a status as either something that can be used to one's benefit, having only instrumental value, or something that has a status independent of its human use, which grants it an intrinsic value. The basic dichotomy between instrumental and intrinsic value is the foundation upon which all moral philosophies and personal ethical calculations are made, and it is the starting point for anyone interested in the moral status of any entity in the human lexicon of ethical evaluation (see NML in Audi 1995, 829–30).

13. In her essay (1992), Harlow defines four senses in which the value of nature might be considered "humanly independent" (28). To quote her "(1) we might want to say that the value of natural objects and processes is not reducible to human interests and preferences; (2) we might want to say that the value of natural objects and processes is not reducible to the value of human experiences or form of consciousness excited by them; (3) we might want to say that the value of natural objects and processes is independent of human good; or (4) we might want to claim that the value of nature and its processes is independent of human consciousness altogether" (28). My argument is that rather than being a classically anthropocentric ethics, Kant's moral and political thought supports the independence of nature on all of these counts. Even the last, which, although it does not make sense in terms of the moral value of nature, which is impossible without human consciousness, makes sense for Kant in terms of the prior independence of time, space, and organic organization in a scientific or theoretical sense (Kant C1).

14. Here "Ecosystem" is not understood as a synonym for nature but is the combination of human systems and natural systems. My use of biosphere is also nontraditional in that it does not equal nature but includes humanity.

15. For a look at world systems, see Jantsch and Waddington 1976.

16. For an examination of how environmental political theory has evolved and how conservation and preservation have defined themselves over time, see Taylor 1992.

17. Lewis White Beck puts it this way: "Nature produced man but brought him to the stage where he can finally assert his independence of her" (1960, 125). For Kant's argument about humanity's transcendence of nature, see Kant UH.

18. Logicians call it a category mistake when one uses a term to connote a quality that a particular class of actors does not have. In this way saying that an animal has rights is like saying snow has a consciousness. Although it can be a logical and moral possibility that a human acted unjustly in killing another living entity, it may make neither logical nor moral sense to say that a wolf acted unjustly when it killed its prey, or should be held responsible for murder.

19. The only specific reference he makes to the mere use of nature is in the use by humans of those natural products that they grow themselves with the help of civil society (Kant MJ, 344–46). These "natural products," which are considered "artifacts" of human social production, are reduced to the status of things only by their existence as artifacts. However, in general, the components of natural systems, especially in the wild, are not classified as artifacts.

20. This might be defined as Kantian sustainability.

21. Kant's treatment of property and human use of it (MJ, 258–71) may hold lessons for the application of the moral law to environmental policy. Specifically, the idea that property is a necessary prerequisite to human freedom is a powerful argument for Kantian conservationism.

22. Two points: First, it is controversial to attribute a "teleology" to nature. I would argue that this is because one is transferring what is a moral, goal-directed, agency-based attribute of a person to natural systems. I will assert here that as Kant has two definitions of intrinsic value, one for humanity and one for nature, he also argues for two concepts of teleology, the human variant having moral content, while the one used to describe nature is functional. For my purposes, "teleol-

ogy" applied to nature simply means that natural systems have dynamic and systemic functional properties that change over time, sometimes to more complexity, sometimes to less. I assume with Golly (1993) that the concept of natural systems evolution does not need to be strictly deterministic, and with Simberloff (1980) and Williams (1966, chap. 5) that natural systems behavior can be assumed to have a stochastic element that can be compensated for by the model used to explain it (O'Neill et al. 1986). This is not unlike the inclusion of stochastic components in statistical models that predict human behavior (see Manheim and Rich 1986; Hanushek and Jackson 1977). Pimm (1991, 131) covers the bases when he argues that "[e]ven the most simple models of population change show a variety of behaviors that include a simple return to equilibrium, cycles, cycles on cycles, and chaos." Perhaps evolution as natural selection is a two-step process where randomness in stage one is combined with tendencies toward natural harmony in step two so that "only that which maintains or increases the harmony of the system will be selected" (Mayr 1976, 24–25). Or perhaps Von Schilcher and Tennant (1984, 72) are correct when they write that "[e]volution can thus be seen as a climb up a mountainside with resting points in sheltered spots; a ratchet-like ridge with stopping places separated by slippery slopes." Overall, from my perspective, teleology or purpose applied to nature is a causal-functional teleology of nature's nonhuman subsystems that finds changes of complexity in natural selection where evolution is progressive while it shows elements of entropy (Brooks and Wiley, 1988).

Second, for years there have been efforts (see Riley 1983) to describe Kant's politics as dependent on his teleology as put forth in the Third Critique (C3). Elsewhere (Gillroy 1992c) I have argued that the politics does not require Kant's teleology but is a direct outgrowth of his moral theory applied juridically. While I still contend that Kant's politics is deontological, I have found a new role for Kant's teleology in building a bridge between the realm of nature and the realm of ends. In this way, consciousness of Kant's two definitions of teleology might be necessary for environmental policy in particular.

23. I will avoid the use of the concept of functional autonomy, since with humanity as an agent-cause, nature is no longer autonomous, though it does have an independent definition of "functional" resilience and persistence or integrity.
24. An environmental ethics like conservationism is one that places the value of humanity at the center and describes all nonhuman entities as having value only to the extent they can be used by humanity (e.g., a tree is only board-feet of lumber and a rain forest ecosystem only present and future drugs for human health) (Taylor 1992, chap. 1). It is therefore both anthropomorphic and anthropocentric. Other approaches, like deep ecology (Devall and Sessions 1985), are only anthropomorphic in that they attribute human characteristics to ecosystems (e.g., rights, duties) but not anthropocentric in that they value humanity and natural systems equally as one natural and interdependent system.
25. It is true that, for eons, nature persisted without humanity. My point is that now, since Ecosystems are made up of the interaction of human and natural systems, each has an effect on the evolution and persistence of the other.
26. Here "reshaping" includes human contact with, and influence and manipulation of the natural world.
27. Let us remember that the physical conditions of the Realm of Ends are achieved through the creation of a just society.
28. One would have to argue that God had merely instrumental value. Kant does not.
29. This has been characterized as *Darstellung*, or "the externalization of morality in the natural world" (Yovel 1980, 70–71).
30. Treating natural systems as having intrinsic functional value involves not only a "negative" policy of noninterference but also a "positive" restoration-and-enhancement policy that empowers natural capacity, ability, and purpose. With-

out the support of humanity, with its scientific efforts to save species and to reinvigorate natural systems processes, one could argue that nature can look forward to a continued diminution of its component subsystems as entropy overcomes ecosystem organization, homeostasis fails, and evolutionary patterns cease. This may be the true basis of mutualism between humanity and the environment.

31. Respect for the functional integrity of the natural system is for the whole, for the connections between organisms and levels of organization and, unlike respect for moral integrity, does not concern each individual organism.

32. The Kantian approach is here more conscious of the unique capabilities of humanity than, for example, deep ecology (Devall and Sessions 1985). For the deep ecologist, humanity is equal to nature and just another class of organism with no special capacities or abilities.

6

Justice from Autonomy: Collective Action

The individual moral agent, struggling for full practical reason, would find challenge enough in seeking and responding to a private search for virtue if it were indeed a strictly private effort. However, Kant recognizes that individuals exist in a social, economic, and political environment, made up of other people making decisions and choices that influence not only their own lives but the lives of others. Moral agency is, as we have seen, a creature of both internal capacity and external ability that together find purpose in moral agency and practical reason. In this chapter we will concern ourselves with Kant's argument about the ideal social contract, property, community, or the collective environment in which this potential practical reasoner perfects his or her moral agency.

Practical Reason and Strategic Rationality

Before we proceed with the constructive argument of this chapter, however, let us take a moment to examine the differences between practical reason and "mere" rationality. The "rational" actor is the basic unit of game theory (Goodin 1976; Taylor 1976, 1987; Luce and Raffia 1957) and the characterization of the individual assumed within the market paradigm. For this reason, the rational agent must be our point of departure for any alternative (in this case Kantian) argument that redefines agency and collective action, setting a distinct normative standard for public choice.

The theory of games is an effort by social scientists and philosophers to understand the interactive strategic frameworks in which people individually and jointly deliberate, choose, and act. These frameworks acknowledge that the outcomes of individual decision making are not directly causal from personal choice but, rather, are the result of the confluence of the choices of one with the choices of others. Each person's payoff in the game, what one gains or loses from the interaction, is a function of how one's choices coordinate or fail to co-ordinate with the choices of others.

All game theory, however, assumes that each person, facing a game environment (one's choices and the choices of others), is rational. This rationality has a common definition and provides the foundation for all further analysis of human collective action. Here, "rationality" is defined as a combination of individual self-interest, personal knowledge of the circumstances of choice, and the aptitude to order and satisfy one's preferences so that individual utility is increased (Sen 1970, chap. 1).

All agents are assumed to have the ability to order their alternative choices so that this order is complete, transitive, and asymmetrical; that is, all alternatives are considered either superior to, inferior to, or equal to all others. This order does not cycle; if X is preferred to Y, which is preferred to Z, then Z is not preferred to X, and no one choice is simultaneously superior and inferior to another. Overall, to be rational, one can place material alternatives in order using one's preferences without internal contradictions or cycles in that order (Sen 1970, chap. 1*; Goodin 1976, 10).

This *economic* rationality (Barry 1978a, esp. chap. 2) is employed within an intellect that considers only what Kant would call hypothetical imperatives. Rationality, as knowledgeable self-interest rendering a preference order, is employed by the individual to ascertain goals or producible ends and the means by which these desires can be obtained. This is a means-ends rationality that seeks to improve the preference satisfaction of the person through recognizing his or her capacity both to know what he or she wants and to get it.

Kant would not call this capacity moral, but heteronomous (C2, 33–34) and egoistic (Sidgwick [1907] 1981, bk. 2), being determined directly by stimulation from the environment with no mediation by the autonomous will. Such a capacity to fulfill one's desires and satisfy oneself, can be described essentially as self-sufficient. Each person is assumed to have the required knowledge to recognize his or her desires, order preferences for those desires, and make decisions to satisfy the resultant wants.[1] Such intellectual operations are considered to be accessible only to the individual and exist without the help or intercession of others in defining desires, goals, or preferences. Each person entering the collective environment is, by definition, rationally self-sufficient (Mishan 1982b, 43–45).[2]

As we have seen, Kant's vision of the "rational" individual is more complex. For Kant, rationality, or "technically practical reason" (Kant AT, 271), is only a preliminary condition for the individual trying to become a practically reasoning moral agent. The capacity to will autonomously and the ability to express moral will in one's choices is a continuous and stressful process of individual struggle for character that may have, at its core, a rationality resembling the "economic" variety, but which requires more from the person than reliance on this primitive form of deliberation.

To achieve the status of a practical reasoner one begins with a basic rationality but also possesses a sense of the moral law and the duties required by it. One is not assumed to have "consumer sovereignty" (Friedman 1984, 27–28) or all relevant knowledge for any decision, but one has a duty to acquire it in moral matters. Nor is it assumed that true moral agency requires or is even supported by self-sufficiency. True autonomy, expressed as moral agency, may require the aid, protection, cooperation, and empowerment of others (Kuflik 1984, 273; Gillroy 1992a, 1992c).

For Kant, character is both ideal-regarding and want-regarding (Barry 1990), composed of both a predisposition to be moral and a predilection toward indulgence of one's self-interest. The practical reasoner handles both categorical and hypothetical imperatives in the struggle for moral agency and must contain the latter to nonmoral questions if self-interest is not to override one's duty in moral matters.[3]

Eventually, one's basic self-interest will evolve into what Kant calls rational self-love (Kant C2, 73) as individuals form stable moral characters built on the application of the moral law to their lives. At this sophisticated level, the individual can do more than order and express preference in means-ends calculation. He can deliberate and express himself as a moral agent in both hypothetical and categorical imperatives. He is a practical reasoner with a deliberative process that can appreciate intrinsic as well as instrumental value.

Therefore, when we speak of strategic rationality in the context of Kant's characterization of collective action, we are speaking about strategic rationality as an element of the deliberative intellect of the moral agent, and not as the totality or complete manifestation of individual reasoning capacity. As the Kantian strategic actor enters life's strategic social environment, she is mindful that what is of critical concern is the effect that joint decision making has on the capacity and ability of each moral agent to transcend his or her mere rationality: protecting, empowering, and refining his or her practical reason in the process of cooperation.

Moral Agency and Collective Action

We have argued that, in addition to one's internal capacity to be autonomous, the human is a strategically rational actor. Elster (1979) maintains that humanity is a unique species because of this strategic ability; that is, being human, the individual can take "account of the fact that the environment is made up of other actors, and that he is part of their environment, and that they know this" (Elster 1979, 18). People can innovate, overcoming the process of natural selection that dictates the behavior of all other species, who have only the parametric rationality to adapt in isolation, without regard for others, to an environment that they perceive to be a constant. In Kantian terms, one might say that humans can create their surroundings as well as be created by them. "We may say that *in creating man natural selection has transcended itself.* This leap implies a transition from the nonintentional adaptation, . . . to intentional and deliberate adaptation (Elster 1979, 16). If we assume that man has the moral capacity that Kant describes as practical reason, as well as the ability to be a strategically rational agent, we are describing an individual who has a prior tendency or predisposition to respect his own and others' humanity. But this person can react to the behavior of others through his expectations, and protect his own basic agency even at the cost of its moral dimension. We can define this as a component of the distinction between agency and moral agency. Although an individual is predisposed to actualize full autonomy and act as a moral agent, one's physical existence and bare-bones strategic rationality, as prerequisites to life, may overcome one's moral predisposition in the determination of choice. Also, one's basic duty to oneself, according to the moral law, involves the preservation of one's "animal nature" (Kant MV, 419–20), so the protection of life has both prudential and moral incentives. Thus, the possibility exists that under stress, a moral agent may find that his or her rationality as well as practical reason make self-preservation a priority.

The expectations a policymaker can take into deliberations regarding any person's ultimate behavior then depend on the expectations each person is perceived to have about the actions of others, and how these will affect their development and expression of moral autonomy. In Kantian terms, a person's behavior involves, not only practical reason, but also prudence (Kant AT, 270–72) in the struggle for character, described in the previous chapter. In a world of fear and uncertainty about the behavior of others, one is tempted to employ self-interest in a prudential effort for self-preservation, even at the cost of personal autonomy. In a world of scarce resources and great competition, one fears the lack of property and opportunity for that expression of positive freedom necessary to survive. Even if one acted morally under these circumstances, one would have no assurance that others will act in a morally autonomous way. Such considerations place stress on one's choice (*Willkür*) to fulfill desire and ignore reason, so that one's existence is made secure, even against the worst behavior of others. Although one may be predisposed to will autonomously, and still could, even in the face of such adversity, the temptation is to err on the side of prudence and protect one's self, even at the cost of one's freedom.

Kant contends that this instinct for self-preservation in an atmosphere of uncertainty breeds a "mania for domination" (Kant AT, 273). Fed by fear and the mistaken belief that the accumulation of power and resources will protect one's security and will compensate for any lost freedom by enriched continued physical existence, the individual forsakes morality and succumbs to the pressure of inclination in the determination of his actions and character. Inclination instructs him to protect himself by gaining as much power over persons and resources as possible so that if anyone is exploited by others, it is not likely to be him.

> This inclination comes closest to technically practical reason, that is, to the maxim of prudence. For getting other men's inclinations into our power, so that we can direct and determine them according to our own purposes, is almost the same as processing other men as mere tools of our will. No wonder that the striving for this kind of power to influence other men becomes a passion. (Kant AT, 271)

Passion, as desire satisfaction, is a contender for the determination of the will in the struggle for character, but one that cannot obtain moral worth for the maxims it recommends. Indeed Kant maintains that the use of others, even in self-protection, is inherently unjust "because it is contrary to freedom under the [moral] law" (Kant AT, 273), which requires that the harmony of wills never treat any one merely as a means to some person's subjective ends. In addition to being immoral, such exploitative behavior is also imprudent in the long run.

Kant points out that denying the freedom of one in the name of another exploits people and "arouses their opposition" (Kant AT, 273), causing breaches of the peace that then disrupt society. In exploiting a person, one fails to utilize one's moral agency in the ethical expression of positive freedom; one violates the categorical imperative. Simultaneously, one denies those they exploit the freedom they require for expression of their full moral agency. If one person exploits another for purposes of his self-preservation, the moral freedom of both parties is undermined. If the exploited become violent, the exploiter will find it necessary to restrict his own freedom more and more, spending an increasing amount of energy and resources defending himself, instead of perfecting his autonomy toward a Realm of Ends as his moral duty prescribes (Korsgaard 1996, chaps. 6 and 7). In addition, his focus moves from predominant concern for public or universal ends to concern for private or unilateral ends, which empowers self-interest in the struggle for character and places the effort toward a just society in limbo, making the failure to cooperate jointly exploitative to all.

If there are both moral and prudential reasons that tell against such behavior and "its manifestation provokes everyone to oppose it" (Kant AT, 273), then how does such uncooperative behavior come about? How does life on earth foil the realization of a Realm of Ends? The answer lies in the strategic considerations each person takes into his dealings with others, and how the struggle for character is affected by the context of one's life as practical reason and strategic rationality vie for domination of the individual's decision process. Hobbes correctly argued that although moral imperatives may hold intellectually, they do not always hold in terms of the ability of an agent to negotiate the realm of civil society and strategic interaction.

> The Lawes of Nature oblige *in foro interno*: that is to say they bind to a desire they should take place: but *in foro externo*; that is, to the putting them in act, not always. For he that should be modest, and tractable, and performs all he promises, in such time, and place, where no man els should do so, should but make himselfe a prey to others, and procure his own certain ruine, contrary to the ground of all Lawes of Nature, which tend to Natures preservation. (Hobbes [1651] 1968, 215)

Though one may be predisposed, in Kantian terms, to observe the moral law, as an objective condition of his freedom and autonomy this can only always be expected to hold *in foro interno*. The reality of the external world, the competition for resources and survival itself, and one's expectations about the priorities of others may cause one to fear that this moral behavior will be exploited by others, causing one's moral and physical ruination. At this point, one's desire for personal security may override reason and determine one's will, compromising one's autonomy. In this way, a person's mania for domination finds that its "origin . . . is fear of being dominated by others: [one] tries to avert this by getting a head start and dominating them" (Kant AT, 273).

The individual's struggle for character and the ramifications of his choices within the strategic environment that sorts and integrates every person's actions can be better understood within the language and formal structures of game theory, where the origin and maintenance of collective action will be defined by the ability of individuals to cooperate in the provision of collective goods.

In chapter 2 we defined the polluter's dilemma as the pertinent metaphor for the collective-action problem within the market paradigm. We also examined the need for central coordination and for anticipatory institutions in the case of freeing the imprisoned rider in environmental-risk cases. Here, we shall see how the prisoner's dilemma differs from the assurance game, and how the latter is a better description of Kant's collective-action problem.

From the Prisoner's Dilemma to the Assurance Game

The polluter's/prisoner's dilemma (see fig. 2.1), identified as the primary strategic metaphor for the provision of collective goods, has been a point of departure for our analysis of environmental risk and market assumptions. Modern theorists (Gauthier 1969; Hampton 1986; Kavka 1986; Kraus 1993) have traced the philosophical origins of the prisoner's dilemma scenario to Thomas Hobbes ([1651] 1968, part 2). The logic of self-interested rationality bringing less than optimal collective outcomes receives its first complete treatment in Hobbes's arguments about the origin of government.

In the move from a state of nature to civil society, Hobbes, in describing this structure of strategic interaction, recommends that men contract with one another to set up a sovereignty that coordinates and maintains an optimal and mutually cooperative equilibrium (R1,C1) rather than the noncooperative status-quo equilibrium (R2,C2), which results from both players choosing their dominant strategy without central guidance. The sovereign establishes the cooperative outcome, but for Hobbes, the problem is to maintain it over time. He assumes individuals merely to be self-interested and therefore always inclined to break the agreed contract and free ride on others' cooperation, if this act will increase their own subjective payoffs. The individual, after all, prefers unilateral defection to joint cooperation.

Kant conceives of the collective-action problem, as well as its assumptions about the individual, their preferences, and what reasonable terms of cooperation might be, differently. When he describes the incentive of the individual to leave the state of nature and move into a civil society, he characterizes it, not as a situation where the "rational" predisposition to be self-interested is the dominant characteristic of the person, but as one where the moral predisposition to cooperate must be protected and empowered in its expression so that self-interest does not overcome it.

Kant argues that for obligations under the moral law to hold, *in foro externo*, one must be assured that an expression of moral agency will not be exploited by the self-interested acts of others. Specifically, Kant is concerned about rightful ownership and the stability of possessions (which are the subject of a future section of this chapter). He argues that the moral law requires property for the expression of positive freedom and that the "mutual obligation" of each to all that creates stability of property, in mutual respect, requires that we leave the state of nature behind and seek a just, civil state of affairs so that we may be assured that our moral actions will not be unilateral.

> I am therefore under no obligation to leave external objects belonging to others untouched unless everyone else provides me assurance that he will behave in accordance with the same principle with regard to what is mine. . . . So it is only a will putting everyone under obligation, hence only a collective general (common) and powerful will, that can provide everyone this assurance. . . . [T]he condition of being under a general external (i.e., public) lawgiving accompanied with power is the civil condition. (Kant MJ, 255–56)

To will remaining in a state of nature is, under these conditions, to act immorally and to do "wrong." The decision against the civil society not only puts one's possessions, which are necessary to one's positive freedom, at risk, but also places one's moral duties to protect and perfect one's essence, one's moral capacities, in jeopardy.

> No one is bound to refrain from encroaching on what another possesses if the other gives him no equal assurance that he will observe the same restraint toward him. . . . Given the intention to be and to remain in this state of externally lawless freedom [a state of nature] . . . they do wrong in the highest degree by willing to be and to remain in a condition that is not rightful, that is, in which no one's existence (essence) as a person is assured against violence. (Kant MJ, 307–08)

The end of seeking justice is therefore, in Kantian terms, the search for assurance against putting one's possessions and one's essence as a moral person at risk in the material world. The search, based on the moral law, finds its origin in the stability and use of property for the expression of positive freedom and requires that one cooperate in the evolution from a state of nature to a just civil condition. The moral law demands that justice assure each citizen that expression of his or her moral essence will not be exploited. While justice protects and empowers the external person, it also encourages the expression of moral capacity and the fulfillment of ethical duty, in one and all, equally. Government, beyond the state of nature, is a necessary juridical or political step to that collective assurance that encourages the full realization of individual morality.

> [T]he citizen's inclination to do violence to one another is counteracted by a more powerful force—that of government. This not only gives the whole

a veneer of morality (*causae non causae*), but by putting an end to outbreaks of lawless proclivities, it genuinely makes it much easier for the moral capacities of persons to develop into an immediate respect for right. For each individual believes of himself that he would by all means maintain the sanctity of the concept of right and obey it faithfully, if only he could be certain that all others would do likewise, and the government in part guarantees this for him; thus a great step is taken toward morality (although this is still not the same as a moral step), toward a state where the concept of duty is recognized for its own sake, irrespective of any possible gain in return. (Kant PP, 376 n)

Kant is not describing a prisoner's dilemma, but an assurance game (Sen 1967, 1973; Elster 1979, 20–22).[4] The preference structure of these games is essentially different. The order of the top two preferences is reversed so that the individual is said to prefer a joint cooperative solution to unilateral defection. However, the worst outcome and the least desirable preference, unilateral cooperation, is the same as in a prisoner's dilemma, for the individual still fears exploitation more than anything else. The uncoordinated equilibrium is still at (R2,C2), resulting from mutual fear of domination (figure 6.1).

A Kantian approach to the collective-action problem assumes that individuals, given proper and equal freedom of choice and unencumbered by extreme pressure of desire, would prefer to act autonomously, self-actualizing their good wills. In the assurance game, the failure of active central coordination and full information to set proper expectations allows fear to dominate one's moral predisposition in the choice of a strategy.

Active regulation and information dissemination is more critical to an assurance game than to a prisoner's dilemma. The assurance game has its greatest challenge, not in maintaining cooperation once established, but at the origin of collective action, which establishes the collectively optimal equilibrium. Because the highest preference of the person is mutual cooperation, once coordination has been established individuals have no further reason to defect from cooperation and free ride.[5] In an assurance game, unlike a prisoner's dilemma, there is no dominant strategy choice (i.e., no strategy that is best no matter what any of the other players choose to do); therefore, it is not always prudent to defect. However, whether one chooses to defect or to cooperate is now dependent on how one agent perceives the expected behavior of the other agents. If she perceives they will cooperate, she will; if the expectation is defection, free riding will ensue. To encourage cooperation, it becomes critical that expectations and information be supplied and supported by central coordinators to assure each person's choice of behavior against the others, and end, or at least control, the "mania for domination" that results when self-interest takes advantage of uncertainty.

In the prisoner's dilemma the requirement of full information is not necessary for the solution to emerge, but in the assurance game the slightest uncertainty or suspicion will make an actor choose [to defect] rather than [cooperate]. Only in a fully transparent situation will the actors converge

Player no. 2

	C1 Cooperate	C2 Defect
R1 Cooperate	1 1	2 4
Defect R2	4 2	3 3

Player no. 1

	Cooperate	Defect
Cooperate	1*	4
Defect	2	3*

Player no. 1
Playoffs in Isolation

The ordinal preferences of each player are:

    (1) Best—Universal Cooperation
    (2) Second—Unilateral Defection
    (3) Third—Universal Defection
    (4) Worst—Unilateral Cooperation

The preference and rational logic of an assurance game:

    The logic here describes a rationality of intention to cooperate with an underlying capacity and ability to exploit. Unlike the prisoner's dilemma, in which exploitation is the best alternative for the player, in the assurance game, the cooperative solution is preferred but the ability to exploit looms as a pertinent consideration of each player's strategic rationality. The worst reality for each player is still exploitation in unilateral cooperation, and even a failure to coordinate at all is a better option than being exploited. Without communication or central regulation to assure each player that he or she will not be exploited in the decision to cooperate (be a moral person) the game can degenerate into a fight for survival and a ruination of collective action as each player, fearing that he or she will be exploited, moves to exploit the other.

    The precarious nature of the intention to cooperate, and the critical nature of outside signals to the individual playing the game, can be seen in the fact that the assurance game has no dominant strategy (see player no. 1's isolated payoffs). If one is assured that the other player will cooperate, then one prefers to cooperate oneself; however, if no such assurance is understood, then one prefers to defect and protect him- or herself. Unlike a prisoner's dilemma, in which each player prefers to defect whatever the other players do, an assurance game lacks a dominant strategy, making one player's payoffs contingent on the decisions of others. The uncertainty of this game, without a dominant strategy, makes the role of central coordination very important and the specter of the "mania for domination" even more real than in the prisoner's dilemma.

FIGURE 6.1
The Assurance Game

upon the collectively rational behavior. Given perfect information, the difference between the two games may be expressed by saying that in the prisoner's dilemma the optimum [(R1,C1)] is both individually inaccessible (no one will take the first step toward it) and individually unstable (everyone will take the first step away from it), whereas in the assurance game it is individually inaccessible and individually stable. (Elster 1979, 21)

In both game frameworks, the need for central coordination is identical, but the fact that the assurance game results in a more stable equilibrium, because of the distinct preference structure, gives the strategic reality of the game a Kantian flavor.[6] The individual in an assurance game gains an inherent moral character denied to him in the self-interested rationality of the prisoner's dilemma. Establishing cooperation focuses less on force and constriction of human freedom and more on the full negative freedom of opportunity and information necessary to the establishment of mutual moral expectations. The collective security resulting from assurance allows moral will to overcome the pressure of fear and exploitation and to determine choice. Kant can contend that a collective situation, if one grants an equal distribution of negative freedom from desire, fear, and uncertainty, will allow a full and equal realization of each person's inherent positive freedom of the will at the social level. Such is the logic of an assurance game.

The Kantian individual is therefore only prudent in self-defense and would prefer to live in a collective condition where he could empower his moral character, and use his practical reason, free from the fear of domination by others. Perfection of one's autonomy and preservation of the physical self are both ethical duties, but as such, these can work at cross-purposes in certain external circumstances, where the duty to preserve one's existence becomes centered, not on perfection of one's autonomy, which would cause one to compromise his life, but on physical security, elevated in importance by the uncertainty and fear one finds oneself dealing with.

A collective environment that encourages individual moral behavior is just. A just government finds a role in the assurance it gives that each person will not have to fear for his life or his basic entitlement in the expectation that he will be dominated by others. A government seeking justice can prevent the situation wherein the fear that one's moral predispositions will be exploited by the choices of others forces one to compromise his exercise of practical reason.

Politics establishes a system of mutual constraints that protects each person against all others, allowing the atmosphere of negative freedom necessary to the full and equal development of each citizen's positive freedom (autonomy of the will). Expectations are then set by a government that establishes justice as a public duty to the moral agency of its citizens according to the moral law, which must recognize and deal with the collective strategic reality of human society if it is to encourage the realization of the Kingdom of Ends.

Therefore, politics is not necessary because of man's evil nature (Williams 1983, 64–66), but because humans live in a world of strategic interaction that can make it difficult for even the best-intentioned individual to coordinate his or her choices with the actions of others without letting his or her reason, his or her moral will, be overridden by negative expectations about one's compatriots. "But since each individual, despite his good opinion of himself, assumes bad faith in everyone else, men thereby pass judgment on one another to effect that they are worth little in point of fact" (Kant PP, 376 n). The strategic nature of an unsolved collective-action problem and not an inherent limitation of the individual corrupts morality for the sake of prudence. In this situation, without the assurance of justice, one may forsake human capacity for animal choice.

> A choice that can be determined by pure reason is called a free choice. A choice that is determined only by inclination (sensuous impulses) would be an animal choice (*arbitrium brutum*). Human choice . . . is the kind of choice that is affected but not determined by impulses. (Kant MJ, 213)

To counteract the power of "animal choice" by taking a moral step would require a Realm of Ends. Kant suggests, however, that a nonmoral step to the same objective can be taken through the establishment of a just government (Kant C1, B373; MJ, 229–34, 354; MV, 388; PP, 376 n).

A just society is a material possibility that supports equal freedom of the will for all, in a jointly cooperative solution to the assurance game that is a juridical move toward moral community. By contrast, the Realm of Ends is a moral or ethical state commanded by the moral law through the categorical imperative, but dependent on each individual's (internal) motivation by a good will. If all individuals were virtuous and behaved freely despite strategic inclinations to the contrary, then the Realm of Ends would be accessible to them. However, one cannot be forced to have a good will because one's virtue is about motivation and is therefore internal to his capacity of reason and not accessible to external coercive efforts to influence it.

Justice, through politics and the policy process that designs its rules and institutions, only consists of external coercion and is not able to create a Realm of Ends by itself. Government's role is to establish justice by solving the collective-action problem presented by the assurance game. This solution requires the state to distribute negative freedom equally and, in this way, to allow each person the best chance at independent moral self-actualization. Politics achieves this by setting a standard for political coordination in a concept of justice drawn from the moral law.[7] In this way, it coordinates by means of a positive law that is just because it is drawn from the categorical imperative.

The collective application of the moral law though the civil law is an effort to create a society in which the harmony of negative freedom of choice empowers the predisposition toward good, generating autonomous thought and agency in every citizen. To set up a political community and provide for its welfare is then an imperative of one's public moral duty. However, this duty is fulfilled, unlike the Realm of Ends, through civil law in the material world. "[T]he welfare of the state should be seen as that condition in which the constitution most closely approximates to the principles of right; and reason, by the categorical imperative, obliges us to strive for its realization" (Kant MJ, 318). Striving for justice is made manifest, first in the ideal contract, which marks the origin of collective action, and then in Kant's theory of property, which defines the persistence of cooperation over time.

The Ideal Contract and the Origin of Justice

Justice finds its full manifestation in the form of the ideal contract, which transports humanity from a state of nature through civil society to a just state and establishes a constitution that "most closely approximates to the principles of right." The ideal contract is that thought device which provides a bridge between the individual in a state of nature and the citizen of a just society; it is a transitional point in the evolution of political and legal justice. Our examination of the ideal contract begins with Kant's concept of the state of nature.

In Kantian collective-action theory, the state of nature is not conceived as an historical reality but as a premoral condition (before the origin of a just or juridical state), where agency is strategically expressed and counterclaims to property become the basis of interpersonal conflict. For Kant, the acquisition and transfer of property take place in the pursuit of individual freedom, as agents express their practical reason through ownership and use of things.

He argues that original possession is in common (Kant MJ, §13, §16) and that private use is moral only when that use is necessary to the positive freedom of the person (Kant MJ, §11, §17). This private acquisition of property for the expression of positive freedom is the source of collective-action problems and requires that private be "rightful" possession for it to be a true expression of freedom and conducive to collective action. However, private "rightful possession" is impossible, within a state of nature, because the public authority necessary to represent the moral law in the "will of all" and to sanction private right does not exist (Kant MJ, §14; Mulholland 1990, 276–77). Therefore, within a state of nature, private acquisition consistently conflicts with the moral law, and the individual is denied an ethical route to that private property necessary to his or her expression of freedom.

Without the framework of a juridical state, the acquisition of property is immoral, unregulated; and the uncertainty and misinformation prevalent in the state of nature leads to the "mania for domination," initiating a vicious cycle that precipitates violence. Collective action fails as desire for use of property, in a state of nature, becomes based on power, fear, and violence. Only with proper distributive rules, derived from the moral law, can private acquisition become "rightful" and collective action be assured. The incentive to the establishment of the civil society is therefore both moral and political. Private right is necessary for the expression of positive freedom, so it is moral, while it is political in that only the assurance of a state and its just rules of distribution can move property from common to private possession through the moral law.

One does not have to acknowledge the "moral law" to understand that without its application through justice, the expression of individual freedom (autonomy) will be a creature of circumstance and fortune; denied arbitrarily to some at the hands of others. While the exploited will have very restricted freedom, even the exploiters, in fear of losing possession of property owing to the violence caused by their exploitation, will also lose their freedom. They will become more anxious for greater control of the wills of the exploited, and ironically, sacrifice more of the very autonomy they are trying to protect. As Kant describes it, the freedom of each person is dependent on the freedom of all people, according to the moral law. A person need not be an altruist, just a practical reasoner, to acknowledge that a state of affairs in which individual freedom finds optimal, equal, and nonviolent expression ought to be preferred to one where strategic conflict causes violence and instability, thereby inhibiting the moral expression and capabilities of all participants (exploiters and exploited alike).

The *ideal contract* is the means by which Kant establishes the just state from the instability of the state of nature. The contract in this case is neither historical nor hypothetical consent under uncertainty (Rawls 1971; Gillroy 1992c; 2000).[8] The Kantian contract is an ideal/critical construction of reason that makes the constitution of the new juridical state compatible with the demands of the moral law (i.e., that which all rational beings ought to consent to, to preserve their and others' status as necessary ends). The contract is made necessary by the social chaos of the state of nature and assures those essential rights that define one's intrinsic value, protecting it from collective harm.

To initiate his argument about intrinsic value, Kant specifically distinguishes between innate and acquired right, the former belonging "to everyone by nature independent of any juridical act" (Kant MJ, 237), and the latter requiring such an act. There is but one innate right: "Freedom (independence from the constraint of another person's choices) insofar as it is compatible with the freedom of everyone else" in accordance with the moral law (Kant MJ, 237). This right is the "one sole and original right that belongs to every human being by virtue of their humanity" (Kant MJ, 237). The innate right to freedom, implies the "innate equality" (Kant MJ, 238) of all persons in their attempt to gain access to full moral agency.[9]

An innate right to equal freedom is basic to the integrity of each person's moral agency, one's intrinsic value, and provides the point of origin for the respect owed as a duty both to oneself and to others. Only a move to a juridical state can secure this right, this critical moral standard, in positive law. Here, the principles of justice (*Recht*) influence the form and content of codified law (*Gerechtigkeit*), and the state takes on a "universal significance" that is "greater" than the "private interests" of the individual (Mulholland 1990, 303–05).[10]

Kant's argument for the necessity of the state is, however, not Hegel's ([1821] 1978). The freedom of the individual is an innate capacity that does not require the sanction of the state for it to exist, but only to grow to its full potential. A human is endowed with both positive and negative freedom as essential capacities. But will he use his freedom to survive in an unjust environment or to flourish in a just one that recognizes his natural right in positive law? The just society is the only proper political environment for the moral agent. The just coercion of government is necessary for the full and equal scope of negative freedom to be assured to all and to overcome problems of strategic/collective action that may inhibit positive freedom's reaching its optimum expression, both individually and collectively.

As a solution to the assurance game, the ideal contract in Kantian ethics does not focus on the distinction between a state of nature (*Natürliche Zustand*) and any civil society (*Gesellschaftliche Zustand*), but on the transition between a state of nature and a certain type of civil society: a juridical or just state (*Rechtlicher Zustand*) that has a system of distributive justice equal to the demands of the moral law (Kant MJ, 306–08). The assurance game is not solved with the advent of a civil society (*Bürgerliche Gesellschaft*), but only with the advent of a just society that assures each that his moral behavior will not be infringed upon or exploited by the behavior of another (Kant RL, 93–98; MJ, 306–08). The contract that solves the assurance game seals a transition between an unjust condition, be it a state of nature or a less than just civil society, and a social condition where the principles of right are applied, through a constitution, to the positive law of the land.[11]

A constitution allowing *the greatest possible freedom* in accordance with the laws by which *the freedom of each is made to be consistent with that of all others*—I do not speak of the greatest happiness, for this will follow of itself—is at any rate a necessary idea, which must be taken as fundamental not only in first projecting a constitution but in all its law. (Kant C1, B373)

The prior role of the moral law in the definition of justice differentiates Kant's theory of collective action from either Hobbes's ([1651] 1968) or Hume's ([1740] 1975). All three use institutions and political processes to settle conflicts of interest and regulate the behavior of individuals so that cooperation and nonviolence secure one person against all others. However, where contract in Hobbes or convention in Hume are concerned with the transition between the state of nature and the civil society, Kant's contract focuses on the transition from an unjust collective situation (politically organized or not) to a just one. In addition, for Hobbes and Hume, politics and justice flow from the will of the sovereign, or from the institutions of convention, as interests relative to a specific population and its circumstances. Kant creates political institutions by defining the objective interests of each and every human being in their freedom and moral agency, independent of circumstances. Kant, within the context of an assurance game, separates the critical morality in justice (*Recht*) from the positive law (*Gerechtigkeit*), granting the former a prior and purely independent point of origin, distinct from the relative origins of convention and the positive civil code, but determinant of it. Human reflective reason and the free ability to become a full moral agent in control of one's own life therefore stand as the objective measuring rods against which all moral judgments about distinct systems of positive law must be made.

Kant also places more demands on the state than either Hobbes or Hume. Hume's state can coordinate conventions and rules of property assignment and transition along any lines that a large proportion of cooperators can agree upon. These norms or conventions are morally just because they are the product of solving the collective-action problem. Hobbes's sovereign is the sole judge of what justice is, and even though a well-adjusted sovereign adopts positive law based on the laws of nature, one's source of legitimate power requires that one approach justice with a singular goal in mind: the continued persistence of cooperation.

In the origin of just collective action, Kant requires that the state fulfill the demands of the moral law by anticipating immoral defection from cooperation and preventing it *ex ante*. In addition, the state is responsible to encourage cooperation and to positively influence the outward expression of moral agency by protecting and empowering moral agency through freedom. The Kantian state must evaluate both intrinsic and instrumental value and seek social harmony. The imperative to seek and maintain the "harmony" of the freedom of each with the freedom of all is timeless and objectively based on the intrinsic value (innate right) of each and every moral agent (Kant MJ, 230–31). This imperative requires not just the origin of just collective action in the ideal contract but the persistence of justice in the ethical (re)distribution of property (Kant MJ, §41).

Property Distribution and the Persistence of Collective Action

Although the ideal contract sets the goals or objectives of collective action in the establishment of a just state, it is with the distribution and redistribution of property that Kant provides the material foundation for both the evolution from the state of nature and the persistence of a just state of affairs, once found. For Kant, property is the material means for establishing the conditions of collective action. As a tangible component of one's moral agency, property is accessible to juridical regulation, and its instability is the reason why assurance is sought and the state of nature abandoned (Kant MJ, §8, §41). Through the (re)distribution of property by the state, a just society persists by its efforts both to establish collective action and to respond dynamically to changing circumstances in an effort to maintain just circumstances over time (Kant MJ, §9, §11, §36, §39, §41). To better understand the interaction between morality and politics, and the extent to which the ability of the latter can empower the former in citizens, thereby solving the assurance game, we will look at Kant's theory of property as the basis of assurance for continued and improving collective action.

Kant describes property as an indispensable means for expressing any person's positive freedom (Kant MJ, 250, 258–59). On the basis of his concept of justice, politics should distribute property in such a way that each person has access to that basic quantity and quality necessary to protect and empower his or her full expression of autonomous capacity. Only then will his or her utilization of positive freedom not be jeopardized by a material restriction on his or her negative freedom caused by the lack of property or the externalities of others' choices.

Kant, like Rousseau ([1762] 1968, bk. 1, chap. 9), distinguishes between two forms of property possession: de jure or *intellectual* possession, and sensual or *physical* possession (Kant MJ 245, 246–57). Only the latter is possible in a state of nature. Consequently, a person who takes private property without a juridical state must physically seize it to obtain possession. Since there are no just rules of transfer of rightful possession, one will be liable to counterclaims and violence by others who compete for the private use of the same property. The insecurity of ownership in such a state of nature necessitates the constant supervision of one's possessions against those who would take them for their own use. Kant argues that prolonged mutual distrust and violence causes individuals to give up their lawless liberty in a state of nature for the assurance of a regulated, but more complete and equal, freedom in a just civil state (Kant MJ, §41).

In order to justify and legally maintain one's possessions without having constant physical control of them, one must solve the collective-action problem by obtaining the cooperation of one's fellow rational creatures, which is possible only through consideration of, and respect for, their freedom and practical reason as moral agents in the assurance game. Then a system of distributive justice can be set up that fairly and equitably encourages individual freedom by regulating private ownership (Kant MJ, §§11–14). Thus, ownership can be set into law and maintained by a system of mutual constraints that,

---

simultaneously, will be an incentive to own property, since it is no longer unstable or allocated in such a way that some individuals' autonomy is sacrificed by others who hold power over excess property.

Kant's theory of property or private right highlights three characteristics: first, property is necessary to freedom and concerns relations between people, not between people and objects (Kant MJ, 261). Expression of individual freedom and protection from violence are the true matters of concern, not the objects of ownership, which are just means to the full realization of humanity as an end in itself. Second, the state of nature establishes original ownership as public, while first (private) acquisition is subject to independent moral and political constraints, which are necessary to avoid instability of property, devolution of collective action, and the advent of violence (Kant MJ, §§13–17). Private acquisition beyond the restrictions of the moral law infringes on the personal freedom of the individual and causes violence and exploitation to all parties who must live in a social situation without just ground rules that would establish a "moral" incentive framework. Third, allocations for private use being subject to these moral constraints, the state is empowered to redistribute property in concern for the prior right of the "will of all" (Kant MJ, §14). In order for anyone to have full access to his or her moral agency and the positive freedom that implies, equal stable access to basic possessions, which secure a person's negative freedom, must first exist. The stability of basic property requires the coordination efforts of political institutions to solve the assurance game through distributive justice (Kant §41).

For Kant, the moral law gives original possession of all property to the "united will of all persons." Common possession is his point of departure for all private ownership, which then bears the burden of proof to show that private use does not violate the assurance and distributive requirements of the moral law as idealized in the standard supplied by the "will of all" (Kant MJ, §§11–14). Each person requires some combination of material objects for the expression of positive freedom, and therefore, the distribution of material things is defined in terms of the equal access of all persons to their full autonomous capacity of will as moral agents. All property appropriated by the choice of a single person for this purpose is legitimate only to the degree that it allows others access to that which is necessary to their full moral agency. Private ownership must respect the prior moral agency and common ownership of all.

> All persons are originally in common collective possession of the soil of the whole earth (*Communio fundi originaria*), and they have naturally each a will to use it (*lex justi*). But on account of the opposition of the choice of one to that of the other in the sphere of action, which is inevitable by nature, all use of the soil would be prevented did not every choice contain at the same time a law for its regulation according to which a particular possession can be determined to every one upon the common soil. This is the juridical [civil] law (*lex juridica*). But the distributive law of mine and thine, as applicable to each individual on the soil, according to the axiom of external freedom [of choice], cannot proceed otherwise than from a primary united will

a priori—which does not presuppose any juridical act as requisite for this union. . . . [I]t is in the state alone that the united common will of all can emerge victorious, determining what is right, what is rightful and what is the constitution of justice. (Kant MJ, 267)

A property right is therefore not necessarily absolute to the individual who has primary physical possession of it. Owing to prior collective ownership, the initial or status quo private allocation of property has no independent moral validity. Kant measures the moral validity of possession in terms of that social reality necessary to the equal access of all persons to their full potential as moral agents, without which any private ownership or status quo is unjust and unstable.

Although no civil/political structure need be assumed in order to understand the concept of the "will of all," any structure then created to coordinate behavior and distribute property must do so only in terms of the "will of all," which stands as the practical standard of the moral law for de jure possession (Kant MJ, 264). Respect for the moral law and the moral ideal of the Kingdom of Ends can be maintained only if the conflicting choices of people are coordinated in such a way that private choice and ownership is harmonized. Ownership, originally public, must be made private only by the will of all, which requires that an individual own property only when this does not violate the access rights of others to that basic property necessary to their own moral agency. This property theory is not based on the concept of equal amounts of property but a common basic amount of property to empower individual positive freedom (Kant TP, 292).

If my ownership does not impose undue restrictions on others' negative freedom of choice, then my private possession is "rightful." My ownership is not based upon labor, power, or wealth, but on that moral distribution of property which positively influences the struggle of autonomous agents for their character (Kant MJ, §15). A state distributing property has an equal duty to each of its citizens to see that their negative freedom of choice is not unreasonably restricted by the property ownership of others.

> [T]he juridically law-giving reason comes in again with the principle of distributive justice; and adopts a criterion of the rightfulness of possession not what it is in itself in reference to the private will of each individual in the state of nature, but only the consideration of how it would be adjudged by a court of law in a civil state constituted by the united will of all. (Kant MJ, 302)

The original *moral* right to common equal possession of the earth is a timeless a priori concept, not historical but ideal, not concerned with the wants of individuals, but with the common moral duty they hold in trust for one another over the material reality of the environment they occupy collectively. Concern for this duty is the only way in which civil law can reflect moral law.

> The possession proper to all persons upon the earth, which is prior to all their particular juridical acts, constitutes an original possession in common

(*Communio possessionis originaria*). The conception of such an original common possession of things is not derived from experience, nor is it dependent on conditions of time, . . . rather it is a practical conception of reason that includes the principle (a priori) alone according to which people can use the place they happen to occupy on the surface of the earth in accordance with the law of justice. (Kant MJ, 262)

In the same way that the political concept of the "will of all" represents the moral law and, in this way, the ethical ideal of the Realm of Ends as a basis for the law of property, so the civil law in a just society represents the moral law by making the transition between private (de facto) possession and real (de jure) ownership contingent upon respect for an a priori collective right over land and resources.

> Right in a thing, is a [temporary] right to the private use of a thing, which I am [timelessly] in possession of . . . in common with all others. For this is the one condition under which it is alone possible that I can exclude every other [would be] possessor from the private use of the thing. . . . By an individual act of my own choice I cannot oblige any other person to abstain from the use of a thing in respect of which he would otherwise be under no obligation. . . . [S]uch an obligation can only arise from the collective choice of all united in a relation of common possession. (Kant MJ, 260–61)

As humans in a material world, where our strategic rationality tends to short-circuit our moral predispositions, we create civil states to assure distribution of property and coordination of private choice in a way that empowers our expression of positive freedom. Otherwise, the power to dominate others might cause some to hold all property and not allow others the basic property necessary to the full expression of their positive freedom, causing fear and generating the "mania for domination." The just state assures equal negative freedom by distribution of property in accord with the "will of all." Such distribution gives each person enough of an entitlement to sustain both the expression and perfection of his or her innate right to equal freedom of choice without allowing any to hoard and exploit the negative freedom of others.[12] In this way, each person's capacity as a moral agent is harmonized by application of the concept of the will of all to the legal and policy decisions of the civil state. The state is, in this case, an artificial construction utilized by humanity in pursuit of personal freedom and the full spiritual and material determination of the moral law in collective action. "Right, as against every possible possessor of a thing, means only the claim of a particular chooser to the use of an object so far as it may be included in the artificial—universal will and can be thought of as in harmony with its law" (Kant MJ, 269). Some philosophers (Nozick 1974; Buchanan 1975; Posner 1983) contend that Kantian autonomy is violated whenever any property is nonvoluntarily taken from the individual by a third party (e.g., the state). They argue that anything one possesses in fact, one has a private, and therefore "rightful," claim to.

Let us assume that, originally, property is either owned by no one or by everyone. In the former case, whoever claims it first rightfully owns it. From this point of view, first possession by a private individual is rightful possession and therefore part of her autonomy, not to be taken away except by her consent. Freedom is in choice, not in capacity, and this approach ignores the role of the moral law in Kantian property theory.

First, freedom for Kant is about capacity, not choice. To the degree property capacitates the individual to express positive freedom, its distribution and assurance are a necessary prerequisite to being fully free. Second, Kant only grants real right to a thing in terms of its relation to all persons' basic equal access to full autonomy. Kant argues that original possession is by everyone. From this point of view, while a person's autonomy involves private ownership as necessary to freedom, it also involves the collective realization that it is in the harmony of private choices and acquisition that autonomy finds its true voice. The Kantian burden of proof is on the private user to justify his or her use, whereas the state, as representative of the "will of all" sets private property regulation standards to protect, empower, and capacitate the autonomy of all its citizens. Distribution and redistribution of property is one of the state's collective duties and, as compatible with the will of all, does not violate any one person's autonomy but supports the harmony of freedom in a just society.[13]

Evolving out of the state of nature and into a just society, where the assurance game finds collectively optimal equilibrium, is dependent upon the logic of Kant's theory of property as the material manifestation of the moral demands of justice. Justice is, therefore, the way in which the moral law works itself out in the world. In writing about virtue, Kant contends that the will legislating for itself is an ideal toward which we, as rational beings, have a duty to strive via self-perfection. In the same way, his idea of justice is practical but utopian in character. Justice sets political goals: what ought to be the civil reality of all rational beings?

But before we consider Kant's fundamental assumptions about the state, let us examine the collective ramifications of practical reason in policy decision making. With a more complex moral agent, in view of both the demands of his practical reason as well as his strategic rationality, the structure of collective interaction involves not just one static strategic reality (e.g., assurance game), but the possibilities of evolution to more sophisticated forms of cooperation or of devolution to less sophisticated ones.

Kantian Practical Reason and Dynamic Collective Action

The Kantian policymaker should assume that an individual moving toward full use of practical reason and faced with moral and nonmoral decision situations is capable of using various levels of reasoning to play a variety of game situations present in any strategic environment.[14] The individual strategic actor is capable of reading his surroundings and applying reason in distinct ways to anticipate different games, strategic choices, and payoffs. This complexity of strategic interaction can be put simply as the individual's ability to apply varying levels of reasoning capacity depending on the strategic reality, the moral weight of the choice, and the demands, or lack thereof, of duty. Since one's ethical duties inform preferences in moral matters and distinguish moral from nonmoral decision situations, one will have distinct preferences, expectations, and responses in any of the variety of game situations open to him or her.

Kant's individual cannot be described as a strictly rational individual with static faculties and capacities, but he or she is a human being with a complex evolving intellect, will, and practical reason seeking moral agency. The purpose of a moral agent is to struggle for his or her character and, in the struggle, to establish his or her practical reason as that complex set of motivations that can distinguish moral matters and respond to him or her from both juridical and ethical imperatives.

Practical reason is therefore both more basic and more complex than mere rationality and, as it is attributed to the player as a moral agent, the responsibilities of public choice also become more complex. Preferences are no longer symmetric in value nor will all be counted equally. The standard of the moral law charges the policymaker with the duty to encourage moral behavior and to establish justice in the name of empowering individual moral agency. Duty therefore eclipses preference as the currency of public choice.

Kant's assumptions about the moral agent's character and motivations add a new dimension and further complexity to the idea of collective action and place even greater responsibility on the policymaker to understand the nature of both individual motivations and strategic expectations so that he may understand what "game" is being played out. This may appear, at first glance, to be a hopeless task from the policy point of view. But while the Kantian assumptions about the individual do add new dimensions to human contact, they also give the policymaker certain predispositions and normative assumptions about moral agents with which to approach the collective-action problems presented by the nested complexity of strategic interaction. Specifically, the game one plays, within the dynamic structure of collective action, is a function of whether the reasoning applied to the choice is *simple* or *complex* and whether the objectives of the players are assumed to be *private/unilateral* or *public/universal*.

Simple reasoning can be defined as coextensive with traditional rationality assumptions. Here, a decision is based on purely instrumental values where the actor's preferences are assumed to be properly ordered, complete, and noncontradictory. The agent is understood to be capable only of hypothetical imperatives and of maximizing his desire satisfaction, which is paramount to his definition of rational action.

Complex reasoning is defined as the practical reason possessed by the moral agent seeking full moral autonomy. This individual has a predisposition toward good, a propensity for evil, and a need to raise her preferences on a foundation of moral deliberation that includes a capacity to formulate and act upon both hypothetical and categorical imperatives, depending upon her analysis of the decision-situation. Complex rationality can contain both instrumental and intrinsic value and accommodate the demands of making tradeoffs between them.

These two levels of reasoning are applied to either *private goals* or *public goals* where unilateral action is stressed in the former and universal action in the latter. For simple reasoning, the motives for private or public action are pure and unbalanced; the individual can be described as having a singular objective in promoting unilateral or universal outcomes. For complex reasoning, the motives involving the ends of action are not pure but mixed. The individual applying practical reason to his strategic environment cannot have a completely singular priority for public or private ends because the struggle for character will always involve both his predisposition for universal action and his propensity for unilateral desires. Here, the policymaker can only make assumptions about which side, in this ethical struggle, is predominant. The ends of action are therefore understood as either predominantly aimed at public ends or predominantly focused on private goals.

The Kantian policymaker assumes that an agent's complex reasoning, and the lack of a dominant strategy, will produce a situation where the predominant end of the agent will be public. This produces the preference structure of an assurance game; the predisposition to cooperate is the highest priority, followed by the ability to unilaterally defect to protect one's moral capacities from exploitation. Since no dominant strategy exists within the assurance game, one's choices are dependent upon the assurance of others' cooperation, which is the responsibility of the coordinating authority.

If the predisposition toward cooperation is subjected to stress, and if one still assumes that complex reasoning is being applied but that the individual goal has shifted from public to private ends owing to the absence of assurance that one will not be exploited, one would, in fact, be replacing emphasis on universal cooperation or defection with unilateral action to gain as much for oneself as possible. Still, no dominant strategy exists and one's choices remain dependent on the signals one receives from the other players, or the policy process, but the individual goal has shifted from primarily universal to unilateral. Still applying one's practical reason, one is cognizant that a duty remains to produce the public good; in fact, the total failure to cooperate (universal defection) is now not an acceptable outcome, as the possibility of social disintegration becomes more probable with the general breakdown of practical reason and the failure of moral predispositions to win the struggle for character. Unilateral defection now becomes the best alternative, while universal defection now becomes the worst.

The predominant role of unilateral action is the shift from the strategic structure of an assurance game to that of chicken and can be more clearly seen if we represent the four possible outcome preferences of the players as ordered in two pairs: primary preferences (the first pair) and secondary preferences (the second pair). If one assumes the preference order of an assurance game as the point of departure (fig. 6.2), then the movement from the northeast cell to the upper right cell, that is, the movement from the victory of public ends in the struggle for character to the predomination of private goals, is the elevation of unilateral preferences over universal preferences in both pairs, representing the shift from the outcome preferences of an assurance game to those of a game of chicken.

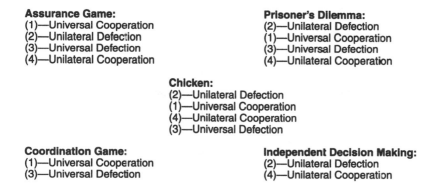

Assurance Game:
(1)—Universal Cooperation
(2)—Unilateral Defection
(3)—Universal Defection
(4)—Unilateral Cooperation

Prisoner's Dilemma:
(2)—Unilateral Defection
(1)—Universal Cooperation
(3)—Universal Defection
(4)—Unilateral Cooperation

Chicken:
(2)—Unilateral Defection
(1)—Universal Cooperation
(4)—Unilateral Cooperation
(3)—Universal Defection

Coordination Game:
(1)—Universal Cooperation
(3)—Universal Defection

Independent Decision Making:
(2)—Unilateral Defection
(4)—Unilateral Cooperation

The games can be understood as being made up of individual motivations and goals. The motivations can be divided into mixed and pure motivations, and the goals can be divided into public and private. This produces a four-cell matrix:

	Goals	
Motivation	Public	Private
Mixed	Assurance Game	Chicken
Pure	Coordination Game	Prisoner's Dilemma

FIGURE 6.2
Preferences, Goals, and Motivations of Dynamic Collective Action

The stress placed on one's predisposition toward good cooperative action causes it to devolve toward a focus on the primarily unilateral goal of coordinating behavior to the private interests of the agent. One's practical reason remains, with the consciousness that collective goods must be provided, but the continued lack of a dominant strategy along with the predominant focus upon private or unilateral ends, and a fear that either none will cooperate or one's own ends will be exploited by cooperating, causes distinct priorities for the strategic reasoner.

The game of chicken is characterized by desperation in terms of joint survival. One can provide the public good for all by allowing oneself to be exploited, but here the imperative to protect one's autonomy and one's predisposition to cooperate in the provision of collective goods come into conflict. There are, fundamentally, the realizations that the collective must be preserved and that the worst outcome is universal defection, where both players are exploited jointly and cooperation destroyed. In such a case, protecting one's freedom (the capacity to reason practically) involves the exploitation of oneself instead of others (as in the prisoner's dilemma) in a strategic interaction with higher stakes (the players' moral or physical survival)[15] and consequently a more critical choice-situation than in an assurance game. Only someone with complex reason and a sense of duty would be able to consider such a choice.

Kant's "mania for domination" takes on a new dimension, as practical reason demands that the collective be preserved at all costs where, unlike the outcome in a prisoner's dilemma, mutual defection (or joint exploitation) is not an acceptable result. Mutual exploitation is an immoral state of affairs, and the dominance of the propensity for evil in a collective-action situation will destroy the moral character of all involved. The failure to act collectively will cause practical reason itself to be corrupted, destroying agency for all. It is therefore not a satisfactory outcome for all to defect. Duty to the survival and perfection of oneself and others causes the individual to contemplate being exploited so that the collective good survives. However, only the consciousness of public ends and one's duty toward them makes this sacrificial act possible. Over time, the experience of self-exploitation will discourage anyone from applying practical reason in the strategic process; the individual agent will utilize pure rationality in a prisoner's dilemma where no mixed consciousness of the need for public-goods provision affects strategic choices. Therefore, with stress on the preference order of an assurance game so that practical reason shifts to predominantly private ends, the preferences of the assurance situation devolve into the preferences and strategic reality of chicken in the upper left cell of our action matrix.

If even more stress is placed on the individual agents, they may forsake their practical reason, their complex motivations, and the struggle for character altogether, allowing a more simple strategic rationality to determine their action. If the goal is purely private, one has the preferences of a prisoner's dilemma, where the dominant "rational" strategy is to defect from cooperation no matter what the other player does. Even with iteration of the game rendering contract by convention (Hardin 1982a), simple reasoning and purely private motives cause cooperation either to be unstable and in constant risk of disintegrating, or with iteration and convention, to produce rules and institutions that have no internal and timeless moral imperatives. Lacking internal moral imperatives to mix the motivations of the players and act as an ethical foundation for preferences, the individual has only the pure rational motive of self-interest. This is expressed in the desire for exploitation of others if possible and in cooperation only if it is advantageous to one's private utility; one is always tempted to defect from cooperation in the hope of being able to free ride. A pure motive for unilateral rational action is the highest preference, and the fear of unilateral exploitation is the worst possible outcome. Unilateral concerns therefore become the center of attention and define the extremes of possible outcomes for the individual in the prisoner's dilemma (lower left cell).

Stress on the assurance game, which produces chicken when complex motives shift from public to private ends and the prisoner's dilemma when complex motives are forsaken for purely self-interested motivations, can also evolve into self-generating cooperative action when simple reasoning is focused upon purely public ends within the context of a pure coordination game (lower right cell).

If one employs simple rationality toward the achievement of purely universal ends, the self-interested agent has but one imperative to receive any payoffs at all: coordinate her choices with the choices of others. The coordinator has only pure rational motivations and pure public goals and therefore has no fear of unilateral exploitation nor desire for unilateral exploitation of others, as these have no payoffs connected to them. In lieu of exploitation or unilateral gain, the universal ends of one's choices are defined by coordination of one's behavior with that of others, which leads to a self-sustaining cooperative equilibrium producing social convention. Lewis (1969) has described this absolute public preference, employing simple rationality to establish convention, as the strategic environment of a pure coordination game.[16]

In sacrificing one's practical reason or complex motivations for simple rationality, one loses the capacity for critical ethical thought internal to the will, categorical imperatives, nonconsequentialist motivation, and any meaningful concern for intrinsic values (humanity or nature).[17] The presence of complex reasoning always allows for critical morality to be part and parcel of the strategic environment. Even within the tension of a game of chicken, practical reason raises the stakes of defection and makes the cost of noncooperation perilous (in moral terms at the very least).

This strategic environment is dynamic because one agent is capable of the iterated play of any or all in succession, given the combinations of reasoning complexity applied to the issues and goals that they have. This combination has an internal source but can be affected, over iterated play, by the institutional or political/strategic environment in which the agent finds herself. The externalities of others' choices and the institutional reality presented to an agent in a strategic situation will either protect and support moral agency over time and encourage continued playing of the assurance game, or allow it to be stressed, causing either the shift of practical reason from universal to unilateral ends (the movement from the assurance game to a game of chicken) or the sacrifice of practical reason to simple rationality. The shift from complex to simple reasoning emphasizing unilateral motives devolves into the strategic framework of a prisoner's dilemma game and either stalemate or the production of conventions that may exploit the agents involved. Simple reasoning emphasizing public goals causes an evolution of the strategic framework to a pure coordination game and self-sustaining social convention.

It is therefore critical that the decision maker, basing policy recommendations on the Kantian paradigm of public choice, be cognizant that his or her understanding of how the rules of the political game and his or her subsequent decisions are constructed will influence how the individual perceives the strategic environment and subsequently influence which iterated game one plays, given this context. The power of the policymaker is not just to assume the assurance game but to support its play by avoiding decisions that place stress on the individual actor to change her goals or forsake her complex practical reason for a simpler and pure rationality where moral imperatives, intrinsic value, and nonconsequentialist motives become difficult and one's exercise of reason is purely rational even if focused on public/universal goals. The imperative for the Kantian decision maker is to support the evolution of collective action toward public ends and to inhibit the devolution of assurance situations into games of chicken or prisoner's dilemmas.

As figure 6.3a shows, it is the responsibility of the policymaker, in seeking assurance and distributive justice, to recognize situations where prisoner's dilemmas exist and change the rules of the strategic reality so that an assurance situation can be generated. One evolves, within the dynamic format, toward stable assurance games by taking the responsibility to provide both the assurance of joint nonexploitation and proper rules of property that acknowledge first common ownership and private use only through the agreement of the "will of all" (path 1).

If one finds current policy creating a prisoner's dilemma situation, as it does in most environmental-facility-siting cases causing NIMBY (Not in My Back Yard)[18] reactions from the public (Rabe and Gillroy 1993), the imperative is for a shift to the politics of assurance (Gillroy and Rabe 1997) and the empowerment of practical reason and one's predisposition toward ethical cooperation. The route to this joint outcome is through the reorganization of institutional practice so that assurance is provided *ex ante* with a proper (re)distribution of property that ensures that one's expression of good will won't be exploited by the immoral choices of others (Gillroy and Rabe 1997, 256).

If the decision maker cannot produce the context of an assurance game in one move, he or she is responsible to make incremental moves in that direction by empowering practical reason sufficiently to make the consciousness of public ends (e.g., hazardous waste disposal) competitive with private self-interest (e.g., protection of neighborhood), moving society from a prisoner's dilemma environment to that of chicken (path 2). At this point the decision maker might, through removing the fear of joint exploitation (e.g., a regional waste-disposal system in which every community plays a part), further transform the game into an assurance situation (path 3).

However, in the same way that dynamic collective action can evolve toward the politics of assurance, it can also devolve from secure assurance equilibria if public policy fails to provide adequate property distribution and the assurance of protection from exploitation for one's moral will (fig. 6.3b). Although a matter may be occasionally nonmoral and unanimously agreed upon as in the public interest (e.g., sewage disposal), thereby promoting the issue into the context of a pure coordination game (path 4), it is more likely that a lack of distributive justice will cause a degeneration within the dynamic format as practical reason gives way to mere rationality and its focus on private gain at the expense of public ends. Whether this degeneration takes place all at once (path 5) (e.g., when a community refuses to cooperate with an unregulated company building an incinerator in their community) or more gradually over time (path 6 + path 7) (e.g., when a community accepts exploitation by initially cooperating in a siting, but then defects when government assurance is withdrawn), the result will be a retreat from the ideal contract, the just constitution, and those political institutions that respect the intrinsic value of humanity and nature alike.

Evolution of collective action, or its devolution into a state of mere "animal" wills (Kant GW, C2, RL, AT), depends on how successful the state is in solving the assurance problem and in making adjustments to allow a solution to persist over time. Solving the assurance problem is Kant's standard for establishing community in the harmony of the choices of one with the choices of others (Kant MJ, 230). But how can community and autonomy coexist?

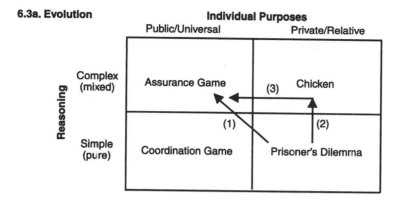

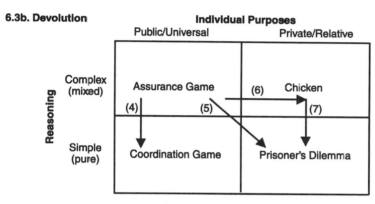

FIGURE 6.3
Evolution and Devolution of Collective Action

Kantian Communitarianism: Juridical Means to Ethical Ends

Kant's concept of autonomy is primarily about one's capacity to choose and not one's choices. Kant's collective-action problem is not focused on the establishment of collective action for its own sake, but upon the specific establishment of assurance through distributive justice and the evolution of dynamic strategies toward a community of ends.

Within contemporary political theory, a debate exists between antithetical points of departure for consideration of justice and "socially better" public policy. This debate is between "liberal individualism" and "communitarianism" (Taylor 1982; Kymlicka 1989, 1990; Avineri and De-Shalit 1992). Where the former considers the individual the basic unit of ethical and political discourse, the latter elevates the community or culture over the individual as both the proper level of reference for making sociopolitical choices and the preferred generator of ethical values and imperatives.

Almost all of the participants on both sides of this debate would place Kant in the liberal individualist camp. However, I contend that a type of Kantian communitarianism exists, based on the ideal of the virtuous individual, that provides a bridge between internal morality and external justice.

Three distinctions segregate Kantian communitarianism from all other approaches to culture and community in political theory. First, Kant's concept of community is based on a concern for the basic moral integrity of the generic human being. Kant is concerned that the categorical imperative/moral law serve the individual as an end "which is also a duty," and that the respect owed to the individual be based upon his or her humanity and dignity as autonomous, self-legislating, practical reasoners. Second, from this definition of individuals as ends, Kant does not consider one's culture as determinant of one's value as a person or as a proper source for one's values in social and political discourse. His communitarianism does not promote culture as a sound grounding for ethical duty but relies on what we have in common as human beings rather than on what separates us into distinct communities, tribes, or "spheres of justice" (Walzer 1984).

The third distinction of Kantian communitarianism is its reliance on an active state to create the optimum "juridical" environment for the evolution of "ethical" community. The just institutional structure for Kant, as well as the just civil law, is based upon our common struggle for character and common striving to become practical reasoners. Kant's ideal community of autonomous individuals can be realized through the intercession in human collective action of a just state that coordinates behavior specifically in terms of the imperatives of the moral law. In this way, we create the political institutions and laws that provide assurance through distributive justice so that no one fears for his or her moral or physical existence owing to ethically irrelevant factors (e.g., culture, race, class, gender).

Kant might argue that although a lack of assurance can affect even the most virtuous of persons for many different reasons, as one falls victim to the immoral choices of others, one's culture, tribe, or specific class or ethnic particularities are the most prominent characteristics that draw discrimination from others and exploitation in a civil arrangement without assurance and distributive justice. If one argues that one's distinct cultural or tribal identity has historically proven to be a focus of injustice and denial of humanity in the person, then how can these characteristics be a sound basis for moral or political community in oneself or others? As morally irrelevant factors, culture must be overcome by assurance and the distributive state in its active social regulation on behalf of practical reason, if social justice is to be established.[19]

In Kant's community no conflict exists between the requirements of the categorical imperative for individuals and the moral law for societies. Justice creates a heterogeneous community of potential practical reasoners where one's humanity is the basis of moral, political, and legal standing. A harmony of striving individuals results where private subjective choices are subject to the basic requirements of the moral law and the respect owed to all because they are human beings. This is not work for a passive state but an active one, whose advocacy is not for any particular group but for humanity as an end-in-itself. The ultimate moral expression of the Kantian community is the ethical Kingdom of Ends. But the juridical/political equivalent is the just state, where regu-

---

lation integrates the choices of one will with those of all others, socially protecting and empowering practical reason.

Kant propels the idea of community beyond the tribe. He argues that morality itself is about how one's individual choices can be universalized, how they affect others as ends, and how they might create a community of autonomous practical reasoners. Juridically, his imperative is to harmonize one's choices with those of others and to obtain private use of things only with the prior assent of the moral law through the "will of all" which has its foundation in common original ownership.

Where the market paradigm has only an aggregation of preferences, Kant describes the just community as the bridge between one's isolated reason and complete moral fulfillment. Without the categorical imperative one has no morality and no duty, but without a consciousness of others and how one's will and choice affect the sociopolitical reality around one, there is no categorical imperative, no justice, no moral law. Therefore, for Kant, the means to virtue is not entirely ethical. Our recognition of duty and our full development of practical reason involve a collective-action problem. To avoid the "mania for domination," assurance and distributive justice must be socially and politically created so that one's capacity or predisposition toward the moral law may find adequate ability or expression in strategic interaction.

In a world where homogenous community is becoming rare and where the just demands of minorities and disenfranchised groups call for integration and participation in political and social institutions, the focus on humanity in the person and the culturally heterogeneous moral community inferred by Kant may offer a better foundation than its culture-based alternative on which to construct a twenty-first-century idea of communitarianism. If we are to cooperate with others and respect them, our common humanity may be a better basis for political constitutions, institutions, and representation than our particular cultures or tribes. Ultimately, if the moral imperative is to adopt others' ends as our own (Kant MV, 450), we need an active state in support of the evolution of moral community. Justice provides the assurance that if we adopt and act upon others' ends as our own, especially when the others are not like us, we will not be politically or morally vulnerable to exploitation by those acting in their own cultural self-interest. We will all be protected and empowered, as human beings, by law.

The imperative of the Kantian state is to harmonize the freedom of each with all, which requires that the state actively create the just environment in which Kantian moral community might be best realized. This brings us to our last fundamental assumption in the Kantian paradigm: the state.

Notes to Chapter 6

1. Some authors (Wolff 1970; Nozick 1974) define autonomy in terms of preference and choice. In chapter 2, I characterized this as, at best, a "thin" theory of autonomy.
2. Each person's ability to satisfy his or her desires, however, depends upon the strategic and game elements that define the environment in which individual choice is

turned into collective outcomes. Outcomes result, not from what we choose, but from how our choices coordinate with the choices of others to produce joint results. Here, individual self-sufficiency meets collective interdependence, and collective-action problems result. These strategic dilemmas are the subject of this chapter.

3. Sidgwick (1907, 496–509) undertakes an analysis of egoism, intuitionism, and utilitarianism and concludes that egoism is not a form of moral argument but immorality, especially when not balanced by other "moral" forces.

4. For a very interesting application of assurance games to public policy, see Chong 1991. This analysis of the civil rights movement in the United States has many Kantian overtones.

5. An assurance situation is not a coordination game where the coordinating agency can disappear once equilibrium is established. The distinction between the assurance situation and the prisoner's dilemma is the degree of coercion, the fact that the coordinating agency must always be on guard for defection, and the fact that in the prisoner's dilemma the regulation is always against prevailing preference, whereas in the assurance game it is in support of the preferred alternative.

6. One might ask how one knows that the assurance is reliable. The approach taken by Kant would lead one to the conclusion that when assurance is found, over time, to be reliable, trust of coordinating institutions will follow. Here, the underlying assumption is that intentions to cooperate will respond positively to protection from exploitation, but as rising distrust of government in environmental-risk cases shows, any betrayal causes widespread defection and the degeneration of the game into chicken or worse. For a full explanation of how stress transforms nested games, read further in this chapter. For more of this argument, see chapter 10. In addition one might examine what Gauthier (1986) has to say about transparent and translucent intentions.

7. Here, I would disagree with the analysis in Riley 1983, which contends that Kant's moral theory and political thought are two distinct systems running parallel and requiring the teleology of Kant's *Critique of Judgment* to act as a bridge between them. I propose that these two parallel systems require no bridge for they are both peninsulas from a common mainland: the moral law or categorical imperative (see Gillroy 1992c).

8. "Ideal" here is distinct from "hypothetical" as it sets a moral standard that is not part of hypothetical contract. Kant, unlike Hume, Hobbes, or even Rawls, is not designing a system of procedural justice that can be constructed upon any foundation that can find agreement or consensus, but requires the "ideal" contract to sustain the demands of the moral law applied to the policy context.

9. The full argument for the connection between freedom, equality, and independence as the juridical attributes of the active citizen will be set out in chapter 7.

10. Mulholland starts off here on the right foot but then his argument degenerates into the traditional contention that Kant supports only a minimal state (1990, 316–19, 323, 328–30). The way in which he deals with Kant's definition of active and passive citizenship (where he claims that Kant will not allow women to be active citizens [329]) is a good example of his unwillingness to take the essential Kantian arguments about freedom to their natural conclusions for collective action, property distribution, and government regulation toward the equal active citizenship of all. I will attempt to consider these entailments as we move through the next two chapters. My argument about active citizenship is in chapter 7.

11. This has ramifications for the traditional view that Kant's moral and political theory come into conflict over subjects like revolution. See Gillroy 1992c.

12. Chapter 7 has a complete argument on this point.

13. This relates to Kant's argument in the *Groundwork* (GW, 430–31), reiterated in part 2 of the *Metaphysics of Morals* (MV, 231), that the moral law sets a standard that

is a "supreme limiting condition" on choice. Under these conditions, the use of coercion to counteract immoral choice is not a violation of autonomy but is required by justice.

14. My ideas related to dynamic collective action have not been formally worked out or mathematically verified; however, they provide a heuristic device for the consideration of how complex practical reason might determine and react to the strategic environments that confront it. This approach runs along the lines provided by Tsebelis (1990, 6–8) and a fuller argument from this perspective can be found in Rabe and Gillroy 2000.

15. The original story behind the game of chicken is that of two drivers in the same lane of traffic driving vehicles toward one another. Whoever weaves out of the lane first is chicken, but someone has to or both lose their lives.

16. Although conventions can be rendered from within the structure of both a prisoner's dilemma (Taylor 1976/1987; Hume [1740] 1975; Hardin 1982a) and a pure coordination game (Hume [1740] 1975; Lewis 1969), the distinction is that coordination within the prisoner's dilemma allows instability of equilibrium because of the dominance of unilateral/private ends and the possibility of exploitation payoffs, whereas conventions established by pure self-enforcing coordination involve no desire for, or fear of, exploitation. The game is one of expectation and anticipation where all rational gain is defined by coordinated public action. This rational imperative to always seek cooperative equilibria is useful, as it establishes conventions where, unlike those in the prisoner's dilemma, the rational goals are quasi-altruistic and therefore have moral weight in the act of coordination, where all gain equal payoffs for their joint action.

17. While the conventions produced from within a prisoner's dilemma can be either immoral and exploitative, such as coordinating a lynch mob, or moral and non-exploitative, such as coordinating a rescue effort, or have the possibility of mixed results, as in a system of property rules, pure coordination conventions will primarily have a nonmoral nature. The ethics of the pure coordination problem is the ethics of consensus, and the seeking of coordination for the collective good is defined as that which can be agreed upon unanimously and which exploits no one. Here, ethics is not metaphysical, but political (Rawls 1993, 11ff), and, unlike the establishment of conventions from within a prisoner's dilemma (Hardin 1982a), the conventions produced by the coordination game have the advantage of not involving exploitation.

18. In chapter 10 there is a complete analysis of NIMBY as a dynamic game environment.

19. This does not mean that culture is not important to the person, in his or her personal search for identity and autonomy, but that for humanity in every person to be the basis of justice, culture cannot be the standard for admission into the moral community.

7

Justice from Autonomy: The Legitimate State

The justice of political institutions begins with the juridical implementation of the moral law as represented in the "will of all." The legitimacy of the state,[1] from the perspective of the moral law, is dependent upon its success in harmonizing the freedom of each with the freedom of all. But what does it mean to harmonize freedom? What role can the state play, in support of collective action, justice, and the moral law, toward this goal?

The Moral Basis of the Legitimate State

Kant, I have argued, is a contract theorist. He utilizes the idea of a social contract to explain how individual morality provides a foundation and a purpose for collective action and public choice. In the transition between the individual and the collective levels of analysis, Kant employs the concept of the "will of all" to represent the moral law in public choice. The will of all is that universal consensus created by the application of the categorical imperative to public life, or what individuals would will collectively if their practical reason functioned flawlessly.

Kant's concept of the "will of all" is the opposite of Rousseau's (Masters 1968; Riley 1986, chap. 5; Ritter and Bondanella 1988, 61–66, 282, 83, 100–101). Rousseau makes a distinction between the "will of all," which is a simple "addition" or aggregation of private interests into a collective preference, and the "general will," which is the "sum of the differences" of individual interests (Masters 1968, 326).

> Far from assuming that the general will is automatically realized by the action of a majority, Rousseau insists that there is an inevitable conflict between private will or interest and the general will within every citizen. . . . Because the tension between private interest and the general will is inher-

ent in political life, art is needed to direct the citizens toward the common good. (Masters 1968, 326–27)

Kant's "will of all" is not a sum of preferences or interests, nor is it really the sum of differences, but the public manifestation of what is universal and necessary to humanity in the person; that is, the collective expression of the moral law in the law and policy of a just society. Kant contends that the will of all holds legislative power prior to all individual interests or exercises of choice in the material world (Kant MJ, 263). The will of all, for Kant, represents the moral autonomy of each and all in agency, the public standard of right that sets the conditions for private use of property and resources as well as the public recognition and protection of private choice (Kant MJ, §§12–14).

For the purposes of policymaking, Kant breaks the macroprinciple of autonomy down into component principles. The key to understanding the will of all, from a policy viewpoint, is to understand these principles, which represent what the moral law guarantees to each citizen and expects in the regulation of collective action by the state. The three "juridical" or rightful attributes of citizenship, and components of autonomy and the "will of all," are: freedom, equality, and independence (*Selbständigkeit*).

> There are three juridical attributes bound to the nature of a citizen as such: first, the lawful freedom to obey no law other than one to which he has given his [moral] determination. Second, the civil equality of having no one among the people superior over him, except a person whom he has a moral capacity to bind to the same degree as the other has to bind him juridically. Third, the attribute of civil independence that requires that one not owe his support and existence to the arbitrary choice of another person among the people in the society but rather to his own rights and powers as a member with common intrinsic character. (Kant MJ, 313–14)

The requirements of these attributes establish the standards within which legitimate state activity will be confined, and provide the policymaker with the material conditions necessary to the political manifestation of the moral law in civil law. They will provide the *principles*, a priori, upon which all civil policy can be judged and justified in terms of the demands of justice as autonomy.

> The civil state, therefore, regarded solely as a just state is grounded on the following a priori principles:
> 1. The freedom of every member of society as a *person;*
> 2. The equality of each person, with all others, as *subjects;*
> 3. The independence of every member with a common intrinsic character, as a *citizen.* (Kant TP, 290, emphasis added)

The imperative to harmonize freedom, as based on the criteria above, involves more than just state noninterference in individual affairs, or simply a minimal state to police individuals so that they do not collide violently with one another

231

(Williams 1983, 164–65, 196; Mulholland 1990, chap. 10). The imperative to recognize the intrinsic value of autonomy and natural-system functioning, combined with the reality of dynamic collective action, presents the state with an active duty to facilitate the moral cooperation of all, the "will of all," so that

232

justice not only protects the negative freedom of the person, but empowers the positive freedom of expression that allows the just society to come about. A legitimate state can materialize only if an active government regulates and supports the quality of life of its population within an incentive structure that assures, through distributive justice, basic material conditions. Only in this way can one's moral agency be fully realized on an individual basis while collective action is facilitated without exploitation. That my agency not interfere with the potential moral agency of another is necessary but not sufficient. Ideally each should develop his or her autonomy so that even one's elective ends are made subject to his or her autonomous will and, in this way, ultimately harmonize with the producible ends of others.

> [I]t is not sufficient that the action not conflict with humanity in our person as an end in itself; it must also harmonize with it. . . . Humanity might indeed exist if no one contributed to the happiness of others, provided he did not intentionally detract from it; but this harmony with humanity as an end in itself is only negative rather than positive if everyone does not also endeavor, so far as he can, to further the ends of others. For the ends of any person, who is an end in himself, must as far as possible also be my end, if that conception of an end in itself is to have its full effect on me. (Kant GW, 430)

Again, we are faced with the collective dimensions of Kant's theory of individualism. For Justice from Autonomy, the duties one has as a matter of virtue are necessary not only ethically, as a matter of conscious and internal reason, but juridically, as political duties in a world where collective-action problems can short-circuit the best intentions of individuals. As previously argued, the role of the state in assuring collective action through distributive justice requires that the state actively protect and empower individual ethical behavior while it sanctions evil and encourages widespread coordination in accord with the moral law.

Kant defines justice (*Recht*) in terms of the translation of the moral law into civil law (*Gerechtigkeit*); in this translation both negative and positive freedom are facilitated in community. Justice is a result of the harmonization of the choices of each with the will of all; it is not the sole responsibility of any one person. It is through the establishment and support of an active state, which has the organizational power and juridical ability to provide that public environment in which nonexploitative collective action is possible, that the moral will of each finds protection and empowerment.

In supporting a just state, one is inherently making others' ends his own. Through just public law, the full moral freedom of each citizen is assured and, in this way, one is supporting others' full autonomy by submitting to the just coercion of the state. Within the regulatory framework of the state, built on the basis of humanity as an end in itself, one can collectively further both his own ends and the ends of others'.

The juridical state, as a mechanism for regulation and coordination of political affairs toward justice from autonomy, is justified, not by liberty, equality, and fraternity, but by freedom, equality, and independence (*Selbständigkeit*). Although two of the three component principles are similar, the third is different and offers insight into Kant's idea of liberalism. The focus of his just state is to support the freedom and equality of all jointly so as to produce morally independent individual citizens. The virtuous person is a collectively fostered phenomenon, the autonomous person in a community of morally autonomous people, where moral autonomy itself is empowered by the collective coordination of individual choices and actions by state use of the moral law to justify its regulatory acts and define the public interest.

The goal of Kantian idealism is equal freedom and individual autonomy based on the moral law, which gives the same imperatives to each person individually, and to all, through the state, collectively. In this way, practical reason grants the freedom to will or create a life, while the state protects the public expression of this will and encourages willed action by providing the freedom that allows individual autonomy to find external expression and harmony with the wills of others.

The principle of autonomy is an integration of freedom, equality, and independence, and these find public expression in a just republican constitution that is a duty for all, as a collective, to strive toward (Kant C1, B373; MJ, 370–73; MV, §21). The justification for this constitution is the moral law (or the "will of all") that presents what is universal and necessary in respect for the intrinsic value of every person: one's freedom actualized and politically harmonized with that of others.

This duty to create and respect the just constitution is a nonconsequentialist imperative to a consequentialist goal: human happiness.[2] However, Kant's concern with happiness is not utilitarian; it is not defined as preference or desire satisfaction, per se. Happiness, for Kant, is something that follows "of itself" from justice and autonomy (C1, B373). Seeking the happiness of others involves their freedom, their moral agency, what the Greeks called the ultimate "Good of Man" (Aristotle PL, 7.1–3; Annas 1993, 43–46).

In terms of comprehensive policy argument (chap. 1), the characterization of the state in our fundamental assumptions requires us to consider the second issue-circumspection question and define *what* principle(s) the state must utilize to set the a priori standards and *ex post* goals for just policy. The moral principle of autonomy can provide this standard; it is played out in three distinct subprinciples: Kant's juridical attributes of the citizen.

The Principle of Autonomy and the Attributes of the Active Citizen

The political principles of freedom, equality, and independence support, and are components of, the moral imperative to provide for autonomy in the moral agency of the citizen. In addition, the three juridical attributes can be seen as mutually supportive and constitutive of the ultimate principle of autonomy.

Protecting Capacity: Individual Freedom through Ecosystem Integrity

The first civic attribute contributing to a detailed definition of Justice from Autonomy is freedom. The concept of freedom exists prior to, and bears upon the construction of, legitimate or just institutions by requiring that the moral freedom or intrinsic value of every person as a human being be a focus of policy decision making. As argued in chapter 5, the moral integrity of the person is perfected only in the protection and empowerment of the functional integrity of the environment. Therefore, the *material condition* of the subprinciple of freedom is in the potential harmony of the world of freedom with the world of causality. This harmony requires respect for the intrinsic value of both humanity and nature, which I shall call *Ecosystem integrity*.[3]

The freedom component of autonomy relates directly to the moral agency or autonomy of the individual and, through this, to the integrity of a functional environment as the requirement of policy to respect intrinsic value in public choice. Freedom, far from being sacrificed to an active state, is assured by the political institutions founded on the basis of the moral law. Respect for the person, as well as for nature, is a function of concern for one's capacity to be a free and autonomous agent. For the state to guarantee freedom, it must protect and empower this autonomy as internal capacity; that is, it must construct an environment of functional Ecosystems, political freedom, and distributive justice that is implied by the moral law through the categorical imperative. Freedom is basic to just policy in the Kantian model, so it is paramount that we begin our examination of state legitimacy by defining the relationship between freedom and the state.

Kant's philosophy, as it relates to the role of the state in individual freedom, is commonly perceived to be primarily concerned with the negative liberty of the individual from state interference (Wolff 1970; Nozick 1974; MacIntyre 1981; Williams 1983; Mulholland 1990). More specifically, this approach defines "autonomy" as requiring primarily that the private choices of each person in the material world be respected, and that each person's self-sufficiency be assumed as part of his or her autonomy (Kuflik 1984). Here, no active state is morally necessary and, in fact, only a minimal state can be justified at all. Such a minimal state has no independent jurisdiction; it is concerned only with adopting policy that gains the consent of its constituents and that is responsive to their preferences. Such is the "efficiency" argument for the state as a surrogate for the market when it cannot function. The minimal state has no independent justification. Not surprisingly, this approach to Kant's definition of freedom degenerates into an argument about anarchy (Nozick 1974).

In this conventional reading, Kantian autonomy is a creature of preference and choice (*Willkür*); negative freedom implies state noninterference with choice as the concept of political liberty involved in making public decisions.

As long as the individual is left alone, and her choices are respected by the central authority, she is free.[4]

When all preference-based choice is autonomous choice, the state's role is to aggregate preferences as the basis of its legitimacy. In effect, the individual must consent, by choice, to all changes in the distributive status quo, which now assumes a moral priority as that distribution of wealth consented to. Each person is assumed by all other parties to be manifesting freedom in whatever choice he makes. No interpersonal, nonrelative standard exists with which to distinguish one choice from another. Each and every choice gains the moral force of autonomous choice. To allow any entity to represent one collectively is equivalent to giving away or forfeiting one's autonomy (Wolff 1970, 14–17). This forfeiture can occur by degrees and over time, but any reliance on government is necessarily a lessening of personal freedom and, therefore, of individual autonomy.

But the association of autonomy with consent and consent with the negative freedom of the individual is akin to what Thomas Hill Green terms the freedom of the savage. "In one sense no man is so well able to do as he likes as the wandering savage. He has no master. There is no one to say him nay. Yet we do not count him really free, because the freedom of savagery is not strength, but weakness" (Green [1881] 1981, 199). Green maintains that real freedom involves "a positive power or capacity of doing . . . something worth doing . . . in common with others" (199). The development of these capacities involves submission of the person to a state framework as "the first step in true freedom, because [it is] the first step toward the full exercise of the faculties with which man is endowed" (199). Freedom for both Green and Kant is "a power which each man exercises through the help or support given him by his fellow-men, and which he in turn helps to secure for them" (Green [1881] 1981, 199).

Kant's concept of freedom is complex. As in Haydn's concept of the sonata form, two unique but interrelated themes combine to shape the full tone and richness of the idea. In addition to negative freedom, Kant's ethics offers the concept of positive freedom, which provides the impetus for which the legitimate state creates a just environment.

Kant's idea of negative freedom is not freedom of the individual from interference by the state, but the independence of one's choices from the choices of others. Negative freedom involves the freedom one has to will a choice, free from the pressures of desire on reason. Desire gains force on one's will through the exploitation and fear caused by the choices others make in the context of the unsolved assurance game. Negative freedom does involve one's choices; with negative freedom one finds the contact point between political action in the material world and the inner will. However, inferring from this that, in Kant's view, the state ought to respect any choice *tout court* and observe minimal interference in its regulation is extreme. For Kant, the politics of negative freedom is inextricably bound with the morality of positive freedom, which is where an accurate investigation of a Kantian theory of freedom and the state must begin.

The primary moral component of each person's humanity is one's positive freedom or autonomy, which concerns one's internal capacity to will what practical reason demands, *prior to choice*. All moral value, and therefore the respect owed to oneself and others, is focused on this capacity. In order to have a full autonomous capacity, however, Kant stipulates that one's will must be free from determination by one's desires, as triggered by the choices of other persons in the material world of collective action (MJ, 229–34). So while autonomy (as the capacity prior to choice) is the proper focus of moral respect, it is dependent on the negative freedom of one's choices from determination by desire brought about by the political behavior of others. Negative freedom is the proper sphere for political action and requires an active state made responsible to protect, and therefore assure, each person that his basic positive freedom as a human being will be supported in collective action and will not be jeopardized by the choices of other strategic actors within the community.

The public coordination or "harmony" of private choices moves us away from a lawless or "savage freedom," where the security of autonomy as an intrinsic moral capacity is left to the whim of chance or markets. In the lawful freedom of a just state positive freedom can be consciously protected and internally encouraged in each person. Harmony requires that each person's "private" choices be assured protection unless they interfere with the freedom of others. This creates public choice that assures negative freedom for the private choices of all, and, in this way, the most widespread expression of positive freedom possible.

A "harmony of freedom" results as one's basic choices, expressing one's will in moral matters, gain the support of central political coercion, so that the subjective ends of others, who may or may not be morally motivated, are in any case prevented from interfering with the full realization of the necessary and objective end of one's humanity. This use of the state's coercion to protect *humanity in the person* and to allow it positive expression will provide the best political conditions within which each person's ethical virtue may find perfection.

The respect owed, as a duty, to the principle of freedom is to the inner capacity of each person as a human being. However, as we argued in chapter 5, this capacity is subject to dysfunction when a choice (*Willkür*) is made that is not in accord with the moral direction of the will (*Wille*). In addition, we are strategic actors in a community of strategic agents. Thus, it falls to the state to regulate private choice and coordinate expressions of freedom so that they are compatible with the moral law. Politics and policymaking are morally valid, and the state is legitimate, depending on how the respect for freedom is made evident in social legislation and regulation.

The mandate of the just state is to protect: to adopt protective measures addressing the moral vulnerabilities of its citizens by acting as their collective political agent.[5] To protect is to empower the intrinsic capacities of humanity and nature as authorized by the moral law, not just by contingent circumstance or instrumental desire.

The state is charged with the quest for the ideal contract and the materialization of the just society as the goal of ethical government decision making.

This mandate is stated in the law of freedom (Kant MJ, 230), and is the sole moral standard by which a policy based on the protection and empowerment of moral agency can be legislated. The law of freedom defines, not only personal responsibility, but the collective duty of government as agent for its citizens in tasks of civic coordination beyond the ability of individuals or subgroups of the society. Civil law, in this way, gains moral force and invokes obligation.

> [The ideal contract] . . . obliges every legislator to frame his laws in such a way that they could have been produced by the will of a whole nation, and to regard each subject, insofar as he can claim citizenship, as if he had consented within the general will. This is the test of the rightfulness of every public law. (Kant TP, 297)

The state's mandate is not to vary its public choices with the individual subjective ends of each of its citizens. The elective choices of citizens are not the primary matter from a moral point of view. Justice should legislate and execute the positive law necessary to the end of human freedom and autonomy, as reflected in the ideal of the "will of all."

The Kantian state does not require that all its citizens have the same producible or elective ends; the focus of public policy is primarily on the promotion and protection of citizens as nonproducible ends in themselves. All potential subjective choices that interfere with the full freedom of each person under government are to be opposed by public law, on the basis of the concept of humanity as an end that is also a duty (Kant MV, 381ff) and therefore the supreme limiting condition of all private choice.

> This principle of humanity and of every rational creature as an end in itself is the supreme limiting condition on the freedom of the actions of each person. . . . [I]t is thought of as the objective end that should constitute the supreme limiting conditions of all subjective ends, whatever they may be. (Kant GW, 430–31)

The task of the government is to oppose nonautonomous expressions of agency that interfere with the moral autonomy of others in the society. Kant assumes that if each person's true expression of positive freedom or ethical choice finds full expression and is not thwarted by external pressure, social justice will necessarily follow. However, the realities of our strategic social environment result in nonautonomous choices being made in moral matters, which requires the regulation or intercession of the state. One may express his agency as he pleases, much of the time, but not when his immoral expressions of private choice cause the exploitation or dysfunction of others as moral ends in themselves.

The harmony of freedom is not about the noninterference of government, but about the requirement of a political society actively regulating and setting limitations on personal choice and, in this way, administering law through the categorical imperative. Here, the material conditions of the principle of freedom require that the policymaker be concerned with intrinsic value. To construct an incentive structure—in which intrinsic value in humanity and nature is protected and therefore each person's access to his or her full autonomy is supported—is the new mandate. Within this political environment, one can pursue subjective ends confident in the knowledge that the pursuit of these choices will not interfere with others' autonomy because of the assurance provided by the regulatory structure of the state as established by the moral law. Only within an active political society can one satisfy preference knowing that the regulation of civil law prevents one from negatively affecting the intrinsic value of humanity or nature.

For example, within the context of American law, I am assured that my actions will not affect others' freedom of expression, as such interference is challengable as an unconstitutional use of agency. Intentionally or unintentionally attempting to interfere with specific expressions of political views is prevented by the state, even to the extent of police protection of unpopular political viewpoints. With a state that protects and therefore encourages autonomous agency, the coordination of choice toward moral ends leads to a harmony of freedom that does not "make" people moral but encourages their predisposition toward moral action. Kant speculates that legislating by the "will of all" will lead to the ethical condition of the "Kingdom of Ends" where we have actualized the "good will" in each and all (Kant GW, 433–41; Korsgaard 1996, 162, 170–71, 209–10, 220 n. 36).

The mutual coercion exercised by citizens through the creation and support of the just state produces freedom in policy by actively counteracting those expressions of nonmoral agency that infringe on the potential autonomy of others. In such cases, coercion is just.

> [I]f a certain use of freedom is itself a hindrance to freedom according to universal laws (i.e., wrong), coercion that is opposed to this (as a hindering of the hindrance to one's freedom) is consistent with freedom in accordance with universal laws, that is, it is just coercion. Hence there is connected with right by the principle of contradiction an authorization to coerce someone who infringes upon it. (Kant MJ, 231)

But nonautonomous choice can affect more than the moral integrity of a human being. It can also transgress the functional integrity of the environment, which we have argued (chapter 5) is a necessary dimension of human autonomy. Our duties to nature, as prescribed by Kantian conservationism and Kantian preservationism, are bound to our own human freedom and require that the functional integrity of our joint Ecosystem be respected.

In terms of Kantian conservationism, the moral law requires that we recognize nature as a necessary ingredient in our own moral agency. Nature ought not to be defined merely in terms of human desires or preferences, but in terms of the juxtaposition of human moral integrity and nature's functional integrity. This dialectic of intrinsic value brings a new dimension to policy argument and promotes essential over instrumental value. We value nature because of its relation to us and for its use, not merely as a means, but as a means that is also a functional end in itself. This makes Kantian conservationism nonutilitarian and nonconsequentialist.

In addition, we have identified a second, stronger argument in respect for nature, Kantian perservationism, where a duty to nature as an independent entity occupies our moral and political deliberations. Concern for nature as a functional end in itself remains, but it becomes an obligation independent of our use or dependence upon it.

Both of these foundations for duties to nature are based on the connection between intrinsic value and the idea of respect for the end-in-itself. In both cases, our obligation is rooted in our capacity to be free and is dependent on our ability to build institutions that protect and empower this freedom.

The positive acts of the state, in accord with the moral law, should be defined in terms of two duties: first, the application of coercion to counteract the unlawful use of agency against the intrinsic value of humanity or nature; second, the assurance and active support for the empowerment and full development of human autonomy and the functional integrity of natural systems. In protecting Ecosystem integrity, we fulfill both of these duties.

With these two expanded functions, the state, as a just commonwealth, becomes the framework for both the perfection of human freedom and the continued evolution of the natural environment from which we came and upon which we are dependent for our continued development. "[A] perfectly constituted state [is] the only condition in which the capacities of mankind can be fully developed" (Kant UH, 27).

The definition of freedom as protection of intrinsic value is made manifest in the material condition of a sound and protected environment. If we assume that nature predated humanity and made us possible, and further, that our freedom is still dependent, both morally and physically, on the integrity of nature, then to protect our own freedom is to also protect the intrinsic value of the natural environment. Thus, to respect the moral freedom of each citizen, the just state needs to be actively involved in the conservation or preservation of natural systems, which, together with humanity and its creations, define Ecosystem integrity within Justice from Autonomy.

Government should not neglect its juridical responsibility for the autonomous capacity of each of its citizens, or allow that capacity to be expended in supererogatory efforts to perfect the self within an insecure and openly hostile social environment. Nor should the state allow the exploitation of nature, for if it does, it allows the duty to nature's capacity, ability, and purpose to be ignored even as it defeats human potential in diminishing the environment in which human capacity, ability, and purpose finds its origin and ultimate expression.

Through the state we must regulate to protect the essential value of nature as we legislate to protect human freedom from the immoral choices of others. This requires anticipation of those choices and acts that would treat the capacities of either humanity or nature merely as a means and not always "at the same time" as an end. The role of the state is to construct that support network necessary for the growth and self-actualization of autonomy in each and every citizen and for the evolution and homeostasis of natural systems. More specifically, the mandate of the state, in terms of freedom as a Kantian ideal, is to provide for the former by active protection of the latter. In protecting our environment, we observe those essential duties related to our freedom and the freedom of others.

Both the protection of individual choice and the empowerment of personal autonomy involve markets and economic entitlement. Kant argues that property and possessions are important to the individual expression of positive freedom.[6] But, uncoordinated, they are a source of instability, as the private choices of some will utilize property to exploit the basic freedoms of others. Basic economic freedom is, then, a necessary prerequisite to full moral freedom, for as long as one is prevented from having a basic material entitlement, one will be more likely, in the resulting atmosphere of insecurity, to compromise his duties to humanity and nature. This compromise will come as choice fails to heed the imperatives of reason and uncertainty motivates desire, in fear of physical demise by the exploitation of others, causing immoral choices to be made. To escape from this uncertainty, to stabilize and distribute property, and to create the assurance necessary to the realization of freedom are the reasons we leave the state of nature for civil society in the first place (Kant MJ, §41).

Property, for Kant, is the conduit for the expression of positive freedom and, simultaneously, the means by which the individual protects and secures his freedom from exploitation by others. The distribution of a basic level of property that assures one against exploitation by others is, moreover, the necessary basis upon which a civil state aspires to be a just state. Kant is not alone in this view.

> For property to achieve its traditional purpose—to guard the citizens' freedom against tyranny . . . property must include guarantees that each citizen can acquire the necessities of life, and not only protection in holding on to existing possessions. (Held 1980, 2)

The freedom of each person's choices (*Willkür*) requires that the state distribute property in such a way that each person's equality as a subject of the moral law is recognized as his or her equal claim to full autonomy (*Wille*). Positive freedom needs a secure, assured, social and natural environment. When basic entitlement is unstable or uncertain, a lack of adequate negative freedom makes positive freedom less accessible to everyone.

Distributing Property: Moral Equality through a Material Baseline

In addition to calling for freedom as a requirement of one's humanity, the moral law, through the juridical attributes, also requires that each person be equally able to express this freedom, which requires property (Kant MJ, 250). Duty therefore requires that the state act as collective agent for the "will of all" in the definition and allocation of property from common to private possession,[7] according to the moral law. The state applies its coercion to counteract the unjust use of agency on the part of some, who, by specifically exploiting others' equal access to that property which allows for mutual coercion and a baseline range of choice, are in fact immorally constricting the expression of their own autonomy and bringing social disharmony to freedom. "Thus the birthright of each individual in . . . a state . . . is absolutely equal as regards his authority to coerce others to use their freedom in a way that harmonizes with his freedom" (Kant TP, 292–93). Equality of power to coerce requires attention to the material position of the individual, but not a strict equality of wealth or "commodity bundles," as a moral duty of a distributively just society. Kant contends that "utmost inequality of the mass in the degree of its possessions" (Kant TP, 291) is consistent with the moral equality of persons. However, Kant's ideal of the moral equality of persons does require equality at a material baseline, consistent with one's ability to "coerce others to use their freedom in a way that harmonizes with his freedom" (Kant TP 293).

For Kant, moral equality requires mutual coercion that has a material dimension related to the equal ability, at a baseline, to express positive freedom. Property is an expression of freedom, and the distribution of property at some threshold level will dictate equal access to one's autonomous capacity. In effect, while discrepancies will exist (even large ones), in the amount of wealth across a population, to avoid moral implications, this inequality must not affect that minimum property allocation necessary to the equal expression of positive freedom. One individual cannot be allowed so much property that others are forced to abandon their autonomy for physical self-preservation. Kant suggests that even if we are not exactly equal in wealth, if we are assured of that basic property that allows us freedom and moral equality, then the greater wealth of one will not give him or her immoral power over anyone else's choices.

In something reflective of the Lockean proviso (Locke [1690] 1988, bk. 2, chap. 5), one cannot justly be allowed jurisdiction over more property than respect for the equal moral worth of one's fellow subjects would allow. Kant thinks it impossible to imagine

> how anyone can have *rightfully* acquired more land than he can cultivate with his own hands . . . and how it came about that numerous people who might otherwise have acquired permanent property were thereby reduced to serving someone else in order to live at all. It would certainly conflict with the above principle of equality if a (positive) law were to grant them a privileged status so that their descendants would always be feudal landowners, without their lands being sold or divided by inheritance and thus made useful to more people; it would also be unjust if only those belonging to an arbitrary privileged class were allowed to acquire land. . . . The owner of large estates keeps out as many smaller property owners . . . as could otherwise occupy his territories. (Kant TP, 296, emphasis added)

Without basic property, one cannot have access to one's full expression of positive freedom or one's full potential autonomy. Only if she has this potential capacity as a moral agent, can she be conceived to have equal authority, as a full citizen, to coerce her fellow citizens, which is the core of Kant's concept of equality. Those who hoard, or who are allowed by the state to gain so much property as to deprive others of that basic entitlement necessary to moral equality, act unjustly. Those who would continue this imbalance over generations do so in further violation of the moral law. In effect, the concept of the "will of all," as that action implied or made imperative by practical reason for collective application, requires that the policymaker invoke the standard of equal coercion to analyze initial or existing distributions of property and justify any and all redistribution by the standard of the "will of all" (Kant MJ, §§11, 15).

Each person, by his or her humanity, has a birthright, an "innate right" (Kant MJ, 237, 326) to that moral equality of position by entitlement that gives him or her access to the expression of his or her positive freedom without fear of exploitation by others. Through the moral law, made real in the just state, political coercion assures each, through real distribution of material goods and support, a baseline equality, where negative freedom is guaranteed against the private choices of others that could corrupt the predisposition toward the good and one's capacity to will the categorical imperative. The harmony of freedom requires that people cooperate in making private choices. Because of the collective-action problems involved, harmony requires the active participation in, and support of, the just state, which, in turn, coordinates one's equal access to personal autonomy.

> In order to be able to participate in the actual law of the land . . . persons . . . require, because they mutually influence one another, a juridical condition of society. That is, they require a condition of society under a will that unites them—a constitution. (Kant MJ, 311)

The institution of a juridical society is necessary because people influence one another's lives, and collective authorities cannot allow one person's equality to be sacrificed for the liberty of others.[8] The just state empowers all citizens by distributing and redistributing to establish and support the baseline at all times and for everyone. Each and all must be morally equal in the capacity to influence all others; the material baseline assures this mutuality.

As I argued in chapter 5, Kant's individual is a practical reasoner, and it is his capacity, ability, and purpose as a practical reasoner that is being protected and empowered. Toward this end, equality, in a Kantian model, is measured by the material condition of property and represents equality against material exploitation (Kersting 1992). Justice requires that each be encouraged to find his or her own life and level of autonomous perfection, assured of the basic material and political conditions of physical and moral self-preservation.

The equality of each in the just society is "equality before the law" (Kant TP, 292); that is, the moral law as made manifest in the civil code. In terms of providing a baseline of material equality, the moral law invokes duties to oneself and others. The duty to oneself involves one's own moral perfection, whereas the duty to others is concerned with their "happiness" (Kant MV, 385–89).

The duty to one's perfection requires personal effort to fully utilize and develop one's autonomous capacity. Possessing a basic entitlement is not related to the happiness of the person, but to the integrity of her moral capacity for autonomy, her moral value as an end (Kant C2, 93). As such, entitlement invokes a duty.[9]

> Adversity, pain, and want are great temptations to transgress one's duty. Thus, it would seem that affluence, strength, health, and welfare in general, which are opposed to those influences, can also be regarded as ends that are at the same time duties; that is to say, it is a duty to promote one's own happiness and not merely that of others. But in that case the end is not happiness, but the *morality of the subject*; and happiness is merely the means of removing the hindrances to morality, permitted means, that is, since no one has a right to demand from me the sacrifice of those ends of mine that are not immoral. It is not directly a duty to seek affluence for itself; but indirectly it may very well be a duty, namely, in order to guard against poverty, which is a great temptation to vice. But then it is not happiness, but the preservation of the integrity of my morality, that is my end and at the same time my duty. (Kant MV, 388, emphasis added)

The moral duty to provide the basic wealth and material support necessary for one's moral integrity is indeed a duty to oneself, but one that can only be generally realized through public duties and collective action in a just society. In a complex and dynamic strategic environment of many people, conflicts, and problems of collective action, the harmony of freedom as well as the equality of each person as an end before the moral law requires the intercession of political institutions to make the moral Realm of Ends accessible in the material world of natural and strategic inequalities. Without such intercession, no assurance exists that the potential of one person or class will not be sacrificed to the exploitation of another. Individually, we must take the first "moral" step to create our lives, but Kant's insight also suggests that we will not be successful in this quest without the aid of others, including the collective "will of all," distributing property within a just state.

The responsibility to support equal access to moral integrity is a duty realized through the nurturing of justice as a collective duty of each to all. Such a duty carries a categorical imperative to protect everyone's moral equality at a baseline and, in this way, empower human moral freedom. Supporting the state is the only practical route to the mutual respect and equal power to which each of us is entitled as a moral agent with common intrinsic value.

A major reason for the involvement of the state in the definition and persistence of a property baseline is Kant's requirement that public policy coordinate individual action. To set up a system of distributive justice in an effort to establish the baseline for all citizens, we cannot depend on voluntary benevolence but must rely upon public policy to coerce compliance. On the one hand, the moral law sets up the state as a collective agent responsible for each and every citizen, and each person supports it in order to realize his or her full and equal potential autonomy. Therefore, the state has a responsibility to each of its citizens in the maintenance of the baseline that cannot be left to chance. On the other hand, it is important that all definitions of distributive justice be sensitive that the burdens of each and every person regarding the support of mutual freedom in the state are equal, for "an unequal distribution of burdens can never be considered just" (Kant TP, 297). The fair distribution of burden requires that not only the poor and middle class, but especially the rich and privileged contribute to the provision of the baseline, as defined and coerced by state regulation as a requirement of justice.

> The general will of the people has united itself into a society in order to maintain itself continually, and for this purpose it has subjected itself to the internal authority of the state in order to support those members of the society who are not able to support themselves. Therefore, it follows from the nature of the state that the government is authorized to require the wealthy to provide means of sustenance to those who are unable to provide the most necessary needs for themselves. Because their [i.e., the wealthy's] existence depends on the act of subjecting themselves to the commonwealth for the protection and care required in order to stay alive, they have bound themselves to contribute to the support of their fellow citizens, and this is the ground for the state's right to require them to do so. . . . [T]he money should not be raised merely through voluntary contributions, but by compulsory exactions as political burdens. (Kant MJ, 326)

The mere existence of a needy segment of society is evidence that the government is unjustly allowing the "gifts of fortune," rather than the moral law, to set policy and distribute property. In a just society, with an active and responsible government, neither those with so much that they could be benevolent nor those with so little that they require benevolence would exist.

> The wherewithal for doing good, which depends upon the gifts of fortune, is for the most part a result of the patronage of various persons owing to the injustice of government, which introduces an inequality of wealth that makes beneficence necessary. (Kant MV, 454)

Unlike charity in the market approach to policy, which is described as a moral act necessary to a functioning society (Sugden 1983), here, charity when needed is a symptom of an unjust society that fails to take responsibility for the distribution of the basic requirements of moral agency to those who have a rightful claim to them.

In Kantian terms, charity as voluntary beneficence is a poor substitute for a just society because it demeans the individual recipient by placing his existence in the hands of other individual persons. Essentially, charity unjustly puts one individual in an unequal position to others in terms of the moral law (his or her equal ability to coerce) and therefore violates his or her innate right (Kant MJ,

237–38). A just society with a moral system of distributive justice would provide baseline support in respect for the individual as an end. Only in a just society, so constructed, can each person maintain his or her equal access to moral agency without humiliation.

> Thus we acknowledge ourselves obligated to be beneficent to a poor man. But this kindness also involves a dependence of his welfare upon my generosity, which humiliates him. (Kant MV, 448–49)

> But if persons were scrupulously just there would be no poor to whom we could give alms and think that we had realized the merit of beneficence. Better than charity, better than giving of our surplus is conscientious and scrupulously fair conduct. . . . Beneficence to others must rather be commanded as a debt of honor than as an exhibition of kindness and generosity. In fact, it is a debt, and all our kindnesses are only trifles in repayment of our indebtedness. (Kant LE, 27:455–56)

Because of the practical strategic reality that people and chance cannot be relied upon to produce justice unaided, it is incumbent on the juridical state to enforce the moral law through civil statute making one's social environment fairer than it might otherwise be.[10] The just state has a duty to represent the "will of all" on a collective level when contingent arrangements provide access to moral agency for some and not others. Public justice, upholding the moral duties of each through its coordination and regulation of interpersonal relations, must respect the freedom of all its subjects equally. This, in turn, means that charity should not be allowed to humiliate anyone when justice could make charity and benevolence obsolete.

> [I]f no one of us ever did any act of love and charity, but only kept inviolate the rights of every person, there would be no misery in the world. The greatest and most common/fertile sources of human misery are due more to human injustice, than to misfortune. (Kant LE, 27:415)

The distributive justice of the juridical state, with its end of equal moral agency for all, is thus mandated by the moral law to assure the basic material conditions necessary so that each person has equal power to coerce others at a baseline. In this way, even if substantial inequalities of wealth exist, a society could remain just, as long as the affluence of some is not attained or preserved at the cost of the baseline freedom and equality of others.

The individual is not assumed to be naturally self-sufficient, but self-actualizing with the equal baseline support of a just commonwealth. Kant would not consider a society in which one is free to starve a just state. He would have the state assure its citizens that boots would be equally available to all before he would expect its citizens to pull themselves up by their bootstraps.

The juridical state is responsible for each person's value as an end-in-herself, independent of any preferences or above-baseline desires the subject might have. To be responsive to, and to base policy on, random preference would make the state the slave of those preferences with more salience, exaggerating the inequalities introduced by chance, markets, and the strategic reality of dynamic collective action.

In a just society, each person ought to be assured that the quest for autonomous expression will be protected and empowered, not made dysfunctional by one's joint occupation of the earth's surface with other human beings (Kant MJ, §16). For one to depend on no one but himself in moral matters (Kant MJ, 388), he should have the assurance that his welfare will not be allowed, by the society he supports, to fall below that baseline that guarantees that his freedom will not be exploited nor his equality, as a moral being, discounted by circumstance.

Virginia Held can be considered Kantian in her claim that moral rights to property extend only as far as the baseline.

> [P]ersons have economic and social rights as well as political and civil rights, but these economic and social rights are to an adequate minimum, or enough for basic necessities or a decent life, but not to a certain share in the whole of the economic product of a society. (Held 1980, 16)

Kant might add that the motivation for the establishment of this baseline is the necessity of autonomy as defined by the equal value of all humans as independent intrinsic ends-in-themselves.

Providing Opportunity: Active Citizenship through Civil Independence

The provision of a baseline entitlement not only results in respect for each person as a moral equal, but also encourages each individual's autonomous capacity by allowing him to achieve an independent civil status with the cooperation of other persons in his political community. The just state therefore is concerned with individual freedom and equal distribution of property at a baseline because it empowers the internal capacities of its citizens. For Kant, independence is not self-sufficiency in an economic sense, but in a moral sense. Nor is independence isolation from the community or alienation from the state, but rather immersion in collective action that supports a community of autonomous persons and creates a state that provides the opportunity for independent critical thought and action. By solving the assurance game, by focusing on freedom and equality, the state provides an opportunity for each person to develop his or her full moral capacities, his or her autonomy. This full development is the essence of Kantian moral independence.

Although autonomy, as an internal capacity of the will, is not accessible to politics, the physical and social environment in which capacities are expressed is the creation of positive law, political institutions, and policy decision making (Kymlicka 1989, 110–11).[11] The constitution of a just state should therefore not only protect the equality of its citizens' access to autonomy, but promote what is best in them by specifically providing for their independence from the influence of others' choices. "[C]ivil independence [is] owing his existence and preservation to his own rights and powers as a member of the commonwealth, not to the choice of another among the people" (Kant MJ, 314).[12] In order to be independent, to develop inner capacity, one must first be assured of access to a baseline entitlement. The individual choices of other persons "among the people" are the greatest threat to independence; therefore, these choices must be regulated by the just state enacting the categorical imperative in positive law. This requires that the collective-action problems involved with personal interaction be solved by a juridical state with a constitution based on the moral law.

> The formal condition under which [one's moral] nature can alone attain . . . its real end is in the existence of a constitution so regulating the mutual relations of men that the abuse of freedom by individuals striving one against another is opposed by a lawful authority centered in a whole, called a civil community. For it is only with this constitution that our natural predispositions [toward autonomy] have their greatest development. (Kant C3, 432)

We do not seek a just constitution to achieve the perfection of man but strive toward a just state because of our collective duty to provide the juridical attributes of freedom, equality, and independence to all, as ends. Kant's politics is fundamentally deontological, not teleological.[13]

The attribute of civil independence is based on the common intrinsic character of each individual under the moral law and gives the state the imperative, not simply to regulate private choice for the sake of freedom or equality, but to encourage the moral self-actualization of each citizen. Under a just constitution, the state has the imperative "not simply to train good citizens but good men who can improve and take care of themselves" (Kant SF, 92).

The state is not only responsible for that distribution of entitlements that will respect the inherent moral equality of each subject, but must also provide the proper incentive structure to empower each person's full development and use of his autonomy. Civil independence, as built upon freedom and equality, provides the best opportunity for moral independence and for the state to be supported by an active and autonomous electorate.

In this way, citizen independence becomes the most important criterion for the establishment and persistence of a just state within a stable democracy. The juridical republic is "the best idea of the state as it ought to be according to pure principles of justice," which provides an "internal guide and standard (norma) for every actual union of persons in a commonwealth" (Kant MJ, 313). There are three organizational forms that can represent justice as institutional political systems: autocracy, aristocracy, and democracy (Kant MJ, 338).

The most complex and ideal form of republic is democratic. In a democracy, the will of all unites to "constitute a people," the will of all independent citizens "forms a commonwealth," and they place at the head of this commonwealth the "united will," in the form of a republican constitution (Kant MJ, 339). The democratic republic with a constitution is achievable only when the juridical attributes are available to all as the state evolves. For Kant, the institutional configuration of the republic is less important than its provision of the civil attributes of freedom, equality, and independence. Kant intimates that only a truly advanced society can become a democracy since it requires the most aggressively distributional state actively providing the attributes of citizens in order that voting represent independent decision making based on widespread autonomous choice. Consent is not sacred, but the consent of an autonomous and independent electorate is the ultimate goal of the moral law in politics.

Even without the full evolution of the democratic republic, however, the state is still responsible regarding the juridical or civic attributes of its people. Any republic ought to govern in regard to the moral law with whatever institutional arrangement facilitates the demands of the moral law, given sociopolitical circumstances.

> The idea of a constitution in harmony with the natural rights of man, one namely in which the citizens obedient to the law, besides being united, ought also to be legislative, lies at the basis of all political forms; and the body politic which, conceived in conformity to it by virtue of pure concepts of reason, signifies a Platonic Ideal (republica noumenon), is not an empty chimera, but rather the eternal norm for all civil organization in general, and averts all war. . . . [I]t is a duty to enter into such a system of government, but it is provisionally the duty of the monarchs, if they rule as autocrats, to govern in a republican (not democratic) manner, that is, to treat people according to principles that are commensurate with the spirit of the law of freedom (as a nation with mature understanding would prescribe them for itself), although they would not be literally canvassed for their consent. (Kant SF, 90–91)

The "will of all" represented in a democracy with independent citizens is Kant's pure (ultimate) republic (Kant MJ, 340). The democratic republic has less chance of slipping back into despotism than either of the other two organizational options (autocracy or aristocracy); it is, in fact, the best long-term solution to the assurance game. However, the democratic republic is realized over time and through the establishment of a government that respects the moral law and legislates according to its requirements, setting up the baseline entitlements and exacting taxes to support every citizen as a free and equal moral agent.

The democratic republic carries the mandate of the moral law to its evolutionary apex and fulfills the spirit of the ideal contract in the practical world. An independent, autonomous, citizenry is the only moral basis for true democracy. Anything else grants power to those without the independence of will to legislate from a Realm of Ends, compatible with the moral law. In this regard, Kant distinguishes between the active and fully independent citizen and the passive citizen whose will is dependent or dominated by others. Because of the lack of civil independence, which is related to one's lack of baseline entitlement and assurance that one's positive freedom will be respected, the passive citizen is said to "lack civil personality" (Kant MJ, 314) and is therefore denied the vote.

The distinction between active and passive citizenship has been identified by some critics (Hicks 1971; Goedecke 1973; Williams 1983; Pateman 1988; Mulholland 1990[14]) as a type of political elitism that disenfranchises women,[15] among others, from the political process by classifying them as passive citizens and therefore ineligible to vote in a democratic republic. To claim this, however, one must ignore both the particular statements Kant makes in the following paragraphs (Kant MJ, 314–15) and the overall logic and structure of his argument. Kant describes an evolution of political institutions where democratic voting is not as critical as the establishment of a republic where the juridical attributes are protected, distributed, or provided to all, regardless of class, race, gender, and so on. He is concerned that someone dependent on the will or property of another (as most women were in the eighteenth century) would, in effect, grant extra votes to those upon whom one is dependent (e.g., one's husband). The critical dimension of politics, for Kant, is providing the environment for the eventual evolution of the ideal democratic republic. But all politics rests upon the moral law, upon the concept of freedom as capacity in every person.

Kant maintains that the natural laws of freedom, one's innate rights, still apply to passive citizens, requiring that a just government recognize them as free, equal, and, at least potentially, independent. In addition, Kant insists that the law of the land respect these innate rights by providing an environment and incentive structure within which the equality of respect for each person and the harmonization of freedom allow "anyone to work up from their passive status to an active status" (Kant MJ, 315). Becoming a voting member of a just society is the goal, but the prerequisites are freedom, equality, and, most critically, civic independence. The just state, therefore, has a mandate to protect and empower each person's capacity, through the baseline entitlement, so that nothing inhibits one's full autonomy except the will of that person him- or herself.[16]

In describing the dependent condition of the passive citizen, Kant defines such dependence in relation to the choices and wills of other individual persons. All "legislative" authority is in the "will of all" that is represented by the state. In its efforts to establish the juridical attributes of citizenship (freedom, equality, independence), the state must provide that policy "reality" where all passive citizens have the opportunity for full and active citizenship.

> The legislative authority can belong only to the united will of all of the people. Because since all right is to proceed from it, it cannot do anyone wrong by its law. . . . Therefore, only the concurring and united will of all, insofar as each decides the same thing for all and all for each, and so only the general united will of all of the people can be legislative. The members of such a society who are united for giving law (*societas civilis*), that is, the members of a state, are called *citizens of a state* (*cives*). (Kant MJ, 313–14, emphasis added)

The imperative of the just state to combat citizens' dependence (Kant MJ, 314–15), combined with the imperative to construct and support a state where passive citizens can make themselves independent and active, commits Kant to a state that is the responsible agent in the definition and constitution of a baseline distribution of entitlements in support of the three juridical attributes and the harmonization of freedom.

In distinguishing between active and passive citizens Kant does not discriminate against the latter, but he highlights their condition and mandates an active state to help them change it. In addition, this distinction plays a role in support of the contention that the active state is responsible to regulate choice and distribute entitlements in such a way that the potential independence of each citizen is guaranteed as part of the solution to the assurance game. The active-passive distinction is therefore one example of the overriding imperative to empower individual freedom, equality, and independence.

Only a politically independent and morally autonomous agent can cast a vote that is a distinct expression of his or her autonomous will. Only in this way can the democratic form of the republic be achieved and protected against the immoral choices of majorities of the population. Those economically, socially, or politically dependent on the will or choices of others have less than full use of their negative freedom and consequently have an incapacitated, "heteronomous" will. By giving a vote to these individuals, the state ignores its responsibility in support of the individual's moral agency by its assumption of self-reliance, no matter the actual circumstances. Such action grants, in effect, an additional vote to those who control the will of the "passive" voter. The policy of such a system would reflect the will of an independent few and would not represent the will of all, making it unjust and immoral. "[W]hatever might be the kind of laws to which the citizens agree, these laws must not be incompatible with the natural laws of freedom and with the equality that accords with this freedom" (Kant MJ, 315). Only an autonomous electorate of free, equal, and independent citizens will, by voting, assure the least conflict between the civil and moral law.

But we must not confuse Kant with Hegel ([1821] 1978). Kant is not arguing that the state grants the individual self-definition. Rather, for him, the state allows the citizen to realize her own definitive self by assuring her of the freedom, equality, and opportunity for independence necessary for the full development of her moral capacity, that, in turn, creates her character. Civil independence is critical to this process of self-actualization.

With independence, the individual can overcome uncertainty and fear and empower practical reason in her consideration of personal and political choices. One gains control of her autonomous capacity, and can align all her subjective goals in such a manner that they promote her ends without interfering with the autonomy or elective ends of others. Although this condition is an ideal, it is one that any political system ought to strive toward, if its policy is to respect the moral law and the intrinsic value of each person as an end.

As long as states spend their wealth and efforts in ways that do not support the distributive baseline, they are "thwart[ing] the slow efforts to improve the minds of their citizens by even withdrawing all support from them, [and] nothing in the way of a moral order is to be expected" (Kant UH, 26).

An economic approach to policy design does not describe this strong and independently defined state that Kant constructs. Proponents of the market paradigm claim that such an active state can be nothing but totalitarian, anti-autonomous and, worse, paternalistic (Nozick 1974; Posner 1983; Paris and Reynolds 1983). However, with Justice from Autonomy, the result of the evolution of government toward the just state is what Kant calls a "patriotic" government. The "patriotic" state intervenes without being paternalistic.

> A patriotic government should not be confused with a paternal government (*regimen paternale*), which is the most despotic of all (for it treats its citizens as children). In a patriotic government (*regimen civitatas et patriae*), the state itself does indeed treat its subjects as members of a family, but at the same time, it also treats them as citizens of the state, that is, in accordance with laws of their own proper independence; and everyone possesses himself and does not depend on the absolute choice of another next to or over him. (Kant MJ, 317)

The just state cannot leave the moral security of its citizens to the whim of other individuals or to the fortunes of markets or chance but must protect and empower its citizens' essential capacity of will. Such a state is patriotic and not paternalistic, however, because this action does not concern itself with all the private choices of its citizens, but only with those subjective choices that infringe on the moral freedom of others in contradiction to the moral law. The objects of politics are not to interfere with the choices people make for themselves, but to support one's prerequisite capacity to make moral choices and to assure, over the long-term, that no one's subjective ends will compromise any person's moral integrity as an end-in-himself.

Toward this end, the state cannot assume that all of one's choices are worthy of respect *tout court*, but it must employ the moral law, as a standard for the civil law, to judge autonomous from nonautonomous choices, respecting only the former. Consistent with the moral law, the state should construct a coordination of individual expression and regulation of interpersonal affairs so that each person can make the most of his internal capacity to will in accord with the moral law. Only at this point are the personal, subjective preferences of the individual worthy of respect. Therefore, a legitimate and responsible state, harmonizing freedom, is not one that is automatically responsive to the preferences of its constituents. But how can a state avoid paternalism and be responsible without being responsive?

Public Trust and the Harmony of Freedom

The role of those (elected and appointed) who make law within the democratic policy process is commonly understood as responding to the preferences of citizens and aggregating these preferences into a collective public choice. "Democratic politics will be improved . . . by a more accurate translation of the preferences of American citizens into public policy" (Jenkins-Smith 1990, 1).

By this definition of public choice, responsive policy and responsible policy are one and the same. In many issue areas, however (e.g., environmental risk), a policy analyst who is strictly responsive to preferences may not be responsible to the citizens she intends to serve. In such cases the need for a morally responsible policy is contingent upon locating a nonpreference standard by which to make the public choice and therefore by which to define the responsible policy as distinct from the responsive policy.

Within the context of environmental-risk policy, how does a responsible state differ from a responsive state? First, we will consider whether responsiveness can also be responsible. Second, in cases of environmental risk, we shall explain how anticipatory policy can be effective, nonpaternalistic, and even necessary to the liberal-democratic polity. In essence, describing the mandate and justification for Kant's "patriotic" government (Kant MJ, 317) will help us to distinguish it from both the limited state of the market and the paternalistic or totalitarian state.

Responsive versus Responsible Environmental-Risk Policy

Environmental risk is a regulatory dilemma because the political requirements of environmental risk and the institutional setting of our democracy do not mesh: whereas the former requires policy *ex ante*, the latter is constructed to produce it *ex post* (Bosso 1993; Page 1978).

The characteristics of environmental risk indicate that once a technology with potential risk becomes part of the environment, hazard is already a zero-infinity dilemma, irreversible, and latent in the environment (Page 1978, 214). Existing in our water, air, or land, hazard may remain undetectable to our senses and may not physically affect anyone until the end of its latency period, when responsive policy will indeed be only a second-best solution.

In order to control risk, one must control the introduction of technologies into the environment. The single most important regulatory act is not banning a technology or cleaning up its consequences (which to a greater or lesser extent is too little, too late), but making a decision about the potential hazard before it is allowed into the environment.

A major reason for the troublesome nature of environmental risk is that decision makers have been forced to deal with it retroactively. Regulation is created only after technologies have shown themselves to be harmful. By harming, the hazard makes its way into people's preference structures and is therefore subject to the responsive aggregation mechanisms of our democracy as part of the agenda of individual citizens, lobby groups, and the electorate in general. At such a late point, little can be done to provide security from technology that exhibits harmful characteristics.

The Clean Air Act (42 U.S.C.A. §§7401–7671q) and Clean Water Act (33 U.S.C.A. §§1251–1387) were responses to dead fish and visible contamination of air and surface water. The legislation meant to control environmental risk is also responsive to perceived problems that required forty years to become evident (Trost 1984). The Resource Conservation and Recovery Act (42 U.S.C.A.

§§6901–92k) as well as Superfund (42 U.S.C.A. §§9601–75) are attempts to control and clean up existing contamination, but they largely depend on insurance, liability law, and those traditional *ex post* compensatory approaches that Talbot Page describes as ineffective in environmental-risk cases (1978, 213). The only legislation that could be described as anticipatory is the 1976 Toxic Substances Control Act (15 U.S.C.A. §§2601–96). This act was passed to *prevent* "unreasonable risk of injury to health or environment associated with the manufacture, processing, distribution in commerce, use, or disposal of chemical substances" (15 U.S.C.A. §2603f). However, as I argued in chapter 3, since its passage any anticipatory dimension of the act has collapsed so that "we are still allowing most new chemicals to enter commerce with little or no toxicity testing" (Trost 1984, 276; Graham, Green, and Roberts 1988).

The influence of the market paradigm in environmental policy argument has generated a fear of false positives; that is, we fear we will condemn a technology that will cause us no harm. Promotion of the "prevent false positives" approach is based on the use of cost-benefit methods that apply the efficiency principle to both the means and ends of environmental policy (Gillroy and Wade 1992, 6). But if the problems that presently face policymakers can be traced to the reluctance of government to regulate risk-producing technologies when they were first synthesized (Trost 1984; Bosso 1987), and if market-based regulation is responsive and can only employ *ex post* regulation, then how is it responsible to be responsive?

The reluctance to establish anticipatory laws, and the propensity to ignore those that are enacted, comes from the perceived preferences of the electorate for a minimal state that allows for an expanding economy and higher production and from the "moral force" of the tie between the market paradigm and our accepted definition of democracy as essentially responsive to individual preferences. Limiting the definition of responsible government to "responsive" government is the core problem.

The "moral" force of the tie between democratic principles and the market relieves the policymaker from any *ex ante* decisions about the potential hazard of any technology. Instead, facing the uncertainty of environmental-risk cases, all she must do is mimic the market, be responsive to the balance between preferences for economic prosperity and preferences for risk, and thus secure our democratic principles. The market provides the policymaker with the imperative to allow the introduction of any technology for which there exists a consumer base; the capacity of a technology to compete in the market is its only qualification for existence. This "moral" argument is based on the ideal that individual consumers know best what they want and that the minimal state is merely responding to the autonomous preferences of these consumers as a market would, by providing as many choices as possible and, in this way, freedom to the self-interested individual and the best possible world for the collective, simultaneously.

If consumers want propellants to make spray cans easier to use, they ought to get them, for they are, by definition, in the public interest. If people want red apples and substance X keeps them red, then substance X should be part of the market, for society will be better for its introduction. Regulation comes only when proof of harm is extensive and *beyond a reasonable doubt.*

The justification for the minimal, reactive state, within a market democracy, is that the production of these technologies provides jobs and an expanding economy that satisfies the wants of the electorate. More weight is given to these preferences when the technologies also give the citizen-consumer more choice and, in this way, a *better life*. Here, democracy, and the minimal institutions it creates, take up the market paradigm as the basic expression of the underlying normative assumptions of the electorate. The continued marketing of the risky technologies is sanctioned by the democratic character of our political institutions. The market provides for the collective interest through the "invisible hand" and for individual freedom by expanding choice to each person.

However, game theory makes us doubt the connection between the invisible hand and the public interest (Goodin 1976; Hardin 1982a; Gillroy 1991, 1992a; Gillroy and Rabe 1997), and I am not alone in questioning the idea that freedom is fully defined simply by quantity of choice in the market.

> I Hate This Supermarket
> But I Have To Say It Makes Me Think
> A Hundred Mineral Waters
> Its Fun To Guess Which Ones Are Safe To Drink
> Two-Hundred Brands of Cookies
> 87 Kinds of Chocolate Chip
> They Say That Choice Is Freedom
> I'M So Free It Drives Me To The Brink
> They Say That Choice Is Freedom
> I'M So Free Its Driving Me Insane
> It's All Too Much For Me To Stand
> So Much Supply and No Demand
> They Say That Choice Is Freedom
> I'M So Free I'M Stuck In Therapy
> (Joe Jackson. 1991. "It's All Too Much" from *Laughter and Lust*)

Current environmental-risk policy is a direct outgrowth of the priority of market efficiency in the policy process. The present regulatory structure, based on the principle of efficiency, would suggest that the only definition of "responsible" necessary to public policy is one that makes it coextensive with "responsiveness." But we need to reassess our criteria of choice and our definition of "democracy." If the responsive policy is not necessarily the responsible one, then it is incumbent on those interested in policy argument and research to routinize the inclusion of other principles that might define the responsible and anticipatory policy, independently of the policy that responds to individual preferences.

For the minimal state, the overwhelming prejudice of its regulatory structure is to prevent a false positive (finding a safe technology hazardous) rather than to protect individuals and the community from false negatives (finding a hazardous technology benign) (Page 1978, 221–49). To responsibly address environmental-risk issues, the active state needs to concentrate on the prevention of false negatives and to create anticipatory institutions that will regulate, *ex ante*, to maintain a sound level of environmental quality, accepting risks only when they prove themselves in the collective interest. But are these institutions democratic? Are they not paternalistic? Will they violate the principles of both individual freedom and collective equality?

Two arguments support the position that an active state applying anticipatory regulation is democratic. First, the definition of "liberal democracy" contains within it the assumption of anticipatory institutions. Second, if the principle justifying these anticipatory institutions involves the prerequisites of one's autonomy as capacity or moral agency, then the institutions cannot be either paternalistic or totalitarian/antidemocratic.

Although the concept of democracy is based on the concept of neutrality (Kymlicka 1989, chap. 5), it has both a "weak" and "strong" definition. The weak definition of liberal democracy makes it coextensive with self-sufficiency, on the assumption that the only way to ensure individual freedom and collective equality is to maintain strictly responsive institutions.

> In a liberal society, the common good is the result of a process of combining preferences, all of which are counted equally. . . . All preferences have equal weight "not in the sense that there is an agreed public measure of intrinsic value or satisfaction with respect to which all these conceptions come out equal, but in the sense that they are not evaluated at all from a [public] standpoint." (Rawls quoted in Kymlicka 1989, 76–77)

But it is precisely because the question of "intrinsic value" is ignored within this definition of economic liberal democracy that it is a "weak" connotation of the concept. We find the roots of the "strong" concept of liberal democracy in its more classical definition.

The classic definition of a democracy (Barry 1989) is structured on the idea that it fulfills two functions. First, a democracy should be responsive to electoral majorities. Second, a democracy should protect the basic rights of each and every citizen, regardless of his or her place in a majority or minority. The liberal democratic imperative is to construct "a political system in which individual rights are given special constitutional protection against majorities" (Barry 1989, 258), relating it directly to the Kantian definitions of the patriotic government and the democratic republic (Kant MJ, 160–63). In Kant's democratic republic, the democratic component is characterized by its responsiveness to the changing will of the majority or plurality, while the republican character of the state sets certain matters apart from majority will as necessary to the intrinsic value or moral character of each citizen and therefore universal and necessary to the polity as a whole. As we saw in the previous chapter, Kant maintains that the existence of a republic is a necessary precondition for any type of just political institutions, including liberal democracy (Kant MJ, 162).

The privileged status of the minimal state and market efficiency within our polity can be traced to a reliance upon responsiveness, the first of these characteristics of liberal democracy. Freedom as choice and the neutrality of democratic institutions in the process of preference aggregation is no doubt one component of democracy, with its own definition of freedom. But what about the other component of liberal democracy and its responsibility to the *ex ante* protection of individual rights and to the good of the community as a whole? By what can we justify a "strong" definition of liberal democracy to act as a foundation for anticipatory institutions, policies, and laws?

One possible foundation comes through Justice from Autonomy by focusing on the intrinsic value of the individual, understood as his or her capacity for autonomous moral agency. Moral autonomy defines intrinsic value for the individual, which becomes the basis for all rights and duties and is therefore worthy of *ex ante* protection within a "strong" definition of liberal democracy. One could say that these *ex ante* protections are necessary to the *ex post* development of one's preference order, which is the focus of all responsive institutions. As such, the provision of those protections that empower positive freedom in each and all individual citizens is a sound justification for responsible public policy and a prior condition for the just aggregation of preferences, and responsiveness to them.

Therefore, in addition to negative freedom of choice, a just state must also consider the internal positive freedom of the individual (Kant MJ; Berlin 1969). We must acknowledge that along with want-regarding principles, like efficiency, which presently form the major part of the decision maker's calculus, there are also ideal-regarding principles. Only the prerequisite existence of regulation, justified by the ideal-regarding principle of Justice from Autonomy, can provide the *ex ante* respect for individual moral agency that environmental-risk policy requires if decision makers are to anticipate hazards to the quality of our lives and prevent them. This want-/ideal-regarding distinction is at the foundation of the Kantian decision maker's justification of anticipatory policy.

> A want-regarding evaluation is one that takes account of the extent of want-satisfaction and nothing else, counting all wants equally regardless of their nature. An ideal-regarding evaluation, by contrast, is one that discriminates among want-satisfactions, assigning a greater value to some than to others, perhaps assigning to some a zero or even a negative value. (Barry 1990, xliv–xlv)

To date, the decision maker has been limited to the application of want-regarding principles to policy issues like environmental risk. This restricts the field of policy argument and limits the definition of responsible policy to that of responsive policy. However, this approach commits the democratic decision maker to the devaluation of the intrinsic character of the individual as well as of any intrinsic value that one might attribute to the natural environment.

But if the autonomy and empowerment of the individual can be a basis for the definition of a responsible policy, as distinct from a responsive policy, then efficiency as an imperative of the policymaker has a competitive principle that can provide its own definition of, and justification for, the just state. But what are the possible counterarguments to state involvement in the origin and persistence of anticipatory institutions as part of liberal democracy? I will isolate three.

First, autonomy as a basis for anticipatory democracy is violated by any action of the state that would remove choice from the individual. This I will call the self-sufficiency argument. Second, any anticipatory action by the state would be paternalistic and therefore antidemocratic. Third, anticipatory action to protect the environment and regulate the economy is "green totalitarianism."

The self-sufficiency argument, examined in chapter 2, contends that, for one's choices to be autonomous, the individual must be self-sufficient and have no interference from the state in his or her decision process (Nozick 1974; Wolff 1970). Any anticipatory action by an active state is therefore an antidemocratic violation of individual autonomy. However, Justice from Autonomy elevates internal capacity over choice in the definition of individual autonomy. The market recognizes only the choice as important and not the internal capacity that informs that choice. Moral capacity, which actually defines the intrinsic value of the individual, needs to become an acceptable definition of freedom for the policymaker. The "strong" definition of liberal democracy, based on a foundation of individual autonomy, needs to transcend the assumptions about the self-sufficiency of choice that are characteristic of efficiency analysis.

Second, it could be argued that any anticipatory policy based upon Kant's definition of a "patriotic" state is by definition paternalistic, as decisions are made by the state for the individual. Two arguments counter this proposition. First, the action of the state cannot be paternalistic if it makes a choice (e.g., to regulate toxic chemicals) that is beyond the power of the individual to make for herself, but which is also necessary for her autonomous capacity, which is, in turn, prior to having a preference order at all. Second, if Mill ([1859] 1947, chap. 4) is correct that the state can act nonpaternalistically to prevent collective harm, then acting to regulate toxic chemicals and prevent a collective hazard is not paternalistic.

The third argument against anticipatory action by the state charges green totalitarianism. The state is totalitarian if it controls individual behavior to achieve a collective ideal. This argument is derived from "myth" surrounding the efficiency analysis of markets as neutral, supportive of individual liberty and the collective good simultaneously. The claim is that to regulate the free trade of individuals, for any reason, would be to violate individual autonomy and the democratic nature of markets, and is therefore totalitarian.

But if the intervention of anticipatory institutions is to protect the intrinsic value of each individual as an autonomous person, then how can it be totalitarian? The action of the Kantian state is to protect that without which one can have no preference order or will to trade, let alone be an active citizen within a liberal democracy. The protection of rights is the imperative of anticipatory institutions and does not mean the diminution of democracy but its enhancement. With autonomy as the basis of anticipatory institutions, active citizens with freedom, equality, and civil independence are produced, and democracy is protected against the forced choices of those who, because of externalities, cannot maintain or satisfy the preferences they would otherwise have. If we further consider that even the nonintervention of the minimal state, allowing risk technologies without prior justification, inhibits the choices of those victimized by environmental risk, then Justice from Autonomy either provides an escape from green totalitarian institutions or can be said to be no more totalitarian than the market.

A responsible policy is distinct from a responsive policy. The former can be justified by the principle of autonomy to support a complete and "strong" definition of liberal democracy that includes anticipatory institutions and an active "patriotic" state.

Public Trust, Civic Attributes, and the Active Citizen

The fundamental assumptions of Justice from Autonomy indicate that what is important about humanity and nature are their respective intrinsic values. The integrity of each, and how they interface, defines the Kantian policymaker's Ecosystem and sets the standard that characterizes the individual level of this paradigm's fundamental assumptions.

Built upon this concern for integrity is the redesignation of collective action from the unidimensional prisoner's dilemma to the politics of the assurance game as a dynamic entity in a complex web of strategic interactions. Because of the dynamic quality of collective action, the role of a representative in the active and anticipatory coordination of citizens becomes more important.

In order to solve assurance situations and avoid degeneration into prisoner's dilemmas, the state becomes a distinct actor with specific tasks, namely, supporting autonomy through freedom, equality, and independence; and creating the material conditions for these principles. The role of the state is to assure the integrity of its citizens by protecting freedom, (re)distributing property to establish a basic moral equality, and providing opportunity of independent status. These considerations, taken as a whole, reflect distinct dimensions of the principle of autonomy, which, as moral agency, is the centerpiece of justice within the Kantian paradigm.

Just as the individual level of consideration for the Kantian policymaker involves a concern for moral and functional integrity, and collective action requires assurance from exploitation by other's choices, the role of the state is to establish just institutions and an atmosphere of trust through the protection and empowerment of humanity and nature. Trust is a product of faith that one's essential self will not be left to its own devices but essentially protected by regulation so that moral agency remains an option for everyone. From this viewpoint, trust is a necessary prerequisite to individual autonomy, social coordination, and political justice.

Trust is an essential element of politics. The capacity of a person to "trust" another allows for cooperation without systematic vulnerability.[17] The Kantian paradigm gives us a motivation for trust in the status of intrinsic value critical to moral agency, providing the policymaker with a means to establish trust in the provision and assurance of autonomy through the juridical attributes of freedom, equality, and independence.

By securing Ecosystem integrity (by protecting moral agency and nature's functional integrity where they interface), distributing property, and providing opportunity for active citizenship, the policymaker is supporting autonomy as the social definition of justice. Assurance establishes the initial atmosphere of trust that then encourages individuals to honor their predisposition toward acting by the moral law. This occurs because the assurance of the juridical attributes limits the role of fear and uncertainty (which are the single biggest contributors to immoral choice, distrust, and social injustice) in the reasoning process of the person.

For environmental risk, trust would be reliable assurance that the fears and uncertainties connected with risk will be anticipated and the intrinsic values involved will be protected and empowered by our responsible collective representatives and institutions. In the moderation of fear and uncertainty, practical reason gains its rightful place in determining individual deliberation so that choice (*Willkür*) follows the legislation of a "good" will (*Wille*) toward a Realm of Ends.

> What provides the basis for trust here is not that we agree necessarily with decisions taken on our behalf, but that we follow the process of moral thinking by which they are reached. We trust the rules of the game, and so distrust is not our automatic response if we regard any particular outcome as undesirable. A public context of accountability provides an essential link between the moral character of rulers and the judgments of their actions and policies made by the ruled. (Johnson 1993, 12)

Kant's concept of the harmony of freedom is precisely the institutional environment where individual character, the public interest, and accountability share the same moral-reasoning structure. If the state is built upon the autonomy of the person and defines itself in terms of the assurance necessary to encourage moral agency in each and all, then values have been coordinated to establish Justice from Autonomy. In effect, trust comes from a harmony of freedom and a shared standard that motivates our shared "process of moral thinking"; that standard is autonomy.

If an active and anticipatory state works to provide the civic attributes of freedom, equality, and independence (as these build upon one another and define autonomy), then we can collectively provide a civic order to encourage and empower the intrinsic value of humanity and nature. But what maxims of choice and methods of analysis can the policymaker use to actualize this objective? Specifically, how do we answer the third process question, and what context model results from the answer?

Notes to Chapter 7

1. When we speak of the "state" we mean government institutions, positive law, and the conventions, practices, and principles of the civil society. For Kant the state is the official legal and institutional structure of government.

2. The "happiness" of others is one's principle duty to others (Kant MV, §§23–25)

3. As it is capitalized, I mean Ecosystem in the Kantian sense of human/nature interface as described in chapter 5, not as a synonym for natural system.

4. This idea of freedom can be traced to concepts like consumer sovereignty (Mishan 1982b). See Gillroy 1992a and chapter 2 of this volume for a detailed exposition of "thin" and "thick" theories of autonomy.

5. See Goodin 1985. Here he dismisses a Kantian standard for protecting vulnerability and adopts a utilitarian approach. The result here is twofold: first, the moral standard has no ultimate basis to compel its purpose. Unlike a Kantian standard, which is compelled by its being a necessary part of one's agency, the utility standard makes "protecting the vulnerable" elective and not necessary to policy decision making. Second, the utilitarian standard is a negative imperative to "protect" but carries no positive imperative to "empower" human capacity and self-protection as Kant's does.

6. For detailed argument about positive freedom, first acquisition, and Kant's theory of property, see chapter 6.

7. Remember that property, according to Kant, is originally owned in common and can only be juridically allocated to individual use by application of the moral law. For the full argument on this point, see chapter 6.

8. Liberty is not freedom in the Kantian sense, but only negative liberty of choice, ignoring capacity in the person, which is the core of Kant's definition of freedom. It is also important here to remember Kant's idea of contract and the possibility that one could have a state that was organized but not just. See chapter 6.

9. In effect, a perfect duty (Kant MJ, 240; Paton 1948, 147–48).

10. Kant might argue that life is not naturally fair, but that we have an obligation, through ethics and government, to make it fairer.

11. Will Kymlicka makes the distinction between political theory and the institutions that are necessary to bring the principals of that theory to fruition. He speculates that Rawls's liberal theory of justice may require socialist institutions to make it happen. Kant's approach is based on the idea that the proof is in the principle. He argues that the institutional configuration of a state is a direct result of the principles it has at its core and their expression. Here, he would agree with Majone (1989), who contends that institutions themselves are arguments, based upon core principles.

12. One should note that Kant specifically highlights the "choices" of other individuals and not the actions of the state as the source of interference with freedom. Throughout the *Metaphysics of Morals*, Kant contends that the state, as long as it legislates by the 'will of all', is not immoral or restrictive of freedom, but necessary to that regulation and distribution that empowers capacity and is justice.

13. See note 22, chapter 5, and note 7, chapter 6 of this volume. Here, I agree with John Ladd's (1984) criticism of Patrick Riley (1983).

14. See note 10 in chapter 6.

15. Schott 1997 is the most recent contribution to feminist criticism of Kant. Although this collection represents diverse points of view on Kant and women, many contributors persist in using obscure references, including Kant's precritical essays (chap. 11), to make the point that Kant's ethics cannot be applied to enfranchise women as equals. One example is the contribution from Annette Baier (1997), which seems, at first, to concede what I will argue here, but then insists that when Kant says "person" he can only mean man. There is no specific evidence for this

contention, only vague references to his *Anthropology* and *Metaphysics of Morals* (307–08), weighed against Kant's ability to choose his words with care.

16. This final obstacle, one's own will, is not a problem if Kant is right that we each have a predisposition toward willing the moral law. In that case, with the political environment limiting the influence of fear and uncertainty in our lives, the Kingdom of Ends becomes only a matter of time and coordination.

17. And, as we remember from chapter 6, even within the assurance game, exploitation is the least preferred outcome.

8

Justice from Autonomy: Maxims and Methods

By answering the third process question, we can complete Justice from Autonomy as a comprehensive policy argument. The "whether" question requires the policymaker to have maxims on which to base decisions and methods of analysis that represent the application of the principles at stake and the moral imperatives inherent in the fundamental assumptions of the paradigm. With a completed paradigm we will also synthesize a new context model.

Politics, Autonomy, and Public Choice

Kant maintains that politics is the association of three concepts: freedom, power, and the statute law.

> A. Statute law and freedom without power [is] anarchy.
> B. Statute law and power without freedom [is] despotism.
> C. Power without freedom and statute law [is] barbarism.
> D. Power with freedom and statute law [is] a republic. (Kant AT, 330–31)

The ideal politics reflects the moral law in a system of regulatory/statute law that protects and empowers its citizens' autonomy and therefore their moral agency. Only in this way will it justly and legally maintain its own power.

The importance of Kant's philosophical politics lies in the essential role played by the concept of "freedom" and how he defines it. Unlike the one-dimensional theory of autonomy as efficiency used by the economic policy analyst, "freedom" as Kant uses it is about the essential capacity of the individual to form and be a self, a morally responsible agent who can use his ability to create the world around him, compatible with the moral law. The distinction between a "thin" theory of autonomy and a Kantian version is the difference between a policy choice based on the subjective and elective utility of the individual consumer and a choice based upon the objective and necessary prerequisites to be-ing a responsible agent for oneself and one's political community.

But what are the political conditions of optimum moral collective action? Kant's approach to Justice from Autonomy is through those material conditions necessary to each individual for his or her autonomous moral capacities to find full potential or actualization. Whereas virtue, in Kantian terms, is the internal application of the moral law to the will of the individual for the purpose of expressing positive freedom, politics is that "just" distribution of material conditions that assures the negative freedom necessary to positively affect the terms and degree of feasible fulfillment in the quest for autonomous expression in a political world. Where virtue exists in one's autonomy, justice exists in the optimal conditions for one's autonomous expression or moral agency. Each supports the other and builds upon it, for as justice secures moral agency on the basis of the principle of one's autonomy, one is free to express one's autonomy in more significant ways and the Kingdom of Ends comes closer to reality. Justice increases the instances of virtue and autonomous choice as it empowers the individual to overcome the power of uncertainty and fear to determine his or her will contrary to the moral law.

Virtue is strategically dependent on the politics of assurance (Rabe and Gillroy 1993; Gillroy and Rabe 1997) because without political collective action in the form of a just state, one's virtue (positive freedom) is too dependent on one's ability to fight off external power and the fear and uncertainty that encourage immediate desire. A starving person has a much higher probability of violating the moral law to survive than a person who is assured that basic food is available.[1]

Moreover, one's fight for virtue is waged under conditions where the unregulated externalities of others cause immorality (through fear and uncertainty) to gain force in determination of the will, exploiting one's propensity for evil. The loss of negative freedom affects the capacity for and expression of positive freedom or autonomy.

The policymaker needs to remember that poverty, exploitation, and unjust treatment cause the negative freedom of the individual to be so restricted that the expression of positive freedom is frustrated in one's uncertainty about physical and moral survival.[2] In order to protect humanity from diminishment by external desire or elective preference, the individual should be collectively free from those conditions in which the temptation to compromise one's virtue is greatest.

The fear and uncertainty generated in such collectively created circumstances can be eliminated only with collective action, that is, with public regulation or public policy. The collective response of policymakers is necessitated by the inability of any single person to coordinate and anticipate the terms of social cooperation and the ability of the state to regulate and coordinate toward a single social goal that is attentive to the basic well-being and opportunity a person requires within the polity.

If a person is considered in isolation, as she would be by the moral theorist, these contingencies are not as important as the assumptions about internal ethical choice. But for political theory and public policy, the collective decision maker is required to assume that the ethically striving person acts within a society where the asymmetries of power, wealth, and opportunity, generated by the strategic environment and the resulting "mania for domination," are real and affect one's ability to empower or express autonomy. In order to assure that the externalities of one person's actions and choices do not preclude another from the material essential to his or her full development of moral agency, it is necessary for individuals to form a regulatory structure of law through public policy to anticipate conflict and compensate for asymmetries in support of the ideals of the moral law. This manifestation of the moral law in the material world is the just state, which, from a policy point of view, is the political (juridical) equivalent to the Kingdom of Ends.

Each citizen's duty to the moral law, from the policy point of view, is a matter of contribution to that political system that has the power to distribute goods (public and private), provide opportunity, and actively support and empower self-actualization in the individual or in his or her fellow active and passive citizens. The maxims of public choice find their roots in the public administrator's duty to protect, distribute, and provide for those conditions that empower citizen autonomy.

The moral autonomy of citizens is not compromised by this concession of power to government, but is strengthened and spread across the board to the entire political community. The coordination necessary to a harmony of freedom is beyond the power or moral responsibility of any one person. Only in public policy can the individual maintain his duty to the moral law, which commands that he treat others as ends and legislate, by his own will, as if all others were free and equal in a Kingdom of Ends. This practical, collective fruition of the categorical imperative requires justice.

Politics does not, however, depend on this moral motivation but establishes coercive civil law (based on the moral law) in the material world for the purposes of protecting and empowering autonomy in each citizen, whether or not he or she is currently motivated by the categorical imperative. Kant's just society does not legislate morality, but the political conditions in which moral virtue can flourish. The assurance game, resulting from the individual predisposed to virtue facing a hostile and uncertain environment, is solved best by a just state. The policy imperative is for a civil society with a sense of distributive justice to coordinate or harmonize the freedom of all by assuring that moral behavior will not be exploited.

Morality is not external to the assurance game as it is to the prisoner's dilemma (Hardin 1982a, chap. 9). Morality is not solely the externally evolved pattern of conventions and norms, imposed on the individual to direct behavior toward cooperation, thereby providing the optimal collective outcome; it is also the prior internal predisposition and reflective capacity of each person. The moral integrity of this capacity is corrupted by the strategic reality, which, unregulated, breeds fear and domination. Politics is not simply the coordinated results of establishing a solution to the prisoner's dilemma, but the use of the moral law as a preplay basis for policy that sets up the external constraints necessary to the empowerment of ethical capacity and its expression by each (now moral) agent. In the assurance situation, the individual player is assumed to have a moral character, an internal or intrinsic moral worth, that is at risk in the strategic interaction.

Governments regulate private choice and the externalities these produce in order to empower freedom as capacity in all its citizens. In order to solve the assurance game and prevent its devolution within the system of dynamic collective action, the civil society must do more than just adopt any rules in order to coordinate;[3] a civil state must seek justice in the moral law which requires the distribution of goods and services in a way that empowers individual practical reason.

Within Justice from Autonomy as comprehensive policy argument, the maxims of public decision making under the third process question (whether?) involve first, the protection and harmonization of human freedom and functional natural systems in the integrity of Ecosystems; second, the (re)distribution of basic property in the name of human moral equality; and third, the provision of opportunity for civic and moral independence or active citizenship. These can be translated into three imperatives: Protect Ecosystem Integrity!, Distribute Property!, and Provide Opportunity!

Principles and Maxims for Public Choice

When the policymaker gathers information to set standards upon which eventually to judge the means and ends of policy and justify his decision, he must, at the most fundamental level, understand the structure of the policy problem, specifically, what is at stake in the decision and the nature of his responsibilities to the collective and the individual. From these considerations the policymaker will form the maxims upon which the policy choice will be made.

We have argued that the duty of the responsible state is to actualize the juridical or citizen attributes of freedom, equality, and independence in each citizen. As the three juridical attributes reinforce one another and define autonomy, so the maxims of action that can be assigned to each attribute reinforce one another and empower Justice from Autonomy in the maxims of the decision maker.

Maxim I: Protect Ecosystem Integrity!

The imperative to protect the intrinsic value of the environment and, in this way, harmonize the world of causality with the world of human freedom[4] is the first maxim to be considered. The ramifications of this maxim are two: first, the interdependence of human and environmental integrity, and second, the ecocentrism of policy planning within this maxim.

As we have argued, the moral integrity of humanity and the functional integrity of nature are intimately tied together. It is within our duties to nature for the individual person to respect the functioning of natural systems and to provide for their essential persistence and continued evolution. This constitutes a duty to nature as a functional end-in-itself and can be characterized as either essentially instrumental, under our definition of Kantian conservationism, or as a duty to the independent intrinsic value of nature as an "other," under Kantian preservationism.

When we humans consider nature as merely instrumental to our own utility, as within the market paradigm, we are considering it only a means to our subjective and elective ends, having no intrinsic value but only use value. As such, we are violating our duties to both ourselves and nature. In fact, we are violating our own freedom by ignoring our moral duties to perfect ourselves and provide for the autonomy of others (Kant MV, 385–89), ignoring our own intrinsic value in this process. By the terms of the imperatives of Kantian preservationism, when we submit nature to our preferences we are ignoring the perfection and harmony of our freedom with the causal world, which invokes a categorical imperative (chap. 5). Without viewing nature as a functional end in-itself, we compromise our duties to that functional causality that created us and of which we are the highest expression. Thus protecting the functional integrity of nature is necessary in and of itself.

This is also true under Kantian conservationism, where the instrumental value of nature is to our intrinsic value and where property is a common possession, of which private use is justified only through the "will of all." One's behavior toward nature, its wanton destruction by subjective preference, weakens one's moral nature, compromises the perfection of one's freedom and the freedom of others, and leads to a violation of one's duties to both oneself and others.

> A propensity to wanton destruction of what is beautiful in inanimate nature (*spiritus destructionis*) is opposed to a human being's duty to himself; because it weakens or uproots that feeling in him which, though not of itself moral, is still a disposition of sensibility that greatly promotes morality or at least prepares the way of it: the disposition, namely, to love something without any intention to use it [e.g., beautiful crystal formations, the indescribable beauty of plants]. (Kant MV, 443)

If we treat other humans merely as means to our ends, we violate our own humanity through this disrespect. The slave owner denies his own freedom in the enslavement of another. In the same way, by enslaving nature we show disrespect of ourselves and others as ends. A functioning environment is not just physically necessary for human survival; the moral importance of nature as the source of our being and our moral life is necessary to the persistent autonomy of each and every person.

The power of nature to inform and define our freedom makes this evident, as when interaction with nature transforms and perfects our reasoning capacities (Norton 1987, chap. 10; Muir [1918] 1992). But nature's contribution to our freedom is also in its independent functioning. Its processes, systems, and propensities inform our own and produce a distinct component of the ultimate good in the harmony of humanity and nature.[5] Nature's intrinsic functioning predates us and requires our respect as a self-generating and self-perpetuating entity. In protecting this functioning, we are preserving nature both for what it can do for us and because it has a unique intrinsic value.

Ecocentrism is implicit for the policy decision maker. By placing natural systems at the core of our definition of human freedom, both intrinsically and instrumentally, we are placing nature at the core of our ethics, our politics, and our economics. Nature is central, not for our prosperity or our utility alone, but, more critically, for our freedom. Nature's status as a core component of our freedom, within Kantian conservationism, as well as its distinct status as a functioning entity that commands respect regardless of its uses and our preferences, makes Ecosystem integrity necessary to sound public policy.

The imperative to preserve human freedom through protecting and enhancing functional natural systems, as both humans and natural systems contribute to the integrity of Ecosystems, has two implications: first, all public choices must grant natural systems priority as they interface with humanity and our wants and needs. Second, humanity is responsible to understand the intricacies of natural systems' functioning in order to define our duties to them within Ecosystems and maintain their persistence in the face of human collective action.

Maxim II: Distribute Property!

In addition to protecting human freedom through Ecosystem integrity, the Kantian policymaker must use her power to distribute material property in such a way as to assure all citizens of those minimum possessions that allow their equality before the moral law.[6] Autonomy, one's positive freedom, is a creature of assurance in matters of private property.

Protecting human freedom through Ecosystem integrity is built on the assurance that government will respect what is essential about humanity and nature in its policy decision making. This respect has two dimensions: first, in respecting humanity and nature, the state encourages participation in politics and markets. Second, by providing assurance, the state encourages private individuals to provide for themselves in ways that reaffirm the harmony of freedom (among humans and between humanity and nature), defeating the "mania for domination."

Participation in politics requires status. Minimum status requires that one have those basic material possessions that allow one to participate in the market and to obtain that material independence that makes one an active citizen. The assurance that one's expressions of positive freedom will not be routinely exploited encourages humans to be active political animals, and it encourages and promotes democracy and active citizenship.

In distributing and redistributing goods the public administrator is removing the fear and uncertainty generated by poverty and extreme risk. In terms of risk to herself and the environment from technology, she is providing assurance that any collective risk accepted is for the intrinsic value of citizens in general and will not damage the intrinsic functioning of the environment.

From the Kantian point of view, public participation results from the respect individuals feel they will receive in speaking out or in taking on collective ends as their own. If individuals are to be shut down or ignored, having decisions made that affect them without their knowledge or participation, then they will answer this disrespect with self-interested and counterproductive behavior. If one cannot be heard at a whisper, one will shout; if one cannot get respect with an argument, one may pick up a gun.

Respect for public cooperation also makes individuals more apt to volunteer for, and participate in, activities that are not in their immediate interest but in the long-term collective interest. In the same way that many sacrifice their lives in a war that they believe will preserve the long-term survival of their nation, some communities will accept a toxic waste site as their contribution to an overall environmental plan that will preserve the integrity of nature and the freedom of future generations.

In addition to the increased public cooperation that comes from assurance, there are also private advantages. If Kant is correct about the individual predisposition to act morally, then assurance will encourage this action in a citizenry. Our private duties of virtue implore us to perfect ourselves and provide for the autonomy of others by making others' ends our own. This, however, assumes that self-interest and immediate desire do not dominate individual choice and action. The fear and uncertainty that fill the social vacuum without assurance produce the "mania for domination" and create that social situation where exploitation of others becomes the imperative.

With assurance, we can prevent the "mania" and can encourage what is best in people instead of what is worst. We can also set the foundation for a society where argument and discussion find general and fair participation and where standards for debate separate the logic and purpose of argument from the self-interest and noise of opinion.

Equality before the moral law, by definition, requires that each individual be able to "bind" another, not be morally subject to him. This equality of power is a function of one's ability to express equally one's positive freedom, which is a function of the distribution of property. One requires basic property for basic expression; without this ability one is not equal to one's fellow citizens before the moral law. By assuring the moral equality of persons through the proper distribution of property, we can most widely express the best in us collectively and individually.

Maxim III: Provide Opportunity!

Autonomy requires that human freedom be protected through environmental preservation, that proper distribution of property assure moral equality and, finally, that one has the opportunity to be an active and independent citizen.[7]

Only an active citizen, with a civic personality, can vote (Kant MJ, §46). The duty of the state is to provide each person with the opportunity to move from a passive to an active status. This conduit to active citizenship and moral autonomy is in the protection of freedom and the distribution of property; its results are public and private trust.

If human beings were considered only in pure isolation by Kant, then the passive/active status distinction would have no context. If the public administrator had no role in providing the political conditions that promote moral agency, then Kant's concern to create the conditions where the passive can become active would be unnecessary.

The imperative to create the conditions in which the opportunity to become active is real to each and all, makes sense only if humans are considered moral creatures in a political world where the survival and full expression of their *noumenal* selves is conditioned by the *phenomenal* reality in which they find themselves. This phenomenal world is the juridical domain of politics and public regulation; within this strategic environment, the manager makes and implements policy. The imperative to empower autonomy is therefore actualized in maxims to protect Ecosystems, to distribute property, and in this way, to provide opportunity for active citizenship to all. Justice from Autonomy creates those circumstances where political power is used to protect and empower what is intrinsically valuable in both humanity and nature.

Implementing Maxims: Two Distinctions

The present analysis of Kantian political argument has rendered a definition of Justice from Autonomy and has provided three maxims derived from the juridical attributes of citizenship that enable autonomy for one and all. The Kantian decision maker is now equipped with guideposts to help him to understand his duties to citizens in Kantian terms. However, these maxims require an administrative redefinition of priorities from the status quo market paradigm that now dominates the way in which policy is designed. The imperatives to protect, distribute, and provide need context, and Kant's philosophical politics suggests certain distinctions, between what the policymaker is accustomed to assuming about humanity, nature, and their interaction and what he needs to know about these factors.

Justice from Autonomy suggests, first, a distinction between concern for critical moral principles and for positive social convention, and second, a dichotomy between rationality and practical reason.

Critical Moral Principles versus Positive Social Conventions

The first dichotomy the policymaker needs to discover is the one between critical moral principles and the positive social conventions that these principles express and pursue. Most discussion surrounding public choices is argued in terms of the values implicit in, or affected by, a particular decision (MacLean 1986; Sagoff 1988; Sugden 1983). The implementation of Kant's maxims takes the analyst a level below the conventions or values espoused by an individual or a society (Hume [1740] 1975) to the fundamental principles upon which the assessment of value is based. In addition to positive social values generated by the evolution of conventions and norms and then socialized by society, the policymaker must accept the existence of a critical intellectual capacity common to all persons as human beings. A political decision maker should assume that this level of critical morality relates to the autonomy of each and every person and that it will be served by collective decisions motivated by Kant's maxims. Aligned with the categorical imperative, autonomy becomes the critical moral principle informing policy, which now has a duty to address humanity in the person, and it is therefore a common ethical (or critical) standard for assessing the generation of new values or the acceptance of a conventional system of values.

"Critical morality" (Hart 1963) has been used to distinguish "the morality actually accepted and shared by a given social group, from the general moral principles used in the criticism of actual social institutions including the positive morality" (20). The critical morality, in Hart's definition, provides a set of standards that act as the ultimate judge of positive laws, practical institutions, and their accepted rules of behavior. It is this standard, independent of established convention, upon which individuals ultimately base their morality and obedience to positive law.

> What surely is most needed in order to make men clear sighted in conforming the official abuse of power, is that they should preserve the sense that the certification of something as legally valid is not conclusive of the question of obedience, and that, ... its demands must in the end be submitted to moral scrutiny. ... [T]here is something outside the official system, by reference to which in the last resort the individual must solve his problems of obedience. (Hart 1961, 205–06)

The fact that law may be valid but immoral, that convention may be accepted but unacceptable to the autonomy of the individual, allows one to be a legal positivist and a critical moralist at the same time.[8] Kant's distinction between civil society and a just society is identical to Hart's dichotomy between a valid law and one that can invoke moral obedience.

Starting from this distinction, the Kantian perspective gives form and definition to this "moral" standard in terms of autonomy. The Kantian policymaker should assume that present law represents one persuasive argument with one accepted paradigm and context model, but that its ability to invoke moral obedience must be considered in the light of whether it empowers moral agency through an application of the critical principle of autonomy. The context of the moral law, the critical standard for the analysis and synthesis of positive law, assumes that ethical principle is independent of and prior to social convention; that principle is the foundation of one's practical reason establishing what is universal and necessary to the individual as a morally autonomous human being.[9] For Kant, the policymaker must separate *who* one is (an autonomous moral agent) from *what* one is (e.g., a White, Anglo-Saxon Protestant) and place the former as the foundation and critical standard of the latter (Taylor 1982, 160–61).

The most important aspect of Kantian critical moral principle is its content: moral autonomy. Most fundamentally, one assumes that the society of which one is part has evolved conventions and norms that exist as a set or competing sets of values necessary to the origin and maintenance of collective action (Hardin 1982a). Kant also assumes that the critical standard to which all these values must be held is the categorical imperative, or the moral law as it defines autonomy as humanity in the person. In order for something to be of moral value it must not violate, but must agree with, support, and empower the universal and necessary requirements of autonomy.

In a Kantian world, cooperation that renders collective action also generates social norms and values that in turn create the ethical experience of each individual citizen. Convention is one level of moral discourse, but not the only one. In addition to the conventional morality that informs our positive law and tradition, a more fundamental level of ethical discourse exists that is defined by autonomy and plays the role of critical morality. Just as Kant distinguishes between justice as positive law (*Gerechtigkeit*) and justice as independent and prior moral principle (*Recht*), he informs the policymaker that the moral character of the individual cannot be gauged solely by the standards of social convention but must be judged as all proper cultural values should be: by the critical moral principle of autonomy.[10]

Autonomy, in this sense, has two dimensions: one private and one social. To empower autonomy, one must address both dimensions. To consider autonomy to be concerned solely with internal freedom is inadequate.

> [A one-dimensional definition of autonomy] fails to recognize that private and public autonomy are equiprimordial. It is not a matter of public autonomy supplementing and remaining external to private autonomy, but rather of an internal, that is, conceptually necessary connection between them. For, in the final analysis, private legal persons cannot even attain the enjoyment of equal individual liberties unless they themselves, by jointly exercising their autonomy as citizens, arrive at a clear understanding about what interests and criteria are justified and in what respects equal things will be treated equally and unequal things treated unequally in any particular case. (Habermas 1994, 112–13)

Within the social milieu, the collective or public requirements of autonomy are debated and the full capacity that is the private autonomous will either becomes fully empowered or dies of neglect and frustration. The social dimension of autonomy lies in the ability of a moral agent to express positive freedom within an environment of social value and convention, where this expression may challenge the status quo and set objectives for its evolution.

Critical morality, therefore, has two roles: judge and agent of change. As a judge of social practice, it acts as the ultimate standard for the assignment of value in the material world. Kant would support the idea of individuals, armed with critical morality, facing the historical, technological, and political reality of the material world and evolving norms and values that make the critical moral standard of autonomy real in their lives and the lives of others (the idea of creating a harmony of freedom through a civil law that reflects the moral law).

As an agent of change, the standard of the critical morality is utilized specifically to test and evaluate current values and practices so that they might be updated and made consistent with the demands of autonomy in light of the realities that confront individuals. Here, context affects ethics. The situation does not determine what is ethical, but circumstances create the dynamic in which convention is judged by critical principle and ethical change defined. Public policy is, then, the acknowledgment that what *is* does not always measure up to what *ought* to be in terms of critical morality. Here, critical morality acts as a moral "rule of recognition" (Hart 1961, 92), defining "good" policy in terms of its consideration of autonomy and its subsequent empowerment of moral agency.[11]

This rule of recognition establishes a standard of moral validity and is decisive as to the ethical standing of any social, political, or economic circumstance. Critical morality is a timeless and universal principle that transforms the material world through the moral agency of individuals and the policy decisions of just states. Critical morality, in the categorical imperative, is always morally conclusive and definitive. Over time those values that do not stand the tests of universality, necessity, and the harmony of freedom lose validity and the power to oblige the individual.

The policymaker trying to harmonize the freedom of one agent with that of another must be concerned with policy that stands the test of the critical morality; he or she cannot allow tradition, convention, or the habits of people to stand in the way of justice. The cultural norms of a time and place are not as important as the evolution of a juridical state and the freedom of each and all, which must be the major source for "good" public policy (Kelman 1987).

Value as a conventional moral concept is therefore a secondary consideration. The moral imperative, even when involved with making policy, rests not on what is of subjective and elective importance to an individual's utility function, but on what is of objective and intrinsic worth to the full development of each individual's reasoning capacities.

This redefinition of value leads to a language of right and duty, which replaces the reliance on preferences or interests and their conflict as the basis of political decision making. The duties demanded by, and the rights so derived from, the critical morality are based upon what is universal and necessary at the most fundamental level: what the individual requires to be an autonomous being. One's humanity, not one's particular culture or citizenship, is the ethical priority.

The rights and duties that promote the harmony of freedom are a necessary prerequisite to any person having subjective preferences or a utility function. How do I know what I prefer if I do not know who I am or what my essential needs are? Can I make real choices or have real interests if I am not a person? Can I be a person without being my own moral master? Can I be my own moral master without being autonomous?

Autonomy is related to basic duties and rights that do not admit to great variation or raise problems with interpersonal comparison. The protection and empowerment of the intrinsic worth of humanity and nature are the subject of these rights and duties, which provide universal and necessary imperatives for public choice.

Overall, the public decision maker should apply Kantian maxims under the proposition that all social values are the product of judging the positive law in terms of the critical morality. This critical level of judgment renders and expresses intrinsic value in policy and can change the positive law by measuring the material world in terms of the categorical imperative. The policymaker should leave sociocultural values, unrelated to human autonomy, to the moral decision process of the individual and concentrate on what the state can do to protect, promote, and empower the moral agency of its citizens. Politically, the root of all value is the critical morality that must provide the standards by which policy will be formulated, recommended, implemented, and evaluated.

Autonomy of Moral Agents versus Preferences of Rational Maximizers

In addition to an understanding of critical morality, and in order to actualize its demands in collective choice, the Kantian policymaker must be able to distinguish between rationality and practical reason. Critical morality is "critical" because it pertains to the power of reason to determine itself practically in the material world. So the administrator should heed the demands of practical reason within a context where expressed preference holds no moral prerogative.

In the second chapter I argued that cost-benefit methods were built to operate on a set of assumptions about individuals, their rationality, and the interests that inform their social choices. These assumptions provide a shorthand for the policymaker and allow decision making, on the collective level, without elaborate theorizing or reference to actual individual choices. The foundation of these assumptions is a definition of rationality that connects three concepts: welfare, preference, and consent (Sen 1982, 66–67).

Introducing autonomy and critical morality changes this set of assumptions and creates a new definition of the individual, her reasoning, and her priorities as a basis for policy choice.

> The autonomy of the will is the sole principle of all moral laws and the duties conforming to them; . . . [T]he sole principle of morality consists in independence from all matter of the law (i.e., a desired object) and in the accompanying determination of choice by the mere form of giving universal law which a maxim must be capable of having. That independence, however, is freedom in the negative sense, while this intrinsic legislation of pure and thus practical reason is freedom in the positive sense. Thus, the moral law expresses nothing else than the autonomy of the pure practical reason (i.e., freedom). (Kant C2, 33)

Concern for distinguishing the critical morality requires that the intrinsic and essential capacities of a person's practical reason, and its translation into action, be elevated over reliance upon the elective value of subjective preference. The policymaker's search for universal and necessary ends will not be satisfied in preferences per se.

Kantian maxims have autonomy for all, empowered through the active moral agency of an active citizenry, as their ultimate goal. Even though it may be possible for one to be an agent without being a moral agent (Gillroy 1992b, 1992c), or a person without a fully developed autonomous will, the moral law requires that the just state create the environment in which even the most passive citizen can become active by his or her own will. But Kant is also making a more important point.

The job of a manager, making collective choices on the basis of the assumptions of Justice from Autonomy, is to consider each constituent as a potential moral agent: to assume that every person is striving to perfect his or her autonomy and to cooperate in a just society. In effect, the operating assumption of the just state is the existence of (at least the potential of) practical reason in each and every citizen. The positive law exists to establish a system of incentives that empower practical reason and punish nonautonomous choice in order to make the possibility of a moral Kingdom of Ends real for a juridical or constitutional society.

The policymaker actuating the critical morality should assume that an individual must be a moral self before she can have, construct, or mentally process a preference order that ought to count positively in the policy deliberations of a just state. The decision maker's duty is to the active citizen and to the passive citizen trying to gain active status. The duty to freedom, equality, and independence is a duty to the elevation of agents to moral agency and is therefore a demand to empower practical reason in every person by encouraging individual autonomy as a prerequisite to preference. That an individual can have preferences and order them into a utility function is contingent, from this point of view, on the precondition that moral agency is protected and empowered. Being "rational" means having autonomous preferences.

The "reasoning" individual should be assumed to have the potential to process categorical as well as hypothetical imperatives and to distinguish between moral and nonmoral decision-situations. This moves past the assumption of economic rationality and toward the more powerful concept of human practical reasoning. The "rationality" of preference orders is not important from a Kantian point of view; just the prerequisites of a fully actualized and morally practical reason are important.

As I have argued, both individual effort and collective coordination through justice are required to make the moral law practical in the lives of active citizens. Practical reason is inherent in all but is a complex freedom that requires collective as well as individual participation in the security and empowerment of each citizen. For Kant, "practical reason is concerned not with objects in order to know them but with its own capacity to make them real" (C2, 90). Knowing what is right is one thing; acting practically in accordance with the demands of one's reason is quite another. "The reason is that in the former it is only a question of the maxim, which must be genuine and pure, whereas in the latter it is also a question of capacity and physical ability to realize a desired object" (Kant C2, 37). The moral imperative to exercise one's practical reason, transferred into the juridical realm, where political duties to oneself and the happiness of others become the individual's focus, creates an imperative to construct the social conditions for the widest possible exercise and expression of practical reason. These social conditions also become the focus of a policy process seeking Justice from Autonomy.

Kant describes the individual, who is the subject of policy choice, as having both reason and desire, and the predisposition to be a moral person. The individual has a complex mind and the capacity to legislate for himself in an eventual Realm of Ends if the political system can provide the just environment for the harmony of freedom.

Here, the policymaker is not interested in why an individual ought to be moral, but only with what he, as a collective decision maker, ought to assume about that individual so that policy is produced that gives the citizen the best chance of actually being, or becoming, morally autonomous. The assumptive structure of policy thought is only concerned with what would be rational and moral to the individual as a fully developed moral agent. The imperative is to assume what is best in the individual and legislate, juridically, on this basis.

The full development of the individual's capacity for autonomy is at stake in the world of collective strategic choice, and the policymaker must be aware of what will affect the integrity of individual freedom. "Dignity" as a concept defined by social convention and the time and place of an individual's social context is not part of the Kantian critical morality and is therefore an unsound basis for policy choice. The priceless, timeless, universal, and necessary "dignity (an absolute inner worth)" (Kant MV, 434–35) of human autonomy is the only fit basis for collective judgments of human value.

In the same way that individual values are superficial and principles central, utility and welfare are elective concerns that are only of consideration to the Kantian policymaker to the degree that they are essential for moral agency. Under these conditions welfare ceases to be a creature of subjective utility, different for each person; it becomes an expression of the demands of making reason practical, which is an objective and universal prerequisite for all moral agents, active and passive alike.

Overall, the decision maker is not choosing policy under the assumption that the citizen is a rational maximizer of his own individual welfare, but on the basis of two axioms: first, that the citizen is an ethically predisposed practical reasoner who requires autonomy that will allow him to exercise his will on the basis of intellectually approved principles; second, that a just state will facilitate this conceptualization of the person and increase everyone's ability to create individual and social lives based upon the moral law. The practical reasoning capacities of the moral agent carry intrinsic value that must be paramount in any public policy calculation.

Having distinguished rationality from practical reason and positive from critical morality, we turn to formulating a methodology to complete our alternative paradigm and answer the "whether" question. The methodology assumes an active and responsible state (examined in chapter 7) as the collective representative of the citizen trying to solve his humanity.

The active state requires that the policymaker have sufficient information about the individual to act in fulfillment of just objectives, based on what is universal and necessary to all citizens regardless of their subjective preferences. Only in this way can the public choice reflect what any autonomous moral agent would legislate and therefore be justified without the actual consent of each citizen.[12] Critical morality provides the policymaker with the tool for active and anticipatory action in defense of individual freedom and the integrity of moral agency that is his duty. The state's role is to protect and empower the cooperation of these individuals and to respect the exercise of autonomy and prevent nonautonomous choices from infringing on the moral development of an active citizenry. Just as Kant sets the ideal of the active citizen as the sole legitimate participant of the republic, he sets the active state (the distributively just state) as the ideal and the sole legitimate reality for the civil society.

Building on the moral law and legislating with regard for what is universal and necessary to all potential moral agents provides the decision maker with a standard for interpersonal comparisons. The rights and duties of the policymaker regarding his obligation to protect and empower the individual are also established, and an independent foundation for anticipatory state action is provided through the material demands of the moral law. The state becomes a distinct institutional entity (parallel to the market) with distinct functions, duties, and responsibilities that reflect the imperatives of the critical morality and the demands of practical reason seeking autonomy in the origin and persistence of the republic and its citizens.

A Baseline Methodology for Justice from Autonomy

Understanding the imperative to protect and empower a citizen's moral agency, the decision maker is still faced with conceptualizing these standards so that they can be applied to real public choices. What specific material conditions will influence the positive development of individual moral character?

Kant's acknowledgment of the strategic reality of collective action and his placement of property ownership as a critical material means to autonomy (chapter 6) concentrate the focus of the just society on the provision of a *baseline* of material goods and services.[13] The baseline provides the minimum material requirements for moral equality and creates individual security through collective assurance, while it supports and reinforces the moral predilection of the actor to recognize and act upon his duties to himself and others (including nature).

Wealth becomes a means to the "preservation of the integrity of my morality," and, therefore, it becomes a duty of virtue to work against the collective-action problems that create poverty as "a great temptation to vice" (Kant MV, 388). Specifically, the collective action necessary to protect, distribute, and provide a baseline of Ecosystem integrity, real property, and opportunity that encourages the harmony of freedom and establishment of a just society must be provided. Private wealth is critical to the baseline entitlement, and, as I have argued, complete freedom as autonomy requires more than being left alone. The active and anticipatory action of the state is required to establish and redistribute goods on behalf of the moral agency of the individual. From the viewpoint of Justice from Autonomy, the connection between wealth and freedom can be seen as quadratic.[14]

In figure 8.1, one is assumed to be born with a minimal, inherent, positive, and negative freedom (F_0) but is unable to have full autonomous freedom (F_1) without a baseline level of wealth and property (W_1). As more material property is acquired, increasing the level of wealth above this baseline, the amount of freedom acquired by the individual also increases up to the point (W_2) where the accumulation of property infringes on the freedom of the individual as he becomes more involved with the wealth as an end-in-itself and not as a means to the full actualization of his moral agency (its only legitimate moral function). Thus, excessive wealth inhibits the freedom of those who accumulate it. If we assume a finite amount of material wealth (W_3) in any society at any one time, then although some basic wealth for everyone is necessary to the expression of individual freedom, excessive wealth for some also inhibits the freedom of others by depriving them of the baseline amount of material property. Redistributing this excess wealth ($W_2 \leftrightarrow W_3$) therefore increases the freedom of both those who have the wealth made available to them and those who have the wealth taken away from them.

Specifically, after the apex point on the curve (W_2), within the range of redistributable wealth (W^{***}), the further accumulation of property gives the individual increasingly less freedom since she spends all her time managing and protecting her wealth instead of perfecting her moral agency. To provide the baseline, the state may redistribute that wealth between points (W_2) and (W_3) to those below (W_1). The imperative is to provide (W_1) for all and allow market forces to allocate wealth between (W_1) and (W_2). Thus, no one has too much or too little property while all are assured of a minimum that allows them participation in the market and the polity as an active citizen with a fully functional practical reason and the ability to express it.

Kant does not propose that all citizens be made exactly equal in material terms. On the contrary, he maintains that inequalities of wealth are not antithetical to the just political system.[15] What is necessary is that all citizens be assured a basic material allocation so that each has use of his or her equal measure of negative freedom, which will empower the full development of his or her positive freedom. At this baseline, no one is destitute or in constant fear for his or her life, nor frustrated in attempts to express or actualize positive freedom by the arbitrary choices (externalities) of others who may have more wealth, power, or position.[16] The distributively just state establishes these baseline material conditions and assures each citizen that attempts to move

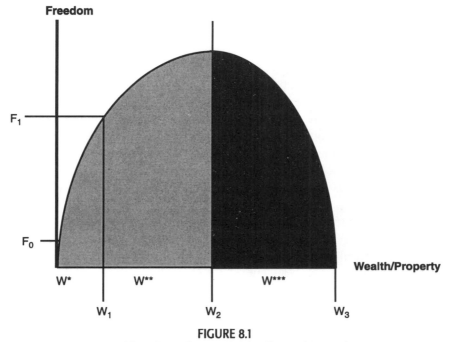

FIGURE 8.1
Wealth and Freedom: At the Baseline and Beyond
W_1 = The baseline; W_2 = Point at which wealth no longer increases positive freedom; W_3 = Maximum amount of wealth to be distributed.

Considering person (i), this curve represents: F = One's core freedom without a just state; (F_1, W_1) = The baseline combination of freedom and property required to protect and empower positive freedom and moral agency in the person; W^* = The baseline range of wealth and freedom which is the primary responsibility of the distributively just state; W^{**}= Range of wealth controlled by markets in a just society (in this range one's accumulation of wealth still increases one's positive freedom) W^{***} = Range of wealth that no longer empowers freedom and is therefore subject to redistribution by the state in its efforts to establish the baseline for others.

from a passive to an active status will not be blocked by anything other than the will of the individual.

Property is necessary for each person's full development as a moral agent. A baseline set of goods and opportunities for expression (the entitlement set) empowers the individual and protects an initial core of positive and negative freedom (F_0) from the ravages of chance or other heteronomous wills. Since government is the only level of human organization that can regulate collective action and act to compensate for economic externalities and social asymmetries that threaten a citizen-agent's equal access to intrinsic moral autonomy, the provision of (W_1) is its juridical duty.

Well-being and assurance that one's access to one's moral agency will not be immorally blocked by others are the core concerns of the just state. Freedom, well-being, and agency are not separate concepts (Sen 1985), but integral components of a single political concern: the full and equal moral agency of all individuals as active citizens. Agency without well-being at the baseline is not moral agency nor is it conducive to the responsible use of one's moral capacity to choose and act publicly. Moral agency, based on autonomy as capacity, will only find widespread and equal expression within the context of a distributively just society created through the methodology of establishing a baseline.

A Kantian justification structure for policy choice values humanity and nature intrinsically. The policymaker, within an active state that has accepted the responsibility to protect and empower individual moral autonomy, is interested in the necessary prerequisite material conditions to assure the integrity of a citizen's autonomous capacity and its expression in moral agency. But how can the concept of the baseline be represented by methodological shorthand for the policymaker?

Baseline conditions will be assumed to be the same for each and every member of a particular society and necessary to the empowerment of the self and to a subjective utility function that does not violate the moral law. Therefore, the baseline will be represented in terms of a *function* that identifies the duties of a just state by the distribution of those goods and opportunities that support the moral agency of the potentially active citizen. The baseline function is political shorthand for both the moral integrity of humanity and the functional integrity of nature. The material requirements of these intrinsic values, designated as an *autonomy function*, imply that the moral law is at stake in the persistence of the baseline. These considerations invoke a language of rights and duties.

After securing the baseline, each individual citizen can be said to have a private right to be respected as a moral agent and a public duty to respect the integrity of others. He will be assumed to have a public right to his baseline function. He will also have a private duty to participate in and support the collective institutions set up to protect and empower his capacity, the autonomous agency of others, and the functional integrity of the environment. Without those institutions, compliance in collective action can be neither expected nor morally required.

If we assume that I will cooperate only on the assurance that others will also cooperate, then reciprocity is required to originate or maintain collective action. This reciprocity is based upon the requirements of the moral law, and therefore, without the assurance of respect for autonomy in my person, I will not cooperate nor can I be morally expected to. Respect for integrity requires assurance that establishes trust and cooperation.

For a policymaker to respect the right of each citizen, he must not evaluate policy just by its gross or net outcomes, but, first and foremost, by its effect on the baseline distribution essential to each person's moral agency. The protection and empowerment of individual moral agency must be considered a collective duty—what we ought to supply to one another—prior to any concern for the wants or preferences of any individual. The primary duty of the decision maker is to assure each and every citizen that his baseline entitlement is secure *ex ante*, from any externalities of chance or others' behavior that might affect it adversely.

The model with which policy ought to be evaluated begins, then, with a specific definition of the baseline. Next, each policy alternative must be examined in relation to this baseline, with the burden of proof placed upon those who would risk the intrinsic value of humanity or nature. Last, those policies that pass the integrity test can then be judged, all other factors being equal, for their satisfaction of individual wants or preferences, their monetary costs, and their welfare effects.

The first step in activating this new paradigm, however, is the definition of the baseline. Although its component parts contain variables that may require adjustment, depending on the technological status of the particular society, the basic components themselves can be assumed to have universal and necessary application to all potential moral agents, as well as the same qualities and categories, no matter the dissimilarities of social reality.

Human moral agency will be considered a function of three components: Ecosystem integrity, property, and opportunity. Ecosystem integrity provides for the quality and long-term security of the first juridical attribute, moral freedom, through the provision of public goods and the regulation of public bads bringing harmony to human–natural systems interfaces. Ecosystem integrity (E^I) is the materialization of the arguments of chapters 5 and 7, wherein the freedom of the individual is tied to the prerequisite of functioning natural systems and provides the conditions under which the human moral duty to nature can be assumed and fulfilled. Duty here is both to oneself and to nature as an "other," but it requires the active state because it must be defined in terms of the provision of a collective good (environmental quality) that requires collective action and social coordination. The component of autonomy that is (E^I) provides the assurance that the world in which one lives will be regulated in an ongoing manner so that our duties to the intrinsic value of nature, and in this way our duties to the intrinsic value of humanity, will not be violated. This is so that each person's freedom can be guaranteed against exploitation by others. A clean and functioning natural environment (e.g., clean air, water, groundwater, public lands, renewable resources [food, building materials]), with exposure to environmental risks consciously limited to a minimum, is part of this baseline component. The role of public regulation and provision of collective goods is to provide coordination that solves the assurance game and protects that solution against those who would overuse natural systems in violation of their moral duties.[17]

The second component of baseline moral agency requires the just distribution of private goods as an entitlement of private property (p_i). This entitlement of the commodity/property bundle represents the private possession of common property necessary to empower one's negative and positive freedom. Three variables are part of this bundle: basic monetary wealth, real property, and sufficient fungible goods to participate in economic markets.[18] This bundle should include a minimum income and enough food, water, shelter, clothing, and other personal possessions to capacitate the individual and make him the moral equal of every other person (at the baseline), fulfilling our duty to the second juridical attribute.[19]

Third, the baseline requires that one have the opportunity set (o_i) necessary to define herself as a morally independent and active citizen. One needs access to a range of possible civil rights and services in a range of specific areas ($1 \ldots N$) that provide a secure set of collective goods now and into the future. This component relates to the third juridical attribute, citizen independence; the existence of these goods and service opportunities allows the full actualization of moral agency through access to: markets without exploitation; education; a just legal system; housing; food; shelter; employment; responsible preventative health care; public transportation; social services (e.g., safe houses); and a range of civil liberties (e.g., freedom of speech, assembly, press, religion, etc.).

Overall, each citizen ought to have an equal baseline autonomy function (A_i) made up of Ecosystem integrity, private resources, and an opportunity set as informed by the collective goods and services necessary to gain independence and moral agency as an active citizen.

$$A_i \ (E^I, p_i, o_i)$$

When each of these components meets baseline distributive requirements, the potential autonomy of each citizen against the exploitation of others will be assured, and consequently, a harmony of freedom generated. When the quantities or qualities of these components fall below baseline requirements, neither humanity nor nature is being respected as an end-in-itself and capacity, ability, and purpose will be unevenly distributed by chance and not universally protected by intentional policy choices and positive law. By chance, nature, or raw expression of power, some individuals may have access to their full moral potential while others will not. For the policymaker, therefore, moral agency is guaranteed and the duty of the active and responsible state fulfilled only under certain necessary and sufficient conditions:

$$\text{For all } (c_i) :$$
$$M_{Ai} = A_i \leftrightarrow (E^I, p_i, o_i) \geq (E^{I*}, p^*, o^*),$$

where (A_i) represents the autonomy of any individual (i), (E^I, p_i, o_i) represents the status of each component for that individual, (E^{I*}, p^*, o^*) the baseline quantities of the vector components, and (M_{Ai}) represents the individual's practical or effective capacity for moral agency. When this biconditional holds for all individual citizens (c_i), then one lives in a just society.

The tasks of the policymaker are to assess how policy alternatives affect these components and then to rank them according to their capacity for protecting and empowering individual moral agency. At this collective level, instead of a social welfare function that accounts for the subjective utility functions of each person in the society, the decision maker is guided, in making public choices, by a social autonomy function (A) that ought to be identical[20] across a society of individuals, and which assures him that individual moral agency will be respected by any proposed policy choice.

$$A (I_1 = I_2 = \ldots = I_i = \ldots = I_N)$$

Justice from Autonomy, in the active moral agency of each citizen, assumes the role as first test and ultimate judge of any political state of affairs or policy argument. The concept of the baseline replaces primary concern for costs and benefits as the methodology of policy analysis and evaluation, with concern for the public support of moral and functional integrity gaining ascendancy over efficiency in setting the ends of public choice.

A two-tiered system of policy evaluation results in which baseline considerations hold priority over above-baseline welfare concerns[21] and tradeoffs within tiers are distinguished from those between tiers. Regulation focuses on the moral asymmetries represented by the threshold between levels; this delineation should be reflected in positive law and public policy. Specifically, the moral justification for baseline trades is a more serious matter of social justice than the economically based calculation of above-baseline trades.

These components of the baseline entitlement should not be considered "primary goods" in the Rawlsian meaning of the term (Rawls 1971, §15). Rawls defines these as "things which it is supposed a rational man wants whatever else he wants" (Rawls 1971, 92). However, whereas baseline entitlement is ideal-regarding, primary goods are want-regarding. The baseline is considered a matter of duty and a universal and necessary prerequisite to a just society regardless of any person's wants. Rawls skirts the question of relative value and universality of these goods to different people with different wants (Gillroy 2000; Barry 1973, 55–56). Baseline entitlements have nothing to do with above-baseline wants or economic exchange but are instead concerned with the ideal of human autonomy and the ability to be a moral agent and an active citizen. The baseline is also ideal-regarding because it sets a standard for sorting wants (Barry 1990) while it focuses upon the generic integrity of the individual that is assumed to be necessary and sufficient (in Kantian terms) to all citizens' moral agency regardless of what wants or needs develop above the baseline. Providing a uniform security package, the baseline activates, protects, and empowers the moral predisposition in humanity and allows the individual the privilege of subjective preferences that are autonomous and moral.

By establishing a baseline and utilizing it as a tool in setting ends for law, all subjective societal welfare goals are made subject to that policy that respects the only necessary ends—human moral integrity and the functional integrity of the environment. The autonomy function can gauge whether a policy initiative is respectful of intrinsic value in humanity or nature and set the proper ends for government policy and the parameters of state regulatory activities.

Once the primary ends of human and natural intrinsic value are protected and empowered, setting the "ends" of the policy, the means of each policy can then be subjected to cost-effectiveness analysis.[22] Cost is a creature of priority.

With the agenda set to provide the baseline, means to those "moral" ends may be the least-cost alternatives. Each citizen has a duty (through the state) to seek justice and the full provision of the baseline, but it is acceptable to judge the most efficient means to the ends specified by Justice from Autonomy so that the highest number of baseline goods and services can be provided. The moral law, administered through the evaluation of the autonomy function, will allow only those actions and allocations that support the freedom of all in harmony. The decision maker need not consider independently what the welfare consequences of his policy choice might be, as long as it respects the moral agency of his constituents *ex ante*.[23]

Asymmetry between present and future generations is also less of a policy dilemma. Although we cannot know the utility function of any future human being, we do know that his or her moral agency will be based on the same considerations as ours. If a baseline is provided for him or her, we can be assured that we are preserving adequate entitlements to protect and empower the future as we protect and empower ourselves. This does not mean that the baseline is static and inflexible to changes in technology or in the complexity of society. The baseline will adapt to the changing demands of individual moral agency by adding or changing material requirements as they are demanded by principle. Adequate housing in the Arctic is different from that in Africa. Baseline food and clothing will vary, given time, place, and climate. But, while the particulars may be different, the overriding imperative is to assure the moral agency of all and the *quality of life* necessary to this end.

The Baseline as Method?

MacIntyre (1977) notes five shortcomings of cost-benefit methods in the evaluation of public policy for which a baseline autonomy function compensates. First, he claims that utilitarianism in the form of cost-benefit procedures cannot limit the number of alternatives to be put to the utilitarian test. Second, MacIntyre posits that cost-benefit analysis lacks a set procedure to classify variables as costs or benefits. The third shortcoming he identifies addresses the question of who will identify costs and benefits. What criteria are used to categorize and rank variables on a cost-benefit scale? Fourth, what counts as a consequence of a policy action is described as problematic. "What are reasonable standards for prediction? How much care and effort am I required to exert before I make my decision?" (MacIntyre 1977, 223). Finally, MacIntyre points to a problem with the time scale (short or long term) used in assessing policy consequences. He concludes that cost-benefit "requires a background of beliefs and of evaluative commitments" if it is to work at all (MacIntyre 1977, 224).

MacIntyre's five criticisms focus on a fundamental fear that cost-benefit methods will not be properly decisive in a particular class of policy questions considered the dominant class of public choices: those involving intrinsic value. The key difference between cost-benefit methods and the use of the autonomy function is that the former is a consequentialist welfare standard, based on the subjective preferences of individuals, whereas the latter is a nonconsequentialist, universal, and necessary standard that removes those material conditions related to human moral agency from the economic-market calculations of monetary cost and benefit and grants them public priority. The autonomy standard replaces the imperative to be efficient with the imperative to be responsible to humanity and nature as ends.

The baseline function is a strong, nonpreference standard of policy choice. As under conditions of Pareto optimality, the individual cannot be dropped below the baseline, whereas, in a departure from Pareto, this baseline is justified by objective, human-scale standards and not by the desires or preferences of individuals. All variables concerning the support of human moral agency and the functional integrity of the environment are accommodated within Justice from Autonomy before any cost process is used. This effectively reduces the procedure to one of cost-effectiveness analysis, which does not undertake to define the benefits or ends of policy but only its most effective and least costly means.

The baseline function removes certain quantities of each component from the market (i.e., cost-benefit) calculation and labels them essentials.[24] The policy process must determine the level at which the provision of the components of the autonomy function are adequate to the baseline (i.e., what levels must be provided in order to establish or maintain the freedom, equality, and independence of each citizen). Once this specific quantitative level is established, the policymaker moves toward the establishment and persistence of the baseline. If we assume that a large number of policy decisions affect the baseline, then only a smaller set of public choices will remain for more comprehensive efficiency testing, and therefore, the use of cost-benefit methods should be easier and less risky to the essential capacities of humanity and nature.

Essentially, the autonomy function delineates and prioritizes a separate stratum of policy concerns. The field of public interest in agency-related goods and services is segregated from the realm of private choice and nonbaseline-related goods, granting the former to state regulation and the latter to market trade.

The baseline function, as a primary policy tool to set the ends of public choice, is nonconsequentialist in nature. It is based on the duty the policymaker has to the autonomy of all citizens. The baseline function would eliminate policy that traded baseline harm or risk for above-baseline welfare (e.g., possible ozone depletion for convenient spray cans) and any policy that led to the exploitation of some integrity functions for the above-baseline welfare of others (e.g., hunger for some, while others stockpile food to drive up the price). In addition, however, the baseline function would, by focusing on autonomy-related matters, set public expectations that immoral choices and actions will be regulated in the public interest so that social integrity is not violated. Even in the difficult cases, policy that traded baseline goods for other baseline goods would be judged by which components of the integrity function are at stake, and which are most critical to the joint moral status of human and natural systems as *Ecosystems*. Tampering with intrinsic value would be justified only by the autonomy function itself (e.g., accepting the environmental risk of pesticides to a natural system when under conditions of impending starvation in order to produce vast crop yield where no less risky alternative is available).

The autonomy function forces the fundamental question of any policy decision to relate to how a particular option affects the baseline, fully established or not. The duty to strive toward the baseline entitlement for all having been included in the deliberations, most political decisions ought to be oriented toward the components of the maxims previously discussed. Like the present decision maker who assumes that efficiency provides an inherently good imperative for policy analysis and choice, the Kantian policymaker can assume that striving toward the provision of the baseline assures the capacity for autonomy and is thereby a timeless element of responsible collective action. Justice from Autonomy provides a safeguard against fear and uncertainty affecting practical reason by respecting intrinsic value and protecting it *ex ante*. Even allowing for the uncertainties of environmental risk, Justice from Autonomy also provides the decision maker with a more ethically accurate definition of the individual, of the collective-action problem, and of the role of the state in establishing justice, so that administrative priorities find a firmer foundation than individual preference alone upon which to base environmental law and policy.

Throughout *Theories of Justice*, Brian Barry suggests that a precept for the assessment of justice is "that other things being equal (in particular where there is no conflict with the interest of others), it is better for people's wants to be satisfied" (1989/1995). This precept has two components: the want-regarding welfarist imperative and the *ceteris paribus* clause. Here, the imperative is determined by the clause. The policymaker must consider whether "other things" are "equal," or it may be unjust for him to consider the satisfaction of people's wants *tout court*.

In justifying and evaluating environmental law and policy, the Kantian paradigm for the active state prescribes a sense of distributive justice at a baseline that assures the equal access of all citizens to their full and active moral agency. I do not propose that the application of welfare considerations has no place in policy evaluation, but that, from a Kantian point of view, it ought to have a secondary role in the decision process. Like the welfare clause in Barry's precept, it can only be a definitive policy standard *ceteris paribus*. A Kantian concern for autonomy is meant to fulfill this *ceteris paribus* condition to welfarist policy decision making so that above the baseline, "people's wants" can "be satisfied" without justice being affected negatively.[25]

In delineating a methodology for Justice from Autonomy, we have now completed an alternative Kantian paradigm for comprehensive policy argument (fig. 8.2). The completed paradigm provides a new strategic tool with which to approach environmental law and policy. But before we move on to the application of theory to case practice in part III of this book, a practical context model that builds upon the foundation of Justice from Autonomy needs to be defined.

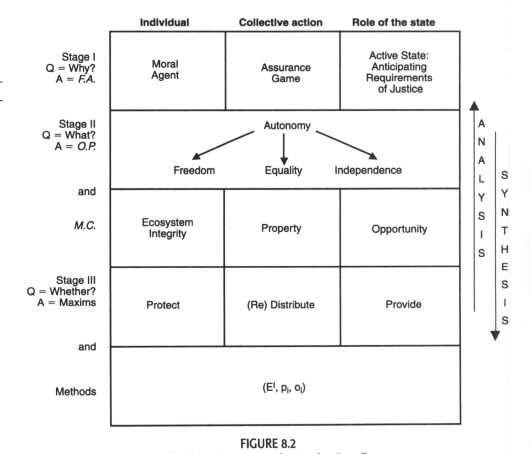

FIGURE 8.2
Justice from Autonomy: The Kantian Paradigm

F.A. = fundamental assumptions; O.P. = operating principle(s); M.C. = material conditions of principle(s).

The Kantian Context Model and "Ecosystem" Design

A context model provides a map of the policy space as entailed by the theoretical paradigm, defining an alternative policy design approach by providing a worldview that sets the priorities, relationships, and parameters of acceptable policy tactics and practical choice. A model of the worldview created by Justice from Autonomy will examine the policy space and the design approach entailed by the Kantian paradigm and will replace the Traditional Sector Approach with a new conceptualization of the human–natural systems relationship.

The context model will be built from the ideas of metapolicy and core/periphery as suggested by Justice from Autonomy, constructing the necessary components and hierarchy as suggested by the fundamental assumptions and principle(s) of the Kantian paradigm. We must remember that the context model is a result of the paradigm and is a map constructed from its preconditions. The hierarchy of the components of the model can be better described as an arrangement of the model's pieces, each of which is defined by the paradigm and placed in relation to all others by the values and conditions inherent in the comprehensive policy argument.

Core and Metapolicy

Chapter 1 suggested that a metapolicy is defined by its inherent self-referential principle that allows one to analyze each metapolicy and its outcomes by its own intrinsic standard. The self-referential standard can also be defined as the core principle of the dominant policy argument within the debate over environmental-risk policy. The principle that defines the core defines the metapolicy and the status quo comprehensive policy argument, whereas competitive arguments exist in a different level of the metapolicy, more peripheral and less central to the definition of the policy itself (see fig. 1.4).

When applied to environmental risk, the Kantian paradigm requires that the intrinsic value of humanity and nature have pride of place in the policy space, when one is assessing the ends of public choice. Specifically, the policymaker should protect Ecosystem integrity in the name of freedom, distribute property to establish moral equality, and provide opportunity for civic independence. The maxims and methods of analysis prescribed for empowering autonomy essentially require that any concern for the instrumental value of human or environmental welfare be supplanted by a universal and necessary concern for the intrinsic value of humanity and the environment, which is a condition of human freedom. Therefore, in placing the intrinsic value of humanity and nature as the core standard for policy choice, and further, by integrating these concerns into the single principle of autonomy, we establish autonomy as the self-referential principle at the core of a Kantian environmental metapolicy. In empowering human autonomy, a policymaker will empower both the moral integrity of human systems and the functional integrity of natural systems. Our context model can be constructed from this new core principle.

Toward a Kantian Context Model

Defining government as a market surrogate supporting and empowering market forces, while facilitating the immediate (TSA-I) or long-term (TSA-II) economic use of nature, within the materials balance, is no longer supportable as a model for Justice from Autonomy. We shall conceive a policy model of nature as a systemic and whole entity in which its components are valuable in that first, they support functioning natural systems, and second, they can be resources or media for human use. On this basis, the legal relationship between humanity and nature requires a holistic approach to law and whole (human-nature) Ecosystems, not separate "natural resources" and "pollution abatement" law. An integrated and systemic Ecosystem law that examines the range of human-environmental interfaces and regulates each one comprehensively is now possible.

Our conception of human systems must also change. No longer will human contact with the environment be measured solely by use. Nor will human actions and artifacts receive automatic priority over natural systems functioning. Within human affairs, a focus on instrumental value will be replaced by an imperative to protect and empower autonomy, and therefore, the burden of proof will be placed upon those who would risk it. Before public choices are made, policy arguments must be persuasively made as to what values (instrumental or intrinsic) are involved, and to whom or what (humanity or nature) these values apply, all to determine what is the best policy to protect the essential value of humanity and the natural world.

The Kantian paradigm requires us to define a responsible state, not in terms of its response to consumer wants, but by its capacity to anticipate harm to intrinsic value and to prevent it. The state is the facilitator of autonomy, and all human systems (including the economy) become part of those artifacts created to enhance the search of individuals for moral agency. We have replaced isolated environmental sectors and human institutions with integrated human and natural systems that have a core responsibility to autonomy, which is the motivation of public policy argument and action.

With autonomy as the core principle, the model will have two major components: human and natural systems. The intrinsic value of each of these components and how they can be enhanced without the major diminution of the other become the occupation and concern of policymakers. Because our duties to nature become tied to our moral duties to humanity, since we are the only strategic and moral agents in the biosphere, the priority of this context model is the protection and empowerment of nature's functional integrity as a prerequisite to an Ecosystemic harmony of ends.

Starting in chapter 4, we redefined "Ecosystem" to include the interaction of human and natural systems, where human moral evolution beyond the confines of nature charges us with a responsibility to natural systems, defined as duties both to ourselves and to nature as a functional end-in-itself. These duties produce a context model where human and natural systems are coequal components characterized by both biotic (organic) and abiotic (inorganic or constructed) elements.

Human systems will now be defined in terms of community, state, and economy, where the state is the major regulator of markets, individual action, and collective ends. We assume that in seeking autonomy, individuals form built communities, synthesize technology, and create economies and political frameworks to operationalize collective action. These artificial constructions form the abiota of human systems, allowing us to generate and transmit energy and define ourselves and our systemic relations as people.

The moral agency of people is the primary biotic value in the consideration of human systems and their evolution. Autonomy defines both the intrinsic value of the person and the political value of law and institutions as they protect and empower humanity in the person. Human beings and their political, social, architectural, and economic constructions define both the biological and artificial substance of human systems.

However, humans are of nature and their freedom begins with, and is perfected through, their basic duties to nature. The other major component of the

Kantian context model is nature, from which we came and to which we owe the genesis of our moral capacities, abilities, and purposes. Natural systems are also described in terms of their biota and abiota, integrating individual natural systems into interconnected sets of Ecosystems as they are confronted with the individual and collective actions of humanity.

Here we have the genesis of the *Ecosystem approach to policy design*. If the interaction of human and natural systems creates the Ecosystems in which we live and interact with nature, then the condition of these Ecosystems ought to define human responsibility and, therefore, determine public policy and environmental law.

Within this reordered context model, all tactical considerations of constraints, feasibility, or pitfalls within policy arguments must consider human wants and needs within the context of a world shared with nature where we bear moral responsibility to the environment as a functional end-in-itself. The burden of proof to show that their use is moral and permissible in view of the duties of the will of all will shift to those who would use the environment. As Kant argued that property is originally owned in common where private use must be justified, so our individual use of nature must be justified in terms of our collective responsibility to the demands of the moral law in creating a harmony between humanity and nature.

Our new paradigm with its redefinition of policy space, metapolicy, and core principle, reorganizes the context of law and public choice. With a new concept of "Ecosystem" that recognizes human and natural systems as protected and empowered by government, and where the priority between these components as well as concerns for constraints and feasibility have both been reconstituted by the shift of the burden of proof to those who would use the environment for private gain, a new context model is created. Specifically, for all the reasons stated above, we can no longer sectorize nature and consider its market uses, but should sectorize our own abiotic interfaces with the environment and harmonize these with nature's integrity and, in this way, our own autonomy.

A Resources to Recovery Framework for Ecosystem Argument

With human and natural systems forming Ecosystems, we have the major components of our practical context model. The model is built on the notion that the contact between human and natural systems, and the condition of these Ecosystems, ought to determine policy. The interface between human and natural systems can be represented by the Resources to Recovery model first suggested in Campbell-Mohn, Breen and Futrell (1993, 51–71).

The Resources to Recovery approach can be utilized to take a natural system's perspective and to examine human contact with nature in terms of those human processes that change or modify nature's functional integrity. Instead of dissecting the environment into species, minerals, and media for use, human contact with the environment is configured into interfaces defined by our choices regarding extraction, production, and disposal. Each of these points of human contact with natural systems (that create Ecosystems) are of concern because they pertain to decisions about how, why, and whether we should use the environment for our own purposes. These points of interface represent ethically critical decision-situations; our duties to ourselves and to nature come into play, and we need to determine our collective policy in terms of the intrinsic value of the human and natural systems involved and how they create resilient Ecosystems.

This approach to our contact with nature needs institutions and laws that reflect this new perspective. The Resources to Recovery context model integrates resources and pollution law, considers all the effects of human action as these affect the functioning of nature as a whole, and replaces the piecemeal and medium-by-medium approach to environmental law with an integrated and systemic approach. Now, all law that pertains to extraction decisions must be considered comprehensively, not species by species or mineral by mineral. All law related to manufacturing or construction and to their pollution and use of nature becomes one concern, and disposal, along with reuse and recycling, becomes an integrated subject because of our effects on nature as a functional whole, and because of the way we regulate ourselves through the law.

We now assume that human systems interface natural systems through three pathways or steps, each having its own effect on functioning natural systems and requiring comprehensive regulatory decision making in terms of preservation or conservation.[26]

> Each of these steps is divided into several parts. The laws that govern extraction are divided into laws defining areas that are off-limits to extraction, laws allocating resources for extraction, and laws governing the extraction process. Laws that govern the manufacturing process are divided into laws governing the process itself, laws governing the products manufactured, and laws governing information. The laws that govern disposal of the product include the laws governing recycling and waste disposal. (Campbell-Mohn, Breen, and Futrell 1993, 53)

In other words, in those decisions that may change the makeup, disposition, or condition of a preexisting natural system (or group of ecological systems), human and natural systems interface, and our duties to nature and ourselves must be considered.[27]

Each of these interface pathways is connected to the other in a hierarchy that originates with the decision to use nature as a resource, continues through the decision of how to use resources while minimizing the technological effects of our manufacturing and construction techniques, and concludes with the decision to reintegrate waste back into the environment.

For extraction decisions, we must define what parts of nature can be considered a resource and what parts represent part of the environmental commons in order that we "preserve the functioning of natural systems" (Campbell-Mohn, Breen, and Futrell 1993, 54). We must also decide who can extract these defined resources and how they can be extracted, and finally, how to keep the process of extraction from becoming too destructive to nature or humanity.

For manufacturing, we need to decide the best way to use extracted resources. What technology will have the fewest effects on nature and what standards will regulate the pollution generated from the processes of fabrication? We must also decide what products are required by human autonomy, under what conditions these products should be used, and which products have the least potential risk. In addition, we must be concerned about what information is provided to assure citizens regarding these products, their use, and what substitutes are available for them.[28]

For disposal, we as citizens, through the just state, are responsible for monitoring disposal and regulating what can be disposed of, when, where, and how. In order to minimize our effect upon nature, we are responsible to reuse and recycle as much as we can and to fabricate long-lasting and nondisposable products whenever possible. We must also be able to regulate risk within a system of law that does not discriminate by size of risk or ease of regulation but only by the moral need to impose the risk and the duties we have to ourselves and to nature in justifying the imposition. Currently, environmental law (specifically RCRA and CERCLA)[29] places a severe regulatory burden on big business and industry, places less rigorous rules on small business, and seems indifferent to individual use and disposal of hazardous products (Percival et al., chap. 3). This variation in regulatory concern is unacceptable within Justice from Autonomy, as it is not the source of the hazard but its potential harm to intrinsic value that is the focus of law and regulation.

The Resources to Recovery approach, as described by Campbell-Mohn, Breen, and Futrell, is amoral. But a close scrutiny of the questions one must ask and the standards one must set to implement it (in order to decide what can be extracted, what manufacturing or production processes are acceptable, and what can be disposed of and how) reveals that it requires a normative foundation, or argument paradigm, to set the moral standards for these decisions. If we build the Resources to Recovery interface from our Kantian paradigm as its context model, then we supply the moral prerequisites of a core concern for intrinsic value, a focus on the autonomy of humanity and the functional integrity of nature, a definition of duty to these values, and the placement of the duty with the only party that can bear it: humanity. The combination of Kantian paradigm, Ecosystems (natural systems and human systems), and the Resources to Recovery interface creates a new view of the world within which policy can be legislated and law codified (see fig. 8.3).

In constructing this fully integrated paradigm and context model, we have defined our Ecosystem Design Approach and provided decision makers with a new strategic orientation for comprehensive policy argument about the environment. We have also redefined the terms of the debate about the environment in some important ways.

The Ecosystem Design Approach suggests a new "truth" about human use of the environment. Instrumental use ought to be made conditional on the demands of intrinsic value and the moral law as represented by the principle of

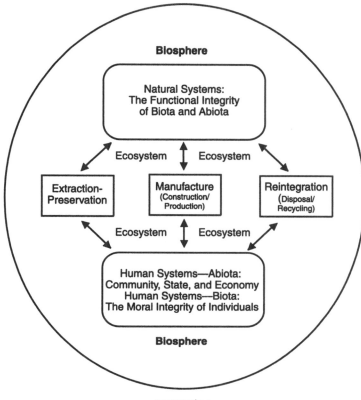

FIGURE 8.3
The Resources to Recovery Context Model

autonomy. Whether we use one another or the environment—and although humans may use both in their expression of freedom—any use must also maintain respect for humans as moral ends and for nature as a functional end-in-itself. Exploitative use, which is the premier preference for the individual deciding within a "prisoner's dilemma" context, is not the predisposition of humanity approaching the environment within the context of assurance and Justice from Autonomy, nor is use of any type the core reason for human interactions with nature. Protection and enhancement of intrinsic value, in a harmony of moral and functional ends, now drives ethics, politics, policy, and law.

Use is best viewed from the perspective of natural systems rather than from the perspective of human economy or market efficiency. If the policymaker is predisposed to protect and enhance intrinsic value, then the instrumental value of nature has less priority than the requirements of its continued persistence. Use decisions are not one-dimensional. Making decisions about morally acceptable use of nature involves prior nonuse choices and consideration of the future (both human and natural, and in terms of the evolution of Ecosystems). Primary questions exist about a priori preservation,[30] and about the right to use nature only as regulated by public and private responsibilities to justice and the moral law. Use is no longer assumed to be normal, while regulation requires justification. The assignment of rights, and therefore of the burden of proof within a policy argument, is now based upon concern for the protection and empowerment of intrinsic value, which places greater weight with natural systems and which requires a persuasive argument and justification in terms of human or natural intrinsic value to segregate any sector of nature for use.[31]

The presumption of nature as a functioning whole worthy of our respect also requires us to anticipate our effects upon nature and to plan to supply the needs of our intrinsic autonomy only when that does not significantly harm natural systems and therefore the Ecosystems we share. What we use, how we use it, and what alternatives exist to natural materials must all be considered necessary questions in making environmental-policy choices. Any other assumption would allow humanity to use nature as a means only, which would violate our duties to ourselves, to other humans, and to nature.[32]

The utilitarian logic that humanity has the moral imperative to use nature all the way to the threshold past which nature breaks down (Goodin 1976) should cease to dominate policy debate. Instead, the moral imperative of Justice from Autonomy interferes in the functioning of nature as little as possible, while providing for our essential needs, the requirements of natural functioning, and therefore, a balanced and intrinsically valuable Ecosystem.[33] If one were to recommend pushing nature to its limits, the only acceptable policy argument would have to identify this alternative as the only way to protect essential autonomy, and we would have to take special care to identify the threshold and not exceed it.

Constructing a Kantian paradigm and context model for Justice from Autonomy concludes part II of our argument. How would the Ecosystem Design Approach make a difference in decision making within concrete legal and public policy cases? On to part III!

Notes to Chapter 8

1. Although one is always morally responsible for his or her actions (Kant C2; Donagan 1977), there is a collective-action problem when preserving one's "animal nature" conflicts with acting autonomously (Kant MV, 421ff.; MV, §6). Concentrating on Kant's ethics to the exclusion of his politics discounts the importance of justice in forming moral persons. See chapters 5 and 6 of this volume.
2. By this I mean the survival of individual moral agency, which can be destroyed, as in slavery, without the physical extermination of the person.
3. Unlike Hobbes or Hume, who are very concerned with process, Kant, in his political theory, elevates the concept of autonomy and the imperatives of the moral law above process, as the only fit standard/principle for civil law.
4. The first juridical attribute.
5. For a complete argument on this point, and those that follow, see chapter 5 of this volume.
6. The second juridical attribute.
7. The third juridical attribute.
8. MacCormick (1981, 160) argues that Hart's legal positivism (1963) is built upon a critical moralism. Hart is said to separate the question of legal validity from the

question of moral duty to the law because the latter is very important and requires separate consideration.

9. Rawls's idea of reflective equilibrium may be valid here (Rawls 1971, 20ff; Gillroy 2000).

10. For a look at political theory where cultural convention is dominant, see Sandel 1982 or the work of his forefather, David Hume [1740] 1975.

11. Kelman (1987, 227–30) makes this same point in defining good public policy as that which contributes to human dignity.

12. Rather than that no democracy exists, this means that the day-to-day decisions of administrators and policymakers go on without electoral input. At present these nonelectoral/nondemocratic deliberations assume the truth of the market paradigm and the principle of efficiency.

13. There are two senses of "baseline" common to the social sciences. The first has to do with the status quo or nonagreement point in a negotiation game: the material point settled for if no solution to the game is found. The baseline in a two-person bargaining game can be of moral significance in that it introduces power asymmetries that affect one's capacity to effect the bargain (Barry 1989), but it has no inherent sense of allocative or distributive justice. The second definition of baseline is the idea of a "security level." This is the minimum payoff a player is willing to take away in any solution to the game and is the definition more compatible with my meaning. Here, however, the baseline is not a noncooperative outcome but a moral standard for individual and collective interest. It requires positive collective acts and finds a solution to the assurance game in the externally enforced, ethically just cooperation among equals (Luce and Raiffa 1957, 114–54, 199–203).

14. The term $4 - x^2 + 5x/2$ approximates this curve.

15. See chapter 7 for a more complete argument about the material requirements of "equality" before the moral law.

16. Also in line with Kantian imperatives, no charity would be necessary in this distributive state of affairs.

17. See chapter 6 for the complete argument on assurance.

18. Whereas the market paradigm assumes no market access but just that individuals will trade, given the limitations of their commodity bundles, Justice from Autonomy characterizes market access as part of the material requirements of an autonomous moral agent.

19. This could be property in the classic sense of real estate, or just material possessions and minimum income assuring active citizenship.

20. Everyone is assumed to have an equal minimum, not an equal overall amount.

21. By baseline considerations, I mean both area (W*) and area (W***) on fig. 8.1. Above-baseline trading is limited to area (W**).

22. See Anderson 1979 for an example of the use of efficiency entirely as an *ex post* cost-effectiveness test and therefore as a necessary policy principle that still allows a different *ex ante* principle to determine public ends.

23. One could see this as a type of ethical Pareto optimality in public choice.

24. In this sense "want" and "need" now have separate definitions pertaining to whether one is above or below the baseline entitlement in the quality or quantity of any particular good or service (Plant 1991, 184–220).

25. The same argument could be made about Jurgen Habermas's idea of discourse ethics (1984, 1996) or John Dryzek's idea of discourse democracy (1987, 1990). These can be analyzed as justice *ceteris paribus*, that is, as long as everyone is invited to the discourse with equal moral capacity.

26. Conservation assumes that we have decided to use but have scheduled the use across time, as in a *sustainable* use policy.

27. We are not responsible, nor do we owe a duty to ourselves or nature, when it is not our agency that is affecting nature. If a hurricane destroys a wetland, we are not

morally responsible to restore the wetland. Dysfunction caused by the interaction of natural systems, as when a lightning storm ignites a forest, is also outside of our moral obligation. Fighting the fire would require considering other than our moral duties to nature. See chap. 9.

28. Information is of special significance for assurance games (Elster 1979).
29. See chapter 3 for details.
30. Preservation can mean both nonuse and the restoration of components of non-flourishing systems.
31. The distinction between intrinsic and instrumental value requires specific assignment of rights to the intrinsic side of the equation, as this is the only way to protect the priority status of human moral integrity and the functional integrity of the environment. Here, I would disagree with Ronald Coase (1960), who describes a world of symmetric instrumental value and suggests that who has the rights, or is assigned the burden of proof, is irrelevant to the proper realization of the "efficient" policy outcome.
32. Use decisions are efficiency decisions and do not require any other standards, but nonuse decisions require a standard that focuses on the noninstrumental value of both humanity and nature and therefore is outside the Economic Design Approach.
33. This may require us to reconstruct nature to encourage its regeneration, as it requires us to substitute natural means for artificial ones (wolves to control deer populations instead of hunting).

PART III

Ecosystem Argument: Applications and Implications

As our case is new,
so we must think anew,
and act anew . . .

9

The Theory of Environmental Risk Revisited: "Rules of Thumb" for Administrative Decision Making

In this chapter, we will examine the theory of environmental risk from the standpoint of Ecosystem Design. In addition, we will assess its theoretical adequacy as an alternative social choice mechanism through the standards set by John Dryzek (1987), and we will examine how theoretical assumptions influence practical policy by analyzing an early EPA groundwater study and its administrative predisposition toward economic analysis. By examining the Environmental Protection Agency's analysis of groundwater contamination and regulation, when it first became a salient policy concern, we can see the "foundational" power of efficiency as a core principle in environmental administration. Thus, we need to explore how the Ecosystem approach to policy argument reorients and redefines the concept of environmental risk and how its application changes both the way in which we characterize risk as a public concern and what aspects of it become central to policy and legal argument.

Twice previously, in chapters 2 and 4, we listed the characteristics of environmental risk as defined by Talbot Page (1978). Initially, we did so in order to critically analyze the market perspective and determine its inadequacy as a basis for risk decision making. Our second use of Page's distinctions defined the moral and administrative requirements of environmental risk so that we could conceptualize a path beyond the market paradigm. To begin applying our new theory to reoriented practice, we shall revisit the characteristics of risk once again to determine how the Ecosystem approach in its developed form addresses environmental policy.

The Theory of Environmental Risk: Uncertainty, Ethics, and Science

The characteristics of environmental risk are divided into those dealing with uncertainty and those dealing with the management of risk. The first dominant characteristic of uncertainty is *ignorance of mechanism*.

From within the market paradigm, ignorance of mechanism is a matter of scientific analysis and the communication of "facts" to the population.[1] In order to allow risk situations to be judged properly as to consequences in terms of individual preferences, science must decipher and quantify environmental risks. Science provides empirical data to fight uncertainty and to allow individual maximizers to factor risk into their expected utility functions (Fishburn 1982). The problem encountered by the market paradigm is the inability of science, in view of ignorance of mechanism, to produce definitive numbers that speak to the actual effects of any potential risk to humans,[2] let alone to the synergistic effects of any one risk generator, given the soup of risks that we face in a modern technological society (Henderson 1993).[3]

Justice from Autonomy offers a different response to ignorance of mechanism. Risk is no longer a strictly empirical or factual matter. Responsibility to the intrinsic value of humanity and nature requires that one's ethical duty be considered in any and all policy deliberations regarding risk. By acknowledging that environmental-risk decisions are, at core, concerns about autonomy, one also acknowledges that one's duty to provide for the moral agency of people and for the functional integrity of the environment, and not welfare consequences, ought to determine policy.

Environmental risk is a matter of trust. The primary question is not about quantity of risk, but about the *capacities* at risk. If the government acknowledges its duty to autonomy, it is required to protect human and natural integrity against both potential and real collective harms—including risk. Ethics can be as potent a weapon to address uncertainty as science and must be employed to maintain trust in situations of great uncertainty (McLaren 1989, 34–35). If people are taught by a trusted instructor to swim rivers so that they can judge current, obstacles, and fords, then they have more faith in their capacity, ability, and the possibilities of a successful crossing than they would otherwise have, even if a river they face is unknown to them or the currents uncertain. It is not the statistical probability of success that is of interest to the swimmers, but their trust in the information passed to them and the confidence they have been taught to have in themselves.[4] Identically, the ethical trust one has in the purity of the food one eats or the safety of one's water supply represents a critical dimension of living in an uncertain world. It is the assurance that one's autonomy is being protected and empowered by collective action, and not the specific probability numbers, that truly matters in gaining individual cooperation in risk decision making.

Numbers are important, but only after assurance and trust are established so that one can examine the scientific "facts" from behind the shield of ethical security provided by a public and a priori respect for one's autonomy. Upon recognizing that uncertainty about the persistence of one's intrinsic value is not within the sole control of any individual, one must depend on the assurance of government, acting as a collective agent for humanity and nature, to provide the information and moral justification for collective policy decisions. If one is uncertain that one's essential value will be considered, protected, and empowered in any collective decision, then one reconsiders cooperating.

Information and argument, in this way, become important prerequisites to citizens' participation in risk decision making. In life, certainty is elusive at best, but by making autonomy a public priority, we can face risk collectively and not fear that our essence will be sacrificed in the name of consumption. This brings us to the second characteristic of risk under uncertainty: its *modest benefits*.

From a market perspective, modest benefits are a controversial expression of welfare. How "modest" is the economic benefit from nuclear power, given its risk? With the substitution of Justice from Autonomy for the market paradigm, the juxtaposition of intrinsic with instrumental values is the basis upon which "modesty" is judged. Examination of the instrumental consumer benefits, or costs, is no longer an acceptable basis for collective decision making. We must understand the intrinsic values involved and judge whether these are at risk in the creation or imposition of risk-bearing technology. Welfare benefits must be justified in terms of the potential harm that they may cause to human autonomy or natural systems functioning. As such, modest benefits cannot be examined without reference to the third characteristic of environmental risk: *catastrophic harm*.

The core dialectic within Ecosystem Design concerns which instrumental benefits or costs are being traded for what intrinsic harms or enhancements. How is the whole Ecosystem (humanity and nature) affected by human action? Human health, the usual concern when discussing environmental risk, becomes only a single dimension of a greater concern for the intrinsic values at stake in policy choice. Our new and more complex tradeoff matrix (see fig. 4.1) requires that we transcend a single, focused concern for increased cancer rates and judge both human harm and benefit through the empowerment of moral agency. Although human health is necessary to moral agency, it is not sufficient to it. The range of material concerns affecting moral agency is greater than just the probability of "excess" cancers in a population. Other health concerns, both physical and mental, as well as increased stress, and even the imposition of fear that can cause one's will to fail in moral matters, are all pertinent to the protection and empowerment of moral agency.

The fear generated by uncertainty, and not the fact of the certainty or uncertainty of an outcome, is essential to the policy choice. When approaching risk in terms of autonomy, the potential fear that could overcome reason and cause bad moral decision making is the highest priority. The responsible state should minimize the role fear plays in the lives of its citizens. The ethical commitment to autonomy and assurance justifies the legitimate power of the state and allows it to bring its influence to bear in the *ex ante* judgment of potential environmental risks.

Remembering that the intrinsic value of human autonomy includes our duties to the functional integrity of Ecosystems as wholes, we find that the decision process becomes even more complex and critical. Calculations of benefit and harm must also focus on the persistence of natural systems and provide for their empowerment, as well. Under these circumstances, catastrophic harm, the third characteristic of risk uncertainty, takes on new meaning.

Even within a market approach, catastrophic harm is a state of affairs where the natural environment is harmed beyond reconstruction and fails to function. However, now we are also concerned with harms that lead to less than total mutation or failure of a natural system. The intrinsic value of natural systems and the interface between natural and human systems that characterizes the Ecosystem Design Approach requires the policymaker to address those essential harms that affect, to any and all degree, the harmony of humanity and nature in Ecosystems.

We need to change the focus of policy choice away from exclusive concern for individual health risks to the synergism that creates a range of risks to human and natural systems. This requires that we not only broaden our collective policy concern from calculation of "excess" cancers to general risk to human moral capacity, but also shift from anxiety about risks to humans to consideration of the ecological effects of artificial and natural agents as they combine to affect the functioning of preexisting natural systems. The health of natural systems and the autonomy of human beings are at stake in environmental law and policy; this requires a shift in the burden of proof for justifying policy to those who would put these essential capacities at risk. Either the proposed technology should be shown to carry no risk to intrinsic value or it should be justified as being worth the risk imposed. The long-term positive effects on the intrinsic values within Ecosystems would have to be worth any additional risk to them.

The government agency or regulatory authority should no longer have to test and decipher risk data to prove that a technology is too risky to allow into the market; rather, those who would market the risk would have to persuade the regulators that the tradeoff between the intrinsic and instrumental values involved is justified. Science then becomes essential to the research and development of environmental-risk-generating technology since before an industry can produce or market it, it needs to justify such technology in terms of its effects upon human and natural intrinsic value.[5]

The last uncertainty characteristic of environmental risk is its classification as a *zero-infinity problem*. Again, we are concerned with how a combination of ethical and scientific "data" can be compiled so that the near-zero probability of an infinitely catastrophic event can be collectively regulated in a reasonable way. In view of the need for "data" on the material conditions of intrinsic as well as instrumental values, the role of science as well as moral argument becomes paramount.

For example, in order to regulate a zero-infinity issue, the functioning of natural systems must be analyzed and understood *ex ante*. An initial step in this process is a "biological inventory" that can be used to define, classify, and map natural systems as well as to assess human impact upon them. The Interior Department's efforts to make an inventory a centerpiece of interagency environmental analysis is a necessary prerequisite to the adoption of an Ecosystem approach to law and therefore ought to be a high priority for public funding.[6]

In Justice from Autonomy, the specific importance of a zero-infinity tradeoff ceases to be its almost zero potential to cause an infinitely serious ecological disaster as weighed against almost certain increases in human instrumental welfare benefits. Policy will now focus on how intrinsic and instrumental values fare in the interface between human and natural systems. Zero-infinity within the context of an Ecosystem Design Approach to policy becomes a larger problem for science but a smaller problem for policy.

Science receives a broader and more comprehensive mandate. Whole systems rather than parts, synergistic soups rather than individual chemical agents, Ecosystem persistence and rebuilding rather than human or natural "health" in isolation, must now be studied. However, with the market now bearing the burden of proof, more money should be available for toxicology study in the lab. With less pressure to judge a particular risk agent in a particular medium, as it, alone, may affect human health, scientists will be able to refocus on systemic data and synergistic effects within whole systems. Science's broader net may be more manageable and may produce more useful policy prescriptions within an Ecosystem Design Approach.

Risk policy is, in the end, a transscience dilemma, in which scientific data is necessary but not sufficient to making the policy choice. In the *zero-infinity dilemma*, the policymaker is concerned with her duty to autonomy that is the imperative of government as it seeks justice. The uncertainty that plagues risk policy as a zero-infinity dilemma is counteracted by a clearer imperative to protect and empower autonomy *ex ante*. Consequences are not the primary issue. Burden of proof to show responsible authorities that such use will not place essential human or natural integrity at serious risk rests on those who would use collective goods like minerals, air, or water for their personal instrumental value. These same public authorities will define "serious," "risk," and "integrity" in terms of the collective interest as defined by the baseline material conditions of autonomy or active citizenship.

Within a Justice from Autonomy paradigm, science is allowed to do what it does best while it cedes the primary authority for defining the terms of risk decision making to civil authorities. Policy requires science, but scientific data is not assumed to be the panacea for uncertainty, as it is in the market model. The "facts" gathered by scientists are evidence for the larger policy argument, which becomes defined in terms of the core principle of moral autonomy and its "certainty" as a representative of what is most important about human and natural systems.

Applying the baseline autonomy function requires that we determine what human actions place natural systems at risk. Here, science plays a key role. Scientific method can describe the physical world and how it functions, or more specifically, it can alert those who would impose a risk as to its potential ramifications on Ecosystem integrity. The functioning of Ecosystems, and more specifically, the persistence of natural systems in cooperation with human systems, becomes the central concern of science within the policy process.

With our new Kantian paradigm, uncertainty in making collective decisions about risk is a more multidimensional problem. The nonconsequentialist focus on duties to autonomy, which includes duty to the functional integrity of nature, provides a need to understand the context and requirements of intrinsic value. By adding ethics to science in the quest for making policy under uncertainty, we redefine uncertainty in terms of fear and assurance, and the public interest in terms of autonomy, while we shift the burden of proof to those who impose risk, and reclassify the role of science in its relation to both commerce and government decision making. The responsibility of the just state to assure a secure environment in which individual autonomy can be pursued becomes the imperative of the public manager.

In addition to the characteristics of risk associated with uncertainty, characteristics are also identified with the management of risk issues. What difference does a Justice from Autonomy approach make in the ramifications of these considerations?

The *stealth* exhibited by environmental risk is the first management-related concern. Within Ecosystem policy argument, the persistence of both human and natural systems, in terms of their intrinsic value, is at stake. Government's responsibilities are to anticipate the violation of autonomy and to provide for the empowerment of humanity and natural systems alike. We have already argued that, with Justice from Autonomy, the burden of proof shifts from those who would regulate a risk to those who would impose it. Within this dynamic, the stealth quality of risk is addressed anew.

Specifically, with a shifted burden of proof, scientific estimation of risk does not occur retroactively, after the introduction of environmental risk into the biosphere, where it affects both humanity and nature. Imposers of risk must justify it in terms of intrinsic value before marketing the product or technology. The policy and science of risk become anticipatory and concentrate on something that is not as stealthy: the moral agency of humanity and the functional integrity of nature.

The stealth qualities of risk are no longer placed in juxtaposition to the tangible and immediate economic gains promised by risk-generating technology. Rather, the tangible, material conditions of the baseline-autonomy function provide the dialectic for consideration of market gain and also provide the standard that guides the decision to allow a risk or prevent it. Thus, in justifying why a certain risk is worth taking, those who would impose it must argue in terms of the real intrinsic values empowered by the technology and not just in terms of its instrumental economic advantages as weighed against invisible future health costs.

Because of the establishment of a baseline function at the core of policy administration, and because the burden of proof has been shifted to the advantage of these intrinsic values, the administrative process of public justification will further reduce any stealth qualities of a technology or product. Proposing to market a product that might generate environmental risk will require that potential risk be fleshed out and scrutinized, first by those seeking marketing approval, and then by those regulators charged with approval of the risk-bearing technology. In effect, although the environmental risk will retain its stealth in physical terms (one will still not be able to taste, see, or sense it), more of its risky dimensions to humanity and nature will be identified in the approval or licensing process, causing the technology to lose most of its stealth in a political and moral sense, thus lessening the overall public fear and uncertainty in terms of policy argument and choice.

The anticipatory responsibilities of the government to protect and empower autonomy are therefore facilitated by the management approval function mandated by Justice from Autonomy and the Ecosystem Design Approach. Although stealth, in physical terms, will always exist, the new imperative to manage it *ex ante* will result in an administrative approval process that takes advantage of a burden of proof favoring intrinsic value and, in this way, manages the uncertainty and stealth quality of environmental risk. Simultaneously, public policy management now encourages dissemination of information about technology and its risks and advantages, as these affect intrinsic value. An incentive to understand potential risks in the research and development phase of new products and technologies is also set into the market, discouraging the expenditure of capital on unessential products with high risks that might not gain approval.

Awareness of potential risk by manufacturers should lead to an economic reality in which government will regulate less and less to protect the autonomy of its citizens and empower their moral capacities. As markets adapt to the regulatory requirements of the baseline function, and as the anticipatory institutions of the state construct the institutional framework for a risk-conscious society, both the fear of environmental risk and its actual effects will wane as the economy moves toward less risky technology as a result of internal price and demand signals.[7]

The risk-conscious society not only provides information to its constituents,[8] revealing the stealth of any environmental risk, but also establishes a regulatory apparatus with which to judge the value of the proposed technology, and retains the power to keep it out of the market if it is judged negatively. Only if the technology can be argued to do more for the intrinsic value of humanity and nature than it potentially harms will it be allowed into our environment. In any case, the justification process will alert regulators and the public to the range of risk, and with required labeling information provide a basis for collective and individual risk decisions that is presently nonexistent.

Turning away from welfare considerations also affects the second management concern of environmental risk: the discrepancy between risk's *internal benefits* and *external costs*.

With the new paradigm, we are no longer concerned strictly with economic costs and benefits. What is internal or external to a market is less important than what is essential and nonessential in empowering Ecosystem integrity. To assure these intrinsic values, Ecosystem law and policy must reclassify economic costs and benefits into intrinsic "empowerments" and "harms." Harms and empowerments judged to be critical to the acceptance of a *conscious* risk affect the demands of the baseline function and its maxims to protect integrity, distribute property, and provide opportunity, no matter whether they are internal or external to markets. The policy imperative shifts from a concern for aggregate quantities of costs and benefits to one for how any instrumental concern creates, or fails to create, the material conditions for the persistence and enhancement of Justice from Autonomy.

Within the Resource to Recovery context model, it is the extraction, production, and disposal interfaces that focus the attention of environmental law. If the dichotomies between external and internal or costs and benefit have any role, it is in terms of the material conditions of the principle of autonomy in the interactions that take place at each interface. Are the empowerments or harms to intrinsic value internal to the interface? To the human systems alone? To the natural systems? Do they increase autonomy or natural systems integrity? Do they cause widespread collective harm in return for private economic gain?

The public choice we make about the *collective nature of risk* is the next management characteristic to be examined. This management imperative, in recognizing that environmental risks are collective, relates directly to the Kantian assumption of property as public trust and to the assurance required, within a complex of dynamic games, to prevent the degeneration of strategic interaction into prisoner's dilemmas and chicken confrontations.

Kant's theory of property asserts the common possession of the land and the need for private right to be justified in the name of the "will of all." The assumption of common possession can be seen, in management terms, as a justification for a primary "public trust" property doctrine (Sax 1970, 1980a, b). Private property is necessary to autonomy. However, as I previously argued, when one amasses property so that it becomes an end-in-itself and usurps autonomy as the moral center of one's agency, then the state must redistribute property in the collective interest. All property must be considered primarily public and allocated privately for moral agency purposes only. In private or public hands, property is a material condition of autonomy and should be provided for as a trusteeship. The humanity in each and every person, over all generations, both morally requires prior public responsibility for property, and ethically justifies private acquisition, ownership, and use. Reconceptualizing public land and public trust helps us to define the collective nature of risk and to manage it.

The power of the state to provide anticipatory assurance requires that it treat both the collective nature of goods and the collective nature of risk seriously. Private property lies beyond government intervention as part and parcel of one's autonomy. It is in the consideration of collective goods, their distribution, and their inherent risks that the state finds its specific responsibility. If the state is to assure moral agency, and assurance is a function of proper material conditions, then the important dimension of environmental risk becomes its collective nature. The risk that one accepts as part of private moral agency (e.g., climbing a mountain) is not a proper subject of public discussion, but any risk imposed as a "nonvoluntary transfer" on all collectively (e.g., toxic contamination, radioactive fallout) is the responsibility of the state in its mandate to provide assurance (Gillroy 1992b, 236–37).

The specific "public trust doctrine" prescribed here is that risks collectively imposed on individual capacity will be consciously regulated; that property will be redistributed in the name of autonomy; and that, in effect, all property not used for the legitimate expression of individual positive freedom will be entrusted to government in the name of the autonomy of its citizens and their intergenerational moral agency. Trusteeship requires that preservation, including mitigation of harm, be the first priority on public lands and that any use be for the collective benefit of all, not for the profit of the few. If all material goods originate in the public trust and are distributed into private hands for the purposes of furthering positive freedom and collective action, then collective risk should be controlled by the anticipatory institutions of the state and not by the responsive mechanisms of the market. One then manages the collective nature of risk by exercising public trusteeship to protect the "commons," regulating collective action and not allowing the imposition of risk without justification in terms of autonomy. Public trust supersedes private instrumental welfare maximization; public or collective interests become necessary prerequisites to the autonomy of the individual and the functional integrity of nature. The conditions of freedom are as critical to autonomy as the expression of that freedom, an expression that requires property, but which cannot impose collective risk without justification in terms of the core intrinsic values involved in Ecosystem persistence and empowerment.

In addition to the public responsibilities to hold property in public trust and to prevent the unconscious imposition of collective risks by private preference, an administrator is also faced with the strategic reality of dynamic games as she manages the *collective* nature of risk. Under the right circumstances and assumptions, assurance games can degenerate into prisoner's dilemmas or games of chicken, or even evolve into coordination games, where less coercion is necessary to establish and maintain cooperation than in assurance games. Holding a public trust to scrutinize the collective nature of risk, the manager must also be mindful that too much exposure to fear and uncertainty generated by environmental risk will lead to a dissolution of faith in public trusteeship. To maintain the persistence of the assurance game, the government, as keeper of the conditions for autonomy, needs to continually protect and empower intrinsic value through its active supervision of collective assets, so degeneration of the game does not occur. Without a full commitment to *ex ante* regulation of public trust lands, strategic degeneration will occur and the increasing requirements of maintaining cooperation will cause increased central coercion and breed distrust as fewer and fewer individuals act autonomously and more turn to Kant's "mania for domination."

If, however, the manager establishes assurance within an active and anticipatory state to protect and empower Ecosystem integrity, then the game will not degenerate. Trusteeship and the prior collective ownership of property makes the degeneration of strategic reality a more remote possibility. The physical "trust" created by the public control over the preservation of property and its transfer into private hands creates a metaphysical trust, on the part of citizens, that the conditions of their freedom as capacity are being protected intergenerationally.

With this assurance, the collective nature of risk is acknowledged by the anticipatory state *ex ante*, and the status of government as the collective agent for the origin and maintenance of the baseline material conditions of active citizenship grants further assurance that any potential private uses of "public trust" property will be authorized only after any potential environmental risks are defined and justified. If all collective risks are consciously anticipated in this way and accepted only in terms of their enhancement of intrinsic values, then one is assured that one's autonomy will not be overlooked in risk decision making. Thus, one's predisposition to be moral and to cooperate is further enhanced. Fear of being exploited by collective risks having been minimized, coordination of autonomous behavior then becomes a probable result of government trusteeship.

The final two management concerns, for which an administrator need compensate, relate to the *latency* and *irreversibility* of environmental risk. A manager should be concerned that risk transferred now, to his constituents, may cause them, or the environment, irreversible harm in the future. Again, the shift in the burden of proof and the anticipatory stance of state regulators manages latency and irreversibility differently. Within a market paradigm and Economic Design Approach, present economic benefits are contrasted with amorphous future harms. This favors present generations and their prosperity over future generations and their potential well-being.

Within Justice from Autonomy, baseline autonomy is the standard for both present and future generations; the latency and irreversibility of a risk are considered with this common threshold in mind. If the responsible state accepts a collective risk because it enhances autonomy at the baseline, this decision may impose risk on the future, but because timeless moral and functional capacity provides the justification for choice, one can argue that it is a risk that future generations would have also taken. With Justice from Autonomy, one does not trade instrumental prosperity now for essential harm later, but works to place essential value at risk only when necessary for the persistence of that intrinsic value. Under these circumstances latency and irreversibility have a timeless and universal intrinsic value standard by which their imposition is judged and accepted or rejected *ex ante*. Potential risks are articulated and analyzed before the technology is accepted by regulators for transfer to citizens. This conscious acceptance of a collective, latent, and irreversible environmental risk is in terms of essential autonomy, not elective welfare, and is a decision that practical reason can approve, making it intergenerationally valid.[9]

In *Rational Ecology*, John Dryzek (1987) examines existing social choice mechanisms for their ability to accommodate environmental policy. He judges markets, administered systems, polyarchy, law, moral persuasion, and international anarchy, finding them wanting on one or more of four criteria: negative feedback, coordination, robustness or flexibility, and resilience.

Negative feedback (1987, 47–48) is defined as the ability of a social choice mechanism to cushion or protect natural systems upon contact with humanity. *Coordination* (1987, 48–51) defines the capacity of a social choice mechanism to recognize the collective nature of public goods and commons problems and treat them comprehensively. *Robustness or flexibility* (1987, 51–52) is the ability of a management system to apply universal and necessary principle across a variety of conditions as well as the capacity to move from one context to the next without undue stress or dysfunction. Finally, *resilience* (1987, 52–54) is the ability of a social choice mechanism to return human and natural systems to their previous course, when "severe" ecological problems cause them to get off track.

The Kantian paradigm provides a social choice mechanism that is sensitive to all of these dimensions of environmental policy. Our context model, which is focused on the interface between human and natural systems, combined with the imperative to anticipate and be responsible for the collective risk involved, as well as with our focus on intrinsic values, makes Justice from Autonomy, unlike the market, a social choice mechanism with an emphasis on *negative feedback*.

The constancy of its moral imperative to protect and empower human autonomy and the integrity of natural systems provide a core principle as a metapolicy that is both *robust and flexible* in facing ecological dilemmas and contexts. Justice from Autonomy is robust because all social choice is determined by a common principle arising from what is essential about humanity and nature. It is flexible because it focuses on autonomy as an end-in-itself, but allows contextual maxims to actualize the baseline. As justice in Kantian terms (*Recht*) produces various systems of positive law (*Gerechtigkeit*), given specific circumstances, so Justice from Autonomy recognizes that the protection and empowerment of integrity will employ various material measures given the context of the decision.

Ecosystem Design, as defined here, is a good *coordinator*, first, because it acknowledges the nature of human interaction from the mixed motives of an assurance game, where human reason is complex and has moral content. Second, it recognizes the collective goods /public trust nature of property and the state's responsibility in redistribution to provide assurance and to protect individuals from exploitation of their autonomy in a world of dynamic games and uncertain interpersonal relations. The nature of the collective-action problem is comprehensive, involving not just human systems or natural systems but "Eco"-systems. Coordination is also made the responsibility of the just state, which is charged with anticipating interruptions in cooperation and preventing them *ex ante*. The risk-conscious society understands the interdependence of human and natural systems and the comprehensive nature of solutions that maintain coordination of human beings in a sound ecological context.

Lastly, Ecosystem Design is *resilient*. To the degree that the courses of human and natural evolution are interdependent and can be deciphered, the imperative of Ecosystem argument is law that keeps the interaction of autonomous choice and ecological evolution on track, utilizing the power of the state to refocus this evolution whenever large-scale problems cause temporary changes.

Unlike the market mechanism, which sectorizes nature into raw materials and waste sinks, the Ecosystem Design Approach, as built upon Justice from Autonomy, recognizes the wholeness of nature and segments human activity in terms of extraction, production, and disposal. Intrinsic value is promoted over use value, and attention is now paid to the collective-action dimensions of human moral capacity, which include duties to nature as a functional end-in-itself. In these ways our alternative appears to take account of Dryzek's criteria and offers a blueprint for a morally informed administrative apparatus that can protect and enhance both human and natural integrity in interdependent Ecosystems. But how might the Kantian manager employ the Ecosystem Approach?

The Kantian Administrator and Ecosystem Design

The specifics of baseline autonomy include not only proper material entitlements, opportunity, and the active support of a just state, but also adequate environmental quality, not just for our own survival, but to respect nature. The Kantian concern with environmental risk is how these cases affect Ecosystem integrity. Thus, the just state has a duty to regulate the development, production, and marketing of toxic chemicals as they threaten the juridical attributes and natural processes at the baseline. Let us consider these in turn.

How does environmental risk affect the material distribution necessary to the juridical attributes of freedom, equality, and independence? Toxic materials in any stage of production or use have the potential to limit an individual's freedom. Limiting baseline security, health, and well-being limits one's moral agency. Toxic substances in the environment have long-term, sometimes irreversible, effects on people. In addition, these threats exacerbate the uncertainty that can cause great fear and personal exploitation as individuals conduct their lives in an environment that they perceive as full of invisible mutagenic or carcinogenic agents. A specific characteristic of environmental risk that increases this effect is its ability to cause great harm with small doses and to exist and spread harm that will only become evident after a long latency period, when it may be too late for a remedy. As I have argued, the free rider is here replaced by the imprisoned rider, who is especially prone to harm within the assurance game under these conditions. Also, prolonged strategic disadvantage or exploitation of the imprisoned rider may cause degeneration of the assurance game into a prisoner's dilemma or chicken situation.

The equality of each person, expressed in moral agency, can be hampered by the private economic choices of a few who market a toxic substance without properly justifying it as advantageous to the intrinsic value of humanity or nature. Testing, evaluating, and justifying potential environmental risks is required by the moral imperative to protect and empower autonomy *ex ante*.

Most environmental-risk problems are caused by complex technology that is almost entirely in the hands of large-scale business enterprise. These individuals and corporations are making most of the critical decisions about the development, production, use, and disposal of toxic material.[10] Without an active state representing the individual's baseline autonomy, the collective as a whole suffers for the economic decisions of the few. Even if a collective risk generates vast instrumental monetary value or increases employment and baseline opportunity, these considerations need to be consciously understood and debated before they are imposed nonvoluntarily upon the Ecosystem as a whole. A potential risk may also bring with it potential good, but we have no mechanisms in place to free the public debate from threats to autonomy before a discourse ensues on, for example, jobs versus clean air.

The just state not only should provide pertinent information to the public on the disposition of toxic substances (or suspected toxins) once they enter the environment, but also should become the premarket advocate for both natural systems and the population at large as fulfillment of a collective moral duty to each person's moral agency. By actively regulating the economic production of externalities through the three interfaces in the context model (extraction, production/construction, and disposal), Ecosystem law and policy can assure that risk and insecurity about exploitation are minimized, and autonomous behavior encouraged. An active state can protect and empower its constituents with both information and the law and can find a solution to the assurance game in the coordination of human and natural systems on the basis of the requirements of their separate, and joint, integrity.

Environmental security becomes an important issue. The independence of citizens is threatened if justice cannot provide security to the individual *ex ante*, in anticipation of harm to selves or natural systems. Only a strong regulatory emphasis, at the national level,[11] preventing toxic contamination, can accomplish this.

The "universality" of law is critical. The activity of the state regarding the baseline is justified by the right of each and every citizen to his or her independent autonomous capacity, ability, and purpose. It is humanity in the person that qualifies each of us for an opportunity for active citizenship; subpolitical boundaries or other geographic or morally arbitrary divisions ought not to deprive any citizen of these basic moral rights. The moral and political/legal communities must be coextensive. As long as humanity is the only qualification for consideration at the baseline (it must be remembered that the functional integrity of natural systems is a part of this baseline function), then the most inclusive governmental level of organization must set the standards and enforce regulation.[12] In the United States, this means that environmental-risk regulation, within an Ecosystem Approach, places primary responsibility for setting baseline standards with the federal government.

Because of the imperative to anticipate the imposition of risk, remedial action becomes a "second-best" regulatory strategy; prevention is elevated to "best" status as a collective duty. Any individual efforts to be an independent and active moral agent will fail if the person, because of fear, uncertainty, or illness, is dependent upon the choices of other individuals for the persistence of his autonomous growth.[13] Only an active government, supporting and empowering the individual, can give the requisite assurance, security, and encouragement within the moral law to control uncertainty and fear as these affect individual lives.

To become an active citizen, the individual needs to have the long-term probability of a baseline quality of life, which is dependent on the integrity of the Ecosystem in which she lives. Only if a person is assured that attempts at independence will have no limits but her own human capacity for thought and

---

action will she have the opportunity to move toward active citizenship in a dynamic republic. The *ex ante* belief that toxic material, or even suspected toxins, will be kept out of the environment until they have been proven benign or shown to have advantages for human or natural intrinsic value is the core of this assurance.

In addition to the confrontation between human moral agency and environmental risk, the effect of toxins on the functional integrity of the environment should also be considered. The synthetic nature of most of the highly toxic threats in risk cases makes this problematic (Brickman, Jasanoff, and Ilgen 1985; Shrader-Frechette 1991, 1993; Trost 1984). The natural environment has no processes by which to break down the harmful effects of this type of contamination, and therefore, entire functioning natural systems may be lost because of induced stress created by synthetic chemicals (Page 1978; Coleman 1992; Goodin 1976).

Overall, the just state should establish a policy-evaluation system that reflects a concern for Ecosystem integrity. This requires generating administrative "rules of thumb," from the principles of the moral law, to help the Kantian manager define and justify the state and its role in people's lives. Justice from Autonomy generates four "rules of thumb":

1. No Harm: Derived from the first juridical attribute and the imperative to protect ecosystem integrity, this rule represents the *ex ante* preservation of human freedom and natural systems functioning, in policy choice.
2. Trusteeship: Derived from the second juridical attribute and the imperative to distribute property, this rule represents the timeless collective use and care of the earth as an intrinsic value.
3. Risk Neutrality, and (4) Technological Compatibility: Derived from the third juridical attribute and the imperative to provide opportunity, these rules of thumb create conditions wherein human and natural intrinsic values will be empowered and made harmonious. Only with these two guidelines is opportunity for both human and natural systems *independence* possible.

These "rules of thumb" or guidelines for choice connect principles and maxims to concrete decisions. Through them, the methodology of baseline autonomy finds everyday application.

With the *no-harm* principle a manager keeps the autonomy function from falling below the entitlement necessary for a baseline quality of life. The imperative to the policymaker in this regard includes the persistence of environmental quality. However, this quality level encompasses more than the moral integrity of humanity. The independent value of nature, and our responsibility as strategic actors, requires that the level of environmental quality also be sufficient for the evolutionary processes of natural selection to flourish. Thus, unique and relatively untouched habitats must be preserved, while the persistence of nature is considered before its use so that its functioning systems and cycles are not corrupted by material that either overloads its natural cleaning ability or is alien to it. This may include the elimination of exotic species, which native systems cannot assimilate without widespread destruction of their own evolutionary variety. To preserve Ecosystem integrity is our duty, and this may sometimes require hands-on management to reclaim nature when we have caused harm to its essential capacities.

As I have argued, the functional integrity of a natural system is holistic, not individual. The interdependence and evolution of systems are at stake in our policy decisions. Habitat, species, and natural cycles invoke moral duties, not individual creatures or components. Nature is represented by unique biological entities and systems tied together by chains of causal interdependence in which each subsystem must be allowed to contribute its part to the complete process of functional evolution, with minimal interference or interruption from humankind. "Harm avoidance is one of the more important components in environmentalist arguments against reckless intervention into natural processes" (Goodin 1983, 15). Possible conflict can occur when a suspected toxin offers the opportunity to support human autonomy while risking a unique natural system or cycle. In such cases, human autonomy, being capable of strategic action and possessing technological ability, has a primary responsibility to find another means to the same end that involves less risk to nature. A moral obligation exists not to trade instrumental for intrinsic values; further, in a choice between human and natural intrinsic values, an obligation exists to err on the side of nature.

Because autonomy is a timeless requirement of moral agency, *trusteeship* adds a dimension to the "no-harm" concept for policymakers as they become responsible to assure Ecosystem integrity for future generations as well as for present citizens. This is accomplished for technological advancement and production by moving to a conscious justification of property use and distribution. It is insufficient to assume that if we *can* use something, we *should* use it. We should consider three categories of human use: what we can use; what we ought to use; and what we ought not to use. If technology creates a by-product or direct output that cannot be assimilated by nature, then we must find another means to the goal under consideration, or find a way of rendering the by-product biodegradable so that we do not threaten the long-term functional integrity of nature. If we can invent a technology that allows less extraction from nature, we ought to adopt it. This conscious consideration of our progress must be undertaken as a moral duty, even if we place our own longevity at risk.[14] A manager needs to recognize that the environmental quality necessary to the long-term functional integrity of nature is also sufficient for the long-term moral autonomy of future generations of humanity. The policymaker ought to aim for the former quality level in consideration of her duties to the coordination of humanity and nature as ends.

A central concern of trusteeship is, therefore, under what circumstances we substitute artificial for natural attributes. This trend would presuppose that if we could place a dome over a city and control the environment, or replace real trees with plastic ones, that we should as long as mankind can gain the same or greater utility from the substitution (Tribe 1974). There are two points I wish to make here.

First, artificial substitution is a short-term and uncertain solution when compared to the persistence of the natural attribute itself. If an administrator has an infinite duty to the future's equal possession of "the whole earth," she can only fulfill this duty if she supports the integrity of the real environment (which is renewable, ongoing, and independently self-generating), not by replacing the natural with the artificial for instrumental reasons like cost. If, however, the substitution of the artificial is considered in order to remove the natural system from instrumental use and preserve it in public trust (e.g., an artificial Christmas tree leaves real trees in the ground supporting other species and natural cycles), then the promotion of the artificial through regulation may be necessary to trusteeship.

The integrity of nature has a priority in the interdependence of moral and functional intrinsic value that humanity ought not to squander without considerable justification.[15] Even if humanity were to eliminate itself from the face of the earth, or move into space, we ought to leave a functioning and evolving natural world behind to proceed with its potential to evolve new forms of life as it evolved humanity itself.

Trusteeship supports the timeless collective ownership of the earth and the responsibility of the state to consider and coordinate human and natural integrity through policy. The persistence of this "public trust," concerned with how the "will of all" protects humanity and nature from the immoral acts of individuals seeking instrumental values that harm long-term capacities, is a moral duty that helps the manager raise the civil law to the standards of its moral counterpart. Trusteeship is, therefore, a rule of thumb concerned with the timeless use and distribution of use value according to the moral law.

Whereas the distinction between the artificial and the natural is one dimension of trusteeship, it is the essence of the third rule of thumb: *artificial-risk neutrality*. In his book on "environmental optimism," Gregg Easterbrook (1995) emphasizes, as one of his major themes, that while the distinction between the artificial and the natural may mean "a great deal to people" it "means nothing to nature" (115). He contends, correctly, that the earth has endured much more abuse, in geological time, from its own creations (e.g., ice ages, climate changes) than it has from human interference. Easterbrook also takes aim, reasonably, at those who wish to elevate the natural over the artificial for having inherently superior qualities. He claims that this focus on the origins of a particular material or risk distracts us from a more important focus on the values and moral "goodness" of individual and collective actions.

> So do it because it's good, not because it's natural. Only standards based on what is good or bad will have universal applicability to environmental decision making. (Easterbrook 1995, 120)

> Judgments about values are exactly what both natural and human society need more of, in order to combat the bad and preserve the good. (Easterbrook 1995, 122)

Mistakenly, however, Easterbrook thinks that the focus on moral values is accessible without a prior *ethical* distinction between the artificially created and the naturally occurring. In maintaining that no difference exists between the natural and the artificial he is also committed to the precept that we have no more moral responsibility concerning that which we create than that which is created by nature without our agency.

Specifically, my counterargument has three components:

1. The artificial is under our control and is therefore our moral responsibility, while the natural is nonmoral and requires our adaptation as strategic agents.
2. Natural risk is causal and creates itself as a matter of natural selection, while artificial risk is consciously created by us and is therefore elective, requiring justification and the application of practical reason.
3. We have an ethical duty, based on our autonomy, to take special care with what our moral agency creates.

In the search for "universal" standards of "environmental decision making," our primary focus should be on the responsibility we have for those artificial risks that we impose both on ourselves and nature.

From the perspective of Ecosystem Design, we would agree that the fact that something is natural does not make it better, but in order to produce the type of value choices that Easterbrook wants us to make, we must understand that an important distinction does exist between natural and artificially generated risk. The significant difference is not scientific, as all chemical substances from sugar to arsenic can be toxic if taken in the appropriate dose (Rodricks 1992), nor is it empirical, as a forest fire started by lightning is as risky and dangerous as one started by drunk campers. It is the moral distinction between the artificial and natural that must concern the Kantian risk manager.

Even if our use of CFCs (chlorofluorocarbons) causes major climate change and widespread mutation, this is not new to nature and may even be something that nature will survive. However, our capacity for morality, for the judgment of good and bad policy, and our ability to strategically assess choices and make them with our duties in mind, require us to segregate any risks we impose through our agency for special attention over any produced by nature itself. Segregation is required by the ethical "fact" that we have a duty to consciously control the former as a product of our individual or collective will.

The difference is moral. There may be no scientific difference between the toxic effects of too much sugar or a synthetic toxin, but in choosing to create the latter and expose ourselves and nature to it we acquire an ethical obligation. That is why we fret more about two people who die from synthetic toxins than about five hundred people who die in a hurricane. The former is our creation, carrying collective moral responsibility with each death, whereas the latter is the effect of natural process and consequently amoral and beyond our autonomous capacities or control. We may mourn the loss, but it is not our fault.

We need be concerned, however, not only with the level of artificial risk imposed on human autonomy, but with how our creation of environmental risk affects the functional integrity of nature. Generation of artificial risk is our responsibility and ought to be *neutral* in terms of its effects upon functioning natural systems unless we have a justification based upon our own or nature's intrinsic value to do otherwise. Artificial-risk neutrality therefore applies not only to the long-term functioning of the natural environment, but also to the lives of present and future generations of human moral agents.

The Kantian public administrator ought to remind citizens that what appears in nature without our technological innovation is part and parcel of ongoing evolutionary function, whereas our "artificial" technologies are part of our abiota and not natural.[16] Our human duty to nature is to utilize our abiota of technology and invention so that we may live conformably with nature without drastically threatening or altering it.

The last rule of thumb for administrators, *technological compatibility*, acknowledges that humans will use nature to support their autonomy but, as a concern for the interfaces between human and natural systems, it sets a standard for proper and improper use.

This standard for policy evaluation requires that human technology be compatible with nature's functional integrity. Humanity should not replace nature with technology in the absence of any advantage to nature; indeed, we ought to design our technology so that it is cooperative with the ends of nature (to paraphrase Kant, humanity's duty is to make nature's functional ends our own). Only in this way can we provide for both our own autonomy and the functional integrity of the environment. A harmony of independently sound human and natural ends is the basis of Kantian preservationism, the primary definition of morally responsible human progress, and the cornerstone of an Ecosystem Design Approach to environmental law and policy.

Harmonizing technology with nature requires at least two considerations. First, we must distinguish between use for baseline autonomy and for above-baseline welfare. We should not impose stress upon the fundamental systemic integrity of a natural resource for our above-baseline welfare, even if these resources can be replaced for future generations of humans. Second, if humanity and nature are to be in harmony, as our duties under Kantian preservationism require, policy should be based on an imperative to both protect and empower nature, first, by maximizing our ability to design technology that is a benefit to both nature and ourselves, and second, by making compensation-in-kind for resources we do use. This imperative might include legal incentives and regulations to encourage technology for selective extraction; reforestation; cleaning of water supplies (of all artificial and human-generated pollution); replacement of fossil fuels with solar power; the development of recycling techniques to allow humanity to reuse previously extracted materials to prevent further use of virgin components from natural systems; and transforming the way we live so that heating, cooling, and conversion to cleaner forms of energy are easier. This last imperative might require containing our growth so that already constructed urban areas are fully utilized before more natural systems are converted for human use. In this way, we can empower nature and our own autonomy simultaneously so that full capacity is possible on both levels of organization and our duties are fulfilled.

Ecosystem Design is based on the assumption that humanity comes from nature but has transcended it. Our transcendent position gives us moral responsibilities to nature that it cannot reciprocate. These duties to nature are inherent to our moral autonomy. Without natural systems integrity, we violate our duties both to ourselves and to nature. Our convenience or instrumental welfare (above the baseline) is not as important as the baseline integrity of Ecosystems. Any technology, product, or risk proposed strictly for instrumental convenience, but which adds to the fundamental stress on natural systems (e.g., a disposable razor) must be justified *ex ante*, before extraction, production, or disposal is allowed. If we limit the exploitation of the environment to those stresses justified by our baseline autonomy (e.g., the medical safety of a disposable syringe), our overall effects on natural systems can be minimized, perhaps to the point where no additional or perceptible stress on natural systems is detectable. We must have the consciousness and practical reason to distinguish between the baseline necessity of a disposable syringe and the above-baseline welfare convenience of a disposable razor or lighter. The duty of a Kantian manager is to help us make the distinction.

Stated fully the four rules of thumb are as follows:

1. The *no-harm* principle makes it a higher priority to avoid a harm to intrinsic value than to provide an instrumental benefit.
2. *Trusteeship* places first ownership and use of the material world in timeless public trust for consideration of how natural functioning and human autonomy might find harmony in distributive justice.
3. *Artificial-risk neutrality* makes humanity conscious of all risk imposed on the environment, and requires justification for "artificial" risks in terms of the intrinsic values involved.
4. *Technological compatibility* creates a technological world where human invention is in harmony with the long-term integrity of whole Ecosystems.

Now we shall move on to the application of these guidelines to policy decision making.

The Predilections and Reorientation of the Public Manager

The market paradigm can be criticized internally for what counts as a cost and whether discount rates are what they ought to be, or, externally, as to the validity of its fundamental assumptions. If Rhoads is correct in his vindication of cost-benefit evaluation against all internal criticism, we shall pose an external question: what is the moral validity of the contention that preferences are the proper foundation for policy?

"RULES OF THUMB" FOR ADMINISTRATIVE DECISION MAKING

> If consumer's wishes are the appropriate standard for policy making, there is no reason to abandon consumer sovereignty for bad principles. . . . If the normative principles on which benefit-cost analysis rests are just and sufficient, the sensible course is to value the benefits of government programs at the best estimate of peoples' willingness to pay for them. (Rhoads 1985, 139)

But what if "consumer's wishes" are not a morally sound "standard for policy making"? The manager using Kantian standards has an incentive to move away from "willingness to pay" and toward the support and protection of moral agency. Social choice is not now a matter of consequences to the average or total utility of a population, but a deontological concern for the obligation one has to empower autonomy at the baseline. If the proposed policy threatens intrinsic value, then policy must move to protect it, regardless of preference. Like the rights articulated in the United States Constitution, the duty of the decision maker to the baseline ought not to be subject to the will of majorities, but ought to be considered a moral entitlement, necessary to each active citizen's capacity as a potential moral agent and a duty that each person ought to provide, through government, to himself and others.

Preferences enter into the deliberation over policy only concerning above-baseline allocations, where efficiency and willingness to pay become acceptable standards for social choice. At or below the baseline, however, the categorical imperative of the moral law sets universal and necessary requirements that must be respected in public choice.

Difficulty arises when one is faced with trading one person's baseline entitlement for another's. For example, a policy that supports the integrity of person X by providing her with a better environmental quality may present a harm to person Y's baseline entitlement, if toxic chemicals are disposed of in his back yard. Under these conditions, if everyone's integrity function cannot simultaneously be protected and empowered, the policymaker must err on the side of those who have had their integrity exploited the most or who are most vulnerable (Goodin 1985). In other words, the waste ought not to be dumped where it affects primarily the old, young, or poor—where it will cause essential harm to those who have not created it, or who have no defensive strategies against it (unable to move)—simply because they are in the minority, or have no political power.

Intrinsic value can only be traded for intrinsic value at the baseline. If the quality of life of all must decline, then the pain ought to be equally distributed, and if only a sector of the population must have their baseline autonomy improved, it ought to be those who have been most severely deprived in the past. The duty to the baseline needs to be consciously assessed and regulated. Assurance cannot be left to chance, power, or ability to pay. To anticipate risk and justify it *ex ante*, is the primary policy imperative. If risk is necessary, it is the duty of policymakers to distribute all burdens of technology justly to those who created them, or if these cannot be found, equally across the population that bears a collective responsibility for the expression of human agency that created the risk (e.g., a comprehensive waste treatment policy that involves many groups and communities in different parts of the plan). The policymaker's concern is primarily with how a particular alternative (including taking no action) affects individuals at the baseline. Here, hard choices must be made and publicly justified in argument.

The major difference between the Ecosystem evaluation system defined herein and standard economic design is that the former is a duty-based theory that assesses policy from the vantage point of independent moral principle. This moral law does not allow government to be a passive actor but charges it with the collective duty or responsibility of supporting the integrity of its citizens.

To illustrate how our new guidelines might be applied to environmental policy, we will now examine an EPA analysis of groundwater contamination. Undertaken when the issue was new to regulators, it illustrates both the predilections of environmental administrators for the market paradigm and the need for a major reorientation toward Justice from Autonomy.

Economic Theory and the EPA Administrator

How do policy administrators actually approach natural systems where human perturbations have caused risk to humanity and the environment? The Davie Landfill, the aquifer beneath it, and the surrounding natural system offer a perfect case study. Located over the Biscayne Aquifer, which is the sole source of groundwater for all of southeastern Florida, the Davie Landfill was opened in 1974 and currently falls under the jurisdiction of the Comprehensive Environmental Response, Compensation, and Liability Act [Superfund] (42 U.S.C.A. §§ 9601–75), listed as number 69 out of 1072 sites on the National Priorities List (40 CFR pt. 300 App. B, 1992, 201).

We will examine the methods and tools government decision makers brought to the evaluation of Davie as an anthropogenic risk perturbation—which, at the time, presented a new regulatory dilemma—to find alternatives to deal with toxic contamination of groundwater *ex post*. We shall argue that EPA's conventional analysis of policy, based on the Economic Design Approach, cost-benefit methods, and the principle of efficiency, is inadequate to the consideration of the intrinsic values involved in the Davie case. With only the consideration of instrumental economic costs and benefits to define the public choice, environmental policy cannot force action to clean up hazardous waste or to restore natural systems or greater Ecosystem integrity. Anticipation, prevention, or conscious justification of intrinsic harm will not influence EPA policy because they are not part of the argument paradigm applied to the issue.

The evidence for our case against the market paradigm as a primary administrative analysis tool is contained within a set of original feasibility studies written by the Environmental Protection Agency and its Benefits Staff at the Office of Policy Analysis in 1983–84 (Geraghty and Miller 1983; Sobotka 1983; Raucher 1983, 1984). Components of a pilot project, these reports have since defined EPA groundwater policy. The objectives of these studies are to "develop and test simplified and low cost approaches to case study analysis of groundwater contamination" (Sobotka 1983, 1), and "to develop a methodology for evaluating the desirability of alternative groundwater protection strategies" (Raucher 1983, 1). The purpose of the EPA effort was to find the best policy option from the "full" efficiency analysis of appropriate alternatives for the Davie toxic waste site.[17]

The EPA analysis of Davie is ideal for our purposes since it is a feasibility study concerned primarily with the "robustness" (Sobotka 1983, 1) of economic strategies for environmental policy decision making. In applying market/cost-benefit analysis (Gramlich 1981) to the Davie case, EPA illuminates its priorities in the confrontation between humanity and nature. EPA also makes it evident that for each "new" environmental issue, like groundwater, which in 1983 was receiving its initial attention from the agency, "analysis" means use of the market paradigm.

Groundwater and Aquifers

Groundwater defines water located beneath the surface of the earth. Specifically, it refers to a store of 97 percent of the earth's unfrozen fresh water, and from 80 to 90 percent of the available water in the United States that supplies one-half of the population with drinking water (Council on Environmental Quality 1980, 84).

Technically, we are not interested in water contained in surface soil (soil water), but only with geological formations capable of transmitting and storing significant quantities of water (Clark and Cherry 1979). Known as *aquifers*, these formations are predominantly made of gravel, sand, or silt. Any geological formation made of porous material, or any heavily fractured rock formation, can also serve as an aquifer. As long as an abundance of voids exists between individual particles of the formation, so that the water can flow around them, the structure can hold fluid and be called an aquifer (National Research Council 1990).

An *aquitard* is the reverse formation of an aquifer and is defined as a geological formation capable of transmitting and storing only negligible amounts of water. Usually made of nonporous material like shale or dense crystalline rock, the aquitard acts as a barrier to water and therefore forms the base of an aquifer to contain the water in a specific area underground.

Groundwater formations are made up of layers of aquifers and aquitards. Aquifers can be categorized as confined or unconfined. A confined aquifer, surrounded by aquitards so that the water is enclosed, is less susceptible to contaminants from surface percolation. Its contents move slowly, so that water in a confined aquifer stays undiluted for long periods of time. Most drinking water is drawn from confined aquifers (Freeze and Cherry 1979). An unconfined aquifer has no aquitard above it and is more vulnerable to contamination from the surface. The water here usually moves more quickly and is a more active part of the hydrologic cycle.

All aquifers seep into surface waters and recharge from rainfall and surface sources. Confined aquifers have specific recharge points that feed the entire formation. At these recharge and seepage points, confined aquifers are especially vulnerable. Unconfined aquifers seep and recharge at a faster rate through the surface of the earth at many points along their length and width (Freeze and Cherry 1979).

The hydrologic cycle "consists of the movement of water between oceans and other bodies of surface water, the atmosphere, and the land" (Pye 1983, 19). Groundwater is a very important part of this cycle, supplying and storing fresh water for natural systems. Groundwater "is not only an important natural resource, but also an essential part of the natural environment" (Pye 1983, 19).

The Biscayne Aquifer in southeastern Florida lies in what is called the Atlantic and Gulf Coastal Plain, which is among the largest and most productive groundwater regions in the United States (McGuiness 1963, 64–77; Conservation Foundation 1987). The Biscayne Aquifer is described as a "highly permeable, wedge-shaped, unconfined shallow aquifer composed of limestone and sandstone underlying the entire [Dade] county."

> In general, the Biscayne Aquifer is divisible, from top to bottom, into three distinct water-producing zones, which are separated by generally dense, clean, silty to sandy limestone and well-cemented quartz sands which act as aquitards. (Singh et al. 1983, 3)

Although a variety of perturbations and specific constituents (both natural and artificial) can lead to the contamination of an aquifer, the most critical type of perturbation concerning the EPA is human, in the form of contamination from synthetic toxins (Fischer 1986). According to John Cherry, the capacity of aquifers to retain water for "many centuries" (National Science Foundation 1983, 14) and the nature of toxins combine to pose a serious and irreversible environmental risk. Toxins in groundwater are zero-infinity risks that are irreversible because contaminants are very hard to filter out before they spread through aquifers and beyond recharge points. Any such risk is, in an important sense, permanent, and a threat not just to the health of human beings, but to their autonomy and to the functional integrity of nature. Toxins can do significant damage to the nutrient and waste-management functions provided by groundwater aquifers to their surface systems.[18] "Synthetic organic chemicals pose a special threat. Many of these are toxic chemicals that cannot be broken down by subsurface microorganisms or filtered out by soils before they reach groundwater" (Epstein, Brown, and Pope 1982, 301). Except for the nonbiodegradable nature of toxins, science has little knowledge of the real toxicity of many contaminants. Mordechai Schechter has argued that "it is estimated that only five to ten percent of the nonvolatile constituents in drinking water have so far been characterized either because no tests have been conducted or because the chemicals were not detected by routine laboratory procedure" (National Science Foundation 1983, 14). The source of these toxins is usually industrial, and affects the groundwater when percolated from toxic waste dumps (landfills or sludge ponds) down into the aquifer. Once in the groundwater, toxins move more slowly than they would in surface water and, over time, an aquifer can accumulate a high concentration of artificial contaminants.

Many toxic organic chemicals are colorless, tasteless and odorless at concentrations at which they occur in drinking water. The concentrations of these chemicals are sometimes orders of magnitude higher in groundwater than they are in surface water, which is a reflection of the lack of mixing and minimal dispersion that occurs in contaminated plumes of groundwater in comparison with surface water. (Pye 1983, 40)

Not only is the Biscayne Aquifer "a very fragile groundwater system" that is "extremely vulnerable to contamination" (Singh et al. 1983, 17), but "there is sufficient pertinent information from animal and occupational studies to infer with reason that the Biscayne Aquifer poses a serious hazard that needs to be addressed" (Singh et al. 1984, 364).

[L]ow to moderate levels of several toxic contaminants are present in groundwater within most of the study area. . . . Contamination of the Biscayne Aquifer was detected in all three water producing zones. The middle and bottom zones had a higher degree (two to three times) of contamination than the upper zone. Most of the production wells (drinking water sources) are in the deep and middle water producing zones. While pumping water, these wells tend to draw contaminants from the upper zone into the two lower zones. (Singh et al. 1984, 362–63)

Within the "study area," where the contamination was discovered, lies the Davie Landfill facility.

The Davie Landfill is located in south Broward County, Florida, within the western segment of the South New River Canal Drainage Basin (Geraghty and Miller 1983, 30). It is bordered by ditches and canals that act to drain and charge the aquifer on three sides, and by land used extensively for agriculture and improved pasture land.

The natural system perturbed by Davie is composed of green grasslands that are part of a greater wetland system that stretches over most of south Florida. Although now primarily pasture land, the grass, plants, and small animals that naturally inhabit this natural system, as well as the domestic animals that graze it, are dependent upon the aquifer to support all levels of organization within the greater Ecosystem (the human and animal populations and communities that coexist in mutual evolution). The processes of photosynthesis and respiration that are the core of nature's persistence are dependent upon energy from the sun, but also on the nutrient systems feeding the food web supplied by the aquifer, which is the most important source of stored and circulating water (Ward, Giger, and McCarty 1985; Downes 1985).

In addition to supplying major nutrients for the grazing cycle of the natural system, the aquifer, with its recharge and discharge, as well as the microorganisms alive in it and its circulating water, are a major waste management system for the surface system. As a participant in the support of both the grazing and detritus cycles, the aquifer is the delicate point of balance for the persistence of evolution. Moreover, the aquifer is the point of balance not only for the immediate surface system, but this single micronatural system can also be understood as a level in a greater Ecosystem of plants, animals, and humans that are part of a wetland and grassland system that stretches across south Florida and includes the Everglades (Pye, Patrick and Quarles 1983).

This entire system is affected by agricultural use, but even with that use the natural system, although perturbed by humanity in this way, was able to persist as long as its energy-waste management system, primarily provided by the aquifer, was left undisturbed.[19] The perturbation that matters, for the purpose of this analysis, is the establishment of the waste site that changed the makeup of the aquifer by introducing synthetic chemicals and pollutants into its water, affecting its capacity both to supply energy for maintenance of the grazing cycle, and to be an active part of the detritus cycle as a waste management system.

Davie is over 70 acres in size and has been operated as both a solid- and toxic-waste disposal facility. A 5.6 acre, nine-foot deep, unlined sludge lagoon exists on the site that has accepted grease trap and septic tank pumpings, municipal-sewer sludge, and industrial waste. Sludge disposal was stopped in 1981, but only after tainted groundwater was discovered under the lagoon. Two levels of contaminated plumes, drawing from the landfill and the lagoon, are moving slowly (about one foot a day) toward the agricultural land and low-density population to the southwest. The plume contains chloride, sodium, and ammonia as well as metals and inorganic toxins that contaminate the groundwater "in excess of drinking water standards" (Raucher 1984, 11–12; Geraghty and Miller 1983, 37–45).

Administrative Analysis and Recommendations

The classification of a benefit for the purposes of the EPA analysis and evaluation of the Davie site is defined in terms of cost avoided. This has two component parts: first, the number of dollars saved on one policy response to contamination rather than another, and second, the statistical cases of cancer, and therefore health costs avoided, by any response action (Sobotka 1983, 3). EPA managers used three policy objectives to analyze the problem (Raucher 1983, 1, emphasis added):

1. *"Prevention"* or *"Containment,"* which includes liner requirement restrictions on land-based disposal, and other methods intended to prevent contamination of the groundwater.
2. *Detection*, which consists of monitoring requirements.
3. *Corrective (Remedial) Action*, which consists of efforts to contain the plume and minimize the damage after the contamination has occurred.

For regulators, the basic question is whether it is more efficient to contain the contamination on-site (option 1), or monitor contamination and respond to it after the fact through remedial action (options 2 and 3). But before considering final policy recommendations, we need to examine the "prevention" option.

The economic market analysis used by EPA is consequentialist in philosophy and outlook.[20] Prevention (owing to its *ex ante* connotation) is therefore a misleading term for the first option. In reality, EPA defines "prevention," not as avoiding contamination of the natural system by toxic waste, but as containment of the pollution on-site, away from large human populations. The goal is not to stop a toxic plume from forming, but to "prevent" it from wandering off-site and causing widespread public health problems. EPA considers the prevention option only after toxic contamination has occurred. To these managers, the pertinent question concerns whether or not it is efficient to contain the pollution. In the context of their efficiency analysis, they must first consider instrumental welfare costs; these are tied, primarily, to the probability of leakage from the site. Within the market paradigm, the concept of prevention becomes synonymous with postponement. Thus, prevention is used here as a point of departure for cost comparison, and as the status quo from which monitoring and remedial action will be judged, not really as an option in itself.

As Talbot Page (1983) notes, prevention in this context does not involve neutralizing the source of the toxic contamination, but is only a concern for the containment of the leakage of the site into adjacent groundwater deposits. "[M]issing are the preventative strategies, such as chemical reaction to transform toxic chemicals, source reduction, and source control" (Page 1983, 1). EPA, however, does not perceive real prevention as a viable policy option.

> We assume that contamination at Davie could have been avoided if the sludge pond had been engineered and operated as a hazardous waste facility, with proper liners and covers since the beginning of operations. This probably overstates the effectiveness and understates the costs of prevention measures. Some contaminant releases would probably have resulted eventually even with a well engineered sludge pond, and trash and garbage landfill operations may also be contributing to contamination releases. (Sobotka 1983, 20)

Detection, the second option, occurs with the failure of the containment strategy and concerns the most cost-beneficial monitoring plan for Davie. Monitoring involves costs in the range of $30,000 for the first year, which includes the installation of wells from which the samples will be taken. Each round of subsequent sampling and testing will cost $2,500 (Sobotka 1983, 45).[21]

The costs of containment and the uncertainty associated with the plume's harmful effects, combined with the real monetary costs of initial set-up and regular water testing, as well as the probability estimates of facility failure as a function of age, conspire to support the official conclusion that monitoring is efficient only for sites where health hazards to large human populations can be proven. However, these containment and monitoring strategies take up the least amount of space in the EPA analysis.

The most attention is focused on assessing the third option, corrective (remedial) action, in which EPA makes recommendations to deal with human perturbations of natural systems. Eight separate remedial courses of action were created and examined for the Davie Landfill; four presuppose closure, four do not. Closure means that the generation of leachate into the groundwater would be stopped. Without closure, "contaminants would continue to be released from the facility indefinitely" (Sobotka 1983, 14). The four policy options that do not assume closure are:

1. *Accept possible health risks permanently.* No action is taken. The plume lengthens over time and moves on to affect an increasingly greater area of the aquifer. More wells and agricultural land become involved. Health and ecosystem consequences of this contamination, whatever they are, are accepted as costs. The degree of cost will depend on the toxic make-up of the plume.
2. *Corrective action to protect drinking water, with reinjection indefinitely.* Recovery wells are dug at the toe of the plume, and counterpumping is begun at a rate high enough to stop the plume. Recovered water is then injected into a deep and unusable sector of the aquifer.
3. *Use of bottled water, permanently.* No action is taken to stop the plume or to protect the groundwater resources. Water from the affected area is replaced with bottled water for drinking purposes.
4. *Replacement of groundwater with municipal water, indefinitely.* No action is taken to stop the plume or to protect groundwater resources. Houses in the area are connected to the water system of the city of Sunrise, several miles north. (Sobotka 1983, 17–18, emphasis added)

The other four remedial policy options assume closure, which can be accomplished at Davie by "digging out the sludge pond and sending the material removed to a secure hazardous waste facility" (Sobotka 1983, 19).[22]

5. *Acceptance of possible health risks and their consequences.* The plume is cut off by removing material from the sludge pond. Until the plume migrates out of the area and dissipates, it will cause contamination and health problems. As with option (1), these costs will be accepted.
6. *Protection of groundwater resources, reinjection.* After the source of the contamination is eliminated, counterpumping and injection (as with response (2)) are instituted. This will continue only until the remnants of the plume are eliminated.
7. *Use bottled water, temporarily.* After the source of contamination is eliminated, and until the plume disappears, bottled water is used by those who might be affected.
8. *Protection of groundwater through contaminant removal.* After the elimination of the contaminant source, recovery wells are used to prevent the migration of the plume. Recovered water is treated and reinjected near the site to flush out contamination. Volumes recovered, treated and reinjected are assumed to be great enough as to allow the elimination of all detectable contamination within twenty years. This is the complete cleanup option for the Davie site, which would restore the aquifer to its former condition. (Sobotka 1983, 18–19, emphasis added)

Utilizing cost figures from Geraghty and Miller (1983), the policy decision makers defined the "lowest cost" remedial action alternative, having considered the costs of prevention and the total cleanup of the site. The efficient option was determined to be option 3: *no closure and the distribution of bottled water indefinitely.* At anything above a zero discount rate,[23] the use of bottled water is most cost-beneficial, whereas the complete cleanup (option 8) is not Kaldor efficient at any discount rate. None of the closure options are efficient under any conditions examined in these studies (Raucher 1983, 2–3).

The economic analysis of groundwater contamination at Davie concludes that neither the closure of the site, which would stop feeding the plume, nor the complete cleanup option that would follow the closure, are warranted as "reasonable" policy. The recommended policy is to take that course of action that minimizes regulation of the market and maximizes the instrumental use of humanity and nature toward this economic objective.

Health risk, as the only "harm" seriously considered in the analysis, is to be accommodated by the adoption of a policy that provides bottled water to the small human population immediately affected. Considering the size of the population at risk, the risk of the groundwater contaminants, and the time periods over which the policy alternatives run, further "remedial responses . . . are not warranted . . . at Davie" (Raucher 1983, 8).

> At Davie . . . the health risks posed are [small] (less than one excess cancer every 12,000 years) because of a very small population. . . . The cost per statistical case avoided by the most efficient remedial response (providing bottled water) is roughly $100 million. . . . [Even] these costs at Davie are more than an order of magnitude greater than observed values that individuals place on reducing the risk of a statistical death ($0.4 to $7 million per statistical fatality). (Raucher 1984, 17)

Ultimately, in the cost-benefit evaluation, site cleanup or containment of the contaminant plume is never recommended as efficient, and therefore "proper," policy. "[T]he case study findings indicate that corrective action will not be supported on a benefit-cost basis for all cases even though contamination may be known to exist and is expected to threaten drinking water supplies" (Raucher 1984, 19). Even with prevention strategies that are weaker than Resource Conservation and Recovery Act guidelines (42 U.S.C.A. §§ 6901–92k) and a remedial response that could have cleaned the site (Canter and Knox 1986, chaps. 3 and 5) by 2003 (Davie option 8), prevention or cleanup is not recommended.

Certain internal characteristics of EPA's analysis produce these results, including the use of high discount rates, short time horizons, and the contribution of uncertainty to the policy choice.[24] The most impressive characteristic of this analysis is that it completely ignores the intrinsic value of human and natural systems. Nature is only counted as an instrumental means for human efficiency goals. The most prominent "cost" considered in these studies, related to the value of nature, is the loss of productive pasture land (Geraghty and Miller 1983). In addition, the only human values in the analysis are focused on excess cancer rates in the small population immediately affected. If human intrinsic value can be defined by something more necessary than cancer rates or more fundamental than one's physical health, then humanity can also be described as subject, primarily, to instrumental value considerations.

To suggest that this EPA analysis is only one possible approach to the policy dilemma is inadequate. These analysts were to measure the "significant" dimensions of the issues involved and propose policy. Assuming that the analytic question pertained to the efficiency value of humanity and nature to market prosperity, they chose to measure the costs and benefits involved. Intrinsic values are not a component in this administrative evaluation of policy options because of the market orientation of the EPA study and its sole concern for instrumental costs and benefits. This phenomenon is a product of the inherent prejudice of economic decision procedures and policy design toward the promotion of instrumental efficiency, which dictates that the benefit of the doubt be given to the unfettered functioning of the economy, its allocation of capital, and its production and allocation of technological products to consumers (Gramlich 1981; Schmookler 1993). From this viewpoint the burden of proof is squarely placed on those who would regulate or interfere in any way with the economic status quo; they must prove that any regulatory action is justified in market terms.

The Davie case, as evaluated by the market paradigm and cost-benefit methods, recommends policy that interferes minimally in the economic status quo and leans toward the least costly action; and away from more radical market intrusions that would clean up or that would recommend the formulation of a more comprehensive prevention strategy that might protect humanity and natural systems before irreversible collective risks are imposed upon them. If Ecosystem argument had been decisive when the siting of Davie was under consideration, minimal interference with the economy would have been weighed against the integrity of humanity and nature, and most of the problems faced in this analysis might have been prevented.

The Davie case provides fuel for those who "fear that in regulatory analysis, the diffuse, long-term, hard-to-quantify benefits of environmental programs may be given insufficient weight relative to industries' concentrated, short-term, readily measurable compliance costs" (Swartzmann, Liroff, and Croke 1982, xii).

Davie: From Economic to Ecosystem Policy Argument

The critical foundation for economic cost-benefit methods is its internal ethical assumptions and prejudices that inform the way the public administrator views the world, decides what variables count in policy considerations and by how much, and, ultimately, how far the market can pursue efficiency. But, regardless of how well a particular cost-benefit study may be done, market efficiency is not the proper principle on which to determine groundwater policy choice. The Davie case makes it evident why the public decision maker ought to move beyond efficiency, and toward Ecosystem Design, in order to establish an adequate groundwater policy.

> Policy analysts typically operate within a social, political, and intellectual tradition that regards the satisfaction of individual human wants as the only defensible measure of the good, a tradition that perceives the only legitimate task of reason to be that of consistently identifying and then serving individual appetite, preference, or desire. This tradition is echoed as well in environmental legislation which protects nature not for its own sake but in order to preserve its potential value for man. (Tribe 1974, 1325)

When moving from the regulation of traditional pollution problems to environmental risk, this criticism seems even more appropriate. With long latency periods, irreversibility, and collective risk, the collective environmental "good" must take precedence over individual human wants or the unfettered functioning of market processes. It is more important than ever to consider the proper distribution of burdens and risk to humans and natural systems alike, to have a standard for the equal consideration of both, now and in the future, and to provide a sense of fairness to whomever or whatever may be harmed if it were not for the *ex ante* protection of environmental law.

Cost-benefit methods assume that the groundwater, as well as the natural systems it supports, has no intrinsic value in and of itself, but has value only as an instrument to man's want-regarding nature (Bagley 1961, 149–50). Consequently, if an artificial technology (e.g., bottled water) serves man as well as the natural environment, then destroying the natural amenity and replacing it with the artificial alternative is morally acceptable. If the level of satisfaction is equal in both instances, the natural and the artificial are considered fungible goods subject to trade and are therefore efficient alternatives to each other. Reliance on preferences to set the standards and values of cost-benefit evaluation relegates all ethical consideration to welfare-maximizing options in which the environment is just another good that can be traded off against others until the costs to man outweigh the benefits.

> By treating individual human desire as the ultimate frame of reference, and by assuming that human goals and ends must be taken as externally "given" rather than generated by reason, environmental policy makes a value judgment of enormous significance. . . . [A]ny claim for the continued existence of . . . wilderness . . . or . . . species must rest on the identification of human wants. . . . As our capacity increases to satisfy these needs and wants artificially, the claim becomes tenuous indeed. (Tribe 1974, 1326)

Like all quantitative decision-making techniques, cost-benefit methodology is "likely to bias conclusions in the direction of the considerations they can most readily incorporate" (Tribe 1972, 97). Those "costs" and "benefits" that normally appear in human monetary terms will therefore be more "readily incorporated" than qualitative variables like human health, natural systems damage, moral good or right, or aesthetic considerations that are not usually analyzed in terms of the "measuring rod" of money. All considerations that do become part of the analysis, however, will be considered fungible in terms of tradable currency.

329

> [T]he objectivist tendency to deny discontinuities by reducing everything to varying levels of smoothly interchangeable attributes (inevitably related to human satisfaction) seriously limits the capacity of the policy sciences to accommodate certain kinds of value . . . values that are intrinsically incommensurable with human satisfaction . . . values with inherently global, holistic or structural features that cannot be reduced to any finite listing . . . of independent attributes . . . [and] values that have an on-off character like . . . integrity , . . . ecological balance . . . or wilderness. . . . [T]he techniques of policy analysis . . . will tend either to filter them out of the investigation altogether or to treat them in ways inconsistent with their special character. (Tribe 1972, 96–97)

Although we may want to retain the prerogative to reject a groundwater policy as inefficient, efficiency as the primary or sole criterion of public choice is insufficient. A policy justification-and-evaluation system based upon alternative principles is needed.

> [P]olicies may be condemned . . . because they threaten parts of the natural environment . . . because they destroy what has intrinsic value . . . things . . . valued in themselves and independently of uses to which they might be put. (Elliot and Gare 1983, ix)

If cost-benefit methods cannot accommodate the "special character" of groundwater law and policy, we should question its ethical validity when used to recommend policy. Perhaps cost-benefit method

> embodies an unacceptable premise, namely that the question to be answered is "What is efficient for society?" rather than "What is good for society?" By all means use the most cost-effective way to achieve the end once the end has been determined, but do not use the cost-benefit analysis to determine the end. (Ashby 1978, 56)

The principle problem in the Davie case is the synthetic nature of most of the highly toxic threats. The Biscayne Aquifer has no processes by which to fully break down the harmful effects of this type of contamination, thus endangering an entire functioning natural system, as well as human lives. In setting a national groundwater policy the decision maker needs to weigh the uncertainty and management characteristics of environmental risk in terms of the integrity of Ecosystems. Among all the expected "costs," intrinsic harm ought to be of primary concern.[25]

The policymaker should establish principles of policy evaluation that reflect the essential values at stake in the Davie case. Overall, in terms of an Ecosys-

"RULES OF THUMB" FOR ADMINISTRATIVE DECISION MAKING

tem Design, utilizing Justice from Autonomy as its paradigm, the imperatives to regulate private human choice as part of the public duty held by government in trust for its citizens involve consideration of both the moral integrity of the present and future generations and the functional integrity of the environment as these are affected by groundwater contamination.

Instead of reliance on efficiency, if the EPA analysis of the Davie situation used an Ecosystem Approach, it would have generated a distinct set of policy imperatives that deal with harm, future preservation, and the distinction between the artificial and the natural. Such analysis would examine technology, not as a means to conquer nature, but as a way to empower human autonomy and our harmony with natural systems. Applying our new rules of thumb suggests a different course of action in the Davie case.

At Davie, the importance of the *no-harm* principle requires that the disposition of toxic waste not be considered in a vacuum. It is inadequate to accept the fact that the plume will form and begin to migrate, or even that the chemical must be introduced into the environment at all. The imperative is to *prevent* a harm, by cleaning up those that exist and assuring that in the future all potential toxic material will be proven safe or necessary[26] to humanity or the environment before it is allowed into the market.[27] This is the substitution of a *risk-conscious society* for a market society. We now have the regulatory apparatus and anticipatory institutions necessary to allow practical reason, rather than unconscious economic forces, to be applied to decisions about collective environmental risk.

Harm must also be considered within a context where physical health is considered necessary, but not sufficient, to human autonomy. Under these conditions, data on "cancer risk" is far too narrow a basis upon which to rest policy conclusions. In addition, harms to natural systems must be deciphered and categorized, and the coordination of human and natural systems within greater Ecosystems becomes the reason for policy and the basis for all assessment of harm.

The market's economic imperatives cannot be accepted unconsciously as having moral priority if intrinsic value is to be protected from harm. At Davie, this requires that the plume be stopped, and that bottled water be distributed until natural systems restoration can be completed (a combination of EPA options 7 and 8). The number of people affected by Davie is not a prime consideration for Justice from Autonomy because baseline autonomy is at risk (Taurek 1977). The groundwater system at Davie must be restored as closely to its former clean condition as is humanly possible. Meanwhile, the plume must be stopped and the landfill site brought up to RCRA specifications so that if toxic waste is ever accepted again, it can be more safely disposed of on-site without affecting the groundwater.

The second precept of *trusteeship* provides a timeless dimension to the prevention of harm. The duty of the policymaker expands to include future generations and the long-term flourishing of the natural system. Market analysis fails to appreciate the duties here. At Davie, humanity's long-term autonomy cannot depend on an artificial substitute for the real aquifer. If the policymaker is responsible to the future, she must be able to guarantee water resources in support of Ecosystem integrity. The long-term availability of the aquifer can be assured only if it is considered a "public trust" that will be protected from essential harm, as an inherent part of the greater Ecosystem, in perpetuity. Intact, the aquifer can provide water to future generations without harm to itself, if its natural process and renewing cycles (functional integrity) can proceed uninterrupted. Bottled water is a poor substitute and will discourage the cleaning up of the aquifer since it draws water from other sources, perhaps debilitating other Ecosystems.

Ignoring the intrinsic value of humanity and natural systems results in the recommendation of a policy that does nothing to prevent further contamination of the aquifer or to clean up the human perturbation of the site itself. The primary recommendation of the EPA cost-benefit analysis is to provide bottled water indefinitely. However, the bottled-water solution violates both human and natural system integrity.

In terms of nature, the bottled water will do nothing to restore the nutrient and waste-management functions of the aquifer. This solution allows the continued degradation of the natural system past its functional capacity to respond. In terms of humanity, agency action needs to respect human autonomy. Respect may be made evident in North Africa by not fouling an oasis or spitting in a well (Baier 1986). A comparable imperative to respect moral agency makes fouling an aquifer and then passing out bottled water an unacceptable policy in the Florida case.[28] In both cases, the "public trust" nature of the water source has been violated by the private preferences of individuals making immoral choices. Therefore, passing out bottled water and allowing the natural source to remain contaminated, without redressing the harm to its intrinsic value and to our own, is not sufficient. Moral responsibility requires that the aquifer be restored, so that individuals and the natural environment are concurrently respected as ends-in-themselves.

The intergenerational and distributional aspects of trusteeship also provide a justification for the absorption of initial cleanup costs by the present, in duty to the future. The timeless nature of our duties to ourselves and our environment requires that we abandon discount rates and accept responsibility for the effects of our technological innovations on essential values.

This brings us to *artificial-risk neutrality*. Our responsibility for artificially created risks builds upon the timeless nature of the environment as a public trust and commits us to the *ex ante* regulation of toxic material so that landfills like Davie do not become problems in the first place. If we take the case as is, artificial-risk neutrality would warrant complete cleanup of the site and prevention-at-source. Risk neutrality recommends that no environmental risk be introduced into the environment unless it is morally justified and fairly distributed. If the moral agent accepts risk as necessary to her intrinsic value, then it may be worth the gamble, but the move from a risk-neutral to a risk-positive state of affairs can only be taken with this *ex ante* moral justification. Once introduced, the risk must be shared, like all collective burdens, by all, and must not routinely exploit one actor (either human or natural system) for the sake of another.

For the Davie site, this requires that a whole new set of questions be asked, and data gathered. What toxins are present? Where did they come from? Is the process that created them necessary to human autonomy? Are there alternatives that would support autonomy but be less harmful to nature and future generations?

The principles supporting Justice from Autonomy make it an obligation of government to protect and empower both its citizens and natural systems through the assurance that all suspected toxins have been completely tested and determined necessary to autonomy before they are allowed onto the market.[29] In a risk-conscious society, it must be demonstrated that an autonomous person, respecting the environment as an end-in-itself, would take the risk. Uncertainty is now confronted by deontic ethics. We take responsibility for our generation of artificial risk, and environmental management refocuses on preventing false negatives rather than false positives.

The final guideline, *technological compatibility*, is also more concerned with prevention of problems like those at Davie, and less with the cleanup of a particular site after the harm is done. The need for cleanup itself is evidence of the fact that we have improper principles determining groundwater policy. The present state of decision making has no imperative to influence the development of technology so that it is harmonious with the natural order while supporting the moral autonomy of humanity.

Technological compatibility requires the active participation of government in the coordination of human innovation, so that an incentive structure is instituted by which the emphasis is placed on biodegradable and renewable technology with minimal waste streams. Here, human invention would be challenged by the task of providing energy, aids to agriculture, transportation, housing, and other baseline goods and services in harmony with the capacity of nature to provide for itself.

In addition, humans would be forced to recognize their interdependence with nature and to respect its functional integrity by treating it as an end-in-itself, worthy of continued persistence. The harmony of the resulting human freedom and natural causality can be seen as the ultimate expression of human intrinsic value; we take responsibility for our artificial creations, conserving and supporting nature in the process of invention. Only under these conditions can progress be considered morally responsible.

Unlike economic analysis, the Ecosystem approach to the Davie case requires that the complete cleanup option be executed. This is the only way that the moral autonomy of individuals and the functional integrity of the environment can be saved from further harm while the human perturbation is completely contained if not reversed. After this primary decision, the baseline can be considered supported; then it is acceptable to find the most cost-effective way of reaching the goal of aquifer restoration (Baram 1980).

Next, in chapter 10, we will demonstrate the revolutionary effects of an Ecosystem Approach on environmental risk, and on overall environmental law and policy, by revisiting the practice of regulation through six concrete cases: wilderness; wildlife; NIMBY; FDA regulation; comparative-risk ranking; and the use of the National Environmental Policy Act (NEPA). These cases will explore the new regulatory environment required by a fundamental concern for the intrinsic value of humanity and the natural environment.

Notes to Chapter 9

1. This explains the fascination of those who support the Economic Design Approach with the subject of "risk communication," as if the specifics of the risk or its ramifications are irrelevant if only one can communicate it properly.
2. There are also "data" and "analysis" problems in the fledging science of ecological-risk assessment (Bartell, Gardner, and O'Neil 1992; Calabrese and Baldwin 1993).
3. This failure to arrive at definitive numbers brings on the constant call for "more research" (Westra 1994), which allows current degradation of the environment by market decisions to continue unabated.
4. This is why Spock always irritated Bones when he would spout statistical probabilities in situations where what was needed was moral courage and the application of practical reason.
5. This is a shift from a false-positive risk regime to a false-negative risk regime. See chapter 3.
6. The U.S. Congress has repeatedly made major cuts in the funds for the biological survey in the name of private property rights.
7. In the epilogue, I will suggest that Proposition 65 in California is evidence for this argument.
8. Although he makes a different point, for different reasons, I believe that the arguments of Ulrich Beck (1992, 1995) on risk perception in society would support my use of the idea of a risk-conscious society.
9. Although circumstances will change over generations, each generation will judge policy decisions by how they affect its baseline autonomy. Each generation can then understand what is, or was, at stake, and its members can assure themselves that they would have made the same decision.
10. Even that risk caused by individual disposal of toxic agents after use originates in the production and manufacturing of the initial product.
11. As I will later argue, since autonomy is a common right, it must be protected at the most universal level of government possible.
12. In a different world, where international or global governments had effective regulatory power, they, rather than national governments would have this regulatory responsibility.
13. In Kant's terms this individual would be sentenced to passive citizenship and, for all intents and purposes, to slave status.
14. This may be the only solution to nonpoint source pollution. If the products that we use are biodegradable, then their nonsource introduction into the environment is not of as much concern. The best regulation here is preventative.
15. One justification, in extreme circumstances indeed, might be the human intervention in the evolution of an ice age that would destroy us as a species.
16. One could argue that since we are "natural," all we do and create is also "natural." However, because we are moral agents and subject to ethical duty, where the rest of nature is not, our will and its results make our actions and choices transcendent of natural causality and therefore "unnatural" and subject to moral thought and practical reason. This is the moral definition of the artificial.
17. The EPA studies actually concern two sites in Florida, but, for space, I have chosen only one. In neither case are complete remedial or preventative options cho-

sen. The EPA recommendation at the 58th Street Site outside Miami is deep-well injection of contaminants to contain the plume.

18. An interesting analysis (Downes 1985) charts the effects on redox reactions and nitrate levels in New Zealand aquifers. These effects are widespread and have serious ramifications both for the water as a source of nutrient and chemical value as well as for its thermodynamic qualities in natural systems energy provision.

19. I assume that the use of the surface space for agriculture has caused some perturbations (e.g., pesticide use, crop planting) but that these intrusions into the natural system are more compatible than the large-scale leakage of toxins into the groundwater caused by Davie.

20. Consequentialist thought finds the moral value of an act or rule in its consequences, whereas nonconsequentialist ethics finds moral value in the act or rule itself and how it considered the rights and duties involved. Not all consequentialist moral theories are utilitarian, but all utilitarian theory is consequentialist. Market efficiency analysis is considered utilitarian. See Sagoff; Gillroy; and MacIntyre in Gillroy and Wade 1992.

21. One needs to remember that all these costs are in 1983 dollars. The specific frequency of testing and the implied costs of setting up the well system depend on the judged toxicity of the contamination involved, the age of the site, the probability of site failure, and the probability distribution of the speed of the plume (Sobotka 1983, 47). Here, the costs and benefits will be discounted over time and imposed only if the probability of risk is enough that the initial costs of the wells and the rounds of testing will produce more health benefits than engineering and labor costs. "The best strategy is to choose the right compromise between the increasing costs of monitoring as the frequency of monitoring rises, and the increasing costs of dealing with larger contaminant plumes as the frequency of monitoring falls. The expected sum of the two kinds of costs arising out of decisions in a given month can be reduced to a minimum by setting the rate of monitoring such that the decrease in monitoring costs just balances the increase in the expected cleanup costs as monitoring is stretched out" (Sobotka 1983, 51).

22. It is assumed that the trash facility is not contributing to the contamination plume. If it were, then closure would be more complex.

23. Discounting assumes that a dollar now is always worth more to person X than the same dollar ten years from now. Like other elements of cost-benefit or efficiency analysis, discounting elevates present preferences over future ones and reduces all considerations to immediate dollar amounts.

24. First, the use of a discount rate and a short time horizon prejudices the analysis against those options with large up-front costs like toxic waste cleanup. With a short time horizon and a zero discount rate, the prevention option is most cost-effective for Davie. With even a 1 percent discount rate, however, the prevention option fails to be least costly. The prejudice is to that policy which stretches the costs of remedial action over the greatest span of time. Second, most of the great uncertainty involved in the cost-benefit evaluation pertains to the benefits of regulation, not to its economic costs. The technical costs of engineering and allocation of funds to the cleanup effort are fairly straightforward and can be estimated with little error (Geraghty and Miller 1983). The benefits of regulation, in contrast, pertain to health costs avoided and effectiveness of remedial or preventive action that involve probability estimation of the concentration, potency, and types of toxicity within the groundwater, as well as the statistical uncertainty of synergistic effects, and the possibility that unknown elements will be toxic that were not discovered in testing. "The concentrations of pollutants over time, the size of the affected population, and the potency of the pollutants are difficult to measure or predict accurately. . . . We used conservative assumptions whenever possible and still found health effects to be low. . . . Despite our conservatism, it cannot be as-

sumed that the health consequences projected in this report definitively represent the maximum possible effects, since some of the plume constituents for which there are no health consequences [also] might not be proportional to the fraction of an individual's life over which he is exposed, and/or synergisms may exist for certain combinations of contaminants" (Sobotka 1983, 26).

25. Harm affects many components of Ecosystem integrity, and "[h]arm avoidance is one of the more important components in environmentalist arguments against reckless intervention into natural processes" (Goodin 1983, 15).

26. Remember that my argument is not for a zero-risk society, but for a risk-conscious society that takes the intrinsic value of human and natural systems into account and decides whether or not a risk is worth taking. If a risk is necessary to moral or functional integrity (if it will feed millions, uniquely solve an energy problem, etc.), it may be worth taking. Today, we proceed if a market exists without any *ex ante* consciousness of the intrinsic values or risks truly involved in the decision. See chapter 4.

27. This assurance would include consideration of the waste stream and the provision of technology to render the waste products of the material harmless as part of the argument for the product's marketing.

28. It is not that bottled water is inherently disrespectful. If no aquifer preexisted, or if natural causes resulted in pollution of drinking water, then respect might require a government to pass out bottled water.

29. This would support the institution of a screening system based more on Food and Drug Administration policy than on the current EPA approach, which has no *ex ante* power to require toxins or pesticides to be judged or morally justified as to their affects on humans and natural systems. See chapter 10.

10

The Practice of Environmental Risk Revisited: Case Studies in Ecosystem Policy Argument

Having derived a new paradigm and context model for policy analysis and argument, and then new rules of thumb from this paradigm, we shall now apply Justice from Autonomy to six case studies grouped in three pairs. Each pair will highlight a specific interface of the policy context model as well as a particular component of the baseline function and will demonstrate how the components of the principle of autonomy harmonize the ends of humanity with the ends of nature.[1] This examination will demonstrate that the moral unity of the principle of autonomy applied to environmental policy produces a coordinated and noncontradictory integration of policy prescriptions in which the components of the baseline function work in unison to a common public end: the empowered intrinsic capacities of humanity and nature.

To streamline the application of the baseline function to the six cases, components of the baseline will be matched with specific rules of thumb laid out in the last chapter that are direct manifestations of the maxims to protect Ecosystem integrity, to distribute property, and to provide opportunity.

First, the extraction/preservation interface in our Ecosystem context model (fig. 8.3) will be examined through the case studies of wilderness and wildlife policy. Although all of the components of the baseline will affect these issues, the first component, Ecosystem integrity (E^I) as derived from the freedom component of the principle of autonomy, is most directly applicable. Therefore, we shall concentrate on the ramifications of the no-harm guideline since it provides the maxim to protect both the moral integrity of humanity and the functional integrity of natural systems through our laws directed at "preserving" wilderness and wildlife.

Second, the disposal (reintegration/recycling) interface from our context model will be examined through the case studies of comparative-risk ranking and the NIMBY (Not in My Back Yard) choice. Here, our primary concern will be the second component of the baseline function, property (p_i), and the dimension of autonomy under scrutiny is equality before the moral law. The tactical rule of thumb of greatest concern at this interface is trusteeship; the timeless preservation of the conditions of moral agency and natural functioning should dictate the ends of risk ranking and the solution to NIMBY and other noncooperative collection-action dilemmas involving our relationship to the natural environment.

Finally, we shall examine the manufacturing (production/construction) interface and the case studies of Food and Drug Administration (FDA) risk regulation and the status of the National Environmental Policy Act (NEPA) as a national planning statute. The baseline component most applicable here is the maxim to provide opportunity for independence (o_i) as part of human autonomy. The applicable rules of thumb are artificial-risk neutrality and technological compatibility, which set standards for the active and anticipatory state as it protects and empowers humanity and nature at the baseline and promotes practical reason within a risk-conscious society.

This chapter will conclude by arguing that the three components of the baseline work with the three interfaces between humanity and natural systems to produce a moral harmony of intrinsic capacity and purpose that fulfills our duties to ourselves and others (including nature). Lastly, using the criteria for political evaluation set up by Brian M. Barry and Douglas W. Rae (1975), the viability of the baseline function as a methodology for policy argument will be analyzed.

Remember that all three baseline components are derived from the same metaprinciple of autonomy, so to achieve the ends of one component in the moral agency of humanity is to enhance the others simultaneously. The ascendancy of Ecosystem Law and Policy Argument requires that we establish a tradeoff scheme between intrinsic values, within which we are responsible to understand consciously and argue about the effects of human agency through the interfaces of our new context model. In making a political decision about the intrinsic values involved, we shall be, in all cases, preserving and enhancing intrinsic value of some sort and will be obliged to sacrifice instrumental value when it conflicts with human or natural integrity. Instead of a lexical order or a conflict of distinct principles (Rawls 1971, 42, 61), our baseline function weighs the necessity of intrinsic values with one another, and, like Kant's three-part categorical imperative, each component supports, reinforces, and adds a dimension to the others without practical contradiction.[2]

Ecosystem Integrity and the Extraction Decision: The Cases of Wilderness and Wildlife

The primary interface between human and natural systems involves the human decision to use the attributes of nature to satisfy human needs and wants. Establishing and maintaining our autonomy requires us, principally, to do no harm and to protect the integrity of nature for itself (Kantian preservationism) and as a component of our own status as moral agents (Kantian conservationism). Our initial case study concerns the extraction from or preservation of natural systems in designated National Wildlife Refuges.

Integrity, Efficiency, and the National Wildlife Refuge

Human use of refuge areas and the impact of these uses on wildlife management are our focus. In addition to this exposition of law, I am also interested in why a wildlife refuge would honor any human use in view of its mandate to protect and preserve species and habitat. Surely it is not counterintuitive to expect that if the intrinsic value or integrity of nature can be accommodated in "resources" policy, it would be through the designation of wildlife refuges. In fact, one might argue that Ecosystem law is best expressed in the wildlife refuge, since the extraction decision is absent, while the baseline imperative to preserve system integrity finds persuasiveness.

However, the principle of efficiency and its TSA context model are alive and well in wildlife law. The history of wildlife law reveals a struggle for jurisdiction between state and federal governments with a single policy end; the primary concern on both levels is the persistence of species as they have instrumental value to humanity. If a concern for other than economic ends arises to affect wildlife law, Congress reacts to reaffirm the principle of efficiency as the core of wildlife policy argument.

The National Wildlife Refuge System is regulated by three statutes: the Refuge Recreation Act of 1962 (16 U.S.C.A. §§460k to k4); the Refuge Revenue Sharing Act of 1964 (16 U.S.C.A. §715s);[3] and the National Wildlife Refuge Administration Act of 1966 (16 U.S.C.A. §§668dd–ee). The three statutes have but one purpose:[4] to provide wildlife (primarily birds) with safe havens for protection and breeding. The protection of species is, however, not protection for the sake of species integrity, but for the purpose of human recreation, study, or other anthropocentric instrumental value.

Nash asserts that, with the enactment of the Endangered Species Act in 1973, species gained rights as part of the moral community in which humans live (Nash 1989). Doubtless, the core element of federal wildlife law is the Endangered Species Act (16 U.S.CA. §§1531 [ESA§2]–1544 [ESA§18]); however, it is less clear that there are any rights or intrinsic value represented in this statute. The mandate to "preserve" listed species and to designate and protect their habitat may be misleading (Switzer 1994, 298–318),[5] for although only scientific criteria can be used in the designation of a threatened or endangered species (ESA §3), economic criteria become a prominent consideration in designating habitat (ESA §4), in writing recovery plans (ESA §4), and in the consideration of exemption from the law under the "economic hardship clause" that appears toward the end of the act (ESA §10). In addition, since the *Hill* case, (*TVA v Hill* 437 U.S. 153 [1978]), Congress has established the "Endangered Species Committee" (ESA §7), which can, for economic reasons, deny a species the protection of the act.

But if intrinsic value is not protected by the ESA, perhaps the refuge system empowers integrity? The specific legislation intended to consolidate and administer a National Wildlife Refuge System also contains a set of mandates that support a concern for economy over Ecosystem integrity and betray the dominance of the market paradigm for wildlife policymakers. In addition to the designation of these lands for "the conservation of fish and wildlife" (16 U.S.C.A. §668dd [a1]), the secretary of the interior is authorized to "permit the use of any area within the System for any purpose, including but not limited to hunting, fishing, public recreation and accommodation, and access" (16 U.S.C.A. §668dd [d1A]). The only restriction is that these secondary uses "are compatible with the major purposes for which such areas were established" (16 U.S.C.A. §668dd [d1A]).

The validity of the "secondary uses" of the Federal Refuge System is first described in the Refuge Recreation Act of 1962 (16 U.S.C.A. §§460k to k4). Here, the "mounting public demand" for the use of wildlife refuges is acknowledged (16 U.S.C.A. §460k), while it is also directed that

> any present or future recreational use will be compatible with, and will not prevent accomplishment of, the primary purpose for which the said conservation areas were acquired or established, the Secretary of the Interior is authorized, as an appropriate incidental or secondary use, to administer such areas . . . for public recreation . . . to the extent practicable. (16 U.S.C.A. §460k)

In the written regulations of the Fish and Wildlife Service (50 C.F.R. chap. 1), the "secondary" and "incidental" uses of the Refuge System take up most of the more than 250 pages of regulations. In addition to allowing hunting (50 C.F.R. §32) and fishing (50 C.F.R. §33), provisions for other land uses such as "feral animal management" (50 C.F.R. §30) and even mineral and oil exploration (50 C.F.R. §29C) are established.

Throughout the regulations, this "balance" of secondary uses with the dominant mandate of species protection appears repeatedly. In dozens of specific regulations for specific wildlife refuges,[6] different species and types of hunting and fishing are specified where the sportsman is constrained primarily by the need for a state license (50 C.F.R. §32.2-hunting / §33.2-fishing). These acts, as regulated, are assumed to be eminently "compatible" with species preservation.

The most interesting and least logical argument for compatibility involves the specific federal regulations concerning the exploration for oil in the coastal plain of the Arctic National Wildlife Refuge.

> It is the objective of this program to ascertain the best possible data and information concerning the probable existence, location, volume, and potential for further exploration, development, and production of oil and gas within the coastal plain without significantly adversely affecting the wildlife, its habitat, or the environment. (50 C.F.R. §37.1)

Consequently, with the proper special permit (50 C.F.R. §§37.11 and 37.23), and the submission and approval of an exploration plan (50 C.F.R. §§37.21–

.22) and a plan of operation (50 C.F.R. §37.24), one can search for oil and gas as a "secondary" and "incidental" use of the Arctic National Wildlife Refuge.[7]

Why does the federal government allow any human use of wildlife refuges? Is it not sufficient that they exist as intact natural systems in order to protect and preserve wildlife? Isn't it counterintuitive to allow hunting and fishing in a wildlife "refuge" where the natural predatory cycles of nature ought to limit numbers and maintain balance, or, at least where species can find protection from human contact and perturbations? How can "land development" uses such as oil and gas exploration and extraction be considered "compatible" with or "incidental" to the designation of a wildlife refuge?

Common sense makes the argument for other "secondary" uses, as compatible with wildlife preservation, counterintuitive. In *Webster's New World Dictionary* (2d ed., s.v. "refuge") a "refuge" is "a place of safety; shelter; protection from danger." To allow hunting and fishing or oil exploration, has the opposite consequence, making these "refuges" dangerous and uncertain places for wildlife.

The rhetoric of "secondary use" becomes reasonable only if one assumes the primacy of the market paradigm in wildlife policy argument. After all, the history of refuge law and the jurisdictional tension between state and federal government over wildlife conservation has not evolved within a paradigm and context model that supports natural systems integrity and the primacy of preservation, but rather has developed from the core principle of efficiency applied to instrumental resource use. The optimal functioning of the materials balance motivates the policymaker; the sector here contains species for use.

The regulation of wildlife in the United States originated in English wildlife law, which was primarily designed around the conservation of wildlife for the purpose of human utilization (Lund 1980; Bean 1983). In English law, wildlife was regulated in a highly centralized manner and by an elite few who controlled real property. These dimensions of English tradition were rejected in America.

American wildlife regulation is decentralized and delegated to the states in what is known as the State Ownership Doctrine (Bean 1983, 12–17). In addition to this doctrine, which gave states almost total control of all wildlife regulation, wildlife conservation by and for the elite was replaced by a democratic ideal to the effect that a wider cross-section of citizens should be able to hunt, fish, and, in other ways, use, extract or "take" wildlife (Lund 1980, 23–25).

The democratization of hunting was so successful that by the end of the nineteenth century, many species were nearly hunted out (Lund 1980, 58). Again, the materials balance was not maintained by the unregulated market under TSA-I, so government regulators entered the scene. The definition of efficiency changed so that, instead of maximum use of a species (e.g., bison), it became "efficient" only to pursue the *optimal* taking of wildlife over time. The state set the number and type of species that could be taken so that their numbers persisted; here again, however, the regulation was not meant to replace economic values with environmental values, but to correct the materials balance for long-term optimal efficiency. The conceptualization of nature had not changed, nor had the motivating principle of "resource" policy moved away from the primacy of extraction. Only the terms of efficiency and the inclusion of government in the regulation of the materials balance were new. The original operating paradigm remained with a modified TSA context model.

The specter of widespread extinction haunted wildlife species from the white-tailed deer on the East Coast to the bison out West (Lund 1980, 60). In response to the propensity of our ancestors to discount the future and overconsume, many state governments and sportsmen's organizations began to regulate "taking" of wildlife with the establishment of "seasons" and "fees" for hunting. Using a conservationist rhetoric, policy argument adopted a principle of sustainability, searching for the optimal yield of animals for present and future generations of sports enthusiasts. This "sportsman's" version of the "market paradigm" dominated American wildlife law and became the conventional status quo that laid the ethical foundation and fundamental assumptions of wildlife policy, even when the federal government entered the picture at the turn of the last century.

Initially, the state had absolute discretion in wildlife law, which seemed to preclude any involvement of the federal government in animal regulation. The only means the federal government had by which to establish its jurisdiction was the Constitution of the United States. So federal wildlife law established federal jurisdiction through the treaty, property, and commerce clauses of our Constitution (Bean 1983, 12).

Over the years, starting with the Lacy Act of 1900 (16 U.S.C.A. §701, §§3371–78)[8] and the *Geer* decision of 1896 in the Supreme Court, and ending with the Endangered Species Act (16 U.S.C.A. §§1531–44) and the 1979 *Palila* decision,[9] the federal government has promoted a more protectionist policy regarding wildlife. However, a preservation argument to underlie this effort has not been successfully introduced, and a new core principle to motivate wildlife metapolicy has not supplanted efficiency. We are not yet promoting and protecting the integrity of species and their habitat as functional ends in themselves. Even in federal wildlife policy, the instrumental value of nature continues to lie at the core of law and the extraction interface.

Efficient human taking remains the key to understanding both the primary and secondary uses of refuges (Bean 1983, 17). Thus, although the conceptualization of wildlife as an economic or recreational resource has been supplemented with the proposition that wildlife serves other ecological and scientific ends,[10] the reliance on instrumental economic value has remained at the metapolicy's core. Concern for science and concern for ecology can be seen as variants of the "efficient use" argument that studies species for their potential contribution to the economy and natural systems for their capacity to feed human growth potential.

The power of the market paradigm can also be seen in the state control of wildlife use. If we considered species and their habitats to have a functional intrinsic value, then our "universal" duties to them could not be satisfied by allowing subnational governments to protect some species in some places while others have no moral status as ends. The focus on state dominance is an outgrowth of dependence on individual preference for welfare or willingness to pay as the ultimate standard for policy choice. It is only reasonable to allow decentralized regulation if wildlife taking is something that ought to be controlled by market or state responsiveness to local human preferences. If all natural systems as well as their components were considered to have intrinsic value, then the most comprehensive level of government would need to be responsible for them in the name of all active citizens. In the U.S. case, this would be the federal government.

The status of wildlife refuges represents a conflict between state concerns for the short-term efficient use of wildlife and their habitat and a federal interest in the longer-term protection of both natural attributes. A federal sustainability ethic, stressing optimal efficiency over time, has been promoted so as to become the dominant use of the Refuge System, but it is still coping with the concerns of the states for ample and immediate sporting and other "use" opportunities. Although we may, as a nation, have decided that long-term sustainability is the central requirement of the Refuge System and we have been able to override state concerns for ample "recreational" uses of wildlife, especially considering endangered species, we also continue to be concerned that this long-term efficiency "not be construed as affecting the authority, jurisdiction, or responsibility of the several States to manage, control, or regulate fish and resident wildlife under State law or regulation in any area within the system" (16 U.S.C.A. §668dd [c]).[11]

Preservation, Conservation, and Legal Wilderness

Within the context of natural resource extraction, the best opportunity for the intrinsic value of nature to determine policy is in the designation of wilderness areas, which are as close as American law comes to recognizing the integrity of whole natural systems. However, here again the concern for efficiency dominates policy. Although a preservationist ethic that includes environmental values is accessible through the idea of wilderness, the American conception of wilderness as foreboding and antithetical to economic prosperity has infused wilderness law and policy with ample veneration for the core value of efficiency and a perception of wilderness as wasted economic resources.

The United States is a settlement colony, founded by people who saw wilderness as frightening and foreboding (Nash 1967; Merchant 1989). The frontier ethic was to maximize economic growth and prosperity and to clear and civilize the wilderness. Security was only to be found in open, organized, and human-dominated spaces (Coggins, Wilkinson, and Leshy 1993, chap. 2). In view of the ethical starting point that associates security with order and disorder and fear with wilderness, that Americans have any legislation that sets aside wilderness areas begs the question of why? Have we converted to an ethic that considers the intrinsic value of wilderness as a central concern or have we just utilized the designation of wilderness as a means for sustaining the materials balance when it otherwise would have failed?

Consideration of the resource uses of designated wilderness areas on public lands may help answer this question. However, the real subject is not resource use, but whether this "use" is at all limited, let alone trumped, by a concern for the intrinsic value or functional integrity and preservation of natural areas in a primitive condition. To fully comprehend the roots and constraints of wilderness law and policy, one must understand the moral dimensions of wilderness as myth and the negative connotation of wilderness "preservation" for Americans.

343

Americans are unique in the world for having legally established wilderness areas.[12] However, our statutes and regulations specifically allow many other resource uses that seem antithetical to wilderness preservation. Our cognitive dissonance results in wilderness law, which pits an ethic of preserving nature against a utilitarian ethic that considers a tree protected as a resource wasted and wilderness without human perturbation as a dark and uncivilized place without light.

Wilderness designation has only been formalized in the last thirty-five years. All wilderness areas on public lands in the United States, like wildlife refuges, are now designated by specific congressional legislation and managed by that public lands agency (Forest Service; Bureau of Land Management; Park Service; Fish and Wildlife Service) which supervised its prewilderness existence (Stegner 1994; Doherty 1992; Anderson and Byrnes 1993, 10).[13] Although the specific management directives and uses for each wilderness area are contained in its enabling legislation, the wilderness preservation system was integrated and codified by a single statute.

The primary piece of legislation to define wilderness in the United States is the Wilderness Act of 1964 (16 U.S.C.A. §§1131–36).[14] Among other things, this statute establishes a National Wilderness Preservation System (§1131[a]), defines wilderness (§1131[b]), specifies how wilderness is designated (§1132), and describes allowable uses of wilderness areas (§1133).

The dominant goal of the Wilderness Act, however, is the promotion and preservation of nature in its primitive state. Like most "resource" law, it reflects the understanding that overtaxing the environment through an unregulated market under TSA-I caused scarcity and a resultant need for the conservation of nature so that its efficient use could be *optimized* over time. But, given this realization, should we not have replaced the market paradigm with other standards and policy assumptions?

The statute originates in the concern that "increasing population, accompanied by expanding settlement and growing mechanization, [should] not occupy and modify all areas within the United States . . . leaving no lands designated for preservation and protection in their natural condition" (16 U.S.C.A. §1131 [a]). Wilderness itself is defined as that "area where the earth and its community of life are untrammeled by man, where man himself is a visitor" (16 U.S.C.A. §1131 [c]).

This preservationist imperative is also evident in the specific regulations that govern the administration of wilderness areas. For example, the rules governing both the Bureau of Land Management (43 C.F.R. §§8500 and 8590, here specifically §8560.0–6) and the Forest Service (36 C.F.R. §293, here specifically §293.2) state that management of wilderness should have three prime directives:

> (a) Natural ecological succession will be allowed to operate freely to the extent feasible.
> (b) Wilderness will be made available for human use to the optimum extent consistent with the maintenance of primitive conditions.
> (c) In resolving conflicts in resource use, wilderness values will be dominant. (36 C.F.R. §283.2)

The primacy of "wilderness values," however, does not mean that other instrumental uses are not allowed or even encouraged by law.

The act has specific provisions for the regulation of aircraft and motorboats as well as action to handle fire, insects, and diseases (§1133 [d1]). "Mineral Activities, surveys for mineral value" (d2) as well as "mining and mineral leasing laws" (d3) are regulated uses of wilderness, as are water utilization (d4), recreation (d5), limited commercial services (d6), and hunting/fishing activity (d8).[15] Therefore, recreation, hunting, fishing, and even mining are allowed in wilderness areas (16 U.S.C.A. §1133) and the wilderness itself is not set aside for its *own sake* but for its "future use and enjoyment as wilderness, and [to] allow for recreation, scenic, scientific, educational, conservation, and historic use" (43 C.F.R. §§8560.0–2).

All of these designated uses and the human-centered, instrumental arguments for wilderness have only two restrictions. First, almost all use is limited to that which existed when the land was designated as wilderness (Pearson 1992, 20; Steen 1992, 18). For example, mining will not be stopped outright with wilderness status, but new claims will be more severely regulated than preexisting operations.[16] Second, each use is immediately made conditional on the primary concern for the "wilderness character" of the land.

> [E]ach agency administering any area designated as wilderness shall be responsible for preserving the wilderness character of the area and shall so administer such area for such other purposes for which it may have been established as also to preserve its wilderness character. (16 U.S.C.A. §1133 [b])

However, even in regulations for a wilderness study area (a prewilderness designation), exploration and mining can be carried out "in a manner that will not impair the suitability of an area for inclusion in the wilderness system" (43 C.F.R. §3802,0–2 [a]). Any mineral leases allowed on wilderness land "will contain reasonable stipulations for the protection of the wilderness character of the land" (36 C.F.R. §293.14 [b]) and all actual mining operations conducted will include, by statute, "reclamation measures." This reestablishment of wilderness character "shall be commenced, conducted and completed as soon after disturbance as feasible . . . and will include . . . (1) reshaping of the lands . . . to approximate original contours; (2) restoring such reshaped lands by replacement of top soil; and (3) revegetating the lands." (43 C.F.R. §§3802.0–5 [a]). Even general access to a wilderness area must be "consistent with the preservation of such wilderness" (43 C.F.R. §§8560.4–3 [b]).[17]

Therefore, other than uses such as mining or grazing (36 C.F.R §293.7) established before wilderness designation, and some hunting and fishing regulated by state law, any future nonpreservation use is strictly regulated. The list of prohibited new acts on wilderness is lengthy and comprehensive. These prohibitions include "commercial enterprises," "temporary or permanent roads," "aircraft landing strips," "use of motorized vehicles and equipment," "landing of aircraft," "dropping of materials, supplies, or persons from aircraft," "structures or installations," and "cutting of trees" (43 C.F.R. §8560.1–2).[18]

It is after wilderness designation that the strictest limitations on economic use go into effect. But how much economic use has already been made of wilderness lands before their designation? Can we truthfully define such lands as "untrammeled"? Are we serious about protecting natural systems in a primitive state or are we simply designating as "wilderness" those lands that have no further resource uses?

Wilderness legislation allows exploration and assessment of resource value, even in designated areas, and the resource status of any proposed wilderness is a major part of the congressional debate over its designation (Lowry 1994, 1998). This should be expected if economic efficiency is the primary motivation of wilderness designation. One might then assume that only lands found to have no "economic" value would receive this distinction. In this way, the stricture that resource use must be very closely regulated to be "compatible" with the primary "wilderness character" of the land has few repercussions in the application of the market paradigm or the maintenance of the materials balance.[19]

The ongoing effort of the Congress to pass wilderness legislation (Satchell 1989; Hamilton 1992; Crow 1993, 32) is marked by a consistent and recurring battle between the forces of economic use and the forces of environmental preservation (Frome 1997).[20] Many in Congress believe that if public land has any present or future economic value, it should not be designated as wilderness. The focus on optimal extraction persists.

Throughout the legislative record, arguments of those opposed to the designation of wilderness are replete with fear generated by the idea of unused natural systems (Lane 1984, 296).[21] Resources, it is feared, will go unexploited; decay and depravation will overtake nature; wilderness as chaos will spread unchecked, causing devolution of the natural world back toward its original status as a "wasteland" or "dark forbidding place."[22] Like many of our ancestors, wilderness skeptics see disorganization, decay, and terror in those areas "untrammeled by man" and seek to limit the spread of "waste" and "darkness" by limiting the amount and degree of outright preservation on public lands.[23]

Even though elaborate regulations exist that allow prospecting and mining in wilderness, and nowhere are they unconditionally prohibited by statute, mining journals argue that once a wilderness is defined "no resource exploration will ever again be allowed."[24] A myth exists that wilderness designation will curtail all resource use forever (Smith 1992, 202).[25] Arguments for this point of view include economic regrets, but also offer a polemic that any prospects for "order" and "good" will be forever precluded with wilderness designation.[26]

With such a primeval ethical position and definition of wilderness, it is not just the economic resources in any tract of land that are of concern, but the idea that property should not be segregated "for all time" as an "untrammeled" natural system. Not surprisingly, legislators opposing preservation saw the 1964 Wilderness Act as particularly "disturbing" because designation of wilderness would mean a victory for disorganization and decay.[27]

Overall, the mythology of wilderness has produced statute and regulatory law with many exceptions, conditions, and authorized uses within wilderness areas, and has assured that little potentially productive land will be designated as wilderness. Nowhere in the law is there any mention of preserving nature for its own sake and, this, combined with a powerful mythology and the conventional fear of loss that "wilderness" suggests, has led to setting aside comparatively little wilderness. Only if future extraction is impossible, or future use inconceivable, is an area obviously fit for congressional designation as a wilderness.[28]

Integrity, Ecosystem Argument, and Preservation

By applying Justice from Autonomy and the Ecosystem context model to these case studies, the core argument and practical recommendations for wilderness and wildlife policy change. To preserve and protect the environment as a functional end in itself is now a duty of human autonomy. Law and policy are now formulated on a predisposition to withhold natural systems from human use unless it can be persuasively argued that the use is necessary for Ecosystem integrity, affirming the intrinsic values of humanity and nature. Justice requires that the intrinsic value of humanity and nature be the primary consideration. With Ecosystem law and policy, the burden of proof is placed on those who would use a natural system to justify that use in the name of the "will of all." Law would require them to demonstrate one of two things in order to use nature at the extraction interface:

1. that human intrinsic value is at stake and that it is imperative that natural systems integrity be put at risk for our own (autonomy-based) needs; or
2. that natural systems functional integrity is not at stake in the extraction and use decision.

At this point, economists usually remind us that without use of the environment modern society would not exist, while to establish priorities like those just articulated would all but force us out of our houses and into caves. A switch of paradigms need not produce such drastic consequences.

First, the comprehensive functional integrity of natural systems is the primary duty of humanity within Justice from Autonomy. Such responsibility means that separate wildlife and wilderness distinctions are not suitable public policy. Each natural system as it constitutes an interconnected web of species, minerals, and media cycles ought to be the focus of public choice. Therefore, the priority of the policymaker is to classify and categorize these natural systems in a kind of biological zoning regime that would separate unique from common systems and "untrammeled" systems from those in which humans already play a major reconstructive role.

Second, most use, if moderate, conscious, and well planned, will not result in significant deterioration of natural systems' functioning and may even enhance their resilience and flourishing. Using natural attributes as a human resource must be justified, but by defining use in terms of Ecosystem integrity, both our own moral agency and nature's functional wholeness will require us to seek solutions to our needs that harmonize nature's ends and our own. This approach argues for clean energy, concentration of human use in areas already reconstructed by humanity (e.g., cities), and production processes that create safe results in safe ways with minimal pollution.

Within Ecosystem law we can designate use that provides what we need and takes from nature where it causes the least harm to the intrinsic values involved, perhaps even allowing us to enhance or reestablish the environmental functioning of a used or abused natural system (e.g., wolves in Yellowstone). Our policy and law will strive for use that affects natural functioning the least, and that is constructive toward our own moral agency because it is compatible with the continued wholeness of the environment.

A single law is needed that designates *wild areas* and *priority natural systems* and that prohibits human use within these designated areas. Such legislation would require a national biological survey and a new natural systems zoning plan that provides the biological, hydrological, geological, and chemical status of each defined system. With this information as a foundation, all prospective uses would have to be justified by the prospective extractor with concern for human autonomy and how it would affect the functioning of pertinent natural systems. Government could, through such a performance zoning scheme,[29] inform prospective extractors of what plots of land, what natural systems, and what components of natural systems were available for use as resources. Each potential user would then be obliged to provide a plan in which extraction techniques as well as quantities and other specifics were detailed. At this point, a government agency would or would not authorize the use.

Any proposed extraction plan ought to be comprehensive and focus on both how the use would enhance our autonomy and what total species and media effects would be forthcoming. It should demonstrate how specific extraction levels and procedures would limit harm to the integrity of a natural system. In addition, such plans would have to specify if the area would be environmentally revitalized *ex post* and how. The more drastic the proposed use, the more complicated and costly the planning should be, but in all cases the costs of extraction must account for both the moral integrity of humanity and the functional integrity of natural systems.

Presumably, wild areas and preserved natural systems would only be one designation in the greater national zoning plan, but it would be the most important designation and should allow no use or only emergency use (if no other alternatives were available and humanity was in drastic straits). From this perspective, natural systems are but one component of Ecosystems, protected and empowered through the baseline autonomy function. Here, the demands of autonomy create our duties both to ourselves and to nature, which, together, require the zoning system to provide evidence for all use justification and extraction decisions.

Humanity must recognize that in protecting wild areas, we are fulfilling our duties not only to nature but to ourselves. The set-aside systems, therefore, must not be "left over" and economically valueless tracts of land, but natural systems designated for their ecological qualities: systems that are intrinsically (biologically) unique or critical to biodiversity (e.g., old-growth forest). In addition, because the larger Ecosystem picture is critical, all natural systems, both urban and rural, must be part of a comprehensive zoning inventory. We should never use nature's functional integrity merely as an elective means to our own ends; this requires us to consider the overall health of functioning Eco-(human/natural) systems as we use any particular environmental component of them. Therefore, we ought to concentrate land use in areas that are already utilized for human habitation and set aside areas that have until now been left relatively undisturbed. The constant human expansion into forests and farm lands for redundant housing is a violation of this duty.

Intrinsic value has priority within this paradigm, and the comprehensive health and dignity of the Ecosystem depends on the harmony of human existence with natural systems. Our use should both cause minimal harm to the intrinsic qualities of functioning Ecosystems as we find them and require us to recognize the present state of those Ecosystems as well as the potential ramifications of any of our extraction plans.

In addition to providing a method for causing the least harm, what do the other rules of thumb and their baseline components add to the analysis of these two cases? The imperative to preserve and empower natural systems functioning places us as trustees of the Ecosystem and its human and natural components. Property within Justice from Autonomy is presumed public and can be transferred into private hands only for the expression of positive freedom. To express autonomy means not violating our duties to ourselves or others (including nature); this requires that private property be utilized only for the greater good of Ecosystems. The regulation of private property for natural systems (or greater Ecosystem) integrity is necessary; use must fit within the guidelines of providing, protecting, or empowering autonomy to give it the moral sanction of the "will of all."

We need to adopt a timeless predisposition to the idea that natural systems and their tangible assets are primarily for the ends of environmental functioning and human autonomy. Our national zoning system, therefore, would be required to focus on classification of wild areas as a public trust, making them unavailable for subjective use based on above-baseline wealth (i.e., recreational as opposed to subsistence hunting) or individual profit (e.g., mining, clearcutting) that systematically exploits either human or natural integrity for elective ends. Although any use of nature that harms its integrity must be justified through the needs of active moral agents, making policy choice by the "will of all" requires the distribution of any such use profits to those who suffer by the use. This includes nature and its reclamation *ex post*. In wild areas these use strictures must be the tightest. Trusteeship can mean nothing less.

In terms of opportunity for independence, artificial-risk neutrality and technological compatibility reinforce the no-harm imperative to protect integrity, and the just state gains an active role in providing both humanity and nature with the opportunity for independent functioning as component parts of Ecosystems. This means that in addition to concern for harmonious cooperation between freedom and natural systems evolution, respect for the specific capacity, ability, and purpose of nature, on its own, is paramount in the choices of human moral agents. This will require anticipatory institutions that set aside places where natural systems progress without human perturbation as part of our moral use and planning of the extraction interface with nature.

In our assessment of nature, we should designate the "untrammeled" systems as wilderness and preserve the functioning and evolution of these spaces with the help of technology. Technology needs to be redefined so that its effects on both humanity and nature become important in the decision process, and we should make policy distinctions between what we *can* accomplish with technology and what we *ought* to accomplish so that invention provides for ourselves and the integrity of nature simultaneously.

We should seek renewable energy, minimal packaging, maximum reuse and recycling, and minimal land use so as to minimize extraction itself. As trustees we should be conscious of our true needs and conserve nature so that its integrity is as intact as possible. This does not mean we move back into caves, but may mean that we drive less, hunt less, have fewer and lighter cars and fewer one-use disposable goods.

If use is secondary to integrity and must be conditioned by it, then our institutions, to provide for moral independence, must also provide for the development of technology that imposes the least risk for the most harmless use of the environment. Here, the shift in the burden of proof, necessitated by our focus on intrinsic value, causes justification and planning for extraction to consider and force the development of technology that is risk neutral and compatible with natural and human capacities. In some natural systems our duty may be to extract resources so as to disturb systemic integrity least or to provide compensation for use in the form of replacement of resources or enhancement of nature for its own sake (e.g., rebuilding spawning grounds).

Overall, the Ecosystem approach demands that practical reason be applied to the earth and its uses. If a natural system is old-growth or supports a unique biodiversity and is relatively untrammeled, it ought to be preserved from use in our zoning system as a wild area (e.g., Tongass Forest). If the natural system has sustained extensive human use, then attention to its empowerment requires us to either concentrate human use in this area or replenish and restore its ecology to the best of our abilities. In all cases, having a market for use of a component or sector of the natural world is no longer enough to justify that use. The extraction interface requires that we treat nature with respect as a functional end in itself and as a component of Ecosystems that require both our active citizenship and our consciousness of moral duty.

Assurance and the Disposal Interface: NIMBY and Comparative Risk

The disposal interface and a concern for property and trusteeship prompt an examination of the comparative-risk process and the NIMBY phenomena. NIMBY results from the failure to provide assurance that all are equal before the moral law. Assuming the NIMBY reaction to be a symptom of the "mania for domination," I will decipher the sources of NIMBY and will analyze the unique approach of Ecosystem policy argument to this issue. Comparative-risk regulation, the second case, will be considered an attempt to move beyond NIMBY and offer a comprehensive look at environmental risk as it affects human and natural systems. Comparative risk seeks to prevent the "mania for domination" by involving a wider population in future planning. In terms of Justice from Autonomy, it is also an attempt to respect the "will of all" by responding to the comprehensive uncertainty that causes individuals to feel less than equal before the moral law.

NIMBY and the Politics of Assurance

The apparent unwillingness of humanity to take responsibility for the waste it creates is a constant problem facing policymakers; indications are that it will worsen every year as fewer necessary environmental facilities are successfully sited.[30] If this imbalance between waste and sites is not solved, the participatory and democratic character of our nation may be at risk as governments force facilities on local communities through eminent domain.

The NIMBY choice will be analyzed from a philosophical point of view; we will examine the basic moral character attributed to the individual by the policymaker within our strategic framework of dynamic collective action. If we investigate the theoretical constructions of policymakers, that is, the theoretical paradigm or ethical and strategic assumptions they make about individuals and their priorities, and the reality policymakers are interpreting in order to suggest policy solutions, this dysfunctional situation might be better understood and solved. The moral underpinnings of the NIMBY situation must be revealed through a concentration on the formal and substantive characterizations of the agents involved and of the collective-action problem, that is, the tense confrontations between citizens, government, and the market that foil the siting of important public works.[31]

I assume that the facility to be sited is a collective good, that the groups opposing one another can be considered reasonable, and that they are involved in a strategic interaction where the choices of both groups produce the resultant outcomes. In such circumstances, the policymaker should ask *why* citizens exhibit low public spirit (Kelman 1987, 10) and reject sitings. Are these defections from cooperation evidence of rational preferences or a dysfunctional preference order caused by the moral dimensions of the strategic interaction?

Two levels of philosophical investigation can partly answer these questions; one is primary and the other is secondary. The decision maker need not decide, at this point, what the philosophical dimensions of the distribution of positive and negative indivisible goods are within a free society. These secondary sociophilosophical questions must be preceded by an accurate construction of the ethical and strategic character of the individual and an assessment of both what is normatively critical about the policy issue and what imperatives explain the evidenced NIMBY behavior. Without first understanding who a person is and why he or she acts in a particular way, it is impossible to talk about policy solutions, define a morally justified distribution scheme, or argue about other philosophical or political issues. Specifically, the NIMBY problem will be examined as a strategic confrontation between the public as a group of citizens, in a specific political jurisdiction, and the forces (e.g., industry) seeking siting. If public policy is a product of the moral and strategic framework within which individual citizens exist and interact, the way in which a decision maker understands this interaction situation will determine his or her approach to the policy issue. Having the wrong representation of this normative and empirical reality will cause dysfunction in the policy process.

For NIMBY, constructing the proper theoretical representation is complicated by the existence of two alternative explanations of the manifest anti-growth preferences of individuals: the market paradigm assumes that the selfish preference is the highest priority of the rational individual, whereas Justice from Autonomy assumes self-interest to be a dysfunction preference of a citizen whose fear of exploitation has overcome his practical reason.

Although, superficially, the NIMBY problem appears to the observer as a classic market-type confrontation of rational agents in a collective goods/prisoner's dilemma (Hardin 1982a) and is handled by the decision maker as one, in essence, I contend that moral agents are confronting uncertainty within an assurance game, unable to protect their moral autonomy and coordinate their behavior simultaneously.[32] In both game situations, the collective good to be provided is identical: a facility that requires a site.[33] It is with the character of the agents and the framework of strategic interaction that the two game situations and the resulting policy prescriptions differ.

What is obvious about a NIMBY situation is the simple rationality and virulent self-interest of the participants. Those who want to site the facility have problems that only the existence of the facility as a collective good will solve; those who oppose the siting may acknowledge it as necessary but do not want it placed near them (Gillroy and Shapiro 1986). The highest priority for each player is to obtain the advantage of the collective good without having to pay for it. The second preference is to cooperate mutually if they have to; their third choice is not to have the good provided at all. Everyone's worst nightmare is to absorb the costs of the good unilaterally, while others benefit collectively and free ride. These preferences define a prisoner's or polluter's dilemma (chap. 2, fig. 2.1).

The prisoner's dilemma is a strategic interaction between rational agents, in which the symmetric payoff structure reveals a situation where the best choice for the individual causes collectively suboptimal outcomes. The prisoner's dilemma is an example of what Hardin calls "the back of the invisible hand" (1982a, 6). Each person pursuing his or her self-interest fails to provide for his or her joint or collective interests.

From within this strategic context, the dominant strategy for each player is to defect from provision of the collective good, whatever choice the other makes. With both agents playing their dominant strategies, the resulting equilibrium will be universal defection. This equilibrium is not Pareto optimal but unstable, and a dilemma for the players as long as they independently prefer universal cooperation to universal defection but collectively produce the latter (Goodin 1976, 166–68).[34]

The NIMBY problem is approached, by the policymaker, as if it were a prisoner's dilemma. This contention is supported by Barry Rabe, who describes the present approach to the problem as if it were a one-shot prisoner's dilemma game.

> [T]he site proponents and local community representatives (potential "hosts") are pitted in a prisoner's dilemma-type situation. For the host, its preferred outcome may be to thwart the proposed site; this may be realized if it resists ("defects") and the site developer withdraws ("cooperates"). Other options, in declining order of host preference, include compensated settlement between parties [universal cooperation], binding arbitration [universal defection], and, finally, developer success in imposing an agreement [unilateral cooperation]. (Rabe 1989a, 6)

The policy analyst, approaching a siting decision through the assumptions of a polluter's dilemma, will assume that the prospective "hosts" of a facility will be utilizing their economic rationality to maximize personal welfare within a preference schedule that desires use of the good without proximity to it; they wish to free ride on the cooperation of whatever others eventually are burdened with the facility.

Under these circumstances only two siting policies are reasonable. In the first, siting is left to the machinations of the free market, where rational agents volunteer for a site if the project and its attached package of economic compensation are perceived as beneficial to the community despite the costs. In the second, communities are coerced to accept sites through law. The former option has not proven effective; the latter has become more typical (Rabe 1988, 1989a, 1989b, 1995; Rabe and Gillroy 1993).

The prisoner's dilemma assumes a nonmoral, noncooperative attitude from the prospective "hosts." Therefore, the analyst could expect that the self-interested demeanor of the rational agents involved will manifest itself in passionate, entrenched interests determined to place the site elsewhere. A rational policy reaction to this assumption is to complete as much of the siting process as possible secretly. If the individuals involved will not cooperate in the provision of the good to be sited, then it is best to keep the plans away from any particular community until it has been decided that they are indeed the best "host," or at least on a short list of acceptable sites. An economic package of "compensation" that might influence the cost-benefit calculations of the community and make its acceptance efficient and rational is also important within this model. The siting policy is formulated to minimize the self-interested confrontation and to maximize the efficiency of material benefits over costs to both parties.

Overall, the prisoner's dilemma assumes a narrowly rational actor with unilateral/private goals who relies on the cost-benefit calculation of personal welfare as the basis of individual choice. If one assumes that siting will always impose material costs of one type or another that will not be overcome by welfare benefits, then cooperation to provide the site is very improbable without coercion. It is improbable but not impossible. Theoretically, if the situation is indeed a prisoner's dilemma, in which welfare efficiency is the major concern of the players, then economic-compensation packages could be made large enough to gain prospective "hosts." Such a perspective assumes that there is nothing inherently "bad" about the site other than the fact that its material benefits to the local residents will not compensate for their expected costs.

In this context, the only hope for cooperation is to iterate the game in order to bargain over compensation and, more importantly, to evolve the norms of cooperation necessary to provide the collective good, over the long term, without central coercion (Hardin 1982a; Rabe 1989a). In this way, a normative character can be introduced into the game and a "moral" connotation granted to the cooperation of the players so that siting decisions become more acceptable to all involved. However, the dominant strategy of the player is to defect from provision of the good, and even in iteration with the evolution of cooperative or "moral" norms, one thing remains true: if the cooperative equilibrium is established, no one agent will have an incentive to make the first move toward it, whereas it is always in every agent's interest to take the first step away, cooperative norms or not.

Under these circumstances the seeming risk-aversion of the agents, their lack of trust, and their unwillingness to listen to policy experts or the "facts" pertaining to a particular siting are attributed to the manifestations of this narrow self-interest in the face of a site that has more welfare costs than benefits to the surrounding inhabitants.

At least one alternative explanation for the behavior of agents in a NIMBY situation exists. The strategic framework of an assurance game (Sen 1967; Elster 1979, 20–21), which I have argued is Kant's definition of the collective-action problem (chap. 6, fig. 6.1), offers another perspective on NIMBY as a dynamic, strategic, and moral confrontation.

The first major difference between a polluter's dilemma and an assurance situation is that the preferences of the agents define the best outcome in terms of cooperation in provision of the collective good rather than of exploitation and free riding on the cooperation of others. Within the assurance game, the ordinal preferences of the players are assumed to be arranged so that the first and second preferences of the agent in the prisoner's dilemma are reversed. In the assurance game the preference with the highest utility is universal cooperation; unilateral defection is second best. Unlike the prisoner's dilemma, where one cooperates only if he cannot free ride, a player in an assurance game will free ride only if he cannot cooperate (see fig. 6.2).

The logic of the assurance situation describes a rationality of intention to cooperate with an underlying capacity, and ability, to exploit. Unlike the prisoner's dilemma, where exploitation of others is the best alternative for the player, the assurance game has a preferred solution of cooperation, but the ability to exploit looms as a pertinent consideration of each player's strategic rationality. The worst reality for each player is still exploitation in unilateral cooperation and, still, the failure to coordinate is better than being unilaterally exploited.

Where information and central assurance that all will cooperate are neither necessary nor sufficient to establish a stable cooperative outcome in the polluter's dilemma (for each player can be expected to free ride whenever possible), they are both necessary and sufficient for the same ends within the assurance game. In fact, within the assurance game, without a commitment to information dissemination, communication, and central regulation to assure each player that he or she will not be exploited in the decision to cooperate and act as a moral person, the game can degenerate into a fight for survival and a ruination of collective action as each player, fearing exploitation, moves to exploit the other in what Kant has called the "mania for domination" (Kant AT, 273, see chap. 6).[35] This situation requires central coordination.

The precarious nature of the intention to cooperate, and the critical nature of external signals to the individual playing the game, are exemplified by the fact that the assurance game has no dominant strategy. If one is assured that the other player will cooperate, then one prefers to cooperate also; however, if no such assurance is understood, then one prefers to defect and protect oneself. Unlike a prisoner's dilemma, in which each player prefers to defect whatever the other players do, the assurance game, in which there is lack of a dominant strategy, makes one player's payoffs contingent on the decisions of others, or on the assurance provided by third parties. The uncertainty of this game, void of a dominant strategy, makes central anticipatory coordination to avoid the "mania for domination" even more important.

Within the confines of NIMBY-related policy, the analyst who recognizes the situation as an assurance game has a completely different assumptive reality than that of the prisoner's dilemma from which to draft policy. The character of the agents is richer because a distinct sense of the collective interest is now the first priority for each person. An internal "moral" recognition exists, in the rationality of the player, that one's self-interest involves the provision of collective goods and cooperation to solve collective-action problems. This elevates the problem from one of narrow calculation of costs and benefits to wider consideration of the necessity of a "collective good" and its relation to the essential nature of the individual as a cooperative moral agent. The character of the "good" to be provided is therefore also distinct and it is incumbent on the decision maker to keep the "public" nature of the collective good from becoming part of the private welfare calculations of any player. With Kant, the policymaker might consider that the principle value informing his deliberations is not efficiency but individual moral autonomy.

> Public policy, then, may not represent an attempt to increase welfare, utility or "satisfaction." It may represent our attempt, rather, to control the conditions under which we pursue happiness—the conditions under which we lead our lives. (Sagoff 1982, 761)

Thus, the passionate self-interest manifest in the NIMBY situation may be an artifact of the fear that, in cooperating without assurance that no exploitation will occur, one's moral integrity could be lost in exploitation. Duty to oneself, particularly to one's physical nature (Kant MV, 421ff), will not allow a moral agent to risk his or her capacity to choose autonomously. Within a NIMBY situation, taking a bad payoff that does not pass a cost-benefit test ceases to be of major concern. The possibility of having one's autonomy as a moral agent exploited by others in a fundamental way is critical. Without assurance that moral behavior will be respected and reciprocated, I will retreat from my predisposition to cooperate and into the "mania for domination" or NIMBY politics.

Within the assurance game, norms of cooperative behavior do not evolve externally, as in the iterated prisoner's dilemma. They preexist, internal to the game, in the moral predisposition of each player to express rational autonomy in choosing to cooperate in the provision of collective goods. The coordinator need not set up a system of norms but simply recognize the norms inherent in the protection and empowering of the humanity of each person and his or her autonomy as a moral agent.[36] Therefore, within the assurance framework, a policymaker's constituents are predisposed to be moral, with *ex ante* assurance from government that this autonomous action will not be exploited by the private market interests of others. This sets up an active role for the public decision maker as representative of the citizens involved in any siting dilemma and concentrates his efforts in the provision of assurance that fundamental intrinsic values will be protected and empowered in any siting decision.

Beyond NIMBY: Comparative-Risk Analysis

Historically, the United States Environmental Protection Agency (EPA) developed the comparative-risk methodology in 1986, and first published a comprehensive analysis of the nation's risk, titled *Unfinished Business: A Comparative Assessment of Environmental Problems*, in 1987. A pilot state comparative-risk project was completed by the state of Vermont five years later (VANR 1991). Meanwhile, in 1989, three of EPA's ten regional offices released comparative-risk studies; the results of these studies encouraged EPA to use the methodology as a tool to help states handle environmental risk.

In addition to Vermont, the states of Colorado (GCAC 1990), Washington (WDE 1990), Pennsylvania,[37] and Louisiana (LDEQ 1991) were among the first to undertake comparative-risk-ranking projects. By May of 1995, twenty-six states were either planning or implementing comparative-risk projects, or had one underway. Seven cities and two tribal groups were also in the comparative-risk process by then.[38] The comparative-risk process is an attempt not only to assess, analyze, and understand the risks posed by the broad range of environmental problems, but to compare and rank risk for the purposes of policy action. It has three phases: *planning, risk analysis,* and *risk management.*

Planning a comparative-risk project normally takes between two and four months. Planning is usually done within the city, state, or agency undertaking the project and begins with an examination of how past projects in other venues have worked best. The needs and priorities of a particular community provide the foundation for comparative-risk planning, and this phase is normally undertaken by professional bureaucrats who initiate the process by identifying a set of priorities while conducting the search for EPA advice and funding (EPA 1993).

The second phase, in reality the initial phase of an authorized and functioning project, involves risk analysis. Traditionally, before the advent of comparative risk, risk analysis consisted of the evaluation of a single chemical or biological agent for its potential risk to human health (see chaps. 2 and 4). Comparative risk, however, goes beyond standard risk analysis in five ways. First, it is an attempt to make judgments comprehensively on all the critical risks facing a community. Second, it ranks the risks, applying the same criteria to all of them, across the board. Third, it assumes that risks to natural systems and to the general quality of human life are as important to policy as human health risk. Fourth, the process assumes that the normative values of the participants are as important to analysis and ranking as the scientific and other empirical "facts" related to the perceived environmental problems. Fifth, comparative risk seeks to improve policy by replacing "crisis management, inertia, and conventional wisdom" with "informed judgment" about what risks are the most serious (Minard 1991).

Some of the inherent strengths and limitations of basic, quantitative, risk analysis carry over into the comparative-risk process. A tremendous reliance still exists on scientific probability data and traditional risk assessment, focusing analysis on health risk in general and cancer risk in particular. Each risk study has a separate technical working group to analyze human health risk, which spends the vast majority of their time concentrating on cancer as the most important potential harm of environmental risk.

Although the technical reports of the individual comparative-risk projects claim that scientific data, or the lack of it, is the central problem with eventual risk ranking (Minard and Jones 1993), the best researched and data-rich component of any comparative-risk project is its scientific "evidence" regarding human cancer risk. The relatively young sciences of risk analysis (e.g., epidemiology, toxicology) originate in a chemical-by-chemical analysis of how environmental agents "cause" cancer in humans. Although most projects have also been concerned with noncancer health risks and sometimes have ranked these highly, the data are predominantly connected to the study of cancer, and it is no surprise that every project has, as its centerpiece for phase two, an analysis of human cancer risks.

Within the risk-analysis phase, the administrative structure of the risk project is created, and this usually requires that technical working groups be formed to come up with assessments and ranking criteria for the risks being studied.[39] In addition to the analysis of human health/cancer risk, however, every comparative-risk project also has at least two other technical working groups involved in risk analysis. One of these considers risk to natural systems (which they call ecosystems). This working group on health or functioning of ecosystems examines risk impact on exposed natural systems, the size of area affected, and the length of effect, as well as estimates of recovery time for these systems. The third working group usually concentrates on nonhealth risks (EPA 1993, 3–9) to humans, which are categorized as quality of life. Here, the focus might concern effects on recreation, aesthetics, economic impact on jobs and standard of living, status of future generations, and many other variables. This phase results in a final integrated ranking of all the risks perceived to be of concern to the participants.

The analysis process, however, assumes first that a list of environmental-risk issues has been compiled which can then be subdivided into health, ecosystem, and quality-of-life categories. In addition, the ranking is assumed to be based upon identical normative and empirical standards. A "scientific data prejudice" has evolved with this assumption.

Comparative risk is part of an evolution from traditional risk analysis, which, as I have argued, concentrates on the empirical testing of animals to determine probabilities of health effects for humans, on the basis of exposure estimates and the deciphering of dose-response curves (Rodricks 1992). Because of the tremendous uncertainties involved in risk questions, the conventional predisposition is to seek "scientific" data on the causal connections between exposure to chemical or biological agent X and its health (particularly cancer) effects.

This bias toward empirical "facts" or "scientific" data to "determine" probabilities and answer risk-ranking questions has been expanded to concerns for risks to natural systems and quality of life within the comparative-risk process. The same quantitative paradigm has been applied to new concerns, and the inclusion of new categories has simply had the effect of raising demands for empirical data, especially economic data, which may be either available but irrelevant or relevant but impossible to obtain. As I have previously argued, ignorance of mechanism is a limitation of risk analysis applied to human health, and the data are still, after years of compilation, incomplete and sometimes inconclusive. The search for factual data in the nonhealth areas will most likely face the same inherent problems, especially since market assumptions and economic data have been singled out as most "scientific." Given the normative character of the market paradigm, how do we estimate the political or moral risks of one technology over another with only market values?

Although the structures set up by comparative-risk projects vary (Minard and Jones 1993), the central goal of all comparative-risk projects, during the analysis phase, is to combine technical expertise and public outreach to list and rank the risks facing a particular population. Comparative-risk projects have increasingly incorporated a wider range of citizens and professionals, made manifest in the evolution of the now-standard three-tiered organizational structure (EPA 1993, §1.2 and §§2.2–2.4).

The first tier, made up of the technical working groups already described, is usually created to decide what risks exist and to gather data and analyze them to determine the effects of the risks on health, natural systems persistence, and human quality of life. Participation in these groups was originally limited to professional bureaucrats or agency personnel (EPA 1990) who had a background in the natural sciences. Although the technical working groups reflect a bias toward physical and biological scientists, in some instances nonscientific personnel or nonbureaucratic scientists have been assigned to these groups (Minard and Jones 1993, 34–41 and 53–65).

Technical working groups are the critical core of the comparative-risk project. In comparative-risk studies these groups are the major force in defining what risks are considered, and they do the preliminary rankings. Each distinct technical working group (health, ecosystem, and quality of life) is responsible, first, to define and rank the risks in their sector of concern, and then, to cooperate in the compilation of a preliminary master list, ranked across the three categories. This tier of administration has the primary data-gathering responsibility and also the primary obligation to rank risks. Although in most cases their rankings are not final (EPA 1993, §§2.2–2.4 and §3.1), they have been very successful in including in the final lists risk items about which they felt strongly, along with the rankings suggested by the "scientific data."

A second level of organization characteristic of the comparative-risk project is the steering committee. This oversight and administrative apparatus facilitates and coordinates activity and has overall authority in the execution of the project. Although many projects stress that the steering committee does not have final authority, the formal and informal power granted to it as a leadership group provides sufficient clout to influence the proceedings and to shape both the technical working groups and any public participation.

The third, and most democratic, level of organization is the public advisory committee (EPA 1987, 1990).[40] Usually asked to analyze the data and recommendations of the working groups, the advisory committee compiles the definitive risk rankings for each subsection (health, ecosystem, and quality of life) and the final comparative-risk ranking that integrates and sets in order risks from all three categories. Because the public advisory committee's responsibility is to encourage a broad input of ideas and, finally, to communicate the findings of the project to the public at large, it needs to be as independent as possible and open to comments and suggestions of all kinds, so that the widest possible range of views is introduced into the process.

The public advisory committee presents the data gathered by the technical experts in the working groups in the final risk ranking for the project, usually released without drastic alterations by the steering committee (Minard and Jones 1993, 2–4). To accomplish their job, the members of the public advisory committee not only have to study the problem in enough depth to understand, and to make a persuasive argument about, the components of the ranking and their assigned place, but also have to communicate the ranking to the general public.

In most instances the public advisory committee is a separate entity appointed by the steering committee. However, in at least one instance, in Louisiana, the steering committee and public advisory committee were merged into a Public Advisory and Steering Committee (Minard and Jones 1993, 43–44). Streamlining the process, participation, and oversight in this way was successful there, and although the committee proved ungainly in terms of its size (sixty-four people), no questions about power over final rankings or the ultimate authority on the direction of the comparative-risk process were asked, as the committee turned to influencing the public policy process.

Comparative-risk analysis and ranking phase are local phenomena, and not all of the subnational entities select the same ranking for the issues under consideration (Minard and Jones 1993). The subnational character of the projects allows each city or state or region to target what it sees as the most serious risks it faces, while it also depends on these local entities to represent fairly the risk "perceived" by them to be critical. Although there are guidelines for and common characteristics of comparative-risk studies, the final decisions on which risks count, how they will be measured, and by whom, are concerns that each individual state or community must answer for itself. This allows the process to be comprehensive and dynamic, while remaining sensitive to the distinct circumstances of each project team. In all cases, however, the comprehensive nature of the undertaking, as well as its focus on policy, are common threads.

The third and final phase of the comparative-risk process is the movement from comparative-risk analysis to comparative-risk management, or the transformation of the risk ranking into a policy agenda for future action. Comparative-risk management assumes that all government entities have limited time and funds to apply to the prevention, regulation, or mitigation of environmental risk. Ranking helps to set political and budget priorities for the purposes of policy redress.

By bringing a diverse group of people together with a variety of experience and backgrounds to debate and rank risks comprehensively, a coalition is constructed that can be utilized to move to the management phase and to apply political action to risk priorities. In addition, by making scientists and nonscientists, technical and nontechnical experts, and practitioners and citizens participate equally in a common effort, a cooperative atmosphere in which a variety of viewpoints and values find common principles and methods to address collective dilemmas should be created. Facing the normative as well as the empirical dimensions of risk, as a collective and comparative exercise, could potentially replace isolated, bureaucratic decision making with integrated and comprehensive public policy argument.

Although some specific projects have claimed to have affected the policy agenda and produced specific legislation (Minard and Jones 1993, 6–8, 66–83), most projects have been unable to translate risk analysis and ranking into environmental law. In some cases the identified priority risks were beyond the control of the city or state level of the federal system (e.g., cleaning up toxic waste dumps). In other cases, ranked risks did not gain an adequate audience to carry over into the legislative process and gain adequate budget authority. In most cases, political or administrative concerns (e.g., a change of administrations or majorities in the state legislature) stalled the final phase of the process and rendered the comparative analysis of risk less valuable, as a policy tool, than it could have been (Minard and Jones 1993).

Trusteeship and the Politics of Assurance

Our concept of trusteeship concerns the timeless nature of autonomy and the timeless requirements of the baseline function. Specifically, we are concerned with that dimension of the baseline that establishes and maintains the distribution of property so that the assurance game persists and civil society evolves toward a just community of active citizens. The dynamic nature of collective action places the public manager in a position to maintain the smooth functioning of government and the persistence of the baseline; or, if collective action is failing to provide for baseline autonomy, it causes the degeneration of social choice into prisoner's dilemma or chicken strategic situations.

The NIMBY reaction to disposal decisions is defined within a context where assurance has not been provided and where, consequently, disposal causes fear and risk, heightening uncertainty and causing the dysfunction of the strategic situation. Treating the game as a prisoner's dilemma misinterprets empirical reality but also is a self-fulfilling act, since the assurance situation devolves into a prisoner's dilemma or worse. Degeneration can also mean a chicken situation in which confrontation between government power and market forces causes widespread disintegration of social cooperation. Within Justice from Autonomy, the "mania for domination" characterizes the NIMBY situation and originates in the widespread neglect of trusteeship duties and the failure of the state to either establish or maintain baseline respect for Ecosystems as a whole. The assurance of moral equality is absent; citizens feel exploited and react to protect their basic capacities. The result is NIMBY confrontation.

Assurance and trusteeship intertwine as the basic prerequisites to the cooperation of moral agents; land or property is the material condition of this component of the baseline. The assurance required guarantees that each citizen has the material property required to express positive freedom and its secure entitlement against the elective preferences of others. Assurance requires that the public trust that distributes property in the name of the "will of all" be timeless and dependable.

The politics of assurance are also the politics of participation, where moral agency is collectively expressed in each person's use of his or her positive freedom as guaranteed by the baseline. Autonomous expression and participation are protected by the just distribution and use of property and encourage each person's predisposition to act in accord with the moral law. Trusteeship requires that the siting process be reconsidered for its effects on Ecosystems, and its respect for the intrinsic values involved. To use property to site an environmental facility ought not exploit human agency or natural systems integrity, and this requires that the policymaker reformulate the entire siting process to prevent the "mania for domination" and NIMBY reactions. Instead of the siting process beginning with a secret feasibility study, then progressing to a siting short list, and only then *ex post* public participation and economic compensation, the siting process recommended by the politics of assurance and Ecosystem Policy Argument would be different.

Public participation is no longer the third step, as it was within the traditional prisoner's dilemma approach, but is now the first step. In view of the critical importance of information in the assurance game and our obligation to one another's moral autonomy, before any facility is picked or a short list of communities is compiled, the public must be involved in all dimensions of solving the inherent environmental problem making the site necessary. *Ex ante* public participation requires active state involvement to establish trust by being the active advocate for trusteeship, property distribution, and more fundamentally, equality before the moral law. The government should not only protect the autonomous choices of its citizens but empower their participation as cooperators by solving the assurance game. The regulator's role should be to encourage the cooperative agency of citizens in matters pertaining to the "public interest," which becomes defined in terms of protecting the autonomy of individual citizens from the exploitation of others. The government should act as "protector" of the public interest, independent of the personal preferences of both "hosts" and "siters."[41] To prevent NIMBY, individuals need to be able to trust the government as a representative of their collective interest, in what is a decision about collective or public goods, not private wants. Only with the full involvement of the active state will facility siting hold collective-goods status, while the government plays its just role as advocate for Ecosystem integrity. A focus on Ecosystems will have the added advantage of making natural systems and their status an integral part of policy discourse, deliberation, and choice.

New step two, the feasibility study, now has a completely different connotation, for it is not a secret study undertaken by experts, but a report of public meetings and citizen input with the conclusions drawn through the combination of expert and civilian policy arguments. Now that the conclusions of the research are the results of a community effort, the feasibility study does not appear to be an external fait accompli but the best recommendations of a greater community to take care of a jointly generated problem. Having the siting study at this point allows it to contain, not only specific siting recommendations for any particular facility, but recommendations for comprehensive waste-management plans to take care of the larger context of the problem requiring the facility. During the public review of a specific hazardous waste facility, for example, the public meetings can also address the waste stream itself, its origins and containment. Subjects such as conservation, reuse, recycling, temporary versus permanent storage, transfer stations, collection points, and long-term justification and use of the particular products that produce the waste (in a search for alternatives) are all logical parts of the siting debate. Within the context of this more comprehensive planning, no one community will feel exploited, but many will be convinced of the importance of taking care of present waste and making plans for minimizing its stream in the future. The assumption, within the assurance problem, is that individuals are not necessarily risk-averse but want to be respected in their choice to accept a risk to themselves and to their community. Each community must believe that it is accepting the site as its contribution to the collective good with the full assurance that it will be protected by government regulators from exploitation both during the siting process and from any resulting facility. Throughout the process, and before any sites are chosen, the risks and burdens must be shared by more than one group of citizens, and the necessity of the site, in terms of human autonomy and natural systems integrity, must be argued to the satisfaction of those involved. Without these preconditions, assurance is not forthcoming, and the process is not about collective goods and the public interest. With the politics of assurance a series of localities can share in the production of the public good and the long-term solution to an environmental problem affecting the integrity of their Ecosystem.

New step three is the short list, which now allows a community or series of communities interested in being part of the collective-goods provision to vote to place themselves in competition for the site. Here, it is no longer the case that communities wake up one morning to find that a predetermined risk-generating facility is going to be placed in their backyard without their advice or consent and in disrespect of their moral autonomy and the functional integrity of their Ecosystem. Instead, moral agents, after due public discourse and recommendation, will have consented to a facility that they had input in defining. The facility has been subject to debate and is being accepted by the community as its part in the cooperative effort to provide the collective good of a quality environment. Siting is now a choice, made by all through the ballot box, with prior and complete information and before any geological or engineering study of their particular community is undertaken. Once a community volunteers for the short list, environmental engineers can begin the process of seeing whether its particular geography is fit for the facility under consideration; but the point is that the decision being made on the actual siting is grassroots, after assurance from the state and full information and participation of the people. The experts go in only after assurance has been given and public trust established by the actions of government. A very important consideration here is the government's lead in discussing the issue, taking responsibility for the problem and for its collective solution. Ecosystem integrity requires tight import/export controls on the waste in order to provide an incentive for facility siting and comprehensive environmental planning.

The fourth and final step in the new siting process remains economic compensation, but unlike the prisoner's dilemma approach to siting that sees this welfare package as the core of the siting decision, the new process sees it as a material compensation for any intrinsic values put at risk or as reward for the "public spirit" of a volunteer community. The compensation package is principally a means by which the qualified community and the experts can engage in bargaining that can make the licensing, construction, and running of the long-term site as smooth and safe as possible. The collective good is already a public trust protected by the central government on behalf of the citizens, who have the decisive power to allow siting only when accomplished in the public interest. After assurance has been given and a site accepted, economic benefits and compensation are no longer bribes but rewards for "public spirit." Policy professionals are not agents of the site proponents, but the representatives of all citizen-agents in the political community involved in the cooperative endeavor. Any site is accepted in full knowledge of its importance and its risks but with the assurance that "free riders" will be regulated *ex ante*. This requires that the government representatives have preexisting law that gives them the power to monitor and control the site, through all its stages.

The critical philosophical distinction between the characterization of NIMBY as a prisoner's dilemma or as an assurance game is that, in the case of the former, all moral and philosophical questions about the siting can be reduced to the satisfaction of wealth preferences. With assurance politics, however, the philosophical dimensions of the problem are more complex. The welfare preferences of the individual citizen become secondary to a primary concern for the protection and empowerment of individual autonomy. Each person is seen to have a "moral character" that is internal and predates the strategic interaction that produces the dilemma. In addition, on a collective level, the assumption that "no rational person would ever accept a siting" changes to one that expects that a number of communities will accept a facility as part of their "fair share" in support of the public interest. For the first time, *fairness* means more than compensatory money and goods, but is reflected in the distribution and sharing of responsibility by the political community as a whole, where active citizens are trustees of their own autonomy and the integrity of the natural environment. Kant argued that the moral agent is willing to be cooperative, and perhaps even sacrifice some personal welfare, if he or she is not exploited by the welfare preferences of others. When facing a siting, individuals do not want efficiency considerations to preempt the protection of their autonomy and the public discussion of the proper division of those collective burdens, goods, and responsibilities under consideration.

If citizens in an assurance situation are confident that the government represents them through the public interest in providing necessary collective goods, and they are allowed full participation in the myriad of decisions relating to the policy problem that necessitates a site before a facility type or site is chosen, then trusteeship for today and the future will be respected, moral agency will not be at stake in the decision, and active citizenship will be encouraged without the pressure of fear and uncertainty. Science can also have more effect, since its evidence for siting can be considered by all, unemotionally, with their moral capacity intact. This is a collective choice, where all are part of the decisions and privy to the information necessary to make the responsible public choice. Here, free citizens, equal before the moral law, and with a fair stake in

both the rewards and burdens of providing for Ecosystem integrity, participate, with a just state, in a politics of assurance.[42]

Baseline trusteeship also affects how we reassess comparative-risk ranking.
Overall, the critical concern of the comparative-risk process is to apply comprehensive normative and empirical analysis to set an environmental-risk policy agenda that establishes priorities for environmental decision makers. The
primary purpose of the process is to inform decision makers as to what risks
are most serious so that they can be politically addressed first. This procedure
moves toward a politics of assurance in that it makes the normative as well as
the empirical dimensions of risk relevant and is set up so that environmental
risk may be anticipated and consciously accepted or rejected *ex ante*. Although
the present administrative structure of comparative risk has its prejudices toward science and has other shortcomings as well (e.g., its focus on residual
risk), the basic approach of comparative risk facilitates the trusteeship dimension of the baseline and the imperative to provide assurance.

Ecosystem law could argue for an enhanced comparative-risk process as the
solution to NIMBY and as a means to provide the timeless trusteeship necessary to assure the continued cooperation of moral agents in a just society. The
basic process is well rounded enough, treating both health and quality-of-life
concerns in relation to humanity and functional integrity as it affects natural
systems. Risk ranking is also comprehensive and recognizes that all environmental problems (i.e., resource and pollution) are different dimensions of one
regulatory responsibility. In this way, the process moves away from TSA and
toward a Resource to Recovery context model.

Adapted to Ecosystem argument, comparative risk can deal with all three
interfaces in an anticipatory way, setting out and ranking those risks that we
will assume as part of our duties to one another and those that we will avoid
on the basis of consideration of Justice from Autonomy. This will require that
we move away from the traditional concentration of comparative risk on *ex
post* residual risk (Minard and Jones 1993) and move toward anticipation of
risk *ex ante*.

If a comprehensive comparative-risk process became a federal mandate to
the states, as part of the national performance zoning-and-classification system, made imperative by our duty to Ecosystem integrity, we would be able to
anticipate waste problems before they happened and to prevent NIMBY. The
assumption here is that what we do not extract from nature we do not manufacture, and what we do not manufacture we do not have to dispose of. The
disposal interface, which we are currently analyzing, is created by the interfaces that precede it. In regulating extraction we not only gain a grasp of the
present conditions of natural and human systems, but understand what the requirements will be for assurance to maintain the baseline in trust for the future
as we move to the manufacturing and disposal interfaces of our context model.

The specific requirements of the disposal interface require consciousness of
what we are introducing into the environment, what the risks to humanity and
nature are, and how we might minimize the artificial risk imposed on the biosphere. The emphasis within Ecosystem law and policy is on recycling and re-

use and the imperative is to hold ourselves accountable for what we define and dispose of as waste, as well as for who takes on the risk and responsibility for waste disposal.

The imperatives of trusteeship include maximum organic reintegration of by-products back into natural systems and maximum reuse, so that dumping potentially risky materials over long periods is minimized and potential NIMBY situations reduced in number and scope. Whatever waste remains requires safe disposal, with respect for both human moral integrity and the functional integrity of the environment in siting the facilities and disposing of the waste. This means widespread public involvement, the active state protecting and empowering the baseline and providing the assurance that what is essential about humanity and nature provides the only fit justification for risk generation and disposition. It is only though a comprehensive and anticipatory understanding of risk, in terms of both what risk we will accept collectively in the first place and what is required for the safe disposal of the risk-generating waste left over, that we can hope to be responsible to our intergenerational trusteeship duties.

Other components of the baseline function reinforce the move toward comprehensive risk evaluation and ranking. The imperative to do as little harm as possible to Ecosystems complements and is preserved by the assurance that the earth, as public trust, is being distributed or used timelessly for the maintenance of moral equality among active citizens. Also encouraged is the minimum use of the environment, as well as the maximum reuse and recycling of necessary products, with a concern for freedom in Ecosystem integrity. This is especially true of virgin resources, which are the most vital to continued natural systems integrity. The minimization of virgin resource use means the minimization of extraction, while reuse produces a minimum amount of waste at the disposal interface. Minimal disposal needs, in turn, require fewer dumps and facilities for permanent storage of risky material (Shrader-Frechette 1993, chap. 9), and fewer occasions for fear, uncertainty, and the subsequent devolution of collective action toward the "mania for domination."

The inclination toward artificial-risk neutrality can be best facilitated by a regime of comparative-risk analysis and ranking that requires risk issues to be fully investigated and ranked *ex ante*. The examination and synthesis of technology compatible with our duties to ourselves and nature can be carried out only if our collective action does not degenerate into a condition where our predisposition to be moral is short-circuited by our desperation to preserve our core capacities.

Overall, the policy requirements of the baseline function, at the reintegration interface, minimize the amount of natural material used that requires permanent disposal and set moral standards for the disposal of what has been generated that maximizes collective action and minimizes immoral public and private choice. Ecosystem law seeks to provide that timeless distribution and redistribution of goods that best assures the cooperation of moral agents and prevents devolution of collective action. Within the reintegration interface, the politics of assurance requires an administrative apparatus like comparative-risk ranking to operationalize a risk-conscious society. The aim is to understand what mix of private and public property will best minimize risk and maximize human and natural capacities so that the apparatus of the state can anticipate failures in the baseline and move to prevent dysfunctional social interactions like NIMBY.

Trust and the Production Decision: NEPA and FDA Regulation

The middle stage of the Resources to Recovery context model translates extraction decisions into reuse or disposal choices. The production decision involves both human manufacturing and construction and includes interactions between the fabrication of material products and the natural environment. Traditionally, this is primarily a pollution-prevention stage of the economic process, but in our context model we can examine the range of issues surrounding manufacturing/construction processes (e.g., land use, risk generation, resource conversion, energy production and transmittal, etc.) that affect the relationship between natural and human systems and, therefore, the moral status of Ecosystems.

These next two cases we shall examine speak primarily to the third component of the baseline function, opportunity for independence, as derived from the paradigm's assumptions about the role of the state. The first case concerns the proper use of the National Environmental Policy Act (NEPA); the second addresses the regulatory regime of the Food and Drug Administration (FDA).

NEPA, Comprehensive Policy Planning, and the Active State

The National Environmental Policy Act of 1969 (42 U.S.C.A. §§4321–4370d) is comprehensive planning legislation intended to "encourage productive and enjoyable harmony between man and his environment" (42 U.S.C.A. §4321). This legislation endeavors to "promote efforts which will prevent or eliminate damage to the environment and biosphere and stimulate the health and welfare of man" (42 U.S.C.A. §4321), while attempting to "fulfill the responsibilities of each generation as trustee of the environment for succeeding generations" (42 U.S.C.A. §4331/ NEPA §101 [b1]).

The vehicle for these goals is an "action-forcing" mandate to prepare documents that chronicle the environmental impacts of any and all significant government acts (NEPA §102). The Environmental Impact Statement (EIS) is required for "legislation and other major federal actions significantly affecting the quality of the human environment" (42 U.S.C.A. §4332/ NEPA §102 [C]). The content of the EIS must not only include the environmental impact expected from the chosen action (C[i]), but must also show evidence that alternatives to the planned action, and their environmental effects, have also been considered (C[iii]).

Tactically, NEPA works by allowing all government agencies to assemble a mutual composite inventory of low-impact actions that are listed (in negotiation between each agency and the Council on Environmental Quality [CEQ]) as having a categorical exclusion from the statute. Actions not on this list must be announced publicly, and an environmental assessment (EA) compiled.[43] This EA determines if it is a major government action with significant impact; if not classified as such, then a Finding of No Significant Impact (FONSI) is filed and the action proceeds. If the proposed action is determined to be major and to have impact, then a sequence starts with public participation and research leading to a Draft Environmental Impact Statement (DEIS), a comment and response period, and, eventually, a Final Environmental Impact Statement (EIS). A Record of Decision (ROD) is then published in the *Federal Register* to indicate the alternatives considered and the final action taken. All disagreements over the ROD are arbitrated by the CEQ, the EPA, the president, and finally the courts.[44]

Superficially, NEPA looks like perfect legislation to move us from a market paradigm and context model to Ecosystem law and policy. However, a closer look at the statute, and the case law interpreting it since its passage, shows that NEPA is essentially a procedural rather than a substantive gatekeeper for Ecosystem integrity.

NEPA is a creature of the market paradigm and context model. The text of the legislation that speaks to natural systems as ends-in-themselves is limited and overridden by more and stronger language seeking to create a stable environment for economic use and human welfare. The true imperative of government action is to

> use all practicable means and measures, including financial and technical assistance, in a manner calculated to foster and promote the general welfare, to create and maintain conditions under which man and nature can exist in productive harmony, and fulfill the social, economic and other requirements of present and future generations of Americans. (42 U.S.C.A. §4331/NEPA §101 [a])

NEPA requires that federal actions help the nation to "attain the widest range of beneficial uses of the environment without degradation" (42 U.S.C.A. §4331/ NEPA §101 [B][3]) and supports the use of cost-benefit methodology as long as the relationship between the results of the economic analysis and other "unquantifiable" environmental impacts are discussed (40 C.F.R. §102.23).

The ascendance of the market paradigm and context model, in which the optimal use of the environment is mandated, was ultimately arbitrated by a string of three prominent federal court cases that sanction the predisposition to use NEPA, not as a comprehensive planning statute based on environmental values, but as a series of procedural hurdles setting optimal efficiency.

Calvert Cliffs Coordinating Committee, Inc. v United States Atomic Energy Commission (449 F.2d. 1109 [D.C. Cir. 1971]) is the first case we shall consider. This decision, which became the most cited NEPA case in its early history (Buck 1991, 23), made a distinction between the "substantive requirements" of NEPA §101, where environmental principles are spelled out, and the "procedural requirements" of NEPA §102, where the requirements of the EIS are listed.

The court found that the congressional declaration section of the statute (§101) "provided a broad, substantive mandate to all federal agencies to use 'all practicable means and measures' to protect the environment," thus "[e]nvironmental values were to become part of a pantheon of values that must be considered before any federal agency acted" (Buck 1991, 23). However, Judge Wright also ruled that the action-forcing section of NEPA (§102) had strict but only procedural requirements. At one level the agency had little discretionary power because performing an EIS was a requirement of the law.

> We must stress as forcefully as possible that this language does not provide an escape hatch for footdragging agencies; it does not make NEPA's procedural requirements somehow "discretionary." Congress did not intend the Act to be such a paper tiger. Indeed, the requirement of environmental consideration "to the fullest extent possible" sets a high standard for the agencies, a standard which must be rigorously enforced by the reviewing courts. (*Calvert Cliffs*, 1114)

This quote can be read in two ways. First, one could say that the procedural mandates of §102 require the full range of environmental impacts and alternatives to be considered by any agency preparing an EIS. In a second possible reading, although the steps outlined in §102 are strict and without discretion, the manner in which they are fulfilled is very much left up to the discretion of the agency involved. If one reads the substantive versus procedural distinction strictly, then the difference between §101 and §102 is that, whereas the first mandates specific and "substantive" content in the considerations of the agency, the second merely requires that a preset procedure be followed any way the agency sees fit to do it. It is the EIS procedure itself that is mandatory in §102, not the environmental content considerations or substance of the analysis itself (which are substantive only within §101). So, although an agency must complete an EIS, the content and considerations within each step of the procedure are left up to agency expertise.

This second interpretation of Judge Wright's opinion may not be what he intended, but it has been verified as the dominant one by a majority opinion of the Supreme Court in the second case we shall now consider: *Vermont Yankee Nuclear Power Corp. v NRDC* (435 U.S. 519 [1978]). Contesting the adequacy of an EIS compiled to construct the Midland power reactors for Consumer Power Corporation, this specific litigation centers on the number and type of alternatives examined in the EIS prior to the construction of the reactors. Specifically, the litigation asks whether the EIS should have looked at power conservation as an alternative to construction of new capacity under NEPA §102 (C)(iii).

In this opinion, Mr. Justice Rehnquist begins by stating that "[c]ommon sense . . . teaches us that the 'detailed statement of alternatives' cannot be found wanting simply because the agency failed to include every alternative device and thought conceivable by the mind of man" (*Vermont Yankee*, 551). He defines the data on energy conservation as "uncharted territory" (*Vermont Yankee*, 553) and associates it with "uncommon or unknown alternatives" concluding that "the concept of 'alternatives' is an evolving one, requiring the agency to explore more or fewer alternatives as they become better known and understood" (*Vermont Yankee*, 552–53). Rehnquist then makes his essential point: even if the data on conservation were more concrete and therefore "feasible," any use of the data in the consideration of alternatives is a judgment that only the agency can make. The courts have a limited role "to insure a fully informed and well-considered decision, not necessarily a decision the judges of the Court of Appeals or of this Court would have reached had they been members of the decisionmaking unit of the agency" (*Vermont Yankee*, 558). To Rehnquist, ignoring energy conservation in an EIS about licensing new nuclear power plants is "a single alleged oversight on a peripheral issue" which "must not be made the basis for overturning a decision properly made after an otherwise exhaustive proceeding" (*Vermont Yankee*, 558).

The conclusion of this case supports our second interpretation of Judge Wright's distinction between substantive and procedural. It states categorically that "NEPA does set forth significant substantive goals for the Nation, but its mandate to the agencies is essentially procedural" (*Vermont Yankee*, 558). Rehnquist added the distinction between goals and mandates to the distinction between substantive and procedural. On the one hand, the goals of NEPA as set out in §101 are substantive and limit discretion but do not involve the EIS process, which is not contained in this section. On the other hand, the policy mandates of NEPA §102 that describe the EIS process and its requirements are not substantive but procedural; while they do not allow the agency discretion in meeting and completing each procedural step, the courts will allow great agency discretion in deciding what goes into any one of these procedural steps.

But even if NEPA is primarily a procedural statute, will the courts allow agencies to ignore basic nonperipheral environmental factors in an EIS? One way to make this judgment is to examine what the Supreme Court has said about two specific tools used to ensure that environmental values have a place in the assessment of human effect on natural systems: worst-case analysis and environmental mitigation planning.

The statute states that part of the EIS must be a "detailed" statement on "any irreversible and irretrievable commitment of resources" (42 U.S.C.A. §4332 [NEPA §102] [C][v]). In addition, the statute requires that "presently unquantified environmental amenities and values may be given appropriate consideration along with economic and technical considerations" (42 U.S.C.A. §4332 [NEPA §102] [B]).

Two of the ways in which unquantifiable amenities find their way into policy analysis are through worst-case reasoning and through the full planning of which environmental mitigation measures are necessary and possible. These answers to the problem of unquantifiability analysis are written into NEPA (§102) and the regulations that implement it (40 C.F.R. §1500.1 and chap. 1). But have the courts said that the procedural quality of NEPA's EIS requirements and the specific granting of discretion to agencies allow them to virtually ignore these environmental tools and their policy imperatives?

The "procedural" nature of NEPA §102, in terms of both the use of worst-case analysis and the failure to produce a complete mitigation plan, is played out in our third and final case: *Robertson v Methow Valley Citizen's Council* (490 U.S. 332 [1989]). In this case the Forest Service planned to grant a "special use permit" (36 C.F.R. §25.50 et seq.) for the construction of a large ski resort in Methow Valley, Washington.[45] This resort was alleged to place both species and natural systems at great risk, but the Court found that the EIS submitted by the Forest Service was acceptable even though it chose the largest and most intrusive resort plan of the alternatives considered without worst-case analysis or a complete mitigation plan for a herd of elk that were severely threatened by the development.

The argument was over whether the EIS had to include a "worst-case analysis" of environmental impacts and a mitigation plan that identified which environmental values were at stake and what could be done to protect or reestablish them. The use of worst-case analysis allows qualitative environmental impacts to be examined for possible and probable maximum environmental degradation and offers a means to understand what is "irreversible" or "irretrievable" in terms of both economic and environmental resources.

Worst-case analysis is one of the primary ways in which "unquantifiable environmental impacts," as mandated by NEPA's regulations at 40 C.F.R. §1502.23, can be assessed. In many situations they provide "the most protective prevention strategy" available to the environmental decision maker (Shrader-Frechette 1993, 86). Although the Council on Environmental Quality and the Ninth Circuit said that the worst-case analysis was mandatory, the Supreme Court disagreed and fell back on their decision in *Vermont Yankee* to justify this choice.[46]

> NEPA itself does not mandate particular results, but simply prescribes the necessary process. . . . If the adverse environmental effects of the proposed action are adequately identified and evaluated, the agency is not constrained by NEPA from deciding that other values outweigh the environmental costs. (*Robertson*, 357)

> In sum, we concluded that NEPA does not require a fully developed plan detailing what steps will be taken and does not require a worst-case analysis. (*Robertson*, 359)

Therefore, within an EIS, the agency must give a "hard look" to all environmental impacts,[47] but its conclusions, defined by its own expertise and choice of tools and methods, are within its discretion, and not a subject for the courts to second-guess.

Mitigation measures for the herd of elk were also defined as discretionary by the Court. *Robertson* states that "[I]t would be inconsistent with NEPA's reliance on procedural mechanisms—as opposed to substantive, results-based standards—to demand the presence of a fully developed plan that will mitigate environmental harm before an agency can act" (*Robertson*, 353). Dealing with the question of mitigation in *Robertson*, the Supreme Court mandated that "more—

not much more—but more than a mere listing of mitigation measures" was all that the statute required of an agency preparing an EIS (*Robertson*, 368).

From the Court's perspective, the actual inclusion of environmental tools or "tests" like mitigation and worst-case analysis, which highlight harm to natural systems, emphasize prevention of harm, and establish the true dimensions of needed harm abatement, are not "substantive" issues. How the environment is protected by a statute that contains no "results-based standards" remains the pertinent question.

The fact is that "except for a single Second Circuit decision, which was reversed by the Supreme Court in *Strycker's Bay Neighborhood Council v Karlen* (444 U.S. 223 [1980]), no appeals court has actually overturned an agency action for violating NEPA's substantive limits" (Findley and Farber 1992, 53). In effect, NEPA has substantive environmental ends (§101) but merely procedural means (§102) to these ends. A statute without teeth,[48] it allows agency discretion to ignore environmental values for economic and technical advantages and puts no practical meaning into its own stated ideals of "prevention," "harmony," or "trusteeship" of the environment (NEPA §101).

Anticipatory Regulation and Social Trust in FDA Regulation

The second case involves the regulatory regime for food additives, drug production, and marketing overseen by the Food and Drug Administration (FDA) under the Federal Food, Drug, and Cosmetic Act (21 U.S.C.A. 301 et seq.).[49] Our examination of FDA regulation focuses on the evolution of premarket approval, the movement toward active state regulation, and the economic and social ramifications of anticipatory collective action.

The origins of the FDA lie in the Progressive Era with the Pure Food and Drug Act of 1906. Built upon social concern about the interstate shipment of misbranded or adulterated food, the act was passed after the publication of Upton Sinclair's *The Jungle* consolidated public opinion regarding the safety of the food supply. In the wake of these legislative and literary events, the Supreme Court, in 1914, decided *United States v Lexington Mills and Elevator Company* (232 U.S. 399). The *Lexington Mills* case established that federal government regulation did not have to prove that food containing "poisonous or deleterious substances" will affect the public health, but only that they may so affect it. In effect, risk was sufficient to justify the national government's regulation in anticipation of harm to the public.

From *Lexington Mills* to the enactment of the Food, Drug, and Cosmetic Act of 1938 and its subsequent reaffirmations from 1941 through 1990,[50] a regulatory regime evolved that is unique to the American experience. The uniqueness of FDA regulation is especially striking after one examines, as we have in this book, the market paradigm regulatory posture of EPA, OHSA, and the Department of Interior.

Instead of an *ex post* risk regime based upon the market paradigm and TSA context models, which protected the economy against false positives (finding a chemical agent to be toxic when it is not), the FDA has evolved an *ex ante* risk regime that protects the public from false negatives (finding a chemical agent innocent when it is toxic) through anticipatory risk regulation. The FDA requires premarket testing and approval for both the safety and efficacy of the products it regulates. Interested as we are in the ramifications of active and anticipatory regulation, as a function of the Kantian state in its provision of opportunity for citizen independence, we will focus on two areas of FDA jurisdiction: food additives and new drugs.[51]

372

Under 21 U.S.C.A. §348 [FDCA §409], the FDA is empowered to require anyone wishing to introduce an additive into the food system to petition the agency for permission (21 U.S.C.A. §348 [FDCA §409] [b1]) and provide, in this petition, a "statement of the conditions of the proposed use of such additives, including all directions, recommendations, and suggestions proposed for the use of such additives, and including specimens of its proposed labeling" (2B); as well as "all relevant data bearing on the physical or other technical effect such additive is intended to produce; and the quantity of such additive required to produce such effect" (2C). Before a food additive can be marketed, it must be tested by those who propose its use. The FDA is only responsible to analyze and verify the testing performed by the producer. The producer's petition must include his or her tests, that is, "full reports of investigations made with respect to the safety for use of such additive, including full information as to the methods and controls used in conducting such investigations" (2E). After this petition is fully compiled and submitted to the FDA, the commissioner will then either approve or disapprove the petition. A petition approval obligates the commissioner to:

> prescrib[e] . . . the conditions under which such additive may be safely used (including, but not limited to, specifications as to the particular food or classes of food in or on which such additive may be used, the maximum quantity which may be used or permitted to remain in or on such food, the manner in which such additives may be added to or used in or on such food, and any directions or other labeling or packaging requirements for such additive deemed necessary by him to assure the safety of such use). (21 U.S.C.A. §348 [FDCA §409] [c1A])

With the food-additive provisions of the Food, Drug and Cosmetic Act, there is a shift in the burden of proof for justification from those who would regulate use to those who would manufacture a risky product and market it.

Specifically, environmental risk in terms of food additives is handled in a two-tier test system. Because of the Delaney Clause (21 U.S.C.A. §348 [FDCA §409] [3A]),[52] added to the act in 1958, no additive is considered safe if it "is found to induce cancer when ingested by man or animal." Therefore, any carcinogenic effect automatically renders an additive unapprovable, as it does not pass the first tier of testing.[53]

The second tier, pertaining to noncarcinogenic agents, requires that an "acceptable daily intake" (ADI) be set for all food additives. This ADI determines the specifics of petition approval and is based upon the estimation of a safe daily intake over a lifetime. For this calculation, only quantitative risk assessment is acceptable (QRA); the economic benefits of the additive cannot be part of the calculation.[54] The FDA requires measures of toxicity in use; the ADI is set by application of a safety factor of at least 100 to the highest "No Observed Effect Level" (NOEL) as identified in the most sensitive animal study (Rodricks 1992, 165–70, 206–11).

Thus, the FDA's approach to food additives reflects an ultimate concern for premarket safety, where risk to humanity is minimized by premarket testing and approval. The burden of testing and proof is on those actors who would produce and market an additive and not on those who would regulate it. Any additive with the potential to cause cancer in "man or animal" is automatically discounted, and noncarcinogenic additives must have "risk only" testing, where daily intakes are set at 100 times the safety level of the most sensitive animal study. The commissioner can approve the petition, but can also specify, not only how and under what conditions the additive may be used, but how it must be packaged and labeled. This is active and anticipatory regulation.

In regulating new drugs, we see premarket testing not only for safety, but also for the efficacy of the product. In 1959, Senator Estes Kefauver, as chair of the Senate Subcommittee on Antitrust and Monopoly, began a series of hearings on the drug business that resulted in the 1960 Kefauver-Harris Drug Amendments to the Food, Drug, and Cosmetic Act.

> His amendments required that before a new drug could be approved by the FDA, it had to be proven both safe and effective. Advertising and labeling of every drug had to include both brand name and the generic name plus warnings of contraindictions and potential side effects. Drug plants had to be regularly inspected by the FDA, and the agency had to be given ample time to evaluate a new drug before approval. (Burkholz 1994, 46)

Kefauver began his hearings in an effort to regulate the high cost of prescription drugs, but this issue was traded away. Instead, the most anticipatory premarket testing scheme in American regulatory law was passed.

The "new drug" part of the statute (21 U.S.C.A. §505 [FDCA §355]) requires premarket approval of a New Drug Application (NDA), which itself requires an extensive regime of preclinical and clinical testing by the manufacturer. Specifically, before an NDA is submitted, a manufacturer must file a Notice of Claimed Investigational Exemption for a New Drug Application (IND) with the FDA. The IND must include the chemical structure and quantitative composition of the drug, its source and method of production, and all preclinical investigations that confirm its safety and efficacy.

Within thirty days after filing an IND, if the FDA has not objected, the manufacturer may begin clinical trials of the drug (21 U.S.C.A. §505 [FDCA §355] [i]). During this three-phase process of clinical trials,[55] the manufacturer may not promote or commercially distribute the drug. Only after the trials are completed, and the drug is found safe and effective by the FDA, are the results of the IND, as well as all preclinical data, submitted with the NDA. Within this extensive premarket process, the producer, through the NDA, fulfills the statute provisions that require "full reports of investigations which have been made to show whether or not such drug is safe and whether such drug is effective in use" (21 U.S.C.A. §505 [FDCA §355] [b1A]).

The regulation of a new drug places the burden of proof on the manufacturer to establish, not only the safety of the drug, but its effectiveness. The producer is required to complete both preclinical and clinical testing of the drug, while the FDA retains many rights, not only in the approval process, but in the resulting manufacturing and marketing process for that drug.

> Once an NDA is approved, the drug's formula, manufacturing process, labeling, packaging, dosage, methods of testing, etc., generally cannot be changed without FDA approval. Any changes to increase safety or effectiveness, however, may be undertaken immediately, without awaiting FDA concurrence. (Worobec and Hogue 1992, 71–72).

Overall, the regulator's imperative is to establish "assurance" that all marketed drugs are both safe and effective and have been properly tested before they are allowed to enter the marketplace (Harris 1994).

The social ramifications of this process include the protection provided to the American people and their resulting widespread trust of the process. For decades, the premarket regulation of the FDA has spared the American people from dangerous drugs that have plagued other nations. For example, the marketing of thalidomide in Europe caused birth defects that were avoided in the United States. "That thalidomide was never marketed in the United States was largely due to the stubborn skepticism of the FDA's Dr. Frances Kelsey, whose doubts about the drug kept it out of American pharmacies" (Burkholz 1994, 43). Even, recently, when the FDA has fallen out of favor with the American people, this lack of trust can be attributed more to the FDA relaxing its regulatory stance in our new era of "small government," rather than to its attention to anticipatory premarket standards (Burkholz 1994).[56]

The FDA experience also demonstrates that an anticipatory scheme of regulation can provide both social trust and economic progress. The economic benefits of drugs remain part of the premarket analysis, and the economic health of the pharmaceutical industry is not significantly inhibited by the active state. Unlike food-additive regulation, which is a "risk only" provision of the statute that does not consider economic benefit per se,[57] risk-benefit analysis plays a prominent role in the approval of a new drug. The FDA can balance the risks and economic benefits of a new drug in assessing the NDA. For all new drugs, the FDA calculates what is called a "therapeutic benefit ratio" (TBR), which measures the difference between the toxic dose of the drug and a therapeutic dose. A benefit ratio of greater than ten is usually required in order to approve the drug.[58]

However, to the degree that the TBR measures economic benefits, the consideration of welfare is not the first, or dominant, consideration in regulatory decision making; it is the third criterion after safety and efficacy have been established. This measure of risks and benefits does not carry the same concerns for Ecosystem law and policy at this point in the process of approval because the intrinsic values involved have already been established as the "trump" standard, driving the process, well before instrumental considerations are brought into the decision. In this way, the use of risk/benefit for NDA, within this false-negative risk regime, is efficiency not as cost-benefit (seeking efficiency of both ends and means), but as cost-effectiveness analysis (seeking efficient means to ends decided by safety and efficacy). This reinforces the mandate to preserve and protect *ex ante*, thereby allowing FDA drug regulation to focus the burden of proof on the industry and its core efficiency principles.

The economic health of the American pharmaceutical industry suggests that the "expense" of premarket testing and the rigor of anticipatory regulation have not caused widespread hardship in the industry. By shifting the burden of proof, the active and anticipatory state internalizes the efficiency decisions of the industry at the research-and-development stage of drug production. Each new drug is considered in light of the demands of government approval and the product's capacity to generate profit, under the regime of these regulatory tests. The efficient products are also those that are safe and effective; efficiency is preserved within the industry while assurance is provided *ex ante* to active citizens in the society at large. In this way, the drug industry continues to be one of the more profitable in the country.

> In the second half of the twentieth century, no major industry has been as stable and as steadily profitable as the legal drug business. . . . [T]he industry is virtually recession-proof. In 1957, the annual sales of pharmaceuticals for human use stood at $1.7 billion, a decade later it had expanded to $3.0 billion, and during that same period the industry sales grew at a rate 10 percent faster than the national output of all goods and services. For the period 1967–1989, the total worldwide annual sales of members of the Pharmaceutical Manufacturers Association grew by more than 900 percent, from $4.9 billion to $50.1 billion, and during the 1980s the industry consistently ranked first in the nation in terms of profitability based on sales. (Burkholz 1994, 31)

All of this growth occurred within the regulatory scope of the FDA and its approval process under the Food, Drug, and Cosmetic Act. In particular, the best returns for the industry, including a 900 percent increase in sales and a strong growth cycle between 1967 and 1989, took place with the Kefauver Amendments as law. Therefore, the consistent growth of this industry and its profit and sales continued to escalate even after efficacy, as well as safety, became premarket tests for any new drug.[59]

Citizen Independence, Trust, and Anticipatory Regulation

Responsible public institutions attempt to mitigate uncertainty through the establishment of trust. If citizens are supported in their quest for full practical reason, and are protected by the adequate establishment of the baseline, then

---

they can trust that greater security is to be had through civil society than in a "state of nature." A just state can make life more equal and fairer than nature provides or anarchy supports. Justice is the quest for opportunity and citizen independence, where the independent citizen is an active citizen applying practical reason without undue fear of the whim of nature or the unregulated actions of other persons in society. The state is responsible to protect citizen capacity *ex ante* and to maintain the trust of citizens by acting as their advocate in the provision of opportunity for independence. The degree to which one assumes that his or her autonomy as a moral agent will not be exploited by forces beyond his or her control (but not beyond the control of the society) is the degree to which one will trust "representative" government.

Trust is a function of the perception of the individual that his or her autonomy (intrinsic value), which includes a concern for Ecosystem integrity, is of primary concern in policy decision making (the trump card). One dimension of this concern is the mandatory information that allows a citizen to understand what risks exist and what comparative statistics accompany alternative policies. The FDA mandate to require labels and to monitor packaging of drugs is a step in this direction; it provides opportunity to educate and assure.

Information is vital to the stabilization of the assurance game that is a prerequisite for the active state. However, although information is necessary, it is not sufficient. Government is responsible to judge and decide what risks are acceptable in view of the intrinsic values at stake. At or below the baseline, government must anticipate harm and regulate it, whereas, above the baseline, the administrator must ensure that producers provide accurate information to aid the practical reasoner in both political and consumer choices.

Generally, the provision of opportunity for independence in terms of environmental risk is assured through two rules of thumb: artificial-risk neutrality and technological compatibility. Artificial-risk neutrality requires the state to monitor and regulate human-created risk in the environment, preventing false negatives. The regulator must be conscious of how much risk any artificial agent produces, whether it affects the capacities of both humanity and nature, and if alternatives exist to generate the same result with less environmental risk.

The concern of the just administrator is to establish a risk-conscious society that examines human technology and our interface with nature so that risk is not imposed without a persuasive policy argument as to its necessity, in light of the intrinsic values at stake. The strategic nature of our rationality, combined with the moral nature of our practical reason, requires that we assume the primary responsibility for limiting the risks imposed on ourselves and on natural systems by our innovation of minimum-risk technology. In this way, artificial-risk neutrality and technological compatibility become dimensions of a single imperative: to use our intellectual power to create technology that harmonizes the functional ends of nature with the moral ends of humanity.

Technological compatibility has both a positive and a negative component in terms of environmental risk. Negatively, technology that will impose risk to intrinsic value without adequate justification should not be created; positively, a system of incentives to encourage invention that enhances both human moral dignity and natural systems integrity must be created by government. The just state aims to create an atmosphere in which human consciousness is enhanced by our ability to create collective institutions with more power and anticipatory capacity than we have as individuals. The planning process then becomes one in which the intrinsic values involved can take center stage while the quest for the security of these capacities becomes the core justification and standard for making policy.

The goal of justice is the widespread development and use of practical reason; this requires that our collective institutions create an atmosphere favorable to its widespread expression. To do this, fear and uncertainty (the great antagonists of practical reason) must be minimized by the active and anticipatory state through planning and impact assessment, thus establishing the possibility for an atmosphere of trust and cooperation. In Kantian terms, trust is a function of a citizen's knowledge that his or her autonomy (i.e., intrinsic value) is the central standard and reason for public policy choice.

One's independence requires that active institutions anticipate and regulate both natural and artificial environmental risk. Responsibility regarding natural risks requires the active state to set up weather and geological services that monitor and predict risky natural occurrences (e.g., tornadoes, hurricanes, and earthquakes); agencies that respond to emergencies resulting from nature (e.g., FEMA); and planning codes to encourage technology that mitigates the effects of natural occurrences (e.g., zoning mandates for earthquake-resistant construction, and a general switch from bulk and density to performance zoning).

In the case of human-generated risk, it should be submitted to a thought and a justification process in which those creating the risk have the burden of proof, and autonomy is the moral standard. Just institutions should provide that state of affairs where the opportunity for independence, active citizenship, and the expression of one's positive freedom are made available to the widest possible number of constituents. Justice assumes that we live in a world of fear and uncertainty that can be minimized by collective action. The expectation of exploitation by others (including nature) must be anticipated and mitigated by our political institutions.

Minimization of fear and uncertainty through artificial-risk neutrality and technological compatibility does not mean that the state will be able to remove all reasons for fear or all of the uncertainty that is a fact of human life. It does mean that trust in institutions will be a function of the amount of security one has in his or her expression of moral agency. In turn, this security is itself a function of the assurance one has that those forces or actions that can affect the autonomy of the person, and are beyond the control of the individual, are being anticipated and controlled to the highest extent possible through public policy. Within this mandate, public policy uses human autonomy (which includes the integrity of greater Ecosystems) as the point of departure for public choice. With anticipatory institutions in place, a policymaker confronting environmental risk holds all human generators of that risk to demonstrate, through argument, that their technology or generation of risk is important to Ecosystem integrity. Thus, our duty to humanity in the person is satisfied through opportunity for independence and active citizenship, while our duty to a flourishing natural world is fulfilled in terms of both artificial-risk neutrality and technological compatibility.

Since the imperative to prevent dysfunctional collective confrontations requires active and anticipatory institutions, the other components of the baseline support and enhance the creation and empowerment of this future-focused, institutional structure. Trusteeship establishes the ideas of public trust ownership as the ultimate justification for the private use of property, while no-harm amends the search for human health and safety with a concern for intrinsic capacity and human-nature interdependence.

Trusteeship and the assurance of property for the expression of positive freedom are institutionalized by the active and anticipatory state. Collective action is regulated by our collective institutions, and the call for trusteeship, combined with the imperative for artificial-risk neutrality and technological compatibility, reinforce one another in the institutional context that must be provided if uncertainty and fear are to be minimized and social trust established. To the concern for prior public ownership, we add the institutional structure that then becomes responsible for the (re)distribution of property and the assurance that positive freedom for each citizen will be respected and empowered in our creation of technology, our generation of risk, and our regulation of human agency to protect the natural environment.

No-harm is enhanced by the idea that the capacities of nature and humanity are at stake in policy choice and now define the public interest. However we specifically empirically measure these standards (e.g., health, safety, resilience, homeostasis), we must not lose sight of the fact that we are concerned with what is, in Kant's words, "universal and necessary" to humanity and nature as ends-in-themselves. No-harm is a call to protect human and natural health; but it is also a call to provide safe and effective products that will not harm the essential dynamic capacities that are the essence of humanity's and nature's inherent value.[60]

In terms of specific policy, the baseline requires that an FDA-type of regulatory scheme be extended to cover all environmental-regulation decisions. A NEPA-like impact analysis is critical to establish and protect the baseline, but we need to recognize the interdependence of human and environmental intrinsic value, and to argue for policy, within the statute, where our duties to nature place "substantive" requirements on the practical components of the EIS. A Kantian EIS will consider the full effects of human interaction with natural systems. Specifically, this would involve alternatives that place less burden on, or pose artificial risk to, Ecosystem integrity; it would also involve the consideration of impacts primarily in terms of autonomy not economy. These planning documents need to cover, not just the actions of the federal government, but "major" actions for the private sector, and all these actions should be considered in light of the national performance zoning map of the nation, made necessary by our concern for not harming Ecosystem integrity. The EIS can be used as a necessary prerequisite to any major action or production of risk, but it must also reverse the current burden of proof.

A planning inventory should include all of the effects of the action but should also consider all of the human and natural needs on which the proposed action will be justified. The human generator of risk should make a persuasive argument that the risk is needed to support intrinsic value and that all other alternatives (especially environmentally friendly ones) have been considered and rejected in terms of autonomy. The baseline may even require the policymaker to take the safety and efficacy requirements of the FDA one step further and require the production of technology or risk to be justified by its unique effectiveness, so that regulators license only those uses of nature that fulfill a unique intrinsic need in the most risk-neutral and technologically compatible way possible.

Ecosystem Policy Argument and the Baseline

Overall, applying the Kantian paradigm and context model to environmental policy argument requires institutional arrangements to be reexamined and new priorities to be set by the combined and self-reinforcing concerns for Ecosystem integrity, assurance, and trust. Instead of a context model in which nature is sectorized and used for human instrumental welfare, a greater Ecosystem is now recognized that sets intrinsic value apart as a public priority. Human contact with the environment is now sectorized into three interfaces where each comprehensively considers all of the environmental and human effects of any proposed policy action, from extraction of resources to production of human artifacts; to recovery, reuse, and disposal of waste. Moral value ceases to be in the outcome of the policy, but exists in how the intrinsic value of humanity and nature are planned for by an anticipatory and active state. Our duties as human beings and active citizens define not only human, but environmental justice.

For a decision maker applying the imperatives of the baseline, the biosphere is a single entity in which humanity's "place" is one evolved from nature, as freedom evolved from causality. Humanity's transcendence of nature is specifically in terms of moral capacities and technological abilities that make us responsible not only to one another but to the environmental capacities that created us. Our capacities and abilities influence each other, since our moral duty drives our application of practical reason to technological innovation.

Institutions need to be streamlined in order to coordinate our expression of positive freedom so that human moral integrity and nature's functional integrity can produce stable and evolving Ecosystems. Justice from Autonomy argues for a more integrated bureaucratic structure to accommodate our duties to nature and an across-the-board "cooperative federalism" in which national agencies are responsible to set the ends of policy, while subnational units cooperate to establish specific means to these ends (Percival et al. 1992, 116–19). Here, bureaucracies can be streamlined around each of the interfaces where the law is coordinated by a single, more comprehensive, agency, with anticipatory mandates operationalized by specific task forces aimed at particular human nature contacts (e.g., a task force on biodiversity, applying extraction law within the public lands trust and disposition section of the Department of the Environment).

Law and policy arguments cease to be primarily questions of above-baseline welfare, but become focused on baseline rights and duties that protect, distribute, and provide for the inherent value of humanity and nature. Rather than one's preferences as a consumer, the status of the person as citizen becomes of primary concern in the determination of public choice. Ecosystem policy argument requires that nature be held in trust for its own functional future and that the law be used to hold the prerequisites of autonomy in trust for all generations of potentially active citizens.

In summation, the establishment of the baseline function as a new standard for public choice may require the following changes, among others, in regulatory theory and practice:

- A Department of the Environment to include all the relevant subagencies from EPA, Interior, and Agriculture.
- The creation of a national Ecosystem performance zoning map to define and categorize human and natural systems and zone them as integrated ecosystems.
- The establishment of substantive EIS requirements for all major public and private collective action.
- The integration of present environmental, natural resources and risk law, and their administrative apparatus within a department of the environment, into three comprehensive laws governing:
  (1) extraction and preservation,
  (2) production and conservation,
  (3) recovery/reuse/disposal.
- A shift in the burden of proof from the agencies to the users of the environment and the establishment of premarket standards for safety, efficacy, and the unique ability of a proposed use to empower Ecosystem integrity.
- A presumption that natural systems are originally in public trust where private use of nature must be justified *ex ante*.
- The establishment of a risk-conscious society in which our duties to intrinsic value in ourselves and in nature set the standards for policy choice and the justification for collective action.

With the establishment of a baseline as the foundation of Ecosystem law, less extraction, more reuse, and more necessary production processes will result, all within a risk-conscious political structure that is responsible to, as opposed to responsive to, its citizens.

The Baseline Standard and Political Evaluation

In their article "Political Evaluation" Brian Barry and Douglas Rae (1975) set out seven criteria as basic requirements of any policy evaluation system. Let us assess the Ecosystem approach using these considerations.

The first test of an evaluative theory is whether it has *internal consistency*. In other words, can it define a socially best policy from a group of alternatives, or will it cycle between options without being decisive? One problem with the Kaldor or Potential Pareto Improvement is its tendency to be indecisive (Feldman 1980, 142–44). Efficiency seeking the greatest proportion of welfare improvements to costs can allow two alternative outcomes X and Y to be Kaldor superior to one another.[61] Substituting Kaldor for Pareto, as a policy analyst must, results in a loss of decisiveness and a loss of meaning for the concept of "socially better."[62]

Justice from Autonomy is decisive at two levels. First, when one alternative involves intrinsic value and the baseline and the other do not, it is decisive for the former. The priority of the baseline trumps any and all preferences for instrumental welfare improvements.

Second, when the inherent worth of nature and the intrinsic value of humanity are both at stake, Ecosystem argument sets standards and assigns responsibilities that make for consistent policy. Because of our duties, humanity must adapt strategically and technologically to minimize harm to nature. The Kantian paradigm defines "socially better" in terms of baseline integrity, property, and opportunity across the population of citizens. The baseline components represent mutually reinforcing second-order principles (freedom, equality, and independence) that are all distinct but integrated manifestations of autonomy. To support one is to support the others in their joint quest to establish the baseline and the anticipatory state necessary to protect, distribute, and provide in behalf of human moral integrity and the functional integrity of the environment. The responsibility of the policymaker is therefore more rigorously defined by a more complex moral system than one would have with the indecisive Kaldor and cost-benefit criteria.

The second test, the *interpretability of evaluative criteria*, must also be considered. Is it possible to sort out reasonable from unreasonable evaluations? Justice from Autonomy assigns different values to that which has intrinsic worth and that which can only be instrumentally valuable over other ends. Kant closes down subjective evaluation of consequences and replaces it with the objective criteria necessary to protect and empower the essential capacities of Ecosystems. These criteria are built upon a foundation of Kant's entire philosophical system. The independent principles that support the concept of autonomy, and the baseline quality of life it represents, yield to a minimum of different interpretations while standing on a solid and elaborate but simple ethical foundation.

Third, can the evaluation system *aggregate its criteria*, so that higher-order criteria will settle any conflicts that might arise? The Kantian paradigm orders criteria internally so that intrinsic autonomy (i.e., freedom, equality, and independence) is elevated over any other considerations. Within the concept of autonomy, the components of the baseline function (i.e., Ecosystem integrity, property, and opportunity) are all equal, while the concept of autonomy includes the interdependent integrity of human and natural systems, the intersubjective equality of persons, and the civic independence of the active citizen as essential to one's practical reason and moral agency. As Kant's three formulas of the categorical imperative reinforce and build upon one another, Rawls's "priority of liberty" problem (1971, 243–51) is supplanted by three sets of material conditions (E^I, p_i, o_i) mutually supporting the functioning of the environment and the freedom of the individual.

Fourth, Barry and Rae ask, does the evaluation system recognize *forced choice?* Within Justice from Autonomy, humanity is involved in an assurance game that must be solved by just government intervention as a collective duty to the moral law. Choice is forced by the definition of justice and the imperative to seek after it, so that it is a failure of duty for a policymaker to allow a status quo that exploits autonomy to remain. The Kantian system also recognizes that the choice made may not be perfectly respectful of all humans as ends-in-themselves. Choice does not define freedom; the capacity to choose does. The "ideal" is a just society of autonomous citizens, the duty is to seek after it, and the imperative to the policymaker is to get the best possible policy that moves his society one step closer to the collective baseline.

Fifth, the system must handle *risk and uncertainty*. Ecosystem law and policy recognize uncertainty as a major foe of practical reason in its struggle for the character of the individual. Utilizing standards generated from the inherent worth of humanity and nature, it sets priorities and standards on the basis of what an autonomous human would accept. This is the only basis on which artificial collective uncertainty can be regulated while a secure environment for the practical reasoner is sought. For risk, we separate public from private and that which affects intrinsic value from that which does not, giving priority to the former in each case (see fig. 4.2). Subjective probabilities, or expected values (Fishburn 1982), are important, not as individual valuations that must be aggregated, but as probabilities applied to the collective expectation of harm that must be calculated by governments as part of their duty to solve the assurance game. The imperative is to secure, that is, protect and empower human moral agency.

Sixth, evaluation must consider the *relevance of time* to the policy choice. Unlike efficiency, which counts upon present preference to aggregate policy outcomes, Justice from Autonomy is sensitive to what is timeless about humanity and nature, placing these capacities at the center of policy justification and motivation as that which defines policy and the just state. In this way, the present and the future are judged on equal and fair terms by identical and timeless means (the baseline integrity function).

Finally, an evaluation system is required to be *relevant to the conditions of individuals*. Ecosystem policy argument forsakes concern for individual happiness or overall welfare, which varies between individuals (both ordinally and cardinally), concentrating on what is universal and necessary to every human and every natural system: integrity as an end-in-itself. The individual can have no strong sense of self or personal priorities that define his happiness, and therefore his overall welfare requirements, if he has no capacity for autonomous practical reason. This capacity for autonomy requires that the functional capacities of nature be respected and empowered, which is a component of moral agency, a requirement of duty, and, therefore, an end of practical reason. The market exists, but only for above-baseline transactions in which instrumental values are being traded after fundamental integrity is assured. Policy consequently leaves concepts like utility, desire, happiness, and "the good" to the individual calculations of agents as above-baseline concerns, whereas the state focuses on those collective conditions that will fully empower capacity and practical reason.

At this level of transactions, after the assurance game has been stabilized, individuals have the capacity to make judgments about what they want, what will truly make them happy, or what is good. At this point one can develop her humanity and discover what brings her happiness or fulfillment, and set her preferences accordingly. This occurs above the baseline, for at or below it, insecure hand-to-mouth existence surrounded by vast fear and uncertainty is typical. Under such conditions happiness and preferences are, in an ethical sense, not one's own.

Justice from Autonomy may yet have trouble in terms of internal consistency and decisiveness since the full complexity of the tradeoffs between values has not been fully analyzed. However, these are disputes internal to the paradigm (as what counts as a cost or benefit and how they are to be measured is an internal dispute within the market paradigm). These concerns notwithstanding, I maintain that the Kantian system sets priorities at least as reasonable and ethically sound as the market approach does, and will be as practical as more minds are put to work fleshing out its complete ramifications. My effort is but a beginning.

Whatever the result, Justice from Autonomy approaches policy analysis differently from traditional political evaluations in which the criteria invoked "are normally concerned not with the intrinsic characteristics of the policies but with the consequences of adopting one policy rather than another" (Barry and Rae 1975, 345). The implications of Ecosystem policy argument are not limited to American environmental policy. The baseline and Justice from Autonomy affect many other public choices, including economic regulation and antitrust, civil rights, energy planning, defense and national security, budget priorities, housing, national health, and education policy, in many nations. In an era when "globalization," with the market paradigm at its foundation, is being recommended, Ecosystem argument may provide an alternative evaluative standpoint from which to analyze the breakdown of national boundaries and the ascendance of "post-industrial ecology" (Sachs, Loske, and Linz 1998), a global economy (Vogel 1995), and international law and policy (Caldwell and Weiland 1996).

Moral agency, and the autonomy that creates it, is at the core of many critical human policy decisions. When Ecosystem integrity is at stake, anticipatory government regulation is a necessary "first-best" solution. To paraphrase Amartya Sen (1970, 1), it is with the application of Ecosystem policy argument to public choice that the "objectives of social policy" will be truly in touch with the capacities, abilities, and "aspirations" of all "members" of "society."

1. I make no claim that the specific interface and baseline components are only connected in the way I portray them here. I have grouped them in a way that allows my argument to have its most critical tests.

2. This assumes that in trading one intrinsic value for another (hostages for hostages, one species for another, a human settlement for a pristine natural system), one is at least trading like entities. This is not the case when life, with intrinsic value, is traded for things with only instrumental value.

3. The significance of this act is that it creates a state-based revenue-sharing formula for National Wildlife Refuges.

4. The primary statute affecting wildlife is the Endangered Species Act (16 U.S.C.A. §§1531–43). However, in addition, other statute law is at the foundation of the refuge system. This law includes the Migratory Bird Treaty Act (16 U.S.C.A. §§703–11); the Migratory Bird Conservation Act (16 U.S.C.A. §§715–715d, 715e, 715f–715k, 715n–715r); and the Migratory Bird Hunting Stamp Act (16 U.S.C.A. §718). In addition one can also consider the impact of specific pieces of legislation aimed at particular refuges like the Alaska National Interest Lands Conservation Act (PL 96–487). As in most cases the National Environmental Policy Act (42 U.S.C.A. §§4321–61) also applies.

5. The Endangered Species Act (16 U.S.C.A. §§1531–44) has distinct sections for designation of species (1533 [a,b]) and designation of vital habitat (1533 [b6C]); the history of the application of the act shows that animals are listed more often than habitat is designated for them. If one assumes that without properly designated habitat the species will have a hard time surviving, the lack of success in designating habitat under the Endangered Species Act makes the refuge system even more vital for biodiversity purposes.

6. The characteristics of the process of designating a wildlife refuge require that a separate piece of legislation be written for each one. This is a unique practice and could be argued to be another hurdle for preservation values. It makes sense, from within the market paradigm, since the land is primarily for extraction and use, and one would want as many safeguards as possible to prevent it from being "set aside" from economic use.

7. The case of the Arctic National Wildlife Refuge (ANWR) is a good example of the conflict between state desires and federal intentions to protect wildlife sanctuaries. Created in 1960 and divided into a combination of wilderness and refuge in 1980 with the passage of the Alaska National Interest Lands Conservation Act (PL 96–487), it is located in Alaska's extreme northwest corner. The refuge includes the Brooks Range and what have been called vital habitats for caribou, grizzly, and polar bear, musk ox, Dall sheep, wolf, wolverine, peregrine falcon, and gyrfalcon (173 *Congressional Quarterly Yearbook* 1988). The Conservation Act created the regulations that govern oil and gas exploration in the refuge (50 C.F.R. 37) and banned oil drilling on the designated wilderness within the refuge but also required the secretary of the interior to study the quantity and quality of the oil and gas reserves in the coastal plane (108 *Congressional Quarterly Yearbook*, 1991). Since then studies have shown that there is an extremely large reserve of oil and gas in this area, "a 95% probability that it contains at least 615 million bbl of oil and a 5% probability that it contains at least 8.8 billion bbl of oil" (Garner 1993, 1). This has set up a contest between the Alaska delegations in the House and Senate and environmental interests in Congress as to whether the entire refuge ought to be designated wilderness and made free from oil exploration or the entire refuge ought to be opened up. This debate has been attached to legislation in 1987, 1988, 1990, 1991, and again in 1993 with HR 1688 (see 315 *Congressional Quarterly Yearbook* 1990 and Bureau of National Affairs, *Congressional and Presidential Activity,*

April 5, 1993). The critical dimension of this debate, for my argument about states' rights and preservation, is that it is the local Alaskan forces that have pushed the hardest for opening oil exploration, while the federal congressional committees have maintained the preservationist paradigm. However, by dividing up the territory between refuge and wilderness, the federal approach has been to allow exploration and state interests to have some "secondary" role in the determination of policy, while the preservation of species and habitat maintains primary value. Here, we have a classic example of federal primary use and state secondary use.

8. This act took one of the initial steps in the preservation paradigm by utilizing the commerce clause of the Constitution to prohibit the interstate transport of any wild animal or bird that was killed contrary to state law. Notice here that state law still plays a significant role as the point of origin for federal concerns. The power of the federal government in bird conservation comes from the propensity of birds to fly across state lines, thereby invoking the jurisdiction of the commerce clause of the Constitution. See, for example, *Geer v Connecticut* 161 U.S. 519 (1896). The *Geer* decision recognized that state jurisdiction went only so far and that it could not conflict with the constitutional powers of the federal government.

9. See *Palila v Hawaii Department of Land and Natural Resources* 471 F.Supp. 985 (D.Ha. 1979) aff'd on other grounds, 639 F.2d.495 (9th Cir. 1981). This decision spread the effects of the Endangered Species Act to its widest venue and defined harm in a most general way that includes harassment and does not require killing or physically impairing the animal. This can be seen as the most significant and widest application of the preservationist paradigm.

10. See the Endangered Species Act (16 U.S.C.A. 1531 [a3]). Although all of these reasons for preservation are anthropomorphic, they exceed what the sportsman's paradigm would consider necessary for conservation.

11. A current policy debate that reflects this tension concerns the Clinton administration's efforts to get congressional support for a national biological survey. Here, the forces for states' rights and private property are allied against the preservationists, and although there is support in the relevant committees for this effort, it is expected that it will have a hard time in Congress. (See *Congressional Quarterly* 1868 [July 17, 1993].)

12. Here I would say *North* Americans, as Canada has also set aside wilderness areas (Lowry 1994, 1998).

13. Since the passage of the Wilderness Act of 1964 there have been specific wilderness bills for many states and specific areas including, for example, North Carolina (PL 98–323, 98 Stat. 259); Virginia (PL 98–322, 98 Stat. 253); New Hampshire (PL 98–425, 98 Stat. 1619); the Arizona Desert (PL 101–628, 104 Stat. 4469); the Mississippi National Forest (PL 98–515, 98 Stat. 2420); and the Vermont Wilderness Act of 1984 (PL 98–322, 98 Stat. 253).

14. In addition to the Wilderness Act and the specific designation legislation for particular areas, wilderness designation is also part of the Multiple-Use, Sustained Yield Act of 1960 (16 U.S.C.A. §§528–31), the National Forest Management Act of 1976 (16 U.S.C.A. §§1600–1614), and falls under the Environmental Impact Requirements of the National Environmental Policy Act of 1969 (42 U.S.C.A. §§4321–61). In addition, the Wilderness Act of 1964 has spawned both second-generation general preservation statutes such as the Endangered American Wilderness Act of 1978 (16 U.S.C.A. 1132) and specific preservation statutes such as the National Wild and Scenic Rivers Act of 1968 (16 U.S.C.A. §§1271–87). For an excellent treatment of the passage of the Wilderness Act, as well as what has happened since, see Frome 1997.

15. The regulations that define and restrict use are found in several places within the *Code of Federal Regulations*; I found them at 36 C.F.R. §§227, 228; 36 C.F.R. 293; 43 C.F.R. §19; 43 C.F.R. 8560; 43 C.F.R. 3802; and 43 C.F.R. 1600.

16. Compare the statute language of the Wilderness Act at 16 U.S.C.A. §1133 d2–3 with the stringent regulations for prewilderness study areas as outlined in 43 C.F.R. Subpart 3802. Here the specific requirements for a "plan of operations" (§3802.1–4) are especially revealing of the greater restrictions on exploration and mining on wilderness, compared with nonwilderness, land (compare with 43 C.F.R. part 3800).

17. The most interesting thing about the case law is the general concern of the judges to maintain wilderness values and to make their judgments of agency action dependent on the argument made for reasonableness, given the preservation standard. See for example, *NAPO v U.S.* (499 F.Supp. 1223, 1980), involving handicapped access to wilderness; *Pacific Legal Foundation v Watt* (529 F.Supp. 982, 1981), involving mineral leasing and the actions of the secretary of the interior; *Minnesota Public Interest Research Group v Butz* (401 F. Supp. 1276, 1975) involving logging; and *Voyageurs Regional National Park Association v Lujan* (1991 WL 3423370 [D. Minn]), which addresses the use of snowmobiles.

18. Exceptions are made for those restricted uses allowed in §1133.

19. The only exceptions to this rule are those refuges that were designated before vast oil or resource reserves were found under them. For example, ANWR has come to be controversial because, since its designation, vast oil reserves have been found that change this barren, frozen, and therefore worthless land into "valuable" land. The effort ever since has been to reclassify the ANWR so the oil can be fully exploited.

20. For summaries of legislative action and debate on wilderness designation, see *CQ Almanac* 1992 at 293. For specific examination of the Colorado Wilderness Bill (HR 631), see *CQ Weekly Reports*, June 19, 1993, at 1564; *CQ Weekly Reports*, July 3, 1993, at 1732; and in the *CQ Almanac* 1992 at 292. For the Montana Wilderness Bill (HR 2473), see *CQ Weekly Reports*, March 19, 1994, at 667; *CQ Weekly Reports*, March 26, 1994, at 732; and the *CQ Almanac* 1992 at 289.

21. This point of view was best set out by James Watt in his efforts to open wilderness to oil and gas exploration rather than let them be "abandoned" to decay and destitution. Although he was unsuccessful, the argument had its origin in the mythology of wilderness as "horrible" waste.

22. "Watt's Reasonable Choice," *Business Week*, March 8, 1982.

23. See Congressman Young's (Alaska) opinion, *CQ Weekly Reports*, July 3, 1993.

24. See "Wilderness Bill 'Compromise' a Blow to Area Exploration," *Oil and Gas*, May 21, 1984, at 59.

25. This can be seen in the debate over the Forest Service RARE reports. These surveys of roadless land for consideration of wilderness designation provide an argument for minimizing that land permanently set aside.

26. *CQ Weekly Reports*, June 19, 1993; *CQ Weekly Reports*, July 3, 1993.

27. *CQ Almanac* 1992.

28. Even the Clinton administration, which has a less dismal definition of wilderness, has been unable to significantly alter this fact.

29. This is a call, not for traditional "bulk and density" zoning, but for performance zoning that plots use in terms of environmental and ecological factors as well as of the geography and geology of a place (Mandelker and Cunningham 1990, 328–30).

30. I assume that, even with maximum recycling and reuse, there would still be radioactive and hazardous waste, as well as plain garbage, that would have to be properly disposed of. I also assume that consciously created storage facilities are better than on-site storage in urban and industrial areas.

31. I would like to acknowledge the work of my colleague, Barry Rabe (1989a, 1989b), especially his research on the Swan Hills site in Alberta, Canada, the success of which we explain with an assurance-game characterization of the siting process (Rabe and Gillroy 1993; Gillroy and Rabe 1997).

32. Here, the NIMBY situation could be related to the Not in Their Back Yard (NITBY) situation, where siting is seen as desirable.
33. This is not to say that the degrees of tension will not vary with the specific facility being sited and its level of risk.
34. Cooperation can be established from within a prisoner's dilemma by iterating the game. However, this cooperation is ineffective without some kind of external constraint (e.g., norms, conventions, law) while the primary preference of each player is to take advantage of the other (Hardin 1982a).
35. One could argue that, within the context of multiple-dynamic games (chap. 6), those who are generating NIMBY dilemmas are in fact causing the devolution of the policy assurance situation into a prisoner's dilemma confrontation.
36. This does not necessitate replacing a concept of self-interest with one of altruism. Kant understood the evolution of one's self-interest to begin with one's animal nature and to end with "rational self-love," which can be defined as the capacity to see one's own real interests in protecting and empowering one's own capacity as a human agent, which entails a further "moral" recognition that cooperation with others as ends-in-themselves is necessary to one's self-interest (Kant C2, 73).
37. The report from Pennsylvania was completed but never officially published.
38. Among the cities undertaking comparative-risk projects are Seattle, Washington; Jackson, Mississippi; Houston, Texas; Columbus, Ohio; and Charlottesville, Virginia. In addition, both the Western and Wisconsin Tribes, and Guam, as well as projects for the Gulf of Mexico and Eastern Europe, have received EPA funding.
39. Some projects have distinct working groups for air or water risk; see Minard and Jones 1993.
40. When the USEPA began the comparative-risk process, this power was concentrated in the hands of government bureaucrats. The national and EPA regional studies were completely organized around professional staff and reflected the "expert" view of risk matters. These staffs were so specialized that, although they felt comfortable dividing themselves into at least two groups to deal with human health risk and ecosystem risk, they would not or could not come together to integrate a single risk ranking. With the initiation of the state and city studies this concentration of power began to decentralize. Although the technical working groups and steering committees reflected agency and governmental expertise, the investment of power in the public advisory committee changed everything.
41. This is accomplished in the Canadian context by the creation of a "Crown Corporation" that oversees siting (Rabe and Gillroy 1993).
42. Barry Rabe and I have done work on successful sitings in Canada that exhibit these properties. See Rabe 1995; Gillroy and Rabe 1997; Applegate, Laitos, and Campbell-Mohn 2000, chap. 10.
43. The need to assemble an environmental assessment in consideration of the definition of a significant action under NEPA §102 was forced by the court's decision in *Hanly v Kleindienst* (471 F.2d 823 [2d Cir. 1972]).
44. The specific guidelines for the preparation of an EIS, and the regulations that govern the implementation of NEPA, are found at 40 C.F.R. §§ 1500–1517.
45. Specifically, the permit was for a facility with sixteen lifts that could handle up to 8500 skier days.
46. The CEQ rule that required the inclusion of a worst-case analysis was rescinded in the 1986 amendments that changed the language from "inclusion of a worst-case analysis in the absence of available information" to simply requiring "inclusion of such unavailable information if the costs of obtaining it are not exorbitant." The CEQ does not define "exorbitant" at 40 C.F.R. 1500 or in the *Federal Register* preamble (at 51 Reg. 15618 et seq.). Even with the CEQ rule withdrawn, many lower federal courts continued to assume that it was part of the EIS process.

CASE STUDIES IN ECOSYSTEM POLICY ARGUMENT

47. The "hard look" doctrine or test originated in *Citizens to Preserve Overton Park v Volpe* (401 U.S. 402 [1971]). In this case the Supreme Court indicated that courts must conduct a "substantial inquiry" into agency decisions to determine whether the agency has taken a "hard look" at the issues. This "hard look" doctrine has become the hallmark of judicial review in environmental law; however, it does not mean that a court can "substitute its own judgment for that of an agency" (Spensley, Freeman, and Marchet 1994, 330).

48. Could NEPA §103 help to shift us toward Ecosystem policy argument?

49. Regulations for enacting this statute can be found at 21 C.F.R. 1–1300.

50. It is uncertain that the 1996 amendments were a "reaffirmation."

51. The FDA also regulates pesticides and medical devices, among other things.

52. Since its inception, the Delaney Clause has come to be seen as too strict, and both the agencies and Congress have tried to get around its provisions (Wargo 1998, chap. 6). My concern here is its original unamended form, as it exemplifies the morality of Ecosystem Policy Argument.

53. The FDA requires, for cancer testing of food additives, that two animal tests be completed and that a virtually safe dose (VSD) be at the one-in-a-million level of risk. Regulation is required at the "no residue" level and not just at the "detectable" level.

54. This makes these provisions of the statute and regulations "risk only."

55. Phase I clinical trials study a few subjects to determine the level of human toxicity, metabolism, absorption, elimination, safe dosage range, and pharmacological actions. Phase II trials again concentrate on a small sample, while Phase III trials are full-scale, controlled clinical studies that are to produce the empirical data upon which the application will be judged.

56. The one exception is the effort by AIDS activists to allow certain drugs to obtain faster clearance for terminally ill patients (Burkholz 1994, chap. 7). However, even though some exceptions are now made for such drugs (see note 55), the courts have been strong in their support of the idea that a terminally ill citizen still requires certain *ex ante* protection. See *U.S. v Rutherford* (442 U.S. 544 1979).

57. Remember (chaps. 2 and 4) that QRA can be used as a surrogate for market assumptions in risk analysis.

58. There is an exception made here for drugs that are developed to treat life-threatening illness (e.g., antineoplastic drugs, TBR = 1).

59. For more on the profitability of the industry, see Teitelman 1989.

60. I assume that, from a Kantian point of view, one's physical health is necessary but not sufficient to the capacity to reason practically. One is not treated justly when one has health but no freedom.

61. Specifically, as long as a hypothetical condition Z exists that has greater surplus welfare, then any one alternative can be made Kaldor superior to another, even if Z is never found or actualized.

62. To remedy symmetry, we can adjust the Kaldor test by use of the Scitovsky criterion (Feldman 1980, 144–45). This test maintains that X is Scitovsky superior to Y when there is a Z, such that Z is preferred to Y by no Q available to the choice, such that Q is preferred to X. Although this removes symmetry between alternative policies, there now exists a transitivity problem between alternative states of affairs.

Epilogue

We must disenthrall ourselves,
and then we shall save our country.

Abraham Lincoln,
December 1, 1862

EPILOGUE

Ecosystem Argument in the States: Act 250 and Proposition 65

The United States of America is at a crossroads. For more than two hundred years the market and its cost-benefit methodology have been the predominant and conventional paradigm from within which we have approached public life. The quest for efficiency creates the language of collective action and defines both the necessary ends and appropriate means of public choice. Market efficiency, transferred into the public sector, has largely defined our idea of "socially better," not only in terms of industrial and welfare policy, but also in terms of our legal relationship with the natural world (U.S. Congress 1979).

The benefit of this focus on market assumptions and methods is a vibrant consumer society; the downside, a neglect, in policy deliberation and choice, of both humanity in the person and the intrinsic value of nature. As this book argues, the time has come for a change of perspective. The market paradigm at the core of our policy deliberations should be replaced with another paradigm that promotes, not the instrumental value of things to persons, but the intrinsic value of humanity and nature coexisting within greater Ecosystems. That we all have inherent value as humans, and that the natural systems surrounding us are valuable as self-generating, living, and evolving functional entities, ought to be promoted into a "trump" position in public discussion, resetting the terms of collective action and public choice. The interface between these intrinsic values is where important "Ecosystem" policy choices are constantly being made; we need to adopt an argument paradigm that promotes these "environmental" values (Paehlke 1989, 1993).

The market paradigm has created a climate of strategic noncooperation that breeds distrust, cynicism, personal and group resentment, racism, and a society of few "haves" and many "have-nots" where the latter would rather anticipate the improbable prospects of becoming rich than deal with the reality of being poor. The competitive, "winner take all" atmosphere created by economic principle, with its dependence on the assumptions of self-interest and its preoccupation with monetary costs and benefits, has produced an environment laced with fear and uncertainty and created, simultaneously, a consumer's paradise and a citizen's purgatory.

This state of affairs is not the fault of the market paradigm, but of our improper application of its "private" assumptions and principles to "public" or "collective" policy. Transferring a set of theoretical tenets and principles that work fine in one framework to a completely different situation does not work because the principles assumed are insufficient to evaluate what is at stake in the decision and therefore cause havoc in their application.

To appreciate the moral dimensions of Justice from Autonomy, we need a new politics that promotes anticipatory government focused on the moral agency of the active citizen and providing the atmosphere of assurance that is required to foster public trust, personal security, and morally practical reason in one and all. Specifically, government is responsible to utilize nonefficiency principles to set the boundaries within which markets function. The task is to create a *politics of assurance* and establish a *baseline*, an *active and anticipatory state*, and a *risk-conscious society* which then may confine markets to above-baseline and private goods transactions. The politics of assurance then creates the background conditions and sets the confines of market operation so that we can achieve prosperity for the individual as a consumer only after citizens are assured of their autonomy through freedom as moral agents.[1]

In this book, I have suggested an alternative to the market paradigm that incorporates intrinsic value into the core of policy deliberation and choice while defining a more appropriate role for markets and their assumptions in private goods transactions. Although other alternatives to the market paradigm should be made accessible to the policymaker,[2] I wish to speculate that my approach is already finding tactical voice in the laboratory of the states.

Federal Policy and State Experiments

The struggle for power between the states and the federal government is a constant theme in American politics. Our politics, our Constitution, and our party system have their roots in the dialectic between state and federal predominance. One of our major parties has always represented the rights of states and localities, while the other supports the role of a federal government, in a republic, as the representative of all of the people to form a common foundation for our rights as citizens. In the 1860s, the new Republican Party filled the latter role, whereas the Democrats occupied the former, and although the federal government prevailed in the Civil War and the locution "the United States of America are" was replaced with "the United States of America is," the dialectic has continued to this day, except, as the century turns, the parties have reversed their philosophical positions.

The Republican Party of free soil, free labor, and free men, which accepted the Federalist tradition and argued for a strong central government guaranteeing the rights of all Americans, has been replaced by a party of the same name, but one with closer philosophical ties to Jefferson Davis than to Abraham Lincoln. The "new" Republican Party of the late twentieth century supports ending federal involvement in a range of policies including welfare and environmental regulation, and devolving these powers and moneys to states in block grants without any mandates or direction from the United States government. The call of "states' rights" that represented the "particular tradition" of slavery, and which tore the country apart in civil war, is again being heard as a clarion call for all-encompassing private property rights, fifty local definitions of environmental quality, and satisfying preferences on the basis of efficiency as the sole fit purpose and motivating imperative of public policy.

Within this concern for commerce and "the efficiency of the economy," the Republican Party, especially in the U.S. House of Representatives, has attempted to completely dismantle environmental regulation and public lands protections by advocating market paradigm solutions, privatization, and the reascendancy of maximum use within TSA-I. Beneath the rhetoric lies complete faith in the market paradigm and its power to provide, not only a "good" consumer economy, but "good" public environmental policy.

If we assume that in times of paradigm shift, the conventions of the status quo, like a faltering light bulb, glow brightest, and that, as the past is replaced by the future, the true believers in the waning paradigm will hold fast to its values and become ever more strident in its defense and evangelical in asserting its truth, this may explain our present reality. But even if we assume a widespread dissatisfaction with private market assumptions and what they have produced as policy (Paehlke 1989; Stone 1975) and we are at the threshold of a shift to a focus on collective life (Hirschman 1982), we do not have a united and concrete image, as a people, of what we want to replace market assumptions with (Shaiko 1999; Kempton, Boster, and Hartley 1995; Gore 1992).

The debate about alternatives, however, is currently under way, and the values that are encompassed and empowered by what I call Ecosystem Policy Argument have achieved some small victories. Pilot projects exist that address environmental issues like land use and toxics regulation but emphasize human and natural intrinsic value by shifting the burden of proof of the merit of their projects to those who would use the environment.

If we view the fifty states, not as the ultimate repository for political power and definitions of the right and the good, but as small experimental stations for the tactical trials of new paradigms and public agendas, we may be able to see the shape of things to come. Specifically, two state-level experiments, Act 250 in Vermont and Proposition 65 in California, lend credence to the relevance of what I have called Ecosystem policy and law.

Vermont's Act 250

For trusteeship to become a transcendent value in environmental law, the just state should regulate the use of land in the public interest with an assumption of prior collective ownership. Without land use regulation at the macro level that places the burden of proof on potential users to demonstrate that their private use has no negative ramifications on the baseline, planning will not have the direct, anticipatory connection to environmental regulation that a just society demands.

Unlike both pollution control law and natural "resources" policy, land use law has not been affected by the evolution from private common law to federal public regulation. Almost all of the land use law in this country occurs on the most local of levels and is accommodated by state authorization statutes and local zoning ordinances (Mandelker and Cunningham 1990). Statewide or regional planning is rare, and federal government land use standards are limited to our public lands (Coggins, Wilkinson, and Leshy 1993).

An exception to this rule came about in 1970 in Vermont with the passage into law of Act 250 (named for its chapter in the Vermont Code). Act 250 requires that "economic development should be pursued selectively so as to provide maximum economic benefit with minimal environmental impact" (10 *VSA* §6042 [6][A]). Toward this end, a state permit must be acquired for all land development and prepossessed subdivision construction (10 *VSA* §6081 [a]). Under its definition of "development," a permit is necessary for any action that involves "more than 10 acres of land within a radius of five miles," for housing projects of more than 10 units, and the "construction of improvements" for municipal or state purposes of more than 10 acres (10 *VSA* §6001 [3]).

The permit system requires a developer to submit five copies of a development plan that specifies "the intended use of the land, the proposed improvements, [and] the details of the project " (10 *VSA* §6083 [a] [2]). Act 250 then creates a number of *District Environmental Commissions* to consider applications and grant permits. One of the responsibilities of a commission is to deny permits where "undue adverse impact" on the environment is probable.

> For purposes of evaluating a proposed land use under environmental impact criteria, an adverse impact on the environment is "undue" if (1) the project violates a clear, written community standard intended to preserve the aesthetics or scenic, natural beauty of the area, (2) the project offends the sensibilities of the average person, or (3) the applicant has failed to take generally available reasonable mitigating steps to improve the harmony of the proposed project with its surroundings. (10 *VSA* §6068 Anno. 5)

In addition, the statute provides specific permit criteria that require a project not to produce "undue air pollution" (10 *VSA* §6086 [A][1]), or harm to the "quality of groundwater" (A). The proposed land use must also provide for adequate waste disposal (C), water conservation (C), the "natural" conditions of forests (C), streams (E), shorelines (F), and protection of wetlands (G) and species habitat ([8][A]).

The importance of this act to our argument is that it reverses the burden of proof on to those who would develop or use the environment (10 *VSA* §6088). By shifting the burden of proof, Act 250 forces those who would define and develop land as a resource to justify their use to the state as collective trustee of the environment. The state is empowered to anticipate the violation of human and natural integrity and stop it *ex ante*. Any potential developer must present and justify his or her private choices in a public forum. The larger community is also involved in the process up front, causing the society to become conscious of the risks and actual harms that may follow a specific extraction decision, as well as of the possibility of harm and the plans for mitigation.

Act 250 requires that citizens make decisions about what land is open to development, what kind of development is acceptable, and under what conditions the actual use will take place. The statute, it can be argued, constructs a baseline and a set of *ex ante* protections for the land, which is then treated as a public resource under collective ownership. Trusteeship is elevated over facilitation of use as a state function and requires that our duties to nature, and to one another, be considered explicitly in the policy deliberation and choice that precede land use.

California's Proposition 65

The Safe Drinking Water and Toxic Enforcement Act of 1986 (California Health and Safety Code [hereafter CHSC] §§25249 et seq.) was adopted by nearly two-thirds of California voters in November of 1986. According to Section 1 of the proposition the people of California have defined the purposes of the act:

> a. To *protect* themselves and the water they drink against chemicals that cause cancer, birth defects, or other reproductive harm.
> b. To be informed about the exposures to chemicals that cause cancer, birth defects, or other reproductive harm.
> c. To secure strict enforcement of the laws controlling hazardous chemicals and deter actions that threaten public health and safety.
> d. To shift the costs of hazardous waste cleanups more onto the offenders and less onto law-abiding taxpayers. (emphasis added)

Proposition 65 requires the governor of California to maintain a list of chemicals "known to the state to cause cancer or reproductive toxicity" (CHSC §25249.5). Entries on this list fall under the regulation of the statute and "no person in the course of doing business" shall "knowingly and intentionally" expose any individual to a listed chemical without "clear and reasonable" warning (CHSC §§25249.6, 25249.10[b]). The only exemption from this warning requirement is if the individual or firm creating the environmental risk can show their product really produces "no significant risk" (CHSC §25249.10 [c]).

In addition to its warning requirements, Proposition 65 also sets an outright ban that prohibits corporations or persons, within the definition of the act (CHSC §25249.11[a]), from releasing listed chemicals "into the water or onto or into land where such chemical passes or probably will pass into any source of drinking water" (CHSC §§25249.5, 25249.9[a]).

Overall, the purpose of Proposition 65 is to force the burden of proof for the justification of the imposition of environmental risk onto those who create and market risk-generating products and technology. With its presumption that a collective right to be protected from nonvoluntary risk overrides a private right to create risk, California moves from a false-positive to a false-negative environmental-risk regime. A manufactured risk is no longer considered innocent and marketable until proven guilty; it is assumed guilty and unmarketable, requiring a public warning, until proven innocent (or noncarcinogenic).

To gain an exemption from the requirements of the law, one must show that "no significant risk" will be inflicted through human exposure (CHSC §25249.10 [c]). To establish at what level "significant risk" occurs, one must generate data that establishes *de minimis* or minimally safe levels of the chemical. However, unlike TSCA or OSHA regulation of risk (see chap. 3), under Proposition 65 regulation the responsibility to find these "safe" levels is assigned, not to state regulators, but to those who would impose the risk on the society at large.

> Proposition 65's fundamental innovation is to take the *de minimis* concept, and simply reverse the burden of proof. Thus, for example, the manufacturer of a product that contains benzene in some small amount, seeking to exempt itself from the requirement of giving a cancer warning, can do so by proving that the level of exposure to the carcinogen is below a "no significant risk" level. This simple-sounding reversal of the burden of proof has profound consequences. Instead of waiting for government to prove that a given exposure (or discharge) is "above the line," regulated industry is faced with the need of showing that the same situation is "below the line"—and is suddenly eager for regulations that will define and quantify those lines. (Roe 1989, 181)

Because manufacturers fear that sales will suffer when a required warning label is placed on a product, industry has responded to the law by eliminating listed chemicals from their products and technologies. The statute-mandated shift in the burden of proof, and the anticipatory role of the state in protecting the public interest in baseline autonomy, has forced private markets to work internally to weed out those products and technologies that generate excess risk and replace them with products that can be shown to present "no significant risk" so as to be exempt from regulation.

Although business fought the adoption of Proposition 65 and protested that the shift in the burden of proof necessitated by the anticipatory regulation required by this act would cause a great decline in the California economy, no major upheaval materialized (Roberts 1989; Roe 1989). Meanwhile, "[t]his simple legal innovation has dramatically accelerated the pace of standard setting and has substantially decreased the amount of litigation over environmental standards" (Pease 1991, 14).

The result has been a drastic reduction of listed chemical use. Within five years after passage, "companies have stopped emitting 6 [of the 44 listed] chemicals . . . [while] . . . emissions have decreased for two-thirds of all chemicals . . . [and] . . . more than 80% of the chemicals with emissions greater than

10,000 pounds per year in 1987 exhibited lower emissions in 1989" (Pease 1991, 16–17).

With the advent of anticipatory institutions, an "unprecedented decisiveness and speed in the applying of uniform principles to the case-by-case issues presented by individual toxic chemicals" have occurred, with relatively little immediate litigation over standards and their application (Roe 1989, 182). "The expectation that regulatory obligations will only increase has been an incentive for companies to audit their chemical use and to institute pollution prevention programs" (Pease 1991, 17).

Justice and Federal Government

Whether the shift in the burden of proof and the authority of the just state to regulate in anticipation of harm to intrinsic value will ever become the core of a new environmental metapolicy at the federal level in the United States is uncertain. However, if it has not yet occurred because of fear that our economy would shut down if these fundamental changes were made, then a combination of the FDA regulatory experience and the state experiments in Vermont and California demonstrate that this fear is ill founded. If the state experiments covered in this epilogue produced the same effects on the federal level, then our economic losses in the new regulatory environment would not be profound. Markets are flexible, industry is creative, and our needs are variable. Disposable razors, or lighters, or pens may disappear and instead of twenty-four kinds of antifreeze, we may only have three from which to choose. But the remaining products will be of higher quality and can be used in the knowledge that the integrity of humanity and nature are intact through their production and consumption.[3] Our freedom, as economic choice, may be more limited, but our more essential freedom, as moral capacity, will be better protected and empowered. Such a tradeoff is necessitated by both the moral law and a just baseline.

In making a transition to Ecosystem Policy Argument and its Justice from Autonomy paradigm, the role of the federal government becomes critical. Essentially, the demands of justice and our duties to ourselves and others (including nature) ought not to tolerate borders, either national or international, that privilege one group of humans or one natural system over others (Braybrooke 1987; Shue 1980; Caldwell and Weiland 1996). To say that the citizens of California have a right to the shift in the burden of proof, while citizens of Pennsylvania do not, has no moral justification. To regulate land use in the public interest and for the greater protection of Ecosystems ought not to be particular to Vermont; it speaks to our duties as human beings, not as residents of specific political jurisdictions.

Justice from Autonomy evolves from a foundation of duty that has, as its core principle, the intrinsic values of human freedom and Ecosystem integrity. These should be regulated, as a public trust, from the federal level, at least in terms of standard setting and enforcement. Eventually, all human beings should be able to live in ethical sociopolitical conditions, but, for now, we ought to be able to have the same rights and responsibilities as active citizens, moral agents, and Americans, living in an environment regulated by national standards, protecting and empowering our autonomy regardless of our particular state of birth. A move toward implementation of Ecosystem Policy Argument and Design would be a first step in the full recognition of both the intrinsic value of the person and the environment in which he or she lives.

Notes

1. Toby Page, in conversation, has characterized this argument as "making the world safe for markets."
2. I not only wish to give the policymaker an additional "tool" with Ecosystem Policy Argument, but open the possibility of using the paradigm/context model logic of chapter 1 to harness other existing philosophical systems (Hobbes, Locke, Hegel, Deep Ecology, etc.) to create additional evaluative alternatives for the analyst's toolbox.
3. Mesarovic and Pestel (1974) might call this a move away from traditional "exponential" growth and an evolution toward "organic" growth for the world economy.

Selected Bibliography

Abrahamson, Warren G., and Arthur E. Weis. 1997. *Evolutionary Ecology across Three Trophic Levels*. Princeton, N.J.: Princeton University Press.

Aharoni, Yair. 1981. *The No Risk Society*. Chatham, N.J.: Chatham House Publishers.

Allison, Henry E. 1983. *Kant's Transcendental Idealism*. New Haven, Conn.: Yale University Press.

———. 1990. *Kant's Theory of Freedom*. New York: Cambridge University Press.

Amy, Douglas J. 1984. "Toward a Post-Positivist Policy Analysis." *Policy Studies Journal* 13:124–25.

Anderson, Charles W. 1979. "The Place of Principles in Policy Analysis." *American Political Science Review* 73:711–23. Reprinted in Gillroy and Wade 1992, pp. 387–410.

Anderson, Larry, and Patricia Byrnes. 1993. "The View from Breadloaf: Fostering a Spirit of Wilderness in the Heart of the Green Mountains." *Wilderness* 56: at 10.

Anderson, Terry, and Donald Leal. 1991. *Free Market Environmentalism*. Boulder, Colo.: Westview Press.

Andrews, Richard N. L. 1999. *Managing the Environmental, Managing Ourselves: A History of American Environmental Policy*. New Haven, Conn.: Yale University Press.

Annas, Julia. 1993. *The Morality of Happiness*. New York: Oxford University Press.

Appelbaum, David. 1995. *The Vision of Kant*. Rockport, Mass.: Element.

Applegate, John, Jan Laitos, and Celia Campbell-Mohn. 2000. *The Regulation of Toxic Substances and Hazardous Waste*. University Casebook Series. New York: Foundation Press.

Aristotle. (PL) 1905. *Politics*. Trans. Benjamin Jowett. Oxford: Clarendon Press.

Ashby, Eric. 1978. *Reconciling Man with the Environment*. Stanford, Calif.: Stanford University Press.

Attfield, Robin. 1983. *The Ethics of Environmental Concern*. New York: Columbia University Press.

Audi, Robert. 1989. *Practical Reasoning*. London: Routledge.

———, ed. 1995. *The Cambridge Dictionary of Philosophy*. Cambridge, U.K.: Cambridge University Press.

Aune, Bruce. 1979. *Kant's Theory of Morals*. Princeton, N.J.: Princeton University Press.

Avineri, Shlomo, and Avner De-Shalit, eds. 1992. *Communitarianism and Individualism*. Oxford, U.K.: Oxford University Press.

Axelrod, Robert. 1984. *The Evolution of Cooperation*. New York: Basic Books.

Bagley, E. 1961. "Water Rights Law and Public Policies Relating to Groundwater Mining in the Southwestern States." *Journal of Law and Economics* 4: 144–74.

Baier, Annette. 1986. "Poisoning the Well." In *Values at Risk*, edited by Douglas MacLean, pp. 49–74. Totowa, N.J.: Roman and Allanheld.

———. 1997. "How Can Individualists Share Responsibility?" In *Feminist Interpretations of Immanuel Kant*, edited by Robin May Schott, pp. 297–318. University Park, Pa.: Penn State University Press.

Baram, Michael S. 1980. "Cost-Benefit Analysis: An Inadequate Basis for Health, Safety and Environmental Regulatory Decision Making." *Ecology Law Quarterly* 8:473–532.

Barry, Brian M. 1973. *The Liberal Theory of Justice*. Oxford, U.K.: The Clarendon Press.

———. 1977. "Justice between Generations." In *Law, Morality and Society*, edited by P. M. S. Hacker and J. Raz, pp. 268–84. Oxford, U.K.: The Clarendon Press.

———. 1978a. *Sociologists, Economists and Democracy*. Chicago: University of Chicago Press.

———. 1978b. "Circumstances of Justice and Future Generations." In *Obligations to Future Generations*, edited by R. I. Sikora and Brian Barry, pp. 204–48. Philadelphia, Pa.: Temple University Press.

———. 1990. *Political Argument*. 2nd ed. Berkeley and Los Angeles: University of California Press.

———. 1992. "Welfare Economics and the Liberal Tradition." In *The Moral Dimensions of Public Policy Choice: Beyond the Market Paradigm*, edited by John Martin Gillroy and Maurice Wade, pp. 325–39. Pittsburgh, Pa.: University of Pittsburgh Press.

———. 1989/1995. *A Treatise on Social Justice*. Vol. 1, *Theories of Justice*. Berkeley and Los Angeles: University of California Press. Vol. 2, *Justice As Impartiality*. Oxford, U.K.: Clarendon Press.

Barry, Brian M., and Douglas W. Rae. 1975. "Political Evaluation." In *Handbook of Political Science*, edited by Fred I. Greenstein and Nelson Polsby. Vol. 1, *Scope and Method*, pp. 337–401. Reading, Mass.: Addison-Wesley.

Barry, Norman P. 1989. *An Introduction to Modern Political Theory*. 2nd ed. New York: St. Martin's Press.

Bartell, Steven M., Robert H. Gardner, and Robert V. O'Neill, eds. 1992. *Ecological Risk Estimation*. Boca Raton, Fla.: Lewis Publishing.

Bartlett, Robert. 1980. *The Reserve Mining Controversy*. Bloomington: Indiana University Press.

Bean, Michael J. 1983. *The Evolution of National Wildlife Law*. New York: Praeger.

Beck, Lewis White. 1960. *A Commentary on Kant's Critique of Practical Reason*. Chicago: University of Chicago Press.

Beck, Ulrich. 1992. *Risk Society: Toward a New Modernity*. Trans. by Mark Ritter. London: Sage.

———. 1995. *Ecological Enlightenment: Essays on the Politics of the Risk Society*. Trans. Mark Ritter. Atlantic Highlands, N.J.: Humanities Press.

Becker, Gary S. 1976. *The Economic Approach to Human Behavior*. Chicago: University of Chicago Press.

Berlin, Isaiah. 1969. *Four Essays on Liberty*. Oxford, U.K.: Clarendon Press.

Berman, Harold J. 1983. *Law and Revolution*. Cambridge, Mass.: Harvard University Press.

Bish, Charles. 1971. *The Public Economy of Metropolitan Areas*. Chicago: Markham.

Boadway, Robin W. 1979. *Public Sector Economics*. Cambridge, Mass.: Winthrop Press.

Bobrow, Davis B., and John S. Dryzek. 1987. *Policy Analysis by Design*. Pittsburgh, Pa.: University of Pittsburgh Press.

Bosso, Christopher. 1987. *Pesticides and Politics: The Life Cycle of a Public Issue*. Pittsburgh, Pa.: University of Pittsburgh Press.

———. 1993. "Environmental Values and Democratic Institutions." In *Environmental Risk, Environmental Values and Political Choices: Beyond Efficiency Trade-Offs in Public Policy Analysis*, edited by John Martin Gillroy, pp. 72–93. Boulder, Colo.: Westview Press.

Braybrooke, David. 1987. *Meeting Needs*. Princeton, N.J.: Princeton University Press.

———. 1991. "A Little Logical Guidance for the Competition of Ideas." Austin: University of Texas, Mimeo.

Braybrooke, David, and Charles Lindblom. 1970. *A Strategy for Decision*. 2nd ed. New York: Free Press.

Breyer, Stephen. 1982. *Regulation and Its Reform*. Cambridge, Mass.: Harvard University Press.

———. 1993. *Breaking the Vicious Circle: Toward Effective Risk Regulation*. Cambridge, Mass.: Harvard University Press.

Breyer, Stephen G., and Richard B. Stewart. 1992. *Administrative Law and Regulatory Policy*. 3rd ed. Boston: Little, Brown.

Brickman, Ronald, Sheila Jasanoff, and Thomas Ilgen. 1985. *Controlling Chemicals: Of the Politics of Regulation in Europe and the United States*. Ithaca, N.Y.: Cornell University Press.

Brooks, Daniel R., and E. O. Wiley. 1988. *Evolution as Entropy*. 2nd ed. Chicago: University of Chicago Press.

Buchanan, Allan, and Gordon Tullock. 1962. *The Calculus of Consent*. Ann Arbor: University of Michigan Press.

Buchanan, James. 1975. *The Limits of Liberty*. Chicago: University of Chicago Press.

Buck, Susan J. 1991. *Understanding Environmental Administration and Law*. Washington, D.C.: Island Press.

———. 1998. *The Global Commons: An Introduction*. Washington D.C.: Island Press.

Burkholz, Herbert. 1994. *The FDA Follies*. New York: Basic Books.

Calabrese, Edward J., and Linda A. Baldwin. 1993. *Performing Ecological Risk Assessment*. Boca Raton, Fla.: Lewis Publishing.

Caldwell, Lynton Keith. 1998. *The National Environmental Policy Act: An Agenda for the Future*. Bloomington: Indiana University Press.

Caldwell, Lynton Keith, and Paul Stanley Weiland. 1996. *International Environmental Policy: From the 20th Century to the 21st*. 3rd ed. Durham, N.C.: Duke University Press.

Campbell-Mohn, Celia, Barry Breen, and J. William Futrell. 1993. *Environmental Law from Resources to Recovery*. St. Paul, Minn.: West Publishing.

Canter, L. W., and R. C. Knox. 1986. *Groundwater Pollution Control*. Boca Raton, Fla.: Lewis Publishing.

Cassirer, Ernst. 1981. *Kant's Life and Thought*. New Haven, Conn.: Yale University Press.

Carson, Rachel. 1962. *Silent Spring*. New York: Houghton Mifflin.

Chong, Dennis. 1991. *Collective Action and the Civil Rights Movement*. Chicago: University of Chicago Press.

Christman, John, ed. 1989. *The Inner Citadel: Essays on Individual Autonomy*. New York: Oxford University Press.

Clark, Edwin H. III., and Philip J. Cherry. 1979. *Groundwater: Managing the Unseen Resource—A Handbook for States*. Washington, D.C.: World Wildlife Fund.

Coase, Ronald. 1960. "The Problem of Social Cost." *Journal of Law and Economics* 3:1–44.

Coggins, George Cameron, Charles F. Wilkinson, and John D. Leshy. 1993. *Federal Public Land and Resource Law*. 3rd ed. University Casebook Series. New York: Foundation Press.

Coleman, James S. 1990. *Foundations of Social Theory*. Cambridge, Mass.: Harvard University Press.

Coleman, Jules L. 1992. *Risks and Wrongs*. Cambridge, U.K.: Cambridge University Press.

Conservation Foundation. 1985. *Risk Assessment and Risk Control*. Washington, D.C.: Conservation Foundation Press.

———. 1987. *Groundwater Protection*. Washington, D.C.: Conservation Foundation Press.

Costanza, Robert, ed. 1991. *Ecological Economics: The Science of Management of Sustainability*. New York: Columbia University Press.

Costanza, Robert, Bryan G. Norton, and Benjamin D. Haskell, eds. 1992. *Ecosystem Health: New Goals for Environmental Management*. Washington, D.C.: Island Press.

Costanza, Robert, John Cumberland, Herman Daly, Robert Goodland, and Richard Norgaard, eds. 1997. *An Introduction to Ecological Economics*. Boca Raton, Fla.: St. Lucie Press.

Council on Environmental Quality. 1980. *The Eleventh Annual Report*. Washington, D.C.: Government Printing Office.

Cranor, Carl F. 1993. *Regulating Toxic Substances*. New York: Oxford University Press.

Crow, Patrick. 1993. "Back To Work: Wilderness and Oil." *Oil and Gas Journal* 56:32.

Davidson, Donald. 1980. *Essays on Action and Events*. Oxford, U.K.: The Clarendon Press.

Deleuze, Gilles. 1984. *Kant's Critical Philosophy*. Minneapolis: University of Minnesota Press.

Devall, Bill, and George Sessions. 1985. *Deep Ecology: Living as if Nature Mattered*. Salt Lake City, Utah: Peregrine Smith Books.

Dickens, Charles. [1854] 1961. *Hard Times*. New York: Signet.

DiIulio, John H. Jr., ed. 1994. *Deregulating the Public Service*. Washington, D.C.: Brookings Institution Press.

Director, Aaron. 1964. "The Parity of the Economic Market Place." *Journal of Law and Economics* 7:1–10.

Doherty, Jim. 1992. "When Folks Say 'Cutting Edge' at the Nez, They Don't Mean Saws: Nez Perce National Forest." *Smithsonian* 23 (September), pp. 32–40.

Donagan, Alan. 1968. "Is There a Credible Form of Utilitarianism?" In *Contemporary Utilitarianism*, edited by Michael Bayles, pp. 187–201. Gloucester, Mass.: Peter Smith.

———. 1977. *The Theory of Morality*. Chicago: University of Chicago Press.

Dorfman, Robert, and Nancy S. Dorfman, eds. 1977. *Economics of the Environment: Selected Readings*. 2nd ed. New York: W. W. Norton

Dower, Roger C. 1990. "Hazardous Wastes." In *Public Policies for Environmental Protection*, edited by Paul R. Portey, pp. 151–94. Washington, D.C.: Resources for the Future.

Downes, C. J. 1985. "Redox Reactions, Mineral Equilibria, and Ground Water Quality in New Zealand Aquifers." In *Groundwater Quality*, edited by C. H. Ward, W. Giger and P. L. McCarty, pp. 94–121. New York: John Wiley and Sons.

Downs, Anthony. 1957. *An Economic Theory of Democracy*. New York: Harper and Row.

Drury, William Holland Jr. 1998. *Chance and Change: Ecology for Conservationists*. Berkeley and Los Angeles: University of California Press.

Dryzek, John S. 1983. *Conflict and Choice in Resource Management: The Case of Alaska*. Boulder, Colo.: Westview Press.

———. 1987. *Rational Ecology*. Oxford, U.K.: Basil Blackwell.

———. 1990. *Discursive Democracy: Politics, Policy and Political Science*. Cambridge, U.K.: Cambridge University Press.

Dunn, William N. 1981. *Public Policy Analysis*. Englewood Cliffs, N.J.: Prentice-Hall.

Dworkin, Ronald. 1980. "Why Efficiency?" In *Law, Economics and Philosophy*, edited by M. Kuperberg and C. Beitz, pp. 123–42. Totowa, N.J.: Rowman and Allenheld.

Easterbrook, Gregg. 1995. *A Moment on the Earth: The Coming Age of Environmental Optimism*. New York: Penguin Books.

Elkin, Stephen L. 1983. "Economic and Political Rationality." *Polity* 18:253–71. Reprinted in Gillroy and Wade 1992, pp. 353–70.

Elliot, Robert, and Arran Gare, eds. 1983. *Environmental Philosophy*. University Park, Pa.: Penn State University Press.

Ellis, Ralph D. 1998. *Just Results: Ethical Foundations for Policy Analysis*. Washington, D.C.: Georgetown University Press.

Elster, Jon. 1979. *Ulysses and the Sirens: Studies in Rationality and Irrationality*. Cambridge, U.K.: Cambridge University Press.

———. 1983. *Sour Grapes*. Cambridge, U.K.: Cambridge University Press.

———. 1989. "Marxism, Functionalism, and Game Theory: The Case for Methodolgical Individualism." In *Marxist Theory*, edited by Alex Callinicos, pp. 48–87. Oxford, U.K.: Oxford University Press.

Environmental Protection Agency. 1987. *Unfinished Business: A Comparative Assessment of Environmental Problems*. Washington, D.C.

———. 1990. *Reducing Risk: Setting Priorities and Strategies for Environmental Protection*, Science Advisory Board. (SAB-EC-90–021). Washington, D.C.

———. 1993. *A Guidebook to Comparing Risks and Setting Environmental Priorities*. (EPA 230-B-93–003). Washington, D.C.

Epstein, Samuel S., Lester O. Brown, and Carl Pope. 1982. *Hazardous Waste in America*. San Francisco, Calif.: Sierra Club Books.

Evernden, Neil. 1985. *The Natural Alien: Humankind and Environment*. Toronto: University of Toronto Press.

Feinberg, Joel. 1973. *Social Philosophy*. Englewood Cliffs, N.J.: Prentice-Hall.

Feldman, Allan. 1980. *Welfare Economics and Social Choice Theory*. Boston: Martinus Nijhoff.

Findley, Roger W., and Daniel A. Farber. 1992. *Environmental Law in a Nutshell*. 3rd ed. St. Paul, Minn.: West Publishing.

Fischer, Frank. 1980. *Politics, Values, and Public Policy: The Problem of Methodology*. Boulder, Colo.: Westview Press.

Fischer, Frank, and John Forester, eds. 1993. *The Argumentative Turn in Policy Analysis and Planning*. Durham, N.C.: Duke University Press.

Fischer, John N. 1986. *Hydrogeologic Factors in the Selection of Shallow Land Burial Sites for the Disposal of Low-Level Radioactive Waste*. Washington, D.C.: U.S.G.S. Circular 973.

Fishburn, Peter C. 1982. *The Foundations of Expected Utility*. Dordrecht, Holland: D. Reidel.

Fisher, Anthony C. 1981. *Resources and Environmental Economics*. Cambridge, U.K.: Cambridge University Press.

Fishkin, James S. 1979. *Tyranny and Legitimacy: A Critique of Political Theories*. Baltimore, Md.: Johns Hopkins University Press.

405

Foot, Philippa, ed. 1967. *Theories of Ethics*. New York: Oxford University Press.

Forester, John. 1993. *Critical Theory, Public Policy, and Planning Practice: Toward a Critical Pragmatism*. Albany, N.Y.: SUNY Press.

Frankena, William K. 1962. "The Concept of Social Justice." In *Social Justice*, edited by R. B. Brandt, pp. 1–31. Englewood Cliffs, N.J.: Prentice-Hall.

———. 1967. "The Naturalistic Fallacy." In *Theories of Ethics*, edited by Philippa Foot, pp. 50–63. New York: Oxford University Press.

Freeman, A. Myrick III. 1993. *The Measurement of Environmental and Resource Values: Theory and Method*. Washington, D.C.: Resources for the Future.

Freeman, Samuel, ed. 1999. *John Rawls: Collected Papers*. Cambridge, Mass.: Harvard University Press.

Freeze, R. Allen, and John A. Cherry. 1979. *Groundwater*. Englewood Cliffs, N.J.: Prentice-Hall.

Fried, Charles. 1977. "Difficulties in the Economic Analysis of Rights." In *Markets and Morals*, edited by G. Dworkin, G. Bermantrand, and P. Brown, pp. 175–95. New York: John Wiley and Sons. Reprinted in Gillroy and Wade 1992, pp. 217–36.

Friedman, Lee S. 1984. *Microeconomic Policy Analysis*. New York: McGraw-Hill.

Friedman, Milton. 1953. *Essays in Positive Economics*. Chicago: University of Chicago Press.

Frome, Michael. 1997. *Battle for the Wilderness*. Rev. ed. Salt Lake City: University of Utah Press.

Galston, William. 1980. *Justice and the Human Good*. Chicago: University of Chicago Press.

———. 1991. *Liberal Purposes*. New York: Cambridge University Press.

Garner, Lynn. 1993. "GAO Confirms Interior Study's Findings on Potential of Alaska's Arctic Refuge." *Oil Daily* 43:1.

Gauthier, David. 1969. *The Logic of Leviathan*. Oxford, U.K.: Clarendon Press.

———. 1986. *Moral by Agreement*. Oxford, U.K.: Clarendon Press.

Geraghty, J., and P. Miller. 1983. "Application of Generalized Containment Option Design and Cost Information to the Biscayne Aquifer, Florida." Washington, D.C.: Environmental Protection Agency, Mimeo.

Gewirth, Alan. 1978. *Reason and Morality*. Chicago: University of Chicago Press.

Gillroy, John Martin. 1991. "Moral Considerations and Public Choices: Individual Autonomy and the NIMBY Problem." *Public Affairs Quarterly* 5:319–32.

———. 1992a. "The Ethical Poverty of Cost-Benefit Methods: Autonomy, Efficiency and Public Policy Choice." *Policy Sciences* 25:83–102. Reprinted in Gillroy and Wade 1992, pp. 195–216.

———. 1992b. "Public Policy and Environmental Risk: Political Theory, Human Agency, and the Imprisoned Rider." *Environmental Ethics* 14:217–37.

———. 1992c. "A Kantian Argument Supporting Public Policy Choice." In *The Moral Dimensions of Public Policy Choice: Beyond the Market Paradigm*, edited by John Martin Gillroy and Maurice Wade, pp. 491–515. Pittsburgh, Pa.: University of Pittsburgh Press.

———, ed. 1993. *Environmental Risk, Environmental Values and Political Choices: Beyond Efficiency Trade-Offs in Public Policy Analysis*. Boulder, Colo.: Westview Press.

———. 1994. "When Responsive Public Policy Does Not Equal Responsible Government." In *The Ethics of Liberal Democracy: Morality and Democracy in Theory and Practice*, edited by Robert Paul Churchill, pp. 177–88. Oxford, U.K.: Berg Publishing.

———. 1995. "Comparative Risk." In *Encyclopedia of Conservation and Environmentalism*, edited by Robert Paehlke, pp. 144–47. New York: Garland Publishing.

———. 1998. "Beyond Sustainability: Toward An Ecosystem Approach to Natural Systems Preservation in Environmental Policy." Paper presented to the Annual Meeting of the American Political Science Association, Boston, Mass.

———. 2000. "Justice from Autonomy: Kant as an Alternative to Rawls in Making Public Choices." *Kant Studien* 91:44–72.

Gillroy, John Martin, and Barry G. Rabe. 1997. "Environmental Risk and the Politics of Assurance: Alternative Approaches to Waste Facility Siting." *Risk Decision and Policy* 2:245–58.

Gillroy, John Martin, and Robert Y. Shapiro. 1986. "The Polls: Environmental Policy." *Public Opinion Quarterly* 50:270–79.

Gillroy, John Martin, and Maurice Wade, eds. 1992. *The Moral Dimensions of Public Policy Choice: Beyond the Market Paradigm*. Pittsburgh, Pa.: University of Pittsburgh Press.

Goedecke, Robert. 1973. "Kant and the Radical Regrounding of the Norms of Politics." *Journal of Value Inquiry* 2:81–95.

Golly, Frank Benjamin. 1993. *A History of the Ecosystem Concept in Ecology*. New Haven, Conn.: Yale University Press.

Goodin, Robert E. 1976. *The Politics of Rational Man*. London: John Wiley and Sons.

———. 1983. "Ethical Principles for Environmental Protection." In *Environmental Philosophy*, edited by R. Elliot and A. Gare, pp. 3–20. Reprinted in Gillroy and Wade 1992, pp. 411–26.

———. 1985. *Protecting the Vulnerable*. Chicago: University of Chicago Press.

Goodpaster, K. E. 1979. "From Egoism to Environmentalism." In *Ethics and the 21st Century*, edited by K. E. Goodpaster and K. M. Sayre, pp. 21–35. Notre Dame, Ind.: Notre Dame University Press.

Goodpaster, K. E., and K. M. Sayre, eds. 1979. *Ethics and the 21st Century*. Notre Dame, Ind.: Notre Dame University Press.

Gordon, George J. 1992. *Public Administration in America*. 4th ed. New York: St. Martin's Press.

Gordon, John C. 1993. "Ecosystem Management: An Idiosyncratic Overview." In *Defining Sustainable Forestry*, edited by Gregory H. Aplet, Nels Johnson, Jeffrey T. Olson, and V. Alaric Sample, pp. 240–45. Washington, D.C.: Island Press.

Gore, Al. 1992. *Earth in the Balance: Ecology and the Human Spirit*. Boston: Houghton Mifflin.

Governor's Citizen Advisory Committee (GCAC). 1990. *Colorado Environment 2000: Final Report*. Denver, Colo., June.

Graham, John, Laura Green, and Marc Roberts. 1988. *In Search of Safety: Chemicals and Cancer Risk*. Cambridge, Mass.: Harvard University Press.

Graham, John, and Jonathan Weiner, eds. 1997. *RISK v. RISK*. Cambridge, Mass.: Harvard University Press.

Gramlich, Edward M. 1981. *Benefit-Cost Analysis of Government Programs*. Englewood Cliffs, N.J.: Prentice-Hall.

Green, Donald P., and Ian Shapiro. 1994. *Pathologies of Rational Choice Theory*. New Haven, Conn.: Yale University Press.

Green, Thomas Hill. [1881] 1981. "Liberal Legislation and Freedom of Contract." In *T. H. Green: Lectures on the Principles of Political Obligation and Other Writings*, edited by Paul Harris and John Marrow, pp. 194–212. Cambridge, U.K.: Cambridge University Press.

Greenstone, David J. 1993. *The Lincoln Persuasion*. Princeton, N.J.: Princeton University Press.

Grim, John. 1983. *The Shaman*. Norman: University of Oklahoma Press.

Habermas, Jürgen. 1971. *Knowledge and Human Interest*. Trans. by Jeremy J. Shapiro. Boston: Beacon Press.

———. 1984. *The Theory of Communicative Action*. Vol. 1, *Reason and the Rationalization of Society*. Trans. by Thomas McCarthy. Boston, Mass.: Beacon Press.

———. 1994. "Struggle for Recognition in the Democratic Constitutional State." In *Multiculturalism*, edited by Charles Taylor and Amy Gutmann, pp. 107–48. Princeton, N.J.: Princeton University Press.

———. 1996. *Between Facts and Norms: Contributions to a Discourse Theory of Law and Democracy*. Trans. by William Rehg. Cambridge, Mass.: MIT Press.

Hacker, P. M. S., and J. Raz, eds. 1977. *Law, Morality, and Society*. Oxford, U.K.: The Clarendon Press.

Haigh, J. A., David Harrison, and Albert Nichols. 1984. "Benefit Cost Analysis of Environmental Regulation: Case Studies of Air Pollutants." *Harvard Environmental Law Review* 8:395–434. Reprinted in Gillroy and Wade 1992, pp. 15–58.

Hamilton, Joan. 1992. "Highly Unusual Politics." *Sierra* 77. July/August, p. 14.

Hampton, Jean. 1986. *Hobbes and the Social Contract*. New York: Cambridge University Press.

Hanushek, Eric A., and John Jackson. 1977. *Statistical Methods for Social Scientists*. Orlando, Fla.: Academic Press.

Hardin, Garrett. 1968. "The Tragedy of the Commons." *Science* 162:1243–45.

———. 1993. *Living within Limits*. New York: Oxford University Press.

Hardin, Russell. 1971. "Collective Action as an Agreeable *n* — Persons' Prisoner's Dilemma." *Behavioral Science* 16:472–81. Reprinted in Gillroy and Wade 1992, pp. 251–67.

———. 1982a. *Collective Action*. Baltimore, Md.: Johns Hopkins University Press.

———. 1982b. "Difficulties in the Notion of Economic Rationality." *Social Science Information* 23:436–67. Reprinted in Gillroy and Wade 1992, pp. 313–24.

———. 1988. *Morality within the Limits of Reason Alone*. Chicago: University of Chicago Press.

Hargrove, Eugene, ed. 1992. *The Animal Rights–Environmental Ethics Debate*, Albany, N.Y: SUNY Press.

Harlow, Elizabeth M. 1992. "The Human Face of Nature: Environmental Values and the Limits of Nonanthropocentrism." *Environmental Ethics* 14:27–42.

Harris, Jeffrey S. 1994. *Strategic Health Management : A Guide for Employers, Employees, and Policy Makers*. San Francisco, Calif.: Jossey-Bass Publishers.

Hart, H. L. A. 1961. *The Concept of Law*. Oxford, U.K.: The Clarendon Press.

———. 1963. *Law, Liberty and Morality*. Stanford, Calif.: Stanford University Press.

Hayek, Friedrich A. 1976. *Law, Legislation and Liberty*. Vol. 2, *The Mirage of Social Justice*. Chicago: University of Chicago Press.

Hegel, G. W. F. [1821] 1978. *The Philosophy of Right*. Trans. by T. M. Knox. Oxford, U.K.: Oxford University Press.

Held, Virginia, ed. 1980. *Property, Profits and Economic Justice*. Belmont, Calif.: Wadsworth.

Henderson, David E. 1993. "Science, Environmental Values, and Policy Prescriptions." In *Environmental Risk, Environmental Values, and Political Choices: Beyond Efficiency Trade-Offs in Public Policy Analysis*, edited by John Martin Gillroy, pp. 94–112. Boulder, Colo.: Westview Press.

Hicks, Joe H. 1971. "Is Kant's Theory of Justice Self-Defeating?" *Southwestern Journal of Philosophy* 2:205–17.

Hill, Thomas E. Jr. 1973. "The Hypothetical Imperative." *Philosophical Review* 82:429–50.

———. 1980. "Humanity as an End in Itself." *Ethics* 91:84–90.

———. 1991. *Autonomy and Self-Respect*. Cambridge, U.K.: Cambridge University Press.

Hirschman, Albert O. 1982. *Shifting Involvements: Private Interests and Public Action*. Princeton, N.J.: Princeton University Press.

Hoban, Thomas More, and Richard Oliver Brooks. 1987. *Green Justice: The Environment and the Courts*. Boulder, Colo.: Westview Press.

Hobbes, Thomas. [1651] 1968. *Leviathan*. Edited by C. B. Macpherson. Pelican Classics. Harmondsworth, Middlesex: Penguin Books.

Hume, David. [1740] 1975. *A Treatise of Human Nature*. Edited by L. A. Selby Bigge. Oxford, U.K.: Clarendon Press.

Hunter, David, James Salzman, and Durwood Zaelke. 1998. *International Environmental Law and Policy*. University Casebook Series. New York: Foundation Press.

Jantsch, Erich, and Conrad H. Waddington. 1976. *Evolution and Consciousness*. Reading, Mass.: Addison-Wesley Publishing.

Jasanoff, Sheila. 1986. *Risk Management and Political Culture: A Comparative Study of Science in the Policy Context*. New York: Russell Sage Foundation.

———. 1990. *The Fifth Branch: Science Advisers as Policymakers*. Cambridge, Mass.: Harvard University Press.

Jenkins-Smith, Hank C. 1990. *Democratic Politics and Policy Analysis*. Pacific Grove, Calif.: Brooks Cole Publishing.

Johnson, Lawrence. 1991. *A Morally Deep World: An Essay on Moral Significance and Environmental Ethics*. Cambridge, U.K.: Cambridge University Press.

Johnson, Peter. 1993. *Frames of Deceit: A Study of Loss and Recovery of Public and Private Trust*. Cambridge, U.K.: Cambridge University Press.

Jun, Jong S. 1986. *Public Administration: Design and Problem Solving*. New York: Macmillan Publishing.

Kant, Immanuel. *Gesammelte Schriften*. Berlin: Prussian Academy of Sciences. [All citations are by academy page, book [BK] or section [§] number where the initials, dates, and volume [V] numbers indicate specific texts. All English translations of the works below reference these academy page numbers. The only exception is the translation of (LT) by Allen Wood and Gertrude Clark (Cornell, 1978), which does not list academy page numbers. For the convenience of the reader, all citations to this work have page references to the Cornell translation.]

(LE) 1755. *Lectures On Ethics*. [V27; V29]

(LT) 1783. *Lectures on Philosophical Theology*. [V28]

(UH) 1784. *Idea for a Universal History from a Cosmopolitan Point of View*. [V8]

(GW) 1786. *Groundwork for a Metaphysics of Morals*. [V4]

(C1) 1787. *First Critique: Critique of Pure Reason*. [V3(A)/V4(B)]

(C2) 1788. *Second Critique: Critique of Practical Reason*. [V5]

(C3) 1790. *Third Critique: Critique of Judgment*. [V5]

(TP) 1792. *Theory and Practice*. [V8]

(RL) 1793. *Religion within the Limits of Reason*. [V6]

(PP) 1795. *Perpetual Peace*. [V8]

(MJ) 1797. *Metaphysics of Morals: Principles of Justice*. [V6]

(MV) 1797. *Metaphysics of Morals: Principles of Virtue*. [V6]

(SF) 1798. *The Strife of the Faculties*. [V7]

(AT) 1800. *The Anthropology*. [V7]

(OP) 1803. *Opus Postumum*. [V21; V22]

Kavka, Gregory S. 1986. *Hobbesian Moral and Political Theory*. Princeton, N.J.: Princeton University Press.

Kelman, Steven. 1981a. "Cost-Benefit Analysis: An Ethical Critique." *Regulation* 10:33–40. Reprinted in Gillroy and Wade 1992, pp. 153–64.

———. 1981b. *What Price Incentives?* Boston, Mass.: Auburn House.

———. 1987. *Making Public Policy: A Hopeful View of American Government*. New York: Basic Books.

Kempton, Willett, James S. Boster, and Jennifer A. Hartley. 1995. *Environmental Values in American Culture*. Cambridge, Mass.: MIT.

Kersting, Wolfgang. 1992. "Politics, Freedom, and Order: Kant's Political Philosophy." In *The Cambridge Companion to Kant*, edited by Paul Guyer, pp. 342–66. Cambridge, U.K.: Cambridge University Press.

Kessler, Winifred B., and Hal Salwasser. 1995. "Natural Resource Agencies: Transforming from Within." In *A New Century For Natural Resources Management*, edited by Richard L. Knight and Sarah F. Bates, pp. 171–88. Washington, D.C.: Island Press.

Knight, Richard L., and Sarah F. Bates, eds. 1995. *A New Century for Natural Resources Management*. Washington, D.C.: Island Press.

Korsgaard, Christine M. 1996. *Creating the Kingdom of Ends*. Cambridge, U.K.: Cambridge University Press.

Kraus, Jody S. 1993. *The Limits of Hobbesian Contractarianism*. New York: Cambridge University Press.

Kuflik, Arthur. 1984. "The Inalienability of Autonomy." *Philosophy and Public Affairs* 13:271–98. Reprinted in Gillroy and Wade 1992, pp. 465–90.

Kuhn, Thomas S. 1962. *The Structure of Scientific Revolutions*. 2nd. enlarged ed. Chicago: University of Chicago Press.

Kymlicka, Will. 1989. *Liberalism, Community, and Culture*. Oxford, U.K.: Clarendon Press.

———. 1990. *Contemporary Political Philosophy: An Introduction*. Oxford, U.K.: Clarendon Press.

Ladd, John. 1984. Review of *Kant's Political Philosophy*, by Patrick Riley. *Political Theory* 12:124–27.

Laitos, Jan G. 1985. *Natural Resources Law: Cases and Material*. American Casebook Series. St. Paul, Minn.: West Publishing.

Landy, Marc, Marc J. Roberts, and Stephen R. Thomas. 1990. *The Environmental Protection Agency: Asking the Wrong Questions*. New York: Oxford University Press.

Lane, L. W. 1984. "Wilderness: We're Losing Ground." *Sunset* 172:296.

Larmore, Charles E. 1987. *Patterns of Moral Complexity*. Cambridge, U.K.: Cambridge University Press.

———. 1996. *The Morals of Modernity*. Cambridge, U.K.: Cambridge University Press.

Larrabee, Mary Jeanne, ed. 1993. *An Ethic of Care: Feminist and Interdisciplinary Perspectives*. London: Routledge.

Lave, Lester B. 1981. *The Strategy of Social Regulation: Decision Frameworks for Policy*. Washington, D.C.: Brookings Institution Press.

410

Laver, Michael. 1981. *The Politics of Private Desires*. New York: Penguin Books.
———. 1986. *Social Choice and Public Policy*. Oxford, U.K: Blackwell.
Layard, Richard, ed. 1972. *Cost-Benefit Analysis*. Harmondsworth, Middlesex: Penguin Books.
Lehman, Scott. 1995. *Privatizing Public Lands*. New York: Oxford University Press.
Leonard, Herman B., and Richard J. Zeckhauser. 1986. "Cost-Benefit Analysis Applied to Risk: Its Philosophy and Legitimacy." In *Values At Risk*, edited by Douglas MacLean, pp. 31–48. Totowa, N.J.: Roman and Allanheld.
Leopold, Aldo. 1977. *A Sand County Almanac*. New York: Ballantine.
Lewis, David. 1969. *Convention: A Philosophical Study*. Cambridge, Mass.: Harvard University Press.
Lincoln, Abraham. [1858] 1989. *Speeches and Writings 1832–1858*. New York: Library of America.
Lindblom, Charles E. 1990. *Inquiry and Change*. New Haven, Conn.: Yale University Press.
Lipsey, R. G., and Kelvin Lancaster. 1956. "The General Theory of Second Best." *Review of Economic Studies* 24:11–32.
Locke, John. [1690] 1988. *Two Treatises of Government*. Edited by Peter Laslett. Cambridge, U.K.: Cambridge University Press.
Lousiana Department of Environmental Quality (LDEQ). 1991. *Leap to 2000: Louisiana's Environmental Action Plan*. Baton Rouge, La., November.
Lowry, William R. 1994. *The Capacity for Wonder: Preserving National Parks*. Washington, D.C.: Brookings Institution Press.
———. 1998. *Preserving Public Lands for the Future: The Politics of Intergenerational Goods*. Washington, D.C.: Georgetown University Press.
Luce, R. Duncan, and Howard Raiffa. 1957. *Games and Decisions: Introduction and Critical Survey*. New York: John Wiley and Sons.
Lund, Thomas A. 1980. *American Wildlife Law*. Berkeley and Los Angeles: University of California Press.
MacCormick, Neil. 1981. *H. L. A. Hart*, Stanford, Calif.: Stanford University Press.
MacIntyre, Alasdair. 1977. "Utilitarianism and Cost-Benefit Analysis: An Essay on the Relevance of Moral Philosophy to Bureaucratic Theory." In *Values in the Electric Power Industry*, edited by Kenneth Sayre, pp. 217–37. South Bend, Ind.: Notre Dame University Press. Reprinted in Gillroy and Wade 1992, pp. 179–94.
———. 1981. *After Virtue: A Study in Moral Theory*. South Bend, Ind.: Notre Dame University Press.
MacLean, Douglas, ed. 1986. *Values at Risk*. Totowa, N.J.: Roman and Allanheld.
MacRae, Duncan Jr. 1976. *The Social Function of Social Science*. New Haven, Conn.: Yale University Press.
Majchrzak, Ann. 1984. *Methods for Policy Research*. Newbury Park, Calif.: Sage Publications.

Majone, Giandomenico. 1989. *Evidence, Argument and Persuasion in the Policy Process*. New Haven, Conn: Yale University Press.

Mandelker, Daniel R., and Roger A. Cunningham. 1990. *Planning and Control of Land Development: Cases and Materials*. 3rd ed. Charlottesville, Va.: Michie.

Manheim, Jarol B., and Richard C. Rich. 1986. *Empirical Political Analysis*. 2nd ed. New York: Longman.

March, James, and Herbert Simon. 1958. *Organizations*. New York: John Wiley and Sons.

Masterman, Margaret. 1970. "The Nature of a Paradigm." In *Criticism and the Growth of Knowledge*, edited by Imre Lakatos and Alan Musgrave, pp. 59–90. Cambridge, U.K.: Cambridge University Press.

Masters, Roger D. 1968. *The Political Philosophy of Rousseau*. Princeton, N.J.: Princeton University Press.

Mayr, Ernst. 1976. *Evolution and the Diversity of Life*. Cambridge, Mass.: Harvard University.

McCloskey, H. J. 1983. *Ecological Ethics and Politics*. Totowa, N.J.: Rowman and Littlefield.

McGuiness, C. L. 1963. *The Role of Groundwater in the National Water Situation*. Washington, D.C.: U.S.G.S. Water Supply, Paper no. 1800.

McLaren, Ronald. 1989. *Solving Moral Problems*. Mountain View, Calif.: Mayfield Publishing.

Meehan, Eugene. 1981. *Reasoned Argument in Social Science*. Westport, Conn.: Greenwood Press.

———. 1990. *Ethics for Policy Making: A Methodological Analysis*. Westport, Conn.: Greenwood Press.

Merchant, Carolyn. 1989. *Ecological Revolutions: Nature, Gender, and Science in New England*. Chapel Hill: University of North Carolina Press.

Mesarovic, Mihajlo, and Eduard Pestel. 1974. *Mankind at the Turning Point*. New York: Dutton.

Mill, John Stuart. [1859] 1947. *On Liberty*. Edited by Alburey Castell. Arlington Heights, Ill: AHM Publishing.

Mills, Edwin S., and Philip E. Graves. 1986. *The Economics of Environmental Quality*. 2nd ed. New York: W. W. Norton.

Minard, Richard. 1991. *Hard Choices: States Use Risk to Refine Environmental Priorities*. South Royalton, Vt.: Northeast Center for Comparative Risk.

Minard, Richard, and Ken Jones. 1993. *State Comparative Risk Projects: A Force for Change*. South Royalton, Vt.: Northeast Center for Comparative Risk.

Mishan, E. J. 1982a. *Cost-Benefit Analysis*. 3rd ed. London: George Allwyn and Unwin.

———. 1982b. *What Is Political Economy All About?* Cambridge, U.K.: Cambridge University Press.

Mishan, E. J., and Talbot Page. 1992. "The Methodology of Benefit Cost Analysis with Particular Reference to the CFC Program." In *The Moral Dimensions of Public Policy Choice: Beyond the Market Paradigm*, edited by John Martin Gillroy and Maurice Wade, pp. 59–113. Pittsburgh, Pa: University of Pittsburgh Press.

Moore, G. E. 1903. *Principia Ethica*. Cambridge, U.K.: Cambridge University Press.

Mueller, Dennis C. 1979. *Public Choice*. Cambridge, U.K.: Cambridge University Press.

Muir, John. [1918] 1992. *The Eight Wilderness Discovery Books*. London: Diadem.

Mulholland, Leslie. 1990. *Kant's System of Rights*. New York: Columbia University Press.

Murphy, Jeffrie G. 1970. *Kant: The Philosophy of Right*. London: Macmillan.

Nagel, Thomas. 1986. *The View from Nowhere*. New York: Oxford University Press.

Nash, Roderick Frazier. 1967. *Wilderness and the American Mind*. New Haven, Conn.: Yale University Press.

———. 1989. *The Rights of Nature*. Madison: University of Wisconsin Press.

National Research Council. 1983. *Risk Assessment in the Federal Government: Managing the Process*. Washington, D.C.: NRC Press.

———. 1990. *Groundwater Models: Scientific and Regulatory Applications*. Washington, D.C.: NRC Press.

National Science Foundation. 1983. *Groundwater Resources and Contamination in the United States*. Washington, D.C.: NSF Press.

Nell, Onora. 1975. *Acting on Principle: An Essay on Kantian Ethics*. New York: Columbia University Press.

Norton, Bryan. 1986. "Conservation and Preservation: A Conceptual Rehabilitation." *Environmental Ethics* 8:195–220.

———. 1987. *Why Preserve Natural Variety?* Princeton, N.J.: Princeton University Press.

Noss, Reed F., and Allen Y. Cooperrider. 1994. *Saving Nature's Legacy: Protecting and Restoring Biodiversity*. Washington, D.C.: Island Press.

Nozick, Robert. 1974. *Anarchy, State, and Utopia*. New York: Basic Books.

Odum, Eugene P. 1975. *Ecology: The Link between the Natural and Social Sciences*. New York: Holt, Rinehart and Winston.

———. 1993. *Ecology and Our Endangered Life-Support Systems*. 2nd ed. Sunderland, Mass.: Sinauer Assoc.

O'Leary, Rosemary. 1993. *Environmental Change: Federal Courts and the EPA*. Philadelphia, Pa.: Temple University Press.

Olson, Mancur. 1971. *The Logic of Collective Action*. Cambridge, Mass.: Harvard University Press.

O'Neill, John. 1993. *Ecology, Policy and Politics: Human Well-Being and the Natural World*. London: Routledge.

O'Neill, R. V., D. L. DeAngelis, J. B. Waide, and T. F. H. Allen. 1986. *A Hierarchical Concept of Ecosystems*. Princeton, N.J.: Princeton University Press.

Ostrom, Elinor. 1990. *Governing the Commons: The Evaluation of Institutions for Collective Action*. Cambridge, U.K.: Cambridge University Press.

Paehlke, Robert. 1989. *Environmentalism and the Future of Progressive Politics*. New Haven, Conn.: Yale University Press.

———. 1993. "Environmentalism: Values to Politics to Policy." In *Environmental Risk, Environmental Values and Political Choices: Beyond Efficiency*

Trade-Offs in Public Policy Analysis, edited by John Martin Gillroy, pp. 44–58.

Page, Talbot. 1973. *Economics of Involuntary Transfer*. Berlin: Springer-Verlag.

———. 1977. *Conservation and Economic Efficiency: An Approach to Materials Policy*. Baltimore, Md.: Johns Hopkins University Press.

———. 1978. "A Generic View of Toxic Chemicals and Similar Risks." *Ecology Law Quarterly* 7:207–44.

———. 1983a. "Intergenerational Justice as Opportunity." In *Energy and the Future*, edited by Douglas MacLean and Peter Brown, pp. 38–58. Totowa, N.J.: Rowman and Littlefield. Reprinted in Gillroy and Wade 1992, pp. 443–64.

———. 1983b. *Biscayne Aquifer Case Studies: Comments*. Pasadena, Calif.: California Institute of Technology, Mimeo.

———. 1986. "Responsibility, Liability and Incentive Compatibility." *Ethics* 97:240–62.

Page, Talbot, and Douglas MacLean. 1983. *Risk Conservatism and the Circumstances of Utility Theory*. Pasadena, Calif.: California Institute of Technology, Mimeo.

Paris, David C., and James F. Reynolds. 1983. *The Logic of Policy Inquiry*. New York: Longman.

Passmore, John. 1974. *Man's Responsibility for Nature*. New York: Charles Scribner's and Sons.

Pateman, Carole. 1988. *The Sexual Contract*. Stanford, Calif.: Stanford University Press.

Paton, H. J. 1948. *The Categorical Imperative: A Study in Kant's Moral Philosophy*. Chicago: University of Chicago Press.

Pearce, David W., and R. Kerry Turner. 1990. *Economics of Natural Resources and the Environment*. Baltimore, Md.: Johns Hopkins University Press.

Pearson, Mark. 1992. "The Private Parts of Paradise: Inholdings and the Integrity of Wilderness." *Wilderness* 56: at 20.

Pease, William S. 1991. "Chemical Hazards and the Public's Right to Know: How Effective Is California's Proposition 65?" *Environment* 33:12–20.

Percival, Robert V., Allan S. Miller, Christopher H. Schroeder, and James P. Leape. 1992. *Environmental Regulation: Law, Science, and Policy*. Boston: Little, Brown.

Pigou, A. C. 1932. *The Economics of Welfare*. 4th ed. London: Macmillan.

Pimentel, David, and Hugh Lehman, eds. 1996. *The Pesticide Question*. New York: Chapman and Hall.

Pimm, Stuart L. 1991. *The Balance of Nature?* Chicago: University of Chicago Press.

Pinchot, Gifford. 1947. *Breaking New Ground*. Washington, D.C.: Island Press. (Commemorative edition, 1998.)

Plant, Raymond. 1991. *Modern Political Thought*. Oxford, U.K.: Basil Blackwell.

Portey, Paul R., ed. 1990. *Public Policies for Environmental Protection*. Washington, D.C.: Resources for the Future.

Posner, Richard. 1977. *Economic Analysis of Law*. 2nd ed. Boston: Little, Brown.

———. 1983. *The Economics of Justice*. Cambridge, Mass.: Harvard University Press.

Power, Thomas Michael. 1993. "The Price of Everything." *Sierra* 78:86–96.

Primack, Richard B. 1993. *Essentials of Conservation Biology*. Sunderland, Mass.: Sinauer Associates.

Pye, Veronica. 1983. "Groundwater Contamination in the United States." In National Science Foundation. *Groundwater Resources and Contamination in the United States*, pp. 17–64. Washington, D.C.: NSF Press.

Pye, Veronica, Ruth Patrick, and John Quarles. 1983. *Groundwater Contamination in the United States*. Philadelphia, Pa.: University of Pennsylvania Press.

Rabe, Barry. 1988. "The Politics of Environmental Dispute Resolution." *Policy Studies*. 16:585–601.

———. 1989a. "The Hazardous Waste Dilemma and the Hazards of Institutionalizing Negotiation." Ann Arbor: University of Michigan, Mimeo.

———. 1989b. "Hazardous Waste Facility Siting: Subnational Policy in Canada and the United States." Ann Arbor: University of Michigan, Mimeo.

———. 1995. *Beyond NIMBY*. Washington, D.C.: Brookings Institution Press.

Rabe, Barry, and John Martin Gillroy. 1993. "Intrinsic Value and Public Policy Choice: The Alberta Case." In *Environmental Risk, Environmental Values and Political Choices: Beyond Efficiency Trade-Offs in Public Policy Analysis*, edited by John Martin Gillroy, pp. 150–70. Boulder, Colo.: Westview Press.

———. 2000. "NIMBY, Assurance Politics and Dynamic Collective Action." Ann Arbor: University of Michigan, Mimeo.

Raucher, Robert. 1983. "The Benefits of Protecting Groundwater: A Summary of Biscayne Aquifer Case Studies." Washington D.C.: Environmental Protection Agency, Mimeo.

———. 1984. "The Benefits and Costs of Policies Related to Groundwater Contamination." Washington, D.C.: Environmental Protection Agency, Mimeo.

Rawls, John. 1971. *A Theory of Justice*. Cambridge, Mass.: Harvard University Press.

———. 1993. *Political Liberalism*. New York: Columbia University Press.

Regan, Tom, ed. 1980a. *Matters of Life and Death*. New York: Random House.

———. 1980b. "Animal Rights, Human Wrongs." *Environmental Ethics* 2:99–120.

———. 1982. *All That Dwell Within*. Berkeley and Los Angeles: University of California Press.

Rhoads, Steven E. 1985. *The Economist's View of the World: Government, Markets and Public Policy*. Cambridge, U.K.: Cambridge University Press.

Riley, Patrick. 1982. *Will and Political Legitimacy: A Critical Exposition of Social Contract Theory in Hobbes, Locke, Rousseau, Kant and Hegel*. Cambridge, Mass.: Harvard University Press.

———. 1983. *Kant's Political Philosophy*. Totowa, N.J.: Rowman and Littlefield.

————. 1986. *The General Will before Rousseau*. Princeton, N.J.: Princeton University Press.

Ritter, Alan, and Julia Conaway Bondanella, eds. and trans. 1988. *Rousseau's Political Writings*. New York: W. W. Norton.

Ritzer, George. 1975. *Sociology: A Multiple Paradigm Science*. Boston: Allyn and Bacon.

Roberts, Leslie. 1989. "A Corrosive Fight over California's Toxics Law." *Science* 237:306–09.

Rodricks, Joseph V. 1992. *Calculated Risks: The Toxicity and Human Health Risks of Chemicals in Our Environment*. Cambridge, U.K.: Cambridge University Press.

Roe, David. 1989. "An Incentive-Conscious Approach to Toxic Chemical Controls." *Economic Development Quarterly* 3:179–87.

Rosenberg, Alexander. 1988. *Philosophy of the Social Sciences*. Boulder, Colo.: Westview Press.

Rousseau, Jean-Jacques. [1762] 1968. *The Social Contract*. Edited and translated by Maurice Cranston. Harmondsworth, Middlesex: Penguin Books.

Ruff, Larry E. 1977. "The Economic Common Sense of Pollution." In *Economics of the Environment: Selected Reading*. 2nd ed. Edited by Robert Dorfman and Nancy S. Dorfman, pp. 41–58. New York: W. W. Norton.

Sachs, Wolfgang, Reinhard Loske, and Manfred Linz. 1998. *Greening the North: A Post Industrial Blueprint for Ecology and Equity*. Trans. by Timothy Nevill. London: Zed Books.

Sagoff, Mark. 1981. "At the Service of Our Lady of Fatima or Why Political Questions Are Not All Economic." *Arizona Law Review* 23:1283–98. Reprinted in Gillroy and Wade 1992, pp. 371–86.

————. 1982. "On Markets for Risk." *Maryland Law Review* 41:755–73.

————. 1983. *The Allocation and Distribution of Resources*. College Park, Md.: Center for Philosophy and Public Policy, University of Maryland, Mimeo.

————. 1985. "Values and Preferences." *Ethics* 96:301–16.

————. 1986. "The Principles of Federal Water Pollution Control Law." *Minnesota Law Review* 71:55–68. Edited and reprinted as "Efficiency and Utility" in Gillroy and Wade 1992, pp. 165–78.

————. 1988. *The Economy of the Earth*. Cambridge, U.K.: Cambridge University Press.

————. 1997. "Do We Consume Too Much?" *Atlantic Monthly*, 279:80–89.

Sandel, Michael. 1982. *Liberalism and the Limits of Justice*. Cambridge, U.K.: Cambridge University Press.

Satchell, Michael. 1989. "The Battle for the Wilderness." *U.S. News and World Report*, Vol. 107, 3 July.

Sax, Joseph L. 1970. "The Public Trust Doctrine in Natural Resources Law." *Michigan Law Review* 68:473.

————. 1980a. "Liberating the Public Trust Doctrine from Its Historical Shackles." *U.C. Davis Law Review* 14:185.

————. 1980b. *Mountains without Handrails*. Ann Arbor: University of Michigan Press.

Schattschneider, E. E. 1960. *The Semi-Sovereign People*. Hinsdale, Ill.: Dryden Press.

Schmookler, Andrew Bard. 1993. *The Illusion of Choice: How the Market Economy Shapes Our Destiny*. San Francisco, Calif.: Harper.

Schneier, Edward V., and Bertram Gross. 1993. *Legislative Strategy: Shaping Public Policy*. New York: St. Martin's Press.

Schott, Robin May, ed. 1997. *Feminist Intrepretations of Immanuel Kant*. University Park, Pa.: Penn State University Press.

Searle, John R. 1967. "How to Derive 'Ought' from 'Is.'" In *Theories of Ethics*, by Philippa Foot, pp. 101–14. New York: Oxford University Press.

Sen, Amartya K. 1967. "Isolation, Assurance and the Social Rate of Discount." *Quarterly Journal of Economics* 81:112–24.

———. 1970. *Collective Choice and Social Welfare*. Amsterdam: North-Holland.

———. 1974. "Choice, Orderings and Morality." In *Practical Reason*, edited by Stephen Korner, pp. 54–67. New Haven, Conn.: Yale University Press.

———. 1979. "Rational Fools." In *Philosophy and Economic Theory*, edited by Frank Hahn and Martin Hollis, pp. 87–109. Oxford, U.K.: Oxford University Press.

———. 1982. *Choice Welfare and Measurement*. Cambridge, Mass.: Harvard University Press.

———. 1985. "Well-Being, Agency and Freedom." The Dewey Lectures 1984. *Journal of Philosophy* 82:169–220.

Sen, Amartya K., and Bernard Williams, eds. 1982. *Utilitarianism and Beyond*. Cambridge, U.K.: Cambridge University Press.

Shaiko, Ronald G. 1999. *Voices and Echoes for the Environment*. New York: Columbia University Press.

Shapiro, Michael. 1990. "Toxic Substances Policy." *Public Policies for Environmental Protection*, edited by Paul R. Portey, pp. 195–242. Washington, D.C.: Resources for the Future.

Shrader-Frechette, K. S. 1991. *Risk and Rationality: Philosophical Foundations for Populist Reforms*. Berkeley and Los Angeles, Calif.: University of California Press.

———. 1993. *Burying Uncertainty: Risk and the Case against Geological Disposal of Nuclear Waste*. Berkeley and Los Angeles, Calif.: University of California Press.

Shue, Henry. 1980. *Basic Rights*. Princeton, N.J.: Princeton University Press.

Sidgwick, Henry. [1907] 1981. *The Methods of Ethics*. 7th ed. London: Macmillan.

Sikora, R. I., and Brian Barry, eds. 1978. *Obligations to Future Generations*. Philadelphia, Pa.: Temple University Press.

Simberloff, Daniel. 1980. "A Succession of Paradigms in Ecology." In *Conceptual Issues in Ecology*, edited by E. Saarinen, pp. 63–99. Dordrecht: D. Reidel.

Simon, Herbert A. 1982. *Models of Bounded Rationality*. Vols. 1 and 2. Cambridge, Mass.: MIT.

Sinclair, Upton. [1906] 1971. *The Jungle*. Cambridge, Mass.: R. Bentley.

Singer, Peter. 1980. "Animals and the Value of Life." In *Matters of Life and Death*, edited by Tom Regan, pp. 218–59. New York: Random House.

Singh, Udai P., 1990. *Animal Liberation*. 2nd ed. New York: Random House.

Singh, Udai P., Norman N. Hatch, J. I. Garcia-Bengochea, and James E. Orban. 1983. "Phase 1 Study of Superfund Sites in Dade County, Florida." *Proceedings of the Industrial Waste Symposia* 56:1–18.

Singh, Udai P., Norman N. Hatch, Jr., Thomas C. Emenhiser, J. I. Garcia-Bengochea, and James E. Orban. 1984. "Remedial Investigation at Biscayne Aquifer Hazardous Waste Sites." *Journal of Environmental Engineering* 110:345–64.

Smart, J. J. C., and Bernard Williams. 1973. *Utilitarianism: For and Against*. Cambridge, U.K.: Cambridge University Press.

Smith, Adam. [1776] 1937. *The Wealth of Nations*. New York: Modern Library.

Smith, Zachary A. 1992. *The Environmental Policy Paradox*. Englewood Cliffs, N.J.: Prentice-Hall.

Snare, Francis. 1992. *The Nature of Moral Thinking*. London: Routledge.

Snidal, Duncan. 1979. "Public Goods, Property Rights, and Political Organizations." *International Studies Quarterly* 23:532–66. Reprinted in Gillroy and Wade 1992, pp. 285–312.

Sobotka, C. 1983. "The Benefits of Avoiding Groundwater Contamination at Two Sites in the Biscayne Aquifer." Washington, D.C.: Environmental Protection Agency, Mimeo.

Spensley, James W., Russell L. Freeman, and Frederic Marchet. 1994. *NEPA Compliance Manual*. 2nd ed. Washington, D.C.: Government Institutes Press.

Steen, Harold K. 1992. "Americans and Their Forests." *American Forests* 98: at 18.

Stegner, Page. 1994. "Red Ledge Province and the Colorado Plateau." *Sierra* 79, March/April, pp. 92–100.

Stokes, Kenneth M. 1994. *Man and the Biosphere: Toward a Coevolutionary Political Economy*. Armonk, N.Y.: M. E. Sharpe.

Stokey, Edith, and Richard Zeckhauser. 1978. *A Primer for Policy Analysis*. New York: W. W. Norton and Company.

Stone, Christopher. 1975. *Should Trees Have Standing? Towards Legal Rights for Natural Objects*. New York: Avon.

Sugden, Robert. 1983. *Who Cares?: An Economic and Ethical Analysis of Private Charity and the Welfare State*. London: Institute of Economic Affairs Press.

Swartzman, Daniel, Richard A. Liroff, and Kevin G. Croke, eds. 1982. *Cost-Benefit Analysis and Environmental Regulation: Politics, Ethics and the Market*. Washington, D.C.: Conservation Foundation Press.

Switzer, Jacqueline Vaughn. 1994. *Environmental Politics*. New York: St. Martin's Press.

Taurek, John. 1977. "Should the Numbers Count?" *Philosophy and Public Affairs* 6:293–316.

Taylor, Bob Pepperman. 1992. *Our Limits Transgressed: Environmental Political Thought in America*. Lawrence: University Press of Kansas.

Taylor, Michael. 1976. *Anarchy and Cooperation*. London: John Wiley and Sons.

———. 1982. *Community, Anarchy, and Liberty*. Cambridge, U.K.: Cambridge University Press.

———. 1987. *The Possibility of Cooperation*. Cambridge, U.K.: Cambridge University Press.

Taylor, Paul W. 1986. *Respect for Nature: A Theory of Environmental Ethics*. Princeton, N.J.: Princeton University Press.

Teitelman, Robert. 1989. *Gene Dreams*. New York: Basic Books.

Thoreau, Henry David. 1985. *A Week on the Concord and Merrimack Rivers; Walden: Or Life in the Woods; The Maine Woods; Cape Cod*. New York: Viking Press.

Tresch, Richard W. 1981. *Public Finance*. Plano, Tex.: Business Publications.

Tribe, L. H. 1972. "Policy Science: Analysis or Ideology?" *Philosophy and Public Affairs* 2:66–110. Reprinted in Gillroy and Wade 1992, pp. 115–52.

———. 1974. "Ways Not to Think about Plastic Trees: New Foundations for Environmental Law." *Yale Law Review* 83:1315–48.

Trost, Cathy. 1984. *Elements of Risk*. New York: New York Times Books.

Tsebelis, George. 1990. *Nested Games: Rational Choice in Comparative Politics*. Berkeley and Los Angeles, Calif.: University of California Press.

U. S. Congress. House of Representatives, Committee on Interstate and Foreign Commerce. 1979. *Hearings on the Use of Cost-Benefit Analysis by Regulatory Agencies*. 96th Cong., 1st sess. Serial 96–157.

Vermont Agency of Natural Resources and Environment (VANR). 1991. *Risks to Vermont and Vermonters*. Waterbury, Vt., July.

Viscusi, W. Kip. 1983. *Risk by Choice*. Cambridge, Mass.: Harvard University Press.

———. 1992. *Fatal Tradeoffs: Public and Private Responsibilities for Risk*. New York: Oxford University Press.

Vlastos, Gregory. 1962. "Justice and Equality." In *Social Justice*, edited by Richard B. Brandt, pp. 31–72. Englewood Cliffs, N.J.: Prentice-Hall.

Vogel, David. 1995. *Trading Up: Consumer and Environmental Regulation in a Global Economy*. Cambridge, Mass.: Harvard University Press.

Von Schilcher, Florian, and Neil Tennant. 1984. *Philosophy, Evolution & Human Nature*. London: Routledge and Kegan Paul.

Walzer, Michael. 1984. *Spheres of Justice*. New York: Basic Books.

Ward, C. H., W. Giger, and P. L. McCarty, eds. 1985. *Groundwater Quality*. New York: John Wiley and Sons.

Wargo, John. 1998. *Our Childern's Toxic Legacy*. New Haven, Conn.: Yale University Press.

Washington Department of Ecology (WDE). 1990. *Toward 2010: An Environmental Action Agenda*. Olympia, Wash., July.

Watson, Gary. 1975. "Free Agency." *Journal of Philosophy* 72:205–20.

Weber, Max. [1922] 1947. *The Theory of Social and Economic Organization*. New York: Free Press.

————. [1956] 1978. *Economy and Society: An Outline of Interpretive Sociology.* Edited by Guenther Roth and Claus Wittich. Berkeley and Los Angeles, Calif.: University of California Press.

Wenz, Peter. 1988. *Environmental Justice.* Albany, N.Y.: SUNY Press.

Westra, Laura. 1994. *An Environmental Proposal for Ethics: The Principle of Integrity.* Lanham, Md.: Rowman and Littlefield.

Williams, Bernard. 1985. *Ethics and the Limits of Philosophy.* Cambridge, Mass.: Harvard University Press.

————. 1989. "The Scientific and the Ethical." In *Anti-Theory in Ethics and Moral Conservatism,* edited by Stanley Clarke and Evan Simpson, pp. 65–86. Albany, N.Y.: SUNY Press.

Williams, George C. 1966. *Adaptation and Natural Selection.* Princeton, N.J.: Princeton University Press.

Williams, Howard. 1983. *Kant's Political Philosophy.* Oxford, U.K.: Basil Blackwell.

Willig, John T. 1994. *Environmental TQM.* 2nd ed. New York: John Wiley and Sons.

Wolf, Susan. 1990. *Freedom within Reason.* New York: Oxford University Press.

Wolff, Robert Paul. 1970. *In Defense of Anarchism.* New York: Harper and Row.

Worobec, Mary Devine, and Cheryl Hogue. 1992. *Toxic Substances Controls Guide: Federal Regulation of Chemicals in the Environment.* 2nd ed. Washington, D.C.: Bureau of National Affairs.

Yaffe, Gideon. 1995. "Freedom, Natural Necessity and the Categorical Imperative." *Kant Studien* 86:446–58.

Yaffee, Steven, Ali F. Phillips, Irene C. Frentz, Paul W. Hardy, Sussanne M. Maleki, and Barbara E. Thorpe. 1996. *Ecosystem Management in the United States: An Assessment of Current Experience.* Washington, D.C.: Island Press.

Yovel, Yirmiyahu. 1980. *Kant and the Philosophy of History.* Princeton, N.J.: Princeton University Press.

Zammito, John H. 1992. *The Genesis of Kant's Critique of Judgment.* Chicago: University of Chicago Press.

Zimmerman, Michael E., J. Baird Callicot, George Sessions, Karen J. Warren, and John Clark, eds. 1993. *Environmental Philosophy.* Englewood Cliffs, N.J.: Prentice-Hall.

Names Index

Page references in italics indicate figures.

A

Allison, Henry E., 159
Anderson, Charles W., 77n15
Annas, Julia, 133
Aristotle, xxxii
Ashby, Eric, 74, 329
Aune, Bruce, 189
Axelrod, Robert, 77n12

B

Baier, Annette, 260n15
Barry, Brian, 285, 337, 380–82
Beck, Lewis White, 197n17
Beck, Ulrich, 333n8
Bentham, Jeremy, 77n19
Berman, Harold J., 26
Bobrow, Davis B., 6
Bones, 333n4
Braybrooke, David, 9, 15, 22, 24
Breen, Barry, 79–80, 137n1
    on human-nature interface, 289–90
    Resources to Recovery approach, 108n4,
        136, 291
Brennan, William, 94
Burkholz, Herbert, 373, 375

C

Campbell-Mohn, Celia, 79–80, 137n1
    on human-nature interface, 289–90
    Resources to Recovery approach, 108n4,
        136, 291
Carson, Rachel, 89
Cherry, John, 321
Clausewitz, Carl von, 6
Coase, Ronald, 76n2

D

Davis, Jefferson, 392
Dickens, Charles, 86
Donagan, Alan, 64, 174–75
Douglas, William O., 110n42
Dryzek, John, 6, 294n25, 299, 310
    Rational Ecology, 308–9

E

Easterbrook, Gregg, 314–15
Einstein, Albert, 9
Elliot, Robert, 329
Elster, Jon, 202
Everenden, Neil, 129

423

Subject Index

Page references in italics indicate figures.

427

Happiness, 172, 233, 260n2
"Hard look" doctrine, 388n47
Hard Times (Dickens), 86
Harm
  anticipation of, 127, 288
  avoidance, 335n25
  vs. benefits, 45–46
  catastrophic, 118–21, 301–2
  collective, 44, 48–49, 118, 300
  compensation for, 75–76
  in conscious risk, 305–6
  vs. costs, 51–52
  definition of, 51–52
  false-positive risk and, 103
  health and, 330
  to integrity, 52
  to intrinsic value, 71
  irreversibility of, 47, 49, 125–28, 308,
    321
  no-harm principle, 312–13, 317, 330, 378
  potential, 251–54, 257, 300
  prevention of, 48–50, 288
  probability of, 92–93, 120
  significant, 93
  unemployment vs. environmental, 91
Harmony
  of freedom, 236–38, 242, 259, 275
  between humans and nature, 191–96
Hazardous waste disposal, 99, 102–3
Health effects, xiii, xiv, 330
  of carcinogens, 356–57, 372, 395–96
  of groundwater toxins, 325–27
  in Quantitative Risk Assessment, 95
  Toxic Substances Control Act on, 101
Heteronomy vs. autonomy, 151, 164, 168,
  196n5
Humanity
  agency of, 51–52, 69, 169–70
  animal data and, 113–14, 138n4
  common, 227
  duty to, 135–36
  in ecosystems, 129, 191
  as an end-in-itself, 152–53, 233
  intrinsic value of, xxxv, 114, *117*, 145,
    187
  nature and, xxxvi, 35n1, 115–16, 128–30,
    181–84, 289–93
  respect for, 161
  self-regulation by, 194
  systems of, 132–35, 288–90
Hunting, 339–41, 344–45
Hydrologic cycle, 321
Hypothetical consent, 60–63
Hypothetical imperative, 64

Ideal contract, 210–13, 228n8, 236–37
Ideal-regarding evaluations, 256, 282
Ignorance of mechanism, 45, 113–16, 299–
  304, 357
Imprisoned riders, 49–50, 52, 71, 118, 125,
  310
Incentives, economic, 24
Inclination, 168
Independence, 247, 281, 349, 377
  in Justice from Autonomy, 142–43, 231–
    33, 246–47, 250
  opportunity for, 366, 376
Individual choice. *See* Choice
Individualism, 232
Individuals
  autonomy of. *See* Autonomy
  in collective choice, xxxiii–xxxiv
  vs. collective good, 41–44, 72
  conditions of, 382–83
  as ends, 152–55, 226, 245–46
  in environmental risk, xxx, 49
  integrity of, 56
  intrinsic value of, 53–54
  in Justice from Autonomy, 140–41, 147–96
  in the market paradigm, 18, 54–55
  the minimal state and, 20
  nature and, 147–79
  in policy design, *16*, 18
  rational, 201–2
  self-welfare motivation of, 18, 21
Inductive reasoning, *8*
*Industrial Union Department AFL-CIO v
  American Petroleum Institute*, 92–94,
  97
Information
  in assurance games, 376
  in collective action, 207–8
  in collective choice, 11, 276
  in risk-conscious societies, 305
Inherent value. *See* Intrinsic value
Innovation, 202
Institutions, central. *See* Government
Instrumental value
  vs. baseline integrity, 317
  benefits of, 118
  definition of, 180
  economic, 71–73, 80
  vs. intrinsic values, 116–18, *117*, 266–67,
    291–92, 295n31, 384n2, 391
  of nature, 135, 180, 182–83
  · of species, 338
  of wildlife, 341–42

National Wildlife Refuges, 338–50
Natural resources
  vs. artificial resources, 314–16
  economics, 86–87
  in the market paradigm, 33, 81–85
  maximum use of, 82–83
  optimal use of, 82–85, 343
  sustainable, 83
  unused, 345
  value of, xiii
Natural selection, 188, 193, 202, 315
Naturalistic fallacy, 132
Nature. *See also* Ecosystems; Wilderness
  causality in, 188
  context of, 116
  definition of, 188
  duty to, xxxvi, 130, 132, 135–36, 179–94
  in the Ecosystem Design Approach, 131–
    32, 291–92
  empirical, 133
  as an end-in-itself, 332
  exploitation of, 189–90, 268
  freedom from, 134
  functional integrity of, 132, 180, 189, 193,
    266–67, 313, 346–47
  human use of, 33–34, 129, 141, 192, 292–
    93
  humanity and, xxxvi, 35n1, 115–16, 128–
    30, 181–84, 289–93
  individuals and, 147–79
  instrumental value of, 134, 180, 182–83
  integrity of, 69, 141, 189, 194, 239
  intrinsic value of, 73, 114, 116–17, 135,
    180–85, 187–94, 266–67
  justice for, 183–84, 289
  Kant on, 179–94
  law of, 156t, 189, 204
  maximum use of, 82–83
  minimal use of, 364
  moral agency and, xxxvi, 123
  morality of, 131–32
  as property, 40
  Realm of, 184–85, 188, 190
  reshaping, 192
  as a resource, 183
  respect for, 183, 191–93
  responsibility to, 116
  rights of, xxxviii, 180–81
  society from, 212
  subsystems of, 51, 188
  systems of, 131–32, 138n4, 347, 357
  technology and, 316–17
  waste assimilation by, 86
  in worldview, 183

Negative feedback, 308
NEPA. *See* National Environmental Policy
  Act
Neutrality, artificial-risk, 314–17, 331–32,
  349, 364, 376–77
New Drug Applications, 373
Newtonian paradigm, 25
NIMBY situations, 350–66
  as assurance games, 353–54, 360, 362–63
  collective choice in, 363–64
  collective good in, 350–51, 354–55, 361,
    363
  cooperation in, 352–54, 363
  ecosystem law in, 364–66
  as a prisoner's dilemma, 351–54, 360, 363
  self-interest in, 351–52, 355
No-harm principle, 312–13, 317, 330, 378
No Observed Effect Level (NOEL), 373
Nonconsequentialism, 334n20
Not-in-my-backyard. *See* NIMBY situations
Notice of Claimed Investigational Exemp-
  tion for a New Drug Application, 373
NRDC v EPA, 95–97
Nuclear power, xiv–xv, 367–69
Nuisance, law of, 86

O

Occupational Safety and Health Administration, 92, 94–95
Opportunity, 57, 144, 246–51, 268–69
  for independence, 366, 376
Optimal Use Model, 81, 83–85. *See also* Traditional Sector Approach model.
Optimization
  efficiency as, 85, 92–93, 95, 98, 106
  of natural resources utilization, 82–85,
    343
  of pollution levels, 84–86
  of wealth, 33
Organic bodies, 185–86, 189
OSHA. *See* Occupational Safety and Health
  Administration
Ought vs. is, 132–33
Ownership, 214–15
  common, 215–17, 314, 378
  prior collective, 215–18, 227, 378

P

Pacific Legal Foundation v Watt, 386n17
*Palila v Hawaii Department of Land and Nat-
  ural Resources*, 341, 385n9

Truth, 35n2
TSA. *See* Traditional Sector Approach model
TSCA. *See* Toxic Substances Control Act
TVA v Hill, 338
Two-tier system, 372–73
Tyranny, 116

U

Uncertainty
  in environmental risk, 113–21, 126, 136,
    299–301
  ethics and, 128
  in Justice from Autonomy, 303
  minimization of, 377
  in policy design, 382
Unemployment vs. environmental risk, 91
*Unfinished Business: A Comparative Assessment
  of Environmental Problems*, 355
*United States v Lexington Mills and Elevator
  Company*, 371
Universalization test, 152
U.S. v Rutherford, 388n56
Utilitarianism, xxxii, 260n5

V

Values, xiii–xiv, xvii–xviii, 291–92. *See also*
    Instrumental value; Intrinsic value
  choice and, 160–62
  in consequentialism, 120
  definition of, 272
  economic, xv, xvii–xviii
  environmental, 35n4
  vs. facts, 131
  functional, 182
  in genetic engineering policy, xvi–xvii
  in harm compensation, 75–76
  instrumental vs. intrinsic, 116–18, *117*,
    266–67, 291–92, 295n31, 384n2,
    391
  judgment of, 187
  nonefficiency, 13
  vs. preferences, 13
  vs. principles, 161
  vs. scientific knowledge, xiii–xiv
  wilderness, xiii, 344–46, 386n17
Vermont Act 250, 393–95
Vermont Yankee Nuclear Power corp. v NRDC,
  368–69
Vinyl chloride case. *See NRDC v EPA*
Virtue
  in autonomy, 173–75
  vs. justice, 176

in politics, 262
Vocabulary, moral, 114–15
Voting, 248–50, 268
*Voyageurs Regional National Park Association v
  Lujan*, 386n17

443

W

Want-regarding evaluations, 256, 282, 285
Waste assimilation, 86
Waste disposal
  case studies in, 336–37, 350–66
  collective good and, 350–51, 354–55
  groundwater and, 323
  laws, 290–91
  market paradigm and, 99, 102–3
Water. *See also* Groundwater contamination
  drinking, 321, 325, 331, 395–97
Water Quality/Effluent Standards, 104
Wealth
  distribution of, 244, 276–77
  freedom and, 277–78
  maximization, 21–23, 33, 59, 85, 126
  optimization, 33
Welfare
  benefits, 118
  consent and, 59–62
  instrumental, 317
  maximization, 60, 63–64
  practical reason and, 275
  preferences and, 67
  self, 18, 21
What questions, 20–22, 36n17
Whether questions, 16–17, 22–25, 36n14
Why questions, 16, 20, 36n14
Wilderness
  case studies in, 337–50
  designation of, 347, 386n20
  economic use of, 344–45
  legal, 342–46
  myth of, 343, 345–46, 386n21
  preservation of, 343–46
  values, xiii, 344–46, 386n17
  as wasted resources, 342
Wilderness Act, 343, 346, 385n13
Wildlife
  case studies in, 337–50
  instrumental value of, 341–42
  law, 338–46
Wildlife refuges
  designation of, 340, 384n6
  human use of, 338
  incidental uses of, 339

INDEX